1870/71 – 1989/90
German Unifications and the
Change of Literary Discourse

European Cultures
Studies in Literature and the Arts

Edited by
Walter Pape
Köln

Editorial Board:
Philip Brady, London · Keith Bullivant, Gainesville
Frederick Burwick, Los Angeles · Mark Galliker, Heidelberg
Joachim Gessinger, Potsdam · Marian Hobson, London
Günter Jerouschek, Halle · François Lecercle, Lyon
Eckhardt Meyer-Krentler, Bochum · Carlo Ossola, Torino
Terence James Reed, Oxford · Elinor S. Shaffer, Norwich
Barbara Stafford, Chicago

Volume 1

Walter de Gruyter · Berlin · New York
1993

1870/71 – 1989/90
German Unifications and the Change of Literary Discourse

Edited by
Walter Pape

Walter de Gruyter · Berlin · New York
1993

∞ Printed on acid-free paper
which falls within the guidelines of the ANSI to ensure
permanence and durability.

Library of Congress Cataloging-in-Publication Data

1870/71–1989/90 : German unifications and the change of literary
   discourse / edited by Walter Pape.
      (European cultures ; v. 1)
      Includes bibliographical references and index.
      ISBN 3-11-013878-6
      1. German literature–19th century–Political aspects. 2. German
   literature–20th century–Political aspects. 3. Nationalism in
   literature. 4. Franco-Prussian War, 1870–1871. 5. Germany–
   History–Unification. 1990. I. Pape, Walter. II. Title: German
   unifications and the change of literary discourse. III. Series.
   PT395.A18   1993
   830.9′358–dc20   93-35566
                                                                      CIP

Deutsche Bibliothek – Cataloging-in-Publication Data

1870/71–1989/90: German unifications and the
change of literary discourse / ed. by Walter Pape.
– Berlin ; New York : de Gruyter 1993
   (European cultures ; Vol. 1)
   ISBN 3-11-013878-6
NE: Pape, Walter [Hrsg.] ; eighteen hundred and
seventy/71–1989/90; GT

© Copyright 1993 by Walter de Gruyter & Co., D-10785 Berlin.
All rights reserved, including those of translation into foreign languages. No part of this book may be reproduced or transmitted in any form or by any means, electronic or mechanical, including photocopy, recording, or any information storage and retrieval system, without permission in writing from the publisher.
Printed in Germany
Typesetting: Greiner & Reichel, Köln
Printing: Gerike GmbH, Berlin
Binding: Lüderitz & Bauer GmbH, Berlin
Cover design: Rudolf Hübler, Berlin

Contents

WALTER PAPE
Cultural Change and Cultural Memory:
The Principle of Hope in the Times of German Unifications 1

History, Education, Language, and National Identity

JAMES J. SHEEHAN
National History and National Identity in the New Germany 25

ALFRED KELLY
The Franco-Prussian War and Unification
in German History Schoolbooks 37

ROGER CHICKERING
Language and the Social Foundations of Radical Nationalism
in the Wilhelmine Era 61

JOHN S. CORNELL
"Dann weg 'mit's Milletär' und wieder ein civiler Civilist":
Theodor Fontane and the Wars of German Unification 79

Literature, Aesthetics, and Literary Market after 1870/71

WALTER PAPE
"Hurra, Germania – mir graut vor dir": Hoffmann von Fallersleben,
Freiligrath, Herwegh, and the German Unification of 1870/71 107

VOLKER NEUHAUS
Friedrich Spielhagen – Critic of Bismarck's Empire 135

ECKHARDT MEYER-KRENTLER
"Gibt es nicht Völker, in denen vergessen zu werden eine Ehre ist?":
Raabe and German Unification 144

Literary Changes Compared – 1870/71 and 1990

KATHERINE ROPER
Imagining the German Capital: Berlin Writers on the
Two Unification Eras 171

DANIEL FULDA
Telling German History: Forms and Functions of the Historical
Narrative Against the Background of the National Unifications 195

1990: The Principle of Hope
or: Nailed to the Cross of the Past?

TERENCE JAMES REED
Another Piece of the Past 233

KARL-HEINZ J. SCHOEPS
Intellectuals, Unification, and Political Change 1990:
The Case of Christa Wolf 251

PHILIP BRADY
"Wir hausen im Prenzlauer Berg": Remarks on the
Very Last Generation of GDR Poets 278

KEITH BULLIVANT
The End of the Dream of the "Other Germany":
The "German Question" in West German Letters 302

Bibliography 321
   Primary Sources 321
   Secondary Sources 336

Notes on Contributors 363

Index 367

WALTER PAPE

Cultural Change and Cultural Memory: The Principle of Hope in the Times of German Unifications

> Ist indeß dem Beobachter nicht ganz erfreulich, wie sich die befreyten Deutschen schon wieder literarisch gegen einander benehmen; so muß man denken, daß dieß nun einmal die Art der Nation ist, sobald sie von fremdem Drucke sich befreyt fühlt, unter sich zu zerfallen. Was mich betrifft, so erlauben mir glückliche Umstände und Ereignisse einen ganz engen Zauberkreis um mich her zu ziehen, in welchem ich, nach alter Gewohnheit, meinen stillen Beschäftigungen nachhänge, das was ich Zeitlebens vorgenommen wieder aufnehme, um das Brauchbare davon meinen zwar wunderlichen, jedoch immer geliebten Landsleuten aufzubewahren.
>
> Goethe to Sara von Grotthus, 7 February 1814[1]

"Literary history in 1970 will look upon the year 1870 as a year of change ('Wendejahr') like literary history of our days looks upon the year 1770, when in Strasbourg Goethe changed from an imitator of the French to a German poet."[2] Not only Eduard Engel, quoted here, but other literary historians too like Richard M. Meyer opposed the years before to those after 1870 as years of political and national change, and of cultural and literary divergence: "The decade preceding the great war like few in our century is poor in literature and in the arts." For Meyer everything since 1870 has changed: "The decade

---

1 Goethe: *Werke* (Weimarer Ausgabe) ser. 4, vol. 24, p. 134. "If it is not altogether pleasant watching how the liberated Germans in the field of literature behave towards another, then one must remember that it is the nation's habit to fall into discord as soon as it feels freed from foreign pressure. As myself I am enabled by fortunate circumstances and events to draw around me a very close magic circle within which, according to old habits, I follow my silent occupations, pick up again what I have pursued throughout my life, to preserve what I find useful for my odd, yet still beloved fellow countrymen."
2 Engel: *Geschichte der deutschen Literatur von den Anfängen bis zur Gegenwart* vol. 2, p. 961.

between 1870 and 1880 has been the most glorious, the richest in substance, that Germany has had in this century."[3] But Meyer is unable to offer examples either for the grandeur of the 1870's or for his conviction that Germany ought to obtain the "supremacy of the new world culture" ("Vormacht der neuen Weltkultur").[4] But, of course, literary or cultural change cannot be attributed to a single political event.[5]

Unlike Richard M. Meyer, Günter Grass in *Unkenrufe* foresees German culture merging into a new world culture. He has Alexander Reschke, his ironic self-parody, answer to the British-educated Pakistani Chatterjee: "Durch völkerverschmelzende Prozesse erhoffe er den endlichen Austausch der Kulturen. Der prognostizierten Weltgesellschaft des Herrn Chatterjee werde eine zukünftige Weltkultur entsprechen."[6] Grass's utopian concept of cultural change is a sort of post-unification aftermath of the leftist discussion in the 1980's: because the balance between 'North and South' and the ecological reforms seem to have ceased to be a subject of German politics or political discussions, his hope of cultural change now resides in an Asian. Europe, and especially the Germans, are preoccupied with their past in a very strange manner: hero and heroine in his *Unkenrufe* are the founders of the German-Polish Cemetery Society ("Deutsch-Polnische Friedhofsgesellschaft"), the task of which is to bring back dead Germans to their former homeland. This parody of reconciliation is brought face to face with an existential and global vision of cultural unification. Günter Grass's *Unkenrufe* satirically answer the commonplace of the 'end of history' which nowadays is a constant theme both in academic and journalistic writing.

1. 1871: "Empire of the Rich" – 1990: "Club of the Rich"

German unification of 1990 was not accompanied by euphoric hopes in a cultural change. 1870, however, was regarded as a "Wendejahr," although the new German Empire and its culture were not considered to be something new, but the fulfillment of a cultural-patriotic and (later) economic desire.[7]

---

3 Meyer: *Die deutsche Litteratur des Neunzehnten Jahrhunderts*, p. 625, 692.
4 Ibid., p. 693.
5 Cf. Daniel Fulda's essay, p. 196 of this volume.
6 Grass: *Unkenrufe*, p. 48. "Through processes amalgamating the nations he looked forward to the final exchange of cultures. A future world-culture will emerge alongside the world-society prophesied by Mr. Chatterjee."
7 Cf. p. 123–24 of my essay in this volume.

Likewise German unification of 1990 (even right wing politicians consciously avoid the term re-unification) according to Willy Brandt's phrase brought together what belongs together ("was zusammengehört"). Both German unifications seem to have been accomplished by "conservative model[s],"[8] they prompt or confirm conservatism in the spheres of culture, politics, and economics.

It is tempting to compare today's breakdown of the eastern communist governments and the disappearance of the GDR with the increasing German capitalism after 1871 and imperialism after 1890. There are some economic parallels: Herwegh's disapproval of the "Empire of the rich" (excluding the lower classes from the 'unity') and Günter Grass's condemnation of the "club of the rich" (excluding foreigners seeking asylum) both deplore the consequences of unification from an engaged 'leftist' point of view[9]. Even a distinguished scholar and maker of economic and monetary policy speaks of the Amfortas wound of German unification[10] – which, one could add, of course cannot be healed only by asking the 'right' question. Unification is a "glänzendes Geschäft" (brilliant business opportunity) for the industry and commerce of the old FRG and a "Totalschaden" (total loss) for those in the former GDR.[11] Hochhuth speaks of the "brutal economic Darwinism of the Treuhand" ("brutalen Wirtschaftsdarwinismus der Treuhand"),[12] and one might compare the Treuhand activities with the "orgy of speculative activity and the crash that ended it in late 1873," as Katherine Roper does in her essay.[13] In his inaugural lecture (1895) Max Weber declared that Bismarck's unification politics was doomed to failure because it led only to an external, not to an inner unification[14]. Unification for Weber was accomplished too early because the social foundation was missing and the industrial revolution had just begun

---

8 Schoefer: "The Attack on Christa Wolf." *The Nation* No. 251, October 22, 1990, p. 448, quoted in Schoeps's essay, this volume p. 273.
9 See p. 134.
10 Hankel: *Die sieben Todsünden der Vereinigung*, p. 10.
11 Ibid.
12 Hochhuth: *Wessis in Weimar*, p. 13. Treuhand is the organization that at first was to preserve the former "Volkseigentum" (state property) in the ex-GDR; the revision of the law of March 1990 in June 1990 altered the purpose decisively: no longer "Wahrung des Volkseigentums" (maintenance of state property), but "Privatisierung und Reorganisation" (denationalization and reorganisation) were the aims of the newly created body; cf. Stefan Heym's statement ibid., p. 11. For a differentiated view on the problems of the Treuhand which has also to cope with billions of debts of the former GDR see Hankel: *Die sieben Todsünden der Vereinigung*, p. 42–53. See also Keith Bullivant's essay in this volume p. 312.
13 See p. 187 in this volume.
14 Weber: *Der Nationalstaat und die Volkswirtschaftspolitik*, p. 27.

in Germany[15]: "We have to understand that Germany's unification was a youthful folly performed by the nation in her old days and which she ought to have refrained from because of its expensiveness […]."[16] Weber indeed was looking forward to some kind of "Arbeiteraristokratie" (aristocracy of the working class) to be the "Trägerin des politischen Systems" (upholder of the political system); even in 1895 he considered the task of social unification too heavy for the bourgeoisie: both the ruling and the rising classes are not prepared for this job.[17]

Likewise the ignorance of modern intellectuals of the need of the lower classes is a nineteenth-century legacy, and condemnations of consumption and the market often turn out to be born of nostalgic conservatism. Wolf Lepenies has denounced the "Großschriftsteller" of the former GDR for their criticizing of the "Konsumsucht" (yearning for consumption) of the lower classes: "The spokesmen of GDR culture had forgotten – or did they ever know? – that longing for immediate satisfaction of needs is a characteristic trait of the lower classes, whereas traditionally the middle class practices the postponement of satisfactions – *deferred gratification pattern* is the sociological term."[18]

In comparing historical phenomena we have to bear in mind the different layers of history: historical changes in constitution and political organizations, the historical survival of attitudes and social behavior. A certain analogy between attitudes after the unifications of 1871 and 1990 is difficult to deny, as is shown below. But as the attitudes both of intellectuals and the broader masses are dominant determinants in politics they can prove stronger than the democratic institutions meant to control their potentially unfavorable influence on political and social life.

2. "No Effective Unity of Mind or Spirit"

When in the years after the unification of 1871 the political unity was not followed by a cultural and social unity the disappointment grew. Both the Kulturkampf, starting very soon after 1871, and the Sozialistengesetze of 1878 are but the most obvious confirmations of the growing suppression of cultural and political progressiveness. As early as 1880 Gottfried Keller

---

15 See also Stern: *The Politics of Cultural Despair: A Study in the Rise of Germanic Ideology*, p. xxviii.
16 Weber: *Der Nationalstaat und die Volkswirtschaftspolitik*, p. 32.
17 Ibid., p. 33, 32.
18 Lepenies: *Folgen einer unerhörten Begebenheit*, p. 36.

remarked: "Für die auswärtigen Freunde und ideellen Anhänger des Reiches fängt es doch an beunruhigend zu werden, daß die Dinge sich nicht schicken zu wollen scheinen und keine durchschlagende Geistes- und Gemütseinigkeit aufkommt [...]."[19] Likewise Adolf Damaschke, alluding to Benjamin Disraeli's *Sybil; Or the Two Nations* (1845), more than half a century after unification emphasized the social discord as a cause of cultural disintegration: "Our people were more and more divided into two nations separated by different notions of the world and the state, celebrating different festivities, carrying different ideals in their hearts."[20] Both cultural and social discord contributed to the increasing "cultural despair" of the years after unification, especially after Bismarck's 'second foundation of the Reich' in 1878.[21] This view was shared by many of the educated ('Gebildeten'):

> It is often forgotten that after 1871 many thoughtful Germans were gripped by a mood of mingled pride and disenchantment: pride in the power and the unity of the Reich, disenchantment with the culture of the Empire, with the fact that beneath the crust of prosperous politics the old Germany was disintegrating, pulled apart by modernity – by liberalism, secularism, and industrialism. Common were the lamentations about the decline of the German spirit, the defeat of idealism by the forces of realism in politics and materialism in business.[22]

Unification and the foundation of the Reich produced a serious crisis of identity that seized many intellectuals and writers: the idea of Germany as a "Kulturnation" (cultural nation) leading to political nation and unification proved deceptive; conversely after 1871 cultural unity was expected to result from state unity: but for a long time the traditional 'Bildungsbürger' opposed all modern tendencies of literature and the arts.[23] The idea of national unifica-

---

19   Keller: *Gesammelte Briefe* vol. 3, 1, p. 450, letter no. 542 to Theodor Storm, June 13, 1880. "The foreign friends and intellectual supporters of the Reich begin to feel uneasy because nothing seems to be falling into place and no effective unity of mind or spirit is emerging [...]."
20   Adolf Damaschke: *Aus meinem Leben*. Vol. 2. Zürich, Leipzig 1925 – quoted from Ritter and Kocka, eds., *Deutsche Sozialgeschichte* vol. 2, p. 392.
21   Cf. Daniel Fulda's contribution to this volume pp. 203–04.
22   Stern: *The Politics of Cultural Despair: A Study in the Rise of Germanic Ideology*, p. xxvi. On history instruction as "the natural focal point of a nationalistic education" see Alfred Kelly's contribution to this volume, pp. 37–60.
23   Cf. Wolfgang J. Mommsen: "Die Kultur der Moderne im Deutschen Kaiserreich." Hardtwig and Brandt, eds., *Deutschlands Weg in die Moderne*, pp. 254–74, esp. p. 254. See also the discussion on aesthetics and politics after 1871 in Middell: *Literatur zweier Kaiserreiche*, pp. 161–202.

tion before 1870 had been born of cultural patriotism and was rooted in an obsolete premodern notion of society. Insisting upon this alternative cultural project in a modern capitalist state was a romantic dream: Heinrich and Julius Hart addressed an open letter in 1882 to Bismarck: "Sollte Deutschlands Kultur jene Höhe erreichen, welche dem Streben seiner besten Söhne gebührt und welche es erreichen muß, um seine Stellung im Rathe der Nationen zu behaupten, so ist es nöthig, ein besonderes *Reichsamt* für Literatur, Theater, Wissenschaft und Künste zu kreiren." These four fields are deliberately called something "Allgemeines, Deutsches" (universal, German) and they have to be controlled not by the different "Partikularstaaten", but by the Reich.[24] And three years later Karl Henckell prefaced the naturalist anthology *Moderne Dichter-Charaktere* by demanding a poetry with a unifying force after the "materialistic mess of the 1870s" ("materialistischer Sudelkessel der siebziger Jahre"): "Wir, das heißt die junge Generation des erneuten, geeinten und großen Vaterlandes, wollen, daß die Poesie wiederum ein Heiligthum werde, zu dessen geweihter Stätte das Volk wallfahrt, um mit tiefster Seele aus dem Born des Ewigen zu schlürfen und erquickt, geleitet und erhoben zu der Erfüllung seines menschheitlichen Berufes zurückzukehren [...]."[25]

Writers' responses to 1870/71 were in general characterized by "sympathy" and those to 1989/90 by "distance," as many contributors to this volume point out.[26] A sort of "cultural despair" seized not only the writers after 1870 but also numerous authors both of the former GDR and the FRG. "History was racing ahead, and the intellectuals were marking time,"[27] thus Lepenies comments on the reaction of German intellectuals to unification. At first glance the debate seems to be a predominantly political one, but – as will

---

24 Heinrich and Julius Hart: "Offener Brief an den Fürsten Bismarck." Ruprecht, ed., *Manifeste des Naturalismus*, pp. 23–27, here p. 26. "Should Germany's culture ever reach the height which is due to its best sons and which it has to reach in order to maintain its position within the council of nations, it is necessary to create a special office of the Reich for literature, theater, science, and the arts."

25 Henckel: "Die neue Lyrik." Preface to Wilhelm Arent, ed., *Moderne Dichter-Charaktere* (1885), quoted from Brauneck and Müller, eds., *Naturalismus*, pp. 353–55, here p. 354. "We, that is the young generation of the great rejuvenated, unified Fatherland, want poetry to be again a sanctuary, a sacred place to which the nation goes on a pilgrimage, in order that it might in its innermost being drink of the spring of eternity and return refreshed, guided, and elevated back to the fulfillment of its human calling [...]".

26 See e. g. Daniel Fulda and Katherine Roper in their articles, p. 227 and pp. 171–94, passim, of this volume.

27 Lepenies: *Folgen einer unerhörten Begebenheit*, p. 35. See also Helmut Peitsch: "West German Reflections on the Role of the Writer in the light of Reactions to 9 November 1989." Williams et al., eds., *German Literature at a Time of Change 1989–1990*, pp. 154–86.

be seen later – it basically is a debate about (post)modern culture and cultural change.

The political role of a writer like Christa Wolf in the former GDR is commented on by Günter Grass in a letter, written to her in February 1993: "Nach meiner Einschätzung hättest Du die Kritik an jener Partei, in der Du Mitglied warst, deutlicher und fordernder aussprechen müssen, auch ohne Angst vor dem oft beschworenen Beifall von der falschen Seite."[28] But in this far more cultural than political debate political issues are often discussed by writers with considerable venom. Even a consciously political author like Günter Grass, carried away by anger, calls unification a "perversion of the constitution" ("Verfassungsbeugung"), although the Grundgesetz does *not* enforce a new constitution after unification has been accomplished; it only regulates what becomes of it *if* a new constitution comes into effect. Regine Hildebrand, the minister of social affairs in Brandenburg, does not dispute Grass's incorrect statement. He also, in using a pun on "Einheit" (meaning both unification and – in compounds – centralization), speaks of the new FRG as a "Einheitsstaat" (centralized state) and neglects the major federalist structures of the FRG.[29] The former GDR was far more centralistic than the FRG. 'Unification' today thus introduces the notion of a unified culture in a negative sense of cultural centralization. But the "new cultural agenda," as Karl-Heinz J. Schoeps called the consequence of the dispute about "Intellectuals, Unification, and Political Change,"[30] is only indirectly the offspring of unification.

Though "the GDR rested its claim to national identity on a moral rather than a legal or cultural basis,"[31] Günter Grass and others are concerned about the "cultural identity" ("Kulturidentität") of the writers and artists of the former GDR. Grass's sarcastic statement that such a thing as "cultural

---

28 Letter of February 9, 1993 – printed in Vinke, ed., *Akteneinsicht Christa Wolf. Zerrspiegel und Dialog. Eine Dokumentation*, pp. 302–04, here p. 302. "I thought you should have expressed your criticism of the party of which you have been a member much more clearly and more insistently and without any fear of that much-invoked applause from the wrong side."
29 Grass and Hildebrand: "Werden Sie Präsidentin, Regine!," p. 20. On the political issues of the German unification see the various essays in Becker, ed., *Wiedervereinigung in Mitteleuropa* (1992).
30 See Karl-Heinz J. Schoeps's contribution in this volume p. 273.
31 James J. Sheehan in his essay "National History and National Identity in the New Germany," p. 28 in this volume. See also the special issue of the *German Studies Review* on *German Identity*, ed. by Harold James. On the myth of the GDR as a 'Kulturnation' during its foundation see Winckler: "Kulturnation DDR – ein intellektueller Gründungsmythos." *Das Argonautenschiff* 1 (1992).

identity" cannot be found in the unification treaty between the two states intimates very delicate questions.[32] If culture is understood in a broader sense, the "cultural identity" of the individual cannot be separated from the forms of property, social order, family as well as economic relations; society and individual form an inseparable cultural unity;[33] there is, according to Talcott Parsons, no change of social structures without a cultural change.[34] In this respect the cultural identities of two opposing social systems cannot be preserved in a unifying process. A narrower notion of culture embraces both the tradition and the present condition of literature and the arts. Since the time of German idealism, since Kant and Wilhelm von Humboldt, Germans are accustomed to oppose (German) culture and (English or French) civilization, mostly excluding from this notion of culture the products of the 'homo faber.'[35] This narrow notion of culture originated in a growing cultural skepticism, and Günter Grass like many others obviously takes up this tradition.

However, the cultural identity of the former GDR writers is inconsistent with the concept of cultural unity (in the narrower sense) to which Germans from Schiller to Grass adhere.[36] Grass's claiming cultural identity for writers and artists of the former GDR contradicts his former enthusiastic advocacy of the idea of an indivisible German culture: "Einzig die Literatur (und ihr Unterfutter: Geschichte, Mythen, Schuld und andere Rückstände) überwölbt die beiden sich grämlich abgrenzenden Staaten. Laßt sie gegeneinander bestehen – sie können nicht anders –, doch zwingt ihnen, damit wir nicht weiterhin blöde im Regen stehen, dieses gemeinsame Dach, unsere nicht teilbare Kultur auf."[37] During the period of the GDR, the concept of a 'Kulturnation'

32　Grass: "Ein Schnäppchen namens DDR: Warnung vor Deutschland: Das Monstrum will Großmacht sein." *Die Zeit* No. 41, October 5, 1990, p. 50.

33　According to Ruth Benedict: *Patterns of Culture* (1934), quoted from Baumhauer: "Kulturwandel. Zur Entwicklung des Paradigmas von der Kultur als Kommunikationssystem," pp. 44 and 48.

34　Cf. ibid., p. 104.

35　Wilhelm Perpeet: "Kultur, Kulturphilosophie." Ritter and Gründer, eds., *Historisches Wörterbuch der Philosophie* vol. 4, cc. 1309–24, here c. 1318. Cf. also Perpeet: "Kulturphilosophie um die Jahrhundertwende." Brackert and Wefelmeyer, eds., *Naturplan und Verfallskritik: Zu Begriff und Geschichte der Kultur*, pp. 364–408, here pp. 365–78: "Die Kultur-Zivilisation-Antithese und die 'Große Stadt.'" See also Peter Gay: "Was ist Kultur?" Hardtwig and Brandt, eds., *Deutschlands Weg in die Moderne*, pp. 45–53, here pp. 46–7.

36　Cf. Grass: "Viel Gefühl, wenig Bewußtsein." *Der Spiegel* No. 47, November 20, 1989, p. 79, reprinted in Grass: *Lastenausgleich*, pp. 13–25, here p. 15: "I like to refer, rather, to Herder's notion of a cultural nation ('Kulturnation')."

37　Grass: "Kopfgeburten oder Die Deutschen sterben aus" – *Werkausgabe* vol. 6, pp. 141–20, here p. 250. "Literature alone (and, concealed within it, history, myths, guilt and other (cultural nation) was regarded by GDR officials and official writers as being directed against the new national identity of the GDR: any reference to a single nation linked by language or history, to a community linked by feeling and destiny was denounced as an expression of FRG-revanchism.[38] But in the years around 1800 Germany was looked upon not only as a 'Kulturnation,' but as a cultural nation with a specific open and cosmopolitan, a 'human' culture. In this respect the question of a specific cultural identity of the former GDR seems to be very doubtful: if culture is linked not with a specific state but with a specific tradition of national, or even European culture there is no need for a western or eastern cultural identity. Grass's ironic parody reducing Hoffmann von Fallersleben's appeal "Germany above everything" ("Deutschland über alles") to "Nothing but western art above everything" ("Nur noch Westkunst über alles")[39] describes the aims of some agents of the FRG cultural system and the (inevitable?) ruin of a culture after social and political change. Yet the very strong bonds between East and West German culture are being neglected.

If we look beyond German borders and consider French social cultural politics of recent years we find something that would cause serious trouble if it had occurred in Western Germany: Jack Lang had no difficulties in striving for an official *and* democratic culture, combining representational state functions, postmodern arbitrariness and leftist striving for power. He asked artists and intellectuals to identify themselves with the socialist government.[40] For German artists and writers such a mixture of state and culture would raise serious problems, because the borders between 'right' and 'left' seem to be blurred. German history and the abuse of national celebrations has made almost impossible a representational function for culture on the French model. The most striking example of cultural change and its democratization can be gained from a comparison of the two celebrations of German unity in

---

remnants of the past) bridged the two states that were bitterly building barriers against each other. Let each continue to exist – they cannot do otherwise –, but impose upon them the common roof, our indivisible culture, so that we are not caught in the rain."

38 Neubert: "Raub bei Schiller," p. 922 – cf. Grawe: "Schillers Gedichtentwurf 'Deutsche Größe'," p. 195. See also John S. Cornell's essay in this volume pp. 84 where he analyzes Fontane's position he "shared with many of his contemporaries": e. g. "a desire for a unified Germany, a belief in the civilizing mission of German culture." (Ibid., p. 102) Roger Chickering in his essay (pp. 61–78, here p. 78) investigates "the centrality of language in the history of radical nationalism during the Wilhelmine epoch."

39 Grass: "Ein Schnäppchen namens DDR: Warnung vor Deutschland: Das Monstrum will Großmacht sein." *Die Zeit* No. 41, October 5, 1990, p. 50.

40 Erwin K. Scheuch: "Kulturpolitik als Problem." Lieser-Triebnigg and Mampel, eds., *Kultur im geteilten Deutschland*, pp. 25–43, here p. 27.

1871 and 1990: the Foundation of the Reich in Versailles, where the nation was excluded, and the celebration or rather party of unification in October 1990 in front of the Reichstag and the Brandenburg Gate.[41]

Thus two issues have to be focussed here: the confrontation of a 'right' and a 'left' culture, and the question of the aesthetic and/or political intention and function of culture.

3. Aesthetics and Politics

Culture in the specific meaning discussed here and in the media since the 'Wende' always has been a phenomenon experienced by a minority ("Minderheitsphänomen"),[42] although since the Enlightenment a steady effort to democratize culture can be observed. Writers of the eighteenth century began to write for 'everyman,' consciously opposing the earlier poetics, which Sigmund von Birken expressed emphatically: "Wer für Herrn Omnis schreibt, / ist der Gelehrt zu nennen?"[43] The failure of the project of Enlightenment nurtured cultural movements against the uneducated 'Volk': Weimar classicism and romanticism were opposed to popular taste.[44] Gert Ueding has discussed the false German alternative which opposes popular literature and literature which follows classical ideals.[45] After 1870, as Eric J. Hobsbawm has emphasized, the belief in a "Kulturreligion"[46] was fostered by schools and universities[47], and the idealistic concept became dogmatized by the conservative German literary establishment.

---

41 Comparing feasts and celebrations on the one hand, and monuments or at least the attitudes towards old and new monuments before and after 1871 and 1990 is an interesting issue not treated in this volume; today socialist monuments especially in East Berlin are removed whereas historic monuments as the Berlin Stadtschloß (Hohenzollern palace) are to be rebuilt; see Sheehan, this volume p. 33. On National Monuments and National Celebrations see e. g. Hansen: *Nationaldenkmäler und Nationalfeste im 19. Jahrhundert.*

42 Eric J. Hobsbawm: "Kultur als Getto." Hoffmann, ed., *"Kulturzerstörung?"*, pp. 60–9, here p. 60.

43 Sigmund von Birken: *Teutsche Rede-bind- und Dichtkunst.* Nürnberg 1679, p. 165 – quoted from Barner: *Barockrhetorik*, p. 231. "He who writes for Mr. Everyman, might he be called learned?"

44 Cf. e. g. Terence James Reed: "Ecclesia militans: Weimarer Klassik als Opposition."

45 Ueding: "Massenware oder stille Kirche: Über falsche Alternativen in der deutschen Literatur." *Neue Rundschau* 104 (1993) H. 3: "Literatur im Abseits – und wie sie herauskommt", pp. 36–43. See also Volker Neuhaus's essay on Spielhagen in this volume pp. 135–43.

46 Stern: *The Politics of Cultural Despair*, p. xxv.

47 Eric J. Hobsbawm: "Kultur als Getto." Hoffmann, ed., *"Kulturzerstörung?"*, pp. 60–9, here p. 62.

When the lower classes tried to adopt the cultural values of the bourgeoisie the loss of function of the arts was already evident: the endeavors of the avantgarde in the years after 1910 were not only aimed at the destruction of traditional mimetic art, language and literature, but also at a new political and social order: But "the negation and sublation [...] of the bourgeois 'institution of art'" did not cause "the transformation of bourgeois society itself"[48] that was aimed at; the artistic principles of avantgarde and l'art-pour-l'art survived. Culture, especially modern literature and modern arts, were narrowed again by many critics into a sort of culture of and for the learned ("*gelehrte* Kultur")[49]. This mostly non-mimetic tradition of modern literature and art was and is opposed by the more popular notion of culture and literature which is not against a broader reading public that expects a sort of mental support and expression of a moral attitude. But some feuilleton-writers – e. g. Ulrich Greiner – deride aesthetics that are not pure and autonomous as "Gesinnungsästhetik" (aestheticized morality), claiming that FRG authors such as Heinrich Böll, Günter Grass, Siegfried Lenz, Erich Fried, Martin Walser, Hans Magnus Enzensberger, Peter Weiss, Heinar Kipphardt, Alfred Andersch use 'extraliterary themes' in their work.[50] These diversely engagé artists are answering public needs; modern and postmodern culture is increasingly alienated, Eric J. Hobsbawm argues, from what the majority expects from literature, culture and the arts – a concern with the problems of their own lives, whether as individuals or as a community.[51] Ten years before the present cultural debate Hobsbawm deplored the destruction of this Enlightenment tradition: thirst for culture (within the lower classes) was once a sign of hope, confidence, and liberation.[52] A great part of postmodern culture has renounced not only the moral and utopian focus of literature but also its social "function as a cultural memory."[53] Postmodern culture has become no more than an immanent semiotic system[54]; a literature

---

48 Huyssen: *After the Great Divide: Modernism, Mass Culture, Postmodernism*, p. 8.
49 Eric J. Hobsbawm: "Kultur als Getto." Hoffmann, ed., *"Kulturzerstörung?"*, pp. 60–9, here p. 66.
50 Greiner: "Die deutsche Gesinnungsästhetik. Noch einmal: Christa Wolf und der deutsche Literaturstreit. Eine Zwischenbilanz." Anz, ed., *"Es geht nicht um Christa Wolf"*, pp. 208–16, here p. 213. See also the contributions of Terence James Reed and Karl-Heinz Schoeps in this volume.
51 Eric J. Hobsbawm: "Kultur als Getto." Hoffmann, ed., *"Kulturzerstörung?"*, pp. 60–9, here p. 67.
52 Ibid., p. 68.
53 Michel Beaujour: "Memory in Poetics." Haverkamp, Lachmann, and Herzog, eds., *Memoria: Vergessen und Erinnern*, pp. 9–16, here p. 16.
54 Ihab Hassan: "Postmoderne heute." Welsch, ed., *Wege aus der Postmoderne*, pp. 47–56, here p. 55.

without "Gesinnungsästhetik" causes what Jean Baudrillard called "some sort of collective vertigo of neutralization."[55] Modern and postmodern literature, as the editors of a recent number of the *Neue Rundschau* complain, has assigned to the reader an unpromising role: his expectations are to be duped, irritated, exposed, and above all disappointed.[56] Likewise Raabe provoked those readers who after 1871 took "little pleasure in such literary manners and mannerisms."[57]

A great part of the former literature of the GDR followed more traditional aesthetics – although there has been a remarkable development of an artistic and literary avantgarde, as Philip Brady points out in his essay.[58] Yet many authors still believe in "motif and theme, symbol and message as well as in the historic claims of artistic form and in the social commitment of art."[59] Though aesthetic and political arguments are confused, the 'case of Christa Wolf'[60] is in essence part of a general cultural debate, in which the media seek to foster a kind of modern and postmodern arbitrariness. But literature seldom is made according to theories nor according to the latest fashion of the feuilleton.

Even in radical (post)modern aesthetics and arts, as Terence James Reed puts it, "'aesthetic' and 'political' cannot be set against each other because they cannot be neatly separated, either in acts of creation or in acts of judgement."[61] Whatever superficial and uncritical feuilleton-writers like Ulrich Greiner, the yuppies of postmodern aesthetics, criticize as 'extraliterary themes,' literary historians try to do more justice to every kind of literature in

---

55 Jean Baudrillard: "What Are You Doing After the Orgy?", p. 43.
56 Busch, Ruge, Wittstock: "Editorial." *Neue Rundschau* 104 (1993) H. 3: "Literatur im Abseits – und wie sie herauskommt", pp. 5–6, here p. 5. See also the other essays in this number, especially those of Ueding (cf. note 45) and Wittstock: "Ab in die Nische? Über neueste deutsche Literatur und was sie vom Publikum trennt."
57 See Meyer-Krentler's contribution in this volume, pp. 144–68.
58 Cf. this volume pp. 278–301; see also Muschter and Thomas, eds., *Jenseits der Staatskultur: Traditionen autonomer Kunst in der DDR*. For a revaluation of GDR literature see now Deiritz and Krauss, eds., *Verrat der Kunst? Rückblicke auf die DDR-Literatur*.
59 Grasskamp: "Die unästhetische Demokratie," p. 71.
60 Cf. Schoeps's essay in this volume pp. 251–77 and Reed: "Disconnections in the 1990 *Literaturstreit.*" – In June 1993 174 American scholars of German literature, culture, and history signed a declaration in favor of Christa Wolf, stressing the point that "DDR-Kultur schlechthin" (GDR-culture as such) as well as the achievements of the GDR in the emancipation of women were being impugned – see Zantop and Wilson: "Das Kind mit dem Bade: Amerikanische Germanisten solidarisieren sich mit Christa Wolf." *Die Zeit* No. 25, June 18, 1993, p. 56.
61 See the present volume p. 248.

the democratic aristocracy of the arts. These aesthetic *and* ethical aspects of literary intention and function might be labelled 'left' and 'right,' but the dominant tendency towards a conservative culture both among 'modernists,' postmodernists and leftist writers was not inaugurated by unification; since the seventies a "Tendenzwende"[62] (change of direction) affects all fields of cultural and political activity. But after unification and after the end of power-politics and of the confrontation between communism and capitalism this neo-conservatism has become influential on the literary scene.

East German writers like Christa Wolf never had illusions about the function of their works even within a socialist society and culture: as early as 1979 she admitted, though in a private letter: "[…] nur dürfen wir uns nicht länger selbst betrügen über unsere Lage als Intellektuelle, dürfen uns nicht vormachen, wir würden für andere arbeiten, für das 'Volk', die Arbeiterklasse: die liest uns nicht, das hat Gründe. Trotzdem bezahlt sie uns, letzten Endes, damit wir uns unsere innern (und äußern) Konflikte leisten können, die sie gar nichts angehen."[63] One would not have expected this frank confession from Christa Wolf, but we are not surprised to read Heiner Müller's antisocialist affirmation: "Kunst ist das Problem einer Minderheit."[64] Many of the former GDR writers are criticized today for their past privileges; but producing culture always has been either a privilege or a curse: Walter Muschg has argued that poverty and suffering (Armut und Leiden) are dominant for many writers[65], whilst Walter Benjamin has emphasized the privileges. The historian who surveys cultural assets ("Kulturgüter") is horrified when he remembers their origins; for what he perceives as cultural assets "dankt sein Dasein nicht nur der Mühe der großen Genien, die es geschaffen haben,

---

62 See e. g. Bohnen: "'Tendenzwende': Zu einer Kulturkontroverse der siebziger Jahre."
63 Christa Wolf quotes this letter in a letter to Günter Grass of March 21, 1993 – printed in Vinke, ed., *Akteneinsicht Christa Wolf. Zerrspiegel und Dialog. Eine Dokumentation*, p. 307. "[…] we should no longer delude ourselves concerning our situation as intellectuals, we should no longer pretend that we are working for others, for the people, for the working class: they do not read our books, for obvious reasons. Nevertheless they pay us, after all, so that we can afford our inner (and outer) conflicts, which are of no meaning to them." – On the role of the writers in the former GDR see also Lewis: "The Writers, Their Socialism, the People and Their Bad Table Manners: 1989 and the Crisis of East German Writers and Intellectuals." *German Studies Review* 15 (1992): 243–66. Lutz Winckler destroys the legend of the GDR as a 'Leseland' (reading country) or a 'Kulturnation', see Winckler: "Kulturnation DDR – ein intellektueller Gründungsmythos." *Das Argonautenschiff* 1 (1992).
64 Müller: "Die Reflexion ist am Ende, die Zukunft gehört der Kunst." Müller: *Jenseits der Nation*, pp. 89–101, here p. 90. "Art is the problem of a minority."
65 Muschg: *Tragische Literaturgeschichte*, pp. 356–441.

sondern auch der namenlosen Fron ihrer Zeitgenossen. Es ist niemals ein Dokument der Kultur, ohne zugleich ein solches der Barbarei zu sein."[66] The same applies to the former GDR and its art.

4. "Progress, Perhaps the Greatest Delusion"

> In der That muß es Nachdenken erregen, daß man beynahe in jeder Epoche der Geschichte, wo die Künste blühen und der Geschmack regiert, die Menschheit gesunken findet und auch nicht ein einziges Beyspiel aufweisen kann, daß ein hoher Grad und eine große Allgemeinheit ästhetischer Kultur bei einem Volke mit politischer Freyheit, und bürgerlicher Tugend, daß schöne Sitten mit guten Sitten, und Politur des Betragens mit Wahrheit desselben Hand in Hand gegangen wäre.[67]

Schiller's cultural skepticism, often overlooked, is given a positive twist in his teleology of history that aims at the final union of culture and freedom. He transforms Rousseau's cultural pessimism of the first discourse[68] into a general principle trying to save the idea of Enlightenment and freedom: "*Ruhe* ist die Bedingung der Kultur, aber nichts ist der Freiheit gefährlicher als Ruhe." Tranquillity mainly was achieved by despotism; if modern times attempt to unite culture and freedom it has to be accomplished differently – by law, "und diese kann der noch freie Mensch nur sich selber geben."[69]

The asymmetrical development of state and culture within a state is relevant to any discussion of GDR and FRG culture and cultural changes after

---

66 Benjamin: "Über den Begriff der Geschichte" – *Gesammelte Schriften* vol. 1, 2, pp. 691–704, here p. 696 (VII). "[…] owe their existence not only to the endeavors of great geniuses who have created them, but also to the anonymous slavery of their contemporaries. There is no document of culture which is not at the same time a document of barbarism."

67 Schiller: "Über die ästhetische Erziehung des Menschen in einer Reihe von Briefen." 10. Brief. *Werke* (Nationalausgabe) vol. 20, pp. 309–412, here p. 339. " One is forced to ponder the fact that in almost every epoch of history where the arts flourish and taste reigns we find humanity in decline and can give no single example where in a people a high degree and a general breadth of aesthetic culture go together with political freedom and civic virtue, where beautiful customs go together with good customs and cultivated manners go together with truth."

68 "[…] mais ici l'effet est certain, la dépravation réelle, et nos âmes se sont corrompues à mesure que nos sciences et nos arts se sont avancés à la perfection." Rousseau: "Discours sur les sciences et les arts." Rousseau: *Schriften zur Kulturkritik*, pp. 1–59, here p. 14.

69 Schiller: "Universalhistorische Übersicht der vornehmsten an den Kreuzzügen teilnehmenden Nationen …" – *Sämtliche Werke* vol. 4, pp. 843–63, here p. 850 (note). "Tranquillity is the precondition of culture but nothing more imperils freedom than tranquillity." – "man still free can give only to himself."

unification. In an interview of May 1993 Heiner Müller was asked: "Wieviel Diktatur brauchen Sie denn zum Schreiben?" And Müller answered:

> Ich brauche gar keine Diktatur; es ging ja gar nicht um mich, es ging um Theater und für Theater ist die Diktatur auf jeden Fall eine bessere Folie. Das sieht man jetzt überall. Keiner weiß mehr, wozu Theater überhaupt noch gut ist. Mein französischer Übersetzer Jean Jourdheul meinte, auch in Frankreich gäbe es diese Lähmung. Er hatte ein simples Schema. Er sagte, früher habe es ein Dreieck gegeben: Die Macht, das Theater und das Publikum. Die Macht ist weggefallen. Jetzt gibt es nur noch Markt.[70]

Totalitarian tranquillity secures the social function of literature as well as it provides the impediments and obstacles a writer needs: "Durch die Zensur in der DDR mußte sich die Phantasie, das Schreiben an äußeren Widerständen abarbeiten. Dadurch entstanden sehr komplexe Texte." Arguing like this seems deliberately naïve: there are other obstacles for writers than censorship, and the only alternative in a society free from censorship, of course, is not Konsalik (the most successful German novelist) as Müller implies.[71] Schiller considers tranquillity guaranteed either by despotism or law as indispensable for culture, Müller looks for nothing but impediments against which art is produced. The dialectical correlation of state and culture, for Schiller a teleological concept of human progress has turned for Müller into nothing but a mechanism to improve the artistic qualities of cultural products. But Schiller is concerned not only with censorship: looking back in history he finds that a high degree of aesthetic culture ("schöne Sitten") is normally opposed by a lack of moral culture ("gute Sitten"). This applies also to literature and literary criticism after unification.

---

70 Müller: "'Es gibt ein Menschenrecht auf Feigheit': Ein Gespräch mit dem Dramatiker Heiner Müller über seine Kontakte mit der Staatssicherheit." *Frankfurter Rundschau*, May 22, 1993, p. ZB 3. "How much dictatorship do you need to write?" – "I myself don't need any dictatorship; it was not a question of me, it was a question of theater and for theater dictatorship always is a better context. You can observe this everywhere. Nobody knows any longer what theater is good for. My French translator Jean Jourdheul believed that there is the same paralysis in France. He said that there used to be a triad of state-power, theater, and public. The state-power has vanished. Now only the market is left."

71 Müller: "Die Reflexion ist am Ende, die Zukunft gehört der Kunst." Müller: *Jenseits der Nation*, pp. 89–101, here pp. 95 and 96. "Censorship in the GDR forced the imagination, forced literature to work against external opposition. Thus very complex texts were created." Friedrich Dieckmann also discusses the problem of censorship and aesthetic quality, questioning the reverse conclusion that censorship fosters the growth of outstanding art: Dieckmann: "Kulturaustausch." *Neue deutsche Literatur* 39, No. 457 (1991), p. 39.

Western culture on the other hand was and is criticized by Heiner Müller and others for its "Americanization" and "computerization."[72] Richard Herzinger has traced socialist criticism of western culture both to conservative cultural criticism and to socialist utopian thinking: civilization and capitalist economics are equated[73]. Friedrich Engels, influenced by Charles Fourier, denounced civilization as advanced by nothing but "platte Habgier" ("plain greed"), the heyday of art ("die höchste Blüte der Kunst") being nothing but a by-product of scientific civilization.[74] In his recent poem, "Mommsens Block," published in late spring 1993, Heiner Müller juxtaposes Nero's Rome, Bismarck's Empire, and Germany after 1990, taking his starting point from the fact that Mommsen did not write the fourth volume of his "Roman History" which was to deal with the time of the Roman Emperors. The 'narrator' understands Mommsen's writer's block[75] when listening to two heroes of modern times ("Helden der Neuzeit"), "lemurs of capital, money-changers and traders" ("Lemuren des Kapitals Wechsler und Händler")[76]. The lemurs – perhaps an allusion to the lemurs in Goethe's *Faust II* (vv. 11515–22, 11531–38, 11604–11) or, more generally, the souls of the deceased – feed the listener with a "nausea at the Here and Now" ("Ekel am Heute und Hier").[77] The poem seems to identify indirectly Mommsen's writing block vis à vis Nero's dictatorship with Müller's own writing block vis à vis west German (dead?) capitalism; and it draws explicit parallels between Mommsen (who welcomed Bismarck's unification enthusiastically, but opposed his politics after 1878) and Müller himself (or the narrator of "Mommsen's block"), who opposes western civilization and economics: "Wissend der ungeschriebne Text ist eine Wunde / Aus der das Blut geht das kein Nachruhm stillt / Und die klaffende Lücke in Ihrem Geschichtswerk / War ein Schmerz in meinem wie lange noch atmenden Körper."[78] Despite Müller's obvious "denunciation

---

72 Heiner Müller: Interview 1986 – quoted from Herzinger: "Die obskuren Inseln der kultivierten Gemeinschaft: Heiner Müller, Christa Wolf, Volker Braun – deutsche Zivilisationskritik und das deutsche Antiwestlertum." *Die Zeit* No. 23, June 4, 1993, p. L 8. See also Herzinger: *Masken der Lebensrevolution: Vitalistische Zivilisations- und Humanismuskritik in Texten Heiner Müllers*.
73 Ibid., p. 97.
74 Engels: "Der Ursprung der Familie, des Privateigentums und des Staats" (1884). Marx/Engels: *Werke* vol. 21, pp. 25–173, here p. 171 (chapter: "Barbarei und Zivilisation").
75 Müller: "Mommsens Block," p. 9.
76 Herzinger in a review of this text points out the christian-antisemitic term "Wechsler" – Herzinger: "Naturschützer im Reich der Transsubstantiation: Zur literaturtheoretischen Einhegung ehemaliger DDR-Schriftsteller." *Frankfurter Rundschau* No. 137, June 17, 1993.
77 Müller: "Mommsens Block," p. 8.
78 Ibid., p. 9. "Knowing the unwritten text is a wound / From which blood is running that

of the West in terms of conservative German cultural criticism,"[79] the pain caused by the unwritten text makes this poem a symbolic and suggestive comment on both unifications and their cultural wounds.

Not only in Heiner Müller but also in Christa Wolf or Volker Braun a criticism of civilization has been observed[80], a socialism suffused with right-wing conservatism. The awkward simplicity of 'right' opposing 'left' certainly cannot be applied either to literature or to theoretical comments. Müller is right in pointing out that the 'right' ("die Rechte") is no unicolored matter; and he is right in referring to Walter Benjamin, for whom revolution did not mean accelerating history but applying the emergency brake[81] – re-volution.

A criticism of civilization that mixes utopian and conservative elements is not uniquely German, but it became prominent after the first German unification. Engels, as we saw, referred to Charles Fourier, and Benjamin likewise criticized the concept of progress by recalling the French utopian socialist.[82] In 1876 Dostojéwski saw western revolutionaries opposing western civilization in silent league with Russian conservatives.[83] As mentioned above, unification and the foundation of the Reich produced a serious crisis of identity; economic and political unity did not produce a cultural identity. The earlier progressive idea of a *whole* cultural nation advanced by many critics of the Bismarck Reich was abandoned because unification once achieved revealed quite a different image: Stefan Breuer in his *Anatomie der konservativen Revolution* quotes from Wilhelm Windelband's 1878 lecture on Hölderlin:

> Die Kultur ist zu breit geworden, um vom Standpunkt des Individuums aus übersehen zu werden […]. Das Bewußtsein des einheitlichen Zusammenhanges,

---

cannot be staunched by posthumous fame / And the gaping break in your work of history / Was a pain in my body breathing – who knows how long."

79 Herzinger: "Naturschützer im Reich der Transsubstantiation: Zur literaturtheoretischen Einhegung ehemaliger DDR-Schriftsteller." *Frankfurter Rundschau* No. 137, June 17, 1993.
80 Herzinger: "Die obskuren Inseln der kultivierten Gemeinschaft: Heiner Müller, Christa Wolf, Volker Braun – deutsche Zivilisationskritik und das deutsche Antiwestlertum." *Die Zeit* No. 23, June 4, 1993, p. L 8.
81 Müller: "'Es gibt ein Menschenrecht auf Feigheit': Ein Gespräch mit dem Dramatiker Heiner Müller über seine Kontakte mit der Staatssicherheit." *Frankfurter Rundschau*, May 22, 1993, p. ZB 3.
82 Benjamin: "Über den Begriff der Geschichte" – *Gesammelte Schriften* vol. 1, 2, pp. 691–704, here p. 700–01 (XII–XIII).
83 Dostojéwski: "Mein Paradox" (1876) – quoted from R. Konersmann: "Revolution, konservative." Ritter and Gründer, eds., *Historisches Wörterbuch der Philosophie* vol. 8, cc. 978–88, here c. 979.

der alles Kulturleben beherrschen soll, geht Schritt für Schritt verloren und die Gesellschaft droht in Gruppen und Atome zu zerfallen [...]. So wird die moderne Gesellschaft mehr und mehr zu einem Bilde der Zerrissenheit, und je schneller dieser Prozeß mit natürlicher Notwendigkeit fortschreitet, um so geringer wird selbstverständlich die Kraft der gesellschaftlichen Ordnung, deren festeste Stütze die Gleichheit des Kulturbewußtseins in den Individuen bildet.[84]

Yet forty-five years later Hugo von Hofmannsthal still dreamt the dream of culture creating "eine neue deutsche Wirklichkeit, an der die ganze Nation teilnehmen könnte," referring to the literature of the French as a model.[85]

German unification and the alleged (or actual) destruction of GDR culture as the only German culture that could (and must) withstand the disintegration and arbitrariness of western mass culture (the roots of which in Nietzsche's cultural criticism[86] should not be overlooked) has not yet initiated a process of actual cultural change but has prompted a reappraisal of cultural values. Public discussion has confused both criteria and values and demonstrated the self-righteousness and arrogance underlying much cultural journalism. If the discussion is carried on in a productive and non-antagonistic manner, the aftermath might be a positive new cultural agenda where memory confirms progress not to be "perhaps the greatest delusion,"[87] but unveils erroneous notions of progress. Likewise in 1956 Walter Muschg deplored the 'destruction of German literature,' not only as a result of Nazism, but by the "collective obtuseness that fancies itself to be progress."[88]

'Mass culture' has been called the agent provocateur of post-modernism;[89] one of the most prominent writers of the old FRG, Botho Strauß, in a highly

---

84 Windelband: "Über Friedrich Hölderlin und sein Geschick," pp. 254–55, quoted in Breuer: *Anatomie der konservativen Revolution*, p. 20. "The realm of culture has grown too large to be surveyed from the standpoint of an individual [...]. The consciousness of a coherence that should dominate all cultural life is gradually lost and society threatens to fall apart into groups and atoms [...]. Thus modern society more and more becomes an image of inner conflicts, and the faster this inescapable process becomes, the more the power of social order diminishes, the strongest support of which is formed by the cultural consciousness shared by all individuals."
85 Hofmannsthal: "Das Schrifttum als geistiger Raum der Nation" – *Gesammelte Werke* vol. [10]: Reden und Aufsätze III, pp. 24–41, here pp. 41, 27. "a new German reality in which the whole nation could take part."
86 Cf. e. g. Krenzlin, ed., *Zwischen Angstmetapher und Terminus: Theorien der Massenkultur seit Nietzsche*.
87 Ball: *Flucht aus der Zeit*, p. 213 (entry 19 April 1918).
88 Muschg: "Die Zerstörung der deutschen Literatur." Muschg: *Die Zerstörung der deutschen Literatur*, pp. 19–56, here p. 39.
89 Norbert Krenzlin: "'Massenkultur' – ein Agent provocateur der Postmoderne." Krenzlin, ed., *Zwischen Angstmetapher und Terminus: Theorien der Massenkultur seit Nietzsche*, pp. 149–64.

controversial essay of February 1993 fiercely castigates "Demokratismus," unlimited dominance of the present ("Totalherrschaft der Gegenwart"), a leftist "cultural majority," and "electronic show business" ("elektronisches Schaugewerbe").[90] Even in his neo-romantic epistemological and poetological essay *Beginnlosigkeit* Strauß cannot refrain from cultural criticism: The German people no longer have any inherent qualities: "Es ist nichts als ein launiger, bequemer Mehrheitspotentat. Ein Auslöscher jeder, aber auch jeder ideellen Kraft. Es spricht nur noch aus Faulheit deutsch, die meisten seiner Regungen und Interessen ließen sich besser auf Amerikanisch ausdrücken."[91] Though Strauß, like artists during the Wilhelminian Empire, also pleads for "courage to secede" ("Mut zur Sezession") and for a turning away from the mainstream ("Abkehr vom Mainstream")[92], his kind of solitary anti-mass-culture with no other perspective than the loner and outsider ("Einzelgänger" and "Außenseiter") clinging to an "unenlightened past" ("unaufgeklärte Vergangenheit"), "historic growth" ("geschichtliches Gewordensein"), and "mythic time" ("mythische Zeit")[93] reveals a sort of intellectual Biedermeier. The obscurity of his essay reflects an (involuntary) intention to murder the German language. Longing for the absence of the present, affecting hofmannsthalian and heideggerian discourse, will not be the chief consequence of unification, but it will be its most characteristic.

5. "The Principle of Hope"

East German literature has for long been part of West German culture: Jurek Becker, Thomas Brasch, Volker Braun, Johannes Bobrowski, Günter de Bruyn, Jürgen Fuchs, Franz Fühmann, Peter Huchel, Hermann Kant, Sarah Kirsch, Günter Kunert, Reiner Kunze, Heiner Müller, Ulrich Plenzdorf, Anna Seghers, Christa Wolf have been part of West German curricula for decades.[94]

---

90 Strauß: "Anschwellender Bocksgesang." *Der Spiegel* 47 (1993) No. 36, February 8, pp. 202–07.
91 Strauß: *Beginnlosigkeit*, p. 122. "They are nothing but a moody, indolent majority. They extinguish every – absolutely every – spiritual energy. They still speak German only out of pure laziness, most of their feelings and interests could be expressed better in American."
92 Strauß: "Anschwellender Bocksgesang." *Der Spiegel* 47 (1993) No. 36, February 8, p. 206.
93 Ibid., p. 204.
94 Cf. Karl Corino: "Vor und nach der Wende: Die Rezeption der DDR-Literatur in der Bundesrepublik und das Problem einer einheitlichen deutschen Literatur." *Neue deutsche Literatur* 39, No. 464 (1991), pp. 146–64, here pp. 148–49. The essay was a contribution to "Überlebenschancen? Die berufliche und soziale Situation der Schriftsteller und die Existenzbedingungen der Literatur in den neuen Bundesländern – Bestandsaufnahme eines

The function of both a large part of West German and East German writers still will be, as Terence James Reed, quoting Heiner Müller, asserts in his essay, "to preserve literature as what it was in the GDR, 'the only place for Utopia.'"[95] Postmodern thinking denounces historic change and believes in the "clôture" (Derrida) of the historic quest for truth.[96] The somewhat arrogant belief in the end of history and the beginning of simulation (Jean Baudrillard) was opposed by Francis Fukuyama's optimistic declaration of the end of history (1989) as the termination of opposing ideological systems and the victory of liberal democracy. Actual political developments reveal that both the notions of 'posthistoire' and of the end of history suggest nothing but the intellectuals' perplexity vis à vis their own theories, or, as Heiner Müller puts it, vis à vis the unsolved Third World problems: "das Ende der Geschichte ist ein Wunschtraum saturierter Eliten."[97] The hope in human progress may be a delusion, but a necessary one.

When Gustav Aschenbach's longing for Tadzio reaches its peak, the narrator comments with sympathetic irony: "Sehnsucht ist ein Erzeugnis mangelhafter Erkenntnis."[98] "Longing for the GDR?" ("Sehnsucht nach der DDR?") was a question *Die Zeit* put to nine East German authors (Klaus Schlesinger, Monika Maron, Friedrich Dieckmann, Hermann Kant, Erich Loest, Adolf Endler, Günter Kunert, Jens Sparschuh and Heinz Czechowski). Some of the answers to this question obscure aesthetic and political issues; but most authors discuss nostalgia about the political past.[99] Important new literary works, however, which represent real or potential worlds, even in the negative, can be written only in a detached mood, at an aesthetic distance. Erich Loest in one of his fictitious post-wall monologues has a "Verdienter Lehrer des Volkes," who at the age of seventeen had entered the "Waffen-SS" and now suffers deeply from the rift within himself, imagine a socialist unification:

---

gesellschaftlichen Problems –. Symposion der Deutschen Literaturkonferenz, Leipzig, 24. und 25. April 1991."
95 Heiner Müller: "Was wird aus dem größeren Deutschland?" *Sinn und Form* 43 (1991), p. 667. See page 249 in this volume.
96 Derrida: *Grammatologie*, p. 169. For a detailed discussion of the postmodern notion of the 'end of history' and the end of innovation and change see Groys: *Über das Neue*, esp. pp. 9–20.
97 Heiner Müller: "Bautzen oder Babylon." *Sinn und Form* 43 (1991), p. 664. "the end of history is nothing but the dream of satiated elites." See also Reed's essay, p. 249, not. 39.
98 Mann: "Der Tod in Venedig" – *Frühe Erzählungen*, pp. 55–64, here p. 612. "Longing is a product of insufficient knowledge."
99 Die Zeit No. 23, June 4, 1993, suppl. "Literatur", pp. 1–2, 4–8. For a harsh comment on the nostalgia of former GDR intellectuals see Gann: "German Unification and the Left-Wing Intelligentsia: A Response." *German Studies Review* 15 (1992): 99–110.

> Manchmal denke ich: Wenn es nun, wie es immer hieß, *gesetzmäßig* verlaufen wäre, wenn der Sozialismus gesiegt hätte und der Kapitalismus verfault wäre, wenn wir, die Sieger der Geschichte, wie wir uns immerfort genannt haben, in die zusammengebrochene Bundesrepublik einmarschiert wären, ob wir dann wohl auf Internierungslager verzichtet hätten. Wir marxistisch-leninistischen Revolutionäre wußten doch, daß man den bürgerlichen Staatsapparat zerschlagen müsse. Parteiführer, Generäle, Millionäre und Wirtschaftshäuptlinge hätten wir hinter Stacheldraht gebracht, ebenso Emigranten, sicherlich auch Sarah Kirsch, die Verräterin, Edzard Reuter von Daimler und Weizsäcker und Lafontaine und Grass und meinen Sohn Hartmut, und dann hätten wir alles mit unseren Leuten sozialistisch aufgebaut. Macht sich kaum einer bewußt, hier nicht und drüben nicht. Wäre ein verblüffendes Argument, wenn hier jemand jammert, daß uns die Westdeutschen übern Tisch ziehen.[100]

Ultimately, as the essays in the present volume show, literature after both unifications *can* prove to be valuable as an act of remembering and as an expression of hope. In spite of postmodern talk and although it seems to be quite out of fashion, one must quote two of the defenders of human hope: according to Herbert Marcuse, memory is the critical yardstick of social change, while according to Ernst Bloch memory is "Mahnung" (warning, re-minding) and "Hoffnung" (hope).[101] Christa Wolf's poem "Prinzip Hoffnung" (The Principle of Hope) evokes the painful dialectic between hope and the past: "Genagelt / ans Kreuz Vergangenheit."[102] The present interest in cultural history and cultural science confirms the important function of the arts as a vehicle for cultural memory, to which this new series, "European Cultures," aims to contribute.

---

100 Loest: "Ich hab' noch nie Champagner getrunken." Loest: *Heute kommt Westbesuch*, pp. 35–64, here p. 40. "Sometimes, I think: if everything had gone according to what they always called the law of history, if socialism had been victorious and capitalism rotted away, if the victors of history, as we have always called ourselves, had marched into the collapsed FRG, we would have done it without internment camps. But we Marxist-Leninist revolutionaries knew that we had to smash the bourgeois state machinery. Party-leaders, generals, millionaires, and captains of industry all would have been brought behind barbed wire, as well as emigrants, surely Sarah Kirsch too, the traitor, Edzard Reuter of Daimler and Weizsäcker and Lafontaine and Grass and my son Hartmut, and then we would have built up everything in socialist fashion with our people. Nobody seems to be aware of this, neither over here nor over there. The idea would perplex anybody complaining that the West Germans had got the upper hand over us."
101 Marcuse: *Triebstruktur und Gesellschaft (Eros and Civilization)*, p. 25; Bloch: *Das Prinzip Hoffnung* chap. 13, pp. 278–85. See also Hans Mayer's distinction between 'hope' and 'utopia' – Mayer: "Nachdenken über Kultur im heutigen Deutschland." *Neue deutsche Literatur* 40, No. 471 (1992), p. 90.
102 Wolf: "Nagelprobe," p. 44. "Nailed / to the cross of the past." See Schoeps's discussion of this poem in the present volume pp. 268–69.

History, Education, Language,
and National Identity

JAMES J. SHEEHAN
Stanford University

National History and National Identity in the New Germany[1]

Abstract: This essay considers the problem of national identity with particular reference to the German experience, before and after the unification of 1989–90. It raises the question of how this new nation will develop a national history to match its past and meet its future.

In the late afternoon of June 16, 1904, Leopold Bloom, a small businessman of Jewish extraction, dropped into Barney Kiernan's public house in search of some light refreshment. Not surprisingly in an establishment of this sort in Dublin, the talk was of politics; it was led by a sinister, one-eyed man known as "The Citizen," who extolled the virtues of Ireland and the villainy of Britain in a style best imagined after several pints of Guinness. Into this overheated atmosphere Bloom brought an unwelcome hint of reason and good sense:

– Persecution, says he, all the history of the world is full of it. Perpetuating national hatred among nations.
– But do you know what a nation means? says John Wyse.
– Yes, says Bloom.
– What is it, says John Wyse.
– A nation? says Bloom. A nation is the same people living in the same place.
– By god, then, says Ned [one of the denizens of the pub], laughing, if that's so I'm a nation for I'm living in the same place for the past five years.

---

1 This essay was first written as an address to the German Studies Association annual meeting in Los Angeles, September 1991 and was published in the *German Studies Review*, *Special Issue "German Identity"*, Winter 1992, pp. 163–74. An earlier version was published as "Zukünftige Vergangenheit. Das deutsche Geschichtsbild in den neunziger Jahren." For some different reflections on "the future of the German past," formulated before unification, see "German Histories: Challenges in Theory, Practice, Technique," *Central European History* 20 (1989), pp. 227–459, a special issue edited by Michael Geyer and Konrad Jarausch.

So of course everyone had the laugh at Bloom and says he, trying to muck out of it:

– Or living in different places.
– That covers my case, says Joe.
– What is your nation if I may ask? says the citizen.
– Ireland, says Bloom. I was born here. Ireland.

To which the citizen responds by spitting onto the floor, an action described with a vividness that has no place in a scholarly journal.[2]

I begin with this passage from Chapter 12 – the so-called Cyclops episode – of *Ulysses* not only because it reminds us that problems of national identity are by no means peculiarly German, but also because I think Joyce provides us with a useful typology of the definitions of nationhood.

The first – and it is the one to which Bloom, a sensible man, is instinctively drawn – is a legal, objective definition: A nation is composed of those living in a particular state. But Bloom, like so many sensible people, is easily shaken by those less sensible than he. Moreover, his initial definition, which seemed to him so reasonable, does not quite fit the groups he himself represents: neither the Jews nor the Irish then had a state of their own, both were in different ways peoples of a diaspora. He moves, therefore, to a second definition, which is subjective and cultural: A nation is composed of those living in different places, but believing somehow that they belong together. If the legal definition is best described in the third person – "he or she belongs," this cultural definition is best asserted in the first person – "I belong." Appropriately enough, the Citizen – whose one eye is supposed to alert us to his fanatical vision – introduces a third definition, which is normative and prescriptive. In this definition, legal residence and cultural identity are not enough; one must also possess certain characteristics – moral, ideological, perhaps racial – that qualify for membership. This definition is prescribed in the second person: you do – or as the Citizen implies in Bloom's case – you do not belong.

The development of most modern nationalisms can be seen as the prolonged effort to fuse these three definitions, that is, the prolonged effort to create a state that would contain all those who could and should be members. National history plays a central role in this process: states as legal entities can, at least in theory, exist without a past; but national cultures and, even more insistently, national norms require historical definition, justification, and

---

2 Joyce: *Ulysses*, pp. 271–72.

defense. As we should expect, the air in Barney Kiernan's was as thick with history as it was with the smell of beer.³

This interaction of history and nationalism had a special place in the German world. As Isaiah Berlin pointed out in his splendid essay on Herder, the very language of nationality was invented by Germans in the eighteenth century. Other scholars have shown how this language shaped Germans' search for nationhood in the nineteenth century and how, after the nation was created, normative definitions of nationalism were used as a political weapon, to weaken, isolate, and eventually to destroy those who were regarded as not being "really German." I mention these familiar facts because they provide the essential backdrop to the main subjects of this essay: first, the deeply problematic relationship between history and identity in the two German states in the postwar period, and second, the future of that relationship now that these two states have, once again, become a single nation.⁴

* * *

In all three meanings of *nation*, 1945 was catastrophic for Germans' national existence. The total defeat and unconditional surrender of the Nazi regime brought the German state to an end as a legal entity; the massive upheavals and population movements that had resulted from the expansion and then the contraction of German power shattered the social and political basis of German culture throughout central and eastern Europe; and finally, the extraordinary crimes committed by Germans and their allies obliterated those claims to moral and cultural superiority which had always been part of German national rhetoric. As a political, cultural, and moral entity, the nation created in 1871 was in ruins. If, as one historian had proclaimed in the 1920s, "Either we have Bismarck's Germany or no Germany at all – Kleindeutschland or Keindeutschland," then German history in 1945 had come to a stop.⁵ And there were those who suggested that it had – in the immediate postwar

---

3 My views on national identity have been especially informed by Ernest Gellner: *Nations and Nationalism* and Benedict Anderson: *Imagined Communities*.
4 I have struggled with the relationship between history and identity in two previous essays: "What is German History?" and "The Problem of the Nation in German History." I attempted to rethink some of these ideas in the middle of the unification process in "Die immer gleiche Geschichte von Verstimmung und Enttäuschung. Der Einigungsprozeß endet nicht mit der (Neube-)gründung einer Nation." *Frankfurter Rundschau* No. 61, March 13, 1990, p. 11, reprinted in Wengst, ed., *Historiker betrachten Deutschland*, pp. 58–61.
5 Erich Marcks, as quoted in Faulenbach: *Ideologie des deutschen Weges*, p. 69

years, some Germans referred to the "loss of history" by which they meant a fundamental break between past and present.

And yet such breaks are impossible: neither individuals nor groups can sever their connections to the past. History does not stop, the power of memory cannot be denied, the search for identity goes on: and, as we all know, this was especially the case in postwar Germany, where one came upon – I am tempted to say, stumbled over – the past again and again, not only in novels and films, but in the lives of everyone one met. The lines of continuity between present and past may often have been obscure, but the past was always powerfully present.

Both of the states built on and from the ruins of the Reich had to create their political, cultural, and moral identities under the shadow of this everpresent past. As we should expect, the German Democratic Republic and the Federal Republic chose very different ways of dealing with the painful legacies of their common history.

Officially, the GDR presented itself as the heir not of German history as a whole, but of its progressive forces, forces that had always resisted the counter forces of reaction and repression. In other words, the GDR rested its claim to national identity on a moral rather than legal or cultural basis. On this moral basis, which had its social location in the working class and its political instrument in the SED, a new, democratic Germany could be built. An essential expression of this moral claim was anti-fascism, which served to distance the regime from the German past and to empower its attacks on those allies and heirs of fascism who continued to flourish in the West.

One got a fine sense of this view of German history in the old Museum for German History whose exhibits once occupied the Zeughaus in East Berlin. These exhibits began with the first human settlements on German soil and continued to the present. In the early sections, the emphasis was on changing modes of production, the driving forces of historical change. Increasingly, one saw the progressives forces at work: the Protestant reformers – especially radical reformers like Thomas Münzer – peasant rebels, German Jacobins, the labor movement, and of course, the German Communist Party. In contrast to the powerful continuities that linked these exhibits, the section on the period 1933–1945 was oddly incomplete and fragmentary. The Nazis, who appear as the tools of capitalists and militarists, were treated very sketchily – there was little about the social basis of the movement, its popular support, or even the full implications of its repression and brutality. Instead, there was a great deal about the Communist resistance and the liberating Soviet army, the two forces upon which the GDR was built. It would have been very difficult to come away from this exhibition with the knowledge that German "fascism" was passively tolerated by an overwhelming majority of the German population and ardently supported by a significant minority.

The political power and historical weakness of the GDR's concept of fascism were joined at the root: anti-fascism may have been an effective way to solidify an international alliance of communist states against an international coalition of fascists and capitalists, but it was not much use in trying to understand the distinctively German features of National Socialism. And this failure in historical understanding left a perplexing gap between the GDR and the national past.[6]

As long as the GDR hoped to be the core of a united Germany, its view of German history was negative and narrowly moralistic. By the end of the 1960s, however, these hopes had been replaced by the need to create a separate, socialist state. One result of this was a somewhat more positive view of German history. The definition of what might count as a "progressive" historical force became rather more spacious: some historical buildings were restored, Frederick the Great's statue returned to Unter den Linden, the Luther Jahr was duly celebrated. Nevertheless, the GDR's relationship to the German past remained largely negative, its continuity with German historical identity, uneven and problematic. Increasingly, the leaders of the GDR seemed to have recognized that its historical identity would have to be created from its own history as an independent state: we see evidence of this in a series of scholarly projects and, ironically enough, in the carefully arranged celebrations of the state's fortieth anniversary, which took place in the fall of 1989. That the GDR had failed to create a convincing historical identity became painfully apparent even before the echoes of this celebration had died away.[7]

The Federal Republic's relationship to German history was no less problematic, but it was problematic in a different way. West Germany both was and was not the heir of the nation created in 1871. On the one hand, the Bonn government presented itself as the only legitimate successor to the German nation state: as its Preamble makes clear, the Republic's Basic Law was promulgated for the entire German Volk, including those who could not participate. Article 116 explicitly denied Leopold Bloom's first definition of nation: citizenship in the Federal Republic was not limited to those within its own borders, but was granted to anyone who had been a citizen of the Germany of 31 December 1937 – and to their descendants. This made Germany

---

6   See Jarausch: "The Failure of East German Anti-Fascism."
7   Compare Geyer: "Die DDR auf dem Weg zu einer eigenen historischen Identität? DDR-Geschichte und Geschichtswissenschaft zwischen Ost und West," and the essays in Jarausch, ed., *Zwischen Parteilichkeit und Professionalität*.

into a diaspora nation by including those – as Bloom put it – "living in another place." On the other hand, however, the Federal Republic represented a new beginning, a dramatic break with those values and traditions that had culminated in the Nazi catastrophe. As a German state, the republic continued national history, while as a member of the European community, a partner in the NATO alliance, and a successful democracy, it was a new Germany, freed from the burdens of the past.

Once again, a museum – or rather museum plans – will help us to see the shape of the official version of the past. As you will recall, four years ago, Germans debated whether or not there should be a museum of German history in Berlin – a western equivalent of the Zeughaus exhibitions I mentioned a moment ago. At the same time, plans were underway for a historical museum to be devoted to the Federal Republic, which was to be in Bonn and was not to be called a museum but rather a "House of History" – presumably for the same reasons that the West German constitution is called a "basic law" rather than a constitution. The coexistence of these two museums suggests the gap that continued to separate the Federal Republic and the German past, a past over which Bonn was prepared to act as a kind of executor: it was prepared to claim control over and sometimes to assume responsibility for German history, but was never quite willing to take full possession of it.[8]

The museum controversy also points towards that persistent sense of historical uncertainty that was part of the Federal Republic's political culture. West Germans never seemed to tire of writing and reading books about their identity problems. In 1980, for example, in a book significantly entitled *The German Neurosis*, Peter Lerche wrote: "A people is able to act only when it can tell the story of its own past and identity with it. Germans today cannot do this, or can do it only with great difficulty. Their identity is thereby endangered." And in a work – again with a significant title, *Our New Arrogance* – published in 1988, Arnulf Baring quoted with approval Dolf Sternberger's lament of 1949: "We don't know who we are. That is the German question." Many observers seemed to assume this problem of identity came from Germans' unsettled relationship to their national past. "Germans of my generation," wrote Martin Walser, Jahrgang 1927, "cannot have an undisturbed relationship to reality – the very basis of our national reality is itself disrupted." And some, like Michael Stürmer, argued that only history could heal this disrupted relationship: as Stürmer put it in his inimitable – and untranslatable –

---

8 On the two museums, see *Protokoll der Anhörung zum Forum für Geschichte und Gegenwart*, Schäfer: "Das Haus der Geschichte," and Stölzl and Tafel: "Das Deutsche Historische Museum in Berlin."

prose: "in einem geschichtslosen Land die Zukunft gewinnt, wer die Erinnerung füllt, die Begriffe prägt und die Vergangenheit deutet" – "in a land without history the future belongs to those who fill memory, shape concepts, and determine the meaning of the past."[9]

Before going any further, perhaps we should pause for a moment and ask if the Federal Republic's identity problems may have been somewhat exaggerated. It seems to me that many of us – and I plead guilty to the charge – took the lamentations of Walser and Stürmer much too seriously. Now that the Federal Republic in its original form has come to an end, we can see that its identity was a good deal firmer that we might have thought. Whatever it might have been in 1949, by 1989 the Bonn republic was not "a land without history" – but rather a state that had created its own historical identity, an identity neither clearly tied nor clearly severed from the history that had preceded it, but firmly rooted in its own shared experiences, values, and institutions.

The Federal Republic was neither the history-less, anxious neurotic its intellectuals often described, nor the sleeping, chauvinistic giant its enemies sometimes imagined. Rather it was a somewhat provincial, largely self-satisfied European state that happened to be tied by the force of history and the force of habit to a national policy which most people had forgotten about. It is, I think, in light of this sense of themselves that we can best understand both the shallow enthusiasm and deep uneasiness with which many West Germans confronted unification. The federal government's absurd promises that unification was possible without much cost came not only from the politicians' fear of this uneasiness among their voters but also from the simple fact that before 1989 no one in Bonn had thought much about the possibility that the GDR would cease to exist.

The degree to which the Federal Republic had established its distinctive historical identity was clear during what was one of the most fascinating public debates on history and identity in recent times: I am referring, of course, to the debate on the Hauptstadtfrage. The first remarkable thing about this debate was that it should have taken place at all. One might have thought the issue settled: by the historical precedent of 1871 to 1945, by forty years of rhetorical gestures and material subvention, and finally, by Article 2 of the

---

9 Peter Lerche: "Nachwort." Peisl and Mohler, eds., *Die Deutsche Neurose*, pp. 238–48, here p. 240; Baring: *Unser neuer Größenwahn*, p. 33; Walser, as quoted by Wolfgang J. Mommsen: "Wandlungen der nationalen Identität", p. 181; Stürmer: "Geschichte in geschichtslosem Land," first published in the *Frankfurter Allgemeine Zeitung* No. 96, April 25, 1986, reprinted in *"Historikerstreit"*, p. 36–39.

Einigungsvertrag between the two German states. But the issue was by no means settled. All during the spring of 1991, the debate went on: it involved the narrowest of economic interests and the grandest of philosophical issues; it pulled to the surface regional rivalries and bad historical memories; it activated confessional tensions and personal ambitions; it cut across party lines and ideological divisions; most of all, it was a debate that was at least as much about the past as it was about the future.[10]

The debate on the Hauptstadt was a wholesome exercise in public reflection. It is understandable why so many Germans were reluctant to move from Bonn, which did, after all, symbolize the best government they had ever had. It was also understandable why people were worried about how much this was going to cost them. It is not at all unfortunate that real estate seems to have been more important than Realpolitik. And it was understandable why the outcome was so close – a mere seventeen votes out of the over six hundred and fifty cast – an outcome that reflected the deeply divided feelings many people on both sides of the debate had about the question. In the end, however, the decision had to be for Berlin. To have decided otherwise would have been to deny history, most immediately the forty years in which the west looked on Berlin as its outpost of freedom and the east as its capital, but beyond that the years in which Berlin stood for so much that was ugly and repressive in German history, as well as for some of what was beautiful and progressive. Lewis Mumford says somewhere that great cities are all museums, instruments of memory that recall and recapture the past. There are few cities so drenched in history as Berlin – not merely in its old buildings and monuments, but also in its fragmentation, its odd empty spaces, and haphazard reconstruction of the past. These spatial breaks and architectural discontinuities are of particular historical interest because they represent the fragmentation and destruction and reconstruction that is so central to the German experience in the modern era. One can only hope they don't all disappear under a monotonous shell of steel and glass – or even worse, under a leaden layer of what is thought to be postmodern wit.[11]

The decision for Berlin, therefore, was – or should be – a decision to appropriate the German past. To say that, however, immediately raises the

---

10 The best place to follow this debate is in the pages of the *Frankfurter Allgemeine Zeitung*, which took a firmly pro-Berlin position. See the collection edited by Mönninger, *Das neue Berlin*. *Die Zeit* was much more ambivalent: see, for example, Theo Sommer's lead article "Noch nicht daheim im deutschen Haus" *Die Zeit* No. 26, June 21, 1991, p. 1.

11 We should look forward to a study of this debate comparable to Pommerin's *Von Berlin nach Bonn*, which will trace the movement in the opposite direction.

question: What past? A question which brings me directly to the issue promised by my title: What is the past that the new Germany will carry into its future?

Perhaps one should start by saying what this past is not: it surely is not the Prussian traditions recently evoked by the reburial of Frederick the Great in Potsdam. One does not know quite what to do with this desperate comedy except to say that there is as little of Frederick's Prussia left outside the coffin as there is of his mortal remains within. Nor can we take very seriously the current campaign to rebuild the Hohenzollern Schloß in Berlin. However much one might applaud the idea aesthetically – it was a fine building, destroyed by an irresponsible act of political vandalism – the project's implications are not very appealing. In any event, the campaign has little enough to do with the aesthetics of architecture and a good deal to with settling old scores against the GDR. In that sense, the discussion of what should be torn down and what rebuilt in the eastern half of Berlin raises a much more serious issue: the need to come to terms with the immediate past, especially with the experience of national division and the legacy of the GDR.

There are two errors to be avoided from the outset. The first is to suppose that the two German states had separate histories, joined only at their beginning and end: Jürgen Habermas seems to have implied as much when he described his own relationship to the GDR as "unconnected" and declared that "their history was not our history." The second error is another version of the first: it is to suppose that there was only one legitimate German history after 1945, and this was the history of the Federal Republic – the history of GDR was ungerman, foreign, a tragic but temporary break in the flow of national development. Both these views make it difficult to ask those questions about the past which are so vital for the future.[12]

The first of these questions concerns the origins of the new Germany: what were the immediate causes of the revolution of 1989? When one talks to people in east and west – in the "new" and "old" federal states – two alternative interpretations begin to emerge. One emphasizes the movement for reform within the GDR, a movement that picked up momentum after the local elections in May 1989 – in which massive fraud was unmistakable – and culminated in the great Leipzig and Berlin demonstrations in the fall. According to this version, the movement towards a democratic, socialist East German

---

12 Habermas, Jürgen: "Die andere Zerstörung der Vernunft: Über die Defizite der deutschen Vereinigung und über die Rolle der intellektuellen Kritik." *Die Zeit* No. 20, May 10, 1991, pp. 63–4. For a reaction from the former GDR, see Dieckmann: "Unsere oder eine andere Geschichte?" *Der Berliner Tagesspiegel*, July 31, 1991.

state was thwarted by the intervention of the West, which used its financial resources and political influence to persuade a majority of easterners that their best chance was a rapid unification with the Federal Republic. An alternative interpretation of the events of 1989 emphasizes the massive westward emigration that began that summer as soon as it became clear that the GDR's eastern neighbors would not close their borders. According to this line of analysis, migration not only forced a series of concessions from the government but also left the West with no real alternative to unification – or, as some put it, the only choice was between a unification of the two states and national unification on West German soil. In this second version, the Federal Republic is not an aggressive seducer forcing its way on a naive and helpless East, but rather a reluctant groom who accepts his penniless bride because neither has a real choice in the matter.[13]

You can see at once that these two stories about what happened in 1989–90 offer two quite different perspectives from which to view the history of the GDR down to its eventual disappearance. Those who favor the first version tend to see the GDR as a potentially progressive country, which might have been a true German social democracy. Tragically, this state fell into the hands of those who betrayed its ideals – these traitors, usually called "Stalinists," became increasingly alienated from their society as they retreated into a realm of private privilege and public paralysis. And then, just as the forces of democracy were coming to life again, they were overwhelmed by the false promises of the West. Those who favor the second version usually see a different GDR: for them, East Germany was not a potentially progressive state ruined by a small group of Stalinists, but rather a fatally and fundamentally flawed system, imposed on a reluctant people by Russian power and sustained by terror and repression. As soon as people had a chance to leave this system, a significant number took it; when they had a chance to vote in favor of unification with the West, a overwhelming majority did so. It is not hard to see how the outcome of this historical debate will be shaped both by what we learn about the past and by what happens in the future.[14]

Closely associated with these two views of the GDR are attitudes about the origins of Germany's initial division – an issue that is bound to reemerge now that the historical era begun by this division has come to an end. Despite the efforts of various "revisionist" historians, especially in the United States,

---

13 For a powerful argument on the importance of emigration, see Naimark: "'Ich will hier raus'."
14 On the future history of the GDR, see Jarausch, ed., *Zwischen Parteilichkeit und Professionalität*. Dieckmann provides the insights of a critical 'insider' in *Glockenläuten und offene Fragen*.

the prevailing opinion in the West is that the division of Germany was imposed on the allies by Soviet intransigence, which broke the "grand alliance" and hardened the temporary division of occupation zones into two German states. Eastern scholars have long taken a very different view of this process. They tend to take seriously various Soviet initiatives for a reunited German state: they regard the Stalin note of 1952, for example, as a serious offer through which a united Germany might, like Austria, have become a neutral nation. Once again, you can see how the question of responsibility for Germany's division affects not only how one views the subsequent history of the two German states, but also how one assesses their end and subsequent unification.

Just beyond the origins of the cold war lies the problem of National Socialism, which has always been and will surely remain the most sensitive and troubling area of German history and historiography. As we have seen, the two German states approached this problem from different perspectives, but for both of them it was always enmeshed with their own rivalries: the concept of "fascism" in the East found its counterpart in the western term "totalitarianism" – both designed to convert the historical experience of Nazism into a propaganda weapon in the cold war. Perhaps now that this war is over, it will be possible to reexamine how this dark chapter fits into German history after 1945. Once again, the future of this past will be shaped by contemporary developments: if the new state remains stable and secure, then it will be much easier to take possession of the Nazi past. The more loudly echoes of this past seem to sound in the present, the more troubling and unresolved it will continue to be, both for Germans and for their neighbors.

Of course beyond the Nazi years stretches the whole expanse of the German past. This too will take on a different shape with the creation of a new nation. Perhaps from the perspective of 1991, the first Reichsgründung will appear still more natural, Bismarck's Germany the only answer to the German question. But it is also possible that, once they have been freed from the political and ideological pressures of national division, German historians will be able to see more clearly the alternatives to unification in 1871 and its limitations in the years thereafter. And how will the creation of a successful democratic Germany affect our views of the national past? Will certain aspects of German history – the powerful participatory element in the Bismarckian Reich, for example – begin to seem more important as time goes on? And will the apparently irreversible drive towards greater European integration cause us to rethink our views on the German Sonderweg, that "special path" which many thought led from Germany's flawed modernization to the catastrophes of 1914 and 1933? Clearly this is not the time to try to answer these questions. But one thing is certain: no aspect of the German past will be left untouched by the new direction of Germany's future.[15]

Let me conclude these remarks in true Joycean manner, by returning to our point of departure, to *Ulysses* – and to what is perhaps the most famous quotation from the book, Stephen Dedalus's bitter comment that "History is a nightmare from which I am trying to awake" – this lament appears towards the end of Chapter Two where it is evoked by some anti-Semitic remarks of his headmaster; thus it is thematically tied to the conversation in Barney Kiernan's pub that I quoted at the beginning. Stephen's view of the past is sometimes cited as though it were Joyce's own; this is, I think, a mistake. Joyce, to be sure, knew enough about history, and particularly about Irish history, to recognize its nightmarish side. But he also knew that history was not only the nightmares that haunt us, it was also the story of who we are – troubling and consoling, a source of conflict and cohesion, difficult to live with but impossible to live without.

We should not, therefore, hope that in their new nation, Germans will awake from the nightmare of history, but rather that they will finally take possession of their past – all of their past, with its nightmares and its dreams, its hopes and failures, its continuities and fragmentations – and that they do so for the only convincing reason there is to appropriate the past: because it is, necessarily and unavoidably, theirs.

---

15 Two preliminary attempts to put the new nation in historical perspective: Meier: "Die deutsche Einheit als Herausforderung." *Frankfurter Allgemeine Zeitung* No. 95, April 24, 1990, p. 36, and Kocka: "Revolution und Nation 1989."

Alfred Kelly
Hamilton College

The Franco-Prussian War and Unification in German History Schoolbooks

Abstract: The Franco-Prussian War of 1870/71 was central to the formation of German national identity. Judging from the pronouncements of pedagogues and officials, as well as the tenor of public culture, one would expect school history, especially after 1890, to glorify the war. Yet instead of promoting chauvinism and militarism, history textbooks use the war as the centerpiece of a kind of German morality play. The war brought out the German virtues of piety, hard work, duty, and discreet patriotism. In this version of history, the Germans loathed war and the bonds of unity were moral and spiritual.

The Franco-Prussian War of 1870/71 was the formative, common national experience of the newly united Reich. To a great extent, the war would define for the new nation what it meant to be German on both a collective and a personal level. This essay analyzes how school history textbooks helped to construct and to sustain the memory of 1870/71 in the minds of millions. In an age when no electronic media competed for children's attention, and when schoolbooks were often found in the home as well as in the classroom, textbook authors were potentially powerful agents of national self-definition. History textbooks – particularly when they deal with the explosive passions aroused by the nation's founding war – are a window on the national soul. As such, they provide the historian an unparalleled opportunity to answer some fundamental questions about German nationalism: Did German schools indoctrinate their students with chauvinistic militarism during the imperial period? Did school history glorify the War of 1870/71 and thus help prepare the way for the enthusiasm of August, 1914?

As in other nations, German leaders had a keen appreciation of the power of education to shape the nation. Shortly after the war, Bismarck himself thanked teachers for their "outstanding contributions" to recent events and called attention to their responsibility for cultivating national feelings in their pupils.¹ These sentiments were more than polite rhetoric. Prussian Minister of Public Worship and Education, Adalbert Falk, echoed the common view of those in power in the new national state when he wrote to his counterparts in other states that the role of the schools was "to strengthen and enliven the German national consciousness."² Not surprisingly, history instruction was the natural focal point of a nationalistic education. Long overshadowed by the three Rs and religion, history first emerged as a separate classroom subject in the Volksschule with the promulgation of the 1872 Prussian curricular plan. Whereas previously, schoolchildren had read a few historical selections in their basic reader, they were now to receive four to eight hours per week of formal history instruction concentrating on Prussia and its rulers.³ Wilhelm himself instructed Falk to make sure that the books emphasized the Prussian kings, as well as the leading men of the Wars of Liberation and the Franco-Prussian War.⁴ The tone was now set for the next two generations of history instruction, which was, in the words of the 1881 curricular plan, designed "to stimulate the keen interest of the students," by concentration on the "charity, justice, kindness, and faithfulness, etc., as well as the heroic deeds in battle and the acts of charity afterwards" of the "outstanding personalities."⁵

To some postwar zealots, the call for a patriotic history stressing rulers and wars justified an overt militarization of the classroom. A. von Rhoden, a Hannoverian officer, argued in 1871 that teacher training ought actually to be taken over by the army; all teachers would be uniformed noncommissioned officers carefully supervised by their military superiors.⁶ No doubt, such a proposal marked the extremity of acceptable opinion. As one critic wrote in 1875 (perhaps with Rhoden in mind), the new chauvinism in the schools would hardly suffice "to establish a 'state of intelligence' and entitle the people to the highest renown."⁷ But there were surely schoolrooms in the 1870s and 1880s where Rhoden's spirit prevailed. Here is how the playwright Gerhart Hauptmann recalled his youthful experiences with reserve-officer teachers in the wake of the war:

---

1 Schleunes: *Schooling and Society*, p. 160.
2 Ibid., p. 172; see also p. 173.
3 Straube: "Die Einführung des obligatorischen Geschichtsunterrichts," pp. 154–55; see also Diere: "Zur Geschichtspropaganda der herrschenden Klassen," pp. 986–87.
4 Berg: *Die Okkupation der Schule*, p. 144.
5 Schallenberger: *Untersuchungen zum Geschichtsbild*, p. 71; see also Berg: *Die Okkupation der Schule*, pp. 143–45.
6 Lemmermann: *Kriegserziehung* vol. 1, p. 29.
7 Berg: *Die Okkupation der Schule*, p. 233.

Wenn der Lehrer die Klasse betrat, schnellten die Knaben von den Bänken und standen so lange steif und stramm, bis das Kommando "Setzen!" in schneidigem Tone erklungen war. Die Art, wie vom Katheder herunter gelehrt wurde, glich genau der Instruktionsstunde beim Militär; […]. Einfache Worte, gütiges Wesen, freundliche Unterstützung des Schülers waren als Sentimentalität verpönt. Sie galten als weichlich, sie galten als unmännlich. Der hinter den Pädagogen Stehende, unsichtbar Maßgebende war nicht Lessing, Herder, Goethe oder Sokrates, sondern der preußische Unteroffizier.[8]

This kind of classroom atmosphere may well have become more common during the Wilhelmian era. Kaiser Wilhelm II fancied himself something of an expert on the education of the young, and on May 1, 1889 he set the Prussian educational bureaucracy to work on a program to assure that Prussian schools would turn out loyal young Germans, immune to Social Democracy.[9] In the Kaiser's view, the state's best weapon in the war for children's souls was "patriotic history" instruction stressing the close bond between dynasty and people. The Kaiser's choice of May Day to issue his orders was intentionally provocative and reflected his alarm at the rapid growth of Social Democracy. His idea to use the schools as propaganda weapons against Social Democracy was, however, not entirely new. Back in 1874, none other than Helmuth von Moltke had warned the Reichstag:

> I believe that the school is the place where we must take action if we wish to protect ourselves against the dangers of socialist and communist aspirations. These dangers threaten us internally as much as an external attack and can only, I think, be removed by social improvements combined with greater and more widespread education.[10]

Although he equated Social Democracy with an external military threat, Moltke probably never intended an overt militarization of the curriculum.

---

8 Hauptmann: "Das Abenteuer meiner Jugend." Hauptmann: *Sämtliche Werke* vol. 2, p. 623. "When the teacher entered the classroom the boys sprang up from their benches and stood stiffly at attention until the spirited command 'Sit!' had rung out. The style with which the teaching came down upon us from the teacher's rostrum was exactly like that of the instructional hours in the military; […]. Simple words, a kindly demeanor, or friendly support for the pupils were scorned as sentimentality. They were considered soft, unmasculine. The controlling spirit standing invisibly behind the teachers was not Lessing, Herder, Goethe, or Socrates, but rather the Prussian noncommissioned officer." Quoted by Höfele: *Geist und Gesellschaft der Bismarckzeit (1870–1890)*, pp. 23–4.

9 Lemmermann: *Kriegserziehung* vol. 1, pp. 13–6; Wenzel: "Sicherung von Massenloyalität," pp. 338–45; Schleunes: *Schooling and Society*, pp. 210–12; Berg: *Die Okkupation der Schule*, pp. 102–05; Goebel: "Des Kaisers neuer Geschichtsunterricht," pp. 709–15; Langsam: "Nationalism and History," pp. 242–44; Meyer: *Schule der Untertanen*, pp. 159–72.

10 Moltke, quoted by Wenzel: "Sicherung von Massenloyalität," p. 336.

During the 1870s and 1880s the schools appear to have been little involved in any systematic propaganda campaign against Social Democracy.[11] What the schools did do was glorify the present nation-state in both daily lessons and on holidays. No child could miss the message that any radical alternative to the present was an anathama to those in authority.

When, in 1889, the young Kaiser Wilhelm II injected himself into education debates, he had no fundamentally new ideas, but he did raise the stakes and set an unprecedented new tone of aggressiveness and stidency. In the wake of the Kaiser's decree, the new instructions on teacher-training in Prussia stressed patriotic history, with the central pedagogical questions being:

> How does the school cultivate reverence for God and King? How does it fill its pupils with gratitude to our ruling dynasty and with love for the fatherland? With respect for the laws of the land, and the morals and arrangements of society?[12]

Making good citizens required full attention to the modern period; history instruction was now to go up to 1888.[13] (Actually most textbooks were already up-to-date.) The Kaiser himself was convinced that studying the French Revolutionary period and the Wars of Liberation was the most effective way to turn out young patriots. At the state-sponsored school conference in December, 1890 he called on history teachers to help rid society of the many "muddle-headed, confused reformers" who "grumble about our government and focus their attention abroad."[14] Pupils, in his view, needed to know above all that the German way was not only different than, but better than, the French way. The new educational spirit of the Kaiser was institutionalized in Prussia in 1891 with the promulgation of the revised curricular plan. With more modern history and, significantly, more gymnastics, the Prussian state sent a clear message about the role of its schools.[15]

Prominent pedagogues joined the call for an education that would produce dutiful citizens and soldiers. H. Rosenberg and C. Reim, who wrote the most popular manuels on school history instruction during the Wilhelmian period, argued that history taught reverence by example. Students learned that revolution is bad by studying the undesirable results of revolutions; that monarchy is

---

11 Ibid., pp. 336–37.
12 "Denkschrift des Kultusministeriums zur 'Ausführung des Allerhöchsten Erlasses vom 1. 5. 1889'", quoted by Wenzel: "Sicherung von Massenloyalität," p. 345.
13 Goebel: "Des Kaisers neuer Geschichtsunterricht," p. 709.
14 *Verhandlungen über Fragen des höheren Unterrichts. Berlin, 4. bis 17. Dezember 1890*, p. 73.
15 Lemmermann: *Kriegserziehung* vol. 1, p. 23; see also Glöckner: *Zur Schulreform*, pp. 65–108; Günther-Arndt: "Monarchische Präventivbelehrung oder Curriculare Reform?," pp. 256–75.

good by studying the great achievements of monarchy. They learned how to act as citizens by studying examples of sacrifice from past wars. Wearing "des Königs Rock" was the noblest and happiest duty of the citizen, for, as Reim said, "This land, fertilized with the blood of heroes, is a holy heirloom."[16] He might well have added, "Don't desecrate it with the sacrilege of Social Democracy." The religious language of high patriotism and ancestor worship was, of course, nothing new, in or out of the schools. Even before 1870 schoolbook history had drawn on an eclectic Christian-Germanic spirit. From Tacitus came the cult of the ancestors; from the Old Testament came the idea of the chosen people; and from the Reformation came Luther as a model for all Germans.[17] This was a vision that valued education as Erziehung (upbringing and character development) more than as Wissenschaft (learning). (It is clearly a masculine-oriented Erziehung, though in the elementary school girls would be exposed to it also.) Neither Kaiser Wilhelm II, nor the pedagogues, nor the bureaucrats invented this vision of education. They merely exaggerated it and tinged it with militarism and vulgar chauvinism.

Certainly, there is some anecdotal evidence to support the interpretation that the schools were, in the words of one historian, under "occupation."[19] One might cite memoirs that depict bygone schooldays like scenes out of Carl Zuckmayer's *The Captain of Köpenick*.[20] One might point to the emphasis on marching in the 1901 Prussian curricular plan;[21] to the frequency of military topics in essay assignments;[22] to the presence of the veterans' newspaper *Kyffhäuser-Korrespondenz* in the Prussian schools, thanks to the Interior Ministry;[23] or to the bombastic Sedan Day celebrations. The perennially popular L. F. Göbelbecker, whose reader *Lernlust* (1893) went through thirty editions and sold 220,000 copies by 1910, may stand as the centerpiece of this interpretation: For him the pupil was a "recruit;" the school "a work community with no strikes allowed, a *monarchy* of the spirit," where learning was analogous to a military campaign.[24]

Militaristic chauvinism did have its opponents, and not just among left-liberals and socialists. At the state-sponsored school conferences in 1890 and

---

16 Langsam: "Nationalism and History," p. 250.
17 Weymar: *Das Selbstbildnis der Deutschen*, pp. 156–58.
18 Olson: "Nationalistic Values," p. 49.
19 Berg's very title, *Die Okkupation der Schule*, suggests her interpretation.
20 Lemmermann: *Kriegserziehung* vol. 1, p. 179; Retzlaw: *Spartacus*, p. 13
21 Lemmermann: *Kriegserziehung* vol. 1, p. 212.
22 Ibid., p. 83; Weber: *Pädagogik und Politik*, p. 83.
23 Lübeck: *Die Rolle der Kriegervereine*, p. 75.
24 Lemmermann: *Kriegserziehung* vol. 1, pp. 136–47; quotation on p. 139.

1900 some participants worried that studying post-1871 history would open the doors for political propaganda. Oskar Jäger, a prominent author of history texts, warned against succumbing to chauvinism, a view apparently shared by many teachers, who were more comfortable teaching the earlier periods.[25] As a group, teachers by no means represented a conservative, monarchical monolith. Though patriotic and loyal to the regime, elementary school teachers in particular were often young liberal idealists whose influence would certainly have vitiated any crude chauvinism in the classroom. Indeed, the *Pädagogische Zeitung*, the official organ of the Deutscher Lehrerverein, carried articles critical of the military, even pacifistic.[26]

There is, then, a real difficulty in judging the degree to which officially sanctioned militarism and chauvinism actually penetrated the classroom. By the time the Kaiser's inchoate and angry wishes had filtered through the various layers of state bureaucracies, teacher-training programs, textbook publishers, and individual teachers facing huge classes, they had lost much of their punch. As the old German proverb has it, "The soup is always cooked hotter than it's eaten." Too often, historians have written the history of education as though official policy equalled classroom reality. While it is true that memoir literature often supports the standard claims of strident militarism in the pre-World War I schools, that literature is itself suspect. Usually writing after the sobering experience of war, those looking back at their Wilhelmian childhoods may well have been prone to select experiences that "predicted" the future. Moreover, the very nature of memory is to polarize and exaggerate; the flashy, exciting story – perhaps totally unrepresentative – simply stores better and is more appealing to relate. What gets lost is the great mundane flow of everyday experience at school, which uneventfully, but inexorably, shapes the lives of millions.

An analysis of textbooks, to which students were exposed daily, does suggest a fairly uniform view of the nation's past, but, as will be clear, that view was by no means blatantly militaristic. Moreover, there was no obvious change in the books after 1890, suggesting that the Wilhelmian chauvinistic bombast may have been more superficial than commonly thought and confounding any simple hegemonic model. Again, one must take care in general-

---

25 *Verhandlungen über Fragen des höheren Unterrichts. Berlin, 4. bis 17. Dezember 1890*, pp. 392–95; see also the 1900 conference, *Verhandlungen über Fragen des höheren Unterrichts. Berlin, 6. bis 8. Juni 1900*, pp. 354–55; Jäger: *Pro Domo*; Goebel: "Des Kaisers neuer Geschichtsunterricht," pp. 713–14; Weymar: *Das Selbstbildnis der Deutschen*, pp. 205–26; Schönemann: "Nationale Identität," pp. 120–22.

26 Olson: "The Social Values," pp. 73–89.

izing, for a tendency towards homogeneity, blandness, and stability over time may be inherent in the textbook genre itself, which is derivative rather than original and aims at a broad constituency. Particularly in a nation as diverse and new as Germany, textbook authors had to take care not to offend any groups. Their books were conscious attempts to integrate the diverse nation by inviting participation in, and celebration of, a standardized past. Even though efforts to create a formally unified elementary school system for the Reich failed (with the Reichstag maintaining as early as 1874 that it had no jurisdiction in the matter),[27] there was fairly rapid agreement that the study of a unified German history should take precedence over the history of individual states. Such a vision was not merely imposed from above by state bureaucrats; it found real resonance among school teachers, for whom teaching German patriotism was as natural as teaching the multiplication table.[28]

Even in Bavaria, where feelings about maintaining state identity were strongest, the Bavarian Teachers' Association pushed hard for the precedence of German history, and "Prussian" textbooks spread widely.[29] As early as 1871, the *Bayerische Lehrerzeitung*, in an article entitled "The War and the Elementary School," argued that the schools must take up the task of cultivating a sense of Germanness, to which Bavarian history must take a backseat:

> The people's historical view cannot be permitted to remain confined in a narrow-minded way to their own little province; we belong to a great and glorious nation, and thus its history, the history of the entire German people, must not remain unfamiliar to the youth.[30]

The same journal routinely gave favorable reviews to Prussian-oriented textbooks. Still, it was assumed that the "fatherland" could also mean Bavaria, and a book that was "too Prussian" would find a hostile reception. As one Bavarian curricular plan put it in 1876, "Special attention is constantly to be given to the history of Bavaria" in discussing the events of 1870/71.[31] Most books approved in Bavaria were more anti-French than specifically pro-Prussian; they stressed the crucial contributions of Bavaria and King Ludwig II in an all-German effort and avoided casting Bavarians in the role of Prussian

---

27 Schleunes: *Schooling and Society*, pp. 173–74.
28 Ullwer: *Der Geschichtsunterricht in der Volksschule*, pp. 21–34; Trapp: *Der Einfluß der Regierungsform*, pp. 192–203; Schleunes: *Schooling and Society*, p. 172; Richard Kabisch uses the term "vaterländisches Einmaleins" (cited by Lemmermann: *Kriegserziehung* vol. 1, p. 166).
29 Ullwer: *Der Geschichtsunterricht in der Volksschule*, pp. 21–2; Trapp: *Der Einfluß der Regierungsform*, pp. 203–07; see also Kennedy: *Lessons and Learners*, p. 248.
30 K. I. Brand, quoted by Trapp: *Der Einfluß der Regierungsform*, p. 196.
31 Ibid., pp. 205 and 210.

agents.³² There were a few grumblings in the Bavarian parliament about "Prussian" schoolbooks, but neither government ministers nor teachers were inclined to support the particularists. By 1886, when German history first joined Bavarian history on the teachers' qualifying exams, Bavarian teachers had already been teaching German history for many years.³³ Bavarian children, like children all over the Reich, were exposed to a fairly standardized version of the German past with the usual heavy emphasis on war. For all practical purposes, then, we may treat the following analysis of textbooks as reasonably representative of the whole Reich.³⁴

Given the patriotic bellicosity of ministerial decrees, curricular plans, and pedagogical texts, it comes as no surprise that school history texts in the Reich devoted a good deal of space to war. One study of the coverage of the period 1864 to 1871 finds that, on average, 25 to 50 percent of the text pages were devoted to war description, with as much as 62 percent in one book.³⁵ With three wars in this period, this coverage may not seem excessive, but a perusal of the books' treatment of the whole sweep of modern history since 1500 reveals that war was indeed the central theme throughout.³⁶ To historians raised in an age when military history is rather in eclipse, these proportions may suggest a sustained propaganda campaign to militarize German

---

32 Kennedy: *Lessons and Learners*, pp. 206–66 passim; Kennedy's generalizations on South German history texts, as well as general readers, suggest that they are little different from those used elsewhere; see her "Regionalism and Nationalism," pp. 11–33; see also Haberl: *Der geschichtliche Unterricht*, pp. 97–109; Scheiblhuber: *Präparationen für den Geschichts-Unterricht*, pp. 249–59; Sattler: *Abriß der bayerischen Geschichte*, pp. 60–3.

33 Trapp: *Der Einfluß der Regierungsform*, pp. 213–23; meetings of the Bayerischer Lehrerverein always opened with a "Hoch" to the Kaiser, though it was not until 1906 that the Bavarians joined the Deutscher Lehrerverein; see Blessing: *Staat und Kirche in der Gesellschaft*, pp. 217–25.

34 Jürgen Kocka uses the phrase "mobilization and deregionalization" to describe the post-1870 process of nation building, including in the schools; see his "Probleme der politischen Integration," pp. 118–36; see also Doerry: *Übergangsmenschen*, p. 101; Schönemann: "Nationale Identität," pp. 122–27.

35 Schallenberger: *Untersuchungen zum Geschichtsbild*, pp. 74–84.

36 Langsam estimates the portion of military history in Prussian texts at two-thirds, and counts 125 military terms in one book; see his "Nationalism and History," pp. 254 and 258. Kennedy's estimate for South German readers is that about one-third of the historical sections are devoted to war, though she did find a Palatinate reader from 1913 where the proportion was two-thirds; see her *Lessons and Learners*, pp. 262–66; on the overshadowing of social themes by war in source books, see Heinel: *Die deutsche Sozialpolitik*, pp. 25–7. Books written specifically for girls' schools usually had less detail about wars. As one author said, girls need "history from the congenial side;" see Mehden, ed., *Vor allem eins, mein Kind*, pp. 111–12.

youth.³⁷ It's all too easy to forget that until relatively recently the vast majority of historians – not just German schoolbook writers – took for granted that the story of dynasties and their wars was the backbone of history. The real issue is therefore not so much the amount of space devoted to war, but rather the attitude toward war. An analysis of how some widely used texts treated the Franco-Prussian War reveals that, whatever the intentions of ministerial officials, the messages about war that came through the books were often ambiguous and ambivalent. To be sure, every book sought to create good Germans who would do their duty for the fatherland, but a good German was not necessarily a budding chauvinistic militarist. The textbook presentation of the Franco-Prussian War suggests that the authors' primary goal was not to glorify the war, but rather to use the war to define the German nation as the heir to the pious earnestness and harmony of 1870, which was, in turn, a revival of the spirit of 1813.³⁸

The centerpiece of this inheritance was the rustic innocence of the Germans in July, 1870. School children were taught that the French war declaration rudely disrupted the idyllic rhythms of field and shop. Germania, as in Ferdinand Freiligrath's poem, suddenly had to exchange her sickle for a sword to defend hearth and home against the impudent peace breakers in Paris. It was as though the war came from nowhere, like a sudden tantrum afflicting the French. Their irrational fears of a Hohenzollern on the Spanish throne were inspired by jealousy at the now inexorable rise of Prussia after 1866. They wanted "revenge for Sadowa," a chance to reassert their historic role as the "grande nation."³⁹ All the books treat the French in a generic, undifferen-

---

37 A notable example is Lemmermann's *Kriegserziehung*.
38 The following discussion of the textbooks is based on a perusal of about one hundred books in the Internationales Schulbuchinstitut in Braunschweig. Many books reappeared with few changes in dozens of editions over generations. And there is surprisingly little difference between the upper levels of the Volksschulen, the Mittelschulen, the Realschulen, and the Gymnasien. What school books are called seems to have little relation to their content, and what appear to be teachers' guides may not be clearly separate from texts for the pupils. In addition to Schallenberger, Langsam, Kennedy, Olson, Schönemann, and Lemmermann, see also König: *Imperialistische und militaristische Erziehung*; Schridde: *Zum Bismarckbild im Geschichtsunterricht*; Tiemann: *Die Vorgeschichte des Krieges von 1870/71*.
39 Andrä: *Erzählungen aus der Deutschen Geschichte*, pp. 156–57; Andrä: *Lehrbuch der Weltgeschichte*, pp. 130–32; Berndt: *Präparationen für den Geschichtsunterricht*, pp. 307–11; Dittmar: *Leitfaden der Weltgeschichte*, pp. 214–15; Fritzsche: *Die Deutsche Geschichte*, p. 298; Fritzsche: *Bausteine für den Geschichtsunterricht* (I. Kursus), pp. 130–32; Hahn: *Leitfaden der vaterländischen Geschichte*, p. 179; Hoffmann: *Handbuch für den Geschichtsunterricht*, pp. 405–07; D. Müller: *Leitfaden zur Geschichte des deutschen Volkes*, pp. 202–03; the same themes quickly made their way into the Prussian reader; see Schleunes: *Schooling and Society*, p. 190.

tiated way, assigning to them the character flaws that had been the staple of nationalist rhetoric since the Wars of Liberation. Subtlety and originality are not the strong points of textbooks. The French as a people were haughty, vain, frivolous, fickle, and disingenuous. There were no reasons why the French were this way, they just were. In an age increasingly dominated by biologistic thought, alleged character traits easily assumed the guise of facts of nature.[40]

What happened between King Wilhelm and the French ambassador, Benedetti, at Ems was not, in this schoolbook view, an isolated incident. It was, rather, a deep expression of the character of the French and Germans. Some books focus on Napoleon III himself as the quintessential Frenchman. It was he personally, the "insidious statesman on the Seine," who was behind Benedetti's outrageous demand that the Hohenzollern candidacy be permanently renounced. By provoking war, Napoleon III sought to rally the French to support his shaky throne. Other books see him as merely weak, a pawn in the hands of a war-mongering clique (sometimes identified as Jesuits) surrounding his devious wife, Eugenie. Still other books see the Emperor as the tool of the rabid Parisian press, screaming for national glory at the expense of German blood.[41] These interpretations – if we may dignify them as such – are really scarcely distinguishable, for they all share an unstated assumption that the psychological traits of a nation are embodied in its leaders, who in turn determine the course of events. The analysis never reaches beyond the realm of personal conflict into a questioning of social or economic structure or even into the intricacies of diplomatic bargaining. Thus, the war was *caused* by the personal insult to King Wilhelm and his manful and dignified handling of the incident. The frequent use of the poem "König Wilhelm saß ganz heiter" underscores this interpretation. Benedetti and all he stood for had previously been a nuisance, but now, with his insatiable demands, he affronted a dignified elderly officer (on vacation, no less) in the person of King Wilhelm. What happened at Ems may be described, then, in language appropriate to a duel between military officers, with Wilhelm representing all Germans in a point d'honneur. Indeed, Wilhelm *is* the nation. In the edifying words of one textbook:

---

40 Examples are Haberl: *Der geschichtliche Unterricht*, pp. 100–02; Hechelmann, ed., *Auszug aus Welters Lehrbuch*, p. 429; Schillmann and Viergutz: *Leitfaden für den Unterricht in der Deutschen Geschichte*, pp. 115–17; W. Müller: *Leitfaden für den Unterricht in der Geschichte*, p. 313.

41 In addition to works cited in notes 39 and 40, see Grube: *Charakterbilder aus der Geschichte und Sage*, pp. 440–42; Scheiblhuber: *Präparationen für den Geschichts-Unterricht*, pp. 249–51; Spielmann: *Der Geschichtsunterricht*, p. 506.

His patience was exhausted. The King did what every German man must see as his inescapable duty. Reduced to the necessity of choosing between war and humiliation, he chose, if the evil neighbor wanted it no other way, war.[42]

If manly honor is at stake, then Wilhelm's actions are transposed into a protected realm above the mundaneness of ordinary selfish motives, exempt from criticism and analysis. The war becomes a decree of fate, as certain as the reality of German honor and French perfidy. To question the war would be to question honor itself.

But what about Bismarck? Was it not he who rekindled what should have been a closed diplomatic quarrel by his famous editing of the account of what had occured at Ems? In the early years of the Empire, the books largely ignore Bismarck, not just because they are more concerned with the dynasty, but also because it was not until the early 1890s that Bismarck's role in the July, 1870 crisis was publicly known. But even during the Wilhelmian period, when about half of the books discuss the Ems Dispatch, Wilhelm still overshadows Bismarck, despite the pivotal role that professional historians of the period were routinely assigning to Bismarck. Bismarck was, after all, a minister, an agent of the King, and ministers come and go. Loyalty to the fatherland, which the textbooks promote, entailed loyalty to a presumably permanent dynasty, not loyalty to a single king's temporary agent. In this respect, Wilhelm I's continuing central role in the school books reveals that the school version of history was beholden to the Prussian dynasty rather than to shifting public opinion. It was Wilhelm II who built up his grandfather as "der Grosse" and denigrated Bismarck as a mere helper. Despite increasing public veneration of Bismarck from the late 1890s on, the schoolbook Bismarck never outgrew the role of agent – a great agent perhaps, but still an agent.[43]

Those books that do deal with the Ems Dispatch are frank, but uncritical, reflecting the prevailing assumption that the war was an inevitable collision of the two national characters. Bismarck could not, in this view, create the war

---

42 Müller: *Leitfaden für den Unterricht in der Geschichte*, p. 315; see also Hoffmann: *Handbuch für den Geschichtsunterricht*, pp. 406–07; Schumann: *Vaterländische Geschichtsbilder*, p. 113; on personality as causation see Schallenberger: *Untersuchungen zum Geschichtsbild*, pp. 71–74; Olson: "Nationalistic Values," p. 53; and Tiemann: *Die Vorgeschichte des Krieges von 1870/71*, esp. pp. 47–60; on "König Wilhelm saß ganz heiter," see Zimmermann: *Geschichtlicher Anschauungs- und Erfahrungs-Unterricht*, p. 27.

43 Schridde: *Zum Bismarckbild im Geschichtsunterricht*, pp. 13–33; Tiemann: *Die Vorgeschichte des Krieges von 1870/71*, pp. 61–6; Kennedy found that texts in Württemberg and Bavaria were more likely to ignore Bismarck than were those in Baden; see her *Lessons and Learners*, p. 213.

for his own purposes; he could only affect its timing, which he had every right to do in the national interest. Accordingly, the editing of the Ems Dispatch is either carefully defended or simply bypassed without comment, with the tacit assumption that nothing remarkable had happened. One teachers' guide offers questions to steer the discussion this way:

> What do we think about Bismarck's actions purely in themselves? What must have enraged Bismarck, like any good German? What had Bismarck known for a long time? How did he intend to anticipate the danger? What was, therefore, the purpose of the Ems Dispatch? Why must we today approve of Bismarck's actions?[44]

This last question is surely not an invitation to critical thought and is not all that different from the heavy-handed approach of another teachers' guide:

> He [Bismarck] pondered, asked Moltke whether the army was ready for war, and wrote the 'Ems Dispatch,' which correctly represented the events in Ems, but in a form that would necessarily offend the French. Is that a 'falsification' by which Bismarck frivolously caused the war? (He knew that the war unavoidably had to come sooner or later; so, as a responsible statesman, he brought it about at the most favorable moment for Prussia; that was not a crime, but rather a great deed of the first rank!)[45]

More important to textbook authors than the exact cause of the war was the way the Germans responded to the French challenge. While the excitable French, in the words of one book, "flew into a war delirium," the earnest Germans "rose up in wrath."[46] The textbooks are unanimous in stressing the unity and enthusiasm with which all Germans rallied under King Wilhelm, the 'Heldengreis,' who embodied all that was noble and good. Weigand and Tecklenburg's ever-popular *Deutsche Geschichte* is typical and worth quoting at length:

> A storm of enthusiasm went through the German land. Once again, the classrooms and the professorial chairs emptied, plowshares and shops were abandoned, and from the grand country houses and tiny cottages everyone rushed to the colors to serve in the same army and fight for the same goal. In every square and street one heard the clatter of arms and the sounds of war, and in quiet chambers clasped hands were raised in prayer. The people and the army congregated in the

---

44 Spielmann: *Der Geschichtsunterricht*, p. 510.
45 Berndt: *Präparationen für den Geschichtsunterricht*, p. 311; see also Kabisch: *Erziehender Geschichtsunterricht*, p. 50; Koch: *Lehrbuch der Geschichte*, p. 157; Neubauer: *Lehrbuch der Geschichte*, pp. 160–61; Schenk: *Lehrbuch der Geschichte*, p. 206.
46 Schumann: *Vaterländische Geschichtsbilder*, p. 113.

houses of God for a universal day of prayer to implore for the help of the Almighty; with faith in God and their hearts steeled for battle, the warriors flocked around their banners. The fiery iron horses drew thousands westwards; and from the cars there echoed "Lieb Vaterland, magst ruhig sein, fest steht und treu die Wacht am Rhein." At every station the soldiers were received with loud cheers; men and women surged forward to offer them refreshments. In a fortnight nearly a half a million soldiers stood ready to meet the enemy, while just as many waited in reserve.[47]

No translation can do justice to the exalted language of schlock patriotism which here reaches a crescendo with every cliche in place: The exhilarating bond of people and army; the cozy inter-class brotherhood; the stout-hearted piety; the banner fetishism; the mighty locomotives spitting fire as they draw westwards their carloads of singing warriors; and the inevitable "once again," connecting all to the Wars of Liberation. The myth of a united people in arms has a tight grip on every textbook, with only an occasional hint that some South Germans might have had reservations to overcome before they committed themselves to the Prussian cause.[48] But in the world of these schoolbooks numbers and facts are secondary. One text, in its exuberant faith in a people's war, puts over a million men in France by early August, more men than during the peak mobilization of the winter.[49] And it is, of course, pure fantasy to suggest that classrooms emptied as schoolboys went off to war. The real number of schoolboy soldiers was vanishingly small, but their stirring example created a poetic reality which soon metamorphosed into a generally accepted fact. Here we confront a paradox, which should give pause to those who would interpret the textbooks as instruments of militaristic propaganda serving the interests of the conservative, monarchical upper classes. The cult of the "people in arms" is indeed a unifying force in the new nation, and it may well help to mold future soldiers. But if the "people in arms" won the war for national unity, then the nation belongs to the people in the spirit

---

47 Weigand and Tecklenburg: *Deutsche Geschichte*, p. 138; typical other examples are in Andrä: *Erzählungen aus der Deutschen Geschichte*, pp. 158–59; Dittmar: *Leitfaden der Weltgeschichte*, p. 216; Hahn: *Leitfaden der vaterländischen Geschichte*, pp. 180–81; Hoffmeyer and Hering: *Hilfsbuch für den Geschichtsunterricht*, pp. 453–54; Jäger: *Abriß der neuesten Geschichte*, p. 108; Fritzsche: *Die Deutsche Geschichte*, p. 298; Fritzsche: *Bausteine für den Geschichtsunterricht* (I. Kursus), p. 131; Neubauer: *Lehrbuch der Geschichte*, pp. 161–62; Schumann: *Vaterländische Geschichtsbilder*, p. 113; Zurbonsen: *Leitfaden der Geschichte*, p. 91.
48 Schillmann and Viergutz: *Leitfaden für den Unterricht in der Deutschen Geschichte*, p. 117; Assmann: *Abriß der Geschichte*, p. 192.
49 Ibid., p. 193; another author claims that 500,000 men fought at Gravelotte; see Krüger: *Die Weltgeschichte*, p. 176.

of the democratic nationalism of 1848. By implicitly denying that the army in 1870 was the professional agent of royal authority, the textbooks deliver the victory, and with it the nation itself, into the hands of the people. To unify the nation emotionally, which the books assiduously seek to do, is to tap into traditions that are inherently subversive of the monarchy.

The mighty "people in arms" cannot be defeated. Rarely do the texts mention the very real fear of a French invasion of Baden or the Palatinate. What really counts is spirit. The Germans have it, the French, as befitting their character, have only a counterfeit version. Thus, the short-lived occupation of Saarbrücken, which caused real concern at the time, is dismissed with lofty scorn as typifying the fakery of French "bravour," which brazenly celebrates the storming of an undefended position.[50] On the other hand, the German spirit is indomitable, for it is the genuine heir of the heroic struggle of the Wars of Liberation. That the enemy is once again corrupt France – indeed, another Napoleon – makes the 1813/1870 analogy an obvious one. But the emotional continuity that the schoolbooks conjure up is focused inwardly on the Germans, with surprisingly little emphasis on the "hereditary foe" themes of popular poetry. The recapture of Alsace-Lorraine or retribution for the hardships of the Napoleonic occupation take a backseat to the two great symbolic gestures linking the generations: King Wilhelm's visit to the tomb of his martyred mother, Queen Luise, on the seventieth anniversary of her death; and the renewal of the iron cross, which had not been awarded in the intervening years. These were highly *personal* royal actions, though carried out in the name of the nation. The old king – the 'Heldengreis' – embodies in himself the memory of the nation. He spans the generations and guarantees that the struggle for national identity will be renewed in pure form. To be loyal to the king is at the same time to be loyal to the memory. Here the books partake of the odd irony of asking children to be true to a legacy, which is itself already secondhand, as symbolized by the preponderance in the books, especially after 1900, of songs from the Wars of Liberation.[51] However noble and sacrificing the Germans of 1870 were, they were still "heir men," assigned by fate to live up to their grandparents' legacy and deprived of the

---

50 Andrä: *Erzählungen aus der Deutschen Geschichte*, p. 160; Hahn: *Leitfaden der vaterländischen Geschichte*, pp. 181–82; Kabisch: *Erziehender Geschichtsunterricht*, pp. 52–53; Koch: *Lehrbuch der Geschichte*, p. 158; Zurbonsen: *Leitfaden der Geschichte*, p. 191.

51 Frank: *Dichtung, Sprache, Menschenbildung*, p. 545; significantly, whereas Fichte and Arndt figure prominently in textbook accounts of the Napoleonic period, little attention is paid to the (dangerous?) popular nationalism of Turnvater Jahn; see Sprenger: "'Strahlte die Jugend für den heiligen Kampf,'" p. 13.

opportunity to contribute anything essentially new to the meaning of Germanness. More than likely, only a few educated people felt the burden of this legacy in 1870; but they wrote the books, assuming – as is only human – that their perceptions were universally shared. Thus are traditions created and passed on in countless new editions of textbooks.

Up through their description of the mobilization, the books are quite homogeneous in both tone and content. When they come to describing the actual combat, however, they begin to diverge, suggesting that there was no single established view of the meaning of combat within the national mythology. Even within the same book the tone and substance may oscillate from the bland, to the heroic, to the gory. A certain unease or uncertainty grips many authors. A large group of books is simply reticent – mentioning troop movements, numbers, engagements, and victories, with few details and little emotional punch. Ludwig Hahn's popular *Leitfaden der vaterländischen Geschichte*, which was already in its forty-ninth edition in 1896, provides this typical account of the Battle of Gravelotte/St. Privat:

> Marshal Bazaine had taken up a fortresslike position with his entire army on the steeply rising heights. Part of the German armies attacked him frontally, while three corps (the Saxons, the Prussians, and the ninth corps) carried out a flanking movement through the mountainous woodland paths and fell upon the right flank of the enemy. The French position was shattered by the victorious fighting of the guard at St. Privat and of the Saxons at Verneville; but at Gravelotte they continued their brave and stubborn resistance against the Germans, who were charging up one hill after another. Until late into the evening the battle fluctuated indecisively; then, at dusk, the Pommeranian (Second) Army Corps advanced on the battlefield after a sixteen-hour march and decided the bloody battle with a final mightly assault, simultaneous with a renewed advance of all the corps.[52]

What is the student to make of page after page of such bland descriptions? Even in translation it's apparent that the passage is garbled (with separate areas of the battle conflated), abstract, vague, impossible to visualize, and therefore simply dull. This is life-killing history, the stuff of dreaded rote memorization, which was such an easy target of contemporary school critics. It certainly does not glorify the war, and it is simply too soporific to militarize the psyche of any child.

---

52 Hahn: *Leitfaden der vaterländischen Geschichte*, pp. 185–86; for other thin and dull descriptions see, for example, Assmann: *Abriß der Geschichte*, pp. 193–97; Nösselt: *Weltgeschichte*, pp. 420–35; Fritzsche: *Bausteine für den Geschichtsunterricht* (I. Kursus), pp. 131–34; Frohnmeyer: *Leitfaden der Geschichte*, pp. 235–41; Haberl: *Der geschichtliche Unterricht*, pp. 100–08; Hahn: *Leitfaden der vaterländischen Geschichte*, pp. 183–99.

A second, perhaps equally large, group of books is less bland and does indeed breathe the spirit of romantic heroism. These books make a smooth transition from the heady days of the mobilization to the actual fighting, often using poetry or poetic imagery to describe the action. As one author remarks, introducing his section on the campaign, "Now came the battles of which the poets speak."[53] "Poetic" battles are, of course, those against the Empire, culminating at Sedan. Not only were these battles decisively won, they could also be viewed as clearly defined episodes in a progression toward a reachable goal. Heroes have to be more than merely brave; they have to accomplish something and then either die a quick and graceful death or return home for their just rewards. Otherwise, there is no structure to the story glorifying their exploits. Here is Gottfried Koch's *Lehrbuch der Geschichte* on the storming of the "impregnable" Spichern Heights, potentially the most romantic battle of the war:

> Using their rifles as supports, sometimes down on their hands and knees, the gallant soldiers clambered up. Ahead of them all, with his sword swinging and the drummer at his side, was General von François – until he sank to the ground, struck by five bullets. His last words were, "What a beautiful death it is on the battlefield; I die happily, for I see that the battle goes forward."[54]

This is a famous story, and most children can see that if the war has a purpose (and that is never in doubt), then General von François died for a purpose. He falls among his men, killed quickly – there is just time to get off a couple of (probably inaudible!) fine lines – with a hint of pain but no revolting suffering to tarnish our image. His example is an inspiration to his men to prove their moral and physical superiority to an astonished enemy. And, one just might be moved to want to emulate him.

We can hardly escape the conclusion that war is glorified here and in other similar passages. Yet it is an oddly precarious glorification. Certainly General von François dies a romantic death in Koch's retelling, but Koch prefaces his account of Spichern with the honest admission that the battle was in fact unintended, the result of confusion.[55] Such admissions of fallibility or high-level disagreements about strategy and tactics, which are common in the textbooks, are the enemy of glory and heroism. It's hard enough to make General von

---

53 Fritzsche: *Die Deutsche Geschichte*, p. 299.
54 Koch: *Lehrbuch der Geschichte*, p. 159.
55 Ibid., p. 158; Assmann says that attacking Spichern was a result of a misunderstanding; see Assmann: *Abriß der Geschichte*, p. 194; Hahn notes that Wörth too was unintentional; see Hahn: *Leitfaden der vaterländischen Geschichte*, p. 183.

François into a hero when he is struck down at a distance by five bullets from strangers he can't even see. But if the whole battle was a mistake, then the perceptive student may well ask whether General von François and his men would have had to die at all had Moltke's plans been followed by his subordinates. Gravelotte too looks different if the "lion's courage of the troops, the proficiency and heroism of the officers, and Moltke's superior tactics" are needed to overcome the "dangerous situation" created by General Steinmetz's "reckless boldness,"[56] for which, as Friedrich Neubauer concedes, he was relieved of his command.[57] Even the revered Moltke is not immune to questioning. Johannes Berndt's teachers' guide invites students to debate Moltke's opposition to the bombardment of Paris and asks whether the bombardment of Straßburg was not "cruel and avoidable."[58] Koch too notes the disagreement about the bombardment of Paris and reprints the popular ditty of late 1870, which admonished, "Guter Moltke, sei nicht dumm, / Mach doch endlich bum, bum, bum!" K. Schenk, on the other hand, sees no moral ambiguity and attributes the delay of the bombardment to "false compassion."[59] Honesty and criticism do have their limits though. No book mentions the great panics at Gravelotte, the disgraceful pilfering of the 'Liebesgaben' (gifts sent from home), or the seemingly pointless drills late in the war. Yet, however muted the criticism, the very admission that some questions are open and troubling vitiates glory and heroism, which demand a primitive sharpness of purpose unclouded by organizational complexity, moral ambiguity, and critical reasoning.

The tenuous grip of war glorification in the pages of the textbooks is further weakened by the juxtaposition of glory with horror. The ubiquitous Heinrich Weigand recommends to teachers as a lesson that they ask their students, "How can you tell that there was a bloody struggle at Mars la Tour and Vionville?" As a follow-up the teacher is to recite Freiligrath's "Die Trompete von Vionville," where death for the fatherland is an aesthetic experience. Weigand's next advice is, then, somewhat jolting:

> At this point a special opportunity is offered to make the students also aware of the terrifying and frightful aspects of war, and to show them that whoever causes a war without cogent reasons commits a great injustice.[60]

---

56 Schenk: *Lehrbuch der Geschichte*, p. 209.
57 Neubauer: *Lehrbuch der Geschichte*, p. 163.
58 Berndt: *Präparationen für den Geschichtsunterricht*, pp. 325 and 328.
59 Koch: *Lehrbuch der Geschichte*, p. 167; Schenk: *Lehrbuch der Geschichte*, p. 213; the latter misinforms students that Moltke favored an early bombardment.
60 Weigand: *Der Geschichts-Unterricht*, p. 403.

Following this advice without breaking awkwardly out of the traditional romantic war narrative is a delicate job. Weigand himself probably strikes the most successful balance. Here he is on Gravelotte:

> With heavy losses, the Germans advance against the entrenchments on the heights; both sides fight with great bravery, the dead pile up on the dead in the ravines, on the slopes, and in the village lanes; the wounded already number many thousands. The deafening roar of the French guns is terrible; the clatter of the mitrailleuses, the whistling of the bullets, the bursting of shells, the wailing of the wounded, and the last sighs of the dying mix in with the dreadful thunder of the guns. Moltke dispatches the order that the attack should not be repeated; already, shattered battalions of our brave soldiers are dashing precipitously down the slope; the French press forward, ever more powerfully. Moltke has quietly ridden off, up on a hill, to look for the Pommeranians, who according to his reckoning, must show up now, and whose help is urgently needed. Then he sees them; they've been on the march since two o'clock in the morning. With a loud Hurrah, they advance against the enemy under Moltke's leadership. Then, through all the ravines and from all the hilltops of the broad battlefield echoes the signal: Advance on all fronts! A loud general Hurrah greets the signal. All advance, ever farther, ever up, and no matter how hard the enemy resists, they must yield, down from the hills, far past Gravelotte and into the fortress at Metz. Out of the tumult of battle comes Moltke, flushed, but riding at an easy pace, and reports to the king: "Your Majesty, victory is ours; the enemy is beaten at all points." Far and wide over the hills and down in the valleys, friend and foe cover the battlefield; their uniforms glow in the cut grain fields like blue corn flowers and red poppies. The dead were buried to the sounds of the song "Jesus, meine Zuversicht."[61]

This passage, which is one of the most detailed battle descriptions in the schoolbooks, is revealing both for what it does and does not say. There is no attempt to disguise the horror and death, though we are distanced from the sickening nature of the wounds and suffering. German victory does seem in real doubt at first, as brave, but shattered, battalions rush back – this an oblique reference to the panic retreat, though implying that the action is in disciplined response to the order not to renew the attack. Up to this point Weigand maintains a tense balance between romance and the realities of modern industrial war, of which Gravelotte is one of the first notable examples. But when the tide of this near catastrophe turns in favor of the Germans, he lapses into a romantic set piece. His Moltke is the stereotype of the brilliant, taciturn, unflappable, and ever-in-control septiginarian, who personally leads his men into battle – never mind that the action takes place over many square

---

61 Weigand and Tecklenburg: *Deutsche Geschichte*, p. 133.

miles and that only a tiny fraction of the men can even see Moltke. The stirring sounds of the signal horns instantly (and inexplicably) revive all spirits, and the French are simply rolled back, overwhelmed by German vigor and courage, which are extensions of Moltke's own virtues. And then, as though it were a second-rate play, the curtain falls on a scene bathed in false pathos and aestheticized death. The dead glow like flowers in a peaceful sun-lit field and were buried (in a distancing shift to the past tense) by hymn-singing survivors. In fact, the battle ended in pitch dark, and the soldiers collapsed in thirst, hunger, exhaustion, and confusion.

In Weigand's account mundane horror and transcendent beauty mix in a bewildering and unsatisfying brew. To be sure, a more skillful writer might do better, but the real problem is more fundamental: Language and experience were lagging behind technological and organizational progress. In the late nineteenth century only a few of the greatest minds (and great minds do not write schoolbooks) anticipated the later laconic cynicism or aesthetics of gore itself, which would be necessary to do justice to Gravelotte. Schoolbook authors are simply not up to the task and, in any case, would have considered an account in the style of, say, Ernst Jünger, in bad taste and unpatriotic. Most schoolbook authors, therefore, either stay with the bland and boring or else punctuate their standard romantic glorifications with unpleasant reminders about how horrible war is. They want the children to experience the glory *and* the horror, but they haven't figured out how to combine them adequately. Thus, Berndt recommends reading the *Fröschweiler Chronik* (a graphic memoir) to impress the horrors on the children, but then immediately adds, "At the same time, we may not allow the heroic deeds of war to be forgotten."[62] Another author, who on one page waxes rhapsodic about the thrills of getting an iron cross, later breaks into the action with this sobering paragraph:

> War is a work of annihilation and destruction. It brings great horrors to a country. Thousands of blossoming human lives fall victim to it. Many who set out in the flower of youth came home as cripples and amputees, with sickly bodies, carrying within them the seeds of an early death. How terrible is the scene of a battlefield! Next to the dead lie thousands of wounded with freshly bleeding wounds and shattered limbs; quick help is urgently needed. In order to mitigate such suffering, Christian love provided care in splendid fashion.[63]

---

62 Berndt: *Präparationen für den Geschichtsunterricht*, p. 313.
63 Hoffman: *Handbuch für den Geschichtsunterricht*, p. 409, quote on p. 440; see also Haberl: *Der geschichtliche Unterricht*, pp. 103–07; Heinze-Rosenburg: *Die Geschichte für Lehrerbildungsanstalten*, p. 75; Hoffmeyer and Hering: *Hilfsbuch für den Geschichtsunterricht*, p. 460; Scheiblhuber: *Präparationen für den Geschichts-Unterricht*, p. 253.

The ambivalence about glory, while hesitantly and ineloquently expressed, remains a major subtheme in the books and is further evidence against interpreting them as self-conscious attempts to militarize the youth. Moreover, it is difficult for any author to glorify the war against the French Republic. As the war dragged on, after it had been won in the traditional sense, it was simply dreary. It's no accident that the schoolbooks, as expressions of "official memory," pay less attention to the fall and winter campaigns, even though there were actually more German soldiers in France in the later parts of the war. Most authors simply acknowledge the war's increasing brutality, while their praise of the early scenic heroism gives way to a more muted admiration for the "tough endurance" of the Germans in a campaign of drawn-out sieges and nasty little skirmishes. The Germans are seen as having the simple strength of character to do a hard unpleasant job. During the seige of Metz, Berndt notes, typus and dysentery take their toll as the men are forced to camp among the all-too-shallow graves of putrid, gas-belching bodies.[64] Toward the enemy the war takes on what one author calls a "bestial character" (caused, of course, by the French), but requiring "inexorable hardness against the French people."[65] Another book recounts the outrages of the franktireurs and then remarks tellingly:

> The Germans took revenge by shooting every captured franktireur. And every village from which Germans were shot at as they passed through was burned to the ground. But excesses such as happened in the Wars of Liberation in France, were not tolerated.[66]

In reality this was the majority of the war, and no amount of imaginative doctoring can turn it into a glorious romp or its soldiers into old-fashioned war heroes. These soldiers are, rather, hard-working survivors of the mundane hardships of diarrhea, cold feet, short supplies, and ambushes.[67]

One reason why this later war is so unglorious is that the French have been stripped of the last vestiges of their heroism as soldiers and have become "rabble,"[68] who fear to show themselves on the field of honor. German glory depends on retaining respect for the French as brave fighters who put

---

64 Berndt: *Präparationen für den Geschichtsunterricht*, p. 324.
65 Mauer, ed., *Geschichts-Bilder*, pp. 537–38; see also Hechelmann, ed., *Auszug aus Welters Lehrbuch*, p. 434.
66 Spielmann: *Der Geschichtsunterricht*, p. 523.
67 See also Neubauer: *Lehrbuch der Geschichte*, p. 166; an occasional exception is the reference to the Battle of Lisaine near Belfort as a "German Thermopylai;" see Egelhaaf: *Grundzüge der Geschichte*, p. 312.
68 Hechelmann, ed., *Auszug aus Welters Lehrbuch*, p. 434.

up a manful struggle. Yet even early in the war, notions that the French as a whole people were degenerate and had deep character flaws carried over to their army, calling into question their soldiers' bravery and thus by extension the majestic grandeur of German achievements. If Sedan was a "judgement of God," as the books maintain, then there was something fundamentally, morally wrong with the defeated enemy. (The books cannot agree about whether Wilhelm said that victory at Sedan came about with God's "leadership" or merely his "indulgence.") The same frivolous, undisciplined behavior that prompted the French to start the war haunted them on the battlefield. Among the captured booty at Spichern, J. C. Andrä tells children, were "upholstered armchairs, carpets, mirrors, rouge pots, fine pastries, and all sorts of costly dainty morsels that the pampered French officers didn't want to do without even in the field."[69] In contrast, even the elderly Prussian king shared the hardships of his men in the field and lived austerely at Versailles, allowing the great palace to be used as a field hospital.[70] It was no wonder, remarks another author, that when pinned inside the fortress at Sedan, the French went to pieces, for "they didn't have enough strength of soul to maintain discipline and order in misfortune."[71] As the war dragged on, the "real" French character emerged more and more, and lying, murder, and betrayal become accepted and routine.[72] Finally, with the Commune, the French go down in an orgy of self-destruction.[73]

French "degeneracy" had always been a two-edged sword for Germans. Textbook authors too faced the delicate task of making the French despicable enough to deserve crushing but honorable enough to make the crushing something to be proud of. (The racist image of the depraved North African Turko – so prominent in the popular imagination – is absent in the schoolbooks, which focus on French soldiers only.) Authors repeatedly stress that the French fought bravely, were well armed with the chassepot, and that defeating them was no easy task.[74] Responsibility for French inadequacies could

---

69 Andrä: *Erzählungen aus der Deutschen Geschichte*, p. 162.
70 Hoffmeyer and Hering: *Hilfsbuch für den Geschichtsunterricht*, p. 461.
71 Kabisch: *Erziehender Geschichtsunterricht*, p. 57.
72 Nösselt: *Weltgeschichte*, p. 422; for other views of French degeneracy see D. Müller: *Leitfaden zur Geschichte des deutschen Volkes*, p. 207; Schumann: *Vaterländische Geschichtsbilder*, p. 114.
73 For harsh language on the Commune see Grube: *Charakterbilder aus der Geschichte*, p. 450; Zurbonsen: *Leitfaden der Geschichte*, p. 97.
74 Berndt: *Präparationen für den Geschichtsunterricht*, pp. 312, 316, 327; Hahn: *Leitfaden der vaterländischen Geschichte*, p. 186; Müller: *Leitfaden zur Geschichte des deutschen Volkes*, p. 206; Neubauer: *Lehrbuch der Geschichte*, pp. 161–62; Schumann: *Vaterländische Geschichtsbilder*, pp. 114–16; Spielmann: *Der Geschichtsunterricht*, p. 528.

be shifted onto the leadership, but not entirely convincingly if the corruption of the French character runs broad and deep. The case of the alleged traitorous behavior of Marshal Bazaine illustrates the problem nicely. If Bazaine was guilty of betraying his troops, then the achievement of defeating those troops is demeaned. On the other hand, if Bazaine was not guilty of betrayal, then the ploy of shifting responsibility for French inadequacies onto the leadership is in jeopardy. It's no accident, then, that texts that do mention the Bazaine case leave open the question of his guilt.[75] Fundamental to this whole issue was that the French had been portrayed from the outset not as evil (for evil can be strong) but as effete; and only so much glory can be extracted from the defeat of the effete. French weakness serves best as a foil to the German character, highlighting German virtues and reminding Germans that "pride goeth before the fall." The textbook version of the war is, then, less a celebration of the glories of battle than a drama about the destiny of the Germans.

That destiny was, of course, unity, which the textbooks take for granted as the outcome of the war. Having already downplayed particularism during the July crisis and mobilization, all the authors go out of their way to salute the indispensable contributions of the various German armies on the battlefield. The brotherhood in arms is unquestioned and sacred, a natural catalyst for unity. Always the focus is on Germans making the nation together, as a people, never on a Prussian-led coalition. Few books go so far as to maintain that the war was absolutely necessary for unity; but the proclamation of the empire at Versailles is smoothly integrated into the war narratives, so that the student is left with no doubt about the bond of war and unity, nor about the relationship between French humiliation and German success. Once again, the role of Bismarck is problematic. A few authors give credit directly to Bismarck, such as in the almost childish: "While the Germans were besieging Paris, Bismarck thought, 'Now it is time for us to get a German Kaiser.' And all Germans thought the same."[76] More common is a focus on Wilhelm as the embodiment of the wishes of the German people or the fulfillment of the Kyffhäuser legend. As Weigand and Tecklenburg say, "The old legend of Barbarossa's return had become a fact."[77] In this view, the Reich and the war that

---

75 Fritzsche: *Bausteine für den Geschichtsunterricht* (II. Kursus), p. 211; Berndt: *Präparationen für den Geschichtsunterricht*, p. 317; Frohmeyer: *Leitfaden der Geschichte*, p. 236; Spielmann: *Der Geschichtsunterricht*, pp. 523–25.

76 Kabisch: *Erziehender Geschichtsunterricht*, p. 59; see also Neubauer: *Lehrbuch der Geschichte*, p. 168; Jöris: *Erzählungen für den ersten Geschichtsunterricht*, p. 85.

77 Weigand and Tecklenburg: *Deutsche Geschichte*, p. 137; see also, for example, Haberl: *Der geschichtliche Unterricht*, p. 109; Müller: *Leitfaden zur Geschichte des deutschen Volkes*, p. 212; Berndt: *Präparationen für den Geschichtsunterricht*, p. 328.

made it possible are lifted from the realm of politics to that of mythological fulfillment, and the 'Heldengreis' becomes the apotheosis of Germanness. The heroic sacrifices in 1870/71, both in the field and on the home front, lay the moral foundations for national identity. Some books do honestly admit that the 'Heldengreis' had reservations about becoming Kaiser and that there was considerable opposition in Bavaria. Berndt even acknowledges that Bismarck wrote the letter that Ludwig II sent to Wilhelm, while another author records the close vote in the Bavarian parliament.[78] Yet even where obstacles are freely admitted, the inevitability and transcendent goodness of the Reich are never in question.

David Müller provides a good summary of the whole meaning of the years 1870/71:

> And for what has bloomed creatively in the German Reich since that time we owe to the old heroic Kaiser, our resurrected Barbarossa; to his glorious son, who proved himself at his side; to the German princes, who, just as in olden times, fought like born generals; to the great statesman and the highly gifted field marshal at the head of Germany; to the heroic German warriors; to the dead slumbering in honor; and to German piety, faithfulness, perserverence, and restraint – may God preserve these virtues along with the German Reich.[79]

What's clear here – and indeed in all the schoolbooks – is that the primary pedagogical purpose is to make Germans in a certain image. The virtues of the war generation – the Germans who beat the French and made their own nation – are *the* German virtues and must be assiduously cultivated and preserved. These are not military virtues as such, though they enable Germans to rise to any challenge, and they are certainly not militaristic. They are really the virtues of a piously Christian willpower, though in their effort to integrate the nation, the books carefully avoid any specifically Protestant overtones. While war may reveal these inherently German virtues, it cannot create them, for modern war is too tainted by materialism – a "French" trait – to be a creative Germanic force.

Unleashed as a historical force, these virtues generate what Nietzsche called shortly after the war "monumental history," a history of grandiose "effects in themselves." As Nietzsche puts it:

---

78 See Berndt: *Präparationen für den Geschichtsunterricht*, p. 329; Stutzer: *Übersichten zur preußisch-deutschen Geschichte*, p. 124; see also Neubauer: *Lehrbuch der Geschichte*, p. 168; Koch: *Lehrbuch der Geschichte*, p. 168; Kabisch: *Erziehender Geschichtsunterricht*, p. 60; Spielmann: *Der Geschichtsunterricht*, p. 529.

79 Müller: *Leitfaden zur Geschichte des deutschen Volkes*, p. 212.

> Das, was bei Volksfesten, bei religiösen oder kriegerischen Gedenktagen gefeiert wird, ist eigentlich ein solcher "Effekt an sich": er ist es, der die Ehrgeizigen nicht schlafen lässt, der den Unternehmenden wie ein Amulet am Herzen liegt, nicht aber der wahrhaft geschichtliche Connexus von Ursachen und Wirkungen, der, vollständig erkannt, nur beweisen würde, dass nie wieder etwas durchaus Gleiches bei dem Würfelspiele der Zukunft und des Zufalls herauskommen würde.[80]

Of course, in Nietzsche's view it would be mostly the "weak and inactive" ("Ohnmächtigen und Unthätigen"), not the "bolder hearts" ("Muthigen") reading schoolbooks. To the majority the real message of the books would be, in Nietzsche's words, "Let the dead bury – the living" ("lasst die Todten die Lebendigen begraben").[81] Time in monumental history is frozen at the grandiose peaks of national experience, when, in response to crisis, the people and their leaders exhibit their noblest traits. To elevate these very traits – the ephemeral products of a unique historical moment – to the status of fixed national characteristics, to Germanness itself, is tantamount to embracing a philosophy of national decline. By so defining the nation, the schoolbooks implicitly assume that their readers are a generation of epigones. What child – what adult – could match the monumental deeds and sacrifices of 1870/71?

The textbooks, then, leave German children an ambivalent legacy about the violent birth of their nation. War is indeed the centerpiece of this legacy, but despite official rhetoric, textbooks writers were not trying to militarize German youth, even after 1890. Rather, they sought to create pious, patriotic, and dutiful citizens who would live up to their grand heritage. To be German was to be worthy of the fathers of 1870/71, who had left field, shop, and hearth to vanquish the foe and to make a nation. If the War of 1870/71 was "great and glorious," it was so because Germans had met the test that horror and death had imposed on their individual and collective wills, not because war itself is great and glorious. Such was the lesson of school history, which millions carried with them into the twentieth century.

---

80 Nietzsche: "Vom Nutzen und Nachtheil der Historie für das Leben." ("Unzeitgemäße Betrachtungen II.") – *Sämtliche Werke* vol. 1, p. 262. Nietzsche: *The Use and Abuse of History*, p. 15: "The events of war and religion cherished in our popular celebrations are such 'effects in themselves'; it is these that will not let ambition sleep, and lie like amulets on the bolder hearts – not the real historical nexus of cause and effect, which, rightly understood, would only prove that nothing quite similar could ever be cast again from the dice-boxes of fate and the future." See also Schallenberger: *Untersuchungen zum Geschichtsbild*, p. 69.

81 Nietzsche: "Vom Nutzen und Nachtheil der Historie für das Leben." ("Unzeitgemäße Betrachtungen II.") – *Sämtliche Werke* vol. 1, pp. 262, 263, 264; Nietzsche: *The Use and Abuse of History*, pp. 16, 17.

Roger Chickering
Georgetown University

Language and the Social Foundations of Radical Nationalism in the Wilhelmine Era

Abstract: This essay surveys recent attempts to employ the tools of linguistic analysis in the study of German nationalism. It then examines the history of the German Language Association (Allgemeiner Deutscher Sprachverein), in order to plead for an inclusive analysis of language – one that is sensitive to both the constituting power of language and its historical contingency. The essay argues that the attempt to purge the German language of foreign words during the Wilhelmine era was based on a belief in the power of language to structure the civic culture, but that this campaign also reflected the social experience and political agenda of a specific milieu.

In the 1920s and 1930s, the unrivalled American center of research on the history of nationalism was Carlton J. H. Hayes' seminar at Columbia University. The role of nationalism in the origins of the great European war dominated its research agenda; and a number of the dissertations that emerged out of the seminar, among them the works of Koppel Pinson, Robert Ergang, and Mildred Wertheimer, left an enduring imprint on the American academic understanding of the pathologies of European, and particularly of German nationalism.[1] In the summer of 1929, Hayes himself delivered a cycle of lectures before the World Unity Council in Massachusetts, in which he summarized the thinking that guided work in his seminar. Two years later he published these lectures in a small volume that bore the title *The Historical Evolution of Modern Nationalism*.[2] Here he spoke of nationalism as an idea, an autonomous spiritual force that had developed everywhere in the direction of more intensity, exclusiveness, and aggressiveness. Its evolution he then traced

---

1 Pinson: *Pietism as a Factor in the Rise of German Nationalism*; Ergang: *Herder and the Foundations of German Nationalism*; Wertheimer: *The Pan-German League*. See also Pinson: *A Bibliographical Introduction to Nationalism*.
2 Hayes: *The Historical Evolution of Modern Nationalism*.

through a series of phases, which he characterized as humanitarian, Jacobin, liberal, and integral (with a nod to Maurice Barrès). His survey led him to a somber question. "Is there something inevitable in the evolution of nationalism which advances its devotees ever faster toward war?" he asked, after an apprehensive reference to Hitler.³

The next European war vindicated Hayes' apprehension, but it was also the prelude to a reorientation in the scholarly study of nationalism. The categories in which Hayes understood his subject reflected a Rankean belief in the autonomy and motive power of great ideas. Although these categories continued to display remarkable vitality in American scholarship on the subject of nationalism, they began in the 1960s to retreat in the face of a new research agenda that reflected the methodological assimilation of Marx and Weber on both sides of the Atlantic.⁴ Impulses from Theodor Schieder's seminar in Cologne and from the proponents of a Historische Sozialwissenschaft helped shape this agenda, whose accents fell on the material and cultural forces that made specific social groups receptive in specific circumstances to ideologies of nationalism.⁵

Had he lived longer, Hayes might have taken comfort in indications of yet another reorientation in the American academy. The study of nationalism has in recent years begun to feature categories of analysis that look remarkably like those he himself promoted. If Hayes attributed the historical evolution of modern nationalism to a logic that inhered in the very idea of the nation, historians have recently brought to bear a new inventory of tools to analyze nationalist behavior in the light of forces apparently no less ideal and a logic no less compelling. The reorientation has come in the name of linguistic theory, which has generated a broad and troubled debate the American historical profession.⁶ Several examples, drawn from recent attempts to employ this theory in analyzing German nationalism, suggest why the debate has proved unsettling.

The first example deals with Québécois rather than German nationalism. It seems fitting nonetheless to consider Richard Handler's work in a broader context, now that Rudy Koshar has recommended it to the attention of Ger-

---

3 Ibid., pp. 303, 311.
4 Kohn: *The Idea of Nationalism*; Schafer: *Nationalism*.
5 See Berdahl: "New Thoughts on German Nationalism;" Düding: *Organisierter gesellschaftlicher Nationalismus*; Wehler: *Bismarck und der Imperialismus*; Dann: *Nation und Nationalismus*.
6 See, for example, Toews: "Intellectual History after the Linguistic Turn;" Harlan: "Intellectual History and the Return of Literature;" Kellner: "Triangular Anxieties: The Present State of European Intellectual History."

man historians.[7] Handler, an anthropologist, presents a penetrating analysis of the social and political institutions, as well as the cultural practices, that have nurtured contemporary Québécois nationalism. It is a remarkable book. One of its remarkable features is the reflections it contains on the author's methodological complicity in his subject-matter, or what Handler calls the correlation between actors' desires and observers' epistemology. He argues that the social scientist who defines Québécois nationalism as an object of study is ratifying the nationalists' own premise that the nation is a bounded, individuated being. More remarkable is Handler's meditation on the phenomenology of nationalism, which he characterizes as "an ideology of what C. B. Macpherson called possessive individualism."[8] This proposition provides the basis for the jarring conclusion to a book that has provided an extended and vivid account of Quebec's recent history. Nationalistic insecurity, the author writes, "is incurable, a function of the logic of possessive individualism rather than the contingencies of national history." "Nationalists are haunted by a vision of totality," he observes, but their vision can never be realized.

> To achieve the totality of a complete and self-contained existence, appropriation is necessary. The collective individual can realize itself only through constant production, through a continual objectivification of what is imagined to be its authentic culture. *But objectivification inevitably unbounds the bounded entity*, deconstructs the desired totality.[9]

This unhappy picture of historical actors sealed off from the contingencies of history, locked – with the author's complicity – in the discursive contradictions of their own enterprise, anticipates to an extent Thomas Childers' recent description of electoral politics in Weimar Germany.[10] In an effort to "provide a fresh perspective" and to move beyond the arid debate over the German Sonderweg, Childers turns to the "social vocabulary of political discourse" in the Weimar era. He finds that this vocabulary was dominated by the rhetoric of the Berufsstand, that all the non-socialist parties addressed potential voters in occupational categories that harbored lingering connotations of corporatist solidarity. The fact that the middle-class liberal parties adopted this vocabulary was especially fateful, for, as Childers explains, the corporatist vocabulary, the "linguistic forms of Stand and Berufsstand," not only had

---

7 Handler: *Nationalism and the Politics of Culture in Quebec*; Koshar: "Playing the Cerebral Savage."
8 Handler: *Nationalism and the Politics of Culture in Quebec*, p. 14.
9 Ibid., p. 194, the italics are the author's.
10 Childers: "The Social Language of Politics in Germany."

"outlived the social and economic conditions" it had evolved to describe; it was also antithetical to liberalism (to say nothing of Marxism) and fed the nationalist intolerance that had come to enshroud corporatist ideas. Hence it "compelled the parties of the left and the liberal center to operate on a linguistic terrain that was far more congenial to conservative or even fascist politics than their own."[11] Language operated as "an independent cultural variable in German political life." Like Handler's nationalists (and like Handler himself), Childers' liberals found themselves constrained by their linguistic practices; they participated in a discourse whose relationship to the "contingencies of history" (in this case "social and economic conditions") was problematic and whose logic defeated the liberal goals these men and women sought consciously to achieve.

A third example invokes a similar analytical perspective, albeit in an interesting variation. It comes from Geoff Eley, who has recently published a second edition of his book on radical nationalism in the imperial epoch. He has equipped the new edition with a new introduction, in order to relieve the misunderstandings sown by reviewers of the book's first edition.[12] The argument of that book, in brief, was that radical nationalism – particularly as it found form in the German Navy League and the Pan-German League – signified a populist onslaught against the established structure of party-politics in Wilhelmine Germany; it represented the self-mobilization of subordinate classes against the narrow conventions of Honoratiorenpolitik, which had excluded these outsiders from influence in the established parties, particularly in the National Liberal party. In his new introduction, the author responds to the charge that the leaders of the patriotic societies in question were themselves recruited from the same social circles as Imperial Germany's Honoratioren and were in many localities in fact the same men who led the National Liberal party. This criticism, Eley explains now, missed the point of his argument, which was to devise a "much stronger form of explanation" than a reductionist, "directly social" approach to politics and ideology – that is, one that "tried to explain radical-nationalist ideology primarily in terms of the social backgrounds of its supporters."

The question is not really pertinent whether Eley is describing now the book he wrote then, although that book's many references to "subordinate classes" and "a new type of petty-bourgeois nationalism" suggest that the author was himself pursuing then what he condemns now as "an explanation from sociology or social history." More interesting are the terms in which he

---

11 Ibid., p. 357.
12 Eley: *Reshaping the German Right*, pp. xiii–xxvi.

has recast the analysis in his new introduction. He proposes to focus on "ideology per se," in order to take radical nationalism "seriously in its own terms." His "much stronger form of explanation" is to be "a political rather than a directly social explanation." And the references in the introduction to deconstructing, discourses, and post-structuralism reveal the extent to which he, too, has built a theoretical scaffolding for this explanation from linguistic theory. Eley evidently wishes to frame the history of radical nationalism within a discourse of German politics. His strictures against sociological explanation invite the conclusion that this discourse must be analyzed on its own terms, that it proceeded autonomously through a series of "discursive moments" until it culminated in 1933. Although its immediate subject is politics rather than language, a compelling discursive logic operates in Eley's analysis, as it does in Childers' and Handler's; and it, too, seems to remain independent of social determination, constraint, or explanation.

All three of these examples bear witness to the growing influence of the "linguistic turn" in the academic community of North American historians. Although the term itself comprehends a bewildering variety of theories and assumptions (by no means all of them compatible), it connotes an interpretive orientation that is founded on the autonomy of language in history. It commonly reflects a preference for an "idealist" theory of language: the function of language is not (or not only) to reflect or mediate a historical reality independently given, but rather to give essential shape to that reality, in other words, to constitute it. Reality, in this view, can be experienced only by means of language – that is, in categories that are linguistically constructed. Language accordingly provides not only the means, but also the limits of knowledge – the substance as well as the forms of experience. The structure of language furnishes the framework for perceiving and interpreting a reality whose claims to ontological autonomy have become problematic. Like the ideas of which Carlton Hayes once spoke, language operates with a force that shapes the very definition of reality.

Two features of this hypothesis – the one epistemological, the other analytical – have had the most immediate implications for the writing of history. The theory demands, in the first place, that the relationship between historians and their subject-matter is constituted in language. The past is intelligible only as a text. The writing of history, the "reading" of that text – or the historian's effort to impose coherence and meaning on the past – is constrained by the rhetorical practices and discursive conventions that structure the historian's own cultural world. It follows then, as a second consequence of this theory of language, that the structuring of that text itself prescribes specific categories of explanation for the historian. Because the experience of historical actors has also been constituted in language, their behavior, too, is to be analyzed in the light of constraints that discursive practices imposed on their thoughts and action.

The three examples cited above suggest some of the possible practical consequences of this theory for the writing of history. Of the three accounts, Handler's is the most self-conscious about the way the historian's (or the anthropologist's) discursive commitments affect the structure of the historical text. All three, however, resort to explanations that feature the constraining force of discursive practice on historical actors. And all three invite objections from social historians who believe in the referentiality of language to social structures and processes.[13] Eley may have evaded a reductionist analysis of politics, but he has made the relationship between ideology and society problematic at the least, if he has not embraced a kind of hermetic, "Lovejoyean" history of politics. Handler's analysis raises the question whether he has not displaced the real issue, which is the nature of the "contingent historical circumstances" that gave rise to ideologies of possessive individualism in the first place. Childers is the most uneasy about the hermetic implications of his approach, perhaps because the logic of his own discourse impels him back into the middle of the Sonderweg debate, where he has to emphasize the role of "pre-modern" factors in the rise of National Socialism and hence to defend a position much maligned, among others by Eley.[14] To test Childers' claims, to relate the "text" of the discourse he describes to its context, would require, as he himself admits, a life's work – a comparative "examination of social structures, modes of political mobilization, and the social vocabulary of political discourse both across national frontiers and over time."[15] An appropriate starting point would surely be the use of the language of Berufsstand in electoral politics during in the early years of the Kaiserreich, when this same social vocabulary apparently comported with an era of liberal ascendency .

A deeper methodological problem is more difficult to address. The self-referentiality of language, a central premise of much of the linguistic theory these historians use, is itself self-referential; it cannot be tested – least of all by historians – through appeal to a historical reality beyond language, whose existence the theory denies. Given the absence of a common forum to which the theory's advocates and opponents can appeal, the debate among historians over the linguistic turn has been as frustrating as it has been empassioned.

---

13 Palmer: *Descent into Discourse.*
14 See Eley: "What Produces Fascism?"
15 Childers: "The Social Language of Politics," p. 357.

The debate has also generated a sense of déjà vue. In significant respects, it has recapitulated epistemological controversies that raged, in Germany and elsewhere, in the social and cultural sciences at the beginning of the present century.[16] Professional historians did not participate much in those controversies, for they were as little equipped then as most are now to engage basic theoretical questions of concept-formation, hermeneutics, metaphysical (or metahistorical) commitment, and the objectivity of historical knowledge. However, the same specters loom again. Theories that today emphasize the power of discursive logic are implicated in Hegelianism, or what was known in the earlier controversies as emanationism, while some varieties of linguistic theory, particularly those known today as deconstructionist, are no less implicated in nihilism (not to say gnosticism).

The methodological reflections of Max Weber provided the most durable reply to Hegel and Nietzsche during the earlier controversies; and it is tempting to argue that they bear on the current debates as well. To be sure, Weber's authority can hardly be invoked against the claims that the role of historians is to "read" the text of the past, or that what passes for historical reality can have only discursive status. But his views do offer practical orientation for historians who wish to navigate amidst or around these claims. In the first place, they suggest the hypothetical, ideal-typical character of all theories that inform historical writing – the fact that theories of whatever order can offer but provisional guidance in framing what might today be called the discourse with the past. Weber insisted, though, that these theories not be regarded as self-enclosed, that they are modified in constant collision with the empirical results that they themselves yield – in other words, with the particulars generated in the discourse itself. The linguistic codes and practices, which in contemporary theories of language frame all discourses with the past, correspond to the interests and value-judgments that in Weber's view govern the observer's choice of ideal-types. Their operation is a powerful constraint on the observer; but it does not preclude a degree of control through the observer's conscientious attention to her own Werturteile. Finally, although the philosophical status of his own preferences was insecure, insofar as they could rest only on his own value-judgments, Weber offered criteria for judging the utility, if not the value of theories, hypothetical constructions, or what one might call modes of discourse. When speaking of history, he once insisted, "one must always think in the broadest sense of the word."[17] Comprehensiveness, the capacity of theory to open and integrate, was, in Weber's view, the meas-

---

16   Hughes: *Consciousness and Society*; Chickering: *Karl Lamprecht*.
17   Weber: "Roscher und Knies," p. 47.

ure of its power. One of Weber's modern-day disciples, the historian Jürgen Kocka, has framed this argument for inclusion in somewhat different terms. To the question of how one assesses the validity of such a construct or model, he poses a practical, negative answer. One should reject a model, he writes, when it is clear that "important features of reality, as these are defined by [the observer's] interests and criteria of inquiry [Erkenntnisinteressen], cannot be comprehended in the model at all, that they fall, so to speak, through its grid, that they fit it neither positively nor negatively, [or] that they are overlooked."[18]

To historians who share these preferences for inclusiveness, linguistic theories suffer to the extent that their analytical force excludes – that it divorces text from context, seals off realms of the past in the hermetic play of language, or blocks analytical access to other realms that scholars, for whatever reason, continue to regard as "important features of reality." To cite the case of Geoff Eley once again, the rejection of a "sociological" approach in favor of a discursive analysis of politics appears to exclude or dismiss historical features of radical nationalism that other scholars have found interesting and significant – such as the social backgrounds of the radical nationalists, the salience of cultural anxiety in their ideologies, their antisemitism, and the very language of radical nationalism.[19] His complaint that other authors "largely talk past the central argument of my own book" is a symptom of the problem.[20]

Analytical exclusion is by no means an inherent feature of these theories, even those that insist on the self-referentiality of language. In fact, many proponents of the linguisitc turn are uncomfortable in the shadow of Hegel; a number of them are social historians who have concluded that explanations built on traditional concepts of social class frustrate the comprehensive ambitions of social history, insofar as these concepts exclude, devalue, or reduce the realms of culture and politics to epiphenomena of class. Some have found powerful succor in the work of Foucault, at least those facets of it that seem to emphasize the bonds among language, symbols, and practice – those that link language to questions of representation and power; despite Foucault's own ultimate intentions, perhaps, understanding language as institutionalized practice has suggested analytical access to ethnography and political science.[21] Social historians have also found theories useful that emphasize the intercon-

---

18 Kocka: *Klassengesellschaft im Krieg*, p. 140
19 Muller: *The Other God that Failed*, pp. 38–39, n. 43; Volkov: "Das geschriebene und das gesprochene Wort," p. 208, n. 30.
20 Eley: *Reshaping the German Right*, p. xxv.
21 Megill: "Foucault."

nection of discourses (or what is being called their "imbrication") – their tropological, structural, or thematic linkages; and some of these theories seem to offer, by means of an expanded, multi-layered understanding of the "text," nothing less than the grounding for a histoire totale.[22]

The question persists, nonetheless, whether these linguistic theories, specifically those that have found employment in recent works on nationalism, are not of necessity so implicated in philosophical idealism that they prescribe an analytical strategy no less exclusionary than those that have led social historians to deprecate class analysis. Privileging language, emphasizing the autonomy of discourse, threatens to reduce social structures and processes to epiphenomena. An inclusive historiography cannot dispense with language; but one might well ask whether the goal of inclusion is not served better by theories that accommodate what one scholar has called the "Janus-faced" features of language.[23] Language, in this view, both mediates and constitutes; the relationship between language and social reality is reciprocal. This approach admittedly skirts issues of ontological priority, but its justification is less theoretical than practical. It addresses interesting historical questions.

The brief remarks that follow represent a plea for such a "Janus-faced" approach to the role of language in history. Their object is an organization whose history begs for close attention to language and discourse, but the historical significance of this organization cannot be understood solely in the light of autonomous discursive practices. Its history touches on central issues in the contemporary scholarly discussion of language and its functions, including the constituent role of language in human affairs, the role of language in forging social identity, and the manipulability of language to political ends.

The pedigree of Sprachgesellschaften in Germany extends back at least into the sixteenth century. The principal significance of these organizations lay in constituting and politicizing a bourgeois public sphere in Germany; after they helped to promote German to the status of a literary language in the seventeenth and eighteenth centuries, they helped, in the early nineteenth century, to establish this language as a foundation of political unification.[24] Their activities included defining common orthographic standards and replacing words of foreign derivation, principally Latin or French, with German equivalents. After unification in 1871, with the campaign for a common

---

22 Jameson: *The Political Unconscious*.
23 Townson: *Mother-Tongue and Fatherland*, p. 212.
24 For a survey and guide to the literature see Olt: *Wider das Fremde?*, pp. 6–45; Ameri: *Die deutschnationale Sprachbewegung*.

orthography largely won, the organizations that made up the so-called Sprachbewegung turned to promoting civic solidarity through linguistic purity, and their attention concentrated increasingly on purging the national language of foreign words.

Several dozen local language societies were active in 1885, when Hermann Riegel, the director of the ducal art museum in Braunschweig, presided over the founding of a national organization, the German Language Association (Allgemeiner Deutscher Sprachverein).[25] The new organization was designed to invigorate, coordinate, and expand local efforts to protect the language. As announced in its statutes, the goal of the Sprachverein was to cleanse "the German language of all unnecessary foreign elements" and to restore and preserve the language's "pure spirit and its unique and essential characteristics [eigenthümliches Wesen]."[26] The growth of the new organization rewarded the expectations of its founder, as the campaign on behalf of these goals enjoyed a broad resonance. Within a year the Sprachverein had expanded to ninety local chapters with a membership of 7,000; by the turn of the century it comprised about two hundred local groups and 20,000 members, and on the eve of the war it had grown to 318 chapters and 34,280 members. The bulk of these members resided within the German Empire, but the network of chapters extended well beyond the frontiers of the state into Austria, Switzerland, Italy, and the United States.

The rapid growth of the Language Association reflected in part the widespread view, which state and local officials shared, that the organization represented a good, patriotic, but harmless cause, and that encouraging it carried little political risk.[27] The organization did in fact often provoke amusement, as national leaders and local activists undertook an energetic hunt for foreign words, which spared neither centers of elegant sociability nor high government offices. Restaurants that offered "menus" instead of "Speisekarten," German diplomats who lapsed into the lingua franca, and the German army, whose designation of ranks betrayed French influence, alike incurred the public opprobrium of the Fremdwortjäger. That the campaign produced its absurdities was perhaps inevitable; and there was widespread de-

---

25 See Dunger: *Die deutsche Sprachbewegung und der allgemeine deutsche Sprachverein*; Bernsmeier: "Der Allgemeine Deutsche Sprachverein in seiner Gründungsphase;" "Der Allgemeine Deutsche Sprachverein in der Zeit von 1912 bis 1932;" "Der Deutsche Sprachverein im Dritten Reich."

26 *Zeitschrift des Allgemeinen Deutschen Sprachvereins* (hereafter cited as *ZADSv*) 1, c. 1.

27 For example: Staatsarchiv Münster, Kreis Tecklenburg (245), Sarazin to Landrat, Berlin, 6 December 1902; Stadtarchiv Freiburg i. Br., C3/362–9, Sarazin to Stadtrat, 8 December 1902; cf. *ZADSv* 15, c. 194.

bate within the organization itself over the wisdom of some of the contortions required to rid the language of foreign imports – like "Zigarre," for which Rauchrolle was the alternative of choice, or "tennis," for which "Rasenballspiel" seemed to offer Ersatz.[28]

These debates spoke to significant disagreements in the Sprachverein about the standards by which to judge the propriety of foreign words, some of which had entered common usage centuries earlier. On the fundamental principle of what might be called the discourse on language, however, consensus reigned in the organization. To the surprise of no modern linguist, this principle was a binary opposition. It was defined by the poles "German" and "non-German" – the opposition between the German language and an entity called, in untranslatable German, "das Fremdwörtertum" or "das Fremdwörterunwesen." This basic opposition informed the commentary and debate in the Language Association's journal and other literature and in the meetings of the local chapters; and in these forums it structured representations of both the language and the organization's own campaign.

The metaphorical variety in which the opposition found expression was one indication of its power. The images were colorful if not entirely consistent. Perhaps the most common were organic metaphors, both animal and vegetable. The German language was portrayed as a living entity, whose growth and health posed both the danger and the great challenge. In this representational framework, foreign words appeared as an "epidemic [Seuche]," a threat to the "healthy development" of the language.[29] They also appeared as "weeds" or "overgrowth [Verwilderung]" in a common variation of this theme, in which the language activists represented the language in metaphors of the garden.[30] That it was no low-maintenance garden was clear in the extended metaphor of one activist, who reflected in 1905 on the rejuvenating functions of folk-dialects. The language in this case was a tree, and the object of this gardener's concern was the dialectical soil in which it grew. Because many a "feeble and dry sprig" appeared on the tree's "mighty boughs and branches," he explained, it was necessary to "loosen the soil carefully," to "turn it over so that light and air penetrate it better and its invigorating fluid streams more vitally up through the trunk to the young leaves and blossoms."[31] Gardening the language could be a strenuous undertaking, and on occasion the metaphors became quasi-military. In 1907 a member eulogized

---

28 See Bernsmeier: "Gründungsphase," pp. 387–88.
29 *ZADSv* 19, cc. 161–66; ibid. 22, c. 166.
30 *ZADSv* 20, c. 1; ibid. 27, c. 176; cf. Ameri: *Die deutschnationale Sprachbewegung*, pp. 118–19.
31 *ZADSv* 20, c. 339.

one of the organization's pioneers, who had saved the language "from the affliction of foreign words" and had undertaken to "remove with a single blow the[se] tiresome recalcitrants [Wildlinge] and to eradicate them root and branch."[32]

In these and other metaphorical variations, the binary opposition between "German" and "foreign" defined the valences in the discourse on language. When one member described foreign words as "pimples" on "the faces that are dear to us," he invoked the aesthetic criteria that reigned in the Language Association.[33] "We are quite certain," wrote another, "that our beloved German language gains in beauty when we drive out the unneeded foreigners [Fremdlinge]." Germans were justified, he continued, "in branding as ugly all foreign words that, by dint of their tonal development, form, or intonation, have an un-German sound." That standards of taste also had ethical connotations became clear when the same writer characterized German words as "upright [bieder]" and foreign words as an "indecent and flashy creature [anrüchiges und geschniegeltes Wesen]." [34]

The allusion to creatures of ill-repute drew from another, more suggestive metaphorical vocabulary, and it suggested the gendered valences that operated in the Sprachverein's self-representations. Many of the images used to describe the German language were feminine. Dialects were, in the characterization of one member, the "simple, down-to-earth mother" of the "proud and eminent daughter," which was the modern, written language.[35] Representing the language in these terms underscored the dangers faced by mother and daughter alike, the vulnerability of their purity as well as their beauty to penetration, or as one activist remarked of German-language instruction in New York City, to "Vergewaltigung" by foreign words.[36]

In its valences and metaphors, as well as in its structural contours, the discourse on language was linked with a number of other discourses in Wilhelmine Germany. One of these was the discourse on foreign policy. In the first decade of its campaign, the principal object of the Sprachverein's vigilance was the infiltration of the German language by French words. By the end of the century, the source of concern had shifted in step with the new priorities and rivalries prescribed in German foreign policy. When one leader warned in 1899 of a "new overflooding of our language with foreign words,"

---

32 *ZADSv* 22, c. 1.
33 *ZADSv* 15, c. 3.
34 *ZADSv* 15, cc. 1–7.
35 *ZADSv* 20, c. 338.
36 *ZADSv* 18, c. 271.

he meant English words, like "tennis."[37] During the same years the discourse on foreign policy became itself entwined in theories of geopolitics, which were cast in the same organic metaphors of growth and health as the discourse on language. The new "science" of race and eugenics likewise drew from this vocabulary, and at this point one might well ask how harmless the efforts of the Language Association really were.[38] It is of some comfort that a preponderance of opinion in the organization rejected the word "race" ("Rasse") as foreign.[39] Nonetheless, calls for "extermination [Ausrottung] of that desolate weed" (the subject was again Fremdwörterunwesen) appeared early and often in the discussion of language in the Sprachverein.[40]

One could perhaps conclude here, by noting this "discursive moment" in a text or linguistic enterprise that culminated in Auschwitz. To do so would leave another order of questions unaddressed. These have to do with power and its social foundations. The interlinking of several discourses pointed toward the broader context of the Language Association's campaign. The object of this campaign was to prescribe the linguistic fundaments – in particular the rigid oppositions between "German" and "foreign" – in which all these discourses were anchored. In this connection, the many small successes that the organization registered in ministries, local government offices, and professional associations were anything but trivial; they suggested the extent to which the campaign to purge the language enjoyed the support of some of the most powerful agencies and groups in the country.[41] Banishing foreign words from street-signs, military ordinances, and menus (and stigmatizing the foreign words that remained) was a hegemonic enterprise; its purpose was, as one commentator has recently noted, to determine via linguistic practices the very "horizons of understanding" through which men, women, and children in Imperial Germany perceived and made sense of the world about them.[42] The members of the Language Association understood their activities in just these terms. The function of language was, in their view, not merely to reflect or mediate reality, but to constitute it. At stake was the mental ordering of the national experience by means of language – the promotion of a basic "mindset," or what in German is called Gesinnung. "Let one only courageously set

---

37 *ZADSv* 14, cc. 249–51; ibid. 27, cc. 130–32.
38 Weindling: *Health, Race and German Politics*.
39 *ZADSv* 15, c. 3.
40 *ZADSv* 1, c. 180; cf. ibid. 22, c. 1.
41 *ZADSv* 25, c. 115–17; ibid., cc. 1–4; ibid. 12, c. 182; Bernsmeier: "Gründungsphase," cc. 381–86.
42 Ibid., c. 377.

out a word," remarked one member about the power of language to structure thinking, "and it will not be long before the desired concept will become connected with it."[43]

It is one thing to emphasize the capacity of linguistic practices to constitute collective identity in this manner; it is another thing to measure the effectiveness of these practices. Binary oppositions are a premise in some varieties of linguistic theory; in historical analysis, they are an interesting problem, particularly when their rigidity encourages the kind of thinking that is known, in another theory or discourse, as dichotomization.[44] Measuring the popular impact of these oppositions, if it could be done at all, would far exceed the bounds of this essay. Here it must suffice to emphasize how few were the people who participated in or cared much about the campaign for linguistic purity in Imperial Germany; the activists were recruited from a narrow social group, and their campaign reflected a specific cultural experience and political agenda.

Hegemony, as theorists of this concept have argued, implies the contestation of a culture's central symbols – a struggle whose object is to prescribe the very meaning of those symbols. The history of the Language Association is testimony to this principle. The prominence of metaphors of struggle and resistance in the language of the Sprachvereinler betrayed an intense awareness of the conflictive aspects of their own efforts on behalf of Imperial Germany's most central symbol. If an aura of confidence had characterized the struggle against foreign words in the early years of the new Kaiserreich, accents of fear and apprehension, as well as a tendency toward conspiratorial thinking, had become salient features of the Language Association's outlook by the end of the century.[45] The images in which these anxieties found expression offered clues to the nature of the conflict, as well as to the cultural issues and social claims at stake in the campaign against foreign words.

In rich variation, these images emphasized infiltration, invasion, impingement, and penetration by hostile forces. The most suggestive of these images employed metaphors of in-fluence – of water, flooding, and storms – to underscore a threat posed by elements out of control, like the myriad ethnic groups in central Europe that "stormed the German language [laufen Sturm gegen deutsche Sprache]."[46] One leader of the Language Association gave expression to the same anxieties in 1914, when he warned against a "flood of

---

43 *ZADSv* 13, c. 230.
44 Chickering: "Der 'Deutsche Wehrverein,'" pp. 7–33.
45 Townson: *Mother-Tongue and Fatherland*, p. 98.
46 *ZADSv* 11, c. 135

laws, ordinances, and publications" written in a "language saturated [durchsetzt] with 'learned' foreign expressions," which was "inundating the German people."[47] The watery images were the most dramatic, but they addressed the same apprehensions as did the other metaphors in the Language Association's repertoire. Whether they were portrayed as a flood, weeds, pimples, or simply as "junk [Kram]," foreign words represented a formidable danger, whose unchecked growth threatened to bring disorder and then chaos to a system of linguistic relationships essential to German culture.[48]

In this light, the German language was itself a metaphor for culture and order, whose custodians had congregated in the Language Association. The garden-metaphors suggested the broader, gendered implications of this proposition. The gardener, the guardian of linguistic purity, represented the agent of discipline and order. The object of his attentions, the garden of the language, was marked in contrast by its receptivity, passivity, and malleability. Foreign words threatened to subvert the quest for structure, order, and clarity, which leaders of the Sprachverein equated ultimately with the achievement of Kultur. Culture meant control. The mark of the Kulturvolk, one leader remarked in 1901, lay precisely in its "creating and dispensing," in its overcoming the receptivity of the Naturvolk.[49] Passivity in the garden boded the most far-reaching practical cultural consequences. The proliferation of foreign words, as one writer observed in 1902, made for unclear, abstract thinking: it encouraged "faded, grey, shadowy, flitting [huschende], foggy, general impressions of flatness and outlines." Eschewal of these words, the same writer continued, revealed a "sharp and exact, well-disciplined – and that means a well-schooled – spirit."[50]

Mention of a "well-schooled spirit" in this connection was not inadvertent; it spoke directly to the social claims that underlay the quest for linguistic purity in Imperial Germany. The language represented both the essential precondition and the guarantee of a specific vision of order. A purified, healthy German language was to symbolize, express, mediate, and constitute this order – and with it the national experience. The critical question was which – or more specifically, whose – language was to symbolize, express, mediate, and constitute German national experience in this fashion. The answer was so self-evident that it hardly required posing in the Language Association. The role, and the authority to which it brought entitlement, fell to those who were

---

47 *ZADSv* 29, c. 1.
48 *ZADSv* 28, c. 99.
49 *ZADSv* 16, c. 308.
50 *ZADSv* 17, cc. 337–40.

known in the parlance of the organization as "sprachverständige Männer," men of insight into language (there was little talk of "women of insight into language"); and these were the men who eschewed double negatives – men whose linguistic practices, grammar, vocabulary, pronunciation, and orthography marked them as being "cultivated."[51]

The salience of Bildung in the ideology of the German Language Association corresponded to the central features of the organization's social profile.[52] A survey of 1,876 men who held local office in chapters in Germany between 1895 and 1914 reveals the overwhelming preponderance of the Bildungsbürgertum. More than two-thirds of the local leaders were "well-schooled" – in the specific sense that they were academically educated. More than a quarter of them also held doctorates. Three-quarters of the local leaders (1,398) were publicly employed. More than a thousand of these public officials, 55% of all the local leaders, were employed in the teaching profession, two-thirds of them as Gymnasiallehrer (who doubtless found that metaphors of the garden spoke to experiences in the classroom).[53] Most of the other public officials in the Sprachverein's cadres were recruited from the upper-level ranks of federal, state, and local bureaucracies, which also required academic training of the men who worked there. Finally, although the evidence is more fragmentary, it suggests that the Sprachbewegung was largely a Protestant phenomenon, and that chapters of Language Association were rare in Catholic Germany.[54] The aspirations of the organization to represent a cross-section of the nation were thus belied by cadres that were largely bereft of women, Catholics, workers, rural folk, and nobles.

This profile of the German Language Association bore a remarkable resemblance to that of the other major patriotic societies in Imperial Germany, such as the Pan-German League, the German Colonial Society, the Eastern Marches Society, and the German School Association. In all these organizations the leading roles fell to Protestant middle-class men who were academically trained and on the public payroll. Fragmentary evidence for these organizations (and the Language Association) indicates that the same generalizations apply as well to the rank-and-file membership, where there was considerable overlap among all the patriotic societies; statistics from Hamburg suggest that amost a third of the members of the local branch of the Lan-

---

51 *ZADSv* 1, c. 180; ibid. 12, c. 237; ibid. 14, c. 6.
52 Bell: "The German Language Association: A Study of Radical Nationalism;" Chickering: *We Men Who Feel Most German*, pp. 314–16.
53 *ZADSv* 14, c. 64.
54 *ZADSv* 19, cc. 97–8.

guage Assocation belonged to one of the other patriotic societies in that city.⁵⁵ These affinities, like the many programmatic parallels, confirmed the location of the Sprachverein in the same social milieu as these other organizations. So does the prominence of rigid oppositions, conspiratorial thinking, and invasive images in the literature of all of them.⁵⁶

These similarities betrayed the campaign for linguistic purity as an instance of what Terry Eagleton has recently called the "inscription of social power within language."⁵⁷ The campaign grew out of the ranks of Imperial Germany's educated Honoratioren, a milieu whose cultural and political prominence gave it power and influence in Imperial Germany far beyond what its numbers might have suggested. The defining mark of this milieu was a common social experience, which featured beleagued claims to cultural authority. The Language Association, no less than the other patriotic societies, was populated in the main by men whose cultural roles were conditioned by academic training and public employment; and these roles demanded that their occupants deal constantly with issues of culture and public order. Here, no less than in the other organizations (although with characterisitic emphasis), the activists participated in what one might call, with Frederic Jameson, the "master discourse" of patriotic activism or radical nationalism in Imperial Germany. This discourse corresponded to the experience of a social group that laid claim to cultural authority in Imperial Germany – men who could plausibly represent themselves as custodians of those German values that underlay culture and order, because their Bildung and their public authority entitled them to do so.

The Language Association, like the other patriotic societies, sought to validate a specific German language and the claims that grew out of the cultural experience of a specific social group. This language no doubt structured that experience, at least in the sense that its rigid oppositions heightened the anxieties of these men and fed their obsessions with the enemies that threatened culture and order in myriad guises – in the form of foreign words, Czech beer, Social Democrats, ethnic minorities, feminists, Catholics, pacifists, or Jews.

However, it is also essential to ask why these men were so receptive to this kind of anxiety-laden language. And one compelling answer is that this language reflected and mediated an experienced world: it made this experience meaningful. The men who used and promoted this language occupied custo-

---

55 Chickering: *We Men Who Feel Most German*, pp. 185–97, 322.
56 Ibid., 81–93; cf. Theweleit: *Männerphantasien*.
57 Eagleton: *Ideology*, p. 196.

dial roles over culture and authority; because of their training and occupations they stood, so to speak, in the front lines of social and cultural conflict in Imperial Germany, for they embodied the public order, authority, and the dominant cultural values that were symbolized in this language.

The history of the German Language Association documents the centrality of language in the history of radical nationalism during the Wilhelmine epoch. Salient features of the campaign to purify the language invite a reading in the light of linguistic theory, for while the success of their campaign is difficult to measure, the Sprachvereinler understood early the significance of linguistic forms in constituting the national experience. But theories that emphasize the autonomy of discursive practices can furnish at best a partial analysis of this campaign, for the history of the Sprachverein underscores as well the historical contingency of language, the fact that language is not autonomous, that it is instead both a contingent and constituent facet of social experience. The designs of the Sprachbewegung were hegemonic; the goal of the Language Association was to establish the civic validity of linguistic practices indigenous to a specific milieu. But the history of this campaign highlights the existence of a plurality of languages, which both reflected and structured a plurality of conflicting social and cultural milieus in the German Empire.[58]

---

58 See Lepsius: "Parteiensystem und Sozialstruktur."

John S. Cornell
Butler University

"Dann weg 'mit's Milletär' und wieder ein civiler Civilist": Theodor Fontane and the Wars of German Unification

Abstract: The wars of 1864, 1866 and 1870/71 were decisive events in shaping Theodor Fontane's identity as a German. This essay examines in detail some of the arguments and attitudes expressed by Fontane in his three histories of the wars of unification. Although disappointed by his failure to gain recognition as a writer for the new nation – a disappointment which fueled his determination to begin writing fiction – Fontane never renounced the German-national position he acquired during these years. The essay argues that this middle period of Fontane's career should be viewed not as an interruption, but as an integral part of Fontane's development as a German writer.

1.

The period of German unification played an important transitional role in the life and work of Theodor Fontane.[1] Throughout the course of his long and productive career, Fontane (1819–1898) never doubted the uniqueness and value of being German. The difficulty was that "being German" was something which Fontane – as did others living at the time – constantly had to figure out and reassess. From Vormärz to the Wilhelmine era, the very conception and political implications of "Germany" changed again and again. During the decades in which Germany emerged as a modern nation-state from the patchwork of the defunct Holy Roman Empire and from the rivalry of Austria and Prussia, German identities shifted dramatically in relation to other modes of self-conception. Fontane, for example, was constantly comparing his sense of being German with his identity, among other things, as a

---

[1] I would like to thank Manfred Horlitz and Peter Schaefer of the Theodor Fontane Archiv, Potsdam, for their indefatigable assistance, as well as Butler University and the German Academic Exchange Service for their timely and generous financial support.

Prussian, as a respectable member of the middle classes, as a European, and as a writer. Like everyone else living in Germany in the nineteenth century, Fontane had to invent what it meant to be German as he went along.[2]

The unification of Germany in the Franco-Prussian War of 1870/71, was a central, defining event for Fontane in constructing his own national identity. Like most other Germans, Fontane greeted the declaration of the empire on January 18, 1871, with elation. To be sure, he did not indulge in the uncritical, chauvinistic "Hurra-Patriotismus" so characteristic of the Gründerzeit. But in later years, he looked back on Germany's achievements with undimmed satisfaction. Fontane is primarily admired today as a keen-eyed observer, even critic of imperial society. This should not obscure, however, the fact that Fontane considered the unification of Germany to be the decisive, dramatic national event of his lifetime. The wars of Prussia against Denmark (1864), Austria (1866), and finally against France (1870/71) had at long last turned "Germany" from an abstraction into a reality. For Fontane – as for many of his contemporaries – these wars played a positive, long-lasting role in shaping what it meant to be German.[3]

The wars of unification also presented Fontane with the most ambitious literary projects which he ever attempted. As a writer and journalist of limited resources and modest renown, Fontane devoted twelve long years from 1864 to 1876 to writing histories of these three wars. The task grew exponentially. What began as a commission for a "popular" military account from the publisher Rudolf Decker,[4] who sent Fontane to survey the entrenchments at Düppel, soon turned into an arduous and, in the end, disappointing mid-life career. Fontane completed his first war book, *Der Schleswig-Holsteinsche Krieg im Jahre 1864*, just in time to head for the battlefields of Bohemia. His account of

---

2   See Hobsbawm: "Inventing Traditions." Anderson: *Imagined Communities* offers theoretical insights to nationalism and individual identity. For a recent extended discussion of German nationalism, see James: *German Identity*.

3   This analysis of German nationalism on the personal level accords well with Kelly's conclusions about collective attitudes, as revealed by German history schoolbooks during the imperial era: "The Franco-German War of 1870/71 was the formative common national experience of the newly united Reich." See this volume, p. 37. My portrait of Fontane parallels Kelly's reading of the textbooks in that "a good German was not necessarily a budding chauvinistic militarist." (p. 45) I found a striking correspondence between the patriotic "high culture" (represented by Fontane) and the wider social culture sampled by Kelly. Specific examples, e.g. downplaying the role of Bismarck in the outbreak of the war, emphasizing the character flaws of the French people, portraying the suffering of war, etc., will be noted below.

4   Fontane: *Werke, Schriften, Briefe*, ser. 4: *Briefe* vol. 2, p. 137.

the *Der deutsche Krieg von 1866* extended to two full volumes. Fontane was still at work on the proofs when war broke out against France in 1870. Because of the prolonged nature of the conflict and its political consequences for both Germany and France, the task of researching and writing this final war book was immense. By the time Fontane finally finished *Der Krieg gegen Frankreich 1870–1871* six years later, it had stretched to four volumes, plus two substantial wartime memoirs. The first, *Kriegsgefangen*, was a very successful account of his six-week imprisonment by the French under suspicion of being a Prussian spy. And the second, *Aus den Tagen der Okkupation*, was a two-volume series of observations based on his trip to France in the spring of the following year. Taken together, these war books constitute the single largest *genre* of Fontane's work – larger than the *Wanderungen durch die Mark Brandenburg*, and more than twice as long as all the novels, verse, and autobiographical works put together.[5]

Length alone is of course no measure of quality. But Fontane himself considered the war books to be a crucial step in his development as a writer. "Ich sehe klar ein," he observed in a letter to his wife Emilie shortly after the publication of *Vor dem Sturm*, "daß ich eigentlich erst bei dem 70er Kriegsbuche und dann bei dem Schreiben meines Romans ein *Schriftsteller geworden bin* d. h. ein Mann, der sein Metier als eine *Kunst* betreibt, als eine Kunst, deren *Anforderungen* er kennt."[6] The extraordinary challenge which the war books presented was to combine many different kinds of material and many different modes of narration into a complete and unified account.[7] Fontane wanted his narrative to be at once detailed and moving, analytical and grand. From a *military* point of view, he compared the tactics, strategy, mobilization, and troop movements of each opposing side. He prepared biographical sketches of major military leaders and assessed the quality of their decisions under fire. He presented sweeping, dramatic accounts of individual battles, notably Düppel, Königgrätz, and Sedan. From a *political* point of view, Fontane sought to determine the causes of each war, giving extensive consideration to history, diplomacy, and public opinion. He also rendered judgments on the responsibility

---

5 Scholarly interest in Fontane's war books has been relatively limited. Hermann Fricke and Pierre-Paul Sagave led the way in modern research. The 1985 reprint of *Der Krieg gegen Frankreich*, with a judicious and admiring forward by Gordon Craig, has elicited comment by, among others, Gudrun Loster-Schneider, Dieter Bänsch, and Christian Grawe.
6 Fontane: *Werke, Schriften, Briefe* ser. 4: *Briefe*, vol. 3, p. 201: "I recognize clearly that I really first *became a writer* with the 1870 war book and then with the writing of my novel, that is, [I became] one who practices his trade as an *art*, as an art whose *demands* he knows."
7 Demetz treats Fontane's narrative strategies in *Vor dem Sturm* with great insight. *Formen des Realismus*, pp. 51–76.

for each war, and assessed its political consequences. Finally, from a *social* point of view (perhaps the most striking departure from the conventions of military history), Fontane strove to include what we could call "human interest" stories from the perspective of war's minor participants, its victims, and its bystanders. He offered glimpses of everyday life among soldiers in camp. He quoted from letters which they wrote home to their families. After describing a battle, he seldom failed to mention the dead and the wounded. When entering territory unfamiliar to his readers, he regularly provided extensive historical background, with sympathetic observations on "Land und Leute."[8] Fontane also sought to capture the shifting moods of popular opinion on the home front: the sober, determined preparations for war as the troops left Berlin, and the jubilant crowds and patriotic speeches which met them upon their triumphant return. In short, Fontane tried to do it all.

His research during these years was substantial and exhausting. His health suffered from the strain of work. Fontane visited battlefields, interviewed participants, and compared published accounts (to his credit, from both sides). He struggled with the war books as with no other literary task before or after. His letters at the time offer poignant testimony of a writer trying to master his material. As one war gave way to the next, and as Prussia's victories turned into Germany's, the story which Fontane was trying to tell became larger, more complex, more fraught with national passions. The difficulty shows.[9]

For all the weaknesses of the war books as literature, Fontane sought to establish with them a claim to being the "vaterländischer Schriftsteller." This ambition to become the "writer for the fatherland" spurred him on when he experienced many travails and few rewards.[10] He had, after all, recounted in a comprehensive, panoramic, and patriotic fashion the epochal events which had led to the creation of a united Germany. However frustrating and burdensome the war books at times became, Fontane felt they would be well worth the effort if he were recognized as a literary spokesman of the new nation.

---

8 For sections on "The Land and its People," see *Der Schleswig-Holsteinsche Krieg*, pp. 4–13, and *Reisebriefe vom Kriegsschauplatz Böhmen*, pp. 36–44.

9 See Kelly's comments on the boring, "dreary" nature of many standard accounts of the war in the present volume p. 56.

10 Fontane: *Werke, Schriften, Briefe* ser. 4: *Briefe*, vol. 3, p. 217. Peter Wruck includes this phrase in the title of an outstanding article on Fontane's ambition and disappointment in this regard: "Theodor Fontane in der Rolle des vaterländischen Schriftsellers." I have incorporated many of Wruck's insights into this essay.

The failure to attain this recognition was a major disappointment for Fontane. The war books found an audience which was neither large in numbers nor loud in its praise. Critical reception was muted. A particular letdown for Fontane was that they were not treated seriously as military accounts.[11] Fontane did receive some official commendations and financial support from the Prussian government, but it was not nearly so much as he felt he deserved.[12]

The purpose of this essay is to examine Fontane's career during the years of German unification, from the outbreak of war with Denmark in 1864 to the completion of his war histories in 1876. First, I shall survey some of Fontane's attitudes towards Germany up until the period of unification. Then I will look in detail at some of the arguments and viewpoints presented in his war books. Finally, I will conclude with Fontane's determination, having failed as a writer of the nation's recent history, to become a writer of fiction. Here he met with great success, and is still admired today for his penetrating portrayals of imperial society. What we should bear in mind at the outset is that the critical observer of later years never obscured the German patriot. Fontane remained, above all, proud of Germany and its accomplishments. His sense of what it meant to be German in the late nineteenth century derived for the most part from the wars which had brought Germany into being.

2.

Part of the reason that "Germany" sounded so good to Fontane is that he, like many others, had strained to hear it all his life. Fontane's personal biography closely parallels the most prominent national events in the nineteenth century. There were, of course, as many different routes to achieving a Germany identity as there were Germans. But Fontane's biography is particularly instructive for having passed through so many familiar stations along the way.

Born in 1819, Fontane grew up hearing his father's stories of the "war of liberation" against the French.[13] As a young man setting out on a career in

---

11 Ibid., vol. 2, p. 280.
12 Fontane's correspondence during these years is filled with reference to personal and pecuniary slights. In particular, Fontane was upset by the withdrawal of a ministerial subsidy in 1868 and by limited support for *Der Krieg gegen Frankreich*. See Fontane: *Werke, Schriften, Briefe* ser. 4: *Briefe*, vol. 2, pp. 196, 226–27, 241–42, 244, 257, 265–66, 292, 310–11, 401–04.
13 A good introductory biography is Nürnberger: *Fontane*. For Fontane's early career and politics, see Nürnberger: *Der frühe Fontane* and Jolles: *Fontane und die Politik*. For Fontane's later political views, see the excellent analysis by Loster-Schneider: *Der Erzähler Fontane*.

pharmacy, Fontane shared with many young Germans an impassioned, politicized, and romantic vision of a united fatherland. There was no contradiction during Vormärz for Fontane between pressing for an end to the division among German states and writing ballads which celebrated the military and aristocratic past of his own native Prussia. Later in life, Fontane viewed the political enthusiasm of his youth with amused, even self-deprecating detachment. "Es kam die Herweghzeit," he wrote to Theodor Storm once his disapppointment over the failed revolution of 1848 had had time to turn into disapproval. "Ich machte den Schwindel gründlich mit, und das Historische schlug ins Politische um."[14]

Fontane's career as an ardent advocate of the German cause reached its climax in the revolution of 1848. Swept up by the enthusiasm of the moment, he found himself on the barricades during the May days in Berlin. Shortly thereafter, he was chosen to be an elector for delegates to the Frankfurt parliament. In a series of ringing liberal-nationalistic essays which appeared in the summer and fall of 1848, Fontane called for the death of Prussia, so that Germany might live.[15] Furthermore, he demanded that German unity be accompanied by political freedoms: it certainly should not come at their expense.[16] In an autobiographical account written in the 1890s shortly before his death, Fontane attempted to dismiss his activities during the revolution as so much idealistic foolishness.[17] The tone of ironic amusement which he adopts, however, does not do justice to the dashed hopes which he experienced at the time for a Germany united in political freedom.

Fontane's route to a national identity next took him abroad. He had already visited England once, on leave from his year of military service in 1844. Longer stays – for five months in 1852, and for over three year from 1855 to 1859 – not only increased Fontane's admiration for that country, but also gave him a greater appreciation for his own homeland, for Prussia. During these years of reaction in the wake of 1848, Fontane clung to a precarious career as a journalist and writer. He made it his business to adapt to the political climate of the times, working on and off in the 1850s for the press office of the Prussian government and, beginning in 1860, for the conservative *Neue Preußische (Kreuz-) Zeitung*. When Fontane had completed his stint as a foreign cor-

---

14   Fontane: *Werke, Schriften, Briefe* ser. 4, vol. 1, p. 376: "Then came the Herwegh period. I went along with the sham completely, and the historical turned into the political."
15   Fontane: "Aufsätze aus dem Revolutionsjahr." *Werke, Schriften, Briefe* ser. 3, vol. 1, pp. 9–16, here p. 9.
16   Ibid., pp. 15–6.
17   Fontane: "Von Zwanzig bis Dreißig." *Werke, Schriften, Briefe* ser. 3, vol. 4, pp. 485–500.

respondent in England, he was determined to discover his own roots in the sandy soil of Prussia. The result was the *Wanderungen*, a rich combination of landscape description, travelogue, historical anecdote, architectural guide, and essayistic commentary which explored the cultural-historical distinctiveness of the Mark Brandenburg. The *Wanderungen* (the first volumes of which appeared in the early 1860s) presage much of the narrative and compositional complexity of the later war books. Throughout the rest of his career, Fontane never ceased expanding and reediting the *Wanderungen*. His fascination for and identification with Prussia continued with the unification of Germany. Being Prussian and being German merged relatively easily for Fontane throughout the rest of his life.

It was the unification of Germany as a result of Prussia's wars which made this dual identity possible. The rapid succession of military victories only intensified Fontane's admiration for Prussia. During the war with France, Fontane widened his loyalties to include the new Reich. Germany, of course, was more than just an extension of Prussia. Fontane, however, would never forget that it was Prussia which had made Germany possible. 1871 succeeded where 1848 had failed.[18]

Fontane finally achieved recognition as a writer in the 1880s – not for his ballads, not for his journalism, not for the *Wanderungen*, not for the war books on which he had set such high hopes, but for his fiction. He first published *Vor dem Sturm* in 1878, and wrote more than a dozen other novels and novellas before his death twenty years later. These are the works which were read and admired in his time, and which are still read and admired today. Fontane proves himself in his fiction to be a trenchant, critical observer of politics and society in the Kaiserreich.

This image of the critical Fontane, however, tends to obscure Fontane's continuing identification with the achievement of 1870/1871. It implies that he grew increasingly dissatisfied with the Kaiserreich, when in fact he remained as national-minded as ever.[19] It has furthermore led Fontane scholars to make a detour around the middle period of his life. Fontane's writings

---

18 Neuhaus (see his essay in the present volume p. 140) portrays Spielhagen's critical stance towards the Kaiserreich and the "lasting congenital defect of the new *Reich*." Fontane, also an heir of 1848, viewed these events quite differently. That Fontane did not become a critic of Bismarck's empire is not so much a failure of political vision as it was a reordering of the principles of 1848, putting unity before freedom. See also Roper's discussion of Rodenberg, this volume pp. 179–82.

19 Contrast my efforts to portray Fontane as more national-minded than his reputation with those of Meyer-Krentler (this volume p. 151), portrays Raabe as less "patriotic" than his reputation.

from the the mid-1860s to the mid 1870s are understandably not of great literary interest. But something else is at work as well. Many of Fontane's readers are put off by the undisguised patriotism of his war books. As a result, these years are viewed as a kind of conservative caesura. Youthful ideals had made Fontane a revolutionary in 1848; experience had turned him into nuanced critic of the Kaiserreich. The pronounced nationalism of the unification period, so the argument goes, was out of character for Fontane.[20]

The problem is that this sort of portrayal explains *away* Fontane's middle years, and prevents us from understanding the war books as part of a consistent, enduring German component of Fontane's personality and political ideals. In the following pages, I would like to examine Fontane's histories more closely in order to reveal the basis in the wars of unification for this German-national identity.

3.

In his first war book, *Der Schleswig-Holsteinsche Krieg im Jahre 1864*, Fontane celebrates, above all, the victory of Prussia in defense of the German cause in the duchies. Although Fontane clearly distinguishes between the interests of the German *nation* and those of the Prussian *state*, the war against Denmark made it easy for him to downplay the potential tension between the two. For a contemporary German observer, Fontane is remarkably even-handed in his treatment of the causes of the war. He systematically sorts through the competing claims upon Schleswig and Holstein: by the Danish monarchy, by Danish nationalists (the Eiderdanes), by the Augustenburgs (German claimants to the duchies), by small German states, and by the two great German powers of Austria and Prussia. Fontane also gives careful consideration to historical tradition and international agreements. In the end, however, Fontane does render judgment: the Eiderdanes, driven by nationalistic stubbornness and greed, pressured Christian XI into incorporating the duchies, thereby offend-

---

20 This is the position of Hans Heinrich Reuter, whose masterful two-volume biography published in 1968 is the centerpiece of modern Fontane scholarship. To Reuter's credit, he does not shy away from the middle period of Fontane's life. But he does draw a giant arc across it, connecting Fontane the revolutionary and Fontane the novelist, and portraying what lies in between as something which Fontane had to get *over* in order to become himself. Reuter portrays the events of Fontane's life up until the late 1870s as a giant *preparation* for Fontane the novelist and social critic. Reuter in fact applies to Fontane the phrase that the novelist used to describe his own father: "Denn wie er ganz zuletzt war, so war er eigentlich." Reuter: *Fontane* vol. 2, p. 34.

ing German national sentiment and breaking the London Protocol of 1852. This forced the German powers to act. Fontane thus attributes the outbreak of war to the unjustified aggression of the Danes and the legitimate indignation of Germans. He minimizes the role played by nationalist sentiment on the German side. If anything, Schleswig and Holstein were threatened by the "Theilnahmlosigkeit des deutschen Volkes. Der Aggression der Dänen, ihrer leidenschaftlichen Hast verdanken wir es, daß das Interesse sich wieder belebte."[21] In Fontane's analysis, "je energischer Dänemark verging, je mehr Hoffnung blieb bei Deutschland."[22] Far from being critical of Prussian policy in 1864 – as Reuter suggests[23] – Fontane seems either unaware of or unconcerned by the active, opportunistic nature of Prussian policy. The hand of an author for whom the interest of Prussia and the interest of Germany easily merged is unmistakeable.

Fully half of *Der Schleswig-Holsteinsche Krieg* is occupied by Fontane's enthusiastic description of the battle of Düppel. As he does for each of the war books, Fontane describes in glowing terms the triumphal entry of the Prussian troops in Berlin at the conclusion of the war and composes a poem dedicated to victory.[24] Fontane draws a parallel between the war against the Danes and the Befreiungskrieg against the French in 1813/1814. The overall tone is one of jubilant satisfaction:

> *Die Herzogthümer waren deutsch, frei.* Ein sechsmonatlicher Krieg, – eine fast ununterbrochene Kette größerer und kleinerer Erfolge – hatte dies glänzende Resultat herbeigeführt, glänzender, als es bei Ausbruch des Krieges die kühnsten Hoffnungen erwartet haben mochten.[25]

---

21 Fontane: *Der Schleswig-Holsteinsche Krieg*, p. 25: "[…] the indifference of the German people. We have the aggression of the Danes and their impulsive haste to thank for the revival of [German national] interest."
22 Ibid., p. 26: "The more energetic Denmark's abuse, the more hope there was for Germany."
23 Reuter: *Fontane* vol. 1, p. 391.
24 Fontane: *Werke, Schriften, Briefe* ser. 1, vol. 6, pp. 238–40, 242–43, 244–46. Each of these poems observes the triumphal entry from the point of view of Prussian monuments in Berlin, either the statue of Frederick the Great on Unter den Linden (1864 and 1871) or the Brandenburg Gate (1866). Other poems commemorating the victories suggest Fontane's attempt to create a new German national mythology. See, for example, "Kaiser Blanchebart" and "Jung-Bismarck," ibid., pp. 243–44, 248–49.
25 Fontane: *Der Schleswig-Holsteinsche Krieg*, p. 373: "*The duchies became German, free.* A six-month war – an almost unbroken string of larger and smaller successes – had brought about this splendid result, more splendid than could have been expected at the outset of the war by even the boldest hopes."

Fontane was undoubtedly more restrained in his expressions of Prussian/German pride than many of his contemporaries. He resists villifying the enemy, and even praises – as he does in each of his histories – the skill and determination of the opposing forces.[26] Part of the motive for this is to increase the honor which attaches to victory, according to the proverb "Viel Feind, viel Ehr."[27] But part of it, as well, is Fontane's very civilian sense of humanity and fairness. Perhaps his unwillingness to indulge in patriotic exaggeration is one reason why his war books generated little public acclaim at the time. It is certainly the chief reason why they are admired today.[28] Nonetheless, it would be a mistake to turn Fontane's understated patriotism into non-partisanship, or indeed into a general critique of Prussian politics and the military. Fontane, for example, concludes *Der Schleswig-Holsteinsche Krieg* on an undeniably expansive note:

> Der 18. April flocht ein neues Blatt in den vollen Kranz preußischer Ehren. Es war ein glänzender Sieg, aber kein leichter und alle die ihn erringen halfen, dürfen in Demuth sich dieses stolzen Tages freuen.
> Und wir mit ihnen! –
> Vor allem aber möge gute Saat sprießen aus dem Blute derer, die gefallen; der Aera des Haders, des stillen und offenen Krieges, folge Friede, Freiheit, frischer Wind und frische Fahrt. Die meerumschlungenen Lande sind unser, werd' es auch das *Meer*. Das walte Gott![29]

4.

In his second history, *Der deutsche Krieg von 1866*, Fontane continues the story of Prussia-helping-Germany – this time against a more formidable opponent and with more decisive results. Once again the fate of Schleswig and Holstein was at stake, and once again the "German question" was uppermost. But

---

26 In his contribution to this volume (p. 57) Kelly observes the same tendency in textbooks of the period, which make the enemy "despicable enough to deserve crushing but honorable enough to make the crushing something to be proud of."
27 Loster-Schneider: "Zur Neuauflage eines Kriegs- und Antikriegsbuches," p. 615.
28 Craig: "Fontane als Historiker," pp. xxiii–xxix.
29 Fontane: *Der Schleswig-Holsteinsche Krieg*, p. 374: "The 18th of April wove a new leaf in the full wreath of Prussian honor. It was a brilliant victory, but not an easy one, and all who helped to achieve it, can humbly rejoice in this proud day. And we along with them! Above all, may good seed sprout from the blood of those who fell; may this era of strife, of secret and open war be succeeded by peace, freedom, a fresh wind, and a fresh voyage. The land surrounded by the sea is ours. May the *sea* itself become ours as well. God grant it!"

now the victors of 1864, Austria and Prussia, were fighting one another. Ostensibly, they were contesting the terms of their joint governance of Schleswig and Holstein. But what was really at stake was leadership within greater Germany.

In a chapter entitled "Wessen ist die Schuld?", Fontane again shows even-handedness and sound judgment in assessing responsibility for the war. He finds fault, or at least grounds for complaint, on both sides. Austria, he argues, is guilty of abandoning its agreements concerning the joint Austro-Prussian governance of the newly won duchies. By recognizing the claims of the Augustenburgs and thereby encouraging the agitation of German nationalists, Austria clearly provoked Prussia. The refusal by Austrian authorities to permit the celebration of Düppel day was, for Fontane, particularly galling.[30] From this point on, Fontane declares, "Das Maß war voll."[31] It is at this moment that Bismarck makes his first appearance in Fontane's histories, demanding to regain "*für unsere ganze Politik volle Freiheit* [...] und von derselben den Gebrauch machen, welchen wir den Interessen Preußens entsprechend halten.'"[32] The chancellor seems to be speaking for Fontane as well.

On the other hand, Fontane admits that Prussia was not entirely free of blame. Prussia had made full use of its prerogatives in the duchies in order draw them more closely into its sphere of influence. From the point of view of the German national movement (which had never accepted the postwar disposition of the duchies), Prussia had overstepped its bounds and threatened to absorb the duchies itself. Fontane was willing to concede that there was no legal recourse between the claims of Prussia and those of the German Bund (backed by Austria). Force alone would decide. Fontane asserts that Prussia naturally had a greater interest in what happened in the duchies than did Austria, and claims somewhat disingenuously that Prussia never intended to annex them. When push came to shove, Fontane leaves no doubt about his sympathy with the Prussian position. Central to Fontane's argument is the notion that Prussia's opportunism was in the service of a higher ideal, that of a unified Germany:

> Unter allen Umständen aber, wenn denn mal gekämpft werden sollte, wollte man die Gelegenheit nicht ungenützt vorüber gehn lassen, unnatürlichen und (für Preußen) unerträglichen Zuständen ein für allemal ein Ende zu machen. Die Herzogthümer-Frage hörte auf die Situation zu beherrschen; der Kampf Oestreichs

---

30 Fontane: *Der deutsche Krieg von 1866* vol. 1, pp. 10–1.
31 Ibid., p. 21: Prussia was "fed up."
32 Ibid., p. 22: "[Bismarck demands that we win] *our complete political freedom of movement*, and to make use of it as we see fit in the interests of Prussia."

und Preußens, wenn er unvermeidlich war, sollte ein größeres Objekt haben als Schleswig-Holstein; aus der schleswig-holsteinschen Frage heraus geboren, sollte er doch zugleich die deutsche Frage zur Erledigung bringen.[33]

This belief in a "greater purpose" meant that Fontane was willing to let Prussia have the benefit of the doubt. He chooses not to dwell on the expansionist elements of Prussian policy, and, thereby accedes to the settling of disagreements by force of arms. Fontane not only accepts the logic of Realpolitik, he also supplies it with a higher national goal. This is a theme which plays a greater role with each successive war.[34]

In addition to favoring Prussia in the war-guilt question, Fontane draws the sharpest possible distinction between the nature of the combatants. The Austrian and Prussian states, together with their peoples, exhibited very different responses to the declaration of war. According to Fontane, the Austrians were eager for it. They allowed dreams of glory to cloud their judgment. In a wave of warmongering by the press and clergy, the Austrians overestimated their resources and lost all respect for their opponent.[35] Fontane's narrative makes it clear that Austria would pay for this foolish and unjustified self-confidence.

On the other side, Prussians responded to war with determination and resolve. According to Fontane, no one made fun of the enemy; no one bragged about a quick and easy victory. Instead, Prussia set about its mobilization in a subdued and disciplined way. Prussia responded to the national emergency with a quiet marshalling of forces, emotional as well as military. Prussians knew where their duty lay – and spoke no more about it. They also benefitted from having leaders of the stature of Bismarck and Moltke.[36] In Fontane's account, in short, Prussia had both might and right on its side. In "the German War" between a boastful Austria and an earnest Prussia, the latter *deserved* to win.[37]

Fontane's second war book is an indictment not only of the Austrian military establishment but also of the entire Austrian imperial system. For Fon-

---

33   Ibid., p. 27: "But in any case, if it should come down to war, then the opportunity should not be lost to put an end to the unnatural and (for Prussia) unbearable state of affairs. The question of the duchies ceased to dominate the situation; the struggle between Austria and Prussia, if it was unavoidable, should have a greater object than Schleswig-Holstein; born of the Schleswig-Holstein question, the struggle [between Austria and Prussia] should also decide the German question once and for all."

34   Reuter argues, by contrast, that Fontane began at this point to develop a critique of nationalism and its political/military concomitants. Reuter: *Fontane* vol. 1, p. 403.

35   Fontane: *Der deutsche Krieg von 1866* vol. 1, pp. 51–3.

36   Ibid., pp. 70–105.

37   Ibid., pp. 63–6.

tane, there were important *moral* elements to Austria's military collapse. He attributes defeat to "jener Fülle von Hemmnissen, die man kurzweg als 'östreichisches System' zu bezeichnen pflegt."[38] Conversely, no single Prussian virtue could alone account for its victory. "Unser Ensemble war unsre Überlegenheit."[39] Fontane resisted attributing victory to mere technological or organizational advantage. "Wir glichen jenen Examinanden, die mit 'gut' oder selbst 'sehr gut' abschließen" – precisely the sort of qualification which many readers found too lukewarm or, indeed, unpatriotic.[40]

As in his first history, Fontane's descriptions of the military aspects of Austro-Prussian War are colorful and commemorative in nature. He adds to the solemnity of the scene at Königgrätz by depicting events from the point of view of the Prussian king. His narrative follows Wilhelm's trip across Prussian territory to take personal command of his troops. Fontane reports the shouts of approval and proud presentation of arms by the troops as the king reviews their ranks. Fontane here becomes not only a reporter of what happened, but also a proud participant.[41] In a short chapter entitled "Vorwärts!", Fontane depicts the moment of victory at Königgrätz, when the tide of the battle turns in Prussia's favor. He records the hurrahs of the soldiers, and the facing page bears an illustration of the shining arms of Prussia placed *over* those of Austria.[42]

Towards the end of his Königgrätz narrative, Fontane cites a letter written by a Prussian soldier of the line. As the smoke clears over the battlefield, the young man sees that the Prussians have won the day. The language is nothing less than that of a patriotic transfiguration:

> Der Nebel, der sich bis dahin dick über dem blutigen Ehrenfelde gelagert hatte, zerriß, und fast plötzlich sah man in weitem, nach Südosten sich öffnenden Bogen die ganze preußische Armee im Anmarsch, Brigade neben Brigade, Bataillon neben Bataillon. Unter klingendem Spiel drängte Alles vor. Mir stürzten die Thränen in die Augen, daß es mir vergönnt war diesen Moment zu erleben. So ist es vielen ergangen. Wiederholt schüttelten wir uns die Hand in innigem Dankgefühl gegen den allmächtigen Geber alles Guten, daß er uns gewürdigt hatte bei so

---

38 Ibid., p. 110: "[…] to this abundance of hindrances which one is used to simply calling the 'Austrian system.'"
39 Ibid. vol. 2, p. 335: "Our superiority was in the ensemble."
40 Ibid.: "We are like those candidates who finish with 'good' or indeed 'very good.'" Reuter cites this and other passage as examples of Fontane's non-partisanship: "Man wird sehr lange in der Kriegsliteratur der damaligen Zeit suchen müssen, bis man auf ähnliche Sätze stößt." Reuter: *Fontane* vol. 1, pp. 392–93.
41 Fontane: *Der deutsche Krieg von 1866* vol. 1, pp. 453–54.
42 Ibid., pp. 608–09.

großer That mitzuwirken, daß er dieses Anblicks uns theilhaftig gemacht […]. Ich blieb halten und genoß in stummer, unsäglicher Freude des ergreifendsten Anblicks meines Lebens.⁴³

The parting clouds, the realization of victory, the tears of joy, the thanksgiving to God – all are calculated to impress upon the reader the solemnity of the moment. Fontane is inviting his reader to join him in consecrating an awesome achievement. This may not be the "Hurra-Patriotismus" of other contemporary accounts, but it suggests that Fontane possessed a genuine reverence for the German cause.

Although Fontane expresses undisguised satisfaction at Prussia's success, he is far from being a gloating victor. He has rightly been praised for his willingness to give credit to the enemy (especially their soldiers, who prove themselves brave and worthy opponents no matter how badly led) and for his touching scenes of the victims of war. These latter include not only casualties on the battlefield, but also local civilian populations. Fontane portrays in a sympathetic fashion people who live in enemy territory. He criticizes his countrymen, including the military, for demanding good will and assistance from a populace under occupation. Prussian soldiers should expect a certain amount of reserve and even hostility.

In a collection of letters from the front published serially in 1866, Fontane develops the theme of Prussian "Überheblichkeit." He points out that the inhabitants of conquered territory, whether Bohemian or Saxon, have their own "Vaterlandsgefühl."⁴⁴ What is more, these peoples have their own habits, history, and culture. During his tour of Bohemia, Fontane expected to find a rude, impoverished, and (by contrast with Germans) an uncivilized Slavic Volk. Instead Fontane came to admire them for their unique and distinctive customs. It would be asking too much, he implies, to expect more than grudging cooperation from civilians under occupation. And with their overbearing ways, Fontane suggested, do Prussian troops really deserve much more?⁴⁵ Fontane's

---

43 Ibid. vol. 1, p. 609: "The smoke, which up until then had lain thick over the bloody field of honor, parted, and almost immediately one could see in a wide curve opening to the southwest the whole Prussian army advancing, brigade after brigade, batallion after batallion. With fife and drums everything forged ahead. Tears came to my eyes, because I was allowed to experience this moment. Many others felt the same way. We repeatedly shook each others' hands in heartfelt thanks to the almighty giver of all good things, that he vouchsafed us to take part in such a great deed, that he let us share in this moment [….] I stood still and enjoyed in silent, ineffable joy this, the most gripping moment of my life."

44 Fontane: *Reisebriefe vom Kriegsschauplatz Böhmen*, p. 42: "attachment to the fatherland."

45 Fontane incorporated some of these sympathetic observations from the *Reisebriefe* into *Der deutsche Krieg*. For this reason, Demetz considers it to be the most admirably humane of

willingness to take his own countrymen to task is one of the qualities which makes these histories remarkable for their time. As Fontane was fond of saying, "Über den Bergen wohnen auch Leute."[46]

Der deutsche Krieg takes for granted, nonetheless, a sense of German cultural superiority. Fontane asserts that Bohemia, settled in part by Germans and surrounded by them, is destined to become a German land. Fontane criticizes many aspects of Czech nationalism as something imposed on the people by outsiders, an artificial political identity not fully rooted in the Volk. With a note of satisfaction – not a sense of loss – he concludes that "so wird an den realen Machtverhältnissen auch das Czechenthum scheitern."[47] Fontane concludes his second war book, as he did his first, on a decidedly expansionist note: "Vor allem […] erfüllt uns die Hoffnung, daß es alsbald in allen Neu-Provinzen von unsrer preußischen Herrschaft heißen möge (wie seinerzeit vom friesischen Hemd): 'erst juckt es, aber hinterher sitzt es warm….'"[48]

5.

Der Krieg gegen Frankreich is a literary monument to German unification.[49] As in the previous histories, Fontane seldom discusses politics consistently or directly. But his analysis of the causes of the war and his attitude towards the conquered provinces of Alsace and Lorraine suggest his underlying German-national assumptions.

Fontane's war books. See "Das Kriegsbuch eines Romantikers" and "Weißer Sklave Fontane," where he writes: "Das heißt aber nicht, daß er des preußischen Patriotismus ermangelte; ihn irritiert nur das leidige Alles-besser-wissen-Wollen, die Xenophobie der Berliner Kleinbürger, die in den Uniformen der Sieger stecken, ihr Mißtrauen gegen Sachsen und Tschechen. Seine Kritik an den Okkupierten ist immer leiser als seine Einwände gegen die Okkupanten." This judgment is echoed by Christian Andree in his Nachwort to the *Reisebriefe*, pp. 91–2: "Fontanes Haltung hebt sich deutlich von einer damals weit verbreiteten Überheblichkeit gegenüber nichtpreußischen Völkerschaften ab."

46 Fontane: "Kriegsgefangen." *Werke, Schriften, Briefe* ser. 3, vol. 4, p. 583: "Those who live over the mountains are also people."
47 Fontane: *Der deutsche Krieg* vol. 1, p. 95: "Czechdom will thus also run aground on the real relations of power."
48 Ibid., vol. 2, p. 335: "Above all, we are filled with the hope, that Prussian rule in all our new provinces will soon be spoken of like the Friesian shirt: 'at first it itches, but then it feels warm.'"
49 Kelly's evaluation of imperial textbooks (p. 45 of the present volume) can be directly applied to Fontane: "[…] the authors' primary goal was not to glorify the war, but rather to use the war to define the German nation as the heir to the pious earnestness and harmony of 1870 […]."

Fontane devotes his opening chapter to an account of the Spanish throne controversy and the diplomatic posturing which produced the notorious "Ems telegram."[50] He knew full well that Bismarck had played an active role behind the scenes in precipitating the crisis, but he nonetheless relegates this particular episode to a footnote. Indeed he praises Bismarck for eliciting a declaration of war by the French at a propitious moment for Prussia.[51] It was the French who picked the fight even though it was Prussia (and Germany) who gained in the end. As in his history of 1864 and 1866, Fontane is willing in 1870 to give Prussia and her leaders the benefit of the doubt.

Like many other Germans at the time, Fontane experienced the outbreak of the war as an outrage against German integrity and honor. He emphasizes this by portraying the events at Ems from the point of view of Wilhelm.[52] In his day-by-day narrative, Fontane induces his audience to feel indignant on the king's behalf. Subject to repeated demands by the French, Wilhelm proves to be remarkably equable and long-suffering. Perhaps he is *too* patient in the face of pressure: the reader can only cheer when Bismarck intervenes to prevent any compromise of the king's sovereignty.[53]

The real, underlying cause of the war, however, was the weakness of the French government and its inability to withstand bellicose public opinion.[54] As with the Danes in 1864 and the Austrians in 1866, the French in 1870 were eager for war. According to Fontane, a wave of hubris swept the French people. By demanding war, they hoped to satisfy their nationalistic delusions of grandeur at German expense.

Fontane blames Louis Napoleon and the elected leaders of the liberal parties for being unable to resist this volatile warmongering. Indeed, with the lone exception of Adolphe Thiers, French leaders shared the "chauvinistischen Rausch" of the people.[55] They were driven to war by the logic of their own patriotic chauvinism, by "dieser eigenthümliche Mischling von Händelsucht, Gloire-Bedürfniß und eitlem aber tiefgewurzeltem Glauben an eine überkommene Mission."[56]

---

50 The account given by Fontane is followed in almost exact detail by Kelly's textbooks. Here, the relegation of Bismarck to a minor role in which he determines only the timing of the war. See Kelly's contribution in this volume p. 46–8.
51 Fontane: *Der Krieg gegen Frankreich* vol. 1, p. 30.
52 Ibid., p. 6–16.
53 For the "personalization" of the outbreak of the war, see Kelly, p. 46.
54 I consider Fontane's judgment that internal political pressures caused the war to be substantially sound. Perhaps the "textbook" version was not so off the mark. See Kelly, p. 46.
55 Fontane: *Der Krieg gegen Frankreich* vol. 1, p. 29: "chauvinistic intoxication."
56 Ibid., p. 22: "this characteristic mixture of a desire to act, an urge for glory, and a vain but deep-seated belief in a traditional mission."

In short, Fontane concludes, France was out of control: "Die Schwäche, die Unordnungen, die *Verlegenheiten* des Kaiserreiches, indem sie dasselbe den nationalen Exaltados in die Arme trieben, *sie* schufen den Krieg."[57]

Fontane is not critical of nationalism *per se*, but only of its abuse. In *Der Krieg gegen Frankreich*, he portrays the German national cause as fully justified. The French declaration of war brought Germans closer together. It was in the struggle against their common enemy, France, that they first achieved their unity. Across the Rhine, "die Begeisterung kannte keine Grenzen."[58] Fontane characterizes those who tried to dampen the German ardor for war as liberal nay-sayers and cowardly particularists. What Fontane portrays as a dangerous and uncontrolled "chauvinism" in the streets of Paris appears as a healthy, natural, and fully justified "enthusiasm" in the streets of Berlin.[59]

As in the war between Austria and Prussia, the two populations differed dramatically in their attitudes towards the war. The French were boastful, arrogant, and all too sure of themselves. They squandered their patriotic feelings in useless displays of bravado.[60] The Prussians, by contrast, harnessed their national energies for the difficult tasks ahead. "Das Charakterische unserer deutschen Rüstungen war die vielleicht nie zuvor Verschmelzung von Enthusiasmus und Ordnung."[61]

Fontane went out of his way – as he had in his other war books – to include words of praise for the common French soldier. During his imprisonment, Fontane gained a very favorable first-hand impression of the many French civilians. He included these observations in *Kriegsgefangen*, knowing full well that good words about the enemy are the last thing in the world many people want to hear in the middle of a war.[62] Fontane consistently kept his eye on human realities. His histories are not blinded by the passions of war.

But it is important not to exaggerate. Throughout his accounts of the Franco-Prussian war, Fontane clings to a decidedly negative assessment of the French people and French values: "[…] aber so angenehm der Eindruck war,

---

57 Ibid., p. 23: "The weakness, the disorderliness, the *embarrassments* of the empire, insofar as they drove it into the arms of the national exultations, *these* caused the war."
58 Ibid., p. 38: "The enthusiasm knew no bounds."
59 Ibid. pp. 29, 38.
60 See Kelly on the "counterfeit version" of national spirit possessed by the French, this volume p. 50.
61 Fontane: *Der Krieg gegen Frankreich* vol. 1, pp. 93–4: "The German mobilization was characterized by a perhaps novel fusion of enthusiasm and orderliness."
62 Fontane: "Kriegsgefangen." *Werke, Schriften, Briefe* ser. 3, vol. 4, p. 582.

den sie als Individuen hervorriefen, so traurig war der Eindruck, den jeder einzelne als Teil des Ganzen machte."[63] It is here that the greater weight of Fontane's judgment lies. Unlike the dutiful Germans, the French have no respect for authority. Neither the state, nor the army, nor the laws of the land, nor even the church commands their loyalty any longer. The problem, according to Fontane, is that the French have broken with their past. The loss of their national history has led them in a futile search for a new one. As a result of their revolutions, the French eschew stability and seek out misbegotten adventures. This makes them a danger to others as well as to themselves. The result is a nationalism which is cut off from its historical roots and therefore dangerous and unhealthy:

> Losgelöst von allem Tieferen, wird auch die Vaterlandsliebe (die dann nur eine gewisse Form persönlicher Eitelkeit ist) leicht zu einer Karikatur, überschlägt sich und gewinnt den Charakter des Hohlen, einer schillernden Seifenblase, eines Nichts.[64]

Why did the French lose the war of 1870/71? There were many contributing factors, but what binds them all together for Fontane is the difference between the German and French national causes. The French were driven by patriotic excess; the Germans, by a *legitimate* nationalism. The Prussian and their allies won by virtue, above all, of their "moralisches Übergewicht."[65]

It was the declaration of the German empire which supplies the Franco-Prussian War with its true significance and meaning. Fontane took great satisfaction in the fact that the war finally convinced the German states to set aside their quarrels in favor of imperial unity.[66] Even Bavaria and other Catholic states which had feared Prussian domination answered the call for national unity in the face of the foreign threat. Smaller goals were renounced in favor of higher ones:

> [A]lles Kleine war abgetan; selbst in den Herzen derer, denen das Jahr 1866 nicht zu Willen gewesen war, schwieg jetzt der Unmut, und die deutsche Empfindung erwies sich mächtiger als jede andere Regung.[67]

---

63 Ibid., p. 583: "[…] however pleasant an impression which they made as individuals, the impression which each individual made as part of the whole was sad."
64 Ibid., p. 583: "Detached from everything deeper, even love for the fatherland (which *then* is only a certain form of personal vanity) easily becomes a caricature, turns on its head, and takes on the character of something empty, of an irridescent soap-bubble, of nothing."
65 Fontane: *Der Krieg gegen Frankreich* vol. 1, p. 89: "moral superiority."
66 See also Kelly, p. 58 of the present volume.
67 Fontane: *Der Krieg gegen Frankreich* vol. 1, p. 48: All pettiness was over and done with. Complaints were no longer heard, even from those who had had their doubts in 1866. The feeling of being German proved itself to be more powerful than any other emotion."

The assertiveness — as well as the humanity — of Fontane's German-national position can best be seen in his attitudes towards the conquered provinces of Alsace and Lorraine. On the one hand (in *Aus den Tagen der Okkupation*), Fontane concedes that the inhabitants of Lorraine have long been French: they speak French; they have a history of ties to France; they do not *wish* to be joined with Germany.[68] The residents of Alsace, though much of their history, language, and culture are German, are also reluctant to become part of greater Germany. Fontane is very critical of the military administration in the two provinces for behaving like foreign conquerers, for trying to compel obedience where they should be trying to earn the citizens' loyalty and trust. The very qualities which produced such brilliant victories on the battlefield, Fontane suggests, threaten to turn the German occupation of Alsace and Lorraine into a miserable failure. The residents should not be treated like a defeated enemy, but like future Germans. Fontane launches on a lengthy critique of "the Potsdams of world history." In these garrison-towns, the military virtues of discipline, loyalty, and obedience too often emerge as administrative vice:

> Das Wesen dieser Potsdamme, sag ich, besteht in einer unheilvollen Verquickung oder auch Nichtverquickung von Absolutimus, Militarismus und Spießbürgertum. Ein Zug von Unfreiheit, von Gemachtem und Geschraubten, namentlich auch von künstlich *Hinaufgeschraubtem*, geht durch das Ganze und bedrückt jede Seele, die mehr das Bedürfnis hat, frei aufzuatmen, als Front zu machen.[69]

These qualities, of course, were the very ones which Fontane did *not* wish to see employed in the occupation of Alsace and Lorraine. Some admirers of Fontane have taken this and similar passages as an indication that Fontane developed a thoroughgoing Militärkritik during the wars of unification.[70] Fontane was, of course, keenly sensitive to the self-satisfied and stultifying nature of much of what passed for patriotism in his country. After reading reports of the Fehrbellin anniversary of 1875, Fontane commented to his wife Emilie

> [...] daß die Pflege des "Patriotischen" in unsrem Lande Sache der Stümper, der Bedienten, der armen Teufel ist. Es hätte dies unter Umständen 'was Erfreuliches;

---

68 Fontane: "Aus den Tagen der Okkupation." *Werke, Schriften, Briefe* ser. 3, vol. 4, pp. 927–28.
69 Ibid., p. 1011: "The nature of these Potsdams, I say, consists in an unhealthy fusion, or also absence of fusion, of absolutism, militarism, and philistinism. A lack of freedom, a quality of the forced and affected, in particular, of a stilted artificiality, pervades the whole, and oppresses every soul needing more to breathe freely than to stand at attention."
70 See, for example, Osborne: *Meyer or Fontane*, p. 7, and "Die Mobilmachung der Kultur," p. 434.

aber überall kuckt das Eselsohr der Eitelkeit, der Wichtigthuerei, der Ordenssucht heraus.[71]

Nor was Fontane overly enamored of military matters. During his captivity in France, he commented on a history of Napoleon's campaigns which he had been reading: "'Solche Bücher,' sagt ich mir, 'schreibst du selbst. Sind sie *ebenso*, so taugen sie nichts. Diese bloße Verherrlichung des Militärischen, ohne sittlichen Inhalt und großen Zweck, ist widerlich.'"[72]

On balance, however, the thesis of Fontane's Militärkritik is untenable. Many scenes from the war books indicate that Fontane supported military action in favor of national goals. He includes in the war books scenes of the troops heading for the front, or returning to Berlin after victory. The parades, the jubilant crowds, the reviewing stand at the Brandenburg Gate, the speeches by civilian and military dignitaries, the wreaths thrown by girlfriends and wives: when Fontane enlivens his story with these details, he does so not with the voice of the critical observer, but with that of the approving participant.

The decisive argument against Fontane's Militärkritik is that he, like many Germans at the end of the war, favored the annexation of Alsace and Lorraine.[73] In the case of Alsace, he favored an active and rapid program of re-Germanification. His main concern was that this be accomplished by consent and not by force.[74] In the case of Lorraine, Fontane admitted there would be difficulties. But he did not doubt that with an enlightened administration, Germany could win the battle for people's hearts and minds.

Fontane did not argue for annexation on the narrow grounds of a military buffer, but rather on the widest possible grounds that Germany represented a superior civilizing principle. The decadent values of the French would have to go. The German values which had proved their worth in the war should replace them. True, Fontane urged fighting this cultural battle through persuasion, and hoped that the residents would themselves choose to become Ger-

---

71 Fontane: *Werke, Schriften, Briefe*, ser. 4, vol. 2, p. 610: […] that the cultivation of the "patriotic" in our country is handled by bunglers, lackeys, and wretches. If need be, [the patriotic] could be gratifying; but everywhere the dog's ear of vanity, self-importance, and the mania for medals flaps out."
72 Fontane: "Kriegsgefangen." *Werke, Schriften. Briefe* ser. 3, vol. 4, p. 603: "'Books like this,' I said to myself, 'you write yourself. If they are *like this*, then they are not worth anything. This sheer glorification of the military, without moral content and a higher goal, is repugnant.'"
73 Fontane's positive assessment of the role of the military in the unification of 1870/71 presents the sharpest possible contrast with the antimilitarism of the post-World War II period. See Bullivant's contribution to this volume, p. 303.
74 See, for example, Fontane: *Werke, Schriften, Briefe*, ser. 4, vol. 3, pp. 191–92, 536.

man. But while the conversion process was going on, Fontane was perfectly willing to leave Germany in control.

> Der französische *Geist* muß erst wieder heraus. Darüber ist man einig. Diesen französischen Geist aber vertreiben wir mutmaßlich weder durch unsere zivile noch durch unsere Heeresverwaltung, was alles auch zu Lob und Preis beider gesagt werden mag […]. [D]as Falsche, Schiefe, Verlogene aufzudecken, gesunde Bildung an die Stelle ungesunder zu setzen, *darauf* kommt es an; diese Aufgabe aber ist eine rein geistige und kann nur durch geistige Mittel gelöst werden. Die Berührung mit dem deutschen Geist allein kann diese Wandlung vollziehen: Lehre, Wissenschaft, Predigt, Lied […]. Das *Allerbeste*, was Deutschland hat, wird dann gerade gut genug sein für – Elsaß-Lothringen.[75]

What was good enough for Germany was apparently good for foreigners as well.[76]

6.

By the time the final volume of *Der Krieg gegen Frankreich* appeared in 1876, Fontane was fed up with the war books. He had spent nearly twelve years researching and writing them. Each successive history brought mounting frustrations. In the fall of 1865, discouraged by delays with *Der Schleswig-Holsteinsche Krieg*, Fontane admitted to his publisher that "*[d]ie Freude an dem Unternehmen ist allerseits längst dahin.*"[77] Indeed, were it not for the fact that he needed the honorarium, Fontane would not have minded scrapping the project entirely. He expressed regret at having devoted "ein bestes Lebensjahr" on "ein vor der Geburt schon gescheitertes Unternehmen."[78]

---

75 Fontane: "Aus den Tagen der Okkupation." *Werke, Schriften. Briefe* ser. 3, vol. 4, pp. 995–96: "The French *spirit* first has to be gotten rid of. We all agree on that. But we are driving out this French spirit presumably with neither our civil nor our military administration, whatever may be said in praise and glory of both […]. It all depends on exposing falseness, perversity, mendacity, and replacing unhealthy with healthy growth. Contact with the German spirit alone can complete this transformation: education, science, preaching, song […]. The *very best* that Germany has is just good enough – for Alsace-Lorraine."

76 Fontane's comments about the French and other foreigners during the wars of unification possess a *confidence* in German culture and accomplishments. Contrast this with the belligerent, xenophobic *anxiety* exhibited by many Germans and patriotic societies in the Wilhelmine era, which Chickering describes – see this volume p. 77.

77 Fontane: *Werke, Schriften, Briefe*, ser. 4, vol. 2, p. 146: "The pleasure in the undertaking is on all sides long gone."

78 Ibid: "[…]. to have spent one of the best years of my life on an undertaking that was dead before being born."

Fontane had a similar experience with *Der deutsche Krieg*. "Die Sache *ist mir keine Herzenssache*," he wrote, comparing the prospects of this second war book to that of writing his novel, *Vor dem Sturm*.⁷⁹ Once again Fontane hoped to finish quickly, but, as he wrote to Emilie in 1868, the work seemed to stretch on forever: "*nur fertig*."⁸⁰

> Mit meinem Buche bin ich nun bald zu Rande und nach länger als 2jähriger, unausgesetzter Arbeit, empfind' ich dies allerdings wie Befreiung von einem Alpdruck. Ich sehne mich nach einem Wechsel in der Beschäftigung und bange doch auch davor.⁸¹

The outbreak of war in 1870 prevented Fontane once again from returning to his novel. He was hardly thrilled by the prospects of another war. As he neared the front, his letters to Emilie reveal his distaste for the military uproar:

> Das ganze wirkt auf mich wie eine kolossale Vision, eine vorübergrausende wilde Jagd, man steht und staunt und weiß nicht recht, was man damit machen soll. Eine durch Eisenbahnen regulierte Völkerwanderung, organisierte Massen, aber doch immer *Massen*, innerhalb deren man selbst als ein Atom wirbelt, nicht draußen stehend, beherrschend, sondern dem großen Zuge willenlos preisgegeben. Es ist, wie wenn es in einem Theater heißt: "Es brennt"; fortgerissen einem Ausgange zu, der vielleicht keiner ist, mitleidslos gedrückt, gestoßen, gewürgt, ein Opfer dunkler Triebe und Gewalten. Manche lieben das, weil es ein 'excitement' ist; – ich bin zu künstlerisch organisiert, als daß mir wohl dabei werden könnte.⁸²

Fontane makes it clear that, whatever his political opinions, he does not share the "patriotische Erregung," which yields "unendlich viel Blech."⁸³

Fontane increasingly came to view *Vor dem Sturm* as a way to escape from the war books. Set on the eve of the German "war of liberation" against the

---

79 Ibid., p. 169: "The whole affair is *not a matter of the heart for me*."
80 Ibid., p. 214: "[I want] *just to be finished*."
81 Ibid., p. 216: "I am just about finished with my book, and after more than two years of unceasing labor, it feels, I must admit, like being freed from a nightmare. I long for a change in activity, and am also afraid of it."
82 Ibid., p. 326: "The whole thing produces an impression on me like a colossal vision, a fearful wild hunt that goes crashing by, I stand and stare and have not the slightest idea what to make of it. A migration of peoples regulated by trains, organized masses, but always *masses*, in the midst of which one is tossed about like an atom, not standing outside self-controlled, but given up against one's will to the great movement. It is like when someone calls out "fire" in a theatre: [one is] carried way to an exit, which perhaps is not one at all, mercilessly squeezed, shoved, choked, a victim of dark impulses and forces. Many like it, because it is "exciting" – I am too artistically put together to feel good about it."
83 Ibid., p. 326: "patriotic excitement," "a lot of endless rubbish."

French, *Vor dem Sturm* was also concerned with a great event in national history. Fontane first conceived the story back in the 1850s, and his earliest drafts date from the winter of 1863/64. But the novel was interrupted time and again by war. Fontane first began writing *Vor dem Sturm* in earnest in the late fall of 1876. By that time, Fontane was only too glad to exchange the ambition of becoming the literary spokesman of the new nation for that of becoming a novelist. "Nur bitt' ich herzlich, mich mit meinem Kriegsbuche erst ins Klare kommen zu lassen, was freilich bis in den November hinein dauern wird. Dann weg 'mit's Milletär' und wieder ein civiler Civilist."[84] The desire to return to "civilian" pursuits increasingly came to be Fontane's highest priority.

The completion of *Der Krieg gegen Frankreich* and the renewed dedication to writing *Vor dem Sturm* was a crucial period in Fontane's personal and professional life. After years of respectable but irregular income, Fontane was offered a post as the secretary of the Prussian Academy of the Arts. He accepted, hoping that the position would stabilize his finances and help make up for the disappointing reception of the war books.[85] After only a few months on the job, Fontane fell afoul of political infighting in the Academy and resigned in disgust. He decided to write *Vor dem Sturm* and take his chances as a novelist instead.

The moment was a risky and decisive one. Having failed to win public acclaim as the narrator of German unification, Fontane gave up his ambition to become the writer for the fatherland, and decided to become just a writer instead. His resignation from the Academy put a great strain on his marriage. Emilie had pinned *her* hopes of respectability and a steady income on just such a position. When Fontane told her of his decision, she packed her bags and went to visit a friend in Silesia. Fontane's letters in late summer, 1876, are moving testimony to the grave disappointment on her part and the gentle but unyielding determination on his.[86] The marriage survived.

Once the historian gave way to the novelist, Fontane never looked back. He had little to say later in his life about his war books. It is primarily as a writer of fiction, of course, that Fontane is remembered today. As he grew

---

84 Ibid., p. 499: "I only ask that you first let me see my way clear with the war book. Then away 'with the military' and again a civil civilian."

85 The pivotal importance of this brief period in Fontane's life has often been overlooked. See Friedrich Fontane: "Theodor Fontanes 'Akademiezeit,'" and Walther Huder, ed., *Theodor Fontane und die preußische Akademie der Künste*.

86 See Fontane: *Werke, Schriften, Briefe*, ser. 4: *Briefe* vol. 2, pp. 536–38, and *Fontanes Briefe in zwei Bänden* vol 1, pp. 424–28.

older and wrote better, Fontane developed into a keen observer of society and politics in the Kaiserreich. In his books and correspondence, Fontane did indeed become increasingly critical of penny-pinching bourgeois, worn-out aristocrats, and pompous reserve lieutenants. He was also deeply suspicious of parliamentary majorities and appalled at times by the pettiness of Bismarck.[87] But for all these complaints, Fontane never second-guessed the founding of the Kaiserreich. The unification of Germany retained until his death in 1898 its overwhelmingly positive resonance.[88]

Despite the fact that the war books paled in literary importance compared to the fiction of his last twenty years, Fontane never repudiated the theme that is central to them all: namely, that the unification of Germany was the event of a lifetime. The Fontane revealed by the war books is, above all, a national-minded Fontane. The "liberal" qualities of Fontane's histories should not be overemphasized.[89] This is not to say that Fontane was a Moltke-Schwärmer, indulging in swaggering expressions of national pride.[90] Far from it. But it is important to recognize that Fontane shared with many of his contemporaries a number of national-political assumptions: a desire for a unified Germany, a belief in the civilizing mission of German culture, an admiration for the military achievements of Prussia, and in the event, a willingness to accede to the Bismarckian solution to the German question.[91] Fontane's war books collectively attest to the satisfaction he took in the accomplishment of a great historical task, the creation of a united Germany – an event for which

---

87 For some of these attitudes see ibid. vol. 3, pp. 25, 97, 125, 142, 314–15, and vol. 4, pp. 121–22.

88 Fulda's observation that writers' responses to 1870/71 were characterized by "sympathy" and to 1989/90 by "distance" is apt. As I have argued, however Fontane was not as ambivalent about victory as Fulda suggests. See this volume p. 227.

89 I am in essential agreement with Loster-Schneider: "Zur Neuauflage," p. 616: "Wird auch auf 'Hurrapatriotismus,' wie Craig einleitend bemerkt, verzichtet, ist doch die ganze Deutung dieses 'erstaunlichen Krieges' national."

90 Gerhard Friedrich over-emphasizes the militarist-monarchist-nationalist aspects of Fontane in his recent biography, *Fontanes preußische Welt*.

91 Though by no means a "liberal" in the party-political sense of the term, Fontane would still fall under the criticism which Pape makes of those writers (particularly Freiligrath) who "had given up their resistance to Bismarck's power politics." See Pape's contribution to the present volume, p. 111. In his essay, Pape (and Neuhaus) emphasizes the extent to which the patriotism of 1870/71 was an abdication of the political responsibility, a failure to stand up for democratic principles, a "confusion of values." (Pape, p. 130.) I have tried to portray Fontane's nationalism in a more sympathetic light, as a typical and by no means so objectionable response to nineteenth-century events. German national sentiment in the wake os 1870/71 should not be made to bear *too* much of the burden for later political developments in Germany.

Fontane had waited the better part of a lifetime. We need to revise our picture of Fontane in order to accommodate this "national" identity. Fontane's later fiction does portray in a critical, ironic fashion many elements of the Kaiserreich. But as for many other Germans during the final quarter of the nineteenth century, 1871 had given Fontane much of what he wanted. "So wurde das Deutsche Reich aufgerichtet und *nur* so."[92]

---

92 Fontane: *Von Zwanzig bis Dreißig*, p. 488.

Literature, Aesthetics, and Literary Market
after 1870/71

Walter Pape
Universität zu Köln

"Hurra, Germania – mir graut vor dir": Hoffmann von Fallersleben, Freiligrath, Herwegh, and the German Unification of 1870/71

Abstract: Later attitudes to the poets of the Vormärz and the Revolution have prevented a critical assessment of their poems on both the War of 1870/71 and Bismarck's Empire. Hoffmann von Fallersleben suspended from his Breslau professorial chair in 1843 because of the publication of his innocuous *Unpolitical Songs*, remained suspect even later to the state, Freiligrath, the former 'trumpeter of the revolution,' became the symbol of the reconciliation of the liberals with the Prussian-German state, Herwegh, however, because of his "villainous insults against persons dear to the entire great Fatherland" (Julius Grosse, 1877) was excluded from literary history for a long time. The poetical outburst of 1870/71 was followed by the 'Götterdämmerung' of the public function of poetry and its 'Sänger.'

1. "Zu preisen gibt es heut nicht mehr viel"

"Ein Volk, das seine Taten nicht besänge, / Es wäre halb nur seiner Taten wert!"[1] With these verses from his epic poem *Sedan* (1875) Ernst von Wildenbruch very conscious of the Reich and of himself addresses one of the dominant functions of lyric in the nineteenth century: lyric, including folk song as well as the poems by individual authors, was meant to represent an apparent cultural unity.[2] As in a dialogue of minds across the centuries, Sarah Kirsch answers him: "Zu preisen gibt es heut nicht mehr viel. / Und deshalb ist des

---

1 Wildenbruch: "Sedan. Ein Heldenlied in drei Gesängen." *Gesammelte Werke* vol. 15, p. 364. "A nation that would not sing the praises of its deeds, would not be worthy of them."
2 Cf. Springer: "Unsere Friedensziele." *Im neuen Reich* 1:1 (1871), p. 696; Springer puts his emphasis on the German "Cultureinheit"; see also Schutte: "Zur Kritik der Volksliedideologie in der zweiten Hälfte des 19. Jahrhunderts," esp. pp. 50–1.

Schreibens müde die Hand."³ The "chronicler" in her poem "Der Chronist" (1992) can do nothing but transfer to paper and to memory a "Strom von Wiederholungen" ("stream of repetitions") and "Grauen" ("horror"). Because there is no teleological structure, no meaningful center to (national) history, it can be looked upon only as chronicle. In 1870, contrariwise, there was a chorus in praise of "das Erschließen der Wunderblume deutscher Einheit und Macht aus dem vergossenen Heldenblut," as the stenographer of the Reichstag and literary historian Eduard Engel remembered in 1907.⁴

Although the public role of lyric since the days of choral societies and men's choirs, since the songs on the first German unification has changed decisively, what Hermann Lingg wrote in 1872 in Paul Lindau's newly founded journal *Gegenwart* is still valid today: "More than ever lyric has become the proclamation of the attitude of a period."⁵ The validity of the statement is confirmed even nowadays when lyric may seem to have lost a social function. Günter Kunert characterizes the situation of lyric poetry in 1981: "The poem has been downgraded not only to a side issue of social interests, but of the whole literature."⁶ The prediction of the demise of poetry has become a cliché of the feuilleton and an ambivalent means of justification by the poets themselves; shortly before the 'Wende' Ludwig Fels wrote a defense of lyric in his foreword to a collection of his poems, in the afterword he gave a prophecy of its end: "Poems are dying out. They don't hold their ground against the daily madness, against the idiots of the apocalypse."⁷ In an inspired essay Hans-Christoph Buch evolved the thesis "that in a historic moment, when nothing in this respect comes to the mind of all the writers of prose and essays because history's wind has swept away their manuscripts from their desks, the poets' bell tolls."⁸ In trying to hold out, German lyric proved its worth after unification in verses like those of Günter Grass, Wolf Biermann (as we will see at the end of this essay), or Sarah Kirsch: "Heul, sag ich, heul! Der Hund / Hilft mir das Jahr / Zu Ende zu bringen."⁹ Such a

---

3 Kirsch: *Erlkönigs Tochter*, p. 16. "There is not much left today to be praised / And hence the hand is tired of writing."
4 Engel: *Geschichte der Deutschen Literatur von den Anfängen bis zur Gegenwart* vol. 2, p. 960. "the unfolding of the wonder blossom of German unity and power through the blood shed by the heroes."
5 Lingg: "Über moderne Lyrik," p. 57.
6 Kunert: *Vor der Sintflut*, p. 10. – Cf. also Volker Hages Essay "Versprengte Tataren" on contemporary German lyrics, published in December 1989 in *Die Zeit*.
7 Fels: *Blaue Allee, versprengte Tataren*, p. 124.
8 Buch: "Die Stunde der Dichter." *Die Zeit* No. 50, December 4, 1992, p. 3.
9 Kirsch: *Erlkönigs Tochter*, p. 5. "Howl, I say, howl. The dog helps me to bring the year to an end."

concord of ontic, social, personal, and creatural experience seems to be the "collective undercurrent" of individual and subjective lyric[10] and hence those poems are more able to give an interpretation of reality in a poetic image than most discursive writers can provide in their essays. Most of the poems written in 1870 and later offered no resistance, they were not in harmony with the collective undercurrent but they did surrender to the ruling currents.

2. "Denken Sie nur was an bisheriger Literatur crepieren wird!"

"Die Einmüthigkeit der deutsch-nationalen Gesinnung, von der sich nur die Vertreter des enghertzigsten Particularismus ausschließen, und die gerechte Entrüstung über den Uebermuth, mit dem Frankreich einen so furchtbaren Krieg vom Zaun brach, wurden alsbald zu inspirirenden Musen der deutschen Nationallyrik [...]. Auch diese Poesie hat indeß ihren, nur außerhalb der Kunstsphäre liegenden Werth als Ausdruck der Gesinnung und als eine in alle Kreise dringende Propaganda patriotischer Gefühle."[11] In these words, five weeks after the beginning of the Franco-Prussian War Rudolf von Gottschall's *Blätter für literarische Unterhaltung* summed up the public political and aesthetic commonsense. Hegelian aesthetics after all was generally accepted: following eighteenth-century poetics, Hegel had admitted only the "ardor of patriotism" as the only kind of political feeling bourgeois subjectivity was allowed to express in a poem.[12]

Emanuel Geibel very early on supported those who wished for a united Germany, excluding Austria, under the leadership of Prussia and Bismarck[13]; he was also the most successful and the most esteemed poet in the second half of the nineteenth century. With his poems written in a late classicistic-

---

10 Adorno: "Rede über Lyrik und Gesellschaft," p. 58.
11 *Blätter für literarische Unterhaltung*. Ed. Rudolf von Gottschall, No. 35, August 8, 1870, p. 556 – quoted from Weber: "Zur bibliographischen Darstellung," p. 41. "The unanimity of the German-national mentality, from which only the most mean-minded advocates of particularism exclude themselves, and the justified indignation at the haughtiness in which France started a such an atrocious war, very soon inspired the German national songs [...]. But the value of this kind of poetry lies outside the sphere of art, being nothing but the expression of the mind and of a propaganda of patriotic feelings suffusing all social groups." See also Osborne: *Meyer or Fontane? German Literature after the Franco-Prussian War 1870/71*, pp. 13–28: "Hurra Germania! Patriotic Lyric, 1870." For a good survey see Sittner: *Politik und Literatur 1870/71*.
12 Hegel: *Ästhetik* vol. 2, p. 474.
13 Cf. also Hinck: "Epigonendichtung und Nationalidee", p. 75.

romantic style he argued against poetry opposing the government. When in 1865, after the Danish-German and before the war between Prussia and Austria, Bismarck was campaigning against the Prussian chamber of deputies, Geibel drew the line not to be crossed by poets in their poems:

> Wenn von außen der Feind uns droht,
> Wohl mit klingenden Saiten
> Im gewappneten Aufgebot
> Ziemt's dem Dichter zu schreiten.
>
> Eisern wie ein geschwungenes Schwert
> Soll sein Hymnus ertönen,
> Bis ihm gnädig ein Gott beschert,
> Siegerstirnen zu krönen.
>
> Aber wo mit Gewalt und List
> Haupt feindselig und Glieder
> Sich befehden im innern Zwist,
> Da verstummen die Lieder.
>
> Eh' sie diente, der Volkspartein
> Zwietracht weiterzutragen,
> Lieber wollt' ich am nächsten Stein
> Diese Harfe zerschlagen.[14]

These verses so devoutly monarchist are entitled "Zur Antwort" ("By way of reply") and are perhaps also reacting to Georg Herwegh's "Bundeslied für den Allgemeinen deutschen Arbeiterverein"; but they are certainly a somewhat late response to Herwegh's appeal "An die deutschen Dichter" (1840). This poem is an impassioned rejection of hymns to princes and it exhorts the poets to take sides with the limbs against the head, in case freedom becomes increasingly jeopardized: "So haltet nur am Schwerte fest, / Und laßt die Harfen uns zertrümmern."[15] The failure of the 1848 German revolution[16] was also detrimental to German literature, because the fatal March seemed to be

---

14 Geibel: *Werke* vol. 2, p. 223. "If from the outside the enemy threatens, the poet has to strut along armed with his resonant cords. // His iron hymn shall resound like a brandished sword, until a God bestows upon him to crown the victors' heads. // But when head and limbs are fighting each other violently and cunningly in an internal discord, songs have to cease. // Rather than using my harp to encourage the discord of the nation's groups I would smash my harp at the next rock."
15 Herwegh: *Werke* part 1, pp. 49–50. "Just cling to the sword, and let us smash our harps."
16 Cf. the objection against the common opinion of the failure of the revolution in Siemann: *Die Revolution von 1848/49*.

nothing but a poetic frenzy[17] and the parliament of the Paulskirche, allegedly comprising mostly scholars and poets,[18] was blamed for its failure. Herwegh is one of the very few political poets who adhered to the former function of political lyric; on the other hand in February 1870 he gave his reply after Geibel had left Munich and got a pension from the King of Prussia; Herwegh maintained his lyrical discourse in – erroneously, but not quite unbefittingly – referring Geibel's poem to the Prussian victory in the German-Austrian War:

> [...]
> Wohl mir, daß ich noch spielen kann
> meine Leier, die alte!
>
> Eh' sie diente, von Königgrätz
> So zu singen und sagen,
> Lieber wollt' ich dem Braun und Metz
> Um die Köpfe sie schlagen.[19]

Braun and Metz were symbolic characters for liberals who had given up their resistance to Bismarck's power politics. Karl Braun (1822–1893), the leader of the liberals in Nassau, after the Prussian annexation of Nassau became a member of the North German Reichstag and of the Prussian Landtag; and also August Metz, one of the propagators of the Nationalverein, now supported the Prussian hegemony formerly opposed by him.

After 1848 and between Königgrätz and Sedan, as German unification was being shaped through wars and through cabinet politics, the political and nonpolitical poets began to play a different role; most of them were not "hard up for a new role," as Herwegh noted in his poem "Tristia."[20] Here, too, Geibel is a symbolic figure: most poets had the choice of escaping into nature or into classical Italy, into unpolitical epigonism or into romantic nationalism. Thus function and appreciation of political lyric in 1870 stood in quite a different context than before 1848. The myriad of lyrical offerings sung in 1870 and 1871 at the altar the fatherland were no longer trying to shape political consciousness as in 1813, but glorifying the present state as a utopia come true. But more instructive and revealing than these hymns from Berthold

---

17 Prutz: *Die deutsche Literatur der Gegenwart. 1848–1858* vol. 1, p. 15.
18 Cf. von Wiese: *Dichtertum,* p. 8.
19 Herwegh: *Werke* part 3, pp. 123–24. "Good for me that I can play the lyre, my old one. Before it served to sing about Königgrätz in this way, I would rather smash it on the heads of Braun and Metz."
20 Ibid., pp. 122–23.

Auerbach to Karl Zettel,[21] the poems (and their reception) of Freiligrath, Herwegh and Hoffmann von Fallersleben (who all wrote poetry of political protest before 1848) can explain some cardinal issues: Why, with the victory of 1871, did "the complete defeat, even extirpation of German mind in favour of the 'German Empire'" begin (Nietzsche)?[22] Why was German unification and German military proficiency invested "with an ideal meaning"[23]? And why did literary historians propagate political judgements in the guise of aesthetic value?

Even Jacob Burckhardt predicted a change of poetical discourse; on New Year's Eve 1870 he wrote to his friend, Friedrich von Preen: "Denken Sie nur was an bisheriger Literatur crepieren wird! [...] was weiterlebt muß eine schöne Portion ewigen Gehaltes in sich haben."[24] And indeed (seen through the eyes of the predominant bourgeois aesthetics) the poetry of political opposition perished, and looking back literary critics even laid claim to the critical literature written before 1848 as such pioneers of the new Reich as Berthold Auerbach did with the radical democrat Ludwig Weidig, contributor to the *Hessische Landbote*.[25] To a great extent the new contemporary literature and the arts had little connection with reality but, as Burckhardt had predicted, turned to eternal values or to what they thought were eternal values: history, classical or Germanic myths, or the transfiguration of the presence of Reich in the mirror of the past.[26]

3. Hoffmann von Fallersleben: "Seit dem Jahre 1848 eine vorwurfsfreie Haltung bewahrt"

In 1843 Hoffmann von Fallersleben was suspended without income from his Breslau professorial chair as a result of the publication of the second part of

---

21 First and last author in the alphabetical index of Franz Lipperheide's edition *Lieder zu Schutz und Trutz* (1871) – See also Zimmer: *Auf dem Altar des Vaterlands*, pp. 71–149: "Religion und Patriotismus in der Lyrik des deutsch-französischen Krieges von 1870/71."
22 Nietzsche: "Unzeitgemäße Betrachtungen I." – *Sämtliche Werke* vol. 1, pp. 159–60.
23 Craig: *Germany 1866–1945*, p. 36.
24 Letter no. 560 – Burckhardt: *Briefe* vol. 5, p. 119. "Imagine what extent of previous literature will perish! [...] What survives must incorporate a good portion of eternal substance." Cf. also Deuerlein: "Die Konfrontation von Nationalstaat und national bestimmter Kultur." Schieder and Deuerlein, eds., *Reichsgründung 1870/71*, pp. 226–258, here p. 234.
25 Georg Jäger: "Die Gründerzeit." Bucher et al., eds., *Realismus und Gründerzeit* vol. 1, pp. 96–159, here p. 98.
26 Cf. Craig: *Germany 1866–1945*, p. 215. – See also Daniel Fulda's essay in this volume, p. 205.

his *Unpolitical Songs*, but unlike other state officials (Beamte) after 1848 he was not reinstated in his office, but merely granted a payment like those state officials who were suspended *during* the revolution. He was still suspect; for a long period he did nothing but his scholarly research, but the deportation from the Kingdom of Hanover, dating from 1848 was not canceled in the following years; on the contrary, on July 28, 1858 the King personally signed a cabinet order concerning the surveillance of Hoffmann and his relations.[27] The suspended professor was never rehabilitated.

Hoffmann shares the conviction of most political poets that poems can influence the political development, but he is one of the few who believe that poems alone are a sufficient means of influence. Obviously he was brought to this conviction, when in the years after 1842 he was a celebrity in Germany, travelling around from pub to pub singing his humorous political songs as a ballad singer or modern strolling minstrel. Thus in 1848 he disapproves of the "Parlamentsgeschichte" (parliamentary affair) and cannot explain to himself why the whole thing has failed: "Es ist manches schöne, aber mehr noch manches übrige Wort für die deutsche Einheit und Freiheit gesprochen, manches Lied gesungen, manches Seidel und mancher Schoppen darauf getrunken, und es hat doch nichts geholfen."[28] Then finally when he was witness of the Baden upheaval in Mannheim 1849 he turned his back on the "Volk": "Es wurde ein schreckliches Trauerspiel vorbereitet. Ich mochte nicht als müßiger Zuschauer warten, bis es in Scene gesetzt war, und wie hätte ich mich beteiligen sollen? Meine Waffe war das Lied, und diese Waffe galt bei dem großen Haufen und seinen Führern, die nur mit roher Gewalt noch etwas auszurichten hofften, gar nichts mehr."[29] In the following year he sees popular sympathy for his role as a singer of political ballads as outmoded by history: "Alles drängt sich der Masse gegenüber Masse zu werden, in der Masse sucht jeder Halt und sich geltend zu machen."[30]

---

27 Andrée: *Hoffmann von Fallersleben*, p. 65. – I am making use here of my essay on Hoffmann von Fallersleben in: Hoffmann von Fallersleben: *Deutsche Gassenlieder. Deutsche Salonlieder*, pp. 79–105.
28 Hoffmann: *Mein Leben* vol. 5, p. 74. "Many a wonderful, and many an engaged word has been spoken in favor of German unification and freedom, many a song has been sung, many a mug of beer and many a glass of wine has been drunk to them, but all to no effect."
29 Ibid., p. 77. "A horrible tragedy was prepared. I did not want to wait as an inactive spectator, until it was staged, and how should I have taken part? My song was my weapon, and this weapon counted for nothing with the vulgar herd and their leaders, who believed in nothing but brute force."
30 Hoffmann: *An meine Freunde*, p. 185, June 8, 1850, to Ludwig Erk. "Everyone goes all out as a part of the mass facing the mass; in the midst of the mass everyone looks for support and recognition."

By 1870 his notion of the people has changed, although in his poetry and in his aesthetics he continues to adhere to an illusory 'folkishness'; now he explains: "Der einzelne ist nur noch etwas, indem er sich am großen Ganzen mitwirkend beteiligt, für des Vaterlandes Einheit und Freiheit sein Bestes tut."[31] Dispensing with individuality in favour of a superior unity reflects the changing attitude of the liberals towards Prussia after 1848 and foreshadows the self-renunciation of the liberals in 1878. Hoffmann was never inclined to break into belligerent song; in 1864, during the German-Danish War, he still thinks it possible to unify Germany with his songs: "So habe ich denn auch jetzt nicht ermangelt, auf meine Weise wieder zu wirken, d. h. durch Lieder. Freilich, diese prosaischen Politiker und politischen Philister glauben eine große volksthümliche Bewegung ließe sich ohne Poesie ins Leben rufen, lebendig erhalten und durchführen. Ich habe an die Leute, welche jetzt an der Spitze stehen, die Lieder geschickt. Gerade *dort* aber ist nicht die mindeste Empfänglichkeit."[32] He had no idea that very soon political poetry (as Geibel had predicted) would do nothing but crown the victors.

Consequently Hoffmann von Fallersleben in 1870 issues his patriotic songs anonymously; banished by Hanover and mistrusted by the ruling politicians, he is nevertheless dedicated to the idea of German unification as still a viable and unchanged goal, and that dedication in spite of its political naiveté accounts for his greatness. When his publisher Ebeling in Hamburg asked his permission to print Hoffmann's song on King Wilhelm "Wer ist der greise Siegesheld" ("Who is the aged triumphant hero") under his full name, Hoffmann explains why he has chosen anonymity: "Ich werde meinen Namen nie verleugnen, wozu ihn aber immer und überall nennen, zumal da, wo Freund und Feind Gelegenheit finden würden, mich eines Gesinnungswechsels zu zeihen."[33]

---

31 Letter to Karl Hirsche, September 24, 1870 – ibid., p. 327. "The individual can only survive if he participates in the integral whole, doing his best for his fatherland's unification and freedom."

32 Hoffmann von Fallersleben: *Gesammelte Werke* vol. 8, pp. 355–56, January 14, 1864 to Carl Gräf. "Thus this time too I have not failed to act my way i. e. through songs. But of course these prosaic politicians and political philistines believe that a great popular movement can be created, kept alive and conducted without poetry. I have sent my poems to those who are now at the head of the state. But precisely *there* not the slightest response can be found."

33 Hoffmann von Fallersleben: *An meine Freunde*, letter No. 136, August 28, 1870, to Theodor Ebeling, pp. 323–24. "I will never deny my name, but why give it always and everywhere, chiefly because friends and enemies will take the opportunity to reproach me for having changed commitment."

Hence his war song "Frisch auf, frisch auf! Zu den Waffen / Rufet uns das Vaterland"[34] (dedicated to a garrison based at Höxter) is printed in the *Kreuzzeitung* with nothing but the note "(Eingesandt)" ("sent in"). Gisbert von Vincke, a forgotten writer of novellas, confirms that the *Kreuzzeitung* would not publish his song celebrating King Wilhelm of Prussia (later on recast and entitled "Kaiser Wilhelm") if his name were put to it. Hoffmann von Fallersleben knew and admitted that as a dismissed and persecuted state official he had a relation "zum deutschen Volke, zu seinen Parteien und zum preußischen Staate" quite different from Freiligrath's. He is convinced that "in einer so großen Zeit nur von einem großen Volke die Rede sein kann, und daß der einzelne in dem gewaltigen Kampfe um Freiheit und Einheit verschwinden muß, wie's auch nicht anders will / Ihr Sie herzlich grüßender / H. v. F."[35]

Just as he does not change his mind, he persists in relying on parody and contrafacture as the pre-eminent strategy of his songs; Hoffmann never directly criticized the political system itself. In his songs published before 1848 he predominantly castigated "secondary subjects of complaint, based on primary deficiencies."[36] In December 1840, shortly after the first part of his *Unpolitical Songs* came out, Campe also published a documentation of the *Breslauer Schillerfest 1840*, containing a long hymn by Hoffmann praising Friedrich Wilhelm IV: "Heil ihm! der nicht allein auf dem Throne thront, / Heil ihm! der auch in unsern Herzen wohnt!" ("Hail to him! who is not only seated on his throne, hail to him, who also lives in our hearts!") Many contemporaries of Hoffmann accentuated Hoffmann's innocuousness: "harmless as a child" Johannes Scherr calls him[37], Ruge speaks of his "harmless humorous songs."[38] Even a satirist is astonished that the singer of the most innocuous popular songs ("Gassenhauer") is persecuted.[39] When finally the German imperial crown comes "in sight" he drinks a glass of punch to the Prussian victors at the Loire, and self-ironically signs a letter to his publisher: "HvF. kaiserlich-königlich preußischer Poet a.D. und Steuercontribuent."[40]

---

34 Hoffmann von Fallersleben: *Gesammelte Werke* vol. 5, pp. 166–67.
35 Hoffmann von Fallersleben: *An meine Freunde*, letter No. 136, August 28, 1870, to Ebeling, pp. 324–24. "with the German people, with its parties and with the Prussian state"; "in such a great time the only question is a great people, and that the individual during this huge struggle for freedom and unification has to vanish, wishing nothing else / yours sincerely / H. v. F."
36 Denkler: "Zwischen Julirevolution (1830) und Märzrevolution (1848/49)," p. 191.
37 Scherr: *Poeten der Jetztzeit*, p. 409.
38 Ruge: *Die politischen Lyriker unserer Zeit*, p. 75.
39 Friedmann: *X.Y.Z. Satyrisch-literarisches Taschenbuch für 1848*, p. 51: "Hoffmann von Gallersleben."
40 Hoffmann von Fallersleben: *Gesammelte Werke* vol. 8, letter to Ebeling, December 7, 1870, p. 359. "HvF. former imperial-royal Prussian poet and contributor of taxes."

After Hoffmann had proved his loyalty to the state with his songs on the war and the foundation of the German Empire, his friend, the principal pastor at the St. Nikolai Church in Hamburg submitted an application to Bismarck and asked for the "Gnade [!] der Rehabilitierung" ("mercy of rehabilitation"). The petitioner emphasizes Hoffmann's constant commitment to Prussia and quotes a pro-Prussian strophe from his *Unpolitical Songs* as well as a toast proposed in 1861 to the King of Prussia on the occasion of his accession to the throne:

> *Der* König, der sich eben jetzt
> Die Königskron' aufs Haupt gesetzt,
> Der muß die deutsche Kaiserkrone
> Einst hinterlassen seinem Sohne.

The application is rejected, though the Prussian Minister of Culture, Education and Church Affairs von Mühler informs the applicant in June 1871 that Hoffmann von Fallersleben "has maintained a conduct without reproach since the year 1848 and that he has done the sciences a great service."[41] Hoffmann's lyrical loyalty to Emperor and Empire is disregarded by the Prussian minister, conceivably also because the war and victory songs of the "most German poet" ("deutschesten Dichters") as he is called by his biographer Gerstenberg[42] through their subdued and non-religious tone stand out from the choir of hurrahs. Hoffmann von Fallersleben gives a very resigned answer in his "Herbstlied" ("Autumn Song"); he knows that he has become aesthetically outdated as a ballad singer yet has remained politically problematic – even his publisher refused to edit a complete edition of his works – but he does not think that he has failed *his* profession:

> Was hilft's, wenn ich noch sing' und sage
>   Vom deutschen Vaterland,
> Und nur für meine späten Tage
>   Ein deutsches Reich entstand?
> [...]
> Doch darum wird mein Herz nicht kühler,
>   Mich freut, daß Gott mich schuf
> Und daß ich nicht wie Herr von Mühler
>   Verfehlte den Beruf.[43]

---

41 Ibid., p. 383. "*That* King, who just now puts the king's crown upon his head, he must leave the emperor's crown later on to his son."

42 Gerstenberg: "Hoffmann von Fallersleben in Schloß Corvey (1860–1874)." Ibid., p. 241.

43 Ibid. vol. 5, p. 184, str. 3 and 5. "What use that I continue to sing about the German fatherland, and that in my old age a German Empire was founded? [...] But therefore my heart

Even his modest longing is not fulfilled: he wishes that "jetzt endlich einmal mein Lied 'Deutschland, Deutschland über alles' zu allgemeiner Geltung gelangte."[44] But this song was obviously no triumphal song, it was in lacking religious patrial metaphors and the ideology of the German Empire; "Einigkeit und Recht und Freiheit" ("unity and justice and freedom") and the fraternal bonds might have sounded to some people too much like "égalité, liberté, fraternité" and the period prior to 1848.

4. Ferdinand Freiligrath: "Diese seltene Einmüthigkeit der Theilnahme und der Zustimmung"

On the 18th of March, 1848, in front of the Royal Castle in Berlin, soldiers fired into the crowd, many people were killed. Shortly thereafter Ferdinand Freiligrath honors the victims in his famous poem "Die Toten an die Lebenden" ("The dead to the living"), where he sets forth his vision of a united Germany. He was arrested, brought to trial, but finally cleared of charges. He describes how German unification should be accomplished:

> Die Throne gehn in Flammen auf, die Fürsten fliehn zum Meere!
> Die Adler fliehn; die Löwen fliehn; die Klauen und die Zähne! –
> Und seine Zukunft bildet sich das Volk, das souveräne![45]

On the 18th of March 1876, exactly 28 years later, Freiligrath dies, and the *National-Zeitung* of the same day publishes the obituary by Julius Wolff:

> Der 18. März der Todestag Ferdinand Freiligrath's! Der weitaus bedeutendste, der begeistertste Sänger der Revolution, den keiner seiner Genossen an Edelmuth und Reinheit der Gesinnung und Gluth der Überzeugung übertraf, legt sich gerade an diesem Tage, über den er hinreißend wie kein Anderer Sturm geläutet hat, zum ewigen Schlafe nieder. Längst war er im Herzen versöhnt; wie immer zu seinem Volk und Vaterland, so stand er auch jetzt fest und treu zu Kaiser und Reich.[46]

---

does not become colder, I am glad that God created me and that I did not, like Herr von Mühler, fail in my profession."

44 Letter to Theodor Ebeling, August 12, 1870 – Hoffmann von Fallersleben: *An meine Freunde*, p. 321–22. "now finally my song 'Deutschland, Deutschland über alles' would be generally accepted."

45 Freiligrath: *Werke* part 2, p. 133. "The thrones burst into flames, the princes flee towards the sea! The eagles flee; the lions flee; the claws and the teeth! – And the sovereign people build their own future!"

46 Quoted from Hellfaier, ed., *Ferdinand Freiligrath – Ein Dichter des 19. Jahrhunderts*, p. 69. "The 18th of March – Ferdinand Freiligrath's deathday! By far the most important, the most

Ferdinand Freiligrath was and is looked upon by many critics as a figure symbolizing the reconciliation of the liberals with the Prussian-German state. In 1882 his biographer asserts: "What was striven for in 1848, has meanwhile become verity."[47] In 1866 after the Prussian victory of Königgrätz that "settled the form of unification"[48] the former revolutionary poet now very skeptical, was not carried away by the "beispiellosen Erfolg der preußischen Waffen," but openly confessed in a letter written in his London exile that

> ich bei allem großen Respekt vor der Tapferkeit des kämpfenden Volkes, dennoch die Resultate des Kriegs nur mit Mißtrauen ansehe. Die Machtstellung Preußens (kann man sagen: Deutschlands?) nach außen ist durch den Krieg sicherlich imponierender geworden, – an die versprochene freiheitliche Entwickelung nach innen glaube ich aber nicht, bis sie endlich da ist. – Trotz Parlament und alledem! Vor der Hand werden wir den schönsten Imperialismus haben.[49]

Half a year later, in April 1867, the *Gartenlaube* published an appeal to all Germans at home and abroad for the benefit of Freiligrath under the title "Auch eine Dotation,"[50] referring to the King Wilhelm's I gift to the victorious Prussian generals and to Bismarck, a total amount of one and a half million talers. The national gift to Freiligrath, as it was called, was initiated by some of his colleagues, by a group of merchants, and the collection finally totalled nearly 60,000 talers, in present-day values one million marks.[51]

When Freiligrath was informed about the collection, he had forgotten his prediction of "the finest imperialism," and faced with this unanimity his skepticism vanished; he thought he had been forgotten, but "nun kommt ein ganzes, großes – ein, will's Gott, bald auch freies und einiges Volk und zeigt mir, daß ich mich geirrt hatte! […] Bei dieser seltenen Einmüthigkeit der

---

> passionate singer of the revolution outclassed by none of his fellows in respect to his noble-mindedness, the purity of his intentions and the ardor of his heart, he lay down to sleep the eternal sleep exactly on that day about which he entrancingly like no one else has sounded the call. He had long since been reconciled in his heart; as then and now he firmly and loyally abides by Emperor and Empire."

47 Buchner: *Freiligrath* vol. 2, p. 202.
48 Craig: *Germany 1866–1945*, p. 1.
49 To Ludwig Elbers – Buchner: *Freiligrath* vol. 2, pp. 366–67. "unprecedented success of the Prussian arms." – "that despite my greatest respect for the braveness of the fighting people I must mistrust the results of the war. The external powerful position of Prussia (can we say: of Germany?) undoubtedly has become more impressive through the war, – but I don't believe in liberal interior development as promised until it is accomplished. – In spite of parliament and all that! Essentially, all we will have is the finest imperialism."
50 Bölling et al.: "Auch eine Dotation." *Die Gartenlaube* 1867, No. 17, p. 272.
51 Vgl. Noltenius: *Dichterfeiern in Deutschland*, p. 195.

Theilnahme und der Zustimmung gewinnt das Persönliche allerdings eine allgemeine, eine höhere Bedeutung! Und das gerade ist's, was mich freut und hebt! In diesem Sinne wage ich es, bei aller Bescheidenheit, mich stolz und glücklich zu fühlen angesichts dieser großen nationalen Kundgebung!"[52]

The political poems Freiligrath had written between 1844 and 1848/49 stand out by their strange and fascinating images and powerful allegories which give visual form to political and social conditions; this ardent commitment to the oppressed and the revolution in his poems written between July 25 and December 1870 is transformed into a combination of unpolitical compassion and a patriotic sense of power. Ten days after the declaration of war, Freiligrath composes his "Hurra, Germania!" about which Theodor Storm raves to his son Ernst on August 8: "Hast Du das wunderschöne Gedicht von Freiligrath gelesen: 'Hurra, Germania!'; das ist ganz der alte goldne Klang wie in seiner besten Jugendzeit, d.h. die ersten fünf Strophen; die letzten drei sind Blech."[53] While harvesting, the peaceful Germania is startled by the "Kriegshorn überm Rhein" ("war horn across the Rhine"), she calls her children "alle Mann! / zum Rhein! zum Rhein! zum Rhein!" ("everybody! / to the Rhine"). And thus from the common threat of the individual tribes (incorporated by the rivers) grows the German unification:

> Vergessen ist der alte Span:
> Das deutsche Volk ist *eins*!
> [...]
> Schwaben und Preußen Hand in Hand;
> Der Nord, der Süd *ein* Heer!
> Was ist des Deutschen Vaterland, –
> Wir fragen's heut nicht mehr!
> Ein Geist, *ein* Arm, *ein* einz'ger Leib,
> *Ein* Wille sind wir heut!

Germania symbolizing the whole German nation was a conventional figure in those days; one may doubt whether Freiligrath was inspired by Heinrich von Kleist's then not commonly known "Germania an ihre Kinder"; in Kleist's

---

52 Letter to Adolf Glaßbrenner, June 24, 1867 – Buchner: *Freiligrath* vol. 2, p. 372. "now there is a whole, a great and – please God, soon also free and unified nation and it proves to me that I was wrong! [...] In sight of this rare unanimity of sympathy and consensus, personal matters actually acquire a broader, a higher meaning! Therefore I feel delighted and elevated! Along these lines I dare (with all due modesty) feel proud and happy in sight of this great national demonstration!"

53 Letter no. 175 – Storm: *Briefe* vol. 2, p. 22. "Have you already read Freiligrath's wonderful poem 'Hurra, Germania!'; that's indeed the old golden tone as in his best youth i. e. the first five strophes; the last three are rubbish."

atrocious ode Germania pitilessly exhorts her children: "Alle Plätze, Trift' und Stätten, / Färbt mit ihren [nämlich der Franzosen] Knochen weiß; / Welchen Rab' und Fuchs verschmähten, / Gebet ihn den Fischen preis; / Dämmt den Rhein mit ihren Leichen [...]."[54] Freiligrath for his part laments in spite of his belligerent appeals and in spite of the refrain "Hurra, hurra, hurra! / Hurra Germania!": "Wohl schnürt's die Brust uns, denken wir / Des Bluts, das fließen wird!"[55] That he is not only deploring German blood is witnessed by a letter to Berthold Auerbach: He mourns the "Zerrüttung eines trotz alledem noblen, tapfern und klugen Volks": "dieses unsägliche Elend, welches (wenn auch durch eigene Schuld) über Frankreich hereingebrochen ist, frißt mir dennoch fast das Herz ab."[56]

Though "Hurra, Germania" is distinguished from the national flood by its moving sounds of misery (on that account one of today's Freiligrath faithful has tried to make him a "poet of peace"[57]), he is the only one of our trio to succumb in his poems to Germany's recent seeming grandeur. As early as 1849 the historian F. C. Dahlmann had declared in the Paulskirche: "The road of power is the only one that will satisfy and calm and appease the yearning for freedom, – for it is not only freedom, the German aims at, for the larger part it is power, which has been as yet denied to him, that he craves."[58] Admittedly, Freiligrath's Germania is not only great and glorious, but also free; the addition "as never before" to all three epithets ("Groß, herrlich, frei wie nie zuvor") destroys the climax that at first sounded so positive and mature. Like Freiligrath's "Hurra, Germania" other political poems written in 1870 and 1871 were part of the transvaluation of the previous liberal notions of freedom and unification;[59] but Freiligrath would never have accepted the bru-

---

54 Kleist: *Sämtliche Werke* vol. 3, pp. 426–33, quotation p. 428. "Dye white all the places, pastures and regions with their bones; whom raven and fox refused, surrender it all to the fishes; dam up the Rhine with their cadavers [...]."

55 Freiligrath: *Werke* part 3, pp. 47–9. "The former conflicts are forgotten the German nation is of *one* mind! [...] Swabians and Prussians hand in hand; the North, the South, *one* army! What is the German's fatherland, – Today we don't ask this question any more! *One* mind, *one* arm, *one* single body, *one* will we are today!" – "The throat tightens if one remembers the blood that will flow!" See also Kelly, this volume, p. 45.

56 Letter to Berthold Auerbach, November 11, 1870 – Buchner: *Freiligrath* vol. 2, p. 413. "ruin of a nevertheless noble, brave and intelligent nation"; "my heart breaks at this inexpressible misery that (though not without their own fault) has befallen France."

57 Freund: "Der späte Freiligrath – ein Dichter des Friedens."

58 Quoted from Meinecke: *Die Idee der Staatsraison,* p. 464; cf. also Craig: *Germany 1866–1945,* p. 57.

59 Cf. Menne: *Einigkeit und Unité. Die Legitimation politischer Vorgänge mit lyrischen Mitteln in den deutschen und französischen Kriegsgedichten von 1870–71,* esp. pp. 296–323: "Die nationale Identität."

tal maxim written in a sonnet by Oswald Marbach (1810–1890) aimed at the "democrats" ("arme Wichte," "empörte Knechte"): "Freiheit ist Herrschaft – lernt euch so betragen, / Wie denen ziemet, die sich selbst bezwungen: / Dient Jedermann und fragt nicht nach dem Lohne."[60]

The complete edition of Freiligrath's work, the termination of which was fostered effectively by the flush of victory in the autumn of 1870, is opened by his "An Deutschland."[61] He is by no means rejoicing ("im Jubelsturm") after the victory at Sedan ("Nun bebt vor Gottes / Und Deutschlands Schwert")[62] like the self-made and acknowledged prophet of Prussia-Germany and of Bismarck, the Kaiserdichter Emanuel Geibel, but he is lamenting Germany: "du wunde, / Du bleiche Siegerin!" ("thou wounded, thou pale victress!") More than half a century later Bertolt Brecht adopts this verse repeatedly: "Deutschland, du Blondes, Bleiches" and "O Deutschland, bleiche Mutter!"[63] However, Freiligrath's pale Germany does not sit "besudelt / Unter den Völkern" ("stained amongst the nations"), but out of the blackness of her mourning she shines ahead of all nations:

> Daß thronend in aller Mitte,
> Du walten magst in Ruh
> Des Rechts, des Lichts, der Sitte,
> Freieiniges Deutschland du![64]

Full of grief Germany is holding court, becomes the judge over the world, immoderate, but in accordance with the delusion of those drunken with the unification: "Du trägst, du wägst in Händen / Eine Welt und ihr Geschick" ("You carry, you weigh in your hands a world and its destiny") – these were words which sounded differently to their contemporaries than Hoffmann's von Fallersleben innocuous songs of triumph. With his mixture of humanitarian sympathy (especially in his "Trompete von Gravelotte") and the German feeling of superiority through unification (without anti-

---

60 Marbach: *Das Halljahr Deutschlands*, p. 52: "An die Demokraten." – "poor dwarves," "rebellious slaves": "Freedom is mastery – learn to behave like those who have mastered themselves: Serve everyone and don't ask for reward." Reference to Marbach in Menne: *Einigkeit und Unité*, p. 321.
61 Freiligrath: *Werke* part 1, pp. 1–3.
62 Geibel: *Werke* vol. 2, pp. 249–50: "Am dritten September." – "Now tremble before God's and Germany's sword."
63 Brecht: *Werke* (Große kommentierte Berliner und Frankfurter Ausgabe), vol. 13, pp. 171–72, vol. 11, pp. 253–54.
64 "That being enthroned in the midst of all at peace you may exercise justice, light, and morality, you free and united Germany!"

French animus), Freiligrath captured the zeitgeist but above all was so precisely in harmony with later German cultural conservatism, especially in schools and universities, that of our trio only he has really survived in German literary history.[65]

5. Georg Herwegh:
"Denn der Lauf der Welt hängt ab vom Lauf der Flinten"[66]

Herwegh on the other hand was the only one of the trio who recognized the causes and consequences of the German victories of 1866, 1870, and 1871. Unlike Hoffmann von Fallersleben and Freiligrath he also perceived Bismarck's coining power. That seems the more astounding because Friedrich Theodor Vischer and Heinrich Heine too had blamed him before 1848, rightly or wrongly, of using windy rhetoric and unrealistic high style; but indisputably he is the only one in the political poets' choir who – from today's point of view – passed a correct judgement on the German unification.

Franz Dingelstedt had declared as early as 1842: "Herwegh has a future if Germany goes through a revolution, otherwise he won't have."[67] A successful revolution failed to come, and Herwegh (in the view of many of his contemporaries and also of many literary historians) had even risked his glory and dignity as a poet (which meant a great deal to him) when in 1848 he tried to join the revolution in Baden with an ill-equipped legion from Paris and failed. Though he was the first poet at the head of an army since the days of Ulrich von Hutten it was not he, but Freiligrath who in 1868 returned home from exile in a triumphal procession and all the richer for the German national endowment of 60,000 talers. Herwegh, in order to come home from Zurich after the amnesty of 1866, had to sell his beloved library and to borrow the travel expenses. Impoverished, he could subsist only by anonymously publishing his contributions to journals. The *Deutsche Schillerstiftung* in 1868 could decide only on one single donation for the friend of Lasalle and the author of the "Bundeslied für den Allgemeinen deutschen Arbeiterverein" because with Herwegh "worthiness and neediness lie so far apart" ("Würdigkeit und Be-

---

65 On the aesthetics of Freiligraths political and unpolitical lyric see my articles (cf. bibliography).
66 "For the way of the world depends on the rifle's barrel." The pun can not be translated. Herwegh's poem "Immer mehr!" (April 1886) closes with these words – Herwegh: *Werke* part 3, p. 97.
67 Letter to Friedrich Oetker – Geiger, ed., *Aus Adolf Stahrs Nachlaß*, p. 44.

dürftigkeit so weit auseinander liegen").⁶⁸ Even Gottfried Keller was skeptical about Herwegh's later poems (which he did not know at all): "Wie steht's jetzt auch mit den neuen Gedichten Herweghs? Da er tot ist, so kann er sie doch wohl nicht mehr zurückhalten [...]. Freilich, wenn neben der unzeitgemäßen Polemik gegen Deutschland und seine Führer nicht ein gewisser Stock rein poetischer Sachen da ist, welche das Bittere versüßen, so könnte die Aufnahme unerfreulich ausfallen."⁶⁹

But when Herwegh's *Neue Gedichte* were finally published in Zurich, in 1877, two years after his death, and immediately banned in the German Empire, the derivative poet and secretary general of the *Schillerstiftung* Julius Grosse, full of indignation, declared that these poems identified the author "nicht bloß als einen politischen Gegner seines Vaterlandes, sondern als eine gemeine Natur"; and he rigorously demands: "Wer im Stande ist, dergleichen Schmähungen auf Kaiser und Reich zu publiciren, dessen Name verdient für immer aus den Annalen der deutschen Literatur gestrichen zu werden."⁷⁰ Before these poems were issued, Rudolf von Gottschall had shown how literary history could redeem Herwegh without taking into serious consideration anything but his early poems; he numbered Herwegh among those poets who have only one magnificent success – in his case the *Gedichte eines Lebendigen* (1841/43). In 1871 Herwegh did not recognize "in these events the dream of his youth."⁷¹

This dream, the idea of German unification, had long been merely a cultural one. The yearning for a unified German nation was part of a cultural-patriotical tradition even before the close of the eighteenth century; for the German, as Schiller expressed it, had "sich längst [über] seinen politischen Zustand emporgehoben," and, in any case, his 'ethical' greatness was revealed not in the form of government but "in der Kultur u: im Character der Nation."⁷²

---

68 According to Ernst Förster's judgement – Kaiser, ed., *Die Akten Ferdinand Freiligrath und Georg Herwegh*, p. 51.

69 Letter to the publisher Ferdinand Weibert, May 20, 1875 – Keller: *Gesammelte Briefe* vol. 3, 2, p. 253. "What about Herwegh's new poems? Dead as he is he won't be able to hold them back. [...]. But of course, if there isn't in addition to the unseasonable polemics against Germany and her leaders a certain stock of purely poetic pieces to sweeten the bitter, the reception might be unfriendly."

70 Grosse in a letter to the Verwaltungsrat der Deutschen Schillerstiftung, February 27, 1877 – Kaiser, ed., *Die Akten Ferdinand Freiligrath und Georg Herwegh*, p. 62. "not only as a political opponent of his fatherland, but as mean character." – "Whoever is capable of publishing such invectives against Emperor and Empire, deserves to have his name stricken from the annals of German literature."

71 Gottschall: "Georg Herwegh," p. 725.

72 Schiller: *Werke* (Nationalausgabe) vol. 2, 1, pp. 431–36, here p. 431. "long since risen above his political conditions." – "in the culture and in the character of the nation." Schiller's

The German bourgeoisie even in the nineteenth century was looking backwards in quest of a national identity;[73] this quest was successful only in the cultural sphere: romanticism, *Germanistik* and the German *Burschenschaften* were the most prominent of its supporters.

The political efforts after 1848 to unify Germany were based on economics and power politics not on politico-cultural considerations. Herwegh had recognized this early. In 1869 in his poem "Tristia" he scoffs at the North German Confederation: "O Einheit, welch ein Schatz bist du! / Einheit im Zoll, Einheit in Waffen! / Das neue Deutschland ist geschaffen." The Bismarckian way to German unification, ushered in by his notorious blood-and-iron-speech on February 29, 1862 before the budget commission of the Prussian chamber of deputies, is hit off aptly by Herwegh:

> Den Leuten, die am besten Schießen,
> Gehört die Welt, das ist erwiesen;
> Und niemals hab' ich noch gesehn,
> Daß die Erschoßnen auferstehn.[74]

Herwegh at first interpreted the Franco-Prussian War positively as a campaign against the despot Napoleon III; in the poem "Endlich!" he exults on August 10, 1870: "Aufgeweckt von deutschen Schlägen / Rührt sich endlich die Justiz."[75] His two great poems of February 1871 ("Der schlimmste Feind" and "Epilog zum Kriege") could only be published in his lifetime anonymously and abroad; the first printing in the *Wiener Tages-Presse* remained unnoticed by bourgeois critics until they were published in the book edition.[76] The two poems of course did not entirely exclude Herwegh from the annals of literary history, but as a matter of fact there is and has been less research on Herwegh than on Freiligrath in the Federal Republic, though not in the German Democratic Republic. Even Friedrich Sengle in his *Biedermeierzeit* merely repeats the nineteenth century's judgements on the two poets: Herwegh was

---

sketch of the poem for the first time was published in 1871! See also Grawe: "Schillers Gedichtentwurf 'Deutsche Größe': 'Ein Nationalhymnus im höchsten Stil'? Ein Beispiel ideologischen Mißbrauchs in der Germanistik seit 1871"; cf. also the introduction to this volume, p. 8.

73 Cf. also the recently published study by Richter: *Hans Ferdinand Maßmann*.
74 Herwegh: *Werke* part 3, pp. 122–23. "O Unity, what treasure you are! Unity of tolls, unity of arms! The new Germany is created." "The world belongs to those who shoot best, It's proven. And I have never seen that those shot dead rise again."
75 Ibid., pp. 128–29. "Awakened up by German beatings, eventually justice stirs."
76 First printing according to Kaiser, ed., *Der Freiheit eine Gasse*, p. 444: February 2 and 14, 1871.

nothing but a show-off ("Angeber"), a Tübingen student run wild ("der wildgewordene Stiftler").[77] At the end of his paragraph on Freiligrath he cites Emanuel Geibel, of all poets, as an unsuspicious witness, agreeing with him that such a visionary is worth remembering.[78] The reception of Herwegh is part of the tragedy of the German mind.

One of the most ardent antagonists of Prussia was Friedrich Nietzsche, though he was a great deal more 'German' than Herwegh and declaimed against "French-Jewish degeneration" ("französisch-jüdische Verflachung"),[79] though he contributed his mite to the patriotic offertory box ("Opferkasten des Vaterlandes") by serving in a military hospital,[80] and though still in June 1871 he expressed his surprise at the "wonderful unexpected discovery" ("schöne unerwartete Entdeckung") of the old Germanic "heroic and at the same time prudent mind" ("heldenmäßigen und zugleich besonnenen Geistes") within the German army.[81] But later (1873) he realized the true reasons for Germany's superiority: Gordon Craig affirms Nietzsche's arguments for the "real reasons for the victory over France": "Strenge Kriegszucht, natürliche Tapferkeit und Ausdauer, Ueberlegenheit der Führer, Einheit und Gehorsam unter den Gefährten," but above all the German army excelled "in dem umfassenderen Wissen der deutschen Offiziere, in der größeren Belehrtheit der deutschen Mannschaften, in der wissenschaftlicheren Kriegsführung."[82] For Herwegh, too, the German victory was nothing but the result of a military superiority, which of course, he morally derided. The foundation of the German Empire, as he observes in his "Epilog zum Kriege," emerged out of "Zerstörung, Tod und Flammen" ("destruction, death, and flames"):

> [...]
> Schwarz, weiß und rot! um ein Panier
> Vereinigt stehen Süd und Norden;
> Du bist im ruhmgekrönten Morden
> Das erste Land der Welt geworden:
> Germania, mir graut vor dir!

---

77 Sengle: *Biedermeierzeit* vol. 2, p. 554.
78 Ibid., p. 548.
79 Letter to Carl von Gersdorff, June 21, 1871 – Nietzsche: *Briefe* vol. 3, p. 203.
80 Letter to the Ratsherr Wilhelm Vischer-Bilfinger, August 8, 1870 – ibid., p. 133.
81 Letter to Carl von Gersdorff, June 21, 1871 – ibid., p. 203.
82 Nietzsche: "Unzeitgemäße Betrachtungen." *Sämtliche Werke* vol. 1, pp. 160 and 162. "Strong discipline, natural braveness, and persistence, superiority of the leaders, unity and obedience among those lead"; "in a more extensive knowledge of the German officers, in better instructed troops, in a more scientific conduct of operations"; cf. Craig: *Germany 1866–1945*, p. 36.

> Mir graut vor dir, ich glaube fast,
> Daß du, in argen Wahn versunken,
> Mit falscher Größe suchst zu prunken,
> Und daß du, gottesgnadentrunken,
> Das Menschenrecht vergessen hast.
>
> [...]⁸³

The antithetical images of this poem contrast most violently; they are juxtaposed to visualize the way unification was only accomplished by force. The German "Denkervolk" ("nation of thinkers") as it is ironically called by Herwegh in his poem "Den Siegestrunkenen" ("To those drunk with victory") had finally obtained power and with power also grandeur. The alleged superiority of the new Germany is also satirized in his poem "Groß" (May 1872) where the "Einheitsbarden" ("Unification-bards") seem to have a wrong notion of greatness, based only on money and soldiers; the former ideal, lacerated and shot to pieces ("zerfetzt nun und zerschossen"), lies in the Prussian hospital.⁸⁴ In Gustav Freytag's *Grenzboten*, Nietzsche's — and thus indirectly also Herwegh's — critique was rejected: "Wann ist Deutschland jemals größer, gesunder, des Namens eines Kulturvolks würdiger gewesen als heutzutage?"⁸⁵ Herwegh comments on the German unification under the Prussian hammer: "Die Wacht am Rhein wird nicht genügen, / Der schlimmste Feind steht an der Spree."⁸⁶ For many a critic, like the art historian Anton Springer, a great centralized and powerful state was hostile to "Bildung"; Springer therefore advocated the traditional decentralization and maintained the German myth of a cultural and educational unity deeply rooted in the German "Volksboden" ("national soil").⁸⁷ Herwegh's and Springer's indictments coincide with Nietzsche's concerns (as early as November 1870) about the "cul-

---

83   Herwegh: *Werke* part 3, pp. 132–33. "[...] Black, white, and red! around one banner the South and the North have gathered; you have become the world's premier country crowned with glory in killing: Germania, I am terrified of you! // I am terrified of you, I almost believe that (under great delusion) you endeavor to parade your false grandeur and that you, drunken with your divine rights, have forgotten human rights."
84   Ibid., pp. 134–5.
85   B. F.: "Herr Friedrich Nietzsche und die deutsche Cultur," p. 109. Reference to this essay in Craig: *Germany 1866–1945*, p. 36, where Craig gives a translation: "When has Germany ever been greater, sounder, and more worthy of the name of a people of culture than today?"
86   "Der schlimmste Feind" – Herwegh: *Werke* part 3, pp. 130–32. "The guard on the Rhine is not enough, the worst enemy stands on the Spree."
87   Springer: "Unsere Friedensziele." *Im neuen Reich* 1:1 (1871), pp. 697, 695 and 696. – Cf. also Deuerlein: "Die Konfrontation von Nationalstaat und national bestimmter Kultur." Schieder and Deuerlein, eds., *Reichsgründung 1870/71*, pp. 226–258, here p. 237.

tural situation to come" and his warning that the new Prussia would be a power highly dangerous to culture.⁸⁸ Theodor Storm too felt so much hatred for "that Prussianism that outwardly wins all these victories," that he refused to contribute to the anthology of war songs *Zu Schutz und Trutz*.⁸⁹

But these were isolated voices against the general conviction that the German Empire's center of power would also become the capital of the German mind.⁹⁰ Foreign travelers to Germany like Xavier Marmier very early (1841) felt their image of Germany clouded by Prussia. Visits to Berlin in 1859 persuaded him to look upon Berlin as a "capitale d'un peuple essentiellement guerrier."⁹¹ And in 1903 the French journalist Jules Huret, then making his tour through Germany, relates the opinion of a lady of very moderate judgement: all over Berlin, quite differently from Paris or London, the names of the sovereigns but not of those engaged in the cultural area are present:

> "Les gymnases s'appellent comme les rois et les reines de Prusse: il y a le gymnase Auguste, le gymnase Frédéric, le gymnase Frédéric-Guillaume, le collège Royal, le collège de l'Empereur-Guillaume, l'école Hohenzollern, le collège Sophie, le collège de la Reine-Louise; j'en passe!
>
> Il y a l'allée de l'Empereur, la place Frédéric, le bois Frédéric, le mont Frédéric, la rue de l'Empereur-Frédéric, la rue Frédéric, l'allée de l'Impératrice-Auguste, la galerie de l'Empereur, la rue Guillaume, la place Guillaume, la rue de la Reine-Augusta, la place de l'Empereur-Guillaume, la place Karl-August. Il y a la rue Royale, la Nouvelle rue Royale, la place Royale, l'allée Royale, le chemin Royal, la porte Royale, le pont Royal, la chaussée Royale.
>
> Les musées, les hôpitaux, les orphelinats sont hohenzollernisés."⁹²

Through later developments, chiefly during the twenties, the French journalist and Herwegh were, for a while, put into the wrong, later again into the right. But this is another German question.

---

88 Letter to Carl von Gersdorff, November 7, 1870 – Nietzsche: *Briefe* vol. 3, p. 155. See also Peter Paret: *The Berlin Secession: Modernism and Its Enemies in Imperial Germany*.
89 Letter no. 175 to his son Ernst, August 8, 1870 – Storm: *Briefe* vol. 2, p. 22.
90 Vgl. Deuerlein: "Die Konfrontation von Nationalstaat und national bestimmter Kultur." Schieder and Deuerlein, eds., *Reichsgründung 1870/71*, pp. 226–258, here p. 240. – See also Katherine Roper's essay in this volume pp. 172–73.
91 Mercer: "From Idyll to Arsenal: The Changing Image of Germany in France As Seen through the Work of Xavier Marmier (1808–1892)," pp. 187 and 190.
92 Huret: *Berlin*, pp. 7–8.

6. Confusion of Values

Treitschke sums up the contemporary verdict on Herwegh: "Als ihm dann endlich, nach kläglichen Heldenthaten im Revolutionsjahre, ein gütiges Geschick beschied, die Tage deutschen Ruhmes zu erleben, da ist er noch lange keifend, schimpfend, höhnend hinter dem Siegeswagen des neuen deutschen Reichs dahergetaumelt, ein Trunkenbold der Phrase, verachtet von den Einsichtigen, vergessen von der Mehrheit der Nation."[93] Herwegh had opposed the dominant political and literary discourse; he had fulfilled in the years before and after the foundation of the German Empire what he had written in 1839 in his essay *Dichter und Staat*: "*Jeder Dichter steht in Opposition mit dem Staate, auch mit dem besten.*"[94]

Of some importance for the reception of the three former "Vormärzler" was their actual civic position *in* this state, the correlation between poetic and civic profession: The never rehabilitated former Royal Prussian professor of Germanistik recognized this quite precisely as we have seen. Even closest friends blamed him for having shifted his commitment ("Gesinnungswechsel"), whereas Freiligrath, the former friend of Karl Marx and member of the *Neue Rheinische Zeitung*, was called home as a result of the collection by his mercantile colleagues in a triumphal procession. As a merchant in his fellow citizen's eyes he could not offend against the capitalist system which he served until his return from his voluntary London exile as the head of a Swiss private bank. What hazardous actions could be expected from him who thanked Marx for sending him the first volume of his *Capital*: "Ich weiß, daß am Rhein viele junge Kaufleute u. Fabrikbesitzer sich für das Buch begeistern. In diesen Kreisen wird es seinen eigentlichen Zweck erfüllen."[95] Treitschke considered Freiligrath "a Westphalian man of soul with the innocent eyes of a child" ("ein westphälischer Seelenmensch mit treuherzigen Kinderaugen") carried away involuntarily in the turmoil of political poetry ("Tendenzpoesie"); for him Freiligrath, in spite of his "radical dreams," remained the good

---

93 Treitschke: *Deutsche Geschichte des Neunzehnten Jahrhunderts* vol. 5, p. 374. "When finally after his miserable heroic deeds in the year of the revolution a kind fate granted him to see the days of German glory, for a long time he tottered behind the wagon of victory, nagging, scolding, sneering, a drunkard of the phrase, disdained by the reasonable, forgotten by the majority of the nation."

94 Herwegh: "Dichter und Staat." Herwegh: *Frühe Publizistik 1837–1841*, pp. 35–37, here p. 36. "*Every poet stands in opposition to the state, even to the best.*"

95 Letter no. 181, April 3, 1868, to Karl Marx – Freiligrath: *Briefwechsel mit Marx und Engels* vol. 1, p. 182. "I know that many young merchants and factory owners on the Rhine are enthusiastic about this book. In these circles it will fulfill its proper purpose."

hearted "always pleasant and cheerful fellow," who "grateful, without pusillanimity, celebrated Germany's newly gained grandeur."⁹⁶

But Georg Herwegh, the son of a cook, expelled from the Stift at Tübingen,⁹⁷ an active revolutionary, who was able to live as a freelance writer only because of his rich wife's dowry, joined (though not with great enthusiasm) the German Labor Movement: This action alone made him suspect to the intellectual exponents of the new Reich. The relation between these and the old campaigners of the revolution is well illustrated in the conversation between the old Buck and Diederich Heßling in Heinrich Mann's *Der Untertan*:

> "Aber wir haben doch, dank den Hohenzollern, das einige Deutsche Reich."
> "Wir haben es nicht," sagte der alte Buck und stand ungewöhnlich rasch vom Stuhl auf. "Denn wir müßten, um unsere Einigkeit zu beweisen, einem eigenen Willen folgen; und können wir's? Ihr wähnt euch einig, weil die Pest der Knechtschaft sich verallgemeinert! Das hat Herwegh, ein Überlebender wie ich, im Frühjahr einundsiebzig den Siegestrunkenen zugerufen. Was würde er heute sagen!"
> Diederich konnte, vor dieser Stimme aus dem Jenseits, nur stammeln: "Ach ja, Sie sind ein Achtundvierziger!"⁹⁸

Hoffmann von Fallersleben and Freiligrath offered their services to the moral spirit ("dem sittlichen Geist") of the German fatherland.⁹⁹ Hoffmann did not have to make a compromise to do so, for the dismissed professor had continued to be true and loyal and did not see through the political conditions and historical correlations, but he reflected truly (as one critic has said) "all mental trends of the German life" ("alle Gemüthsströmungen des deutschen Lebens").¹⁰⁰

---

96   Treitschke: *Deutsche Geschichte im Neunzehnten Jahrhundert* vol. 5, pp. 376–77.
97   His family background and uncompleted studies led to a negative assessment of him and his works even in later literary histories, cf. Riha: "Georg Herwegh – in rezeptionsgeschichtlicher Sicht."
98   Mann: *Der Untertan,* pp. 117–18. "'But, thanks to the Hohenzollerns, we do have the unified German Empire.' 'We don't,' said the old Buck and with an unaccustomed swiftness rose from his chair. 'For we ought to follow a will of our own in order to prove our unity; and are we able to do so? You assume unity, because the pestilence of slavery becomes more common! Herwegh, a survivor like me, in spring 1871 shouted this to those drunk with victory. What would he say today?' Diederich confronting this voice from the other world could nothing but stammer: 'O well, you are a forty-eighter!'"
99   Carriere: *Die sittliche Weltordnung in den Zeichen und Aufgaben unserer Zeit. Rede gehalten am 3. September 1870 in einer Volksversammlung zu München*. München 1870, pp. 3–4 – quoted from: Bucher et al., eds., *Realismus und Gründerzeit* vol. 2, p. 517.
100 Anonymus (Rev.): "Unpolitische Lieder von Hoffmann von Fallersleben"; quite similar Karl Gödeke: *Deutschlands Dichter von 1813 bis 1843*, p. 310: "Ohne besondere Tiefe faßte er die Ansichten des überwiegendsten Theiles seiner Zeitgenossen in singbare epigrammatische Gedichte […]."

Freiligrath on the other hand succumbed to the "confusion of values," confounding military technical knowledge and economic power with intellectual greatness. Gordon Craig's summary of this problem can serve even today as an admonition, although this unification was ushered in very differently:

> No one was ever to have reason to doubt German proficiency. It was demonstrated repeatedly in many fields of endeavor in the seventy-fifty years that followed the war with France. But the tendency to invest it with an ideal meaning, to confuse it with virtue and morality, and to make it the basis of claims of superiority, continued to be its concomitant.[101]

The reactions to the war and unification expressed by these three pre-revolutionaries and the way, in turn, that posterity has responded to them, show the essential dilemma: Freiligrath has a museum dedicated to him; Hoffmann von Fallersleben got (besides long existing memorials) a new museum in the castle of Fallersleben; the Herwegh archive, however, is located in Switzerland, and on the tombstone of the Stuttgartian Herwegh in the *Swiss* town of Liesthal, erected by Swiss and German workmen who collected the money, is written, like a posthumous slap in the face for Bismarckian Germany: "Hier ruht, wie er's gewollt, in seiner Heimat freien Erde Georg Herwegh."[102]

7. "Jeder Dichter steht in Opposition mit dem Staate, auch mit dem besten"

The German unification of 1871 led – as is seen in the example of Herwegh – to discrimination against all those who stuck to the ideals of 1848 and viewed the new German Empire and Bismarck's power politics since 1866 with skepticism.[103] In today's Germany too Jürgen Habermas diagnoses a discrediting of the critical intelligence. He does not, however, focus on the writers, but claims that the state socialism in the GDR has discredited progressive ideas as such: "Die Entwertung unserer besten und schwächsten intellektuellen Tradition ist für mich einer der bösesten Aspekte an dem Erbe, das die DDR in die erweiterte Bundesrepublik einbringt."[104] These are the

---

101 Craig: *Germany 1866–1945*, p. 36.
102 The text is *not* by Herwegh – cf. Kaiser, ed., *Der Freiheit eine Gasse,* p. 425. "Here lies, as he wished, in his homeland's free soil, Georg Herwegh."
103 See also Volker Neuhaus' remarks on the causes of the oblivion of Spielhagen in this volume pp. 136.
104 Habermas: "Die andere Zerstörung der Vernunft: Über die Defizite der deutschen Vereinigung und über die Rolle der intellektuellen Kritik." *Die Zeit* No. 20, May 10, 1991, p. 63. "The devaluation of our best and weakest intellectual tradition is one of the worst aspects of the heritage the GDR has brought into the enlarged Federal Republic."

most precarious parallels to 1871 and the years after, though the 'intellectuals' then and now contrasted profoundly as to the yearning for unity as such. One should not directly connect Auschwitz and the German 'unification' of 1938 with those of 1871 and 1990, but one should speak of the cultural wound of Germany which, of course, ultimately reaches as deep as the Holocaust and its 'cultural' grounds.

Then and today for government, parliament and people alike unification was not a question of culture, but of politics and economics. Because the solution of economic problems affects the basic existence of many people, especially in the eastern provinces, there is no question but that the issues are economic ones – if only issues were not again being confused, both by politicians and by intellectuals.

A predominant feature of German poetry since the 'Wende' seems to be a sort of melancholy,[105] a sort of utopia only in the act of writing. A disconsolate "defiance" determines much of the current lyric poetry, including Sarah Kirsch's poems in her new volume *Erlkönigs Tochter* (*Erlking's daughter*), her first book published since the 'Wende.' Many of her nature poems are still political, some of them even more explicitly than her earlier poems; though sensitive Sarah remains somewhat nebulous: Seven poems "From the Haiku region" ("Aus dem Haiku-Gebiet"), open the collection with her most candid statements:

> Das neue Jahr: Winde
> Aus alten Zeiten
> Machen mir Zahnweh.
>
> [...]
>
> Wie der Schnee sie auch
> Verklärt – meine Heimat
> Sieht erbärmlich aus.
>
> Den Mond über der Havel
> Hatte Schalck wohl
> Zurückgelassen.[106]

That is not a spectacular response to German unification; reference to the 'we' of the whole society is preserved in the representative subjectivity con-

---

105 See also Konrád: "Die Melancholie der Wiedergeburt."
106 Kirsch: *Erlkönigs Tochter*, p. 5. "The new year: winds / from old times / cause my toothache. // However the snow / transfigures my home country / it looks miserable. // The moon above the Havel / must have been left / behind by Schalck." Schalck: an allusion to Schalck-Golodkowski, the former GDR government's principal foreign-exchange-dealer.

soling everybody because a vague and enigmatic sadness is put into such beautiful images.

Sensitive subtleties like Sarah Kirsch's seem to be made only for posterity; for an instant and immediate impact they are too weak. Wolf Biermann with his crude and earthy humanity or Günter Grass with his aggressive and desperate obsession do better – Grass in keeping open the wound of German unity by memory, "beset by song and pain" ("vom Lied und Leid im Lied besessen"), in his thirteen *Novemberland*-sonnets,[107] Biermann in cutting down German sufferings to their proper proportions in view of threatening global catastrophes. By severely castigating the "two-third majority" ("Zweidrittelmehrheit") unified only by fear Grass returns, in the chaste severity of a sonnet, for the first time to the forms and tendencies of his collection of political poems *Ausgefragt* (1967), but the former humor becomes darkly grotesque:

> Die Angst geht um, November droht zu bleiben.
> Nie wieder langer Tage Heiterkeit.
> Die letzten Fliegen fallen von den Scheiben,
> und Stillstand folgt dem Schnellimbiß der Zeit.[108]

The dead of November and the unification without mercy ("die keine Gnade kennt"),[109] merge into an apocalyptic Novemberland, transforming itself into a fortress by means of a new right of asylum, secure from "Roma, Schwarzen, Juden und Fellachen" ("Romanies, blacks, Jews, and fellahs") a building, sweated out by calculating fear ("hat planend Furcht ein Bauwerk *ausgeschwitzt*").[110] The grave pun amalgamating the problem of asylum and the Holocaust recalls the horror Herwegh felt at the new German Empire.

Wolf Biermann, no lyrical poet in a modern and postmodern sense, but more like a relic of those days when poetry, especially if it was sung, had an overt social function, complains that "wir Deutschen […] uns wieder verloren / Noch eh wir einander fanden," but raises his eyes from the "puddle of tears" ("Tränenpfützen") of the continuous rain in November land:

> Mir aber lacht das Herz, ich weiß
> Bald heilt auch die deutsche Wunde

---

107 First printed in *Die Woche* No. 9, February 25, 1993, p. 30; then published in March by Steidl. Quotation: Grass: *Novemberland,* p. 13.
108 Ibid., p. 21: "Andauernder Regen." "Continuous rain": "Fear circulates, November threatens to continue. Never again serenity of longer days. The last flies fall down from the panes, and standstill comes after the fast-food bar of time."
109 "Bei klarer Sicht." Ibid., p. 29.
110 "Die Festung wächst." Ibid., p. 23, italics are mine.

> Nur eines ist dumm, ganz nebenbei
> – die Menschheit geht grade zugrunde[111]

Antagonists of Grass or other East or West German writers and their way of opposing the unification should remember the fatal "strategy of integration"[112] of the Hurrah-poets of 1870/71 who closed their eyes to the social and cultural polarization of those days. The unifying effect of the 1813 lyric (to recall the first national lyrical movement) was respected also by French critics because it arose from an emotion the sacredness of which should not be doubted: "l'amour de la patrie."[113] The patriotism connoted here is not the egoistic one that would deteriorate into nationalism and chauvinism, but the republican patriotism of the French Revolution that was no contradiction to cosmopolitism,[114] the one which in a French expert's view in 1871 was replaced by the egoistic nationalism relying on common origin and fate.[115]

Adolf Damaschke's (1865–1935) depiction of the years after 1871 disprove a harmonious unification, a 'community of fate'; between then and now there are certain parallels concerning society and mentality:

> Auf der einen Seite ein Massenelend furchtbarster Art, auf der anderen Seite ungeheure Gewinne ohne jede volkswirtschaftliche Gegenleistung. Da entstand das bekannte Lied von Georg Herwegh, das in Arbeiterkreisen bald von Mund zu Mund ging: Achtzehnhundert siebzig und drei, / Reich der Reichen, da stehst du, juchei! […]. Es wuchs bald in Hunderttausenden von Arbeiterherzen ein Zweifeln, ein Verzweifeln an diesem vor kurzem noch mit höchster Begeisterung begrüßten Deutschen Reiche […].[116]

---

111 "Dideldum" – Biermann: *Alle Lieder*, pp. 435–38, here p. 438. "we Germans lost another, before we found together." "It warms the cockles of my heart, for I know the German wound will heal soon. But, by the way, what idiocy – mankind perishes at the same time."
112 Schutte: "Zur Kritik der Volkslied-Ideologie," p. 51.
113 Martin: *Poètes contemporains*, p. 205.
114 H. J. Busch/U. Dierse: "Patriotismus." *Historisches Wörterbuch der Philosophie* vol. 7 (1989), cc. 207–17, here c. 211.
115 Montégut: "La démocratie et la révolution. Les transformations de l'idée de patrie," pp. 440–41.
116 Adolf Damaschke: *Aus meinem Leben*. Vol. 2. Zürich, Leipzig 1925, pp. 50–4 – quoted from Ritter and Kocka, eds., *Deutsche Sozialgeschichte. Dokumente und Skizzen* vol. 2, p. 390. – Damaschke's quotation of Herwegh's "Achtzehnter März" has been corrected according to Herwegh: *Werke* part 3, p. 143. "On the one side the most appaling misery of the masses, on the other side the enormous profits without any economic responsibility. In these days Georg Herwegh wrote his well known song, that passed among the workers by word of mouth: Eighteen hundred seventy and three, / Empire of the rich, there you are, hurrah […]. In hundreds of thousands laborers' hearts doubt and despair about the German Empire shortly before welcomed with the highest enthusiasm […]."

Herwegh's 1873 recollection of the March revolution and its promises of twenty-five years before promptly excites the (of course very problematic) play with historic parallels: Herwegh's "Reich der Reichen" ("Empire of the rich") and Günter Grass' "Club der Reichen,"[117] the 'revolution' and utopias of 1968 and the 'revolution' and the – alleged – loss of utopias in 1993. But unlike after the first unification, when critical writers and intellectuals were alienated from the state and a conflict between politics and unpolitical culture began to emerge,[118] at least in poetry, there is no such change today.

At the time of the first German unification poetic forms were very traditional, the gentle revolution of naturalism or Liliencron's impressionism was yet to come. Eduard Engel, looking back in 1907 at the 'Sänger' of the 1870s, could do nothing but enumerate the poets who then had a great reputation: e. g. Julius Wolff, Rudolf Baumbach, and – following the great lyrical poets Fontane, Conrad Ferdinand Meyer, and Friedrich Theodor Vischer (!) – Heinrich Vierordt, one of the most derivative neoclassical writers of that time.[119] Actually there was no visible change in poetic diction; on the contrary, the representational function of poetry and its 'Sänger' was demonstrated in 1870 and the years immediately following, before the 'Sänger' and their poems lost their public function. Indubitably the hollow unison of national and lyrical grandeur turned out to be the 'Götterdämmerung' of traditional lyric.

We should therefore reconcile ourselves to the fact that nowadays the Herweghs outnumber the Geibels, though one might doubt or even reject a skepticism about German democracy such as Günter Grass's and agree, rather, with Gordon Craig's conviction that the German democratic constitution, a jurisdiction in conformity with the rule of the law, and capable political leaders will take history in a very different direction from that pursued after 1871[120]; still, we have to understand and to defend Herwegh's wise word, because it is, even today, a promise of utopia: *"Jeder Dichter steht in Opposition mit dem Staate, auch mit dem besten."*

---

117 Grass: "Sturmwarnung" – Grass: *Novemberland*, p. 15.
118 Christa Berg and Ulrich Hermann: "Industriegesellschaft und Kulturkrise. Ambivalenzen der Epoche des zweiten Deutschen Kaiserreichs." Berg et al., eds., *Handbuch der deutschen Bildungsgeschichte* vol. 4, pp. 1–56, here p. 18.
119 Engel: *Geschichte der Deutschen Literatur von den Anfängen bis zur Gegenwart* vol. 2, pp. 963–68. On Vierordt see my article in Killy, ed., *Literaturlexikon* vol. 12, p. 25.
120 Craig: "Gervinus und die deutsche Einheit." Craig: *Die Politik der Unpolitischen: Deutsche Schriftsteller und die Macht 1770–1871,* pp. 191–208 here pp. 207–08.

VOLKER NEUHAUS
Universität zu Köln

Friedrich Spielhagen – Critic of Bismarck's Empire

Abstract: Friedrich Spielhagen (1829–1911), both the most popular and equally aesthetically well-regarded contemporary novelist of his time, treats the Prussian German development of the 1848 Revolution from the Prussian constitutional conflicts to Bismarck's foundation of the Reich and its consequences. He becomes therefore for posterity one of the most important literary representatives of a liberal Germany which would be ruled through political participation and democracy. That research today hardly deals with this writer stems from two particular causes: Those who should have established him as a figure of literary repute in the public eye were members of the "skipped over" generation at the time of Friedrich III, who had nothing yet to say under Wilhelm I and nothing more to say under Wilhelm II. The other reason is that Spielhagen became a victim of literary homicide on the part of the jüngstdeutsch Hart brothers. This essay illustrates Spielhagen's plan, in view of his major works, of a German statesmanship which was actually inferior but in the end superior alternative to the policies which were conducted by Bismarck and later by Wilhelm II.

In his time Friedrich Spielhagen was Germany's most popular novelist but was also considered by his colleagues – among them Theodor Fontane – to be an aesthetically high ranking author of novels in which he presents his outspoken political convictions, the legitimate heir to the Young German Movement. In his abundant epic oeuvre he critically deals with Prussian history from the revolution of 1848/49, the constitution struggle of 1863/66 to the foundation of Bismarck's empire and its consequences. Though his own involvement with party politics remained marginal – a disguised account of it may be found in *Freigeboren* (1900) – he sympathized openly with the *Fortschrittspartei*, which, in opposition to the National Liberals, refused to come to terms with Bismarck's policies. Sometimes he came close to the left Lasker-wing of the National Liberals. For posterity he becomes the most important representative of a liberal Germany standing for government by the people, democracy and social justice.

One might call Spielhagen the novelist of a generation tragically skipped over by history, the generation of emperor Friedrich III, who was almost of the same age and an ardent admirer of Spielhagen's craft. Because of the old Kaiser's extremely long life, Friedrich's early illness and his reign of only 99 days, a whole generation of liberal politicians lost the chance of ever entering onto history's stage. To them Werner Richter dedicates his biography *Kaiser Friedrich III*:

> This zealous and optimistic, self-confident and successful, outstanding and humane generation, perhaps one of the best, which Germany had produced, has had no voice in German political history. Throughout their whole lives they were ever active on in apolitical spheres of activity, this generation has left behind to their children a wealthy, blooming and in all material respects a very powerful country. To assume control of the political formation of their existence was, however, denied to them just as it was to their Emperor.[1]

Spielhagen's political friends, as portrayed in *Freigeboren*, were identical with the crown prince's chief advisors. In Spielhagen's autobiography *Finder und Erfinder* Friedrich III ist mentioned with warmth and respect. In direct contrast with that portrayal, Spielhagen's special adversary, the national liberal author Gustav Freytag, who had spent the Franco-Prussian War as Friedrich's personal guest in his headquarters, published a derisive pamphlet against his former host and benefactor immediately after the emperor's death.

The label 'author of the – in this tragic way – lost generation' explains how his tremendous success – in 1876 his novel *Sturmflut* was serialized in five newspapers from St. Petersburg to Elberfeld – was followed by a speedy consignment into oblivion among the general public. But he remained a favourite author in workers' libraries even into the twenties of our century. Leo Löwenthal concludes his study on Spielhagen with the sentence: "Therein lies the story of his fame – they hushed him up."[2] and in his preface to the reedition in 1971 he names those he held responsible for the "Totschweigen" – "the reactionary literary establishment."[3]

Obviously Spielhagen is a victim of the national liberal tendencies of late 19th century German philology with its concept of a timeless classic literature removed from reality. This concept arose with the subsiding of the Vormärz tradition and continued to prevail well into the 1960s. Accordingly the true poet has to stand on a higher platform than the ramparts of a political party, as Freiligrath put it. Today it is still painful to read that even his friends and

---

1 Richter: *Kaiser Friedrich III.*, p. 11.
2 Löwenthal: *Erzählkunst und Gesellschaft*, p. 175.
3 Ibid., p. 9.

admirers distanced themselves from the political tendencies of his novels, while his adversaries, particularly Julian Schmidt and Gustav Freytag with their journal *Grenzboten*, which was widely read and very influential among the national liberal bourgeoisie, preferred to ignore him blatantly. Schmidt published a critical study on Spielhagen in *Westermann's Monatsheften 1870/71*, which culminates in the false pity, that Spielhagen regrettably stayed with the flag of democracy, which prevented a renewal of his talents.[4]

Even more fatal was the literary manslaughter of Spielhagen by the brothers Hart. There is not a mention of our author in recent works of literary history that does not refer to this critical attack. Again and again one repeats with satisfaction how completely the Harts dealt with this author – so that we do not actually have to read him. In the Harts' case it is the widespread phenomenon of manslaughter within the familiy, almost of parricide. The jüngstdeutschen strict realists wanted to earn their laurels by annihilating their predecessor, the leading representative of the jungdeutsche tradition of a realistic, politically engaged liberal literature. At the same time we find a strong testimonial to Spielhagens influence on the young Heinrich Mann. He portrays him in *Im Schlaraffenland* as novelist Waldemar Wennichen, formerly famous and widely read and now earning merely half his former royalties, "da er seit fünfzig Jahren immer dieselben Romane verfaßte, die niemand mehr las […]. Auch heute noch lebte Wennichen unter braven freisinnigen Kaufleuten, die mit übermütigen Junkern und pfäffischen Finsterlingen in edlem, uneigenmütigem [sic!] Kampfe lagen."[5] But when Mann himself praises the 48er Buck sen and denounces Diedrich Heßling, he stands on Spielhagen's shoulders. His very technique of alluding to the emperor while deriding the *Untertan* is prefigured in Spielhagen's *Was will das werden*, where Bismarck is criticized for his ardent admirers and toadies who become his ridiculous caricatures.

Due to the lasting result of the Hart attack, Spielhagen was passed over when the tradition of political and social criticism in German literature was rediscovered, the main interest focused on the Vormärz. The author of the 'lost generation' again was skipped over – like his generation by history. To the public – among them leading historians[6] – Gustav Freytag today seems to

---

4 Cf. Schmidt: "Friedrich Spielhagen."
5 Mann: *Im Schlaraffenland*, p. 48. "[…] for fifty years he had been writing the same novels, which no one ever bothered to read anymore […]. Even today Wennichen still lived among the worthy liberal merchants, who sided with arrogant Junkers and sanctimonious, sinister characters in noble, selfless struggle."
6 Zinken quotes Hans-Ulrich Wehler's words about the realistic novelist "Ferdinand Spielhagen", cf. Zinken: *Der Roman als Zeitdokument. Bürgerlicher Realismus in Friedrich Spielhagens "Die von Hohenstein,"* p. 11, n. 2.

be the only literary representative of 19th century German bourgeoisie, while the *citoyen* Spielhagen is ignored.

A close study of three novels of contemporary history by this popular and widely read author deepens our insight into the mentality of German bourgeoisie after the foundation of the empire. Spielhagen embodies together with many other authors, among them Berthold Auerbach, the program, that Ernst Keil 1867 proclaimed for his *Gartenlaube*, in which later Spielhagen would publish his *Was will das werden* – not to sacrifice liberty, the most important value of all, for unity.[7]

My thesis will concentrate on the three novels *Sturmflut*, *Was will das werden?* and *Ein neuer Pharao* (book editions 1877, 1886, and 1889). They were published in Bismarck's *Reich* which at the same time serves their background. "Sturmflut" tells of the Gründerkrise of 1873, *Was will das werden?* is the autobiography of a young man before and during the decade after the unification of Germany, and *Ein neuer Pharao* tries to give a vivid picture of the empire's leading society at the time of the two attempts on Emperor Wilhelm's life in 1878.

Within this limited space I can only deal briefly with the earliest testimony of Spielhagen's criticism of Bismarck's politics. In 1863, during the Prussian constitutional struggle, Spielhagen publishes his novel about the 1848/49 revolution, *Die von Hohenstein*. The weekly publication suddenly stops – probably because of reasons of censorship, and the book edition appears in 1864. In her dissertation Rosa-Maria Zinken has demonstrated that the novel on one hand wants to preserve the positive heritage of 1848/49 and on the other tries to assert a democratic-revolutionary influence on the actual constitutional conflict between the royal government and the elected assembly[8].

This prelude is characteristic: In all the novels mentioned here generally the heritage of 1848 serves as a foil to contrast positively the so-called 'achievements' of Bismarck's politics. When Leo Löwenthal accuses Spielhagen, whom he otherwise treats with great respect, of being diffuse – "the first, or if one will, the last" is "any sort of spiritual, not further deducible existence"[9] – it is only the Marxist's contempt for the 'so-called civil rights', to which mankind returns since 1989 on a large scale. For these civil rights Spielhagen uses the somewhat unsharp terms "Idealismus" und "Humanismus", but the equation with the ideals of 1848 stresses his point: He fights for the human rights of the late 18th century, which probably really are "not further

---

7 Cf. Keil: "Photographien aus dem Reichstag IV," p. 268.
8 Cf. note 5.
9 Löwenthal: *Erzählkunst und Gesellschaft*, p. 165.

deducible" (Löwenthal) for which reason the fathers of the USA called them "self evident" – liberty and equality, participation of all citizens in a democratic state under the rule of the law.

For his claim of this heritage without any cutbacks in all three novels Spielhagen with certain variations and modifications makes use of the same device: An old 48er, who has been persecuted, mutilated, imprisoned, or even sentenced to death for his ideals criticizes Bismarck's *Reich* from his point of view. I compile these basic points of criticism before dealing with the changes following the changing of times and consisting in a growing scepticism and radicalism. So I concentrate on the political contents of the novel and must do without an analysis of Spielhagen's narrative technique. Still well known is his own theory, that the narrator should remain objective and should not judge his characters. To make up for this seeming 'objectivity', Spielhagen makes use of a special 'rhetoric of narration': Unpleasant characters are sentenced to death by their creator, political opinions are discussed at large from different standpoints and the reactionary or pseudoliberal participants denounce themselves by stupidity and ridiculousness and the absurdity of their convictions.

The persistance of the traditions of 1848 itself diminishes Bismarck's achievements – and that at a time of an unlimited Bismarck-worship in all regions of society: Bismarck did nothing other than to reap the harvest sown by thousands of patriots, who were imprisoned and shot for their endeavours. Lothar Gall, the Bismarck scholar, whose biography I use as a modern foil for Spielhagen's opinion, stresses the same point: Bismarck realized the political platform of the kleindeutsche liberals[10]). In the graphic words of a 48er in *Sturmflut*: Bismarck took that German crown from the shelf where it had been placed by Friedrich Wilhelm IV as a sign of his contempt for it in 1849. But more and more he is considered as the hero who created this crown out of nothing, as we read 1889 in *Ein neuer Pharao*.

It is decisive, how he took this crown from the shelf: by means of *Blut und Eisen*, by unscrupulous power politics, for which only success counts, without people's participation, and as a crown 'by the grace of God', which is metaphysically founded without being democratically legitimized. "In the heart of the occupied country, in the circle of generals, courtiers and diplomats, the German princes committed the kleindeutsch unification"[11]. From Hoffmann's von Fallersleben demands for "Einigkeit und Recht und Freiheit", for

---

10 Cf. Gall: *Bismarck: Der weiße Revolutionär*, p. 271.
11 Ibid., p. 450.

which the 48ers had fought, bled and died, only the demand for "Einigkeit" has been fulfilled and nevertheless more and more citizens – i. e. 'subjects' – are content with this result, among them the national liberals.

From these facts a lasting congenital defect of the new *Reich* results for Spielhagen: An empire uses the very means by which it was created to preserve and protect itself. The empire's birth in the midst of a war leads to an absurd exaggeration of the military complex. A pampered warriors' caste, recruiting itself from an already privileged class, is esteemed in its fighting strength as the decisive force in protecting the state against its external and internal enemies. To justify this esteem an enduring concept of an enemy is necessary: Outwardly Germany is surrounded by the notorious Welt von Feinden, inwardly it is undermined by democrats or worse, social democrats. Whoever pleads for changes, for a stronger element of a people's army is *per se* an enemy of the state, a vaterlandsloser Geselle.

As in natural history this superannuated outdated outdying species of overprivileged warriors luxuriates: Spielhagen's novels abound with arrogant, self-assertive, extravagant hopelessly indebted, duel-crazy and trigger-happy lieutenants.

The realization of German unity by means of a policy without any scruples or principles legitimated solely by its success has led to a complete disappearance of scruples and principles from all sectors of society. They are replaced by sheer immoral success, which justifies itself. According to Bismarck's definition questions of law are questions of power, and this principle more and more pervades interior politics and economics. This development is precipitated by a modern legislation on commerce and economics. That is not an unwilling concession to the national liberals, but a strengthening of the empire's fundaments: A prospering bourgeoisie will stabilize the state, while at the same time social welfare becomes divided from political progress which were till then considered inseparable[12]. Spielhagen warns against the tendencies hidden in that policy: A permanent stress laid on economic independence and self-responsibility of the individual may lead to an economic and social Darwinism, which the author insightfully diagnoses in the Gründerzeit. The same principle of economic appeasement without political participation Spielhagen sees at work in Bismarck's attempts to win over the working class for the empire. Bismarck had sketched out his plans, which he started to force in 1878/79, as early as 1871[13]: welfare measures on one hand, enforced oppression of political articulation on the other up to the imprisonment of

---

12 Cf. Ibid., p. 495.
13 Cf. Ibid., p. 497.

their leading figures. In that, too, Spielhagen, like Lothar Gall later on, denounces Bismarck's typical "combination of contempt for mankind, disdain for alleged principles and for purely positive ways of thinking".[14]

The legitimation of the new crown 'by the grace of God' leads to an officially enforced devoutness in the upper class, mostly affected, which in *Ein neuer Pharao*, influenced by the experiences with Wilhelm II, is denounced as *Byzantinismus*. In Spielhagen's continual attacks on Catholic priests, Vatican-influenced crypto-Jesuits, and the priest-ridden popish Zentrumspartei Bismarck could not agree more with him, only that our dyed-in-the wool liberal would lead his Kulturkampf also against Protestant ministers like Hofprediger Stöcker.

A last point of Spielhagen's criticism is a growing hyper-Germanness as a consequence of the victories of 1870/71, comparable to the awakening of Teutonism around 1813. All these subjects listed here are constants in Spielhagen's works about the Bismarck era. They are only subject to change so far as our author grows more and more pessimistic and at the same time radical. *Sturmflut* of 1877 ends with the hope that the deluge of the Gründerkrach has washed away for good the cynical materialism without any principles and that the people will return to traditional human values. 1886, at the end of *Was will das werden* a high-ranking nobleman and officer is thoroughly cured of his nationalism and royalism and confesses to an alliance of liberals and social democrats as the only hope for any kind of future.

In 1889, in *Ein neuer Pharao* this aim has almost disappeared from the horizon. For the contemporary reader the title was an allusion to the new emperor Wilhelm II, who had ascended his throne in 1888, when the short reign and early death of Friedrich III had buried the last liberal hopes – "now there arose up a new king [in Luthers translation "ein neuer Pharao"] over Egypt, which knew not Joseph" (Exodus I, 8). An old 48er returns a generation later to Germany and does not recognize it any longer. The reigning spirit does not know the better traditions of a Germany struggling for freedom. Bismarck's bad example has his followers chiefly among the younger generation. Obsessed with their careers, devoutly worshipping success and unscrupulousness they consist mostly in boring caricatures of the Iron Chancellor, from the boots up to the very moustache, the brutally empty eyes and the cropped hair. They even run around with the chancellor's favourite dogs, great Danes. Spielhagen's bitter view of German youth is supported by the crown prince's complaint in 1882: When he would some day ascend his throne he would

---

14 Ibid., p. 224.

hardly be able to accomplish anything – the generation of his son being hopelessly reactionary.¹⁵

Bismarck's motto is said to be "L'état, c'est moi!" and he was successful in establishing it in every layer of society. The higher officials of the former novels, who made their decisions by the principles of law and effectiveness, have disappeared and have been replaced by toadies – 'cyclists' in German, bowing to their superiors and and treading on their inferiors like the pedals of a bike. These creatures only want to learn the chancellor's will, bow to it and relentlessly carry it out by treading on their inferiors underfoot. Bismarck hated the old constitutional tradition of officials adhering to the laws – according to his own words he used to dream of a shoot where the kill consisted exclusively of Kreisrichter and Regierungsräte. After these experiences disappointed and disillusioned the 48er leaves Germay, while an old comrade of 1848, completely cured of his national liberal tendencies will keep on trying to continue the fight for some time.

In Spielhagen's later novels only Lassalle's ideas of a radical economic, social, and political reform have a promising future. In spite of many reservations against his enigmatic personality various characters of Spielhagen see in Lassalle Bismarcks's equal and in one point even his superior: He too is unscrupulous and craving for power, but he fights for important values: "die Emanzipation, die Vermenschlichung des vierten Standes; die Übersetzung der papierenen Menschenrechte von 1789 in die Wirklichkeit des neunzehnten Jahrhunderts."¹⁶

The female protagonist and narrator of Spielhagen's last novel about his contemporary society, *Freigeboren* (1900), is certain that Lassalle's ideas will survive the imperfect vessel that carried them and will be victorious some day, when the German people have overcome Bismarck's errors of crude materialism, of the "gesteigerte Streber- und Junkertum, den Imperialismus und seinen greulichen Begleiter: den Byzantinismus."¹⁷ But that these fatal errors may lead into a horrible catastrophe is clearly pronounced by the old 48er of *Ein neuer Pharao* – and his prophecy has sadly come true:

> Ich glaube, vielmehr: ich bin fest überzeugt, daß die politische Reaktion ihr Versprechen, selbst wenn sie es ehrlich meint, nicht einlösen kann; daß diese nationale

---

15 Cf. Ibid., p. 647.
16 Spielhagen: *Was will das werden (I) – Sämtliche Romane* vol. 21, p. 447. "[…] the emancipation, the humanization of the Fourth Estate the translation of the human rights of 1789 which had only existed on paper into the reality of the 19th century."
17 Spielhagen: *Freigeboren – Sämtliche Romane* vol. 29, p. 315. "of intensified pushiness and Junkertum, imperialism and its heinous companion: servility."

Politik, welche nur danach strebt, die Nation mächtig zu machen und vorherrschend vor den andern, nichts weiter ist als das alte Manchestertum von dem Markte des Handels und Wandels auf die großen Verhältnisse der Völker und der Menschheit übertragen. Das muß aber in seiner Konsequenz und Verallgemeinerung – denn die andern Nationen machen es ja nicht anders und nicht besser – zu einem Weltenbrande führen. Die in sich glück- und friedlosen Völker werden, der Angst, die sie beklemmt, Luft zu machen, sich nach außen wenden, einander in den gräßlichsten Kriegen zerfleischen, deren Frucht der Tod der Gesittung, der Untergang aller der Errungenschaften der Bildung sein wird, ohne die denn freilich auch das Leben nicht mehr wert ist, gelebt zu werden.[18]

The German people did not cluelessly stumble into the "Weltenbrand" Spielhagen so clearly predicted in origin and result. There were warners and exhortators, and they were heard and read, but in the end they remained a minority. But a history of German literature does well not to forget them.

---

18 Spielhagen: *Ein neuer Pharao – Sämtliche Romane* vol. 20, p. 137. "I believe, rather: I am wholly convinced that this political reaction, even if it truly intends to, cannot make good its promise; that this national statesmanship, which is only striving to make the nation mighty and superior to other countries is nothing more than the old Manchester economics of the trade and change to carry over to the great relationships of the peoples and humanity. That must, however, in its consequences and generalization lead to a world-wide confligaration since other countries certainly do not do otherwise or better. They become peoples who are hapless and unable to find peace, they are unable to give voice to the fear which weighs upon them, they turn outwards, rending one another limb from limb in the most hideous of wars. The fruit of these conflicts will be the death of the civilized mode of behaviour, will prove the destruction of all the achievements of education, without which life is admittedly not worth living."

ECKHARDT MEYER-KRENTLER
Ruhr-Universität Bochum

"Gibt es nicht Völker, in denen vergessen zu werden eine Ehre ist?": Raabe and German Unification

> Bouillon im Wirthshaus. Abf. nach dem Bahnhof. Am Schalter "Nicht zanken, wir sind jetzt alle Brüder!" 2 Stunden auf den Zug wartend. Abf. 2 Uhr.12[1]

Abstract: The case of Wilhelm Raabe reveals a combination of politics, prevailing mentality, the literary market, poetic criticism of contemporary issues, and aesthetic program. Before 1871 Raabe was thinking of and writing on behalf of national unification. In 1871 he was expecting an upturn in both the nation and literary life. For him, however, this upswing did not occur. He was ignored by the general reading public. Raabe placed the blame on the "German nation." This lead to the fundamental critique of the German Gründerzeit in Raabe's later work and to a new aesthetic program: in the history of prose narrative it is the end of Poetic Realism and the beginning of Modernism.

July 19, 1870. Smack in the middle of the mobilisation for the Franco-Prussian War, the breakthrough to German unity, a German writer set out with all his goods and chattels, lock, stock and barrel, in the opposite direction. Wilhelm Raabe,[2] one of the more prominent young prosaists, made his move from

---

[1] Diary 19 July 1870. – "Bouillon in the tavern. Dep. for the train station. At the ticket counter: 'Don't quarrel, we're all brothers now!' Two-hour wait for the train. Dep. at 2:00 a.m."

[2] All quotations from Raabe's works and letters refer to the Braunschweiger Ausgabe (Göttingen: Vandenhoeck & Ruprecht) in 20 volumes, abbreviated as BA, followed by the pertinent volume number (1–20), or, for the supplementary volumes, BA E, followed by volume number (1–5). Quotations from the notebooks give dates as provided by Raabe or deduced. Raabe's diary (Tagebuch, 1857–1910) is cited according to the manuscripts in the Brunswick City Archives (Stadtarchiv Braunschweig), in the edition currently being produced by the present writer. Dates given after titles in this article refer to the first printing.

Stuttgart to Brunswick, from Southwest Germany to North Germany, from a literary metropolis to the boondocks, from the outlands to his homeland, from the realm of petty states to an empire which was just beginning to coalesce. It was a somewhat precipitate move: he left behind him a career as a popular novelist, and before him lay years of failure, of struggle for his daily bread, of writing against the grain and of critical awareness of his political and cultural ambience. His was to be a development away from his status as the 'national' author of the *Chronik der Sperlingsgasse* (1856), and of *Der Hungerpastor* (1863/64), the latter a book held in extraordinary esteem by German readers until the fifties of the present century. Instead, he was transformed into the modern, critical Raabe, discovered by scholars and the general public only in the sixties, but increasingly valued since then, the author of works like *Zum wilden Mann* (1874), *Pfisters Mühle* (1884), *Unruhige Gäste* (1885), *Das Odfeld* (1888), *Stopfkuchen* (1891), and the fragmentary *Altershausen* (1899–1902).

Raabe's move in 1870 was motivated by professional and political considerations, as well as by personal factors. It divides his private life (1831–1910) and his literary œuvre (1854–ca. 1900) into two unequal halves. The popular author turned into a critical author, and the adherent of political utopias became a skeptic who could do no more than mock and scorn.

In both phases, Wilhelm Raabe was interested in politics, even though he was rarely actively involved, and he underwent all the hopes and disappointments connected with the national ideal, its realisation in 1870/71, and with the quite different development of the following decades.

But this thoroughly normal biographical experience takes on a special interest through his particular field of activity. Raabe considered the "Volk," and the "Nation" to be his "Customers," for whom he wrote and whom he treated with consideration – or inconsideration.

Hence the questions: How did Raabe establish himself in the vanguard of the Empire, and how did he subsequently establish himself in the Empire itself? How did he react as a writer to the national agenda, and how did he later react to the fact of German unification? How did he define his literary mission in these different phases, and how are his aesthetic and political experiences related?

The answers to these questions can only be suggested in the following, for Raabe is a very complex case. His private life and his experience of politics reveal symptomatic traits which, however, are hardly pertinent to his works.

Rolf Parr subjected this article to his critical scrutiny. Rosemarie Schillemeit provided me with documentation from the as yet unpublished fifth volume of BA E 5. William Walker translated the article into English. My thanks to all of them.

And yet he provides an example of the fact that an author must not necessarily be a committed member of the political opposition in order to carry on authentic critical analyses of his times through the development of his writing. This critical posture is not only a matter of assuming a respectable and honorable position in political questions; it also involves the connections between his political opinions, his professional situation as a writer, and his use of literary motifs. And it has to do with the way in which all these elements are elaborated in his literary texts, with poetological and aesthetic skill and with relevance for the future.

1. Political Opinions

A very brief survey of Raabe's personal political development is now in order.

Several geographical and political stages in his life are of importance, since they show that he was both a North German and a wanderer across the variegated crazy quilt of petty German states. Raabe was born in 1831 in Eschershausen and grew up in Holzminden and in Stadtoldendorf, an enclave of Brunswick in Hanoverian territory. As a child, he personally experienced the Hanoverian tax barrier erected against the Customs Union. This experience alienated him for his entire life from the Hanoverian Guelphs and made him an adherent of Prussia and national unity. In 1845 his family moved to Wolfenbüttel, and in 1849 Raabe went to Magdeburg as a bookseller's apprentice, a course of training he never completed, moving on in 1854 to Berlin, where he registered as an auditor at the University in 1856. It was in Berlin that he wrote his first novel, the *Chronik der Sperlingsgasse*, after which he returned to Wolfenbüttel, where he stayed until 1862, when he married and moved to Stuttgart. In 1859 he was active as one of the organisers of the Schiller Festival. The centennial of Schiller's birth, lavishly celebrated throughout the country, marked the elevation of Schiller to the status of a 'national' author and was a crucial experience in the process of discovery of a sense of national identity.[3] In 1860, Raabe joined the "Nationalverein," a majority of whose members desired a unification of Germany with Prussia at the helm, and which accordingly resisted the efforts of Hanover to become diplomatically involved in the process.[4] Raabe attended the first general assembly of

---

3 Cf. Noltenius: *Dichterfeiern*, pp. 113–43; Noltenius: "Die Einheit Deutschlands." – Cf. also: Raabe: *Der Dräumling. Mit Dokumenten zur Schillerfeier 1859*.
4 Cf. Hartmann: "Gutmanns Reisen."

the Nationalverein in Coburg in 1860, and the second in Heidelberg in 1861, without making himself the least bit politically conspicuous. He did, however, rework these experiences in his writings, as we shall later see.

He retained his passive political interests in Stuttgart, but shifted in 1866 away from the position of a post-1848 democrat[5] and became instead an ardent supporter of Bismarck and the "Deutsche Partei," which promoted an imperial unification of petty German states. This brought Raabe into conflict with the dominant public opinion in Württemberg[6] and made him into an unpopular foreigner whose residence permit seemed likely to be lifted[7] – one of the reasons behind his return to his native North.[8]

But in retrospect, this seemed a period of private, professional, and even political fulfilment. Not 1871, but the earlier year, 1866, seemed to Raabe the decisive date, an opinion not entirely without historical justification. With benefit of hindsight, he perceived it as follows:

> In der Litteraturgeschichte soll das meine "pessimistische Epoche" gewesen sein, weil ich Abu Telfan und den Schüdderump von 1867 bis 70 schrieb, und – es war doch mit meine glücklichste Lebenszeit.

---

5 For Raabe's democratic position in the post-March period cf. Siemann: "Bilder der Polizei." For Raabe's political attitude in general and its literary expression cf. Denkler: *Wilhelm Raabe*, pp. 182–84; Manthey: "Raabe und das Scheitern des Liberalismus."

6 Cf. Diary 28 June 1866 (after an Austrian victory shortly before the defeat at Königgrätz): "Dreadfully depressed mood over the South German rejoicing."

7 Diary 7 August 1866: Raabe learns that someone – whose name is blacked out in the diary – "[ihn] auf der Polizei als 'Spötter über Schwaben,' Verräther an Heer u Vaterland denunziert und zur Ausweisung empfohlen [habe]." ("has denounced [him] to the police as a 'reviler of Swabia,' a traitor to the army and the fatherland, and recommended expulsion.")

8 Cf. the letter to his mother of 11 September 1866 / BA E 2, No. 110: "Was unsere einstige Rückkehr nach Norddeutschland betrifft, so ist's damit noch dunkel und unbestimmt. Wenn sich die Verhältnisse hier weiter entwickelt hätten, wie es gleich nach dem Kriege den Anschein hatte, so würde uns wohl nichts anderes übrig geblieben sein, als so schnell als möglich aufzupacken; wenn wir nicht sogar von Polizei wegen ausgewiesen wären. Letzteres hätte sehr wohl der Fall sein können; denn ich glaube ziemlich sicher zu wissen, daß ich der hiesigen Sicherheitsbehörde anonym als ein der schwäbischen Wohlfahrt sehr gefährliches Individuum denunzirt bin. Die Leute könnten sich aber doch die Finger nicht wenig verbrennen." ("As far as our eventual return to northern Germany goes, plans are completely up in the air. If conditions here had turned out as it appeared they would in the time just after the war, then there would probably have been no choice for us but to pack up and leave as fast as possible, assuming the police hadn't thrown us out first. This last was a very real possibility, because I am pretty certain that I was anonymously denounced to the forces of law and order here as an individual posing great danger to the wellbeing of Swabia. But these people just might be in for a nasty little surprise.")

> Das Jahr 1866 hatte alle meine politischen Wünsche erfüllt, meine Frau war noch jung, mein Kind gesund und mit dem Geldbeutel stands ausnahmsweise auch einmal nicht ganz übel; was wollte ich mehr von der Welt? Ja, ja, es ist ein eigen Ding um die Litteraturgeschichtschreiberei, und wenn einer davon nachsagen kann, so bin ich's! –⁹

So for Raabe, 1866 meant not only the end of the Austro-Prussian War and the foundation of the North German Federation, but at the same time the establishment of his great sympathy for Bismarck; one can hardly see in this a feeling of affection for Prussia, but rather his political bias in favor of the nation-state and against the system of petty states he had suffered under in his youth. Raabe took approving note of the Prussian annexation of Hanover in 1866 as an accomplishment of Bismarck.¹⁰ Shortly thereafter he acquired a photograph¹¹ and in 1871 even a bust of the Iron Chancellor, which from then on helped to furnish his study.¹² His veneration for the great statesman continued unperturbed, through Bismarck's resignation, death, and beyond.¹³ It remained intact, separate from his bitter criticism of the realities of German unification. Raabe accepted unification "from the top down" as the correct policy and reserved his criticism for the people *en masse*, the German

---

9 Letter to Karl Geiger, 16 January 1910 / BA E 2, No. 486. – "This is supposed to have been the 'pessimistic epoch' in my personal literary history, because I wrote Abu Telfan and Schüdderump between 1867 and 1870, and yet it was the happiest time of my life. The year 1866 had fulfilled all my political wishes, my wife was still young, my child healthy, and I also wasn't doing too badly in the financial department. What more could I have asked of the world? Oh yes indeed, the writing of literary histories is a curious business, as I know better than anyone else!"

10 Cf. Diary for 17 August 1866: "Graf Bismarck legt der Kammer das Einverleibungsgesetz von Hannover, Kurhessen, Nassau u Frankfurt vor." ("Count Bismarck submits to the [parliamentary] Chamber the law prescribing the annexation of Hanover, Kurhessen, Nassau, and Frankfurt.")

11 Diary for 21 September 1866: "Bei Käser Photograph. v. Bismark u Blumenthal gekauft." ("Purchased photographs of Bismarck and Blumenthal at Käser's.")

12 Diary for 9 May 1871: Raabe acquires a bust of Bismarck. Later, given its removable spiked helmet, it served as a keyholder. Cf. Denkler: *Wilhelm Raabe*, p. 8.

13 Raabe noted Bismarck's seventieth birthday in his diary, and on his eightieth he wrote with obvious outrage: "Der deutsche Reichstag lehnt den Glückwunsch an Bismarck z. 80st. Geburtstag ab!! Lewetzow legt den Vorsitz nieder. Telegramm Kaiser Wilhelms nach Friedrichsruhe." ("The German Imperial Parliament refuses to send its congratulations to Bismarck on his eightieth birthday!! Lewetzow resigns as presiding officer. Kaiser Wilhelm's telegram sent to Friedrichsruhe.") Diary for 23 March 1895. In 1901 (!) Raabe buys Bismarck's "Gedanken und Erinnerungen" (Diary for 7 October 1901) as well as Bismarck's "Briefe" (Diary for 9 December 1901). Diary for 9 October 1902: "Vor 40 Jahren Bismarck Preuß. Ministerpräsident!" ("Forty years ago Bismarck became the Prussian Prime Minister!")

"Volk," who had shown themselves unworthy of Bismarck's mighty political deed.

At the outset, however, Raabe invested high hopes in the rosy dawn of national unification beginning in 1866. These are revealed in numerous private details, as, for example, the fact that in 1867 the Raabes spent their first long summer vacation on Sylt, the very island snatched from the Danes and now transformed into "German" territory.[14]

Subsequently, in 1870, Raabe was in full support of the political and military events, without lapsing into the wilder sort of enthusiasm. Directly after his arrival in Brunswick he wrote to his friend Schönhardt in Stuttgart:

> Die Franzosen werden sich übrigens doch wundern. Dies Norddeutschland rasselt wahrhaftig in Waffen; und die ernste Ruhe, mit der sich Alles dem einen großen Zweck und Ziel zuwendet, ist wahrlich schauerlich schön![15]

And as late as October 1870, Raabe was still hoping, on the eve of unification, for a literary as well as a political boom. On October 7, 1870, Raabe wrote to Friedrich Notter, a Stuttgart friend and ideological soulmate who was much more active politically than Raabe himself. He describes the private chaos brought about by his move but includes his hopes for better prospects. His positive outlook derives both from the current reports from the battlefields and from the "world-historical starting point for the happiness of our people," i. e., the geographical setting of the war with Denmark in 1864, which he had viewed with patriotic fervor. The passage culminates in the hope "that along with everything else, the literary life of our people will experience such a flowering from now on that nothing will ever be lost to it":

> Lieber Freund!
> Dießmal antworte ich umgehend auf Ihre herzlichen, erquicklichen Briefe. Sie können mir glauben, daß meine Stuttgarter Briefschulden schwer auf mir gelastet haben, aber die bösen Mächte des Lebens haben uns bis jetzt derart verfolgt, daß ich trotz der großen Zeit allem Licht u Verkehr des Daseins am liebsten Valet auf immer gesagt hätte. Seit d. Anfang Augusts ist unsere kl. Elisabeth lebensgefährlich kranck gewesen, und selbst jetzt noch wird das Kind von zwei Ärzten behandelt. Dazu waren wir in Ermangelung eigener Wohnung auf die engsten Räume beschränkt: ohne die Telegraphie des norddeutschen Bundes und die officiellen Nachrichten vom Kriegsschauplatz wäre ich rettungslos verloren gegangen.

---

14 Cf. Diary August 1867.
15 To Karl Schönhardt, 29 July 1870 / BA E 2, 141. – "The French are in for quite a surprise. This North Germany is truly bristling with weapons; and the sober calm with which everything is concentrated upon the one great goal and purpose has a really fearful sort of beauty!"

Hoffentlich haben wir nun das Schlimmste hinter uns. In den nächsten Tagen beziehen wir unsere Wohnung am Salzdahlumerweg N^{ro} 3. Ich bekomme meinen Schreibtisch wieder – und – vielleicht giebt es doch noch andere Gefühle in der Welt als die eines auf den Rücken gefallenen Käfers! –

Was soll ich Ihnen aber aus Braunschweig melden? Der Enthusiasmus und der Lärm werden sich wenig von dem Stuttgarter Wesen unterscheiden. Wir halten 600 Franzosen in der Aegidienkirche eingesperrt, haben die Hospitäler voll Verwundeter und wollen unser Theil von allem Guten u allem Bösen, was der Nation beschieden ist.

Im vorigen Monat habe ich Jensen in Flensburg einen Besuch abgestattet, habe den welthistorischen Ausgangspunkt unseres Volksglücks, das Schloß Glücksburg besucht und die alten Schlachtfelder Düppel, die Insel Alsen und Oeversee gesehen. Auch die Seebefestigung durch Torpedos ist mir von Interesse gewesen; es ist übrigens ein bängliches Ding, zwischen den Bestien hindurch zu fahren.

Herzlichen Danck für Ihre Stuttgarter Nachrichten! Ihre Schilderungen der politischen Wandlungen bei den verschiedenen guten Bekannten sind höchst ergötzlich. Daß der Druck des Dante's wieder sistiert ist, ist unangenehm; aber ich hoffe, daß mit allem Andern auch das literarische Leben in unserm Volk von jetzt an einen solchen Aufschwung nehmen wird, daß hierin noch nichts verloren ist. Gerade Arbeiten wie die Ihrigen wird die ernster gewordene Nation jetzt mehr zu würdigen wissen. –

[…] Wird denn das Kränzchen bald zusammentreten? Es wäre doch Schade, wenn dieses segensreiche Institut in den Kriegeswogen zu Grunde ginge. Ich meine, der Stoff zur Unterhaltung sei seit unserer letzten Zusammenkunft mächtig angewachsen. […]

Nun – Deutschland und unsere alte Freundschaft für immer!

Möge es Ihnen und den Ihrigen stets wohl und immer besser gehen. Bitte, schreiben Sie recht bald wieder!

    Ihr getreuer WilhRaabe.[16]

---

16 To Friedrich Notter, 7 October 1870 / BA E 2, No. 145. – "Dear Friend! This time a prompt answer to your cordial and stimulating letters. Please believe me when I say that my epistolary debts from the Stuttgart period have weighed heavily upon me, but the evil powers of life have persecuted us so that despite these stirring times I would have really preferred to bid farewell forever to all the radiance and bustle of existence. Since the beginning of August our little Elisabeth has been very dangerously ill and is still being treated by two doctors. In addition to this, we were squeezed into the most cramped quarters, since we had no apartment of our own: without the telegraph service of the North German Federation and the official reports from the battlefield, I would have been lost without hope.

I hope the worst is now behind us. In the next few days we will move into our apartment in the Salzdahlumerweg No. 3. I will get my desk back, and, just maybe, I'll begin to feel like something other than a beetle flipped over on its back!

But what can I report to you from Brunswick? The enthusiasm and noise are surely little different from that in Stuttgart. We've got 600 Frenchmen locked up in the Aegidius

Despite all expectations to the contrary, Raabe never did recover from the feeling that he was like "a beetle turned over on his back." Everything took on a different aspect once the unification had become a daily fact of life. Clearly the hopes that Raabe had placed in the new national dignity of the body politic and of the "Volk" – though without succumbing to the most egregious excesses of patriotic euphoria – went unfulfilled, most especially in Brunswick, whither he had moved with such a sense of optimism. It was obvious that little had changed here in everyday life as a result of unification. On the contrary, Raabe felt himself plunged from the cultural vitality of Stuttgart into the dark night of the backwoods. Both in the private and professional spheres, Raabe, at any rate, got no benefit at all out of the "flowering" in "literary life" that he had been so confident would come with unification. There was no "nation grown more serious" that might have been capable of appreciating this native writer, whose critical sense had grown ever sharper since 1866, to the degree he would have wished.

From this time on, Raabe held back from any sort of committed partisanship in his private life. He turned into a decidedly uncommitted person. His political experience flowed into his attraction to Schopenhauer's philosophy, which had begun as early as the mid-1860s. He adopted a "Philosophie des Stillehaltens, Stilleseins, Stillebleibens."[17]

Things were quite different in his life as a writer. After 1871 Raabe wrote and spoke differently about the "German people" in general and about the

> Church, the hospitals are filled with the wounded, and we want our portion both of the good and the bad now granted to the nation.
>
> Last month I paid Jensen a visit in Flensburg and saw the world-historical starting point for the happiness of our people, Castle Glücksburg, and toured the old battlefields at Düppel, the island of Alsen, and the Oeversee. I also found the use of torpedos in the sea defenses of interest; it is, I can tell you, a queasy feeling to sail through the midst of those monsters.
>
> Many thanks for your reports from Stuttgart! Your descriptions of the many political shifts going on among various close acquaintances are most entertaining. It is unpleasant that the printing of the Dante has once more been held up; but I hope that along with everything else, the literary life of our people will experience such a flowering from now on that nothing will ever be lost to it. Works like yours, especially, will now be better appreciated by this nation which has grown more serious. Is the Club going to get together again soon? It would really be too bad if this blessed institution succumbed to the tumults of war. It seems to me that there is a great deal more material for conversation since our last meeting. And so – Germany and our old friendship forever!
>
> May you and yours flourish and prosper ever more. Please write again soon!
> Your faithful WilhRaabe"

17 Raabe's Notebooks for 1889; quoted from (and in the reading of) Denkler: *Wilhelm Raabe*, p. 89. – "philosophy of keeping quiet, being quiet, staying quiet."

series of crucial political events in 1859, 1860, 1864, 1866, and 1871. Again and again his literary works took up the theme, as a secondary or as a central concern, but never again in order to promote the national idea. His intention now was to heap scorn and mockery upon its failure.

It comes as no surprise that German readers took little pleasure in such literary manners and mannerisms. This is not merely due to the ignorance of the reading public, as Raabe himself always claimed, but is a necessary condition of controversial writing. Raabe sometimes quite deliberately provoked such responses. After his skeptical conversion, laboring under the impression of political reality in a united Germany, he repeatedly offered his readers poetic identifications which were illusory, in order that the identifications could then be all the more devastatingly disavowed. As time went on, this became a major theme of the late Raabe: depriving the German reader and philistine of "Behagen," his sense of contentment[18] and identity rooted in the "Gründerzeit." Raabe's specific discontent with the new empire and with the role expected of him as a writer within it is the beginning of a path leading to the literary articulation of existential discontent in a way that makes him a forerunner of the twentieth century.

2. Literary Reflections

What sort of path led Raabe to this late destination? And what was the literary end result of his political perceptions?

To begin with, Raabe never wrote "political" novels or novellas in the narrow sense, certainly not with reference to current political events. Even so, a political connection to his times is always tangible, both in the historical narrations and in those with contemporary subjects. I shall now concentrate on several texts which reflect the prominent political events during various phases of his life and work, from the Schiller centennial of 1859, through the General Assembly of the Nationalverein in Coburg in 1860, down to the founding of the Empire in 1871. They reflect these events both more and less directly, initially in their striving for the unification of the fatherland and subsequently in their critique of the founding and of the entire "Gründerzeit" and its characteristic modes of behavior.

---

18   On Raabe's lifelong use of the word "Behagen," cf. Meyer-Krentler: "Elektronische Einsichten," pp. 53–4.

Narration before the Founding of the Empire

Let us begin with *Die Schwarze Galeere*. This is a story notorious as one of the set pieces of German Literature courses at German secondary schools, from the turn of the century right down to the sixties. It ensconced Raabe, by means of formal education, as a patriotic author. The teacher's aids produced for this text reveal the changing emphases, from military basic training, through national-socialist conditioning against everything "foreign," to a boyish passion for adventure, with which its classroom treatment, even in the postwar period, was hypocritically justified.[19] The didactic apparatuses make no bones about its potential political applications in a given period. A very clear instance occurs in Brather's commentary of 1917, in which he says that the Schwarze Galeere reminds him of the "unforgettable Emden." He further associates the conquest of Antwerp with the victorious German campaign of 1914.[20]

These are monstrous elaborations upon a novella conceived initially as a private love story, of the kind that Raabe turned out like hotcakes in his early years. Raabe left the manuscript on his desk in Wolfenbüttel in the summer of 1860 and hastily finished it upon his return from Coburg.[21] This accounts for the somewhat abrupt political and heroic stylisation, which comes across as an obvious discrepancy in the text. Still riding his high from the Coburg Assembly of the Nationalverein, Raabe gave free rein to his heroic and nationalist emotions and thereby exalted the private love story to a treatment of the historical and political theme of the liberation of the Netherlands. The idea of national unification as a contemporary political agenda in Germany is the obvious subtext of this historical theme.

What would nowadays (and especially after 1871) seem merely embarrassing had its purposes in 1860, namely, the forging of a nation out of the various outlanders in Swabia, Saxony, Bavaria, Prussia, Holstein, Lippe, Hanover,

---

19 The first hint of this unwritten chapter about the dubious reception at the school level of Raabe's works is to be found in Peter: "'Wilhelm Raabe kommt in den bundesdeutschen Lehrplänen nicht vor.'" – For teacher's aids with obvious political tendencies cf. in Meyen (BA E 1) the following numbers: 3143 (Adler, 1903), 3144 (Luther, 1910) 3145 (Grupe, 1913), 3147 (Brather, 1917), 3148 (Lorenz, 1919/20), 3149 (Sommer, 1928), 3150 (Ehrentreich, 1938), 3152 (Ulshöfer, 1953), 3153 (Rosebrock, 1958 / [4. A. 1976]). – Even in the schools of the German Democratic Republic (for foreigners with English as their mother tongue!) Raabe found his place with this text; cf. Raabe: *Die schwarze Galeere*. Leipzig 1969. – There are, on the other hand, hardly any respectable scholarly analyses of this text.
20 Brather: "W. R's Erzählung 'Die schwarze Galeere'." – Cf. also Brather: "Unsere Feinde."
21 Cf. Diary for 1860.

and Brunswick, despite their special interests, and the emphasizing of their common interests.

The dire necessity (and literary task) of creating a "nation" in the hearts and minds of people from disparate "lands" or "states" as a prerequisite for a functioning political union has once again arisen as a consequence of the second German unification of 1990. In the present case it is obviously a need noticed only in the sobriety after the party, as a rent through the nation defined in terms of 'Ossi' vs. 'Wessi,' and one not easily stitched together. One reason among many for this state of affairs is no doubt that in contrast to the pre-1871 period, there was no common journalistic and literary public, and no common literary market, prior to 1990, and hence no means by which the creation of a national consciousness (in literary taste or any other respect) could take place. The present (1992/93) war in the Balkans shows how dangerous it is if such a process does not occur in due time. And however skeptically we nowadays regard this older "national" idea, we must admit that the historical achievement of national unification in the period *before* 1870 was not least an achievement of literature.

As in this early novella, so too in other texts of Raabe, for instance, the *Chronik der Sperlingsgasse*, in which motifs from the Napoleonic Period, the Wars of National Liberation, the reactionary phase after 1848/49, and the great wave of emigration to America are woven into the text, all of them national as opposed to regional experiences. Instead of a long disquisition, let us present a passage which proceeds from the problem of emigration to a great exhortation to the national consciousness. This is a passage which is utterly inappropriate to the otherwise resigned tone of the *Chronik's* narrator, Wacholder, and instead issues a summons to advance, in a spirit of *Realpolitik*, towards the national future[22], and in so doing stresses the special assignment of the "poets and writers," the "preachers and guardians of the people":

> Es ist nicht mehr die alte germanische Wander- und Abenteuerlust, welche das Volk forttreibt von Haus und Hof, aus den Städten und vom Lande, die den Köhler aus seinem Walde, den Bergmann aus seinem dunkeln Schacht reißt, die den Hirten herabzieht von seinen Alpenweiden und sie alle fortwirbelt, dem fernen Westen zu: Not, Elend und Druck sind's, welche jetzt das Volk geißeln, daß es mit blutendem Herzen die Heimat verläßt. Mit blutendem Herzen; denn trotz der Stammzerrissenheit, trotz aller Biegsamkeit des Nationalcharakters, der so leicht sich fremden Eigentümlichkeiten anschmiegt und unterwirft – worin übrigens in

---

22 Along the same lines cf. Siemann: "Bilder der Polizei," p. 88. Siemann sees this passage in the context of the aboutface, for reasons of "Realpolitik," of many journalists in the period of the mid-1850s.

diesem Augenblick vielleicht allein die welthistorische Bedeutung Deutschlands liegt –, trotz alledem hängt kein Volk so an seinem Vaterland als das deutsche.

In englischen Schriften läuft Deutschland öfters als "the fatherland" κατ' ἐξοχήν. Das wird zwar mit einem gewissen "sneer" gesagt, aber es ist eine Ehre für unsere Nation, und wir können stolz darauf sein.

O ihr Dichter und Schriftsteller Deutschlands, sagt und schreibt nichts, euer Volk zu entmutigen, wie es leider von euch, die ihr die stolzesten Namen in Poesie und Wissenschaften führt, so oft geschieht! Scheltet, spottet, geißelt, aber hütet euch, jene schwächliche Resignation, von welcher der nächste Schritt zur Gleichgültigkeit führt, zu befördern oder gar sie hervorrufen zu wollen.

Als die Juden an den Wassern zu Babel saßen und ihre Harfen an die Weiden hingen, weinten sie, aber sie riefen:

"Vergesse ich dein, Jerusalem, so werde meiner Rechten vergessen!"

Die Worte waren kräftig genug, selbst die zuckenden Glieder eines Volkes durch die Jahrtausende zu erhalten.

Ihr habt die Gewohnheit, ihr Prediger und Vormünder des Volks, den Wegziehenden einen Bibelvers in das Gesangbuch des Heimatdorfs zu schreiben; schreibt:

"Vergesse ich dein, Deutschland, großes Vaterland: so werde meiner Rechten vergessen!"²³

---

23 BA 1, pp. 166–7. – "No longer is it the ancient Germanic lust for wandering and adventure that drives the people from hearth and heath, from city and countryside, that tears the charcoalburner from his woods, the miner from his dark pit, that calls the shepherd down from his alpine pasturage and propels them towards the distant West: rather it is need, misery, and coercion that now scourge the people to leave their native land with bleeding hearts. With bleeding hearts; for despite the disunity of the tribes, despite all the malleability of the national character, which so readily embraces and succumbs to foreign idiosyncrasies, and which is perhaps the sole world-historical significance of Germany at the present time, despite all this, no other people is so devoted to its Fatherland as the Germans.

In English writings Germany is frequently termed 'the fatherland,' no more, no less. This is, to be sure, uttered with a certain 'sneer,' but it is an honor for our nation, and we can be proud of it.

Oh you poets and writers of Germany, say and write nothing to discourage your people, such as you, who bear the proudest names in poetry and learning, have, alas, so often done! Curse, scorn, and scourge as you will, but refrain from promoting, let alone summoning up, that feeble resignation which leads, one step further on, to indifference.

When the Jews sat down by the waters of Babylon and hung their harps upon the willows, they wept, but they also cried:

'If I forget thee, Oh Jerusalem, let my right hand forget her cunning!'

These words were powerful enough to sustain the trembling members of a people even through the millenia.

You are accustomed, you preachers and guardians of the people, to write a verse from the Bible in the hymnals of the hometowns, dedicated to their emigrant citizens. So write this one:

'If I forget thee, Oh Germany, great Fatherland, let my right hand forget her cunning!'"

Raabe subsequently portrayed the discovery of national identity within a larger framework, the literary form of the Bildungsroman, in his *Hungerpastor*, similarly to Gustav Freytag in *Soll und Haben*. Both in Raabe and in Freytag the portrayal is at the expense of the Jewish antitypes, and in Raabe's case is constructed by means of a methodical excursion through various German landscapes and social classes to the last outpost of the Empire and culture, the "Hungerpfarre" (starvation parsonage) in the village of Grunzenow on the shores of the Baltic, where the hero finds his calling as the "Hungerpastor." Another instance is *Im Siegeskranze* (1866): here it is not hard to see parallels between the Wars of National Liberation and the contemporary political situation in 1866 – or to see a message to the reader, especially the female reader. In this case, too, there is a private love story, and the patriotic death of the groom transcends the grief of his bride. It is no wonder that this novella was also a favorite classroom text for many years.[24]

The same applies to *Des Reiches Krone*.[25] Raabe wrote this story in the early summer of 1870, his last work before his move, and published it immediately in the magazine *Über Land und Meer*, whose very title conveys powerful associations with the idea of a national entity.[26] This narrative too has a historical theme which is connected to a "private" love story, but which simultaneously establishes a strong link to contemporary events. The background consists of the efforts at the time of the founding of the Empire to reactivate the long-vanished pomp and ceremony associated with the Kaiser, and specifically to recover the crown of the Holy Roman Empire. Crown Prince Friedrich Wilhelm of Prussia (in 1888 Kaiser Friedrich III) attempted through diplomatic channels to persuade the House of Habsburg to relinquish the Imperial Treasures, but ran up against resistance from his father[27], who rejected, out of Protestant Prussian sentiment, any traditions smacking of the medieval, the Catholic, and the ultramontane. In 1871, at the convocation of the Imperial Parliament, he nonetheless took his seat on the bronze throne of the Salian Emperors from Goslar, an imitation of the throne of Charlemagne.[28] This

---

24 Cf. BA 9/2, p. 470 as well as this title of the greatest significance for the national education of women: Brather: "Wilhelm Raabes Erzählung 'Im Siegeskranze' (1919)."

25 Cf. Brather: "Raabes Erzählung 'Des Reiches Krone' (1919)."

26 This is not at all uncommon in the genre of the magazines devoted to serialised novels in this period. One has only to think of titles like *Deutsche Rundschau*, *Nord und Süd*, or *Vom Fels zum Meer*.

27 For the attitude of the party on the side of the Crown Prince in 1870, cf. Fehrenbach: *Wandlungen*, pp. 64–6.

28 In a similar way, then, the black-white Prussian eagle dominated the new Imperial arms, but above it hovered the "Crown of Charlemagne" (in reality a creation of the Saxon period).

whole question of whether and to what extent Prussian-dominated Germany should take over the medieval imperial concept in the form of its surviving symbols was a topic of passionate public debate in 1870 and 1871. Literary figures, among them Gustav Freytag, threw themselves into the discussion.[29] And so the question with which Raabe's novella concludes was easy for the contemporary reader to answer. It is an undisguised call to political action: "Des deutschen Reiches Krone lieget noch in Nürnberg – wer wird sie wieder zu Ehren bringen in der Welt?"[30]

As noted, Raabe deemed all of this to have literary and political meaning as long as the forging of the nation was still in the offing. This principle is also found in more critical texts before 1870, for instance, in the novel *Abu Telfan oder die Heimkehr vom Mondgebirge* (1867), in which discontent with German provinciality, with the crass philistinism of Bumsdorf and Nippenburg as observed by the traveler upon his return from Africa, still leaves room for the utopian agenda of an expansive national unification. In this work, the agenda can still be conveyed with all seriousness, with the sincere conviction that it is a literary and political mission.

After 1871: the "German People" as an Ungrateful Reading Public

But then came the turning point of 1870/71. Anyone who continued to write in such a way after this point was, in Raabe's view, a lackey to the preservation of the status quo. This charge can certainly not be laid at Raabe's door.[31] But his political disappointment and his expression of it are unmistakably commingled with his disappointments in the literary marketplace, which did not fulfil his expectations, but became less promising.

Our first example is *Der Dräumling*, the book whose first draft Raabe packed along when he moved in 1871, but, given the new conditions in the "swamp"[32]

   On this entire issue, cf. Schieder: *Das deutsche Kaiserreich*, pp. 154ff. [Exkurs III: Die Reichskleinodien und das Kaisertum von 1871]; Fehrenbach: "Über die Bedeutung der politischen Symbole im Nationalstaat," pp. 346–50. – On the political significance in the eighteenth and nineteenth centuries (1759 to 1871) of the Imperial Treasures preserved in Nuremberg see: Winckler: "Die deutschen Reichskleinodien."
29 Freytag: *Der Kronprinz*.
30 BA 9/2, p. 378. – "The Crown of the German Empire is still in Nuremberg – who will restore it to a place of honor in the world?"
31 On this topic I have not yet been able to take into account Schrade: *Kontinuität*.
32 Cf. Raabe to the Jensens, 11 April 1971 / BA E 3, No. 118: "If I were finished with the Dräumling, I'd be quite happy; I've been sitting in that disreputable swamp since April of last year!"

of Brunswick, did not complete until May of 1871 or publish until 1872. In this novel, Raabe, making extensive use of his diary over long passages, describes the Schiller centennial of 1859 once again, this time in the setting of a godforsaken North German dump called Paddenau, which is literally and figuratively "in a swamp." The Schiller festivities are presented as trivial rather than edifying, with an emphasis on the comical elements. This is a farewell to the passions of the earlier period, now seen as misplaced, and at the same time a critique of the present attitude of the nation, which, in the form of the reading public, is called upon to justify its behavior.

Raabe brings this point home when he writes to his brother Heinrich:

> Was die Leute dazu sagen werden, kann ich nicht sagen; denn das Werk ist im geraden Gegensatz zu der jetzt oft so widerlich hervortretenden Selbstverherrlichung des deutschen Philisterthums geschrieben.[33]

Here we clearly see that the tone of political skepticism is suffused with Raabe's disappointing experiences on the literary market, experiences which he was about to endure yet again: For like every one of the books Raabe produced in his critical phase, *Der Dräumling* failed with the public. And as the failures mounted up, Raabe's attitude hardened into dogma: the German "Volk," which had frivolously wasted the chance posed by the unification of 1870/71, was the same people who now callously deserted him, the critical writer. Disillusionment in both areas of life. He expresses this in 1873 in a cynical remark to his friend Jensen, who had made him a birthday present of some punch glasses:

> Punsch?! – Großer Gott, Wasser, Wasser, – Wasser ist das einzige Getränk, das das edle deutsche Volk nach dem Jahre Siebenzig Unsereinem zu trinken gestattet. Und ihr ironischen Leute schickt Einem eine Reihe Punschgläser zum Geburtstage! ......[34]

This is the fundamental tone throughout the following years. The critical Raabe is the Raabe misperceived by the German people.

---

33 Raabe to Heinrich Raabe, 20 April 1871 / "Aus Braunschweiger Briefen Wilhelm Raabes," pp. 15–6. – "For my own part, I have no idea what the German people will say about it; for this work is written as a direct contradiction of that self-glorification of German philistinism which is nowadays so often and so disgustingly manifest."

34 Raabe to Marie und Wilhelm Jensen, 3 October 1873 / BA E 3, No. 173. – "Punch?! – Dear God, water, water, – Water is the only drink that the noble German people grant to the likes of us after the year seventy. And yet you ironic folks send a man a set of punch glasses for his birthday! ......" – Punch was the drink notoriously served up on festive

And this tone is recorded in his notebooks, with great persistence, whenever the topic turns to the German nation. For example:

> Diese Deutsche Nation gibt mehr für papierne Vatermörder und Halskragen aus als für *bedrucktes* Papier.[35]
> Den richtigen "Lesepöbel" hat allein das Volk der Dichter und Denker aufzuweisen.[36]
> In Deutschland hat mehr als in irgendeinem andern Lande der Welt nur der Pöbel Geld und wendet es in seiner Weise an.[37]

Here and there we find attempts to rescue the high concept of the nation from its parasites:

> Die Pflanze deutsches Volk. Die grünen dazu gehörigen Blattläuse, die von Zeit zu Zeit den Hintern hervorheben und da einen Saft von sich geben: Junker-Pfaffentum, Parlamentarismus etc. Der Glaube an die Pflanze und nicht an die Parasiten.[38]

And then hopes for the generation after that of the founding:

> Es gibt zweierlei Art von Büchern. Die einen lesen die Leute, weil sie wollen, die andern, weil sie müssen. Die letztere Art ist die wahre. Die Generation, welche nicht gewollt hat, ist hin; jetzt kommen die Geschlechter, welche müssen.[39]

---

occasions, in a punchbowl, generally in private circles, and presented by the host. This is confirmed by the total of sixty-one references to 'Punsch' in Raabe's narratives. Raabe himself was in the habit of drinking punch at the 'Kleiderseller' evenings, and his comical complaint is in contradiction to his own practice."

35 Raabe: Notizbuch 4, ca. 1874/75 / cited in Hoppe: "Aphorismen Raabes," p. 95. – "This German nation spends more money on the paper in collars – both for people and dogs – than it does for *printed* paper. – One should remember that the 'aphorisms' collected by Hoppe are not true examples of the form; Raabe's notebooks instead collected quotations which he could later incorporate into his works."

36 Raabe: Notizbuch 5, 24 August 1876 / cited in Hoppe: "Aphorismen," p. 103. – "Only the people of the poets and thinkers has a true 'reading rabble.'"

37 Raabe: Schreibmappe, 6 December 1876 / cited in Hoppe: "Aphorismen," p. 104. – "In Germany, more than in any other nation of the world, it's only the rabble that has the money and spends it as it pleases."

38 Raabe: Schreibmappe, 5 December 1880 / cited in Hoppe: "Aphorismen," p. 112. – "The German people as a plant. And then the green aphids that go along with it, and from time to time raise their rear ends and spray out some juice: the Junkers and their ecclesiasts, parliamentarianism, etc. Faith in the plant, and not in the parasites."

39 Raabe: Schreibmappe, 30 April /1 May 1889 / cited in Hoppe: "Aphorismen," p. 115. – "There are two kinds of books. People read the one kind because they want to, and the other kind because they have to. The latter are the true kind. The generation that didn't want to is gone; now come the races who are going to have to."

And repeatedly we find complaints about the insufficient readiness of the German people to support its writers:

> Wenn ein Franzose so das innerste französische, ein Engländer das innerste englische Wesen gekannt und beschrieben hätte wie ich das deutsche, dann würden denen ihre Völker mit Jauchzen zugefallen sein. Die Deutschen wollen von dem, was sie selbst haben, nichts wissen. So habe ich einen schweren Kampf durch mein ganzes schriftstellerisches Leben hindurch führen müssen – gegen Frankreich selbstverständlich – gegen Kalifornien, gegen Norwegen, Rußland usw. usw. – gegen alles, was dem deutschen Volke weit her, also desto sympathischer ist und die Buchhändler billig haben können.[40]
>
> Sich selbst will das deutsche Volk nie.[41]
>
> Der Horizont des Geschlechts, das nach 1870 gekommen ist, ist *nicht* weiter geworden.[42]
>
> Das deutsche Volk preßt seine Zitronen bis zum Äußersten aus.[43]

In all these laments for the wretchedness of the German people, Raabe retains his awareness of the underlying masochism:

> Es ist ein verflucht süßes Gefühl, sich als Märtyrer zu fühlen, welches nur die Edelsten in der Menschheit leider nicht kennenlernen.[44]
>
> Es kann eine Welt geben, in der es eine Ehre ist, gehängt zu werden, und also auch zu einem Vergnügen werden kann.[45]

For Raabe there is a general interconnection of political and aesthetic aberrancy, and the German nation and its reading public are united, in the negat-

---

40 Raabe: Schreibmappe, 6 August 1892 / cited in "Aphorismen," p. 117. – "If a Frenchman had perceived and described the innermost being of the French, or an Englishman of the English, as I have of the Germans, then their respective peoples would receive them with rejoicing. The Germans have no interest in learning what they have. And so I have had to fight a hard battle throughout my whole life as a writer – against France, of course – against California, against Norway, Russia, etc., etc. – against everything which is distant from, and hence pleasing to, the German people and which the booksellers can get ahold of cheaply."

41 Raabe: Notizbuch 7, 1895 / cited in Hoppe: "Aphorismen," p. 119. – "The German people never desires itself."

42 Raabe: Notizbuch 7, 1895–1903 / cited in Hoppe: "Aphorismen," p. 122. – "The horizon that opened up before this nation after 1870 is *not* a more expansive one."

43 Raabe: Schreibmappe (undated) / cited in Hoppe: "Aphorismen," p. 127. – "The German people squeezes every last drop out of its lemons."

44 Raabe: Notizbuch 4, 18 October 1874 / cited in Hoppe: "Aphorismen," p. 93. – "It's a damned sweet sensation to feel oneself a martyr, and one which, alas, only the noblest of humanity fail to experience."

45 Raabe: Schreibmappe, 1 February 1879 / cited in Hoppe: "Aphorismen," p. 93. – "Possibly there is a world in which it is an honor, and therefore also a pleasure, to be hanged."

ive sense. But the missing link between his political critique and his aesthetic position is provided by his bad experiences in the literary market place.

Raabe employs some powerful images in order to describe the special position that the "German people" has forced upon him. For example, he asserts that he has been crammed into a Procrustean bed. In 1887 he writes to Marie Jensen in response to her commentary on his just published book *Im alten Eisen*:

> Schönen Dank für Deine freundlichen Worte, Marie, über das alte Eisen. Ich liege beim deutschen Volke so sehr darin, daß mir allgemach alle Gliedmaßen von dem saubern Bett wehthun. Und der Versuch mich auf die andere Seite zu drehen ist mir eben wieder einmal total mißlungen. Das wird ein sauberes Jahr werden![46]

This connection between literary ambition, writerly failures, and the scorn of the nation becomes transparently clear in the case of *Pfisters Mühle* (1884), which was returned to Raabe in 1884 by a prominent publisher with the comment that it stank too much in the mill to be acceptable to the German people. Raabe subsequently sent the book, published despite this reaction, to Marie Jensen for Christmas in 1884 and requested her to "smell" it with her discriminating nose. Marie wrote back:

> Das deutsche Publikum soll nur zufrieden sein mit Deiner Weihnachtsgabe; – es riecht selber tausendmal schlechter.[47]

And Wilhelm Jensen added:

> […] ein Volk von 45 Millionen, von dem 99% so zum Himmel stinken, darf sich wahrhaftig über etwas mehr oder minder penetranten Geruch aus Pfisters Mühle nicht aufhalten. Doch für unsere sittlich-ästhetischen Zeitschriften muß Alles Familienparfum prima Qualität sein, um den großen öffentlichen Gestank, wenn nicht zu verdecken, doch für die Nasen und Näschen zu überräuchern. Der Teufel hole alle ihre Schnauzen![48]

---

46 Raabe to the Jensens, 31 December 1887 / BA E 3, No. 388. – "Many thanks for your kind words, Marie, about the 'alte Eisen.' I'm so well tucked into that clean bed of the German people that all my limbs are starting to hurt me. And the attempt to turn myself over on my other side has failed once again. This is going to be some year!"

47 Cf. Raabe to the Jensens, 22 December 1884 / BA E 3, No. 343. – "The German public ought to be satisfied with your Christmas present; – they smell a thousand times worse themselves."

48 The Jensens to Raabe, 23 December 1884 / BA E 3, No. 344. – "[…] a people of 45 million, of whom 99% stink to high heaven, truly should not be put off by the more or less penetrant odor emanating from Pfister's mill. But our moral-aesthetic periodicals have got to have everything in a cloud of familial perfume of the finest quality, so that the enormous public stench, even if it cannot be covered up, can at least be smoked and flavored for all the noses, great and small. The devil take all their snouts!"

So far so good; the three friends were in agreement. However, Raabe could not leave it at this, but insisted upon acting as if he had known it all as early as 1870, and so reproached his friend for having shown excessive patriotism back then:

> Was Du lieber Freund über den gegenwärtigen übeln Geruch im deutschen Volke sagst, muß Dir freilich aus mißmuthig-betrübter Seele kommen. Ich für mein Theil habe Dich schon Anno 1870 gewarnt, unsere Nation nicht zu sehr zu loben. Wenn mir etwas in meinem Autorleben eine Genugthuung gewähren könnte, so wäre es dieses, daß ich damals über all' dem Augenblickspathos gelassen den Dräumling habe schreiben können. Wir sind am Feiertag wahrlich nicht besser als andere Völker und am Werktag wahrhaftig auch nicht.[49]

The Poetological "Missing Link": Triviality of Existence

This brings us to another crucial concept, one denoting the poetological point of connection between political critique and literary representation: this is the description of the "workaday world," everyday life, and the renunciation of poetic exaltation and pretty surface appearances – even when the focus shifts to the festive aspects of life. For Raabe's critical perspective consists not only of political skepticism, but of a poetic concept which he had made his own even before 1870.

As early as the mid-1860s Raabe had bid farewell forever to the agenda of "poetic realism"; he no longer considered it his task to use literature to show the better potential of an imperfect world. He ceased to portray things as they ought to have been and described them as they were, in all their triviality, wickedness, and injustice, without the amelioration of "poetic justice."[50] The new manner begins after the *Hungerpastor* (1863/64), and his first book written in it is *Drei Federn* (1865), the second *Abu Telfan* (1867).

The new element added after 1870/71 consists solely in the forced humoristic tone, a posture of lighthearted indifference to reality as found. This

---

49 Raabe to the Jensens, 31 December 1884 / BA E 3, No. 346. – "What you, dear friend, say about the present foul smell in the German people surely derives from a gloomy and depressed state of your soul. For my part, I warned you as early as 1870 not to praise our nation too much. If anything in my life as a writer could ever give me satisfaction, it is this, namely, that I was able to write the Dräumling then in a tranquil spirit, despite all the high emotions of the moment. During our holidays we are truly no better than other peoples, and the same applies to us during the rest of the week."

50 For a more detailed account of this turning point see Meyer-Krentler: *"Unterm Strich,"* pp. 40–4 and passim.

too is a logical development: once his political utopia had turned into sordid reality, once the utopian refuge was lost, humor was his sole means of accommodation with a present now perceived as incorrigible. This at least was Raabe's reckoning.

Jensen, who did not share this attitude, but to Raabe's displeasure held true to the concept of poetic beauty[51], saw at once what was happening when the *Dräumling* appeared, and criticised it. He was also aware that he was completely in line with programmatic "poetic realism" and its main defender, Julian Schmidt:

> Das Leben ist allerdings ein Dräumling, auch dasjenige, das aus seinen mehr oder minder flugkräftigen idealen Gedanken stets mit den Schwingen wieder zum Herab- und Eintauchen in den Sumpf genöthigt wird – so fasse ich die Idee des Ganzen auf – allein dieser Gedanke von nachdenklicher Ernsthaftigkeit kommt mir fast nur von seiner komischen Seite zum Ausdruck, oder liegt unter dem Lächerlichen so verschleiert, daß er dem Leser kaum zum Bewußtsein gelangt. Da habe ich wahrhaftig einen Satz geschrieben, als hätte Julian Schmidt mir über die Achsel gesehn [...].[52]

The ludicrous, purely comical elements had now come to dominate every attempt at a serious discussion of the contemporary political state of the nation. These elements were developed into Raabe's general strategy of concealing "more serious matters behind humor,"[53] as this was the only way left of articulating them. This applies to such apparently superficial popular novels as *Christoph Pechlin* (1873) or *Der Lar* (1889), whose very titles anticipate their tone. Whereas titles like *Im Siegeskranze* (1866) and *Des Reiches Krone* (1870) were fraught with dead-serious nationalistic pathos, these later titles fly the patriotic flag ironically, if at all. In the texts themselves, patriotism is treated

---

51 Cf. Meyer-Krentler: "Stopfkuchen – Ein Doppelgänger," pp. 187–8.
52 Jensen to Raabe, 5 March 1872 / BA E 3, No. 136. – "Life really is a 'Dräumling' [the name applied to the swamp by the local inhabitants] and this includes the life that is constantly forced down from its flights in the realm of idealistic thoughts into the murk of the swamp. This is how I conceive the overall idea, but this notion of contemplative seriousness seems to me to occur almost exclusively in its comical form of expression, or else it is so well concealed behind the cloak of the ridiculous that the reader can hardly be aware of it. Now that last sentence sounds just as if Julian Schmidt had been peering over my shoulder."
53 Raabe to Emil Sträter, 29 May 1889 / BA E 2, p. 267 (on the publication of Lar); cf. Meyer-Krentler: *"Unterm Strich,"* pp. 15–6. – Cf. also: Raabe to Jensen, 20 September 1879 / BA E 3, No. 274 (as a response to an article about Raabe by Jensen in *Westermanns Monatshefte*): "Von dem Wirklichen, dem was unter dem Spaß liegt, hast Du so Manches fein herausgefunden." ("You have very acutely discovered a good deal of the reality that lies hidden behind the humor.")

even more ironically, as the most trivial of trivialities. We might cite *Deutscher Adel* (1878/79), a book set in a lending library, from whose frog's-eye view the campaign in France of 1870 is presented with obvious skepticism. And as early as 1873, the story *Deutscher Mondschein* takes a similarly clear position: here a German civil servant appears as a thoroughly comical figure, suffering under the German summer moon at a guesthouse.

It is indeed not all that easy to make out the serious element behind the humor, but it consists in the fundamental conviction that the world is a trivial place, constructed of inessential elements, and that elevated emotions are no longer appropriate to reality. Raabe saw the public discussions of politics from this perspective, and accordingly he relegated such topics in his literary writings to the status of offhand remarks. For example, we find in *Der Lar* (1889) a passage in which the editor-in-chief of a newspaper is posed the utterly banal question, shortly before Christmas, as to whether he has bought his Christmas tree yet:

> Der Oberleiter, der eben auf der andern Seite des Redaktionstisches im verkniffensten Eifer das Zentrum mit den Deutschfreisinnigen multiplizierte, die Sozialdemokraten subtrahierte und die Konservativen und Deutschkonservativen durch die Nationalliberalen dividierte, ließ einen Klecks auf die ganze saubere Berechnung fallen und sah den Frager mit so freudiger, aber zweifelnder Überraschung an, als ob er ihn selber eben zum Heiligen Christ als eine noch nie dagewesene Attrappe geschenkt kriege.[54]

And repeatedly Raabe's critique of the state of the German nation and the world of the Philistines is connected with the motif of the failed writer. *Der Lar*, a piece of light fiction consciously composed as such, once more refers this connection explicitly to the literary man in Raabe's situation. Raabe, at a low point in the practice of his vocation, serves up the whole topic of his involuntary career as a comical literary entertainer.[55] The central figure, a writer who has descended to the level of a journalist, is exhorted by the editor-inchief of the local newspaper to write the rubbish that the nation deserves and in fact demands of him, namely, the columns in the "local section" (i.e.,

---

54 BA 17, p. 300. – "The Chief, who was absorbed at that moment on the other side of the editorial desk, with furious concentration, in multiplying the Center by the German Free Thinkers, subtracting the Social Democrats, and dividing the Conservatives and the German Conservatives by the National Liberals, spilled a drop of ink onto his immaculate calculations and scrutinized his interrogator with an expression of joyful but skeptical surprise, as if the man himself were a Christmas present in the form of a dummy he was seeing for the first time."

55 Cf. Meyer-Krentler: *"Unterm Strich,"* passim.

"Unterm Strich," literally, "below the line") of the paper, a kind of writing for beneath his own standards of excellence:

> Wenn du es mal über dem Strich bei uns versuchen willst, Kohl, – mit Vergnügen. Aber was hast du von der Langweilerei? Bleibe du mit den übrigen Besten der Nation unterm Strich. Sieh mal, das deutsche Volk will es ja so. Es will seine Besten unter dem Striche haben. Ich versichere dich, lieber Freund, die sechzig Millionen edelster Menschenrasse gestatten sich nur sehr selten den Luxus, durch Druck vervielfältigten Geist ganz jenseits unseres Striches. Du hast Geist, Kohl, und du bist uns damit willkommen; aber ich rate dir gut: gib ihn unter unserm Striche aus.[56]

The triviality of existence also applies to the higher levels of politics. In *Gutmanns Reisen* (1891) Raabe turned one last time in a direct way to the national theme, presumably because of Bismarck's resignation in March of 1890. This is a detailed rehash of the history of the founding of the Empire, appended to the Coburg General Assembly of the Nationalverein in 1860. The story is historically a precise rendering of his own diary entries from 1860 – so precise, in fact, that his politically aware contemporaries praised it as a serious treatment of those long past events.[57] Here, as in the early stories and even in the later Raabe, the "big" theme is interwoven with a private love story. In this case, there is a patently obvious metaphorical allusion to the "greater" and the "petty" German solution, in that the North German lover is granted a smashing victory over his Austrian rival!

But even so, this is not a book which celebrates the historically fateful meeting in Coburg as we would expect from a historical or political novel. The private sphere is no longer elevated by the great national concept. On the contrary: history in the larger sense is left on the sidelines, and emerges only in terms of private history. The love story takes precedence over all the political babbling and modulates it to the level of triviality.

---

56 BA 17, p. 283. – "Kohl, if you want to try out with us in the national and international department, be my guest. But why bore yourself to death? Stick with the rest of the best and brightest in the nation – namely, with the 'town and country' news. Look here, this is what the German people want. This is the department where it wants to keep its best and brightest. I'm telling you, my friend, these sixty million finest specimens of humanity only rarely permit themselves the luxury of reproducing their intellect in print in the other department. You've got brains, Kohl, and they're welcome here; but take my advice, and don't show them off except in the local news."

57 Cf. Henrich: "'Wunsiedel und die Gründung des Deutschen Nationalvereins.'" – F. Henrich and the present author are preparing a separate edition of Raabe's diary and travel book passages on the General Assemblies of the Nationalverein in 1860 and 1861, with a detailed commentary by Henrich on the participants and the political background.

The theme of the "literary marketplace and the German nation" also puts in an appearance. In the first third of the text, the narrator indulges himself in a short excursus:

> Was könnte dieses herrliche deutsche Volk an dieser Stelle für eine wundervolle Bekanntschaft an seinem wackern Volksgenossen, dem Schneider Daniel in Koburg, an dessen Frau und dessen Hauswesen machen, wenn es das Geld dafür hätte! Aber ich fürchte leider, das Buch von Gutmanns neuen Reisen wird ihr, der edlen deutschen Nation, der edelsten der Welt, jetzt schon zu dick und zu teuer. Ergeben, aus alter Erfahrung ergeben in die "pekuniäre" Armut der Denker- und Dichterrasse ziehen wir doch seufzend hier einen Strich durch den Reichtum unseres diesmaligen Quellenmaterials. Was ihm auch im Schoße der Zeiten verborgen liegen mag, dem deutschen Volke: in dieser Hinsicht können wir ganz ruhig sein, da kriegt keiner es unter. Ja: "Bildung macht frei", sagte Meyer in Hildburghausen. "Aber billig muß sie sein", sagt das deutsche Vaterland, und beide haben vollkommen recht.[58]

3. Extensions: The Critique of the "Gründerzeit" in Raabe's Late Works

When we look for Raabe's literary response to the founding of the Empire, it is not enough to examine his more or less direct comments on political events. Raabe had no interest in articulating a concrete political critique; what

---

58 BA 18, pp. 257–58. – Cf. note 57 – "What a splendid acquaintance this glorious German people could make with their brave fellow citizen, the tailor Daniel in Coburg, with his wife and all the members of his household, if only they had the money to pay for it! But I fear, alas, that the book about Gutmann's new travels will be too thick and too expensive for it, for the noble German nation, the noblest in the world. Resigned, resigned from long experience to the 'pecuniary' poverty of the race of poets and thinkers, we now cross out, with a sigh, all the wealth of our present source material. Whatever else may lie hidden in the womb of time for the German people, we may rest assured that in this respect, at least, there is no defeating them. True: 'Education liberates,' said Meyer in Hildburghausen. 'But it has to be cheap,' says the German Fatherland. And they are both absolutely right."

See also the similar passage in the introductory chapter of *Deutscher Adel*; in the description of the staff of the lending library we find the selfsatisfied assertion (BA 13, p. 174): "Ganz umsonst können es die Musen leider immer noch nicht tun; aber das muß man ihnen lassen, Rücksichten nehmen sie, und so billig wie die deutsche Nation ist noch keine andere auf Gottes Erdboden zu dem Rufe eines Kulturvolkes gekommen!" ("Too bad the muses still can't perform their function completely for free; but you have to admit that they show great consideration, and no other nation on God's green earth ever acquired the reputation of being cultivated so cheaply as the Germans!")

And with regard to the librarian Achtermann (BA 13, p. 180): "Daß er ein ästhetisches Gewissen besaß, konnte man nicht behaupten; aber er gab darin seiner Nation nicht das mindeste nach." ("No one could truthfully assert that he had an aesthetic conscience, but in this respect he did not lag an inch behind the rest of the nation.")

he found important was the crass transformation of the social milieu and of the modes of behavior in the "Gründerzeit." This theme, thoroughly worked over by Raabe, has been discussed so often in the secondary literature from the 1960s to the 1980s[59] that a few brief remarks will suffice here. We will concentrate on the development from his specific critique of social behavior to his fundamentally new aesthetics of narration.

The theme of social behavior in Raabe appears across a broad spectrum of variants. In *Zum wilden Mann* (1874), for instance, the specific topic is financial speculation in the "Gründerzeit" and the desolate moral condition of the nation. In *Meister Autor* (1874) he deals not only with the destruction of the suburban idyll in this period through roadworks and industrialisation, but also with the change of mentalities – a theme taken up anew both in *Pfisters Mühle* (1884) and the *Akten des Vogelsangs* (1896). To take another example, in *Horacker* (1876) we see the shift from the kindly old schoolmaster in the person of the "last corector, Dr. Werner Eckerbusch" (BA 12, p. 296) to the rigid, Prussian, and not very pleasant headmaster Dr. Neubauer;[60] like so much else in Raabe, these characters are very keenly observed, as the historian Friedrich Meinecke confirms in his memoirs:

> Raabes Horacker zeichnet sehr gut die verschiedenen Typen von Lehrern an den höheren Schulen in der Zeit nach den großen Kriegen, den etwas zerfahrenen, aber herzenswarmen alten Lehrer, in dem Humanist und Mensch zusammengewachsen waren, und den schneidigen, philologisch gedrillten jungen Lehrer mit dem Rezept: "Immer stramm, stramm, stramm, alles über einen Kamm." Der große Philologe Hermann Diehls, dem ich dies einmal erzählte, bestätigte mir, daß genau so in seiner Frühzeit um 1870 sich die Generationen der Lehrer geschieden hätten. Nicht ganz genau so, aber ähnlich waren auch die Typen, die ich kennenlernte.[61]

---

59 With reference to the political context, see, for example, Manthey: "Raabe und das Scheitern des Liberalismus." It is necessary to sharpen Manthey's thesis to refer specifically to the failing hope that imperial unification would lead to a national renewal. Raabe quite frequently presented the view that the generation of 1848 was dead and gone, despite all his sympathy for them, as in the figure of Felix Lippoldes in *Pfisters Mühle* (1848).
60 Cf. Thunecke: "Verhinderte Dichter"; Weber: "Lehrerfiguren."
61 Meinecke: *Erlebtes*, pp. 65–6. – "Raabe's Horacker is a very good delineation of the different types of teacher at secondary schools in the period after the great wars, on the one hand the somewhat abstracted, down-at-heels, but warmhearted old teacher, who combined the best qualities of a humanist and a human being, and, on the other hand, the clean-cut, philologically drilled young teacher who followed the motto: 'Always in fighting trim, and the same standards for everybody.' The great philologist Hermann Diehls, to whom I said this, confirmed that there was exactly the same difference between the generations of teachers that he had known in his early years around 1870. And the types that I came to know were, if not precisely the same, at least similar."

In Horacker we also find the art instructor Windwebel. Like the others, he is not only a sharply delineated character study, but also symptomatic of the aesthetic problem: when he encounters the "robber" Horacker, he discovers that the act of drawing, of creating an artistic simulacrum, of the person before him precludes any true contact. This parallels Raabe's own growing problem, namely, that it is impossible to observe reality aesthetically without distorting it.⁶²

The problem of the misapprehension of reality in narration subsequently appears in a whole series of Raabe's characters. Here we will mention only the figure – described in the third person – of the academic and parlor aesthete Dr. Albin Brokenkorb in *Im alten Eisen* (1887). The same development is obvious in first-person narrators, whose defective presentation of reality amounts to a fundamental disavowal of "realistic" narration. The prime examples are the first-person narrators Eduard in *Stopfkuchen* (1891) and Karl Krumhardt in *Die Akten des Vogelsangs*. Their antagonists Stopfkuchen and Velten Andres yank the carpet of middle-class selfconfidence, so characteristic of the "Gründerzeit," out from under them. What began for Raabe as a concrete critique has now become an existential critique of the consciousness of one's times as well as a critique of his preferred literary form, the realistic narrative.

There is no need to document this in detail.⁶³ As we proceed from 1870 it becomes increasingly clear that Raabe saw himself even in the Philistines he describes. He recognised himself not only as the contemporary and critic of the generation of the "Gründerzeit," but also took himself to task in some of his figures for being a Philistine. His identification with the Eduards, the Brokenkorbs, and the Krumhardts took place willy-nilly: there was no escape.

Irony of ironies, Raabe lets the unappealing Dr. Blechhammer of *Horacker*, a German of the new generation, pen an aphorism which he had recorded in his notebook in reference to himself, and not without sympathy:

> Gibt es nicht Nationen, in denen unbekannt zu bleiben oder von denen vergessen zu werden eine Ehre ist?⁶⁴

---

62 For more details see Meyer-Krentler: "'Wir vom Handwerk,'" p. 222.
63 Cf. the chapter on Raabe in my study: *Der Bürger als Freund*.
64 BA 12, p. 302. – "Are there not nations in which it is an honor to remain unknown or to be forgotten?" – Cf. Raabe: Notebook 4, März 1875 / cited in Hoppe: "Aphorismen," p. 97: "Gibt es nicht Völker, in denen vergessen zu werden eine Ehre ist?" ("Are there not peoples, among whom it is an honor to be forgotten?") – But along with this, as a positive counter-formulation, we find (Notizbuch 5 / 29. Nov. 1875 / BA E 5, p. 355): "Ruhm ist, mitgedacht zu werden, wenn an ein ganzes Volk gedacht wird." ("Fame consists in being thought of, when one thinks of an entire people.") – In the sketches for *Deutscher Adel* we find this turn of phrase once again, but it was not taken over into the final version (!).

Literary Changes Compared – 1870/71 and 1990

KATHERINE ROPER
Saint Mary's College of California

Imagining the German Capital: Berlin Writers on the Two Unification Eras

Abstract: Both eras of German unification gave rise to extended discourse among Berlin writers about the city as a convergence point for multifarious issues. The central question of whether the newly unified populace actually shared a national commonality became interwoven in Berlin literature with concerns about divisive ideological legacies, the physical transformation of the city by opportunists and speculators, the moral effects of unbridled capitalism, and an idea of a Germany that encompassed the visible presence of non-Germans (or people perceived as such). The literary images produced by Berlin writers of the 1990s suggest numerous points of contact with their literary forebears of the 1870s. The prevalent literary pessimism over the second unification, however, attests to the increased difficulties of imagining a national community in light of the moral and political tumult separating the two experiences. Despite current controversies over literary engagement, the long-standing legacy of such engagement will likely impel Berlin writers to continue to use their works to grapple with urgent social and political questions that connect Berlin to German experience.

A pivotal moment of the demonstrations of November 1989 came when crowds in the German Democratic Republic changed their chant of "Wir sind das Volk" to "Wir sind ein Volk." But after the euphoria of those days passed, upwellings of doubt about the existence of genuine national community swept through both Germanies. A shocking testament to such pessimism occurs in a juxtaposition of images assembled by Berlin poet Brigitte Struzyk (b. 1946). At the center is the bungee-cord jump an entrepreneur erected on the bare expanse of Potsdamer Platz, so recently a no-man's-land. For Struzyk, the adventurers who make the 50-meter leap are paying to indulge in an "as-if" death fantasy before they bounce safely upside down on the cord. Germans, the passage continues, are similarly indulging in an "as-if" fantasy with their leap into unification, with the "as-if" secured by an imagined cord of brother- and sisterhood. But what if that cord does not exist? The appalling possibility is contained in the narrator's revelation that her daughter had taken her own life the preceding spring, that she had leaped from the same height as the bungee tower – only with no cord to bounce her to safety.[1]

The search for "ein Volk" beneath Struzyk's "as-if" question resonates through the literary discourse surrounding both German unifications. Berlin is central to that discourse, not just as the capital of the new German state but as the convergence point for a multitude of disparities that make up German experience. The city bombards writers who gravitate there with profuse material to be transformed into imaginative visions of their times and their nation.[2] Or, in the grim words of Günter Grass (b. 1927), Berlin serves as a permanent open wound whose ruptures are the ruptures of German history.[3] The dual experiences of unification are surely two such ruptures, both provoking vivid imagery in the writings of Berlin *Literaten*.

The novel of November 9, 1989, has yet to be written, but writers' consciousness about the revolutionary changes has spilled already into a torrent of article collections, fictional pieces, poetry, and interviews.[4] The intense awareness among today's writers that Germany has been through unification before has helped to quicken their desire to get on with understanding the experience. Taking the experience of 1871 as our guide, we can see that they are beginning a process of literary imagining of Berlin and the new Germany that will likely continue for two decades – or longer. According to a recent study, Berlin writers of today have scant knowledge of their literary forebears of the first unification era,[5] but woven into the current concerns are clear legacies of perceptions about Berlin as central to questions about the prospects for genuine German unity.

In both eras these perceptions developed in the context of controversy about Berlin as the political and cultural capital of Germany. In 1871 the political issue involved less debate than simple resentment from other German

---

1 Struzyk: "Im Niemandsland," p. 57.
2 The most comprehensive bibliography of representations of Berlin in literature is contained in Glass et al., eds., *Berlin: Literary Images of a City*, pp. 188–210. See also Reuleke: "Das Berlinbild"; Charlotte Jolles: "Berlin wird Weltstadt." Glass et al., eds., *Berlin: Literary Images of a City*, pp. 50–69; and Roper: *German Encounters with Modernity*, pp. 1–8.
3 *Das Berliner Autoren-Stadtbuch*, p. 8, "[…] weist die Brüche im Verlauf deutscher Geschichte nach." Two other good sources on the literary society of Berlin in the 1980s are Funk and Wittmann: *Literatur Hauptstadt* and von Mangoldt: *Berlin Literarisch*.
4 Buch: "Die Stunde der Dichter." *Die Zeit* No. 50, December 4, 1992, Literaturbeil., p. 3. "Der große Roman über die Berliner Mauer ist bis heute nicht geschrieben worden," much less any sort of 'Bestseller' "über den Tag, an dem die Mauer fiel."
5 Funk and Wittmann: *Literatur Hauptstadt*, pp. 429–30.

cities, but many criticized Berlin's cultural pretensions as those of a parvenu city that could not sustain German cultural legacies. Inexorably, however, no other city could establish itself as a feasible alternative to Berlin.[6] After 1989, aside from the practical considerations of moving the government from Bonn, the political debate focused on Berlin's historical legacy, with opponents pointing to the city's role as capital of a succession of disastrous German regimes and proponents countering with its tradition of democratic opposition reaching back to 1848.[7] As to the cultural debate, most acknowledged the role of Berlin as a cultural showcase for each of the former German states, but the parvenu controversies of the 1870s have echoed in recent talk about commercialization and fears of Berlin becoming a soulless *Megastadt*.[8] After a close vote in the Bundestag in 1991, it became clear that not even Bonn provided a genuine alternative to Berlin as the political capital. Nor, despite flourishing cultures in many other cities, could any possibly challenge Berlin's status as the cultural capital of Germany and, potentially, of the new Europe.[9]

Of greater interest in the literary discourse than the question of *whether* Berlin should be capital are the questions about *how* Germanness is being molded within that capital. Among problems common to both eras, the overriding one is the search for a German commonality suggested by Struzyk's bungee-cord image and the concomitant fear that fragmentation *(Zerrissenheit)* relentlessly divides Germans from one another. These notions extend far more broadly than the simple fact of the Wall to include themes of crisscrossing social divisions among immigrants, refugees, and inhabitants of East and West; of psychological ambivalences growing from the day-to-day stresses of urban life and appealing mythologies of a bygone past; of tensions between the cultural establishment and its challengers; and of ideological disunities of conflicting visions of the German past, present, and future.[10]

Radiating from this central concern are other basic questions about ways in which these German rifts might be bridged. How might genuine freedom

---

6   See Faden: "Berlin: Hauptstadt?" and *Das Hauptstadtproblem in der Geschichte*, pp. 111–65. Despite the connotations of his book's title, Detlef Briesen provides statistical evidence that Berlin far outranked other German cities as Germany's cultural center and that it achieved this status during the era of the first unification. Briesen: *Berlin, die überschätzte Metropole*, pp. 33–80. See also Sheehan's essay in the present volume, pp. 31–2.
7   Cf. *Berlin-Bonn, die Debatte*.
8   See, for example, a review of Berlin theater during the second half of 1991: Merschmeier: "Guten Abend, wir sinken."
9   See Langguth, ed., *Berlin: Vom Brennpunkt der Teilung*, esp. pp. 226–35, and pp. 273–93.
10 A good recent treatment of this theme is in Keith Bullivant: "The Divided City: Berlin in Post-War German Literature." Glass et al., eds., *Berlin: Literary Images of a City*, pp. 162–77.

become the foundation of German unity? How might the German past be used to build such unity (or, in current discourse, how is *Vergangenheitsbewältigung* to be achieved)? How can German unity be detached from the rampant materialism unleashed by unification? How can notions of Germanness be reconciled with the presence of perceived non-Germans – whether Jews of the 1870s, foreign immigrants of both periods, or asylum seekers of the 1990s? And, finally, to what extent is the writer morally or artistically responsible for confronting these dilemmas in literature? Manifestations of these questions, densely interwoven into profuse imagery of the two unifications, will provide our focus here.

Berlin writers' grappling with things German preceded actual unification in both eras. Two such novelists, Friedrich Spielhagen (1829–1911) and Peter Schneider (b. 1940), were among those who produced works showing Berlin as the place in which the pieces that make up the German nation come into unique contact. In each of their novels, *In Reih' und Glied* (1866) and *Der Mauerspringer* (1982), a writer character attempts to imagine how those pieces fit together even as he confronts both internal and external obstacles to German community in his own life.

Consider a scene near the end of Spielhagen's *In Reih' und Glied*, which joins three elements of literary discourse – the writer, Berlin, and Germanness – into a political critique and a democratic vision for the German future. A sedate – even somber – engagement celebration is underway in a Berlin pension; the makeup of the small gathering is democratic, notes the narrator, including a humble tailor and his wife as well as a pair of aristocratic sisters. Invoking one of his frequent conventions, Spielhagen uses two toasts as a vehicle for his political message. The first, by Dr. Paulus, a guest who is a liberal member of the chamber of deputies, commends the heroic stance of the fiancé Walter Gutmann, who now faces a six-month prison sentence for having published a novel judged to be a threat to family, state, and church. Walter's work, Dr. Paulus urges, is an important contribution to the cause of leading their nation from its medieval constraints "to freedom and to light." Walter responds with a toast praising all those present for their commitment to a free and just Germany in the face not only of persecution but of political attacks on them as unpractical dreamers.[11] Berlin, in this novel, is clearly the arena in which the political and cultural struggle for German freedom is being waged, and by having the scene end with Walter being taken into police custody, Spielhagen emphasizes the repressive regime that must be overcome.

---

11   Spielhagen: *In Reih' und Glied – Sämtliche Werke* vol. 6, pp. 397–400. On Spielhagen and German unification see also Neuhaus, this volume pp. 135–43.

Numerous autobiographical parallels suggest Walter as Spielhagen's alter ego and mouthpiece. It is he who explicates the novel's title in a vigorous exchange with his activist cousin Leo Gutmann (a forceful character bearing parallels to Ferdinand Lassalle). Admonishing Leo about trying to impose his revolutionary leadership on people and situations, Walter declares that liberation can be realized only with individuals committing themselves to march "in rank and file" in a great army striving for freedom as one people.[12] Unity, in this view, begins with the people, who, only when united in common cause, can effect the transformation that failed in 1848. Leo's fierce rejection of what he sees as Walter's fuzzy dreaming causes their estrangement. Leo's intricate political intrigues lead to his complete alienation from the masses and also to a fatal end. Walter, released from prison, will presumably remain in Berlin and will continue to use his writing to awaken Germans.

One hundred twenty years later, Berlin writers from both East and West, although they continue to seek a democratic German commonality, are more perplexed than Spielhagen about where to find it. A major part of the pessimism before 1989, of course, came not just from the fact of two militantly opposed German political systems, but from the vast human divisions they created. Among numerous novels that ask what sort of Germanness could span the chasm, Peter Schneider's *Der Mauerspringer* offers the most intricate network of representations of imaginings about what sort of Germanness might transcend the Berlin Wall.[13] A succession of "stories" combining fanciful situations with images of everyday life on both sides of the Wall allows Schneider to explores a spectrum of responses to the perplexing fact of Berlin's existence as a "Siamese-twin" city. His narrator, a writer who settled in Berlin from West Germany, is consumed by the need to overcome the Wall. His tales about wall jumpers provide literary expression for his quest, but its personal expression are his regular pilgrimages to visit friends and places in East Berlin. As his quest unfolds, however, he seems only to become more "West German" and to become more estranged from those to whom he seeks to build bridges.

A striking instance of this unwanted estrangement occurs in a café on Kurfürstendamm, where the narrator is sitting with his friend Robert, a recently arrived writer from the GDR. A crowd of demonstrators converges and shatters a line of elegant display windows. The pair gets into a nasty argument after Robert offhandedly attributes the fracas to a masterplan by the

---

12 Spielhagen: *In Reih' und Glied – Sämtliche Werke* vol. 5, pp. 266–67.
13 A good survey of attempts in fiction of the 1980s to come to terms with Germanness in the face of the Berlin wall is Saalmann: "'Deconstructing' the Berlin Wall."

government and the narrator lashes back at his friend's easy presumption. Soon they are "striking out at each other with weary, weighted blows, angrily babbling our lessons, true to the states whose influence we no longer recognize."[14] Pondering this and other quarrels, the narrator realizes that the system in which each was reared had instilled irrevocable assumptions.[15] Like Spielhagen's Walter Gutmann, Schneider's narrator sees a friendship falling victim to ideological conflicts, but he is conscious, as Walter is not, of having internalized the values of the society he is criticizing.

Like Walter, this writer also finds in his quest for a German commonality stymied by a repressive system. On one of countless journeys to East Berlin, he banters with the border guard, who is making an unusually thorough search of his car. How, he asks the official, can he hope to know what contraband he might becarrying in his head? Suddenly his passport is handed to him, and he is told to return to the West: "You have not been granted permission to enter the DDR. In accordance with international protocols, no information will be disclosed regarding the duration or grounds for this measure."[16] This episode, like Walter's arrest in Spielhagen's novel, represents the collision of a writer's ideals with actualities of German society, with Berlin as the setting for such collisions.

Schneider's vision is more unsettling than Spielhagen's because he confronts his inability to know where the state ends and his own self begins.[17] If the state has pervaded one's being, then where are the connections between Germans from opposing states? A fleeting answer that they lie in their common language is belied by countless instances in the novel in which Easterners and Westerners talk past one another. In an article written in the spring of 1989, Schneider suggested a more ironical basis for commonality when he

---

14 Schneider: *The Wall Jumper*, p. 93. "[…] mit müden, schweren Bewegungen aufeinander einschlagen, zornig unsere Lektionen lallend, gehorsam den Staaten, die nicht mehr in Sicht sind." Schneider: *Der Mauerspringer*, p. 91. On differing eastern and western perspectives on German history see Sheehan, pp. 33–4.

15 Schneider: *The Wall Jumper*, p. 94. East Berliner Klaus Schlesinger (b. 1937) similarly pondered in a 1982 piece: "was wäre aus dir geworden, wärst du fünf Kilometer weiter, statt im Nordosten, im Nordwesten geboren worden, statt im Prenzlauer Berg, der später zum sowjetischen, im Wedding, der später zum französischen Sektor Berlins gehörte? Welche Eigenschaft, welche Charakteranlage fördert die eine und welche die andere Gesellschaftsform…?" Schlesinger: *Fliegender Wechsel*, p. 272.

16 *The Wall Jumper*, p. 138. "'Die Einreise in die DDR kann Ihnen nicht gestattet werden. Über die Dauer und Gründe der Maßnahme wird keine Auskunft erteilt, wie es internationalen Gepflogenheiten entspricht.'" *Der Mauerspringer*, p. 134.

17 *The Wall Jumper*, p. 125. On perspectives of East German writers about this problem see Reed (pp. 237–40) and Schoeps (pp. 261–64).

quoted a West German diplomat assigned to East Berlin as saying, "Sometimes I think the Wall is the only thing that still keeps us Germans together."[18] The Wall allowed Germans to believe in an imagined nation that might no longer exist.

On November 9, 1989, it was inconceivable to the thousands of celebrants that the opening of the Wall could expose a breach in German community, but in the resulting chain of events jubilation yielded to a profound sense of loss to those with loyalties grounded in the socialist ideals of the vanished GDR. The first unification similarly involved not only the creation of a new Germany but the loss of particularist traditions, including Berlin's old Prussian identity. It is no accident that the ideologies of writers who express the most acute sense of loss in the two unifications are at opposite ends of the political spectrum, for they are the strongest adherents to the ideals they perceive to be passing.

The novel that most explicitly articulates grief over Bismarck's unification came from the pen of Ludovika Hesekiel (1847–1889) daughter of arch-conservative Berlin writer Georg Hesekiel. *Von Brandenburg zu Bismarck* (1873) recounts the struggles of fictional counterparts to the author and her father on behalf of an ideal of freedom that rests in the harmonious union of all Prussian subjects in loyalty to their king. Reacting against the revolution of 1848, the novel develops arguments that popular rule will bring destructive competition and that a cohesive Prussian society can result only from a strong monarchy. Ironically, this very strength became the precondition for Prussia's merging into the German Reich: "If Prussia had fallen to democracy [after 1848]," the narrator comments, "we would not have a united Germany today!"[19]

A major dimension of Hesekiel's novel is a paean to *bürgerlich* values that, in her view, are being undermined by modernity's intrusion into a once humble and unpretentious city. Descriptions of two such settings – Wilhelmstraße and Kreuzberg – are replete with phrases contrasting "then" (1849) with "now" (1870s). Wilhelmstraße of 1849, "this most original of all Berlin streets," for instance, epitomizes the harmony of the old stratified society,

---

18 Schneider: "Was wäre, wenn die Mauer fällt." Schneider: *Extreme Mittellage: Eine Reise durch das deutsche Nationalgefühl*, pp. 157–76, here p. 158. "Manchmal kommt es mir so vor, als sei die Mauer nach vierzig Jahren Teilung das einzige, was die beiden Deutschlands noch verbindet." The English translation is from a reworked version of that article in Schneider: "Before the Fall." Schneider: *The German Comedy: Scenes of Life after the Wall*, pp. 3–19, here p. 4.

19 Hesekiel: *Von Brandenburg zu Bismarck* vol. 1, p. 154. "Wäre Preußen damals in die Hände der Demokratie gefallen, wir hätten heute kein einiges Deutschland!"

with the quietly elegant palaces on the northern end merging into the unpretentious houses and shops on the tree-lined southern end.[20] The charming, comfortable house of Dr. Thurn, the protagonist's father, exemplifies bygone ways, "as only the old Berlin knew them and which are inexorably being lost in the imperial capital."[21]

Hesekiel similarly uses Kreuzberg, a beloved destination for Sunday outings, to show a small-town Berlin of old threatened with domination by rowdy masses of the new era. The occasion, a royalist celebration of the Prussian victory over the 1849 uprising in Baden, that draws families from across Berlin society up the hill beyond Hallesches Tor. Not yet flanked by villas, the narrator comments, this modest spot was a place where the celebrants could revel in the Berlin traditions of Weißbier, buttered sandwiches, and spirited patriotic songs. An uneasy tone, however, is conveyed by Dr. Thurn: "This is offensive to me, [...] this patriotism of beer and shouting."[22] A journalist friend replies that the patriotic noise is essential to their own ends: "we have to scream into the people's ears what they should love and honor."[23] Indeed, the whole novel suggests that, however distasteful it might be, loyalist writers must devote themselves to building such popular support for their king.

Despite the vast chasm in ideologies between Hesekiel and literary supporters of the GDR, their expressions of loss bear clear similarities. To be sure, in contrast to Hesekiel, East Berlin writers welcomed events such as the mass demonstration on Alexanderplatz on November 4 as evidence that the citizens of the GDR had overcome their speechlessness and would transform their state into a genuine socialist democracy. But for many these hopes quickly faded after the opening of the Wall. Lamenting his fellow citizens' shopping sprees in West Berlin, for example, East Berlin author Stefan Heym (b. 1913) betrayed an aversion to perceived mass rowdiness similar to Dr. Thurn's.[24]

A latter-day version of Hesekiel's contrast between the humble values of old Berlin and the ostentatious displays of the new pervades discourse about the disappearance of the GDR. Even some of the strongest critics of the former society suggest the slower tempo and simpler ways of its people might

---

20 Ibid., p. 34. "[...] dieser originellsten aller Berliner Straßen."
21 Ibid., p. 35. "[...] wie sie nur das alte Berlin kannte und die der Kaiserstadt immer mehr verloren gehen."
22 Ibid., p. 119. "Mir ist's zuwider, [...] der Patriotismus mit Bier und Geschrei."
23 Ibid., p. 117. "[...] was das Volk lieben und verehren soll, muß man in die Ohren schreien."
24 Heym: "Ash-Wednesday." Berlin writer Monika Maron issued a sharp criticism of Heym's apparent blindspots for the material deprivations his privileged status had allowed him to avoid. Maron: "Writers and the People."

be seen as a kind of freedom unknown in the frantic world of the capitalist West.²⁵ Monika Maron (b. 1941), however, rejects any idea of regret for the loss of such freedom, arguing that once one admits that "a closed society was the precondition for these idyllic features," then it must be also admitted that "the GDR has nothing to bring with it into unity. It has nothing to preserve."²⁶ Many authors similarly caution against sentimentalizing life in the GDR and urge their colleagues not to allow feelings of loss to overshadow the demise of a corrupt dictatorial regime.²⁷ Recognizing that corruption, however, does not obliterate the fact articulated by Elisabeth Wesuls (b. 1954) on the day before unification, that the country in which she was born would disappear tomorrow.²⁸ Moreover, other authors emphasize that the vanishing of a way of life has profoundly affected not just writers but a whole citizenry. Poignant testimony to their bewilderment is the plaintive statement of a 60-year-old postoffice worker quoted by East Berlin writer Friedrich Dieckmann (b. 1937): "I am upset that all of a sudden everything that existed then is now supposed to have been garbage."²⁹

Contemporary writers trying to come to terms with what has been lost thus are coming up against painful complexities unknown to their forebears of the 1870s. The same holds true for literary attempts to depict national community as emerging in the experience of unification. Two moments that symbolize these experiences are June 16, 1871, when victorious troops returned to Berlin from France, and November 9, 1989, when a low-key announcement brought the opening of the Wall. Two attempts to incorporate these events into a fictional quest for Germanness are Julius Rodenberg's novel *Die Grandidiers* (1879) and Botho Strauß's drama *Schlußchor* (1991). Despite sharply differing approaches, both authors use the mass euphoria in Berlin as a background against which to wrestle with divisive conflicts impeding

---

25 See, for instance, Ahrends: "The Great Waiting," p. 46.
26 Maron: "Writers and the People," pp. 40–1. See also Maron: "Zonophobie," a scathing piece about what she perceives as the pettiness and self-pity of those who lament the end of life in the GDR.
27 As Peter Schneider noted, at a Writers Union conference in (East) Berlin in March 1990, a funereal atmosphere prevailed. Schneider: "Some People Can Even Sleep through an Earthquake." Schneider: *The German Comedy: Scenes of Life after the Wall*, pp. 66–91, here p. 84; "Man kann sogar ein Erdbeben verpassen." Schneider: *Extreme Mittellage. Eine Reise durch das deutsche Nationalgefühl*, pp. 54–78, here p. 74.
28 Wesuls: "Landeswechsel," p. 159.
29 Dieckmann: "Staatsräume im Innern Berlins: Ein Streifzug," p. 559. "Ich bin entsetzt, daß das alles auf einmal Mist gewesen sein soll." One of many thoughtful discussions about the identity of GDR citizens in the new Germany is developed by Schlesak: "Zweimal Deutschland."

national solidarity. Woven into both works are efforts to explore how the German past pertains to these moments.

In *Die Grandidiers* Rodenberg (1831–1914) interweaves the euphoria of 1871 with imagery of the Hohenzollern rulers and the revolutionary legacy of 1848 to create a basis for national solidarity. In the process he gives literary expression to compromises over ideals of freedom that allowed him and many other liberals to embrace Bismarck's unification as the realization of a genuine German community. In one scene a skeptical old 48er, impressed by Bismarck's Reichstag address at the outbreak of the war, asserts that Bismarck will achieve the German fatherland they wanted in 1848. The narrator expands this judgment into a vision of German community:

> The king of Prussia had himself raised the banner under which there would no longer be party differences, no gulf between the people and the army, no opposition between North and South [...]. [T]hose who had tarried in faraway lands came hurrying back or sent generous contributions to the war being fought for the rebirth of the German people.[30]

With such passages and their re-imagining of the ideals of 1848, Rodenberg thus dissolves the question of democratic freedoms into the achievement of German unity.

Many other divisions beyond the hostility of revolutionaries of 1848 toward the Prussian regime are depicted, and with all of them Rodenberg shows the patriotic delirium as the impetus for transcending *Zerrissenheit* that ranges from the alienation an artistic son and his business-minded father, to the divided loyalties of the community of Huguenot descendants, to the antagonisms between immigrant workers and their native Berlin counterparts, to the growing gulf between the humble old *Kleinbürger* and the ostentatious new bourgeoisie.[31] Common sacrifice to the war becomes the universal cure for all these divisions.

June 16, 1871, however, also becomes a time for two characters to contemplate what has taken place. One is an Alsatian immigrant whose ambivalence at the beginning of the war gave rise to the comment that Berlin in

---

30 Rodenberg: *Die Grandidiers*, p. 360; see also p. 227. "Der König von Preußen hatte selber das Banner erhoben, unter dem es keinen Unterschied der Parteien, keine Trennung von Volk und Heer, keinen Gegensatz von Nord und Süd mehr gab [...]. [W]er noch verbittert bisher an fremden Küsten geweilt, eilte selber herbei oder sandte reichliche Gaben zum Kriege für des deutschen Volkes Wiedergeburt." See also the essays of Cornell (pp. 85, 102–03) and Pape (pp. 111–18).

31 See Roper: *German Encounters with Modernity*, pp. 44–7. See also Cornell (p. 96) and Kelly (pp. 49–50).

mourning would divide ("zerreißen") his heart as much as Berlin in jubilation.³² Indeed, although convinced his homeland has been liberated by Germany, he is melancholy because of the human tragedies wrought by the war. Although the novel clearly asserts the necessity of these sacrifices, with this character Rodenberg raises the question of what measures can justify the end of national greatness. In another corner of Berlin, away from the crowds on Unter den Linden, a second character makes a pilgrimage to lay flowers at the statue of the Great Elector, who first invited the persecuted Huguenots to Berlin. Rodenberg thus grounds the new German identity in imagery of Berlin as a centuries-old haven for exiles and immigrants. German *Zerrissenheit*, he suggests, had to do with competing loyalties that could be resolved when Germans affirmed Prussian history as their own.

Botho Strauß's (b. 1944) *Schlußchor*, produced in Berlin's Schaubühne in 1991, is far removed from Rodenberg's novel in that it makes no attempt to construct a coherent narrative, to weave the fates of characters together, or to create self-explanatory dialogue. And yet in juxtaposing fragments of everyday life, in portraying an array of divisions among the parade of characters, in alluding to underlying questions about Germanness and German history, and in using a pivotal historical experience in Berlin as backdrop, the drama offers significant parallels to Rodenberg's treatment of the first unification. Strauß, too, warns that national solidarity can be built only upon an understood German past, but since for him the Nazi past occupies center stage, he depicts the celebrations of November 9 not as fulfillment of German community but as a facile excuse for abandoning the difficult work of national remembrance.

The first two acts depict a jumble of encounters that might be set in any country, except for the fleeting German memories of the postwar years that pop up in the disjointed dialogue of the play's conglomeration of characters. Another explicit allusion is the unexplained cry, "Deutschland!" which occurs seemingly randomly in each act.³³ In the third act issues of Germanness come into sharp focus. Set in a West Berlin restaurant on the night of November 9, the act focuses on Anita von Schastorf, who has met with her mother to commemorate the ninetieth birthday of their husband/father. Soon a bitter quarrel breaks out over the circumstances of his being shot by the Nazis in mid-1944 and over her mother's role in covering up what actually happened. Their argument, which brings *Vergangenheitsbewältigung* to the family level, draws in friends as well as other patrons.

---

32 Rodenberg: *Die Grandidiers*, pp. 361 and 431. On other signs of writers' ambivalence toward the war see Cornell (pp. 80, 98), Kelly (pp. 52–6), and Pape (pp. 124–26).
33 Strauß: *Schlußchor*, pp. 15, 29, 50, 73.

The backdrop for all this is the opening of the Wall, first intimated when a "Crier" pokes his head in from the street and shouts "Deutschland!" to the puzzlement of all in the room. He returns shortly to exclaim that the Wall has opened, that people are pouring into West Berlin, that Vopos are dancing on the watchtowers. The whole city is one great party, he cries: "Don't just keep hunkering at your tables! You'll never again see such jubilation."[34] This news provokes an an ominous comment from Patrick, one of the patrons: "they want to drive the last demons of the postwar era out of the land with fireworks and the popping of champagne corks."[35] As people in the restaurant run out into the streets, Anita and Patrick remain inside, continuing the argument. Anita had accused her mother of covering up unsavory details about her father's life and death, but now Patrick castigates her for doing the same thing by editing his wartime diary to cast him falsely as a resister. "You would have better served the memory of your father if you had not crept around the truth!" he admonishes and strides outside.[36] Surely this line is Strauß' admonition to his German audiences as well. The strains of Beethoven's chorus ("Schlußchor") are heard offstage, its message of universal brotherhood an ironic counterpoint to the bitter divisions in the restaurant. The final scene depicts not the euphoria of thousands of Berliners but Anita's descent into fatal madness, as she battles an eagle she releases from the zoo.

Strauß cannot celebrate an exultation he believes to be founded on a collective will to forget the Nazi past. In light of the 120 years of history since Rodenberg's portrayal of Berlin's first celebration of German unity, Strauß' pessimism is understandable. Indeed, a modern-day reader of *Grandidiers* is tempted to identify with the melancholy of the Alsatian character. Despite their differing reactions, however, both Rodenberg and Strauß share the belief that genuine German unity must be built on an understanding of a shared German past.

The halting process of *Vergangenheitsbewältigung* will be slow, as Germans attempt to come to terms with two dictatorial regimes. In the meantime, however, now, as with the first unification, Berlin has begun a physical transformation whose visible signs quickly appeared in literary discourse as ironic or critical comments on the effects of unification. Two particular targets of

---

34 Ibid., p. 89. "Bleiben Sie doch jetzt nicht an Ihren Tischen hocken! Nie wieder werden Sie einen solchen Jubel erleben."
35 Ibid., p. 90. "[…] mit Feuerwerk und Korkenknall die letzten Dämonen der Nachkriegszeit aus dem Land getrieben werden." See also Bullivant (p. 313).
36 Ibid., p. 94. "Sie hätten dem Andenken Ihres Vaters besser gedient, wenn Sie um die Wahrheit nicht herumgeschlichen wären!" See also Bullivant (p. 316).

writers are the forms of memorialization that sprouted and the pellmell construction by which a throng of speculators sought to enrich themselves.

The mania for memorials, or for getting rid of them, evokes sharp comments from Friedrich Spielhagen and Stefan Heym. In Spielhagen's *Sturmflut* (1877) a Berlin sculptor describes how the onslaught of commissions for victory statues has caused him to resort to dusting off an old statue of Homer he once sculpted and replacing its head with a rendition of Germania. The fabrication seems an apt representation of German unification, retorts his friend, an aging 48er who despises Bismarck and his political work.[37] In 1991 Stefan Heym commented similarly on a current "monument problem." Noting the irony of Lenin's statue having been cleared away from the square that bears his name, Heym suggested that the bare spot is a more painful memory than the statue itself. Instead of removing it, Heym continues, perhaps they should substitute a Bismarck head, or, better yet, personify the new Germany with the head of Wilhelm Busch, creator of Germany's favorite mischief makers, Max and Moritz. But please save the old heads for possible future "changes," Heym cautions about his modest proposal, revealing not only his dislike of the Kohl regime but his own faint hope that socialism will be given another chance in some future era.[38]

Far more disruptive than the refurbishing of statues is the helterskelter construction in Berlin as it expands into its new role as German capital, and, again, writers of both eras reacted with vivid imagery. Witnessing the effects on Berlin of the five-billion franc indemnity paid to Germany by the French, writers of the *Kaiserzeit* wavered between condemning the fervor to tear down old Berlin and admiring the dynamism of the emerging metropolis. Conrad Alberti expresses both sentiments in his novella "Im Rechtsstaat" (1887) in a scene in which an expatriate returns to look at the city he left years earlier. He can hardly get his bearings because the "spirit of the times has stalked so destructively" through the streets: "Before him spread out a desolate huge expanse of debris, a whole city dedicated to demolition." But as he looks beyond the piles of rubble and the gaping cellars of vanished houses, he sees a new Berlin: "the city of grandeur, of youth, of magnificence, through which pulsated the powerful stream of worldwide commerce."[39] Most Berlin writers

---

37 Spielhagen: *Sturmflut – Sämtliche Werke* vol. 13, p. 123.
38 Heym: *Filz*, p. 34.
39 Alberti: "Im Rechtsstaat," pp. 322–23. On the 'destruction' of Berlin in this era of expansion, see Kiaulehn: *Berlin*, p. 58. "Da breitete sich jetzt ein wüstes, ungeheueres Trümmerfeld aus, eine ganze der Vernichtung geweihte Stadt." "[…] das moderne Berlin […], die Stadt der Größe, der Jugend, der Pracht, in der der mächtige Strom des weltbeherrschenden Verkehrs pulsierte."

of these years similarly concluded the energy of the modernizing city outweighed the loss of the old. Still, however, they tended to be harshly critical of what they saw as architectural embodiments of the materialistic spirit of the age.

The Berlin of 1989, of course, quickly underwent a more dramatic transformation: the demolition of the Wall, begun by what Peter Schneider described as an international brigade of people hacking away at the resistant concrete with tools of all shapes and sizes.[40] If the creation of victory monuments symbolized sculptors' opportunism after the first unification, the unbridled trade in pieces of the Wall suggests a popularized version of such artistic enterprise. Schneider describes a proliferating species of "Mauerspechte" (wall peckers) begetting a subspecies of new entrepreneurs with vending tables displaying multi-colored fragments of the graffiti-covered expanse to buyers whose tools or time did not suffice to chip their own souvenirs. "There was no telling when concrete from the Berlin Wall would reach parity with gold," Schneider commented, "but surely, once the Japanese got into the act… Only the East Germans sold cheap, unaccustomed as they were to the free market."[41]

Other signs of speculative furor have set Berlin on the road to becoming what one journalist described as the "biggest building site in Europe."[42] Darryl Pinckney, an American observer, invoked imagery similar to Alberti's, but without the awe, when he commented in *Neue Rundschau* that Berlin "is once again the German Chicago, just like Mark Twain saw, a boom city, boiling over with secrets, deals, smugglers, entrepreneurs, contracts. Rents are skyrocketing in Kreuzberg; politicians and investors are manipulated like speculators."[43]

Debates about the future of the newly reunited Berlin reveal fears/anger over the rush to build upon the bare swath left by the Wall, with the most in-

---

40 *German Comedy*, p. 20; *Extreme Mittellage*, p. 13.
41 Schneider: "East-West Passages." Schneider: *The German Comedy: Scenes of Life after the Wall*, pp. 20–41, here p. 21. "Es steht nicht fest, wann der Berliner Mauerbeton den Goldpreis erreicht, aber wenn erst die Japaner ins Geschäft einsteigen … . Nur die Ostdeutschen, an freien Handel nicht gewöhnt, verkaufen billiger." Schneider: "West-Östliche Passagen." Schneider: *Extreme Mittellage. Eine Reise durch das deutsche Nationalgefühl*, pp. 13–32, here p. 14.
42 Nawrocki: "Angst vor Schutt und toten Zonen: Streit um die Hauptstadt: Die Berliner betrachten die Neubauwut und Abrißideen der Bonner Regierung mit Skepsis." *Die Zeit* No. 1, January 1, 1993, p. 22.
43 Pinckney: "Nicht länger Hongkong," p. 16. "[…] ist wieder das deutsche Chicago, genau, wie Mark Twain es sah, eine Stadt des Booms, brodelnd von Geheimnissen, Deals, Schmugglern, Unternehmern, Verträgen. Die Mieten steigen in Kreuzberg; Politiker und Investoren werden behandelt wie Spekulanten."

tense controversy focusing on Berlin's most valuable piece of vacant real estate: Potsdamer Platz. The mere mention of the site evokes myriad layers of historical memory beneath the transience of the absurd bungee tower: the desolate expanse of sand that for 28 years stretched eastward behind the Wall; the bombed out ruins of 1945; Europe's busiest intersection flanked by some of its grandest department stores; the square as entry into the elegant Tiergarten district of the 1870s; and the gate through the old city wall that once opened onto the country road to Friedrich II's beloved Sans Souci in Potsdam.[44] The recent outcry over the scandalous sale of this site at bargain prices to Daimler-Benz and Sony had no effect, noted Berlin novelist Dieter Hildebrandt (b. 1932) in a mournful article in the *Berliner Tagesspiegel*. Contemplating the forthcoming architectural catastrophe of densely packed office buildings, he appealed to fellow Berliners to use the precious time of bareness that remains for a "spiritual inventory," and to embrace for one last time the vision of "our empty Berlin, our marvelous urban steppes, our unrestorable historical prairie."[45]

A particularly striking point for comparison of images of Berlin's metamorphosis lies in two treatments of the razing of a Berlin palace and its replacement by a spot for popular entertainment. Robert Springer (1816–1885) provides the first instance in his semi-autobiographical novel, *Banquier and Schriftsteller* (1877). Searching for an apt representation of the triumph of greed over tradition, Springer describes the demolition of an elegant little palace in Charlottenburg that once belonged to the Gräfin Lichtenau. The graceful building fell so quickly "to the picks and sledgehammer of speculation," Springer laments, that no one thought to photograph it or its interior reliefs by Gottfried Schadow.[46] In its place arose the "imposing Flora Establishment, financed by a huge stock offering." A glass structure of lavish halls filled with palm trees and sumptuous appointments, it became the gathering place of crowds of well-to-do Berliners. The Flora came to symbolize the precariousness of much post-unification construction, when, as Berlin historian Annemarie Lange reports, a beam in the main hall collapsed, and so shaky was the financing of the enterprise that it went bankrupt, bringing countless unwary investors to grief.[47]

---

44 On the implications of Potsdamer Platz for past and future, see Sack: "Schmelzendes Packeis" *Die Zeit* No. 38, September 11, 1992, p. 61–2, and also Marcus: "Berlin: Into the Future." *New York Times Magazine* Part 2, October 18, 1992, pp. 16, 84–93.

45 Quoted in Sack: "Schmelzendes Packeis," p. 13. "seelische Inventur [...] unser leeres Berlin, unsere wunderbare Stadtsteppe, unsere unwiederbringliche Geschichtsprärie."

46 Springer: *Banquier und Schriftsteller*, p. 169. "unter der Picke und dem Mauerbrecher der Spekulation," "großartige, auf Actien gegründete Etablissement Flora."

47 Lange: *Berlin zur Zeit Bebels und Bismarcks*, pp. 192–95.

Contemporary Berlin has its counterpart to the Palmenhaus Flora in its Palast der Republik. This expansive glass and marble building is also built upon the site of a former palace: the vast Hohenzollern residence, described by Robert Springer as "the center of Berlin's most important historical and political memories."[48] Unlike the Lichtenau manor, however, this palace was demolished not in an era of German unification but in 1950 by the Ulbricht regime. Whatever political expediency lay behind the rationalization about irreparable war damage, more than a quarter of a century passed before the new building rose on the site. Even more than the Flora, the Palast der Republik became a thronging public center, having received 70 million visitors to its concert hall, theater, restaurants, kiosks, and cafés since its opening in 1976.

This building, like the Flora, has been made into a symbol for corruption, in this case, of the SED-regime, a connotation that has given rise to a proposal to tear it down and reconstruct the Hohenzollern palace. Critics have argued strenuously against the notion of trying to undo the destruction of the palace in 1950 with a far more expensive wrong: the reconstruction of an unusable royal residence of some 1500 rooms at an astronomical cost.[49] Whatever the outcome of the debate, it points to more intricate issues than simply old landmarks versus showy new buildings. As Friedrich Dieckmann commented, the fate of the "Volkshaus" will not be decided by the people who paid for it to the tune of 100 marks for every man, woman, and child, that is "by the inhabitants of that zone now hyphened with the word 'former.'"[50] Yet, Dieckmann reminds readers, it was they who thronged to its multifarious events and they who watched their first freely elected parliament debate their state's future there in 1990. At the heart of Dieckmann's discussion lies the loss of one visible source of pride for a citizenry otherwise united only by oppression. He thus uses its proposed demolition to show the impulsiveness with which today's counterparts to the founders of the 1870s wish to transform Berlin.

Beneath writer's denunciations of victory statues and of helter skelter construction plans in both unification eras lies a widespread perception of materialism sweeping over the city and the nation. The central symbol of this after the first unification was the *Gründerzeit* (founder's era), which referred to

---

48 Springer: *Berlin*, p. 97. "[...] den Mittelpunkt für Berlins wichtigste historische und politische Erinnerungen."
49 Sack: "Das Berliner Schloßgespenst." *Die Zeit* No. 52, December 18, 1992, pp. 43–4. See also Seehan (p. 33).
50 Dieckmann: "Staatsräume im Innern Berlins," p. 559. "[...] von den Bewohnern jener Zonen, die mit dem Wort ehemalig apostrophiert werden."

the hundreds of joint-stock companies founded in the boom years following unification. This orgy of speculative activity and the crash that ended it in late 1873 came to be portrayed by German writers as an overriding national failure (even though the crash originated in Vienna and New York). Because the speculative maelstrom in Germany centered in the *Börse*, Berlin became the obvious setting for literary depictions of the crash that followed. The best-known literary treatment of the *Gründerkrach*, Friedrich Spielhagen's best-selling *Sturmflut* (1876), weaves the story an intricate railway scheme (patterned after the vast Strousberg project) with images of a glittering Berlin society feasting on paper profits of speculation. Karl Gutzkow (1811–1879), in his last novel, *Die neuen Serapionsbrüder* (1877), gives an even more sarcastic depiction of the effects of an epidemic of profit-seeking on Germany as is evident when he has one character proclaim: "Let our millions go into the stockmarket! Into buying and selling of railroads and whole city blocks. Taking part in whatever swindle comes along will bring in more money than any dallying with national purposes or the good of the people we might have promised!"[51] Such cynical imagery recurs in countless other Berlin novels, linking anti-capitalist mythology with perceived threats to national well-being.[52]

Since 1989 numerous writers have similarly represented the reunification of Berlin with bitter anti-capitalist imagery and have linked it to notions of a failed national community. If the Strousberg railway project came to symbolize the *Gründerzeit*, its contemporary counterpart is surely the Treuhandanstalt, the establishment set up in 1990 to undertake the privatization of state-owned property of the GDR. Surrounded from its inception by charges of corruption and ineptitude, its members subjected to unremitting criticism and even murderous attacks, the institution has come to symbolize the uncontrollable sway of capitalism. A poem and three drawings by Günter Grass, for instance, depict the Treuhand as gathering its booty like dead flies and strewing them over the land.[53] Friedrich Dieckmann extended the negative symbolism by noting that Treuhand was housed in the complex built by Goering for his air force ministry and added that the previous occupant was the bureaucracy that planned the GDR's economy into bankruptcy.[54] And Stefan

---

51 Gutzkow: *Die neuen Serapionsbrüder* vol. 2, p. 102. "Unsere Millionen gehen lieber an die Börse! Kaufen und Verkaufen von Eisenbahnen und Straßenvierteln. Sichbetheiligen an allem Schwindel, der auftaucht, bringt mehr Geld ein als alle langen Geschichten mit Nationalzwecken und Volkswohl – die wir versprochen hatten!"
52 For further treatment of this, see Roper: *German Encounters with Modernity*, pp. 55–72 and Forderer: *Die Großstadt im Roman*, pp. 161–73.
53 Grass: "Treuhand."
54 Dieckmann: "Staatsräume," p. 554.

Heym growled that the citizens of the GDR handed themselves into the power of the new masters – and got the Treuhand in return. Indeed, he suggested, the marauding of GDR property by the Treuhand might be compared with the American invasion of Grenada except for the fact that the Americans were not attacking their own brothers and sisters. Although professing no tolerance for "real existierenden Sozialismus," Heym thus denounced the arrival of "den real existierenden Kapitalismus."[55]

Such denunciations, with their implications of national moral failure, are echoed in less ideologically virulent terms by Peter Schneider in imagery of two-way German venality. From the East came maneuvers ranging from petty scams over bus tickets to claims that West owed the GDR populace 650 billion marks in restitution for its postwar economic suffering. From the West Schneider invoked images of an eastward parade of Mercedes disgorging their occupants to snap up cultural treasures at bargain prices. Even West Berlin bloodbanks got into the mood of things, reported Schneider, with offers of quick payment for blood donations, which provoked a Berlin headline that proclaimed, "West-Vampire saugen DDR-Blut."[56] In short, reactions against the perceived "onset of supermarket culture" can be interpreted as sequels to literary reactions against the wave of speculation after the first unification. What recent writers have seen as "the final victory of Western materialism over German culture: the triumph of *Macht* over *Geist*," echoes from the earlier era.[57]

Imagery of the East being colonized by the West suggests another deeply rooted theme of Berlin writing: its division into East and West. Despite its prominent Cold War incarnation, this dichotomy originated in the 1870s, with the East symbolizing the traditional values of the *Kleinbürger* and the West epitomizing Berlin's identity with a parvenu bourgeoisie.[58] Paul Lindau's

---

55 Heym: *Filz*, pp. 99, 45, 71. Heiner Müller provides another image of invasion, comparing the capitalist colonization to the earlier colonization of Stalinism. Domdey: "Feindbild: BRD," p. 67. On "utopian anti-capitalism" see also Bullivant (p. 309) and Reed (p. 241).

56 Schneider: "The Deep-Freeze Theory and Other Hypotheses." Schneider: *The German Comedy: Scenes of Life after the Wall*, pp. 137–72, here p. 148; "Gibt es zwei deutsche Kulturen? Die Kühlschranktheorie und andere Vermutungen." Schneider: *Extreme Mittellage. Eine Reise durch das deutsche Nationalgefühl*, pp. 120–56, here p. 163. Quoted from *die tageszeitung*, January, 29, 1990.

57 See Brockmann: "Introduction: The Reunification Debate," p. 30. On western "colonization" of the east see also Bullivant (p. 311) and Schoeps (p. 269).

58 On the theme of westward expansion of Berlin in literature see Modrow: *Berlin 1900*, pp. 57–67. Scheffler's *Berlin* is filled with imagery of parvenuism; see, for instance, pp. 18, 143–46, 154, 178, 189.

(1839–1919) wildly popular *Der Zug nach dem Westen* (1886) was not the first novel to suggest the contrast but was surely the most influential. The title is explicated by a character who links the city's east-west migration of those made upwardly mobile by new wealth to a larger movement of migrants arriving in the city from eastern provinces to seek their fortune.[59] In other novels of the *Kaiserzeit* the westward march continues through "Berlin-W," extending the length of Kurfürstendamm and finally into the lavish villas of the farflung Grunewald district.

East and West Berlin continue to evoke these connotations, intensified, of course, by the clashing ideologies of the postwar German regimes.[60] A quintessential depiction of these two Berlins is contained in a piece by Hans Joachim Schädlich (b. 1935), entitled, "Ostwestberlin."[61] Opening with the question, "Wo fängt der Qdamm [sic] an?" the piece proceeds without punctuation, spilling out a cascade of visual impressions and their ideological connotations. Although written two years before the opening of the Wall, Schädlich's dizzying description of consumer society on display anticipates the impressions of the thousands of Easterners who poured westward in November 1989. Schädlich's torrent of street numbers and buildings devolves into profuse lists of commodities with prices, opening hours of the stores in which they are sold, and the spectrum of colors and styles in which they are available. Advertisements for hotels – with all their amenities – are piled against travel bureaux' enticements for bargain tours. The possibilities for indulgence are infinite: lists of ice cream flavors are followed by lists of drink menus, then by newspapers at kiosks, pizza combinations, beauty salon treatments, 170 sorts of tea at a café – and a naming of 33 makes of cars plying the boulevard. Suddenly shifting to East Berlin, the narrative erupts into lists of the multitude of sights offered by the capital of the GDR. Schädlich compresses successive incarnations of German history into this Berlin:

> Behind the Kaiser WilhelmKarlLiebknechtBridge arches the Cathedral restored on the right in long-standing alliance with the National Front for the further cultural flourishing in the city and country on the left the Palace of the Republic contain-

---

59 Lindau: *Der Zug nach dem Westen*, pp. 73–4. See also Scheffler: *Berlin*, pp. 145–48.
60 On East Berlin literature before 1989, see Tate: "The Socialist Metropolis? Images of East Berlin in the Literature of the GDR." Glass et al., eds., *Berlin: Literary Images of a City*, pp. 146–61, and Dorothy Rosenberg: "Berlin: Backdrop, Stage, or Actor?" Haxthausen and Suhr, eds., *Berlin: Culture and Metropolis*, pp. 206–18.
61 Schädlich: "Ostwestberlin."

ing instead of the [Hohenzollern]palace the People's Chamber works with plans with rules with living socialist democracy[.]⁶²

A multitude of such juxtapositions ensue, ending at Brandenburger Tor, which, it is noted, lost its function as a gate in 1865 when the demolition of the city wall left it standing alone. The last sentence fragment trails off into the existing Wall (of 1987), leaving the reader to ponder what will stand alone when this Wall, someday, is demolished.

Brandenburger Tor now does stand alone, and since November 1989 it has been the center of many celebrations. In at least one instance, on August 6, 1991, it provided an ironic counterpart to earlier scenes of triumphant German troops passing through its Doric columns. When a throng of Berliners gathered to celebrate the 200th anniversary of their beloved landmark, Berlin writer Christoph Dieckmann (b. 1956) captured the astonishing incongruity of Bundeswehr soldiers marching across this so recently-barricaded spot when he recalled that Ulbricht justified building the Wall "to prevent the Bundeswehr from marching through Brandenburger Tor with ringing tones. 'And now: the marching band of the Bundeswehr!' *That's the Berlin Air Air Air.* Along with us the old times are returning."⁶³

It is also a new time, and images of the marching band recede before those of the countless thousands who have flocked through this gate without walls. Such movement is not restricted to Berliners who are citizens of the new Germany but involves hordes of new arrivals as well as an existing "foreign" population. Once again Berlin is a city colonized by outsiders – migrants from German-speaking communities throughout Eastern Europe, arriving to claim the German citizenship guaranteed by the Basic Law; asylum seekers and refugees from the collapsed communist regimes, fleeing from persecution, war, and economic catastrophe; and a spectrum of "guest workers" from the former two regimes, ranging from the long-established Turkish population in Kreuzberg to thousands of Vietnamese who had been settled throughout the GDR, following a 1980 agreement with Vietnam.⁶⁴

---

62 Schädlich: "Ostwestberlin," p. 177. "Hinter der Kaiser WilhelmKarlLiebknechtBrücke wölbt sich der Dom rechtswiederhergestellt im bewährten Bündnis der Nationalen Front für das weitere Aufblühen in Stadt und Land links der Palast der Republik anstatt des Schlosses enthaltend die VolksKammer arbeitet mit plant mit regiert mit lebendiger sozialistischer Demokratie[.]"

63 Dieckmann: "Mit uns zieht die neue Zeit," p. 88. "[…] daß sonst die Bundeswehr mit klingendem Spiel durch Brandenburger Tor zöge. 'Und nun das Blasorchester der Bundeswehr!' *Das ist die Berliner Luft Luft Luft.* Mit uns zieht die alte Zeit."

64 See, for instance, Schneider: "In Deutschland hat Saigon gesiegt. Vietnamesen in Berlin." Schneider: *Extreme Mittellage. Eine Reise durch das deutsche Nationalgefühl*, pp. 92–108, trans-

Although the immigration crisis extends throughout Germany, Berlin has the densest concentration of differing peoples, and it has a long historical identity as a haven for the persecuted.

Writers of the *Kaiserzeit* laid foundations for the literary representation of immigrants to the city, as the above discussion of Rodenberg's *Grandidiers* attests. In another such instance, Fritz Mauthner (1849–1923) opens the first novel of his "Berlin-W" trilogy, *Das Quartett* (1893), with two couples enjoying an evening together. Each of the four, it turns out, is a migrant to Berlin, and they discuss how they typify the population of the burgeoning *Weltstadt*.[65] Imagery of immigrations devolves in this novel, as in many others, into depictions of Berlin as a parvenu city overrun by opportunistic outsiders. At the opposite end of the social spectrum are literary depictions of wretched newcomers such as the family of Eastern Jews described by Berlin naturalist Conrad Alberti (1862–1918) in opening scene of his novel *Die Alten und die Jungen* (1889). Through the eyes of the protagonist, a young composer heading to Berlin in a fourth-class train compartment, readers see middleclass distaste for these woebegone occupants, who he realizes are, like him, journeying to Berlin for its opportunities.[66] In addition to such uneasy expressions of aversion, Alberti and other authors also used their novels to criticize signs of intolerance toward outsiders, particularly the anti-Semitism that spread in Berlin after unification.[67]

Similar ambivalence toward outsiders is evident in recent descriptions of people arriving from eastern Europe. Early in 1989, as travel restrictions were lifted, Berlin checkpoints began to be crossed by decrepit cars filled with Poles, eager to sell their meager goods for hard currency and return home with chocolates and other foodstuffs to sell on the other end. As other communist regimes disintegrated, the invasion multiplied. In a series of vignettes entitled "Marktplatz Berlin" author Renée Zucker (b. 1954) invokes the invasion with an incantation that recurs throughout the piece: "The smell of humanity pervades Kantstraße."[68] Like Alberti's protagonist, Zucker's narrator

---

lated as "In Germany, Saigon Wins: The Vietnamese in Berlin." Schneider: *The German Comedy: Scenes of Life after the Wall*, pp. 92–108.
65 Mauthner: *Das Quartett*, pp. 3–5. See Scheffler: *Berlin*, pp. 22–3.
66 Alberti: *Die Alten und die Jungen* vol. 1, p. 6.
67 See, for instance, Mauthner: *Der neue Ahasver*, and Jacobowski: *Werther der Jude*, both treated in Roper: *German Encounters with Modernity*, pp. 146–63.
68 Zucker: "Marktplatz Berlin." "Es riecht nach Mensch auf der Kantstraße." See also Schneider: "Before the Fall." Schneider: *The German Comedy: Scenes of Life after the Wall*, pp. 3–19, here pp. 4–7.

ponders her own distaste for figures huddled at U-Bahn entrances or blocking sidewalks with their pathetic merchandise. In confronting their ambivalences, Berlin writers have assumed the role of conscience, as their forebears did with similar portrayals. Similar moral questions are being raised about the role of Berlin's Turkish community in the reunited city. Kreuzberg's exotic markets and people are depicted not just as local color, but a growing body of literature by writers like Aras Ören (b. 1939) shows Turkish feelings of *Zerrissenheit* about a city that has taken them in but also has excluded them from its German identity.[69]

Although Berlin has been spared the worst of attacks against foreigners since unification, the concentration of foreigners in the city and the hostility they experience will surely command intensified literary attention. The ironic comment of Darryl Pinckney, an African American observer in Berlin, will have to be tested: "Maybe hatred of foreigners is an unavoidable byproduct of national reconciliation, like the rise of the Ku Klux Klan in America after its civil war."[70] As if to belie that assumption, however, on November 8, 1992, 300,000 Berliners from East and West converged at Brandenburger Tor for the first mass protest against attacks on foreigners in their city and country.[71] Will Berlin writers find ways to build on such instances to rediscover the city's legacy of tolerance?

At the heart of that question lies the question of the future of literary engagement among Berlin and, more widely, German authors. Authors disillusioned in the aftermath of the pellmell rush into German unification have articulated doubts about the appropriateness of such engagement. For instance, Christoph Hein (b. 1944), responding to a question about his plans for future political writing, stated that such subjects could best be left to historians, and elsewhere he emphasized that the literary representation of events would be the province of a future generation.[72] Whether Hein's sentiments imply a re-

---

69 See Heidrun Suhr: "*Fremde* in Berlin: The Outsiders' View from the Inside." Haxthausen and Suhr, eds., *Berlin: Culture and Metropolis*, pp. 219–42. Ören's most recent German book is *Wie die Spree in den Bosporus fließt*. See also Dieckmann: "Ali Baba und die Mörder." *Die Zeit* No. 1, January 1, 1993, p. 54.
70 Pinckney: "Nicht länger Hongkong," p. 17. The English translation is my own, from the German translation of Pinckney's piece: "Vielleicht ist Fremdenhaß ein unvermeidliches Nebenprodukt nationaler Versöhnung, wie der Aufstieg des Ku-Klux-Klans in Amerika nach dem Bürgerkrieg."
71 See Hartung: "Ein Spaziergang der Demokraten." *Die Zeit* No. 47, November 13, 1992, p. 2.
72 Thiele: "Engagiert – wofür?," p. 80, and Janssen-Aimmermann: "Perspektiven. Perspektiven?," pp. 157–58.

treat into aesthetic concerns is not clear, but others, such as literary critic Ulrich Greiner, have proclaimed that, indeed, the postwar tradition of engaged literature has become outmoded.[73]

A heightened impetus for this conclusion has been a fractiousness that has reverberated through literary society and extended to the wider public. The most recent manifestation are revelations that Christa Wolf (b. 1929) and Heiner Müller (b. 1929), two of East Berlin's most venerated writers, made reports to the Stasi. Wolf's stay at the secluded Getty center on the California coast has given rise to further talk about the retreat of writers tainted by ideological sins.[74] Günter Grass' resignation from the SPD because of its compromises over asylum seekers has also been interpreted as a sign of the end of an era of engagement.[75] These and a plenitude of other signs of the "raw nerves" and "frayed tempers" described by Andreas Huyssen,[76] might be seen to suggest a resounding "no" to Brigitte Struzyk's question about German brother- and sisterhood with her bungee-cord metaphor. Other Berlin writers, however, such as Jürgen Fuchs (b. 1950), emphasize the inevitability of feelings of anxiety and disillusionment as Germans from both east and west confront new situations, and they insist on the need for patience.[77] The present contentiousness, from this perspective, is but the first stage of transition to a new literary society that will continue to contribute to the redefining of a radically new German nation.

The tradition of engagement in Berlin literature, reaching back to the first unification era, would seem to make a universal retreat into new inwardness ("Innerlichkeit") unlikely. As Klaus Ziegler once noted, Berlin is an excellent corrective for this German tendency.[78] The city will continue to inspire its writers with imagery of the meeting place of the former two states, of the cultures that converge there, and of the capital of unified Germany. It will inspire them to search for the signs of German community whose existence Struzyk morosely questioned. Berlin writer Helga Königsdorf (b. 1936)

---

73 See the history of this controversy in the introductory essay to Anz, ed., "Es geht nicht um Christa Wolf." See also Reed (p. 248–49) and Schoeps (p. 274–77).
74 Raddatz: "Von der Beschädigung der Literatur durch ihre Urheber: Bemerkungen zu Heiner Müller und Christa Wolf." *Die Zeit* No. 5, January 29, 1993, pp. 51–2. See also Reed (pp. 244–48) and Schoeps (pp. 264–66).
75 Greiner: "Kassandra, arbeitslos. Günter Grass verläßt die SPD." *Die Zeit* No. 2, January 8, 1993, p. 41.
76 Huyssen: "After the Wall: The Failure of German Intellectuals," p. 109. This article provides a good introduction to the *Literaturstreit* surrounding Christa Wolf.
77 Fuchs: "*– und wann kommt der Hammer?*," p. 132.
78 Ziegler: "Die Berliner Gesellschaft und die Literatur," pp. 47–8.

acknowledges that such community must be grounded in the experiences of lost wars, the Holocaust, and failed regimes. But, she continues, community can also be built on 1989, the first successful German revolution. And it can rise from venerable traditions ranging from the cultural heritage of Goethe to the legendary German efficiency ("Tüchtigkeit"). Let Germans set to work, she concludes.[79]

---

79 Königsdorf: *Aus dem Dilemma eine Chance machen*, pp. 83–99. See also Hoffmann: "Die schiefen Türme."

DANIEL FULDA
Universität zu Köln

Telling German History:
Forms and Functions of the Historical Narrative
Against the Background of the National Unifications

Abstract: After having constructed a genre model which allows for an appropriate handling of the singular relationship between political developments and historical narrative, the paper aims to present Gustav Freytag's historical works as an example of the 'national-liberal' historical narrative which was closely connected with the historiography and shaped by a national historical teleology, narrative illusionism and a belief in the ability of the middle-class to act effectively in history. The conflicting positions with regard to historical theory, aesthetics and ideology in Meyer, Fontane and Raabe show the decline of the integrative force of national unification. German history is at the moment predominantly 'to be dealt with' ('zu bewältigen'). The historical narrative participates in a tendency among historians towards a 'historicization' of National Socialism. The historical theme of reunification in various narrative texts reveals conflicting attitudes towards the radical changes in 1989/90.

When Gustav Freytag observed Prussian regiments during the Franco-Prussian war in 1870, he involuntarily associated them with Teutonic hordes.[1] This image gave him a sudden insight into that strange mixture of continuity and change which he understood as national history and which gave him the idea for the cycle of novels *Die Ahnen*. He meant to trace the stages of the rising evolution of the German nation from the migration of the people (Völkerwanderung) to his own century. 119 years later, however, in another "year of history," Peter Handke in his search for jukeboxes withdrew to a little Spanish town and the news he received there about the radical changes in Eastern-middle Europe could only renew his "horror of history."[2] Do we

---

1 Cf. Freytag: *Erinnerungen*, p. 347. – Stefan Möller and Muzafar Ali Qazilbash translated the article into English.
2 Handke: *Versuch über die Jukebox*, pp. 26, 124 ("Grauen vor der Geschichte").

thus have to do with an "ahistorical origin" or even negative historical experiences, which made the nation-state appear obsolete to many contemporary writers,[3] and on the other hand with a nationalistic and optimistic historical awareness?[4] The handing-down and interpretation of (national) history which is inherent to historical fiction will be analyzed in order to add the necessary differentiations to such sweeping statements because neither did purely uncritical and patriotic affirmation follow in the wake of the foundation of the Reich, nor did writers, as has often been said, pass over reunification in silence.

1.

The reasons for the changes in the historical narrative at the time of both unifications, the subject of this paper, can hardly be attributed to a single political event. The poetics of the genre 'historical novel' has not yet developed an adequate model which sufficiently allows for the integration of a variety of influences. Literary theorists regard the historical novel on the whole as a "hybrid genre, sad to behold."[5] People had already criticized its (alleged) irresolution between history and literature when Walter Scott established the genre: "The historian interferes with the poet and yet again, the historical truth cannot assert itself over poetry."[6] More or less strong ties with a subject-matter external to literature are still viewed with suspicion because of the repercussions of an epistemology which dismissed empirical knowledge as random truth[7] and of an aesthetics which aimed at the highly mediated connection of the 'ästhetischen Schein' (Schiller) to reality. The influence of history over the present, however, even in a poetic guise, is a precondition for the genre 'historical novel.' As early as in 1828, Wolfgang Menzel acknowledged that "his-

---

3   Ibid., p. 25 ("Herkunft aus der Geschichtslosigkeit"); Patrick Süskind: "Deutschland, eine Midlife-crisis." *Der Spiegel* No. 38, September 17, 1990, pp. 116–25, here p. 123, quoted from Korte: *Über Deutschland schreiben*, p. 71.
4   Most of the eminent writers were rejoiced over the foundation of the Reich. Cf. Freytag: *Erinnerungen*, p. 377, he calls the German Reich the "supreme achievement of my life" ("höchster Gewinn meines Lebens"); cf. Meyer: *Sämtliche Werke* vol. 8, p. 150; letter to Schönhardt, October 14, 1870, Raabe: *Sämtliche Werke* suppl. 2, p. 159; Loster-Schneider: *Der Erzähler Fontane*, p. 258. For Fontane see also John Cornell in this volume, p. 80.
5   Harro Müller: "Possibilities of the Historical Novel in the Nineteenth and Twentieth Century." Roberts and Thomson, eds., *The Modern German Historical Novel*, pp. 59–70, here p. 60.
6   Immermann: *Werke in fünf Bänden* vol. 1, p. 548.
7   Cf. Meran: *Theorien in der Geschichtswissenschaft*, pp. 37–42, 46–8.

tory" must not be a "mere vehicle for certain philosophical and moral ideas" but should also be treated "by the poets for its own sake."[8]

This genre-specific historicism does not necessarily entail a flight from the present. Since Herder, people have attributed to historical education a source of insight into future developments, since the present, because of the historicity of human beings and their institutions, can only be understood from its past history. The criticism of the historical novel which aims at its latent escapist tendency ignores furthermore the fact that history can be productive for the present and the future in various ways. According to Nietzsche, not only a critical dealing with history but also an antiquarian and monumental one can be beneficial for life.[9] In the historical narrative past events are indirectly connected with politically relevant subjects and thus given a contemporary character. In this case, Döblin's famous dictum has to be modified: The historical novel is in the first place a novel and in the second place history.[10] Hence, it does not make sense to look at the genre as autonomous fiction whose poetological problems alone merit discussion. To save the suspicious genre by choosing 'other' historical novels, which are interesting by dint of their epistemological potential for the hermeneutics of the presentation of history,[11] undermines its representational function with regard to the past as well as to the function of history in the author's present.

Thus, I would like to describe the domain of the historical narrative as a field in which three different points of reference (Orientierungen) function. While historical narrative basically participates in general aesthetic developments (1), it is subject to genre-specific influences of 'history' (2), by which are rather understood the *historiae rerum gestarum* than the *res gestae*. The historical subject-matter finally entails a specific connection with the present (3) where the author brings the 'objective' authority of historical processes to bear. I will not treat the *res gestae* as a point of reference in its own right – often treated

---

8 Wolfgang Menzel: "Die deutsche Literatur." Lämmert et al., eds., *Romantheorie 1620–1880*, pp. 277–84, here p. 278.
9 Cf. Nietzsche: "Vom Nutzen und Nachtheil der Historie für das Leben." *Sämtliche Werke* vol. 1, pp. 245–334, here pp. 258–70.
10 Cf. Döblin: "Der historische Roman und wir." *Schriften zur Ästhetik, Poetik und Literatur*, pp. 291–315, here p. 298. An approach to historiography via this definition should be unproblematic for the literary critic since it has already been identified as "an essentially poetic act" (White: *Metahistory*, p. x).
11 Cf. Geppert: *Der "andere" historische Roman*, pp. 11–2. Limlei, too, raises important objections to Geppert's conception: *Geschichte als Ort der Bewährung*, pp. 23–5. Limlei explains the genre in terms of liberal need for reconciliation of individual and society. As ideological fiction it must particularly not reveal its constructivistic character (cf. ibid., pp. 51–68).

somehow naively as established facts – since they are imparted to writers of historical novels mainly by professional historians and even for the 'study of sources' in a more restricted sense they are available only through (predominantly narrative) texts. Historiography itself influences historical fiction by requiring delimitation but also by providing stimuli in the form of new subject-matter as in the case of Scheffel, Riehl or Ebers, or in the question of technique and interpretation as to how and why the narrated past should be oriented towards the present. Thus, it is less a 'hiatus' between fiction and the highly problematic 'factuality'[12] than the tension between depictions of history in literature and historiography which I hold to be constitutive for the genre. The latter functions in any case as a point of reference for the historical narrative also beyond the history-fixated 19th century. At the close of the twentieth century, historians maintain a firm position in the public awareness of West Germany, which is first of all shaped by the Nazi crimes in a political and moral sense. Examples in the fourth part of this paper are proof of the extent to which the literary historical narrative is tied to this constellation.

The plurality of tendencies in the historical narrative, stated above, requires an explanation through the reasons for its changes into a discourse which goes beyond literature and which has been so far neglected by research into the historical novel[13]. Thus I will try (2.) to outline a national-liberal discourse on history which was jointly conducted by literature and historiography with Gustav Freytag as its main proponent in literature. I would then like to look into poetological positions which, despite similiar national political points of departure, distinguish Fontane, Meyer and Raabe from the pro-Prussian historical narrative and its intended effects (3.). From the various forms of historical fiction in the present I will then single out a few examples of the way in which National Socialism is dealt with in literature. These are closely connected with the way Germans see themselves and recent tendencies in historiography (4.). Works by Heym, Walser, Grass, Delius and Maron attest to the share of historical fiction in the discussion concerning the development of the nation before, during and after the changes in 1989. In closing, I will draw a short comparison between 1870 and 1990 (5. and 6.).

---

12 Cf. David Roberts: "The Modern German Historical Novel. An Introduction." Roberts and Thomson, eds., *The Modern German Historical Novel*, pp. 1–17, here pp. 2–3.

13 The only work worth mentioning (Limlei: *Geschichte als Ort der Bewährung*) at least relates the nineteenth-century historical novel to social history. Limlei unfortunately too readily accepted important dates of political history as decisive points in the history of the genre, cf. note 39. The most recent study of the historical novel (Kebbel: *Geschichtengeneratoren*) is aimed at a poetics of the genre, which is based on a theory of discourse and thus does not take historical references into consideration.

2.

Freytag is virtually the epitome of the genre-typical link between literature, scholarly historiography and, through his political activities, orientation towards the present. He is regarded as *the* "poet of the middle-class,"[14] he and Julian Schmidt were the editors of the *Grenzboten*, the mouthpiece of Northern German liberalism and Literary Realism, he was the author of the five-volume social history *Bilder aus der deutschen Vergangenheit* (1859–67) and a member of parliament for the national-liberals in the North German Reichstag. Even though he held no leading position in literary criticism, historiography or political journalism, Freytag could envision himself as being in its centre. The foundation of the Reich confirmed his awareness "that I was in the battles of my time on the side of those who were awarded the greatest triumphs."[15]

In the spirit of literary theory at that time, which insisted on delimitation from historical sciences, Freytag denied that aesthetic consequences might arise from his mediatory position. His cycle of novels *Die Ahnen* (1873–81) was meant to be "free and modern literature" so that everything real or historical was a burden to him.[16] *Die Ahnen* is, however, not in the least devoid of historiographical gestures that explain historical and cultural details and emphasize historical otherness[17]. The closeness of *Die Ahnen* and *Bilder aus der deutschen Vergangenheit* raises even stronger doubts about Freytag's claims concerning the autonomy of the novel. It is less important that the latter often provides the historical and cultural basis for the former than that the narrative techniques come together in a central point: The reader of *Bilder* is asked to empathize with the feelings "of our ancestors." The perspective of "the average human being" will, it is hoped, to make the course of history visible.[18] Both texts are characterized with regard to ideology and narratology by the following observation: In Freytag's opinion, a citizen basically represents the nation in a social respect; historical and cultural rather than political developments shape its life. Moreover, it is he and not the aristocratic political leadership who makes decisive contributions to a historical evolution, namely of

---

14 Herrmann: *Gustav Freytag*, p. 297.
15 Freytag: *Erinnerungen*, p. 4.
16 Ibid., pp. 349–50 ("freie und moderne Dichtung").
17 For example the couple, which is evidently meant for each other, kisses in a romantic atmosphere. But a little later, the narrator breaks the illusion by declaring that "the kiss at that time was no proof of love" ("Nun war zu jener Zeit ein Kuß noch kein Beweis von Liebe.") (Freytag: *Gesammelte Werke* ser. 1, vol. 5, pp. 369, 372).
18 Freytag: *Bilder aus der deutschen Vergangenheit* vol. 1, p. 15; vol. 3, p. 658.

education (Bildung). As a consequence, the individual emotional and spiritual life become more important than the external plot.[19]

Hence, both works represent an early example of a history of mentalities which is, however, inevitably ideologically constructed, since this is the impression a historian who confines himself to the lives of a certain Müller from Friaul or a false husband from the Languedoc receives of the great span of time between the Teutons and the present century. The *Bilder*, however, are based on common historistical premises in their assumption of a continuous historical evolution which leads to the education of the nation and of the individual.[20] It is the poetical bonus of *Die Ahnen* that the supra-individual historical link finds its visible expression in a succession of generations over 1600 years: Nine young men from the lineage of the Ingo are tied into structurally similar plots. The fact that there is an overriding link between individuals, contrary to the liberal conception of man and society, reflects the precedence of 'unity' over 'freedom' in the days of the foundation of the Reich.[21] Since Freytag's illusionistic and objective style never emphazises the fictitiousness of the references – often in the shape of implausible motifs – his literary and historiographical oeuvre claims to show, like Ranke, 'wie es eigentlich gewesen' ('how things really happened').

Whereas past events are concretized diachronically as 'history' through the idea of an evolution, they are constituted within a particular era by the perspective of a protagonist in each volume. Minor characters and their environments also function to that end. In the third book of *Die Ahnen*, the hero Ivo, despite the great distance he travels, keeps meeting the same persons in different parts of the Reich, in Sicily, in the Holy Land and the Vistula area. Eventually, the bad meet their deserved ends and the good find happiness or at least a satisfying mission in life. Freytag regarded the terminability of the plot and "the inner coherence of its parts" as "structural principles of the historical novel," which are essential if a particular effect is intended. It is hoped that the reader "completely grasps the reasonable interrelation of events" so that he "gains the pleasant feeling of security and freedom,"[22] i.e. he is supposed to learn to assess his possibilities of operating within history. The optimistic assumption that one can get insights into the evolutionary direction

---

19 Cf. ibid. vol. 3, p. 581; pp. 656–57; vol. 1, p. 483; *Gesammelte Werke* ser. 1, vol. 5, p. 575; *Erinnerungen*, p. 277.
20 Cf. Droysen: *Historik*, p. 12 (ed. Hübner), p. 11 (ed. Leyh).
21 Cf. Limlei: *Geschichte als Ort der Bewährung*, p. 154.
22 Freytag: "Willibald Alexis: Isegrimm." Bucher et al., eds., *Realismus und Gründerzeit* vol. 2, pp. 285–87, here p. 285.

of history finds its concrete political expression in Freytag's praise of patriotic and Prussian tendencies in Alexis' *Isegrimm*. Thus, Freytag's poetology ultimately has a political intention.

His narrative technique, aiming to concentrate on one main character and to bring a concise plot to a satisfactory conclusion, is rooted in the ideology of liberal historism which began to dominate historiography and the 'kleindeutsch' (the idea of a German Reich excluding Austria national movement after 1848[23]) with Heinrich von Sybel's discourse "Über den Stand der neuen deutschen Geschichtsschreibung" as its typical manifestation. Sybel hails the new partiality of historians as a "most considerable progress" which was meant to be a bias towards the inexorable course of history.[24] The lost battles of the revolution appear from this point of view as an unsuccessful attempt to forestall an organic evolution. Supported by historical thinking, 'Realpolitik' aimed at a 'sensible' coming to terms with tradition and politically with Prussia. To participate in a tradition established in this spirit in *Die Ahnen* was no longer a liberal 'Fall'. As early as 1230, the Teutonic Knights, who conquered Prussia in the following decades, stood for an honest and brave policy of statesmanship of which the emperor and the princes were incapable. In the fifth and sixth volume of the book, the König family fights for Prussia and thus ultimately for Germany's freedom. National-liberal literature and historiography jointly set out to trace Prussia's 'Beruf' (vocation and profession) through history. Willibald Alexis' *Hosen des Herrn von Bredow*[25] preceded Droysen's academic elaboration in 1855, whose voluminous scholarly 'historical novel' and quasi-literary allegory *Geschichte Alexanders des Großen* (1833) anticipated the German unification through Prussia in the Greek one through Macedonia. In this piece, literary arrangement and scholarly consolidation of the Prussian view of history were, in fact, no longer clearly distinguishable.

Thus, the narrative poetics of Freytag's historical fiction and the 'kleindeutsch' historiography merge in an orientation towards political positions they see on the current agenda of history. Sybel also praises the new "clearly defined artistic form" and makes out a new, somehow national-liberal standard style as a direct result of the political reorientation[26]. With his firm, political realism,

---

23   Cf. Iggers: *The German Conception of History*, p. 91.
24   Sybel: "Über den Stand der neueren deutschen Geschichtsschreibung," p. 349; cf. Hardtwig: *Geschichtskultur und Wissenschaft*, pp. 224–44.
25   Cf. Alexis: "[Vorrede zu] Die Hosen des Herrn von Bredow." Lämmert et al., eds., *Romantheorie 1620–1880*, pp. 315–18, here p. 317; Hardtwig: *Geschichtskultur und Wissenschaft*, pp. 111–13.
26   "feste Kunstform." This aspect is also not taken into consideration in a most recent study *Geschichte des Historismus* by Jäger and Rüsen. Some of the aspects of contemporary historio-

the historian is in a position to abstain on the one hand from moralizing reflections of Old Liberals like Schlosser and on the other hand from seeing past events from the point of view of a ruling statesman, who has to be judged by his motives as well as by ethical standards.[27] This clearly corresponds to concurrent tendencies in the 'realistic' novel as they were discussed in the context of Freytag's *Soll und Haben* (1855). In Realism, objectivity is understood as the absence of narratorial comments, as an illusion where "facts speak for themselves"[28]. This understanding is the exact equivalent of the historiographical attempt to let history itself teach "practical lessons."[29] The guise of objectivity, however, serves an even more resolute bias in both variations. The fact that the narration of the historian is supposed to concentrate on an individual personality in order to give it a clear-cut outline reflects the displacement of Gutzkow's and Alexis' 'Vielheitsroman' by Freytag's unifying and singular hero.[30] By linking the attempt to understand a historical personality from his motives to the validity of eternal ethical principles, Sybel accepts the literary tendency of a figural narrator while maintaining a cosmos of "eminent eternal laws."[31]

The fact that a representative middle-class writer agrees on the whole with the 'kleindeutsch' historiography in its conception of the present, of history and narrative techniques, relates the historical novel more significantly to the political events of the 1870s and its social and intellectual driving forces than a few affirmative quotes from the text. Freytag's oeuvre is an integral element of middle-class culture and attitude of mind, which saw in the foundation of the Reich the "wonderful fulfilment of all its wishes and aspirations."[32] The unity of national culture and national policy, which had been sought since the 1850s and (allegedly) achieved in 1866/67, differs fundamentally from the sometimes severe disagreements over the present foundation of a nation-

---

 graphy (forms of art and political orientation towards the present) that Julian Schmidt discusses in his *Geschichte der deutschen Nationalliteratur* vol. 3, pp. 383–476, prove that there was an awareness of the unity of historiographical and literary discourse.

27 Cf. Sybel: "Über den Stand der neueren deutschen Geschichtsschreibung," pp. 356–58, quotation p. 350.
28 Robert Giseke: "Soll und Haben. Roman in sechs Büchern von Gustav Freitag. Eine Charakteristik." *Novellen-Zeitung* Ser. 3, 1 (1855), pp. 311–18, here p. 314, quoted from Steinecke: *Romanpoetik*, p. 158.
29 Sybel: "Über den Stand der neueren deutschen Geschichtsschreibung," p. 355.
30 Cf. Steinecke: *Romanpoetik*, pp. 34–8.
31 Spielhagen: "Der Held im Roman," pp. 98–9 ("große ewige Gesetze").
32 "alles Wünschen und Streben […] in so unendlich herrlicher Weise erfüllt." Sybel's letter to Hermann Baumgarten, January 1, 1871, Fenske, ed., *Im Bismarckschen Reich*, p. 37. Consequently, the first volume of *Die Ahnen* (1872) was met by the literary public with a much greater response than any other historical novel up to that point. Cf. Eggert: *Wirkungsgeschichte*, p. 176.

state. This unity becomes particularly clear in the field of the historical narrative since politics and the historical novel both return to history for purposes of identity formation as does historiography.

But to what extent are Freytag's works oriented towards the desired national reunification? The *Bilder* begin and end with a glance at the emmenent fulfilment of a middle-class historical tradition, which had been developed in this text, whereas *Die Ahnen* abstains from a portrait of the war of unification with France even though Freytag saw in it the pinnacle of national history.[33] The possible celebration of a collective achievement is briefly alluded to in the prediction of Ernst König, a veteran of the war of liberation, that "the grandsons will contribute to new victories." His son Victor sees the Germans still "being occupied with building the new house of their state."[34] The author's own reasons for leaving out the fate of the present generation, which is the final point in his ancestral line, are contradictory[35]. The decisive factor apparently was that a novel about the foundation of the Reich had to be written in about 1880, thus at a time when essential ideological preconditions for a 'realistic' poetics of transfiguration were no longer covered by the realities of society.[36]

In the last chapter of *Die Ahnen*, the assumed unity of the historical process and the intended synthesis with tradition become apparent in the genealogical research by the König family and a double marriage between the aristocracy and the bourgeoisie. Bismarck, however, ousted the Liberals in 1878 from their participation in the government and implemented a 'second foundation of the Reich.' The pride of the Liberals in the foundation of a nation-state was thus exposed as a misjudgement of the factual balance of power. Not only were government and middle-class party again in opposition, but the Liberals themselves split up and revealed their claims to represent the whole nation as illusory[37]. Since for Freytag the incomplete unity could not

---

33 Cf. Freytag: *Bilder aus der deutschen Vergangenheit* vol. 1, p. 14; vol. 3, pp. 654–58; *Erinnerungen*, p. 371.
34 Freytag: *Gesammelte Werke* ser. 1, vol. 5, pp. 641, 645 ("die Enkel werden bei neuen Siegen helfen," "über der Arbeit […], das Haus seines Staates zu zimmern").
35 Freytag on the one hand asserts technical problems since, as he said, he could not cope with an event as complex as this war by means of a fictitious hero, who is inevitably in a subordinate position. On the other hand, he sees in "the poetry in the course of history" ("Poesie des geschichtlichen Verlaufs"), which he implicitly denied, an adequate substitute for any novel; and this substitute, according to Freytag, has been accepted by the Germans (*Erinnerungen*, pp. 371–72).
36 Cf. Holz: *Flucht aus der Wirklichkeit*, pp. 188–89.
37 Cf. Born: *Von der Reichsgründung*, pp. 131–37. As to the relation of liberal national movement and the unification of the Reich "from above," cf. now Dann: *Nation und Nationalismus*, pp. 140–52.

be achieved without the Liberals, the years 1878/80 meant for him "a disaster of unforeseeable consequences."[38] His historical optimism oriented towards the middle class suffered a blow that undermined his firm nationalliberal poetics. After the liberal disaster, middle class heroes, indispensable in Freytag's view of history (to the effect that he had to create 'substitute citizens' in the volumes dealing with the Middle Ages), could only hold failed political beliefs. The cycle of novels ends in museum, a place of dead history, and with it Freytag's poetic works, though he himself lived until 1895.

A break in the poetics of the historical novel can thus be related to Bismarck's overtly conservative, 'second foundation of the Reich' rather than to the national unification in 1871.[39] In his growing silence, Freytag represents both national-liberal historiography and historical narrative. The same period saw the decline of the Prussian school of historians. Treitschke and Mommsen began to acknowledge the tension between the authoritarian nation-state and liberalism, which had been denied so far for the sake of harmony, even though the consequences were different. Both left the national-liberal group in the Reichstag, the former turning to the right, the latter to the left.[40] The national-liberal standard style broke down exactly at the point which Sybel had regarded as central in 1856: a tendentious Prussian perspective which had been cultivated in the works of Häusser, Droysen and Sybel was now criticized by Baumgarten in Treitschke's *Deutsche Geschichte im 19. Jahrhundert* because it harmed the inner unity of the Reich.[41] This confirms that the unanimity of the dominant faction of German historiography was tied to a political aim that was aggressively supported. The national-liberal standard style

---

38 Freytag: *Erinnerungen*, pp. 308–09.
39 Limlei: *Geschichte als Ort der Bewährung*, p. 197, who relates the development of the genre to the history of German liberalism, regards the foundation of the Reich as a "stylistic boundary." For this purpose, he has to include *Die Ahnen* in the "historical novel after the 1848 revolution." Moreover, he suggests a premature date for the shift of subject-matter to earlier ages, cf. below p. 205. On the other hand, Limlei characterizes the tragic heroism in Felix Dahn's *Kampf um Rom* (1876) accurately as post- and antiliberal (cf. ibid., pp. 200–02). The periodization of the historical novel corresponds, generally speaking, to the assessment of liberalism: Limlei locates the break – on the basis of Baumgarten's *Selbstkritik des deutschen Liberalismus* (1866) – at the moment of the compromise with the Prussian government (thus not in 1871) while I prefer to take seriously the national-liberal view that the foundation of the Reich meant a partial fulfilment of their own objectives. Cf. also Langewiesche: *Liberalismus*, pp. 106, 111, 164–67, 175–76, and Nipperdey: *Deutsche Geschichte*, pp. 314–18, 326, who sees neither in 1866 nor in 1871 a capitulation of the National Liberals to Bismarck and locates their "disaster" as late as 1878/79.
40 Cf. Iggers: *The German Conception of History*, pp. 122–23.
41 Cf. Baumgarten: *Treitschke's Deutsche Geschichte*, p. 40.

in literature and historiography was bound to disintegrate after its fulfilment since its unifying concept was superseded by political and social developments, such as, for example, the rise of the labor movement.

A closer look at the widely-held opinion that the foundation of the Reich entailed a significant change in the subject-matter of the historical novel confirms the view that 1878/79 was the more important turning point than 1870/71 from the point of view of the middle-class historical narrative since subject-matter that smacks of escapism (ancient cultures, Teutons, migration of the people as well as the Middle Ages) occurs increasingly only after 1880. A comparison of preferences for certain epochs in the 1870s and the 1880s reveals that earlier ages become more popular while interest in recent ones declines. The centuries before 1500 are apparently more attractive than the modern ages in the 1880s.[42] The treatment of these "exotic" subjects was unlikely to produce the political effects intended by the Liberals. With regard to the second foundation of the Reich the Liberals also lost supremacy in the bid for history.

Heinrich Laube's *Waldstein* (1864)[43] proves, however, that the form rather than the subject-matter is crucial to a monumental interpretation of national history since even though the novel is set in the Thirty Years War, a time of internal discord which is considered to be a national catastrophy, it has a vivid 'kleindeutsch' bias in its handling, explanation and assessment of the disaster through constellations of characters and plot. Waldstein (=Wallenstein) appears in the beginning as the innovator of the "German Reich," who envisages a strong empire as the political centre[44]. Historically, however, the treacherous commander fails ignominiously and hence definitively for the novelist, too. Only by portraying him as the victim of scheming foreigners, was Laube able to make national capital of this failure.[45] Taking Walter Scott as an example, Laube, however, adds a fictitious character to the historical one and nevertheless succeeds in remaining faithful to political intentions as well as to his-

---

42 Cf. Eggert: *Wirkungsgeschichte*, p. 209.
43 The triology *Der deutsche Krieg* with the three-volumed *Waldstein* as its middle part was among all historical novels the greatest public success of a famous author before 1870, cf. Eggert: *Wirkungsgeschichte*, p. 196. Laube is like Freytag a "representative of a specifically middle-class mentality," which after 1849 related its claim to the leadership of its own social class based on education to a 'politically realistic' Anschluss to Prussia, cf. Huesmann: "Jungdeutsches Bildungsbewußtsein und bürgerliche Krisenerfahrung," esp. p. 28.
44 Laube: *Waldstein* vol. 1, pp. 90–3. The fact that a seventeenth century emperor had to be a Habsburg is ignored and neutralized in a pro-Protestant spirit by a strong anti-Jesuit tendency.
45 Cf. ibid. vol. 3, pp. 68, 214, 305.

torical factuality. Hans Starschädel, a Northern German Protestant, remains loyal to the "great purpose in life, the Fatherland." In the end, he passes the political and moral judgement on the declining Waldstein, saying that he has "no heart for any ideal," that he is "no German." The narrator adds the current political lesson: the presumptuous commander lacked "precise plans for the German Reich" as well as idealistic willpower.[46] Laube, a former member of the Paulskirche parliament, strongly recommends that 'Realpolitik' and a sense of liberal principles should complement one another.

In *Waldstein* we find what Freytag avoided: a fictitious tradition of a national striving for unity. Authors and (some) readers are aware of this anachronism[47] which, of course, is ignored, when the strong national political intention is taken into consideration. For even a methodically conscious historian like Droysen did not refrain from depicting the medieval Hohenzollerns as German patriots.[48] Laube's anachronisms ask the reader to realize finally the unity which perniciously remained unachieved in history while Droysen assures the reader that the Prussian rulers had long since taken this business in hand. Freytag, however, need no longer call for action or seek for followers – a change which the foundation of the Reich had achieved despite the similar points of departure of the authors.

Die Ahnen also owes its existence to a different attitude towards history, thus to a different model for the novel than Laube's *Waldstein*. The fates of the commander, of the the page Leo Steinwald as a 'mediocre hero' and of various minor characters are constructed in keeping with common narrative patterns[49]. Traditional political and military history is only of minor interest. The factuality of the plot may not be important for the historicity of a historical novel since Freytag invents the plot almost completely, but it is built on a broad historical and cultural basis out of which grows a whole host of descriptions, many contemporary characters and some motifs. Freytag's contemporaries[50] already saw in this broad basis the work's characteristic feature. With regard to *Waldstein* and *Die Ahnen*, national attitude and its anachronistic

---

46 Ibid., pp. 109, 244, 97 ("großer Lebenszweck, [das] Vaterland," "kein Herz für irgend ein Ideal," "kein Deutscher." "bestimmte Pläne fürs Deutsche Reich").

47 Cf. Laube: "Erinnerungen." *Ausgewählte Werke* vol. 8, p. 51; Adolf Stahr: "Rez. über Willibald Alexis: Ruhe ist die erste Bürgerpflicht." *National-Zeitung* 11./12. 5. 1852, quoted from Steinecke: *Romanpoetik*, p. 36.

48 Cf. Droysen: *Geschichte der preußischen Politik* vol. 1, pp. 3–4, 457.

49 Leo enters as a 'pure fool' the service of his illegitimate father (!) Waldstein and two love plots, his own and Starschädel's, are subject to frequent changes. In the end, Leo has gone through an education which allows him to become a conscientious citizen.

50 Cf. Eggert: *Wirkungsgeschichte*, p. 177.

incorporation into the plot of the novel functions in an inverse proportion to a historical and cultural footing. It is no coincidence that the more committed novel was written before, the more historistical one after the foundation of the Reich. As a result of its de-politicizing effect, the success of Scheffel's and Ebers' historico-cultural novels also did not begin before 1875,[51] even though *Ekkehard* and *Die ägyptische Königstochter* had already been published in 1855 and 1864. *Waldstein* and *Die Ahnen* thus represent two variations of national-liberal historical fiction whose differences are rooted in their date of origin before or after the foundation of the Reich. Yet, as a late testimony of national-liberal historicism, Freytag's novel is closer to the intentions of the time before 1870 than to its escapist successors.

3.

Fontane's political ideas, unlike Freytag's, did not suffer under Bismarck's break with the Liberals in 1878, since the chancellor was absolutely central to.[52] Fontane, however, despised the bourgeoisie and particularly its pursuit of profit which had been immortalized in Freytag's *Soll und Haben*.[53] Freytag was confident that the moral force of "ordinary people" would enable them to act in history while the ingenious Bismarck convinced Fontane of the contrary: "the individual decides everything, is allowed to do everything, as long as he is equipped for it."[54] In Conrad Ferdinand Meyer's historical fiction, Bismarck's eminent personality became a determining subject. His *Jürg Jenatsch* (1874/1876) is supposed to be a partial justification of a politician who liberated his people from foreign rule, though by morally dubious means. While writing the novel, Meyer had to decide in view of his wealth of material whether he wanted a strict artistic form or a loosely built novel.[55] Thus, there was at the same time a choice between having a dominant protagonist and having one who is relativized by many characters. In a remark about Bismarck, Fontane notes, as it were, about this relation that "in the presence of

---

51 Cf. ibid., p. 210.
52 Cf. Loster-Schneider: *Der Erzähler Fontane*, p. 237.
53 Cf. Stefan Greif: "'… dieses gleich sehr zu hassende und zu liebende Preußen!' Der Altpreuße Theodor Fontane zwischen bürgerlicher Revolution und Wilhelminismus." Scheuer, ed., *Dichter und ihre Nation*, pp. 290–310, here p. 293.
54 Freytag: *Gesammelte Werke* ser. 1, vol. 5, p. 575 ("kleine Leute"); letter to his wife, June 6, 1879, Fontane: *Sämtliche Werke* ser. 4, vol. 3, p. 25 ("der *Einzelne* bestimmt alles, darf alles, wenn er der Mann danach ist").
55 Cf. Osborn: *Meyer or Fontane?*, pp. 93–4.

such a tyrant only second- and thirdrate characters will serve."[56] In keeping with this insight into the correlation between protagonist and character-constellation, Meyer's yearning for greatness made him write a novel possessing the rigidity of a novella.[57] Since he also wanted to discuss "epoque-making subjects: [...] the conflicting principles of law and power, politics and morality," only a responsible statesman and not a fictitious 'mediocre hero' is eligible for the role of the protagonist.[58] The need for representativeness is complementary to the concentration of characters and plot since *Jenatsch* is not intended to be merely Swiss regional history[59].

Meyer was concerned about the similarity between his Jenatsch and Bismarck ("Bismarckähnlichkeit"),[60] and not without reason, since his 'will to form' had aestheticized Jenatsch's character to such an extent that his life is to be read as a historically unspecific example of demonic excessiveness. Its gruesome end can only be understood in terms of tragic categories like hubris and nemesis[61]. Meyer, following his own classical poetics, saw in that end an example of the "eternally-human nature"[62], but it would be more precise to talk of a consistent subsumption of historical conflicts under poetological interpretative patterns. The fact that the view of history in his work is ultimately an ahistoric one[63] relativizes Meyer's affection for Bismarck, which is hardly founded politically, and its reflection in narrative technique. In Meyer's opin-

---

56 Letter to Eulenburg, March 12, 1881, Fontane: *Sämtliche Werke* ser. 4, vol. 3, p. 125 ("daß neben einem solchen Despoten nur unselbständige Naturen und Kräfte zweiten oder dritten Ranges dienen können").
57 Cf. letter to Rodenberg, April 21, 1880, Meyer/Rodenberg: *Briefwechsel*, p. 66.
58 Letter to Haessel, September 26, 1866, Meyer: *Sämtliche Werke* vol. 10, p. 277 ("die jetzt die Welt bewegen: [...] den Conflict von Recht u. Macht, Politik und Sittlichkeit").
59 Cf. letter to Haessel, September 5, 1866, ibid., p. 276. The great European policy is in fact mentioned. However, Meyer excessively strains his stylizing efforts with the etiquette "The Wallenstein from the Grisons. The Thirty Years War epitomized in a single character." ("Der bündnerische Wallenstein. Der dreißigjährige Krieg in einer einzigen großen Gestalt verkörpert.") (Meyer in a publisher's brochure in 1880, ibid., p. 302).
60 Letter to Rodenberg, March 28, 1891, Meyer/Rodenberg: *Briefwechsel*, p. 297.
61 Cf. Meyer: *Sämtliche Werke* vol. 10, pp. 236, 256, 263, 268. Moreover, the fact that Jenatsch does not pursue any longer at the peak of his power a realistic policy and instead toys with his friends and enemies and claims that he has to sacrifice his roots in the country (his Protestantism) to his political rise distinguishes Meyer's Bismarck allegory from the "myth Bismarck" whose structure was reconstructed by Rolf Parr in terms of discourse analysis. Moreover, *Jenatsch* implies a criticism of the assumption of the 'mythic Bismarck' that there are "points of contact between antagonistic paradigms" (Parr: "*Zwei Seelen*," p. 194).
62 Letter to Luise von François, May 1881, François/Meyer: *Briefwechsel*, p. 12 ("das Ewig-Menschliche").
63 Cf. Lutz: *Vom Ereignis zur Erzählung*, p. 31; Meyer: *Sämtliche Werke* vol. 10, pp. 261–62.

ion, history has "existential significance" in a sense that is only remotely related to politics and it appears to him as a symbol-laden space where the human life, subject to the law of crime and punishment and orientated towards death, becomes visible again and again.[64]

Bismarck drew not only the attention of Meyer and Fontane towards "men [...] who made history"[65] but also that of many historians. The trend resulted in a rising number of historical biographies, wherein many historians "likewise arrived at the conviction [...] that heroic power is essential for the great turning-points in history."[66] Like Meyer, historians were intrigued by the "enigma of the personality,"[67] whose solution might require an increasing use of literary procedures. This tendency once more unified literature and historiography. The poet's orientation towards the uncertain 'eternally human' helped him not to lose sight of ethical principles, while historians like Sybel exempted the successful genius from a moral judgement even though he resorted to violence.[68] A character like Walser who succeeds in the course of the story and settles down in a comfortable middle-class life allows a critical reading of such respect for authority. While he is uneasy in the beginning about Jenatsch's "unrestrained will," Walser later exempts the murderer and the one who broke the treaty from any human jurisdiction since he "acted for the welfare of the fatherland."[69] The reader witnesses the fascination of power and violence for the petit bourgeois when Walser and Jenatsch meet after that incident. The fact, however, that Jenatsch finally falls victim to Lucretia Planta's revenge beneath a statue of the goddess Justice puts the beguiled Walser likewise in the wrong.[70]

Fontane's admiration for the historically eminent politician Bismarck did not tempt him into monumentalizing historical personalities. In *Vor dem Sturm* the relation between historical protagonists and fictitious characters is dissimilar to 'classic' historical novels or to *Jenatsch*. The peasants, bourgeois and noblemen in Fontane's first novel can be subsumed under those who were

---

64 Moos: *Dasein als Erinnerung*, pp. 142–43.
65 Treitschke: *Politik* vol. 1, p. 6.
66 Otto Hintze on Reinhold Koser's biography of Frederick the Great, quoted after Schleier: "Reichsgründung und Geschichtsschreibung bis 1914," p. 528 ("wieder zu der der Überzeugung geführt, [...] daß zu den großen Wendepunkten der Geschichte immer eine heroische Menschenkraft" gehört); cf. ibid., pp. 528–34.
67 Treitschke: *Politik* vol. 1, p. 6; cf. Jacobson: "Jürg Jenatsch," p. 88.
68 Cf. Iggers: *The German Conception of History*, p. 119.
69 Meyer: *Sämtliche Werke* vol. 10, pp. 35, 251 ("unbändiger Willen," "zum Heil des Vaterlandes notwendige Taten").
70 Cf. ibid., pp. 253–54, 268.

affected by history without playing a decisive part in it. They are not mediators of 'great' history and in this respect similar to Freytag's characters, but they act independently and contribute to the Prussian uprising, even against a irresolute and weak king. The only one of all the characters who dies heroically is the "somewhat stiff and pedantic" deputy rector Othegraven.[71] Thus, in his definitively patriotic novel, Fontane offers a counterpoint against an increasing fixation on historical and political awareness about the Hohenzollerns.[72] His protagonists as well as Freytag's are fictitious, but on an entirely different basis. Fontane's preference for biographies, memoirs and anecdotes enabled him to shape a great number of characters upon existing models.

The use of material from local history points to the *Wanderungen durch die Mark Brandenburg* as the point of departure of Fontane's narratives. The novel retains the specific technique of evoking historical duration. In *Vor dem Sturm* the narrator's comments on various strange objects in village churches and in castles echo those in the travel-journals and result in a historical deepening of the novel's present, which goes back as far as the days of colonizing Cistercians[73]. This is, however, a method which amounts to nothing more than a selective and anecdotal evocation of historical events. Fontane's portrayal of history focuses only on selected moments, particularly since the plot of sevenhundred pages concentrates on two months. The style of his historical thinking is exactly the style of telling a single story like *Vor dem Sturm*. The way of telling the story, similar to genre paintings, is familiar and the fact that its eight areas of life are only loosely put together with few figural interferences is not neutralized by narrative techniques such as anticipations and interconnected symbolic relations. A dispute within the novel as to the correct way of telling history confirms these findings. Lewin von Vitzewitz gives a comprehensive account of Napoleon's flight from Moscow whereas his sister criticizes the didactic tone and the tiresome striving for completeness. The fact that *Vor dem Sturm* specifically meets Renate's expectations of a historical narrative is only concealed by Lewin's mocking comments since what else does Fontane offer other than "historical snap-shots" (Guckkastenbilder) which appear at first sight "comfortable" and "handy"?[74] The "connection" claimed by Lewin is only alluded to in history and fictitious story. Historical thinking

---

71 Fontane: *Sämtliche Werke* ser. 1, vol. 3, p. 587; cf. p. 706.
72 Cf. Hardtwig: *Geschichtskultur und Wissenschaft*, pp. 149–52.
73 It retains the air of a tourist's guide, cf. Fontane: *Sämtliche Werke* ser. 1, vol. 3, pp. 14, 54 (*Vor dem Sturm*), ser. 2, vol. 1, pp. 753–54 (*Oderland*).
74 Ibid. ser. 1, vol. 3, p. 49.

and poetology correspond to one another in *Vor dem Sturm*, and the latter finds its justification in the former.[75]

Anecdotes form the centre of both. They not only shape Fontane's conception of how to discover and to write history – an anecdote is "the best of all histories" – but also his narrative technique, since his characters would most enjoy stringing together an infinite number of anecdotes.[76] From this technique ensue no continuous and stringent courses of history, but an "incomplete vividness" which Fontane already saw as typical of his *Wanderungen*.[77] He learnt as a contemporary journalist and historian that the historiographer, too, has to construct hi*stories*[78]. His fictitious historical work is, however, not so much shaped by the reflection of the constructivistic character of every historical narrative, but by an abstention from a rigid narrative unity. And yet Fontane reaps aesthetic profit from this historiographical and poetological retreat since gaps allow interpretation. Dubslav von Stechlin's principle applies here, too: "There are no unassailable truths and if there are any, they are boring."[79]

Since Fontane does not pursue the political aesthetics of national-liberal historicists, he feels entitled to reject a dramatically intensified plot "with only one hero." In his opinion, the "'Vielheitsroman' with its extensiveness and obstacles, its masses of portraits and episodes" is "equal to the 'Einheitsroman'."[80] *Vor dem Sturm*, however, does not reopen the socially and politically

---

75 For Osborne: *Meyer or Fontane?*, pp. 134–35; "Theodor Fontane," pp. 428–31, Fontane's genre style deals with the disillusionment of the 1870 war, where the feuilletonistic character apparently ironizes the usual glorification of the gruesome events. The selective representation of history in *Vor dem Sturm* cannot sufficiently be explained in terms of this intention, but is rooted in the technique of the *Wanderungen*. Compared to the latter, *Vor dem Sturm* is in fact the more concise work, cf. the integration of the Derfflinger episode in Gusow (*Oderland*, Fontane: *Sämtliche Werke* ser. 2, vol. 1, pp. 732–47) and Guse (*Vor dem Sturm*, ibid. ser. 1, vol. 3, pp. 132–34).

76 Fontane: *Sämtliche Werke* ser. 3, vol. 4, p. 413 ("das Beste aller Historie"); cf. letter to Wichmann, June 2, 1881, ibid. ser. 4, vol. 3, p. 135; ibid. ser. 1, vol. 3, p. 198.

77 Ibid. ser. 2, vol. 1, p. 547 ("lückenhafte Anschaulichkeit").

78 Cf. ibid. ser. 1, vol. 6, p. 387, "Historiography: [...] Stories and history / Grow and change when they are written." ("Geschichtschreibung: [...] Geschichten und Geschichte / Wachsen und wechseln im Entstehen.")

79 Ibid. ser. 1, vol. 5, p. 10 ("Unanfechtbare Wahrheiten gibt es überhaupt nicht, und wenn es welche gibt, so sind sie langweilig.").

80 Letter to Heyse, December 12, 1878, Fontane: *Vor dem Sturm* (Aufbau Edition) vol. 1, p. 369. Among historians, Burckhardt is particularly close to Fontane and contributed to his refutation of historical linearity. Cf. Stefan Greif: "'…dieses gleich sehr zu hassende und zu liebende Preußen!' Der Altpreuße Theodor Fontane zwischen bürgerlicher Revolution und Wilhelminismus." Scheuer, ed., *Dichter und ihre Nation*, pp. 290–310, here p. 296.

important, debate about the poetics of the novel which had been decided twenty years earlier by *Soll und Haben* against the 'democratic' novel of 'coexistence' (Roman des 'Nebeneinander')[81]. With *Schach von Wuthenow* Fontane had already gone on to narratives which focus on a single protagonist and which include a 'coexistence' only when seen together with the 'cycle of Berlin novels'. His own remarks tend to display a preference for "lovable characters" and an interest in "all sorts of human beings," which appear to be the nucleus of his attempt to evoke the reader's empathy for as many characters as possible.[82] Consequently, he does not find fault with the fact that in *Die Ahnen* each book revolves around one particular individual. Instead, he sees its main flaw in the unsubstantiality of the characters.[83]

The contrasts between Fontane's and Meyer's historical fictions which depict a vigorous hero within a dramatically intensified plot in *Jenatsch* and Bernd von Vitzewitz as a finally humanistic squire and a heroic deputy rector among many other characters, who are calmly observed by the narrator, in *Vor dem Sturm* are not meant to be looked at from the aspect of ideological implications arising from a poetics which has not even been made explicit[84]. Both have to be viewed against the 'Prussian' historical novel from which they differ ideologically in the way they handle Bismarck's impact; one must also consider Fontane's different narrative structure. They do not use the relevance to the present of a historical subject-matter provided for by a historical continuum. Their view of history excludes a cooperation with national-liberal historiography from which they dissociate themselves through the topoi of historical fiction.[85] Fontane depicts faith in the unconditional Prussian excellence, which others, chiefly historians, regard as the real national failing.[86]

Even though Freytag, too, declares his novel to be 'pure' poetry, the aesthetic aspect controls the other points of reference of the historical narrative only in Meyer's and Fontane's works. Thus, the foundation of the Reich influenced their development as artists: for they were forced to cope with the war experiences in their literary works such as *Huttens letzte Tage* (1872) or *Krieg*

---

81 Thus Steinecke: *Romanpoetik*, pp. 42–3; Humphrey: "The Napoleonic Wars in the Historical fiction," p. 119; Eggert: "Der historische Roman," p. 354.
82 Letter to Hertz, June 17, 1866, Fontane: *Vor dem Sturm* (Aufbau-edition) vol. 1, p. 328; cf. *Sämtliche Werke* ser. 2, vol. 1, p. 14.
83 Cf. Fontane: "[Rezension von Gustav Freytag:] Die Ahnen." *Sämtliche Werke* ser. 3, vol. 1, pp. 308–25, here p. 322.
84 For a contrary view see Osborne: *Meyer or Fontane?*, p. 104.
85 Cf. Spitzer: *Untersuchungen*, pp. 182–83. Cf. the ironical treatment of a "universal history in a big way" in *Vor dem Sturm*, Fontane: *Sämtliche Werke* ser. 1, vol. 3, p. 173.
86 Cf. ibid., p. 616.

gegen Frankreich (1873–76). The break of 1878/79 thus did not need to have the same disastrous effect as it had on Freytag. Fontane certainly depicts the divisions of a class society in his Berlin novels, which are no longer historical ones, while clinging to the "glorifying duty of art."[87] Meyer continued in his historical novellas to pursue the course he had already taken in *Jenatsch* of a continuous aesthetization of history.

A genuine literary criticism of the nineteenth century form of relating history was not brought about until Raabe's *Odfeld* in 1888. The hi*story*'s origin in the subjectivity of the author becomes apparent where it plays with the reader's claim for authenticity. The narrator first offers a 'plausible' explanation of why the cave on the Ith, which is crucial to the plot, cannot be found again, before claiming possession of this cave for himself and to the incidents which occur therein.[88] Setting and action have thus been declared fictitious since they owe their existence to a conscious decision on the part of the author. The usual delimitation from historiography through forewords and other personal testimonies (commonly glossed over, in fact, in the novel by an illusion of referentiality indistinguishable from historiography) is incorporated into the text in a way which anticipates the self-reflexivity of modern literature despite its roots in the comic narrative. Thus, Raabe achieves "a realism of narration rather than of the narrated."[89]

Raabe's ironic play embraces even more stereotypes of the 'realistic' historical fiction. Whereas descriptions of weather play a decorative role in Fontane's novels, these images assume a decisive function in the plot of Freytag's novels.[90] Raabe's narrator, however, explains the various means, like cloudbursts or Prussian canons, which God as the master of history uses to influence the events.[91] Thus he treats ironically the usual externalization and objectification of narratorial intrusion and comments. The drawing of "world history" on Master Buchius' table with the help of chalk, a loaf of bread, a herring and a tureen ridicules the attempt to focus locally 'great' history in the historical novel, as can be observed in Meyer.[92] As when the old man in the final scene is no longer able to tame a raven he has kept in his room and has to release Odin's horrifying bird, a ghostly messenger of death, through the

---

87 Fontane: "[Rezension von] Paul Lindau: Der Zug nach dem Westen." Ibid. ser. 3, vol. 1, pp. 561–70, here p. 569.
88 Cf. Raabe: *Sämtliche Werke* vol. 17, p. 149.
89 Sammons: *Raabe*, p. 337.
90 Cf. Freytag: *Gesammelte Werke* ser. 1, vol. 4, pp. 315, 318.
91 Cf. Raabe: *Sämtliche Werke* vol. 17, p. 109. Cf. Meyer-Krentler: "Homerisches und wirkliches Blau."
92 Raabe: *Sämtliche Werke* vol. 17, p. 50.

window,⁹³ Raabe's tale from the Seven Years War reflects a contemporary boom in heroism, particularly in the Teutonic historical novel. In Dahn's *Kampf um Rom* (1876), the defiantly heroic Goths were shown the way "to the North, towards Thule!" by a falcon which had been released toward the heavens under a transfigured evening sky.⁹⁴

There is also a political dimension in Raabe's aesthetic criticism of the illusory historical novel. By revealing the traditional reconciliation of individual and society, of private life and world history as a narrative construct, he changes its ideological function. It no longer serves the social and political interests of the bourgeoisie and instead reveals their illusions. By disclosing his poetical techniques, Raabe within his own works entrenches himself too deeply, however, in the field of autonomous fiction to be able in his works, according to Brewster, to reveal "the contradiction between heterogeneous components of the genre [in Geppert's sense]" or to reveal the 'historiographical truth' as fiction and illusion⁹⁵, particularly since the narrator in *Odfeld* sympathizes as well with his protagonist's understanding of history. The old scholar adheres to a historia magistra vitae. When he evokes classical examples, any historicity fades away, leaving behind "only a difference in the course of time and in the costume." The narrator consequently dissociates himself from nineteenth-century "empirical sciences."⁹⁶ Thus, the signifier and the signified of poetical signs in *Odfeld* paradoxically diverge from a historical point of view. The negation of an unequivocal meaning goes beyond the historical narrative of the century but protagonist and narrator try to take refuge in pre-modern historical thinking. However, this retreat also leads to the establishment of basic narrative forms which subject the 'realistic' coherent narration to an inherent criticism: "Repetition, circular movement, a void diachrony with incidents which go beyond the moment, characterize history in *Odfeld* in a double sense (narratio, historia) and neither the one nor the other guarantees an unequivocal meaning."⁹⁷

Thus, Raabe holds in the second half of the nineteenth century the aesthetically most advanced position in the field of historical fiction. The three points of reference no longer act in combination as in Gustav Freytag's na-

---

93 Cf. ibid., pp. 217–20.
94 Dahn: *Ein Kampf um Rom*, p. 953.
95 Brewster: *Raabes historische Fiktion*, pp. 143, 16a. Brewster comes closer to my position when he admits that Raabe's narration is not based on "hermeneutical reflection" and does not contain an implicit theory of historiography (cf. ibid., pp. 161–62).
96 Raabe: *Sämtliche Werke* vol. 17, pp. 103, 29 ("nur ein Unterschied in der Zeitenfolge und im Kostüm," "empirische Wissenschaften").
97 Brewster: *Raabes historische Fiktion*, p. 299.

tional-liberal historism. The later Raabe is sceptical about the epistemological and interpretive claim of historiography[98] and rejects the idea that a part of history can be rationally orientated towards the present. This historical turn becomes even more obvious since Raabe, too, tried before 1870 to "raise the ghosts of the past in order that the hopeful faith in a happy and proud future should not be lost."[99] Like Freytag and other Liberals, he still saw in the national unification the resolution of "*all*" contradictions."[100] In *Odfeld*, however, the belief of the middle-class in their own ability to act in history is literally buried because young Thedel von Münchhausen, who remains on the Odfeld after the battle, is the last survivor of those hopeful 'mediocre heroes' who epitomized the liberal optimism about history in the first half of the century that was still present in Freytag's works.[101] In the 1880s national unity, the objective that previously had been both longed for and hotly disputed, loses its glorious appeal, which formerly integrated various social groups and cultural disciplines.

4.

The three points of reference of our genre-model, i.e. aesthetic innovation, examination of scholarly historiography and political commitment, can also be seen to converge in one contemporary author – Günter Grass. He can be compared to Gustav Freytag. Grass' publication of the *Blechtrommel* in 1959 coincided with the beginning of the exploration of National Socialism by historical research. His novel represents in its transformation of historical conflicts into narrative structures a new type of historical novel. Moreover, Grass sees his model of historical fiction as a corrective of a naively objectivistic historiography which conceals individual perspectives and social processes.[102] In activly supporting the Social Democrats Grass was standing for one of the most influential political forces in the 60s and early 70s.

---

98 Cf. Daemmrich: "Raabe's View of Historical Processes," pp. 108, 112.
99 Raabe: "Kleist von Nollendorf," p. 520 ("die Geister der Vergangenheit heraufzuholen, daß der siegesfreudige Glaube an eine glückliche, stolze Zukunft […] nicht verloren gehe."). For a treatment of Raabe's role as a propagandist of German unification see Meyer-Krentler in this volume, pp. 146–52.
100 Manthey: "Raabe und das Scheitern des deutschen Liberalismus," p. 89.
101 Cf. Limlei: *Geschichte als Ort der Bewährung*, p. 68.
102 Cf. Neuhaus: *Grass*, pp. 39–40; Durzak: "Geschichte ist absurd," pp. 15–7; Brode: *Zeitgeschichte im erzählenden Werk*, pp. 76–91, esp. p. 89.

Historical fiction in the decade of reunification is characterized by a concurrence between playful aesthetic experiments and a reappraisal of national history, particularly of the Third Reich, while some eminent authors turn away from German history to the impending apocalyptical end of humanity or its mythical beginnings (Grass, *Die Rättin*, Christa Wolf, *Kassandra*).[103] Literature did not comply with political claims that national identity should be boosted by a positive memory of one's own history. Rather the critical dealing with the past has been crucial to the formation of an identity in West Germany. The search for self-definition by identifying with forces of resistance and with the victims of tyranny logically entailed a negative assessment of the nation, the nation-state and its history.[104] Literature dealing with National Socialism formed a new narrative pattern at the close of the 70s – the 'Väterliteratur', moving thus from the analysis of history and society to the personal guilt of individuals and the dismay of post-war generations.[105] As a consequence, the relationship between literature and history is largely characterized by "opposition." In an age of catastrophic fears "where history seems to have become impossible," literature could see itself as a "poetic counter-action."[106] The less history was understood in terms of tradition and promise of progress, the more it was open to post-modern play and experimentation. Wolfgang Hildesheimer, for instance, tells the story of an English lord – who meets Goethe – and discusses his avant-gardist position in the psychoanalytical analysis of art, even though the lord never lived (*Marbot*). Attempts at an approach to past realities instead of turning away from them were most likely to be sustained in "exotic," historical themes or in 'Vergangenheitsbewältigung' (coming to terms with the past) in literature.

The literature about National Socialism appears to be most sensitive to stimuli from historiography, particularly since the 'Historikerstreit' – the debate about the 'singularity' of the Holocaust – had a remarkable publicity among recent historiographical disputes. A more far-reaching effect in his-

---

103 Cf. David Roberts: "The German Historical Novel in the Twentieth Century: Continuities and Discontinuities: II – The Postwar Generation." Roberts and Thomson, eds., *The Modern German Historical Novel*, pp. 171–80, here pp. 179–80.

104 Cf. Michael Zimmermann: "Negativer Fixpunkt und Suche nach positiver Identität. Der Nationalsozialismus im kollektiven Gedächtnis der alten Bundesrepublik." Loewy, ed., *Holocaust*, pp. 128–43, here p. 136.

105 Cf. Ehlers: "Erinnerungsarbeit," p. 226; Briegleb: "Vergangenheit in der Gegenwart," pp. 89–95.

106 Schnell: "Zwischen Geschichtsphilosophie und 'Posthistoire'," p. 354. Fritz Martini gives a superficial account of "Über die gegenwärtigen Schwierigkeiten des historischen Erzählens."

toriography can already be attributed to the 'historicization' of National Socialism that Martin Broszat, then the director of the 'Institut für Zeitgeschichte,' called for in 1985 and which was also welcomed by Jürgen Habermas[107]. Since the 'Vergangenheitsbewältigung,' according to Broszat, "had been for some time reduced to rhetoric without providing energy and imagination for a new morally stimulating historical reflection," National Socialism should on the one hand be looked at in a more distant, thus 'historical' way, and on the other hand made accessible to the historical experience by a lively, realistic narration and concretization[108]. This historicization does not affect the political and moral verdict on the Third Reich. It is the special narrative technique of a historicization such as is suggested by Broszat that makes it so important for historical fiction: He calls, for instance, for "a multi-dimensional story inhabited [...] by powerful and psychologically plausible characters" and examples of resistance and persecution, which provide the reader with "historical insights" and facilitate a "subjective acquisition," an emphatic "comprehension of past deeds, despair and errors."[109] This goes beyond a general return in historiography to narration[110] and suggests parallel developments in literature and historiography comparable to those in the national-liberal discourse on history.[111]

---

107 Cf. Johann Baptist Metz: "Für eine anamnetische Kultur." Loewy, ed., *Holocaust*, pp. 35–41, here p. 36; Habermas: "Eine Art Schadensabwicklung." *"Historikerstreit,"* pp. 62–7, here p. 72. Cf. Henke and Natoli, eds., *Mit dem Pathos der Nüchternheit*, esp. pp. 155–71. Hella Ehlers: "Erinnerungsarbeit gegen Vergessen und 'Entsorgung'. On the Treatment of the Experience of German Facism in Prose Works of the Last Decade in the Federal Republic." Williams, Parker, and Smith, eds., *German Literature at a Time of Change 1989–1990*, pp. 225–42, however, puts the narrative pattern of the "Väterliteratur" forward against 'revisionist' tendencies.

108 Broszat and Friedländer: "Um die 'Historisierung des Nationalsozialismus'," p. 349; cf. ibid., pp. 349–51; Backes, Jesse, and Zitelmann: "Was heißt 'Historisierung'?," pp. 26–8, 36–9; Broszat: *Nach Hitler*, pp. 159–73. James Sheehan, too, uses the notion 'historicizing' for the way of dealing with NS history recommended by him, cf. "Zukünftige Vergangenheit," p. 282.

109 Broszat and Friedländer: "Um die 'Historisierung' des Nationalsozialismus," pp. 340, 349, 351. His principles found expression in the vol. 6 of Broszat's series *Bayern in der NS-Zeit*, Fröhlich: *Die Herausforderung des Einzelnen. Geschichten [!] über Widerstand und Verfolgung*. It has to be noted that our specific interest in narratological problems is only one aspect of a historiographical 'historicization'.

110 Cf. Kocka: "Zurück zur Erzählung?"

111 The precarious character of a reconstruction of the minds of those who lived in the Third Reich and the political misunderstandings which may arise from that became apparent in 1988 when the President of the Bundestag, Philipp Jenninger, lost his position because a few sentences in his speech quoting culprits and fellow travellers were interpreted not as

The 'Vergangenheitsbewältigung' in literature is in fact also shaped by a tendency towards 'historicization'. Ludwig Harig's "novel about my father" *Ordnung ist das ganze Leben*, which was published in the year of the "Historikerstreit," can be read as a revision of 'Väterliteratur.' It provides a detailed description of the nationalist and militarist character of his father and his petit-bourgeois mentality – a life that is not judged but is depicted in all ambivalence. Another novel by Harig, *Weh dem, der aus der Reihe tanzt* (1990), aims directly at the centre of the fascination of the Third Reich, namely at the question: "How was it possible that the Germans hailed Hitler, that adolescents were intrigued by Jungvolk and Hitler Youth, that people were unaware of terror and extermination?" The inclusion of sayings and mottoes into chapter headings of the autobiographical novel, which reveal their meaning only to those who are initiated into the socio-cultural context, suggests that Harig wants to come to a better understanding of a mentality. His life as a student, a member of the Hitler Youth, a confirmed Protestant and a worker (Arbeitsmann) as well as the influences upon him are, however, hardly ever evoked in longer passages because the author intrudes on the experiences by refering to a qualitative historical distance and by describing and reflecting upon the process of remembering. Harig's narration of his own childhood moves in a triangle of memories, investigations and the historical plot. Moreover, the triangular structure basically corresponds to a trinomial in historical sciences which consists of the recollection of historical tradition, rational research and a re-narration of the past.[112] Both literature and historiography, which shared their illusionism in the nineteenth century,[113] feel thus obliged in the present to reveal their procedures, be it with regard to poetics or to methodical research.

The two time levels allow Harig certain historical insights, which on the one hand confront former convictions – like, for instance, the enthusiasm for the war in 1939 – with the sober insights of the older man. On the other hand, the child-like experience, avowedly devoid of reflection,[114] is subjected to the supremacy of a critical reviewing of the past. Thus its earlier seductiveness could only be said to win out in few cases. For instance, when the narrator is reminiscing about the film "Hitlerjunge Quex," the immediacy of the experience which he conveys makes possible an emphatic understanding of

---

'erlebte Rede' (narrative monologue), but as representing his own views. Cf. Jenninger: "Von der Verantwortung."
112 Cf. Rüsen: *Lebendige Geschichte*, pp. 71–3.
113 Cf. Brewster: *Raabes historische Fiktion*, pp. 91–3.
114 Cf. Harig: *Weh dem*, p. 111.

that time for the reader. According to Harig, it is ultimately impossible to understand a brutal ideology: "Was everything – colours, song and uniform – nothing but a temptation without meaning and reason? […] I want to know. I do not know. I have to know. No, I do not know."[115] Harig's break with National Socialism takes place, however, in passing – "as if nothing had happened."[116] There is no reply in his account of the member of the Hitler Youth to the overriding question of why the Germans let themselves be lead into war and mass murder. What an autobiographical memoir like *Weh dem, der aus der Reihe tanzt* ultimately makes us aware of is the gulf between the innocuousness of the individual, his feeling for freedom, and his operating in a barbaric machine,[117] which can only be reconstructed from different sources by those who remember. The scouting games did not stand for a war of aggression, 'Judenseife' does not express anything about the idea of genocide to such young persons. Thus, Harig's retrospective and individual perspective on history does not only confirm the productiveness of Broszat's suggestions but also illustrates the bounds of intelligibility. The fact, however, that the historical background has been considerably reduced is due to Harig's technique of remembering – nothing but his own experiences are real for him,[118] in contrast historiography does not subject itself to this restriction.

In the final sentence of Harig's novel we find the 'bone of contention' in the shape of *the* Hitler quotation on the German youth: "For the rest of their lives, they won't be free any more."[119] Two years later, Bernhard Haupert and Franz Josef Schäfer chose the same motto for their biography of a member of the Hitler Youth who became a tank-driver: *Jugend zwischen Kreuz und Hakenkreuz*. In their attempt to apply the methods of Oral History and hermeneutical sociology to an exemplary life under National Socialism, something "individual" serves as a "foil for the understanding of historical courses" in an even more consistent way than suggested by Broszat.[120] There is a striking reference to Harig's novel in that the protagonist comes from a village in the neighbourhood of Harig's Sulzbach. But history in this book is not seen from the point of view of a contemporary. Instead, the authors reconstruct the self-evident, hence unstated sociocultural factors in a biography,

---

115 Ibid., p. 76 ("War alles, Fahne, Lied und Uniform, nichts als eine Verführung ohne Sinn und Verstand? […] Ich möchte es wissen. Ich weiß es nicht. Ich muß es wissen. Nein, ich weiß es nicht.").
116 Ibid., p. 244 ("als ob nichts gewesen wäre").
117 Cf. ibid., pp. 102–03.
118 Cf. ibid., p. 62.
119 Ibid., p. 5 ("Und sie werden nicht mehr frei, ihr ganzes Leben.").
120 Haupert and Schäfer: *Jugend zwischen Kreuz und Hakenkreuz*, p. 229.

before approaching the innermost feelings of a deceased person. By choosing the method of an 'objective and hermeneutical analysis of photographs,' historiography apparently seeks to compete with literature in a field which it had traditionally left to the latter, namely the insights into the character of an unknown individual.[121]

But the analysis of six photographs of the tank-driver Josef Schäfer amounts to nothing more than a few suggestive question and simple physiognomy[122]. Even though the theory presents "internalized models of normality" as the point where individual aspects and those that are typical of society meet, the character-analysis never goes beyond the ordinary: "He dreamt of seeing the world, of travelling to far-off shores, of becoming an engine driver, of leaving the confines of his village."[123] While the thouroughly researched portrayal of the place of origin leads to a better understanding of the attitude of the people under National Socialism than Harig's childhood memories, the attempted approach at Josef's character and his individual view of the world fails since it does not succeed in combining various clues into a narrative portrayal. Thus, as an application to an exemplary character, the linguistically clumsy account by a former member of the Hitler Youth of how he enjoyed the premilitary training is only followed by the remark: "As usually Josef's enthusiasm for shooting [...] was positively supported by the Hitler Youth."[124] While the apolitical horizon of a young man sets the limit for Harig's retrospective technique, Josef Schäfer does not gain the desired measure of personality and literary stature.

Ulla Berkéwicz's *Engel sind schwarz und weiß* (1992) offers a purely poetic evocation of growing up in the Third Reich. According to the publisher's advertisements, the novel is specifically meant to be a product of the discussions about a history of mentality and of everyday life, which Broszat wanted to use for his new approach to the Third Reich. Within fiction, Berkéwicz (b. 1951) reveals to the reader the most immediate perspective of an adolescent who, born in 1923, belongs like Harig, Schäfer and Broszat to the Hitler Youth generation. Do we finally get to know "the spell which was sung in the innermost cup of the brown flower?"[125] There is no lack of evocations of such

---

121   Cf. Droysen: *Historik* (ed. Leyh), p. 239.
122   Cf. Haupert and Schäfer: *Jugend zwischen Kreuz und Hakenkreuz*, pp. 238, 246, quotation p. 250: "Josef's facial expression [...] indicates a introverted man with a distinctly emotional life."
123   Ibid., pp. 16, 250.
124   Ibid., p. 153.
125   Berkéwicz: *Engel sind schwarz und weiß*, p. 133 ("welcher Zauber im innersten Kelch der braunen Blume gesungen" wurde).

linguistic kitsch. The reader, however, is not given vivid descriptions of those consecrations of the flag, campfires and mid-summer celebrations that captivated the 'Pimpf' Reinhold Fischer.[126] Moreover, the hero is only a half-convinced National Socialist and he offers the reader a potential for identification because of his *rejection* of Nazi violence. Whereas Harig's narrative mode disrupts his own juvenile enthusiasm and thus opens up a second, critical perspective, Berkéwicz imposes a shattered existence upon her hero, who is at the same time Nazi leader and resistance fighter as well as a Wehrmacht soldier and a hide-out fellow of Russian Jews. That is why her story loses any plausibility. To evoke the fascination of National Socialism and to offer at the same time an ideologically correct identification is bound to go beyond a novel which focuses on a single character.

The above-mentioned examples of recent literature on the Third Reich indicate the problems of historicization. However, these do not affect the explicitness of the verdict on National Socialism, rather but the literary and historiographical (narrative) techniques of depicting history. There is no discernable impact of reunification, particularly since a "casting off of the German past" (Wehler) which was feared in some quarters, has not taken place. Historicization in the 80s began at a time when national unity was beyond political expectations. Interaction between the historical novel and historiography can be found, just as at the time of the foundation of the Reich, in narrative techniques and in the choice of subject-matter. The program 'historicization of National Socialism' combines both aspects. The fundamental dissociation in both disciplines of poetology and historical theory, however, should not be overlooked. If the academic character of historiography were made up of structural transparency and self-reflexivity rather than of theory and generalizations about social groups and structures, a point that has been raised in the discussion about the history of everyday life or micro-history, it could well be compatible with literature which was guided by the same principles in the modernist period. However, other features of literary modernism like the dissolution of a coherent plot run against the conception of a single 'history'.[127] And although there has been talk of an "unstoppable approximation to the individual"[128] in the history of everyday life, our literary and historiographical examples emphasize specific points in the continuum of the individual and the 'general' and seem to be incapable of escaping it.

---

126 Cf. ibid., pp. 71–2.
127 Cf. Rüsen: *Lebendige Geschichte*, pp. 74–5.
128 Zang: *Die unaufhaltsame Annäherung an das Einzelne*.

5.

The decade before the reunification with its many new museums, best-seller historical biographies and novels, academic and public debates about Prussia or about the 'Barfußhistoriker' (amateur historians) was very conscious of the past,[129] which does not necessarily contradict the critical attitude of literature towards history, since both come together in their criticism of German history. The history boom concentrates on earlier ages, the Middle Ages in particular, and is characterized by a "need for any identification whatsoever"[130] rather than by being based on national thinking as in Freytag's and Giesebrecht's times. Gisbert Haef's novel on *Alexander* (1992) highlights the withdrawal from a positively national ideology observable since the Second World War, particularly in comparison with Droysen's *Alexander*. In its accentuation of narrated history the text seems to choose precisely the present problems of 'inner unity' as a point of reference. The impending internal battles after Alexander's death determine its perspective even though the first volume that has been published so far has the sub-title *Roman der Einigung Griechenlands*. The dispute of the generals concerning riches can be read as an allegory on the current battles about the distribution of wealth in Germany.

New questions about a national and West German 'identity' in the 80s were provoked by the increasingly established separateness of the two German states and by the threat of nuclear wars at the interface of super-power blocs.[131] A historically evolved cultural people ('Kulturnation'), first and foremost supported by literature, would, it was hoped, prove to be a common bond.[132] As a German alternative to 'capitalism' as well as to dictatorial communism, utopian 'third ways' were suggested, as for example in Stefan Heym's novel *Schwarzenberg* (1984), where the utopia is embedded in reality because of its historical basis. The district of Schwarzenberg in the Erzgebirge remained unoccupied after the Second World War and a handful of German anti-fascists take over the provisional government. For one of them, a permanently independent Schwarzenberg opens up the opportunity of a social

---

129 Cf. Wichert and Heinemann: "Zwischen den Zeiten," p. 3.
130 "vagabundierender Identifikationsbedarf," Weidenfeld: "Politische Kultur und deutsche Frage," p. 23. Cf. Voltmer: "Das Mittelalter ist noch nicht vorbei," pp. 221–25; Fuhrmann: *Das Interesse am Mittelalter*; Althoff: "Sinnstiftung und Instrumentalisierung," pp. 4–5; Ralf Schnell: "History in the Contemporary German Novel." Williams, Parkes, and Smith, eds., *Literature on the Threshold*, pp. 9–28, here p. 27.
131 Cf. Honolka: *Schwarzrotgrün*.
132 Cf. Korte: *Über Deutschland schreiben*, pp. 48–53; Anonym: "Die deutsche Literatur der Gegenwart in Ost und West," p. 777.

experiment amidst two political systems. However, these utopian dreams come to an abrupt end when the Americans pull out of Central Germany and Soviet troops move to the West. The district which was unoccupied for six weeks is an odd historical fact different from its fictitious role as a political model. Consequently, the foundation of a new social order which was hoped to unite freedom and socialism, individual and state, spirit and power has to be confined to the nightly constitutional sketches of the fictitious sociologist and philosopher Max Wolfram in order not to go beyond the paradoxical closeness of utopia and history.

Even when he is later arrested by the Russian secret police, the very force he believed to have assembled in the spirit of his own ideas, Wolfram still hopes "for a new Schwarzenberg, built by different people in a different time."[133] Its utopian potential would have made *Schwarzenberg* a dissident novel in the GDR had it been allowed to be published there. Wolfram is convinced that freedom must not be usurped for a didactic purpose by a group or a party which claims to possess the truth; it is particularly this principle that calls the idea for leadership by "the working class and the Marxist-Leninist party" into question.[134] Heym's utopia of non-alignment, however, also went against the national status quo that had been accepted by West Germany and was consequently rejected as an extravagant disruption of the 'step by step policy' pursued by Social Democratic and Christian Democratic governments.[135]

In the wake of the changes in 1989, *Schwarzenberg* turned from a countermodel into a model. Intellectuals like Heym, committed to the civil rights movement and having a democratic *and* socialist society in the spirit of Max Wolfram in mind, began to remember old "anti-fascist and humanist ideals."[136] Heym's novel and the dissident manifestos in the GDR were very much alike even in their precautionary statement about a failure. Similar to the impending Russian occupation of Schwarzenberg right from the beginning, "influential circles in West German industry and politics" that are likely to crush the "independence of the GDR" and the "vision of a democratic socialism […] in embryonic form" were already identified in November 1989.[137]

---

133 Heym: *Schwarzenberg*, p. 246 ("auf ein anderes Schwarzenberg irgendwo, das andere Menschen zu errichten haben würden in einer anderen Zeit"), cf. p. 259.
134 Cf. ibid., p. 133; the first article of the East German constitution (1974). The official, East German interpretation of the events in Schwarzenberg does not recognize a difference between the aims of the local 'antifascists' and the factual development, cf. Heydick, Hoppe, and John, eds.: *Historischer Führer*, p. 292; Groß: *Die ersten Schritte*, pp. 8–11, 88–91.
135 Cf. Bölling: "Kleine Schritte statt großer Sprünge," p. 36.
136 "Aufruf 'Für unser Land', 28. 11. 1989." Wolf: *Im Dialog*, pp. 170–71, here p. 171.
137 Ibid., p. 170; "Aufruf zum 'Hierbleiben'." Ibid., pp. 169–70, here p. 170.

Among the indicators of the fictiousness of the text, which claims to be authentic, is the repeated recollection of the origins of the miniature republic: an American lieutenant and his sergeant tossed a twentyfive cent coin to decide whether the district of Schwarzenberg was affected by ambiguous advance orders. The two American soldiers play a theatrical role in the whole novel. Thus, a farcical situation and farcical characters form the only link between factual history and the existence of a "third way" "in Schwarzenberg of all places."[138] The poetical context thus indicates out that the good faith and the optimistic concepts of the characters are not immediatley applicable to political reality. In this respect, *Schwarzenberg* could have been read as a warning against utopian hopes in 1989/90.

Since reunification, the assessment of national history has become a contested political issue among writers, too, since here, in a historistical sense, the past was supposed to judge the present, namely the establishment of a new nation-state. As early as 1988, Martin Walser admitted to a "feeling for history" that made the German division appear unnatural to him. For that he was almost pronounced unsound.[139] In the following year Walser was pleased that the Germans, too, finally "succeeded with history," while his colleagues, apart from a few exceptions (de Bruyn, Monika Maron, Kunert, Hochhuth), could not rid themselves of a "deep-rooted, specifically German national trauma."[140] For Günter Grass, the most obstinate opponent to unification, Auschwitz marks the absolute fixed point of the historical awareness in German history – in its absoluteness in fact outside history – which annuls the human right of self-determination and excludes a nation-state.[141] Consequently, there has not been until now a resurrection of historical fiction which would refer to the nation-state in a way Freytag and Meyer did. The various possibilities of historical fiction in the present converge in one point: literature does not avail itself to history in order to justify state and nation. Writers, on the whole, have accepted the nation-state as a political frame of reference

---

138 Heym: *Schwarzenberg*, p. 98.
139 Walser: *Über Deutschland reden*, pp. 99–100; cf. Becker: "Gedächtnis verloren – Verstand verloren." *Die Zeit* No. 47, November 18, 1988, p. 61. For the debate among writers about identity and nation that had already taken place in the former Federal Republic of Germany see Helmut Peitsch: "'Antipoden' im 'Gewissen' der Nation? Günter Grass' und Martin Walsers 'deutsche Fragen'." Scheuer, ed., *Dichter und ihre Nation*, pp. 459–89, whose antinational standpoint turns even Günter Grass into a dangerous nationalist. Cf. Keith Bullivant in this volume, pp. 304–6.
140 Walser: ibid., p. 115; Kügler: "Positionen," p. 4.
141 Cf. Grass: "Kurze Rede eines vaterlandslosen Gesellen." *Die Zeit* No. 7, February 9, 1990, p. 61, "Schreiben nach Auschwitz." *Die Zeit* No. 9, February 23, 1990, p. 19.

to a lesser extent than, for instance, historians, where some of them have, after all, revised their call for a post-national age (Kocka, Winkler)[142]. This reservation considerably limits the possibilities of literature to contribute to the expected formation of the nation, of an "all-German community with a common will and a common feeling of solidarity." The historian Otto Dann has just pointed out that the historical legitimation of the reunification is even more important since, in contrast to 1870, it has not been preceeded by a national movement.[143] The historical embeddening of the regained unification, which literature has achieved so far, hardly meets these claims.

A supporter of reunification, Walser pays only little heed to national history in his latest novel *Die Verteidigung der Kindheit* (1991) since the detailed portrayal of the irritations that came along with the German division for the individual and the echo of important war-time and post-war evants are always part of the private destiny of Alfred Dorn, a neurotic fixated on his mother.[144] Meanwhile, Grass chose an even bolder means than historical fiction in order to express his fears: in *Unkenrufe* (1992), a historical novel set in the future, as it were, a German-Polish cementery project set up in the spirit of reconciliation degenerates in the course of the 1990s into a new type of a German occupation of land in the East, this time with the help of German marks, an occupation Grass warned against already in the year of reunification.[145] There are significant modifications of the familiar historical novel. In Walser's novel, the importance of the historical and political constellation is not as successfully developed as the emotional realm, while Grass fails to prove on the basis of the West German past that super-power attitudes and a new 'drive towards the East' can be expected from reunification. The genre virtually functions here as a touchstone for emotional and private concerns, for a polemical and utopian view of history, and for their transformation into literature.

The way in which another little short narrative thematizises history intrinsically also discredits its historical assessment of reunification. In Friedrich Christian Delius' *Die Birnen von Ribbeck* (1991) a Ribbeckonian tells "Wessis" (pejorative term for West Germans), who have invaded the village for the planting of a new pear tree, the true story of the village, which the "swindler"

---

142 Cf. Hacker: *Deutsche Irrtümer*, pp. 365, 370–71; Wengst: *Historiker betrachten Deutschland*.
143 Dann: *Nation und Nationalismus*, p. 319.
144 Cf. Walser: *Die Verteidigung der Kindheit*, p. 33 (June 17, 1953), 318 (August, 13, 1961).
145 Cf. Grass: *Unkenrufe*, p. 246; Grass: "Ein Schnäppchen namens DDR. Warnung vor Deutschland: Das Monstrum will Großmacht sein." *Die Zeit* No. 41, October 5, 1990, p. 50.

Fontane distorted to make it acceptable for the educated classes.¹⁴⁶ The famous pears, he says, were sour and the villagers had always done badly anyway, whether under Prussian squires, Nazis or socialist bureaucrats. However, the basic constellation that those 'down there' had to suffer under the yoke of those 'up there' has been the same in all ages so that they become indistinguishable from one another.¹⁴⁷ History is reduced to a cliché – Delius also lacks with Fontane's precise observations and descriptions – in order to brand the impending unification as a take-over of power.¹⁴⁸ Delius de-historizes history even more than Freytag's bourgeois and national teleology.

Reunification resulted in an entirely new function only for the historical fiction of East German writers. In the GDR, the historical novel was particularly affected by state regulations for literature. A prescriptive theory of history and an established view of history committed writers to depict the regular structure and the teleological character of every part of narrated history, preferably in the dawning consciousness of an exemplary protagonist.¹⁴⁹ Christa Wolf's *Kindheitsmuster* makes a shift towards a subjective and individual recollection of history in the GDR. As a criticism of a coherent and illusionistic narration of history, childhood memories, a return to the scene and narratorial reflexion form in this novel a triangular structure that can later be found in a simplified form in Harig's work. Christa Wolf's inquiry into the continuing 'fascist' character of East German society was bound to provoke a constitutionally 'anti-fascist' state. Due to an enlarged notion of the heritage in the 80s,¹⁵⁰ the historical novel had access to additional, until that time 'irrelevant' subject-matter and was able to handle them in a sophisticated manner. Yet the October 1989 volume of the *Weimarer Beiträge* warned against a playful, allegedly destructive and meaningless treatment of the past in the West.¹⁵¹

After the collapse of socialism, a second German 'Vergangenheitsbewältigung' has become a further mission for the historical novel.¹⁵² The pattern of

---

146 Delius: *Die Birnen von Ribbeck*, p. 27. For the content of this story see Bullivant in this volume, pp. 314–15.
147 Cf. ibid., pp. 7, 16, 32, 50, 61, 65.
148 As to the denunciations the unification was subjected to by West German intellectuals, cf. Bullivant in this volume, p. 309–319.
149 Cf. Haase: "Individuum und Geschichte"; Rosellini: "Zur Funktionalisierung des historischen Romans," pp. 70–9; Warm: "Zum Verhältnis von Vergangenheit und Gegenwart," pp. 68–70.
150 Cf. Hanke: "Sozialistischer Neohistorismus?," pp. 58–62. J. H. Reid rates high "The Recent Historical Novel in the GDR." Williams, Parkes, and Smith, eds., *Literature on the Threshold*, pp. 61–75.
151 Cf. Haase: "Individuum und Geschichte," p. 1721.
152 Cf. Mitter: "Die Aufarbeitung der DDR-Geschichte"; Hoffmann: *Stunden Null?*, pp. 205–80.

'Väterliteratur,' has become productive again, along with autobiographical accounts about the Stasi and reports from 'Stalin's camps.'[153] In Monika Maron's short novel *Stille Zeile Sechs* (1991), the daughter of a hardened, staunch communist takes the high-ranking former official Beerenbaum, who employs her as a secretary for his memoirs, as a substitute in the battle against her late father. In the awareness of the fact that the domineering and dictatorial character of men like Beerenbaum and her father created the authoritarian GDR, which made a fulfilled life in freedom impossible for her, she contradicts Beerenbaum's "life legend"[154] made up of empty ideological formulas and his consciousness of being a former victim of fascist persecution. Monika Maron's novel is exceptional in not asking 'how' and 'why' everything could have happened. Thus, the novel ridicules a widely-held account of ideological orientations in social history when the female protagonist makes an exact guess at Beerenbaum's origin and party career without knowing his name.[155] Maron's communist variant only quotes in a shorthand fashion what is expanded in Berkéwicz's novel into social kitsch where the reader presumes to know everything from the story of the lower middle class storm-trooper to the Hitler Youth leader, who is a Hölderlin and Nietzsche enthusiast. How ideology deforms human beings is captured in a few insistent images: For instance, her father's conviction that he was always in the right as a communist was so dominant that he never thanked her for the lemon cream she made for him.[156] If Maron's novel seems better suited to its task than Berkéwicz's, it may credit part of its success to the fact that the reassessment of the second German dictatorship does not yet have to fight against the ritualizations of the literature about National Socialism.

6.

It can be seen that the basic position of most writers, apart from a few exceptions in both cases, was characterized in 1870 by sympathy and in 1990 by distance. The supporters and the creators of the national movement saw in the foundation of the Reich the fulfilment of a crucial political objective and

---

153 Cf. Korte: *Über Deutschland schreiben*, pp. 70–1; Wolf: *Was bleibt*; Kunze: *Decknahme 'Lyrik'*; Loest: *Die Stasi war mein Eckermann*, *Der Zorn des Schafes*; Roland: *Wie eine Feder im Wind. Meine Zeit in Stalins Lagern*. For Kunze see Terence Reed in this volume, p. 239–40.
154 Maron: *Stille Zeile Sechs*, p. 148 ("Legende seines Lebens").
155 Cf. ibid., pp. 26–8.
156 Cf. ibid., p. 159.

of their life's purpose. In our days, however, the nation-state has first of all to be accepted as the constitution of a democratic society, although this type of a nation-state in Western Europe can look upon an unbroken tradition since the French Revolution.

The impact of unifications on literature, the historical narrative in our case, could until now be assessed only for the past century where the nation-state as a desired and much-debated political objective was particularly productive for literature but lost its integrative force after its foundation. A joint political purpose united the national-liberal historical novel and historiography in a working unit which declined with the fragmentation of the Liberal Party together with its narrative illusionism. While Freytag tried to combine historiography and fiction in the interest of a national teleology, the increasingly disillusioned Raabe insisted on the autonomy of fiction and treated ironically artificial meanings that are based on a single, perfectly clear and manageable history. The historical optimism in the days of the foundation of the Reich, which already suffered a fragmentation in the later Freytag, was relativized by the description of the ambivalence of victory and violence in Fontane and Meyer and has only an individual and ethical rather than a socio-political dimension in Raabe.[157] However, this self-reflexive and ideologically critical tendency in the historical narrative after the foundation of the Reich goes together with Dahn's Teutonic heroism or the 'professorial novel' as popular works which support the status quo.

Even though unification in 1990 was not preceeded by a national movement, literature in particular kept the awareness of a continuous cultural and national unity alive. The boom in a 'cultural people,' however, was linked with an increasingly widespread notion of the factual separation. The question of the German nation arose not so much from a feeling of political responsibility as from problems with the self-identity of the poets.[158] A fundamental change in the conception of society and history becomes apparent: the current historical narrative, as compared to Freytag's days, no longer anticipates historical progress nor asks the individual to fit into society. The scope of the historical narrative, however, is often unfavourably limited by the retreat into the personal. Nevertheless, the recollection of National Socialism and its crimes in literature made a significant contribution to the shaping of political and historical awareness. This memory is part of the German identity even

---

157 Cf. letter to Korth, July 19, 1894, Raabe: *Sämtliche Werke* suppl. 2, pp. 357–58; Sammons: *Raabe*, p. 52.

158 Cf. Korte: *Über Deutschland schreiben*, p. 49; Steinfeld and Suhr: "Die Wiederkehr des Nationalen," p. 389.

after the re-establishment of the nation-state, since because of the familiar course of German history, the subject-matter and orientation of historical fiction have to assume a critical attitude towards national history. This attitude, however, is no clear-cut contrast to 1870 because Fontane did not take part in the weaving of a legendary Prussian 'Beruf,' but searched for a humanistic potential in old Prussian ways of life, while Meyer pointed out the problems arising from an amoral historical greatness. Even *Die Ahnen* with its middle-class tradition implies a criticism of semi-feudal political and social structures in the Empire and avoids an enthusiastic celebration of the foundation of the Reich. The discussion about historiographical and literary forms of dealing with the Third Reich are affected by reunification only in so far as East Germany has to catch up on it since an ideological anti-fascism impeded until recently an effective 'Vergangenheitsbewältigung'. The latter should involve a reassessment of the communist dictatorship in order to prevent any form of political extremism.[159]

The collapse of an empire in 1989/90 that was regarded as unshakeable created a new environment for the historical narrative. Conservation in the sense of a 'cultural poeple' and utopian models like Schwarzenberg were no longer a satisfactory response to the German question. According to our findings, the historical narrative has difficulty finding appropriate answers to the new nation-state. It is not easy to estimate whether experiences with history in progress are more likely to lead to horror as in Handke's case or to an increased interest. Since the Federal Republic of Germany is democratically legitimized and strives for European integration, a united Germany is not in the least interested in a return to a nationalistic and leader-centred conception of history. Nevertheless, Grass', Walser's, and Delius' attempts reveal the difficulty in connecting German history with current questions, in such a way that the past in fictitious presentness forms a 'narrative argument' beyond clichés and subjective perspectives.

Also from an aesthetic point of view historical fiction of that kind would not lead back to the nineteenth century since on the one hand referentiality satiated with facts does not exclude narrative modernity and on the other hand most of the above mentioned texts are told in a traditional way. Some of the well-founded texts dealing with older subject-matter refute in particular the continuing effect of the law of an idealistic aesthetics which states that the poeticity of a text stands against its referential function. Dieter Kühn's and Horst Stern's works on the Middle Ages (both 1986) open up a wide range of possibilities. Kühn's *Parzival des Wolfram von Eschenbach* takes up the aesthetic

---

159 Cf. Mitter: "Die Aufarbeitung der DDR-Geschichte," p. 381.

imperative of narrative self-reflexive as a chance of bringing the epistemological potential of fiction and sciences into line, and he amuses himself by playing an almost post-modern exaggeration with his right of disposal over the past and the present.[160] The reader of Stern's *Mann aus Apulien* is presented with the expertly reconstructed autobiographical perspective of the Emperor Frederick II. A poetological reflection upon the mimetic potential of language and its tendency towards autopoiesis and stylization has been entirely transferred into the historical character by dint of the separation of the experiencing I and the narrating I.[161]

Historical self-reassurance through a romanticizing return to the two constituent states has been present for some years among West German writers and now among East German writers as well.[162] However, a permanent clinging to the existence of two constituent states would deprive literature of the possibility of accompanying the evolution of the nation in a critical way which is also connected with the present. We can see after 1870 that more important writers divorce historical narrative from affirmative conceptions of history, and it is clear that they were reacting against the tendency to align the genre with the national movement. On the other hand, it might nowadays be desirable for literature to move closer again to the subject-matter of the nation-state and its history.

---

160 Cf. Kühn: *Parzival*, pp. 70, 249, 262, 292, 296, 297, 301, 303, 305, 313, 322, 384, 387.
161 Cf. Stern: *Mann aus Apulien*, pp. 97–100, 110–18, 144–47, 164, 248, 313, 331, 358, 424.
162 Cf. Korte: *Über Deutschland schreiben*, pp. 81–82, 85; Kunert: *Sturz vom Sockel*, pp. 10–3.

1990: The Priciple of Hope
or: Nailed to the Cross of the Past?

TERENCE JAMES REED
University of Oxford

Another Piece of the Past[1]

Abstract: The essay places the events of 1989/90 in the sequence of historical upheavals and catastrophes that typify German history; looks back briefly at the evolution of literature in the GDR; surveys the responses of (mostly East) German writers – Volker Braun, Heiner Müller, Walter Janka, Reiner Kunze, Stefan Heym, Heinz Czechowski, Thomas Rosenlöcher, Christa Wolf, Friedrich Christian Delius – to the concluded GDR past and the 'unified' present; and questions the arguments and motives of West German critics in the 'Literaturstreit.'

The point of my title is that, more than with any other country, the German past comes in pieces – pieces of territory, pieces of time. First there were the three hundred pieces in the jigsaw of the Holy Roman Empire, which at least lasted all the way from the Middle Ages till 1806, when Napoleon abolished it. For sixty-five years after that there were the thirty-odd separate pieces decreed by Napoleon, but kept on after his defeat in 1815. Then comes the span from 1871 when Germany first existed as a state in the modern sense, though only for seventy-four years. And that itself splits into three pieces: the forty-seven years of the Wilhelmine Empire, the fifteen of the Weimar Republic; the twelve of Hitler's Thousand-Year Reich. Then there is renewed division for the forty years from 1949. Finally there is a single Germany again, for the shortest time-span yet: since reunification began on October 3, 1990.

In other countries, the present is more continuous with the past. Their history may split into time-units each with a character of its own, but only in

---

[1] This paper was originally the Cheltenham Lecture given on 14 October 1991 at the annual Festival of Literature, which for the first time was devoted to continental writing, and subsequently published in the volume *Geist und Macht: Writers and the State in the GDR*, Special Number of *German Monitor*, edited by Axel Goodbody and Dennis Tate, Amsterdam and Atlanta 1992. The lecture offered an overview of recent developments by a non-specialist for a non-specialist audience. One or two footnotes contain material that post-dates the lecture.

Germany has the form of the nation been both so long delayed and so often and radically undone; and only in German history are the break-points between periods so uniformly catastrophic: defeat in 1806, defeat in 1918, tyranny in 1933, defeat in 1945, tyranny again in half the country from 1949. Only 1989 has broken that pattern, though it is itself – after initial euphoria – not a wholly happy event.

Catastrophes and reversals challenge literature. Much German writing duly engages the past, recounts the latest upheaval, tries to explain or assign responsibility for it, or at least to commemorate the past and make the backwards link which is an essential part of a society's continuing life in the present. In the 1880s, Theodor Fontane's fiction probes the mentality of Prussia whose defeat gave Napoleon power over Germany, and which later, in Fontane's own day, won the victories that made Germany a fateful power in Europe. Near the end of the Wilhelmine Empire, Heinrich Mann writes a satire on the cynical opportunist type, to show what made that society tick. In the twenties, Alfred Döblin captures the chaos of a nation in defeat with a novel called *November 1918*. For the Nazi period, you can choose between the psycho-history of Thomas Mann's novel *Doktor Faustus*, whose hero is an avantgarde composer, and the earthier music played by Günter Grass's Oskar on his Tin Drum. And many more besides: the Nazi past has inevitably been a compulsive theme in German post-war writing.

Now literature has another piece of the past to cope with. Where, this time, do we begin? In the East, obviously, although parts of this talk will be about West German reactions and the worsening relations between East and West. Nothing, it seems, divides people like unification. That is one reason, besides the need for ease of reference, why I shall say simply 'East German' and 'West German' whether I am talking about pre- or post-unification. Germans are currently hung up on awkward formulations like 'the former GDR' 'the ex-GDR', 'the acceded area', the 'new federal states', 'the old federal states', 'our new fellow-citizens', not to mention other more abusive terms. I should also say that the view I am going to offer is sympathetic to East German writers and critical of West German responses: the critic has a first duty to enter positively into the works he treats. But, for the record, let me say some of my best friends are West Germans.

Upheavals bring people back to the roots of literature in experience: recording, reacting, remembering, in diary and memoir and personal reflection. These may not necessarily be sharply distinct from more formal prose or even poetry. In 1989 East Germans had the exhilarating new experience of seeing their old experience become a closed chapter. But however grim that old experience had been, they also then had the traumatic experience of seeing their present, with all its institutions bad and good, dissolve along with their past as the unification process absorbed them. The response to all these things was direct, partly because East German writing, for all its difficulties with the censor, has always been close to experience and direct expression. That was so because these things had to be defended. From the start a declared 'socialist literature' raised problems, because it demanded that writers should state and illustrate certain fixed truths, and no literature worth the name can go on for long without freedom to question and explore and discover. What was worse, the truths also appeared less and less true as Stalinist ideology and political practice gradually killed people's early hopes, until it became impossible for honest writers to go on proclaiming the bright vision of this socialist state. Individual experience became the touchstone for what was real, a defence against propaganda, a deflator of ideological statements, the only reliable form of truth. Stating it directly became a vital task. Against pressure from the Party, East German writers recorded authentic experience and maintained the individual standpoint against false collective norms. Freedom of expression became itself a theme, whether it was independent thought, or literary utterance itself, or the less elevated but in its way vital freedom of teenagers to wear jeans or play a guitar in public. Jeans, says the hero of Ulrich Plenzdorf's *Neue Leiden des jungen W.*, are an attitude, not a pair of trousers; and one of the most controversial works of GDR literature, Reiner Kunze's *Die wunderbaren Jahre*, is a collection of bitter real-life episodes which show how the authorities at every level tried to extinguish the spark of independence in schoolchildren and teenagers.[2]

Inevitably, such writing had problems with the Party, which was still demanding wholly positive views of the development of GDR society. The trouble was that it hardly did develop; and one reason was that the Party would not tolerate the open dialogue any society needs for constructive change. Brecht stated the principle in a late poem:

> Ich benötige keinen Grabstein, aber
> Wenn ihr einen für mich benötigt
> Wünschte ich, es stünde darauf:
> Er hat Vorschläge gemacht. Wir
> Haben sie angenommen.
> Durch eine solche Inschrift wären
> Wir alle geehrt.[3]

---

[2] Kunze: *Die wunderbaren Jahre*.

[3] "I have need of no gravestone, but supposing / you need to have one for me, / Then I'd like to have on it this: / He made suggestions. We / Accepted them. / An inscription like

Brecht's word "Vorschläge" (suggestions) is shorthand for any social input based on the real experience of individuals. When they emphasised this experience, writers were not arrogantly claiming a special value for their own, but attempting to open up, at all levels of power and in all contexts, the dialogue Brecht had spoken for. There was a brief moment of hope in 1971 when Erich Honecker declared that there need be 'no taboos' for writers commited to 'firm socialist positions'. But the Party's practice hardly changed. 'No taboos' for writers would have meant the Party admitting its mistakes and taking politically unacceptable steps to correct them. A reform programme can hardly be conceived which would have removed the authoritarian instinct Kunze's *Die wunderbaren Jahre* traced everywhere.

Honecker's 1971 proviso of a commitment to 'firm socialist positions' may in any case seem a hefty one. Yet despite the decades of disillusion since 1949, it made sense in its context. Critical literature in the GDR was never in principle *dissident* literature, which is how – in good faith or for consciously political reasons – West German criticism commonly read it. Virtually to the end of the GDR, writers had a critical commitment to the society which, whether they were real socialists or not, they happened to live in and which as far as they could see (and, it is important to remember, as far as everyone else could see too) was a permanency. What made them appear dissidents was the Party's refusal to listen. A political interpretation by the West then hardened positions, which in some cases drove writers to leave the GDR, even though the West was not their ideal and they would have preferred, for better or worse, to stay where they were. Long after the emphasis in writers' critical commitment had shifted heavily from 'commitment' to 'critical', the idea still persisted that things might change in this society and make it more of a real community. The idea of true community – Utopia, if you will – persistently appeals to the liberal imagination. In the end it only ever came into being on any scale among the crowds on the squares of Leipzig and other less publicised towns who chanted "wir sind das Volk." 'I' had at last, really if briefly, become 'we'.

Against this background we can understand a writer like Volker Braun who sees that his criticism has helped undo the society he lived in, while his commitment has lost all meaning now that the society has vanished:

> Da bin ich noch: mein Land geht in den Westen. […]
> Ich selber habe ihm den Tritt versetzt.

---

that would be / A credit to us all." Brecht: *Werke* (Große kommentierte Berliner und Frankfurter Ausgabe) vol. 14, p. 191–92.

> Es wirft sich weg und seine magre Zierde.
> [...] Und unverständlich wird mein ganzer Text [...].

'Text' here means his past writing, perhaps even his whole life as a writer. His lines mingle self-criticism and historical regret as East Germany is swallowed up by its aggressively individualistic big brother, and the social ideals the GDR professed but never realised are now nowhere even professed. The poem's last line is: "Wann sag ich wieder *mein* und meine alle."[4]

This, if you like, is socialist or at least communitarian nostalgia. A more radical self-criticism is possible, as in this poem by Heiner Müller, the leading East German dramatist, though typically more performed outside than inside the GDR. The problem is again things written in the past, but not because they are 'incomprehensible':

> Meine Herausgeber wühlen in alten Texten
> Manchmal wenn ich sie lese überläuft es mich kalt Das
> Habe ich geschrieben IM BESITZ DER WAHRHEIT
> Sechzig Jahre vor meinem mutmaßlichen Tod
> Auf dem Bildschirm sehe ich meine Landsleute
> Mit Händen und Füßen abstimmen gegen die Wahrheit
> Die vor vierzig Jahren mein Besitz war
> Welches Grab schützt mich vor meiner Jugend[5]

In a time of political change and instability, this seems to me firm poetic utterance, measured and lucid, movingly direct, a view of history private and public which is sensitive to the writer's responsibility. Hypersensitive, in fact, because Müller was not one of the Party faithful who ganged up to prescribe what their colleagues should write, to muzzle them when they wrote something different, to expel them from the Writers' Union with its professional privileges, and sometimes finally to hound them out of the country. Yet he is surely right to be hypersensitive: he has been associated, at whatever remove, with the practice of tyranny. Morally, his hypersensitivity puts him in the

---

4 "Here I am still: my country has gone west / [...] / I myself helped kick it down the road / It's thrown itself and its meagre charms away. / [...] And my whole text's incomprehensible. / [...] When shall I again say 'mine' and mean us all?" Volker Braun: "Nachruf." Chiarloni and Pankoke, eds., *Grenzfallgedichte*, p. 109.

5 "My editors are rummaging in old texts / Sometimes I shiver when I read the things / I wrote IN FULL POSSESSION OF THE TRUTH / Sixty years before my likely death. / Now on the screen I watch my countrymen / Voting with their hands and feet against the truth / That was my possession forty years ago. / What grave will now protect me from my youth?" Heiner Müller: "Fernsehen 3: Selbstkritik." Chiarloni and Pankoke, eds., *Grenzfallgedichte*, p. 55.

honourable tradition of Thomas Mann, who in a similar time of political accusations and self-justifications perceived proto-fascist elements in his own early work and confessed them in his *Doktor Faustus*. That is the subjective side. Objectively, and again like Thomas Mann, Müller is pointing to a basic intellectual or psychological aberration (not of course the same one Mann saw at the root of fascism) from which all the other evils of the political system followed. Believing you possess the truth leads to ruthlessness, the end is held to justify the means, dissenters can be removed, debate is disallowed. No wonder the greatest of German debaters, Lessing, declared that he would decline an offer of the truth from God himself. Men's minds were in every sense partial; absolute truth was too perilous a possession for them.

I have dwelt on a few lines of poetry because poetry can go to the heart of the matter. The first personal account by a victim of East German injustice of those evils that followed duly carries the title, again with a Brecht echo, *Schwierigkeiten mit der Wahrheit* (Difficulties with the truth). Readings from it at a Berlin theatre on 28 October 1989 were a significant event in the midst of *the* events. Its author Walter Janka, ran the leading East German literary publishers (the Aufbau Verlag) till 1956, when he was arrested, given a show trial, and sent to the infamous Bautzen jail for five years. He had been there before as a communist in the Third Reich, part of an impeccable Party record which also included concentration camp and fighting at the front line in the Spanish Civil War. Why he was framed is not clear. The methods are brutally so. Things he had said, done, and written with the backing of the Minister of Culture, the poet Johannes R. Becher, were made into charges against him. His friend the Minister knew he was innocent; so did his friend Anna Seghers, the most celebrated East German novelist of the older generation, whose prestige surely made her secure. Neither helped him; Seghers sat there in the courtroom silent.[6] In every sense Janka's disillusionment with the state was more painful than that of the writers who merely failed to change things through dialogue. Because Janka was a Party man, he was shocked to find himself a victim of the Party. Yet because he was a Party man he must have known the drill. He knew what the Party had done to left-wing deviationists in Spain virtually alongside him. He had heard Becher say of earlier frame-ups that "these things are bound to happen in politics. Justice has always been a political instrument";[7] Becher called them the "developmental difficulties" of communism.[8] Janka's

---

6 Hans Mayer attempts not very fully or, therefore, persuasively to defend her. See his *Der Turm von Babel*, p. 203.
7 Janka: *Schwierigkeiten mit der Wahrheit*, p. 14.
8 Ibid., p. 21.

disillusionment, his "shame that such procedures are possible under socialism"⁹ need not have waited till it was his turn.

Janka's account will not sound new. Worse has come out of the Soviet Union, where the victims of show trials were shot. But novelty is not a criterion here. Every liberated society has its own truths to make public about the tyranny that followed from the "possession of truth." All over Eastern Europe facts are being unearthed, and often more than facts.

One new angle has however been found. A police state has the ironic virtue of exhaustively documenting itself – if you can get to the documents before someone shreds them. The poet Reiner Kunze did, and published a selection from his twelve State Security files, 3491 pages, under the title they used for him: *Deckname "Lyrik"* (Codename "Poetry"). The book is sub-titled "a documentation," but is halfway to being literature. It makes a montage of the crude reality and weaves themes from one lump of officialese to another. That is a finer revenge than merely revealing the Stasi's intricate and malicious routines, though it does that too. We watch the writer's work being frustrated, publication hindered, his every move observed, his most trivial details recorded, his readings blocked or packed with Party members; he is offered bribes and then threatened, his wife's career is damaged, the family is systematically harassed, until they finally leave the country. There is a particularly nauseating report by the agents who bugged his flat. This worries the neighbour whose party wall is to contain the bug. What about *his* privacy? He is assured that "there is confidence in return for confidence," and that this is the way to defend "our humanist social order."¹⁰ All very much what we might expect, except perhaps for the grotesque lengths observation could go to. The light in the poet's room is regularly observed not going out till 22.00 or even 22.30, he is up there and has "apparently been working," no doubt on more of his dangerous poems.¹¹ And at the end of the book, when he has emigrated to West Germany, the Stasi have thirty pages of his known contacts to follow up, each one a potential set of files, a new centre from which to spread tremors through a society where on the surface everyone was supposed to use the friendly form of address, 'du', and it was all meant to add up to the brotherly 'we'. How much of it would the tremors leave intact?

Especially as the operation was only made possible by large numbers of 'inoffizielle Mitarbeiter', i.e. citizen informers. In Nazi Germany or the Soviet

---

9 Ibid., p. 108.
10 Kunze: *Deckname "Lyrik,"* p. 74.
11 Ibid., p. 41.

Union a relatively clear line separated the population from the Gestapo or the KGB. In East Germany people never knew who was reliable. They might think they did, but Kunze's documents show how wrong they could be, himself included. We hear someone saying in a student English club that at least here it is safe to talk – and we are reading it in a report someone at the club sent in. Another one is about a poetry reading in church where everyone present had been personally vouched for by someone else. But who did you trust to do the vouching? And how could they be sure? Who did you really know? Who could you ever trust fully? Virtually no one. Kunze found his files contained the detailed layout of his flat, provided by a friend of the family; a farewell letter of warm thanks to close friends written when the family emigrated; details of a heartfelt inscription he wrote for another friend in a volume of his poems. The theme Kunze's montage carries is the destruction of trust which means the death of decent human society. The Stasi was indeed, in Volker Braun's grim joke, the 'Ministry of State Insecurity'.[12]

The logical conclusion of this ever-widening 'conspiracy' (that was the Stasi's own approvingly-meant word for their work) is drawn in a story by Stefan Heym about an underling in the local Stasi head-quarters during the tricky days of 1989 when a Citizens' Committee might burst in and offer violence at any moment. While his smarter superiors keep well clear, he is left to hold the fort – he is, in the boss's words and the story's title, "one of our most reliable people." When the visitors duly come and scatter the files everywhere, he is shocked to find one on his wife. It is built up wholly from little sayings of hers, everyday bits of old-fashioned moral good sense that he has casually quoted at work. Again, nothing was ever off the record, he should not have trusted his colleagues. Failing to realise that was what made him indeed one of their most reliable people.[13]

The bitter little irony is symbolic of a worry common in East German minds: how far have I let myself get drawn into the system, by slackness, gradual drift, or inadvertence, even when it wasn't putting me under direct pressure. For, again in comparison with Nazism, GDR oppression (for all the imprisonments and the shootings at the Berlin wall) was not as hideously brutal: for many citizens it was no more than what one writer calls "Mini-terror," such that "in the last ten or twenty years we always had more respect than the actually mild repression really required."[14] That made it all the easier to drift. You could go along with the steady small pressures, could sit in a room listen-

---

12 Braun: "Monströse Banalität." *Die Zeit* No. 48, November 22, 1991, p. 63.
13 Cf. Heym: "Der Zuverlässigsten Einer." Heym: *Auf Sand gebaut*, pp. 7–20.
14 Rosenlöcher: *Die verkauften Pflastersteine*, pp. 31, 22.

ing to people mouth the required lies, and find that one of them was sitting in your seat.¹⁵ The final person you could not rely on was yourself.

The 'reliable' underling also stands for the ordinary people who in Stefan Heym's view will lose out under any system. The seven short stories in his volume *Auf Sand gebaut* (Built on Sand) are all set in the chaotic interim between the communist collapse and German unification, when after the "moment of beauty" on the streets and squares of Leipzig and other cities and the party at the Berlin Wall,¹⁶ hardline politics gave way to hard-nosed economics – and the latter's own form of hardline politics. One of Heym's satires tells how the democratic slogan "Wir sind das Volk" was turned into "Wir sind ein Volk" by an ex-German advertising genius from Madison Avenue. He is now worried by what he has set going: the story is called "The Sorcerer's Apprentice." Another tale shows the beginnings of a shift from democracy to plutocracy, from the East German "We are the people," via "We are one people," to the West German "We are the money."¹⁷ We see the Western companies move in and the smart East German careerists move out of Marx and into markets.¹⁸ Beneath Heym's sardonic humour is the serious suggestion that the forces taking over are not so benevolent and, for the ordinary man, not structurally very different from the old ones. Looking at East Germany as it now is, one can't altogether dismiss this as the exaggeration of satire.

Stefan Heym was one of the group of writers who wanted a new democratic GDR rather than a sell-out to the Federal Republic, and were shouted down by the crowds, those ordinary people of Heym's who turned out to be keen to go west, lured by a more glittering kind of Utopia. To the sceptical eye watching them acclaim the Federal Chancellor, it seemed historically more of the same, as in Heinz Czechowski's poem "Historical Reminiscence":

> Was hat man uns nicht
> Alles eingeredet: daß
> Uns Monokulturen bekömmlicher sein solln
> Als Vielfalt und daß die Versteppung des Landes
> Uns erst dessen wahre

---

15 Cf. Fuchs: "Die Lüge." Fuchs: *Gedächtnisprotokolle, Vernehmungsprotokolle*, p. 37.
16 Cf. Königsdorf: *Ein Moment Schönheit*.
17 Cf. Humann, ed., *Wir sind das Geld. Wie die Westdeutschen die DDR aufkaufen*.
18 In the story "Rette sich wer kann" (Sauve qui peut). Cf. the account of Bertelsmann moving into the ex-GDR: "[In Berlin] another Bertelsmann agency had meanwhile been established, managed by one named Eberhard Reimann who, until recently, had been the right-hand man of the since fallen ex-GDR Minister of Culture." Kaufmann: "A Cultural Clearout." *Index on Censorship* 21[:1] (1992), p. 20. Stefan Heym's volume, as it happens, was published by Bertelsmann.

> Schönheit offenbare … Heute, so scheint es,
> Ist wieder ein Tag,
> Wo man uns einreden will: Nun
> Wird alles gut!
> […]¹⁹

These sceptical reservations among East German writers have not, to put it mildly, endeared them to West German critics. There is little understanding in West Germany generally for what it feels like to be taken over wholesale and for the most part insensitively; little realisation that the process of clearing up one set of social and psychological problems is generating a third. The sense that another piece of history is already being made, and made badly, is stronger in the East, where historical consciousness was part of the ideological education and the Party was always making grand historical claims that contrasted grotesquely with what was in front of your eyes. The last piece and the new piece of history can even seem a fated continuity: "A great mass of errors and failures lies behind us, and new guilt is waiting for us to fall into its traps."²⁰

It is of course possible to meet history with a sense of humour rather than high rhetoric, to spot life's little ironies and see the ridiculous side, even of the West's commercial takeover. Already the writer records the first sighting of an empty coke can in his garden; and while he waits on a 12 DM fee for a poem printed in the local paper, his brother has ambitions to be big in birdfood, he has been in touch with the Western firm "VOGELVITAL" and is all set "to build up a Saxon budgerigar empire." Nothing is untouched by change. Even the official organ of the Party, *Neues Deutschland*, is not what it was, one day it even carries a headline "THINKING NEEDED."²¹ Where once he used to thumb lightly through its daily reports of undiluted socialist triumphs, now he has the *Frankfurter Allgemeine* to cope with, which with supplements and all weighs like a kilo of roof-tile; when you spread the pages out, it turns you into an orang-utan, you need an athlete's stamina just to hold it open, punctuated by cracklings of potency as you turn the pages over, you only have to sit reading

---

19 "Think of the things / That they've made us believe: that / Monocultures were better for us / Than variety, that turning / Our country into a steppe / Would bring out its true / Beauty … Today, it seems, / Is one more of those days / When they want us to believe: Now / Everything's going to be all right." Heinz Czechowski: "Historische Reminiszenz." Chiarloni and Pankoke, eds., *Grenzfallgedichte*, p. 74. This appears to be at least partly a case of emotion recollected in tranquillity. For Czechowski's immediate reaction, see Thomas Rosenlöcher's account of the Kohl visit in *Die verkauften Pflastersteine*, pp. 81–82.
20 Heiduczek: "Elegie des Vergehens." Heiduczek: *Im gewöhnlichen Stalinismus*, p. 227.
21 Rosenlöcher: *Die verkauften Pflastersteine*, pp. 95, 93, 35.

a Western newspaper and you feel important.[22] The coinage too is heavier, and he has to peer and count it out awkwardly like a tourist, "a foreigner in my own land, which of course never did belong to me."[23] When he goes on a visit to "Schicki-Micki-Land," i.e. West Germany, the glittering range in a department store produces mild nausea, yet draws him repeatedly in, though not to spend: how can you choose anything when each single thing is claiming to be Everything? In any case, "the elation western money arouses goes well beyond the attraction of actual things." He finally buys a ballpoint pen: "they're always right."[24] But the humour is mixed with seriousness. Alongside the self-deflating account of his unheroic GDR past and his non-decisive part in the 'events', there is the anger over lost life-time, "the theft of the years in the name of a future that always evaporates";[25] and once again, that leitmotif of East German experience, the feeling that the changes are bringing more of the same, a new orthodoxy as rigid as the old, imposed in a similar way. This time it is a meeting of East German writers with forty of their Western colleagues:

> Forty-fold self-righteousness round the tables. The ones who live in affluence must be right. Word for word to the assembled press, which of course has *always* been right. Near me a seated giant directs his entourage with an ironic raising of the brow. I'd never have thought western intellectuals could turn out to be such massed bands of yes-men. Three or four residual left-wingers, stuttering a few words against the Great Acceptance. And what about me? Just the same as it always was. Like being at a Party meeting: not capable of the least objection. Sweating with cowardice under the overbearing pressure of the unification proposals.[26]

The unchanged cowardice shows up the (essentially) unchanged pressures towards 'Einheit', a unity that means conformity. With election time, there are posters everywhere, a shiny surface symbolically papering over the decaying grey walls like an "advance fulfilment of all promises."[27] At the end, our hero confronts power, rather like the conformist meeting the Kaiser in Heinrich Mann's *Untertan*, or crazed Eugene addressing Peter the Great in Pushkin's *Bronze Horseman*. Here it is a larger-than-lifesize placard of Helmut Kohl set up

---

22 Rosenlöcher: *Die Wiederentdeckung des Gehens beim Wandern*, pp. 10–11. The phrasing of this passage has become a touch less sharp im comparison with the pre-publication "Leseprobe" sent to the Cheltenham Festival organisers.
23 Ibid., p. 10.
24 Rosenlöcher: *Die verkauften Pflastersteine*, p. 56.
25 Ibid., p. 65.
26 Ibid., pp. 100–101.
27 Ibid., p. 99.

in the park, with crocus beds and all the stars of the European Community behind him. "'Rosenlöcher', he says, 'your ideas are all just dreams. People over here have long since seen what it's really all about. Just look around you. There's nothing better than what I have to offer.'"[28] But was that all the 1989 revolution was about? To cap it all, the neighbour's hated dog springs out from behind the placard and our hero hastily departs, disappearing pathetically into the distance like Charlie Chaplin.

The whole situation has echoes of Brecht's late poem "Der Radwechsel" (Changing a Wheel):

> Ich sitze am Straßenhang.
> Der Fahrer wechselt das Rad.
> Ich bin nicht gern, wo ich herkomme.
> Ich bin nicht gern, wo ich hinfahre.
> Warum sehe ich den Radwechsel
> Mit Ungeduld?[29]

East German writers did not much like it where they had been, nor where they were going. They felt helpless at the roadside while the driver made the changes, somewhere on a route from one dystopia to another. But it was the population at large who were impatient. Now they too are belatedly realising it was not a short route to the easy life.

I said there has not been much understanding in West Germany for the critical reservations of East German writers. The insensitivity of the takeover in practical areas has been, if anything, even greater in literary journalism. Not much sign of 'humane letters' here. The controversy has centred on Christa Wolf's short novel *Was bleibt*. Like most of her work, it has a directly autobiographical base. It narrates her experience of being put under surveillance by the Stasi in the late '70s. Christa Wolf was always committed to the East German state, a Party member and at one time a candidate for the Central Committee. She was no enthusiast for the West, but highly esteemed there for the values her fiction explored and defended. Against collective values she had defended since 1965 the view that art "necessarily proceeds from particular cases [...] and cannot give up being subjective."[30] Her book *Nachdenken über*

---

28 Ibid., p. 113.
29 "I sit by the roadside. / The driver changes the wheel. / I don't much like it where I come from. / I don't much like it where I'm going. / Why do I watch him change it / With such impatience?" Brecht: *Werke* (Große kommentierte Berliner und Frankfurter Ausgabe) vol. 12, p. 310.
30 Quoted in the *Hansers Sozialgeschichte der deutschen Literatur*, vol. 11: Schmitt: *Die Literatur der DDR*, p. 48.

Christa T. (The Quest for Christa T.), published in 1969, narrated a young woman's attempt to live out individual self-fulfilment despite collectivist pressures, before her early death of leukemia (or as Marcel Reich-Ranicki put it, typically of Western critics, what she suffered from was the GDR). Though this individualist line earned Wolf a lot of criticism from Party orthodoxy, her reputation grew at home and abroad. The GDR could not do much about authors of international standing – indeed, it could not do without them;[31] she was accepted, in East and West, as an ornament of GDR literature. So surveillance came as a shock. It was almost certainly part of the crackdown after 1976, when the satirical poet and performer Wolf Biermann was expelled from the country, and Christa Wolf was among the writers who issued a public statement inviting the government to reconsider.

Was bleibt is a close study of the woman writer's morale under stress – an unheroic sequence of fear, depression, and nervous crisis. By the end, friction with the authorities and supportive contacts at a public reading have given her the courage to go on. But the work also has two other obvious strands. First, it tries to achieve a literary understanding and a new language that will embrace the 'other side' – from the young Stasi operatives with their lunchboxes parked all day outside, to the controller of the operation, who she imagines is a renegade intellectual she knows, someone who envies her ability to know fully the human beings she portrays and who lusts for total knowledge of a flesh-and-blood human being instead. Secondly, the book is a frank and rather bleak look (the mood of her fiction has steadily darkened over time) at where she now stands, with her materially easy life and her increasingly blunted response to the constraints of East German society. This in contrast to two radical young writers who seek her help; one has been in prison and the other is likely to end there because they will not compromise. Whereas she is already asking "what remains" from her life and work, what achievements and memories she can retire with,[32] they do not ask that brooding, small-minded ('krämerisch') question, they are spontaneous and single-minded. Has she a duty, or a right, to stop them "running on to the knives" of the Party?[33]

Christa Wolf herself ran on to another set of knives because her book had a fatal flaw, its publication date. It was written in 1979, and if it had appeared

---

31 See the comment of Ulbricht's secretary Otto Gotsche after the publication of *Nachdenken über Christa T.*: if Christa Wolf were not such a good writer, she would have been "long ago put through the mill." See Drescher, ed., *Dokumentation zu Christa Wolfs "Nachdenken über Christa T.,"* p. 209.

32 Wolf: *Was bleibt*, p. 79.

33 Ibid., pp. 56, 77.

then it would have been hailed as another indictment of the police state. Instead, she kept it back, then revised it in 1989 and published it in 1990. A chorus of criticism rejected it as too late. Worse, it was an attempt to pose as a victim of the regime which she had been happy to live under and to live off. Scales, it seems, fell from the eyes of Western critics who had said nothing against her work over the years; suddenly, it had always been worthless. Where she had been respected as a gentle but insistent voice speaking for individuals and sanity, now it was clear she had all along had a deep psychological impulse to conform to the authoritarian state.[34] What counted now was not the values she had stood for, but all the political occasions in recent years when she had not made a public protest. And where she had, as in the Biermann affair, this was devalued by rumours that her protest had later been withdrawn.

Christa Wolf thereby became the main defendant in a journalistic show trial in which prominent East German writers generally (not the Party hacks and prompt fulfillers of cultural decrees, but all the serious claimants to the title of writer) were declared to have 'stabilised the regime' with their works, their success, their prestige, – in other words, simply by their decision to stay in the GDR and go on writing.

Those parts of the accusation that have any substance are already admitted in Christa Wolf's self-scrutiny – her life of relative luxury, the tiring of her radical impulse. It is also an obvious paradox not peculiar to her time and place that the literature of an independent and even protesting voice may gradually and insidiously get absorbed into the affirmative culture around it. But beyond that the charge fails, and makes the accusers look crass. To stay in East Germany and attempt critical dialogue did not mean condoning the regime. One might as well say that Nadine Gordimer 'stabilised' the South African government and sustained apartheid by staying on there and continuing to write books, only three of which (out of eighteen) the authorities felt they had to ban. What, realistically, were East German writers to do? Emigrate to the West? Some in the end had to. Yet the notion that individuals should leave behind the place they are attached to and all its problems[35] itself arguably rests on a typical Western assumption that total freedom of choice takes precedence over any form of social responsibility. It is known that Christa Wolf considered leaving and decided against, partly because she did

---

34 Schirrmacher: "'Dem Druck des härteren, strengeren Lebens standhalten'. Auch eine Studie über den autoritären Charakter. Christa Wolfs Aufsätze, Reden und ihre jüngste Erzählung." *Frankfurter Allgemeine Zeitung* No. 127, June 2, 1990, "Bilder und Zeiten" [p. 5].

35 Evidence of this – hardly surprising – human attachment is contained in some of the interviews in Königsdorf: *Adieu DDR*.

not think she could write outside the society she knew. That explains why she did not publish the novel when she first wrote it: in the climate of 1979 she would have been forced to go.

But why then did she publish it in 1990? Perhaps she was naïve enough to expect sympathetic understanding. Her work had always been warmly received in the West. All artistic value aside, it was a record of the problems and stresses of living in East Germany, and was avidly read as such. She may have thought that this text too belonged in the record now that she was free to release it. If so, then she forgot (and it is surprising a German writer could forget) that the way the last piece of history is read is a crucial factor in the next piece that isalready in the making. As one of her denigrators wrote with unashamed ruthlessness: "What is at issue is the interpretation of the literary past and the pushing through of a reading. That is not an academic question. If you control the way things were, you also control what comes next."[36] It must have given Christa Wolf a bitter home-from-home feeling when her work met not with literary criticism, but denunciation.

You may wonder what motives lay behind the denunciation, and since Wolf's assailants indulged in some amateur psychologising at her expense, we may also speculate a little. For years the GDR extorted good money from the Federal Republic in return for allowing visits between families divided by the Wall. The GDR also had to be recognised and to some degree courted as part of a larger *Ostpolitik* aimed at reducing European tension. Then again, compassion was constantly in demand for the brothers and sisters in the East, and especially for those in conflict with the authorities, which often meant writers and intellectuals. That extended to their books and gave them a paradoxical advantage in public interest and sympathy, what was called the 'GDR bonus.' The Federal Republic was always giving. Yet now, after the 1989 revolution, here were many East Germans wanting to live in their own fashion, dragging their feet over unification, having independent ideas about other ways in which society might be run democratically and humanely, instead of handing things over at once to the established Western political parties.

Enough accumulated resentments, perhaps, to account for the outbursts of the more illiberally-minded critics, – to account, that is, for a U-turn as sharp as any that East German 'Wendehälse' have been accused of as they disowned their past and slipped into new careers.

---

36 Greiner: "Die deutsche Gesinnungsästhetik. Noch einmal: Christa Wolf und der deutsche Literaturstreit." *Die Zeit* No. 45, November 2, 1990, p. 59. I take a closer look elsewhere at the principles underlying the journalistic practice of Greiner and others. See "Disconnections in the 1990 *Literaturstreit*."

But the attack then widened not just beyond Christa Wolf to East German writers generally, but beyond specific writers to the question of what literature should be about and how it should be judged. Denunciation, in other words, was followed by the decreeing of a new line, yet another ironic echo of communist practice. The new doctrine was that all writing or critical judgement which has politics or principles as its motive was to be out; 'aesthetic' values were to be in. That went for West German writers too, who for years have tried to be the conscience of the Federal Republic – Heinrich Böll, say, or Günter Grass. Grass, incidentally, annoyed proponents of unification by declaring flatly against it. Enough is enough, said the *Frankfurter Allgemeine*. The irony here is that the attack on political values is itself political, part of the politics of taking over the East and writing off virtually everything that was ever done or thought there.

Even without that to cast doubt on its credentials, the argument is altogether too simple. 'Aesthetic' and 'political' cannot be set against each other because they cannot be neatly separated, either in acts of creation or in acts of judgement. For example, in that confessional poem of Heiner Müller's the form grows out of the ethical self-questioning, which is shaped by the political situations of two different times; we move between these levels and integrate them as we read. There *is* no 'aesthetic' quality above or apart from the poet's effort to shape that complex and our effort to understand it. The same would apply to that much larger text of Volker Braun's life and work, which will not be 'incomprehensible' in a more balanced time to readers of broad interests and sympathies (if indeed it is now); and it will certainly turn out to include at least one classic.[37] It is too easy to dismiss East German works of similar stature simply because their themes – the individual and society, power and freedom, rigidity and change, integrity and corruption – arose from a political situation and *can* be labelled 'political'. To denigrate such writing and call for pure 'aesthetic' writing and judgments can only lead to the impoverishment of literature, as the pursuit of the aesthetic for its own sake always has in the past.[38]

East German writers have not taken all this lying down. Acutely aware of the controversy's political nature, they have declared that their function will go on being the same despite, or even because of, unification: still to ask awk-

---

37 Cf. Braun: *Unvollendete Geschichte*.
38 If 'aesthetic' has any useful role in this controversy, it is in Kant's sense of a 'disinterested' reading: that is, deeply absorbed in everything the work of art enacts for us, but not moved by practical, local, topical interests. That mental attitude does not depend on the work's subject. Unfortunately there are few such dispassionate readers in Germany at present.

ward questions; to undo ideology (now above all that of the market); to prevent a complacency that takes the end of the Cold War for the end of all conflicts; and to preserve literature as what it was in the GDR, "the only place for Utopia."[39]

If I have talked too much about politics for your taste, I can only plead that German history as I described it at the start makes these conflicts and arguments unavoidable. So unlike the home life of our own dear literature, which one sometimes thinks might as well be happening in Utopia itself.

To end with something more conciliatory. There have been notable defenders of East Germany and its literary achievements.[40] Perhaps even more important, there has been one fine work of fiction by a West German writer, that tries to enter into East German feelings. Friedrich Christian Delius's *Die Birnen von Ribbeck* (The Peartrees of Ribbeck) is a stream-of-consciousness monologue – in a prose, incidentally, of high 'aesthetic' quality – spoken by an old Prussian farmworker as he looks back over his lifetime, from the feudal days of Wilhelmine society, through wars and Nazism and Communism, to the events of 1989. Now a crowd of West Germans have brought the village a new peartree, to renew the legend of a generous lord of the manor whose gifts of fruit to the village children inspired a famous nineteenth-century poem by Fontane. They make a day of it, they bring lavish Western food and drink with them, there is much Western back-slapping and talking and not listening, the tree is pushed straight in without anyone stopping to ask exactly where the traditional place is. But this is not quite satire: the Westerners are friendly and well-meaning, and who would notice satire? They are so full of the present, and the present is so full of them, that the past is overlaid, except as a pretext for a party. Soon the village will no doubt be a theme-park based on the legend, and will support its inhabitants so they no longer have to sweat in the fields. All of which has been made possible by a revolution which was a

---

39 Müller: "Was wird aus dem größeren Deutschland?" *Sinn und Form* 43 (1991), p. 667; see also Heiner Müller: "Bautzen oder Babylon." Ibid., p. 664, where he insists on the acuteness of unsolved Third World problems: "das Ende der Geschichte ist ein Traum saturierter Eliten." Similarly Volker Braun, quoted by Wallace: "Zu Volker Braun," promising to be a critic of the new compromises and illusions and to encourage rational thought on a world scale.

40 Walter Jens: "Plädoyer gegen die Preisgabe der DDR-Kultur. Fünf Forderungen an die Intellektuellen im geeinten Deutschland." *Süddeutsche Zeitung* No. 136, June 16, 1991, pp. 14–6. Also a speech by the Swiss writer Adolf Muschg: "Rede an einen abgefahrenen Zug. Nachtreten auf bereits Liegende als neue deutsche Feuilleton-Lockerheit." *Frankfurter Rundschau*, December 8, 1990. See also, outside the literary arena, the humane and sensible analysis of the new German citizenship and its problems in a small book by the ancient historian Christian Meier: *Die Nation, die keine sein will*.

triumph of the East, though the programme for celebrating it is now organised by the West.

But the village already has its own pear-tree, a local wild growth, though the bearers of the new tree did not want to hear about it. Might it possibly take a graft from their more refined species? Perhaps:

> da müßte ein Experte anreisen und klären, ob die beiden Pfropfpartner einander vertragen, müßte beiden Bäumen Wunden zufügen mit Kopuliermesse und Kopulierhippe, und bei der Stärke unseres Baumes müßte er die Kopulation mit Gegenzungen vornehmen, damit wegen der größeren Festigkeit, der größeren Berührungsflächen eine innigere Verwachsung erreicht wird.[41]

You could only try it, and wait and see.

In the newly-united country of which Willy Brandt hopefully said "jetzt wächst zusammen, was zusammengehört" – what belongs together is now growing together – the process has cut deeper and more woundingly than anyone expected. I have tried to describe the somewhat bitter fruits of a first season.

---

41 "an expert would have to be called in to say whether the two grafting-partners were compatible, he would have to cut wounds in both trees with his grafting tools, and in view of the strength of our tree he would have to make the graft using tongue-wedges for greater firmness, so that the contact surfaces grew more closely together." Delius: *Die Birnen von Ribbeck*, p. 40.

Karl-Heinz J. Schoeps
University of Illinois

Intellectuals, Unification, and Political Change 1990: The Case of Christa Wolf

Abstract: Christa Wolf's celebrity status in both East and West Germany before the German unification of 1990 and the subsequent attacks made by West German critics on her after unification make her a particularly suitable example for the position of GDR literature before, during, and after unification. Loyal but critical East German writers like Wolf expressed dissatisfaction with the Communist regime in their works and received severe criticism from party functionaries in the East and high praise from Western critics. After unification, in a surprising turn of events, a number of Western critics proceeded to attack these same writers, especially Christa Wolf, for supporting a corrupt system. According to these critics, the second German unification also brought an end to post-war German literature in both East and West and the opportunity for a totally 'new' German literature.

For over forty years, West Germans and western politicians had called for unification but when it came in 1990, no one was prepared. Even after the opening of the wall on 9 November 1989 immediate unification did not seem to be on the cards. First calls for unification were heard in the streets of Leipzig on 22 November, when the chant of the Monday demonstrations changed from "Wir sind *das* Volk" (we are *the* people) to "Wir sind *ein* Volk" (we are *one* people) thereby changing the entire nature of the demonstrations. On 28 November 1989 Chancellor Helmut Kohl of West Germany unveiled his ten point plan for a confederation of the two German states, envisioning eventual unification. But events moved so rapidly that the West German government decided to drop the quickly outdated 10-points-plan and move the unification process ahead. The process was accelerated with the introduction of the West German mark on 1 July 1990 and ended with the official unification on 3 October 1990. In the unification process – which had really begun with the massive flight of people via Hungary and Czechoslovakia in the summer and fall of 1989 – the people determined the speed of events, not the politicians or intellectuals. How did the intellectuals, especially the writers in

East Germany, fare in the unification process? Christa Wolf's case may serve as an example of the fate of the critical but loyal majority of East German authors. Wolf's celebrity status in both East and West Germany before unification and the attacks of West German critics on her after unification make her a particularly suitable example for the position of GDR literature before, during, and after unification. Her "case" rose to a "cause célèbre" in 1990, and in any discussion of cultural ramifications of the second German unification the Christa Wolf debate cannot be ignored.

In the summer and fall of 1989, when thousands of East Germans left their country and headed west, a number of concerned East German citizens appealed to them to remain in their country, the German Democratic Republic (GDR). One of those appeals, published on 8 November 1989, one day before the opening of the wall, was signed by a diverse group of people, including representatives of civil rights groups such as Bärbel Bohley of the "Neues Forum" (New Forum) and Gerhard Poppe of the "Initiative für Frieden und Menschenrechte" (Initiative for Peace and Human Rights), the conductor of the Leipzig "Gewandhaus Orchester" Kurt Masur (now also the conductor of the New York Philarmonic Orchestra), as well as the writers Christoph Hein and Christa Wolf.[1] In the brief period of change from the old GDR to the new united Germany, a number of people ranging from writers and artists to dissidents and reformers at the newly created democratic "round tables" saw a chance for the reconstruction of a socialist democracy "from below." With the benefit of hindsight, their efforts now seem to have been somewhat naive and unrealistic, yet in the wake of the dramatic changes taking place in 1989 and the massive demonstrations in various cities of the GDR, it was their hope to create a truly democratic and socialist society which had eluded them during forty years of SED-decreed socialism "from above."

One of the largest rallies took place on 4 November 1989 on East Berlin's Alexanderplatz under the motto "Für unser Land" (For Our Country); the featured speakers included Christa Wolf. As she said almost three eventful months later in Hildesheim where the local university awarded her an honorary degree on 31 January 1990, Wolf saw this giant rally as the result and culmination of years of opposition literature, including hers. This literature had attempted to encourage the people of the GDR to resist lies, hypocrisy and resignation. But in this speech she also conceded that their hopes for a renewal of the GDR were unrealistic and that the efforts to achieve it came much too late. Christa Wolf recognized that the main function of GDR liter-

---

1 Wolf: *Im Dialog*, pp. 169–70.

ature – providing information – would now be taken over by a free press, and she was uncertain as to the future role of literature:

> Wer wird die Trauer, die Scham, die Reue vieler Menschen, die ich aus ihren Briefen herauslese, in ihren Augen sehe und auch in mir selbst finde, noch öffentlich ausdrücken wollen, wenn alle mit der Verbesserung der materiellen Lebensbedingungen beschäftigt sein werden? Wer wird es auf sich nehmen, Widerspruch anzumelden gegen bestimmte menschliche Konsequenzen eines Wirtschaftssystems, dessen Segnungen verständlicherweise von den meisten herbeigesehnt werden.[2]

Wolf expressed concern at the disorientation and depression she witnessed in many people and wondered what would happen if people's expectations were once again disappointed: "Wohin werden sie politisch treiben?" she asked.[3] But she also remained hopeful that after some years a desire for utopian thinking would rise again.

In order to understand Christa Wolf's attitudes and positions during and after unification it is necessary to take a look back at her personal development and her position in the cultural life of the GDR. Christa Wolf was arguably one of the most prominent and respected representatives of GDR literature in both Germanies. Born on 18 March 1929 in what was then called Landsberg/Warthe (today Gorzow Wielkopolski) she experienced the Nazi period from childhood to adolescence and became an ardent member of the "Bund Deutscher Mädel, BDM" (Union of Young Maidens), the female version of the "Hitler Youth." Along with millions of other Germans, she and her family were forced to leave their homes in 1945. They found a new home in the Soviet occupation zone of Germany, from 1949 to 1990 known as the GDR, and Christa Wolf's eyes were then opened to the crimes of Nazi Germany. Wolf (and countless others like her) became a convinced socialist and fervent supporter of the East German "anti-Fascist workers and peasant state," whose leaders included a number of survivors from exile, concentration camps, and Nazi-prisons who had experienced the cruelties of the Nazi regime first hand. The beginnings of Wolf's reeducation process are vividly depicted in her story "Blickwechsel" (Change in Perspective) of 1970, and in her novel *Kindheitsmuster* (Patterns of Childhood) of 1976.

---

2   Ibid., p. 162. "Who will express the sadness, the shame, the remorse of a great number of people which I find in their letters and also in myself when everyone is preoccupied with the improvement of living conditions? Who will take it upon himself/herself to oppose certain negative effects of an economic system, the blessings of which are now understandably devoutly desired by most people?"; my translation. All further translations in the text are my own unless otherwise noted.

3   Ibid., p. 160. "Where will they drift politically?"

"Blickwechsel," a precursor to *Kindheitsmuster*,[4] was Christa Wolf's contribution to a volume that commemorated the 25th anniversary of the liberation from Fascism.[5] The story depicts the experiences of a sixteen year old girl at the end of the war. The title has a double meaning: it refers not only to the change from girlhood to womanhood of the main character but also to the change of her political orientation. The narration, presented in the typical Wolf style of reflection and remembrance, contains a great deal of autobiographical material. In both *Kindheitsmuster* and "Blickwechsel," Wolf describes in fictional form her traumatic awakening from youthful innocence; in both works the main characters are are laboring under feelings of guilt. "Blickwechsel," from the narrative perspective of 1970, describes how a group of German refugees, including Christa Wolf and her family, fled before the advancing Red Army in the spring of 1945. A central passage in this description is the analysis of the feelings the main character and her fellow refugees have when they encounter a group of concentration camp victims, survivors of the death march from the concentration camp Oranienburg:

> Trotz allem, was wir einander und was wir uns selber beteuerten: Wir wußten Bescheid. [...] Wir wußten: Diese da, die man zu Tieren erklärt hatte und die jetzt langsam auf uns zukamen, um sich zu rächen – wir hatten sie fallenlassen. [...] Und mit Entsetzen fühlte ich: Das ist gerecht, und wußte für den Bruchteil einer Sekunde, daß wir schuldig waren.[6]

At first, the German refugees kept a fearful distance since some of the former prisoners were armed in order to defend their newly-won freedom. But then one of the former prisoners joined the refugees at the campfire to share their meager meal of simple soup. When asked why he was incarcerated he replied: "Ich bin Kommunist."[7] Nelly, the main character in *Kindheitsmuster* and Wolf's alter ego, was perplexed that someone could accuse himself of being a communist because so far she had always heard the term "communist" in connection with the term criminal. The communist's reply came "ohne Vorwurf, ohne besondere Betonung: Wo habt ihr bloß alle gelebt."[8] This key

---

4 See Schoeps: "Wandel und Erinnerung: Christa Wolfs Erzählung 'Blickwechsel'."
5 Schmidt, ed., *Der erste Augenblick der Freiheit*, pp. 329–52.
6 Wolf: "Blickwechsel," p. 100. "Contrary to all reassurances to others and to ourselves we knew the truth. [...] We knew: those people who had been declared animals who were now approaching us to take revenge – we had deserted them. [...] And with horror I felt: this is justified, and for a fraction of a second I knew that we were guilty."
7 Wolf: *Kindheitsmuster*, p. 430; "I'm a communist" (*A Model Childhood*, p. 332).
8 Ibid., p. 431. "Without reproach, without special emphasis: Where on earth have you all been living" (*A Model Childhood*, p. 332). As Christa Wolf pointed out in remarks concerning

sentence determined both Nelly's – and the author Christa Wolf's – future course of life: "Natürlich vergaß Nelly den Satz nicht, aber erst später – Jahre später – wurde er ihr zu einer Art Motto."[9] This theme could also be called "Writing under the shadow of Auschwitz," a theme Günter Grass – born two years before Christa Wolf in 1927, but like Christa Wolf a child of lower middle class shopkeepers and "fellow travellers" of the Nazi party from an area which is now part of Poland – claimed as a dominant force behind his entire oevre although he wrote under different personal, social, and political circumstances.[10] Both authors wrote (and continue writing) under the shadow of Auschwitz, but while Grass was able to find his way out of the shock he experienced when his eyes were opened to the Nazi crimes without relying on any kind of ideology, Christa Wolf "fell from one ideology into another."[11] In a discussion with Aafke Steenhuis on 11 December 1989 Wolf vividly described her high hopes during the early years of the GDR:

> Meine Generation identifizierte sich schon früh mit der entstehenden Gesellschaft, weil wir hier in den vierziger Jahren gezwungen waren, uns intensiv und radikal mit der faschistischen Vergangenheit auseinanderzusetzen, schärfer als das in der Bundesrepublik der Fall war.[12]

Later, when it became evident to her that socialism as practiced in the GDR was less than ideal, she was still full of hope that people would prevail who had preserved the dream of socialism.[13] Her existential shock ("existentieller Schock") came with the Warsaw Pact invasion of Czechoslovakia in 1968. And yet she refrained from open opposition, because as a young person

---

her work as a writer, Nelly's experiences resemble those of her creator very closely: "I experienced […] that it is something different to hear people whispering the term 'communist' always in connection with 'criminal' and then suddenly on a cold night, after many weeks on the road, after many images not thought possible to sit by the fire next to a German communist in concentration camp clothing." ("Ich erfuhr, daß es etwa anderes ist, […] das Wort 'Kommunist' immer nur im Zusammenhang mit 'Verbrecher' flüstern zu hören, als plötzlich, in einer kalten Nacht, nach vielen Wochen auf der Landstaße, nach vielen nie für möglich gehaltenen Bildern, neben einem deutschen Kommunisten in KZ-Kleidung am Feuer zu sitzen". Wolf: *Die Dimension des Autors*, p. 80.)

9   *Kindheitsmuster*, p. 431. "Of course Nelly didn't forget his sentence, but only later, years later, did it become a kind of guiding principle for her" (*A Model Childhood*, p. 332).
10 Günter Grass: "Schreiben nach Auschwitz."
11 See Günter Grass: "Aufhören, auf leere Hoffnungen zu setzen," p. 27.
12 Wolf: *Im Dialog*, pp. 134–35. "My generation identified itself early on with the new society just being created because an intensive and radical preoccupation with the Fascist past was forced upon us in the forties that was much more thorough than in the Federal Republic."
13 Ibid., p. 135.

raised under Fascism she had developed strong feelings of guilt, and she felt a great reluctance to oppose people who had been in concentration camps during the Nazi time.[14]

In 1949, in the belief that she was participating in a great venture to construct in East Germany a truly humane and anti-fascist society, Christa Wolf joined the Socialist Unity Party (SED), the ruling party in the GDR, a party she did not leave until the summer of 1989, even though it was this very same party which also caused her great problems and difficulties. First indications of problems ahead arose with the publication and the troubled reception of her first novel *Der geteilte Himmel* (The Divided Heaven) in 1963; no lesser a figure than Horst Sindermann, later president of the People's Chamber (Volkskammer) of the GDR, initiated the attack on *Der geteilte Himmel* in the Halle newspaper ironically called *Freiheit* (Freedom).[15] In particular, GDR hardliners criticised Wolf's alleged distortion of socialist reality and bourgeois skepticism in her novel. The critical reactions and vituperative accusations culminated in an uproar when her novel *Nachdenken über Christa T.* (Quest for Christa T.) was published in 1968. In the light of what happened to Christa Wolf after the German unification of 1990, the complicated reception and publication history of *Nachdenken über Christa T.* is worth a brief review. The debate about *Nachdenken* was already documented by Manfred Behn in 1978.[16] But with the demise of the GDR and the opening of archives, new and additional materials, including private notes from Christa Wolf herself, have been made available in a very informative volume edited by Angela Drescher.[17] In a letter to Angela Drescher, Christa Wolf expressed some concern about Drescher's documentation, since it could again provide grist for the mills of (West-) German feuilletons, resulting in reactions similar to those Christa Wolf had experienced after the publication of her story *Was bleibt* (to which I will come later):

> Du kennst meine Skrupel angesichts dieser Publikation, die im ungünstigsten Fall, mit dem zu rechnen ist, (wieder nur) einer feuilletonistisch-moralisierenden Betrachtungsweise Vorschub leisten wird und der Bestätigung der vorgefaßten Erwartungen.[18]

---

14 Ibid., p. 136.
15 See Drescher, ed., *Dokumentation zu Christa Wolf*, p. 22.
16 See Behn, ed., *Wirkungsgeschichte von Christa Wolfs "Nachdenken über Christa T."*
17 See Drescher, ed., *Dokumentation zu Christa Wolf*.
18 Ibid., p. 189. "You know my reservations concerning this publication which, in the most unfavourable scenario (which is likely to occur) will give rise (again) only to a superficial and moralizing view confirming precast expectation."

For Christa Wolf, the publication of this documentation was difficult, and she felt that the attacks on her in the West surpassed anything she had ever experienced in the GDR: "Es fällt mir nicht leicht, in die jetzt fällige Entblößung der Eingeweide, in diesen Wirbel von Beschuldigungen, Selbstverteidigung, Verschleierung, Gewissenserforschung, Selbstverleugnung, Lüge und Verschweigen die nüchterne Darstellung eines solchen vergleichsweise geringfügigen Vorgangs hineinzuwerfen."[19] But it was her hope that the documentation would help to correct the phantom image that threatened to replace the GDR's concrete history. After the end of the socialist experiment in Germany this documentation, and the novel *Nachdenken über Christa T.*, seemed to Christa Wolf to come from a different world.

The novel *Nachdenken über Christa T.*, dealing with the self-realization of the individual in a collectivized society and a plea for socialism with a human face, was begun as Christa Wolf's immediate response to the disastrous 11th plenary session of the Central Committee of the SED on 15–18 December 1965 which officially condemned "skepticism" and "liberalism." The main targets in Erich Honecker's address to the plenary session were the writers Werner Bräunig, Stefan Heym, Heiner Müller, and especially Wolf Biermann. After his attacks on individual writers, Honecker summarized the criticism of unwanted "-isms" such as liberalism, skepticism, and subjectivism:

> Das Charakteristische all dieser Erscheinungen besteht darin, daß sie objektiv mit der Linie des Gegners übereinstimmen, durch die Verbreitung von Unmoral und Skeptizismus besonders die Intelligenz und die Jugend zu erreichen und im Zuge einer sogenannten Liberalisierung die DDR von innen her aufzuweichen.[20]

The only attempts at defense came from Anna Seghers and Christa Wolf, but to no avail. As a result, Christa Wolf wrote the novel *Nachdenken* to overcome these traumatic experiences. The main motivation for the fictional Christa T. to write was "to overcome things by writing,"[21] and this, of course, applies equally to the author herself:

---

19 Ibid., pp. 189–90. "It is not easy for me to give an objective account of a relatively minor event in an atmosphere of expected confessions, in this vortex of accusations, self-defense, protection, protestations, obfuscation, soul-searching, self-denial, lies, and silences."

20 Franke: *Literatur der Deutschen Demokratischen Republik* vol. 1, pp. 139–40. "It characterizes all these phenomena [liberalism, scepticism, subjectivism] that they are in objective agreement with the enemy in their efforts to influence our young people and the intelligentsia through distribution of amorality and scepticism in order to weaken the GDR from within."

21 Wolf: *Nachdenken über Christa T.*, p. 122 "... daß ich nur schreibend über die Dinge komme!" The sentence is repeated several times throughout the novel.

Ich brauchte anscheinend ziemlich scharfe, schwere Geschütze, damit Verdrängtes in einer heftigen Eruption hervorkommen konnte. Danach aber war ich offener und hab mit einer neuen Unbefangenheit schreiben können, über die ich mich heute fast wundere.[22]

The complicated publication history of *Nachdenken* is outlined in detail by Christa Wolf, herself, in diary notes of the time and in a letter dated 8 February 1991 which she wrote to Herbert Wiesner, occasioned by the exhibition "Censorship in the GDR."[23] According to these sources, the manuscript was finished on 1 March 1967 and was submitted at that time to the Mitteldeutscher Verlag, Christa Wolf's publisher in Halle, GDR. After four different "expert" opinions, the permission to publish was given with 31 March 1969 as date for publication of the first edition of a projected 15,000 copies. But in December 1968 the publishing process was interrupted for some time because a number of party functionaries (some of whom had not even read the book) objected to its contents. A much smaller number of copies than earlier envisioned was eventually published in the GDR in 1969, although the sales were handled in a rather restrictive manner. [A second edition (backdated to 1968!) did not appear until 1972 when Ulbricht had retired and Honecker had promised a more liberalized cultural policy.] But despite the limited publication in 1969, the debate went on. In a letter to the official SED party newspaper *Neues Deutschland*, dated 15 May 1969, even the publisher turned against his own book. While all this was happening in the GDR, the West German edition appeared withoutdifficulties in April 1968 where it made the bestseller lists both in *Die Zeit* and *Der Spiegel*. However, it did not help matters in the GDR when on 23 May 1969 a very positive review of the book appeared in the West German weekly *Die Zeit*, written by Marcel Reich-Ranicki, a critic who could under no circumstances be accused of being a communist sympathizer. This review, entitled "Christa Wolfs unruhige Elegie" (Christa Wolf's Unsettling Elegy), praised the novel very highly ("ein höchst erfreulicher Fall"[24]), and it contained the crucial sentence "Christa T. stirbt an Leukämie, aber sie leidet an der DDR" (Christa T. dies from leukemia but she suffers from the GDR).[25] Reich-Ranicki's laudatio, and particularly this sentence,

---

22 Drescher, ed., *Dokumentation*, p. 9. "It seems I needed strong and heavy guns so that repressed feelings could emerge in a violent eruption. But afterwards I was able to write more openly and with a newly found ease which surprises me even today."
23 See Ibid., pp. 25–8. See also Christa Wolf's diary notes in Drescher, ed., *Dokumentation*, pp. 193–213.
24 Ibid., p. 104, "a highly pleasing case." Reich-Ranicki had read the West German Luchterhand edition that was published in April of 1969 without a hitch.
25 Ibid., p. 105.

caused Wolf even more problems. A number of SED functionaries took Reich-Ranicki's review as a point of departure for their attacks on Christa Wolf, and she came under a variety of pressures. Thus she was "advised" to relinquish her candidacy for a leadership position in the East German writers' union, which she refused to do. Another complication arose when Wolf withstood a great deal of pressure and refused to change her opposition to the Warsaw pact invasion of Czechoslovakia. In a speech during the writers' congress at the end of May 1969, Max Walter Schulz, vice president of the GDR writers' union and director of the "Institute for Literature" in Leipzig, severely criticized the ideological position of *Nachdenken*, quoting extensively from Reich-Ranicki's review to prove what great service Christa Wolf had done to the "class enemy" in the West. Even harsher was Otto Gotsche, Ulbricht's secretary in the cultural section of the Central Committee, and one of Christa Wolf's arch enemies ever since she defended the vilified authors at the 11th plenary session of the Central Committee of the SED in 1965. Also referring to Reich-Ranicki's review, he told Christa Wolf that her book was miserable from an ideological point of view, even worse than *Der geteilte Himmel*, and that her tendency towards doubt and tragedy could never lead to positive results[26] – as was expected under the doctrine of socialist realism.

In a meeting with officials of the writers' union and a representative of the Central Committee of the SED (a man by the appropriate name of Hochmuth, English "arrogance"), Wolf was asked to declare that she would never again write a book like *Nachdenken*, and she was told to stay closer to the party line in the future. Again she refused, fearing that it would be the end of her ability to write if she were forced to say what she did not mean. But she also realized that by not giving in to these demands, she might bring an end to her career as a writer and be forced to look for another profession.[27] As Christa Wolf told Therese Hörnigk in an interview in 1987, the acrimonious attacks on *Nachdenken* in 1968–69 almost ruined her life:

> Meine Existenz in diesem Land als gesellschaftliches Wesen wurde in Frage gestellt, ich habe danach längere Zeit gebraucht, um wieder schreibfähig zu werden. [...] Ich begriff auf einmal, daß ich *nicht* dasselbe wollte wie sie, daß sie sich durch mein Buch bedroht fühlten und darum so heftig reagierten.[28]

---

26 Wolf's diary in Drescher, ed., *Dokumentation*, pp. 208–09.
27 See Wolf's diary notes in Drescher, ed., *Dokumentation*, pp. 202–04.
28 Hörnigk: *Christa Wolf*, p. 32. "My existence as a social being in this country was called into question. After that, it took me a while to be able to write again. [...] until I realized that I did *not* want the same things they [the functionaries] did, and that they felt threatened by my book, which explained their harsh reactions."

The attacks marked a turning point in Wolf's life and career as a writer. Once Wolf had come to terms with the division that existed between herself and the cultural representatives of the SED, she was no longer distracted from her course:

> Aber jedenfalls war ich nun nicht mehr abzudrängen von dem, was ich machen mußte, ich erwartete nicht mehr, hier öffentlich akzeptiert zu werden, ich erfuhr später auch, wie es ist, ausgegrenzt zu werden – eine nützliche, wenn auch sehr schmerzhafte Erfahrung.[29]

Yet in this ideological struggle – the literary quality of her book was never in doubt – Wolf could also count on the loyal support of some friends and colleagues. Thus Robert Havemann, former cell-mate of Erich Honecker in Brandenburg prison under the Nazis and at that time one of the major dissident figures of the GDR, wrote to her on 21 July 1969:

> Ich habe *Nachdenken über Christa T.* gelesen. [...] Es ist ein wahrhaftiges Buch, ohne jede Lüge, ohne jede Feindschaft, so, wie wir diese Sache lieben und doch fast an ihr verzweifeln könnten. Ich hoffe aber, daß Sie diesen unverzeihlichen Mut, den wir brauchen, trotzdem nicht verloren haben.[30]

Christa Wolf remained steadfast; despite increasing odds, increasing pressures, and increasing hopelessness, she retained the same style and approach that had brought her both glory and grief with *Nachdenken* throughout her career as a writer in the GDR. As the publication histories of her later works show, none of them had smooth sailing through the maze of the GDR political and cultural bureaucracy. Yet she also deflected applause from what she considered the "wrong side" (i. e. the West) when she felt it was warranted, and she emphasized her strong belief in socialism. In a letter to the Swedish publisher of *Nachdenken*, for example, she pointed to a sentence in her novel that she thought best illustrated Christa T.'s (and her own) ideological position: "Unter den Tauschangeboten war keins, nach dem auch nur den Kopf zu drehen sich lohnen würde."[31] This letter was written on 1 July 1969, and throughout the years, despite great difficulties, Christa Wolf never abandoned her hope for a socialist utopia that was never realized.

---

29 Ibid., pp. 32–3. "But in any case, I was not to be pushed away again from what I felt I had to do. From then on I did not expect to be officially acceptable in this country, and later I learned what it means to be excluded – a useful, if very painful experience."

30 Ibid., p. 147. "I have read *Nachdenken*. [...] It is an honest book without lies, without hostility, exactly what we need for our cause which looks so hopeless at times. But I hope that you have not lost this unpardonable courage which we all need."

31 In a letter to Thomas von Vegesack, 1 July 1969, in Drescher, ed., *Dokumentation*, p. 136. "Under the alternatives was none for which it was even worth turning my head."

What came instead was the collapse of the GDR – despite the urgent appeals of Wolf and others for a new and rejuvenated socialism in the GDR. The first book Christa Wolf published after the disappearance of the SED regime was the story *Was bleibt* (What Remains). The story was originally written during June and July 1979, and revised in November of 1989. It depicts the surveillance of a writer by the Stasi, the dreaded state security police, and the agonies it caused her. The story is told in first person narrative and, in typical Christa Wolf style, is permeated with reflections and reminiscences. Similar to *Nachdenken*, the story is also a quest for self-identity:

> Ich selbst. Wer war das. Welches der multiplen Wesen, aus denen "ich selbst" mich zusammensetzte. Das, das sich kennen wollte? Das, das sich schonen wollte? Oder jenes dritte, das immer noch versucht war, nach derselben Pfeife zu tanzen wie die jungen Herren da draußen vor meiner Tür?[32]

The story is a quest for identity in a changing political world, and a document of the psychic effects of police surveillance. What got lost in the political and ideological debate ensuing its publication was the fact that *Was bleibt* – like most of her works – is not pure autobiography but a fictionalized account of a tormented character with whom countless others could identify, a fact that very few critics acknowledged. One who did was Herbert Lehnert who examined the complex relationship between author and narrator of the story.[33] According to Lehnert, author and narrator are by no means always identical, and the events depicted in *Was bleibt* may not have occurred in just that way or in just that sequence. Therefore the text should not be read as the author's self-justification but as a dialogue between the author and a fictitious narrator for purposes of self-examination and deepened self-understanding. In this context already the title "Was bleibt" raises a number of questions. The German title (without question mark) is ambiguous since it could be a statement meaning "something remains" as well as a question meaning "what will remain?" What is this something that remains? A psychological wound? Or the hope that something of the socialist utopia will carry over into the new and united Germany? Or is the question an indication of doubt that anything will

---

32 Wolf: *Was bleibt*, p. 57. "I, myself. Who was that. Which of the multiple beings which constituted the self. That which claimed to know itself? That which wanted to protect itself? Or the third one that was still tempted to dance to the same tune as those young men outside my door?"

33 Lehnert: "Fiktionalität und autobiographische Motive," pp. 423–44. See also the discussion of Christa Wolf in Terence James Reed's article "Another Piece of the Past" in this volume pp. 244–47.

remain? In the story, Wolf, herself, comments on the missing question mark that is so crucial for the ambiguity of the interpretation:

> Fragezeichen. Die Zeichensetzung in Zukunft gefälligst ernster nehmen, sagte ich mir. Überhaupt: sich mehr an die harmlosen Übereinkünfte halten. Das ging doch, früher. Wann? Als hinter den Sätzen mehr Ausrufezeichen als Fragezeichen standen?[34]

Thus, the missing question mark is much more than a mere linguistic game; the ambiguity caused by its absence signifies a world view that has been shaken to its foundations.

Was bleibt is not the only Wolf story dealing with paradise lost. There are close thematic links to other works of hers, especially to *Sommerstück* (Summer Piece), in its earliest versions dating back to 1979, and also to *Kein Ort. Nirgends* (No Place. Nowhere), also written in 1979. These texts, all written or begun in 1979, deal with the loss of utopia, a term that, in its German (or English) translation, even provided the title to the story "No Place." On the surface, *Sommerstück* seems to be about the author's escape, together with her family and friends, from the city of Berlin to the idyllic rural landscape of the province of Mecklenburg. But this is deceiving. In the country, the author does not find the longed-for solace. Instead she is pursued by nightmarish dreams (among them a dream of a congress; a reference to the disastrous writers' congress of 1979 – see below). Moreover, the seemingly idyllic calm is overshadowed by the cancer-death of the narrator's close friend.[35] As in *Was bleibt*, the writer in *Sommerstück* suffers from "writer's block" from which she sees no way out. She has lost her self-confidence, the ferment she needed in order to be able to write; it was completely taken away from her.[36] This "writer's block" was caused by the loss of of illusions; her "former enthusiasm" has turned into "disappointment." What remains could be viewed as capitulation: "Was bedeutete es denn aber, wenn diejenigen, die sich einst der Veränderung verschrieben hätten, nun schlicht aufs Land gingen? Kapitulation?"[37] It is in this story, long before the publication of *Was bleibt*, and the ac-

---

[34] Wolf: *Was bleibt*, p. 12. "Question mark. I told myself that in the future I must take punctuation more seriously. In any case: adhere more closely to the harmless agreements. At one time, that was possible. When? When there were more exclamation marks than question marks after sentences?"

[35] The characters are clearly modelled after real people: writer Ellen and family after Christa Wolf and family, the dead friend after Maxi Wander, another friend after Sarah Kirsch.

[36] Wolf: *Sommerstück*, p. 72.

[37] Ibid., p. 95. "But what does it mean when those who once were dedicated to change now simply escape to the country? Capitulation?"

cusations hurled against Wolf, that she exercised the kind of soul-searching her critics expected from her after the collapse of the GDR in 1990:

> Die Unfähigkeit zu handeln als Schuld. Schuld, daß sie ihre Pläne, Entwürfe, da man sie ihnen mit mehr oder weniger Aufwand, mehr oder weniger plump abgeschmettert hatte, einen nach dem anderen zurückgezogen, beiseitegelegt hatten. Auf kleiner Flamme kochen, nannte man das wohl. Sich in eine Umgebung zurückziehen, die einem nicht mehr melden konnte, wieweit man sich durch Selbstaufgabe verfehlte.[38]

What really pained the author was that she, like anyone else, had grown accustomed never to do what she wanted to do, never to say what she wanted to say, and not even to think the way she wanted to or should.[39] Yet rather than attempt to fault the circumstances in which she lived, the author blamed herself for her lack of honesty and uprightness: "Und nun fang bloß nicht an, deine Veränderung auf die Umstände zu schieben. Und dich auf Ausflüchte einzulassen. Das fehlte noch. Dann wärst du geliefert."[40] The result of this soul-searching was the question that formed the title of her much maligned story *Was bleibt*. In the face of her friend's death the question assumes an existential quality:

> Was bleibt, Steffi. Was bleibt. Ich seh uns dahinschmelzen wie unter zu starker Strahlung, ein zeitgemäßes Bild, ich weiß. […] Ich sehe unsere Umrisse sich auflösen. […] Unser alter Trieb nach Höhlen, Wärme, Miteinandersein ist zu schwach gegen die Weltraumkälte, die hereinströmt.[41]

As in *Was bleibt*, the lack of a question mark after "what remains" here again creates ambiguity between statement and question. But then Christa Wolf also provides the following answer to the question: "Was bleibt, sind Bilder."[42]

---

38 Ibid., p. 95. "The incapacity to act as guilt. Guilt because they [the would-be reformers] had withdrawn or stowed away one plan and one concept after another since they [the functionaries] had rejected all of them [the plans and concepts] with more or less ado and clumsiness. Putting them [the plans] on a back burner, as the saying goes. To withdraw to an environment where it became impossible to know the extent to which one had given up oneself."
39 Ibid., p. 99.
40 Ibid., p. 99. "And do not start to blame your change on other circumstances and rely on excuses. Do not let it come to that. That would be the end of you."
41 Ibid., p. 202. "What will remain, Steffi. What will remain. I see us melting away as if we were under too much radiation; a timely image, I know. […] I see our outlines dissolve. […] Our drive to seek out caves, warmth, company is too weak against the universal cold coming in." The "timely image" of radiation refers to the story *Störfall (Acccident)* Wolf wrote after the Chernobyl accident in 1986.
42 Ibid., p. 203. "What remains are images."

The writers Ellen in *Sommerstück* and Christa T. in *Nachdenken* fail in their efforts to write, but Christa Wolf, their alter ego, succeeds as a writer by writing about their failure. Thus "was bleibt," taken as the statement meaning "that which remains," also refers to her literary work, or as the poet Friedrich Hölderlin's well known phrase has it: "Was bleibet aber, stiften die Dichter"[43] (What remains is what poets create), a phrase Christa Wolf surely had in mind when choosing this title.

As we have seen, attacks on Christa Wolf and her works were nothing new for her. As long as the GDR still existed, the attacks on Wolf always came from the East because she was not loyal enough to the party cause. At the same time, however, she was amply honored and celebrated in the West. But in a surprising turn of events, the attacks on her and her work after unification came no longer from East German functionaries but from a number of West German critics who accused her of having been too loyal to the party cause. In their view, her service as a faithful stooge of the SED regime even contributed to the stabilization and prolongation of the system. In both cases, the critics' arguments were made essentially on ideological rather than literary grounds.

The attacks on Christa Wolf were spearheaded by Ulrich Greiner in *Die Zeit* of 1 June 1990, followed by Frank Schirrmacher in the *Frankfurter Allgemeine Zeitung* of 2 June 1990, and Karl Heinz Bohrer in *Merkur* 44, 10/11 (October/November 1990). Schirrmacher was not primarily interested in an evaluation of Christa Wolf's literary merits which, in his view, were vastly overrated anyway: "Ihr schriftstellerischer Rang [wird] weit überschätzt."[44] For him, Christa Wolf was a political case. Schirrmacher's article is much more than a mere review of *Was bleibt*; it is a journalistic reassessment of the ideological position of GDR literature in general, and Christa Wolf's oeuvre in particular. According to Schirrmacher, Christa Wolf had pleaded the case of the SED-GDR ever since the publication of *Der geteilte Himmel* in 1963; she enjoyed all the privileges accorded to her and never actually realized that she lived in a totalitarian system. In Schirrmacher's opinion, Christa Wolf was incapable of understanding complex social systems; for her, the model of society was the authoritarian bourgeois family to which a member is wedded for better or worse:

---

43 So Friedrich Hölderlin in the last line of his poem "Andenken" (Remembrance), written around 1803.

44 Schirrmacher: "'Dem Druck des härteren, strengeren Lebens standhalten': Auch eine Studie über den autoritären Charakter: Christa Wolfs Aufsätze, Reden und ihre jüngste Erzählung *Was bleibt*." *Frankfurter Allgemeine Zeitung* No. 27, June 2, 1990. "Her literary rank [is] vastly overrated."

Sie [war] unfähig, die moderne Gesellschaft als kompliziertes System konkurrierender Gruppen zu verstehen. Sie hat die Gesellschaft, in der sie lebte, allem Anschein nach immer nur als größere Variante der kleinbürgerlichen, autoritär aufgebauten Familie verstanden.[45]

In condemning virtually all GDR writers (except presumably those who emigrated to the West) Schirrmacher makes no difference between Kuba and Christa Wolf, Erik Neutsch and Volker Braun, Günter de Bruyn and Hermann Kant. He is correct in viewing Christa Wolf's political development in the context of Germany's Nazi past, but he then proceeds to "de-legitimize her biography"[46] by accusing Wolf and all GDR authors of the same shameless opportunism that in his view permeated Germany in an unbroken line from Imperial Germany to Nazi Germany and the GDR. By using the Nazi term "Dienstverpflichtung" (obligation to serve) for all GDR intellectuals, he places Wolf, de Bruyn, Robert Havemann, Stefan Heym and others next to Nazi authors such as Hanns Johst, Gerhard Schumann, Edwin Erich Dwinger, or Hans Zöberlein. He accuses Christa Wolf of lack of courage for failing to speak out during the East German uprising of 17 June 1953 or the construction of the wall in August 1961, as well as of defending the Warsaw pact invasion of Czechoslovakia in 1968 [which she actually opposed], and he downplays her protest of Wolf Biermann's expulsion in 1976. His discussion of *Was bleibt* concludes his lengthy invective against Wolf. Had the publication of this book come 10 or even 5 years earlier, according to Schirrmacher, it would have been significant; in 1990 it was simply meaningless, even ridiculous. In his view, instead of discussing her guilt and responsibility, Wolf talks vaguely about a new language and similar nebulous concepts with which Nazi authors some forty-five years earlier had attempted to conceal their involvement with a criminal regime. For Schirrmacher, *Was bleibt* is nothing but a book exposing a guilty conscience.

In *Was bleibt*, Ulrich Greiner finds the same "idyllic refuge from reality" that he finds so typical of Christa Wolf's works in general. Like Schirrmacher, his major argument against *Was bleibt* runs almost entirely along ideological lines. He condemns the book as an attempt on the part of Christa Wolf to whitewash herself after being accused of having been a "Staatsdichterin," a loyal author in the service of the SED. (Ironically, this accusation was first

---

45 Ibid. Wolf "was incapable of conceiving modern society as a complex system of competing groups. Apparently she viewed the society in which she lived as a larger variant of the petit bourgeois and authoritarian family."
46 See Wolf Lepenies's article "Alles rechtens – nichts mit rechten Dingen." *Die Zeit* No. 51, December 11, 1992, pp. 87–8.

levelled against Christa Wolf in 1987 by Marcel Reich-Ranicki, the same critic whose positive evaluation of *Nachdenken* in 1968 served East German functionaries as a pretext for their attacks on Christa Wolf.) For Greiner, Wolf seems to be saying: "Seht her, ihr armen, von der Stasi um Ansehen und Zukunft gebrachten Mitbürger und ehemaligen Genossen, auch ich wurde überwacht, auch ich war ein Opfer, ich bin keine Staatsdichterin, ich bin eine von euch."[47] It is the date of publication that arouses Greiner's particular ire. Before the opening of the wall and the demise of the SED, the publication of this story would have taken courage, now he finds it merely embarrassing ("peinlich"): "Daß sie ihn jetzt veröffentlicht, verrät einen Mangel an [...] Aufrichtigkeit gegen sich selbst und die eigene Geschichte, einen Mangel an Feingefühl gegenüber jenen, deren Leben der SED-Staat zerstört hat."[48] It mattered little that in the same issue of *Die Zeit* Volker Hage published a very positive assessment of Christa Wolf and her story *Was bleibt*, since most other critics who began to dominate the media after the demise of the GDR sided with Greiner and Schirrmacher. For Karl Heinz Bohrer, Christa Wolf's *Was bleibt* was simply "Gesinnungskitsch" (kitschy way of thinking), and he hoped that the times of quasi-religious adoration of writers such as Grass and Wolf, and the drug-like effects their works had on their community of worshippers, were now gone.[49]

As demonstrated in Schirrmacher's review of *Was bleibt*, western critics expected to hear an instant "mea culpa" from Christa Wolf; her earlier acts of defiance in the GDR (such as her defense of colleagues under attack at the 11th plenary session of the Central Committee of the SED, her protest of the Warsaw pact invasion of Czechoslovakia, or her protest against Biermann's expulsion) were almost entirely ignored. Yet long before Western critics raised questions of guilt and responsibility, Christa Wolf, herself, had dealt with those issues as we have already seen in a relevant passage from *Sommerstück* quoted above (p. 263). Thus we read in *Störfall* (Accident), written between June and December of 1986 in the wake of the Chernobyl disaster:

> Nicht zuviel – zuwenig haben wir gesagt, und das Wenige zu zaghaft und zu spät. Und warum? Aus banalen Gründen. Aus Unsicherheit. Aus Angst. Aus Mangel an

---

47 Greiner: "Mangel an Feingefühl." *Die Zeit* No. 23, June 1, 1990, p. 63. "Look at me, poor compatriots and former comrades now deprived of reputation and future by the Stasi, I, too, was a victim, I am not a 'Staatsdichterin,' I am one of you."

48 Ibid. "The fact that she published it now betrays a lack of honesty toward herself and her own history as well as a lack of sensitivity toward those whose lives were ruined by the SED state."

49 Bohrer: "Kulturschutzgebiet DDR?"

Hoffnung. Und, so merkwürdig die Behauptung ist: auch aus Hoffnung. Trügerische Hoffnung, welche das gleiche Ergebnis zeitigt wie lähmende Verzweiflung.[50]

In another portion of the same book, Christa Wolf explains the deceitful nature of this hope:

> Treiben die Utopien unserer Zeit notwendig Monster heraus? Waren wir Monster, als wir um einer Utopie willen – Gerechtigkeit, Gleichheit, Menschlichkeit für alle –, die wir nicht aufschieben wollten, diejenigen bekämpften, in deren Interesse diese Utopie nicht lag (nicht liegt), und, mit unseren eigenen Zweifeln, diejenigen, die zu bezweifeln wagten, daß der Zweck die Mittel heiligt?[51]

These are indeed prophetic words of self-examination, and that more than three years before the fall of the Berlin wall and after years of painful soul-searching. If she had done this soul-searching openly and in public after the demise of the GDR, some of her critics might have welcomed her candor but in the atmosphere of western self-congratulating and gloating over the "victory over socialism," Christa Wolf did not find it appropriate to bare her soul to a hostile public.

For one thing, the acrimonious debate left little room for objective and rational discussions. For another, Wolf simply had not come to terms herself with the demise of the socialist experiment in which she had invested so much. She said as much herself in a speech she delivered in France after receiving the title "Officier des Arts et des Lettres" on 12 September 1990:

> Immer sind meine Gefühle bei solchen Gelegenheiten zwiespältig – ganz besonders in dieser Zeit, da ich mich in einer Phase der Selbstprüfung und Selbstauseinandersetzung befinde –, ein normaler Zustand für jeden Schreibenden, enorm verstärkt natürlich durch die Fragen nach den Ursachen des Zusammenbruchs jenes Staates, für dessen grundlegende Verbesserung ich mich lange eingesetzt habe. […] Es wäre eine andere, längere Rede, mir selbst und anderen klarzumachen, daß und inwiefern wir uns an Unmöglichem abgearbeitet haben. Der Preis dafür ist hoch.[52]

---

50 Wolf: *Störfall*, p. 68. "We have not said too much – rather too little – and that little bit too timidly and too late. And why? For banal reasons. Because of insecurity. Because of fear. Because of lack of hope. And, strange as the claim may be: because of hope as well. Deceitful hope, which produces the same results as paralyzing despair" (*Accident*, p. 60).

51 Ibid., p. 37. "Do the utopias of our time necessarily breed monsters? Were we monsters when we, for the sake of a utopia we were not willing to postpone – justice, equality, humanity for all – fought those in whose interest this utopia was not (is not), and, with our own doubts, fought those who dared doubt that the ends justify the means?" (*Accident*, p. 30).

52 Wolf: "Dankrede," p. 148. "On such occasions my feelings are always ambiguous, especially in these times in which I find myself involved in a phase of self-examination and self-criti-

Or should we take Christa Wolf's brief text "Nagelprobe" (The Acid Test) as a reaction to her western critics? This text, a sort of "Nachdenken über Nägel," observations on a variety of meanings and expressions about nails, was written in December of 1991 in connection with an exhibition by Günther Uecker in St. Gallen and a visit to Matthias Grünewald's Isenheim altar in Colmar. The text contains some revealing sentences when placed in the context of the debate surrounding *Was bleibt*, for example: "Manche treffen den Nagel auf den Kopf. Manche treffen immer jeden Nagel auf den Kopf. Oder sie treffen unfehlbar jeden Kopf. Unfehlbar immer jeden anderen Kopf, denke ich. Manche sind unfehlbar, sage ich."[53] Could this be an ironic comment on the self-righteousness of her critics? In another passage from this text, she raises questions of guilt and innocence in her description of a the sculpture from the Congo of a wooden head with hollow eyes, a wide open mouth formed in a silent scream, and one side of the head covered with nails. This supposedly magic sculpture serves to protect the innocent and to punish the guilty; each nail has its own story.[54] The text concludes with a poem inspired by Grünewald's depiction of the crucifiction; it is entitled "Prinzip Hoffnung" (The Principle of Hope), borrowed from Ernst Bloch. The brief text reads:

> Genagelt
> ans Kreuz Vergangenheit.
>
> Jede Bewegung
> treibt
> die Nägel
> ins Fleisch.[55]

These ambiguous lines allow a number of interpretations. But in the uncertain times of change, the author seems to feel herself held captive by a past that neither her own thoughts nor her critics will allow her to escape. Perhaps

---

cism. This is a normal condition for any writer but now it is enormously enhanced through questions concerning the reasons for the collapse of that state, the fundamental improvement of which had been the object of my endeavours for years. [...] It would be a different and much longer speech, to explain to myself and to others that, and to what extent, we labored to accomplish the impossible. The price for that is high."

53 Wolf: "Nagelprobe," pp. 35–6. "Some hit the nail on the head. Some always hit every nail on the head. Or they unfailingly hit every head. Unfailingly every other head, I think. Some are infallible, I say."
54 Ibid., pp. 38–9.
55 Ibid., p. 44. "Nailed/ to the cross of the past./ Each movement/ drives/ the nails/ into the flesh."

these short lines from "Nagelprobe" contain more significant and more thoughtful reflections than the lengthy essays of acid-tongued critics.

Strangely enough, it was not Hermann Kant, or other writers like him who were much closer to the center of SED-power who were attacked by western critics, but Christa Wolf who had always had problems of her own with the SED. But then, Kant and some of the others were clever enough to avoid the limelight after the end of the GDR – until recently (1991), that is, when Kant published his defensive autobiographical book *Abspann* (End of a Journey).[56] In West Germany, very few colleagues came to the defense of Christa Wolf; among those who did were Walter Jens and Günter Grass. In a discussion with a *Spiegel* reporter, Grass castigated the acrimonious tone of the debate which he labeled "poisonous." It reminded him of the Inquisition and self-righteous pharisees arguing from a safe haven.[57] It was Grass as well who severely criticized the Federal Republic's "colonization" of the GDR. In a speech he delivered on 27 August 1990 in Oslo at the conference "Anatomy of Hate" (organized by Elie Wiesel), he stated:

> Denn nicht eine Einigung findet statt, vielmehr erweitert der größere Teil Deutschlands seinen Markt. Der kleinere Teil jedoch, dessen Bewohner soeben noch froh waren, sich endlich frei von staatlicher Bevormundung begreifen zu dürfen, erfährt nun das Diktat profit-orientierter Kolonialherren.[58]

Grass saw this kind of "colonization" at work also in the cultural field.

Another voice of sympathy for Christa Wolf came from France where people had little use for the "typically German" debate about Wolf. After awarding her the title "Officier des Arts et des Lettres," Jack Lang, the French Minister for Cultural Affairs, praised Wolf's "courage and clearheadedness" in "difficult times," and he proceeded to criticize her German critics:

> Die Veröffentlichung Ihres letzten Buches, *Was bleibt*, hat in einigen Zeitungen zu einer Polemik geführt, deren Echo bis nach Frankreich gedrungen ist. Ich möchte Ihnen heute abend sagen, daß uns diese Kampagne als ungerechtfertigt erscheint,

---

56 A term difficult to translate; "abspannen" means to unharness the horses at the end of a journey.
57 Grass: "Nötige Kritik oder Hinrichtung?: *Spiegel*-Gespräch mit Günter Grass über die Debatte um Christa Wolf und die DDR-Literatur." *Der Spiegel* No. 29, July 16, 1990, pp. 138–43, here p. 143. ("Ich habe Angst, daß ein Ton einreißt, der vergiftend ist und inquisitorisch und pharisäerhaft, zumal vom sicheren westlichen Port aus geurteilt wird.")
58 Grass: "Gegen den Haß." *Neue Deutsche Literatur* 38:11 (1990), p. 6. "It cannot be called unification because the larger part of Germany merely expands its market. The smaller part, however, whose inhabitants were happy to have shaken off the tutelage of the state is now coming under the dictatorship of profit-oriented colonial masters."

ungerechtfertigt, weil dieses Buch, ein sehr schönes Werk der Erinnerung, des Schmerzes und der Ironie, nicht wie ein Leitartikel beurteilt werden kann, wie eine Petition oder ein Pamphlet. Ungerechtfertigt auch, weil die Neunmalklugen von heute leichtes Spiel haben, wenn sie die denunzieren, die, obwohl sie das Schlimmste erdulden, ihre Jugendideale nicht aufgeben; aber diese Neunmalklugen, was wissen die von der täglichen Wirklichkeit im realen Sozialismus, was wissen die von der Schwierigkeit zu schreiben, was wissen sie von der Gefahr, die in den Worten liegt? [...] und wir wissen, daß wir auf sie zählen können, liebe Christa Wolf, wenn wir das Schweigen zurückweisen, daß Ihnen gewisse Leute vielleicht auferlegen wollen.[59]

The question of why Christa Wolf was trailed by the secret service in the first place never arose during the entire debate. In order to answer this question we have to go back to a cultural-political event in 1979 which caused even more anguish and bitterness than the expulsion of Biermann in 1976. For Joachim Walther, the events of 1979 belong to the darkest chapters in the cultural policies in the history of the GDR: "Nach der Ausbürgerung Wolf Biermanns im Herbst 1976, dem Protest und Exodus von Künstlern, Schriftstellern, Schauspielern und Regisseuren gen Westen eskalierte die Situation im Sommer 1979 erneut."[60] What had happened? The summer of 1979 saw increasing attacks on East German writers who were arguing for greater liberalization in the cultural field. For example, in a letter to Erich Honecker, published in the SED party paper *Neues Deutschland* on 22 May 1979, Dieter Noll, East German author and loyal SED party member, assured Honecker that there were only "einige wenige kaputte Typen wie Heym, Seyppel oder Schneider, die da so emsig mit dem Klassenfeind kooperieren,"[61] while the

---

59 Lang: "Rede zur Verleihung des Titels 'Officier des Arts et des Lettres' an Christa Wolf," p. 147–48. "The publication of your latest book *Was bleibt* has lead to such polemics in some papers that their echo reverberated in France. Tonight I would like to tell you that we feel that this campaign is unjustified. It is unjustified because this book, a wonderful document of remembrance, of pain, and of irony, cannot be judged like a lead article, a petition, or a pamphlet. It is unjustified also because the know-it-alls of today have an easy task to denounce those who do not want to relinquish the ideals of their youth even when they suffer severe consequences. What do these know-it-alls know about the daily realities in the socialist states; what do they know about the difficulties of writing under those circumstances, what do they know about the dangers embedded in words? [...] and we know that we can count on you, dear Christa Wolf, when we reject the silence that certain people might want to impose on you."
60 Walther et al., eds., *Protokoll eines Tribunals*, p. 7. "In the summer of 1979, after the expulsion of Biermann in the fall of 1976, after the protest and exodus of artists, writers, actors and directors to the West the situation worsened again."
61 Ibid., p. 97. "A few burnt out types like Heym, Seyppel, and Schneider who cooperated with the class enemy."

vast majority of East German writers, in Noll's view, supported the cultural policies decided upon at the 8th and 9th party congresses which opened new avenues of "artistic freedom." The campaign against "dissident" writers reached an unprecedented low point when the leadership of the Berlin section of the East German writers union decided to expel from the union nine writers including Kurt Bartsch, Adolf Endler, Stefan Heym, Karl-Heinz Jakobs, Klaus Poche, Klaus Schlesinger, Rolf Schneider, Dieter Schubert, and Joachim Seyppel. For the 7th of June 1979 chairman Günter Görlich had called for a general meeting to sanction the expulsions. Most of the members present dutifully complied, and the Central Committee of the SED was duly notified of the result. The main accusations against all of them were connections to the "class enemy" and agitation against the GDR. Their "crime": since they were denied publication opportunities in their own country they had passed a letter to the western press in which they expressed their concerns about the repressive cultural policies following the expulsion of Biermann. At this meeting, there was little discussion, although Stefan Heym rose to express his opinion in his customary direct manner. The vast majority of those present voted for the expulsions but there were 50 votes against, among them those of Stefan Hermlin and Christa Wolf. While Hermlin, too, openly spoke against the expulsion, Christa Wolf remained silent. However, on 10 June 1979 she wrote a letter to the writers' union of the GDR with the request that the expulsions not be confirmed:

> Ein solcher Ausschluß so vieler Kollegen – ohne Beispiel in der Geschichte des Verbandes – wird verhängnisvolle Folgen haben: nicht nur für die Betroffenen, auch für den Verband, für unser kulturelles Leben, für jeden einzelnen von uns.[62]

Instead of expulsion, Christa Wolf suggested that it would be more useful to examine the motives of those colleagues and to get to the bottom of the conflicts which many writers, including herself, experienced with increasing acuteness. In the letter, Christa Wolf sympathizes with colleagues who feel that they have no other choice but to publish their criticism in western media since they are denied all opportunities to do so in the GDR:

> In den letzten Jahren hat eine Reihe von Kollegen – auch ich – Briefe oder andere Schriftstücke an verschiedene Redaktionen, Organisationen, Partei- und Staatsstellen gerichtet, um ihre Bedenken über bestimmte Entwicklungstendenzen in der Kulturpolitik zu äußern. Nie wurde auch nur eine Seite eines solchen Schriftstücks

---

62 Ibid., p. 116. "The expulsion of so many colleagues – without precedent in the history of the union – will have disastrous consequences, not only for the individuals concerned but for the entire union, for our cultural life, for each one of us."

– sofern es zur Veröffentlichung bestimmt war – in unserer Presse gedruckt, nie die Richtigstellung oder Verteidigung eines Autors auf öffentliche Angriffe gebracht, nie aus einem dieser Briefe öffentlich zitiert.[63]

She accuses Hermann Kant of quoting in public from private letters not even addressed to him, while remaining silent when asked where she, Wolf, could publish her opinion: "[…] aber die Frage, wo ich zum Beispiel bei uns meinen Standpunkt zu diesen letzten Vorgängen meinen Lesern in der DDR darlegen könnte – worauf ich großen Wert legen würde – könnte er mir auch nicht beantworten."[64] For Christa Wolf, the result of this act of solidarity with those nine punished authors resulted in the Stasi surveillance described in *Was bleibt*, and one must bear in mind that the story was originally written in 1979!

The divisions and ill-feelings among East German authors that resulted from the Bierman affair and the 1979 expulsions last to this day; they are one of the legacies of the former GDR carried into the new Federal Republic. Even Hermann Kant, for example, in his anecdotal and defensively autobiographical book *Abspann* regrets the differences between himself and Christa Wolf as a result of the events of 1976 and 1979: "Es war einmal ganz anders zwischen Christa Wolf und mir, und die jetzige Vergiftung unseres Lebens gehört zum Schlimmsten, was bei der immer noch nicht beendeten Biermann-Affaire herausgekommen ist."[65]

For some, the debate about Christa Wolf, in particular, and guilt and responsibility of East German artists, writers, and intellectuals, in general, that was conducted after the demise of the repressive SED regime was reminiscent of the acrimonious debate that raged through German papers after the defeat of the criminal Nazi regime. Rolf Schneider, one of those authors punished with expulsion at the writers' congress in 1979, was one of the very few GDR writers who, in a *Spiegel* article of 29 October 1990, openly discussed his share of guilt and responsibility for supporting the GDR regime. Although he criticizes the arrogant tone of the debate, he basically feels that the debate

---

63 Ibid., p. 116. "In recent years a number of colleagues – myself included – have addressed letters and other written materials to different editorial offices, organizations, organs of the party and the state, in order to register concern about certain developments in cultural policies. To the extent that they were meant for publication, not even one page of such documents, not one correction, not one defence of authors who were publically attacked, not one quote of those letters was printed in our media."

64 Ibid., p. 117. "He could not answer my questions as to where within the GDR I could publish my views of recent events – something that is of great importance to me."

65 Kant: *Abspann*, p. 409. "There was a time when things were quite different between myself and Christa Wolf, and the present poisoning of our lives belongs to the worst remnants of the Biermann affair that still lingers."

about the role of East German writers and the extent of their involvement with the SED regime merits discussion, and he regrets that this debate was started by Western critics rather than by the East German authors themselves. He reminds his readers of the controversy between Thomas Mann and Walter von Molo when Thomas Mann raised the question of guilt and the responsibility of writers who had stayed behind in so-called "inner emigration" during the Nazi period.[66] Schneider felt that the position in which most GDR authors found themselves after the end of the GDR rather closely resembled that of Walter von Molo and like-minded authors at that time. A closer inspection of this parallel would probably reveal the flimsiness of this argument – writers like Ernst Wiechert, Reinhold Schneider, Jochen Klepper, Walter von Molo were no Nazis and certainly did not want to see an improved Nazi state, whereas most of the East German writers, including Schneider himself, were committed Marxists who, far from wanting to abolish communism, worked for a better socialist system in the GDR. But Schneider is correct in pointing to the rapid change of attitude that befell most people after the demise of both the Nazi and the SED systems, and their "inability to mourn" in both instances; after 1945 and after 1989, the number of instant turn-coats without memory was equally substantial.[67]

Schneider also sees parallels between Stalinism and Nazism, although he is quick to distance himself from the historian Ernst Nolte who claimed that Stalin bears the main responsibility for Hitler's atrocities. It seems that the "Literaturstreit" (literature controversy) that ensued in 1990 in the wake of the publication of Wolf's story *Was bleibt* attempted to achieve in the field of literature what the "Historikerstreit" (history controversy) some five years earlier attempted for history: a re-evaluation of the recent German past. In both instances, people such as Nolte and Schirrmacher attempted to equate Marxism with National Socialism.[68] Christa Wolf clearly received unfair treatment when she published her story *Was bleibt* after the change. But then her case was only a point of departure for a new cultural agenda. As Christine Schoefer remarked in an article published in *The Nation* of 22 October 1990:

> This literary campaign reveals the hidden agenda of the conservative model of German unification, which is intent not only on doing away with the Communist

---

66 For more details about this debate see Grosser, ed., *Die grosse Kontroverse*.
67 Schneider's article, entitled "Volk ohne Trauer" ("A People Without Grief") is heavily indebted to Margarete and Alexander Mitscherlich's essay "Die Unfähigkeit zu trauern" ("The Inability to Mourn"), first published in 1967.
68 For parallels between "Historikerstreit" and "Literaturstreit" see also Irene Heidelberger-Leonard: "Der Literaturstreit – ein Historikerstreit im gesamtdeutschen Kostüm?" Deiritz and Krauss, eds., *Der deutsch-deutsche Literaturstreit*, pp. 69–77.

East but on erasing the history of the GDR and the very idea of socialism itself. Wolf is a sacrificial lamb in a larger project: the ideological shaping of unified Germany.

The reasons the critics singled out Christa Wolf, at least according to Schoefer, had probably less to do with the fact that she is a woman than with the fact that she was one of the most prominent writers of the GDR who enjoyed great respect in the west as well, at least while the two states still coexisted: "Why Christa Wolf? The fact that she is a woman may be coincidental. But it goes without saying that if one of East Germany's most respected writers is discredited, all East German writers who shared her vision will be silenced."[69] This is not to say that there was a concerted campaign or a conspiracy afoot with Greiner, Schirrmacher, or Bohrer as agents. But the literary debate fits well into an overall pattern of discrediting everything from the former GDR, including literature and the arts.[70]

The culture debate of 1990 was by no means restricted to the former GDR. Again it was Schirrmacher who took the lead, and, in addition to the literature of the GDR, he also consigned the literature of the former Federal Republic to the dustbin of history with his article "Abschied von der Literatur der Bundesrepublik" (Good-bye to the Literature of the Federal Republic) in the *Frankfurter Allgemeine Zeitung* of 2 October 1990. And again he was supported by Greiner in *Die Zeit* of 9 November 1990, who condemned what he called the "Gesinnungsästhetik" (politically correct thought) of the politically committed literature of the FRG represented by authors of "Gruppe 47" (Group 47) such as Heinrich Böll, Günter Grass, Siegfried Lenz, Erich Fried, Martin Walser, Hans Magnus Enzensberger, Peter Weiss, Heinar Kipphardt, Alfred Andersch:

> Die Gesinnungsästhetik ist das gemeinsame Dritte der glücklicherweise zu Ende gegangenen Literaturen von BRD und DDR. Glücklicherweise: Denn allzusehr waren die Schriftsteller in beiden deutschen Hälften mit außerliterarischen Themen beauftragt, mit dem Kampf gegen Restauration, Faschismus, Klerikalismus, Stalinismus et cetera.[71]

---

69 Schoefer: "The Attack on Christa Wolf." *The Nation* No. 251, October 22, 1990, p. 448.

70 For example, Siegfried Gohr, director of the Ludwig Museum in Cologne, refused to display any paintings from the GDR because he did not consider them art, and the former East German painter Georg Baselitz replied when asked about East German painters such as Bernhard Heisig or Wolfgang Mattheuer: "No artists, no painters. None of them have ever painted a picture." Protzman: "Germany Slow to Embrace Its Eastern Artist." *The New York Times* No. 48, 469, January 3, 1991, pp. 15–6.

71 Greiner: "Die deutsche Gesinnungsästhetik." *Die Zeit* No. 45, November 2, 1990, p. 63. "Politically correct thought was the common denominator of the now fortunately defunct

Karl Heinz Bohrer came close to the infamous epithet "kaputte Typen" (burned out types) Dieter Noll had used in 1979 for the East German writers Stefan Heym, Joachim Seyppel, and Rolf Schneider when he, Bohrer, labelled Jens and Grass as "politisch und intellektuell aber schon seit längerer Zeit überfordert," who, in tandem with their like-minded East German companions, were vainly attempting to save what they could of bygone utopias.[72] The aim of the entire debate was to get rid of not only all books and authors from the GDR:

> Liquidiert wurden [...] fast alle Bücher und Autoren aus der DDR: Exilanten und Antifaschisten der ersten Stunde ebenso wie die Systemreformer der mittleren Jahre, die Ewig-Gestrigen unter den Ausgebürgerten und die grün eingefärbten Alternativen vom Prenzlauer Berg.[73]

– but also all leftist intellectuals and all kinds of utopian thought in the West as well. Neo-conservative critics advocated consigning all books and photos of the members of the Gruppe 47 to Kohl's historical museum in order to make room for a new all-German literature in which literature could again be literature, without pushing any social agendas. If anything, this literature should celebrate "new German pride and greatness" free from all self-pity and pacifism. And free especially from the typically German tendency to retreat into an idyllic corner, which these critics saw amply demonstrated in the works of Heinrich von Kleist, Christa Wolf, and even Anna Seghers's novel *Das siebte Kreuz* (The Seventh Cross).[74] So far this new concept of German literature exists only in the pages of publications such as *Merkur* or the *Frankfurter Allgemeine* – unless one wants to resort to literature from earlier periods of presumed German "greatness," or to the works of Ernst Jünger as Karl Heinz Bohrer advocates.[75] It remains to be seen to what extent the writers will heed the call of these critics.

---

literatures of the FRG and the GDR. I say fortunately because writers of both halves of Germany were overly concerned with extra-literary themes such as the fight against restoration, Fascism, clericalism, Stalinism, etc." The article is reprinted in Deiritz und Kraus, eds., *Der deutsch-deutsche Literaturstreit*, pp. 139–45.

72 Bohrer: "Kulturschutzgebiet DDR?" *Merkur* 44 (October-November 1990), p. 1015–18. "Having been politically and intellectually overtaxed for some time now."

73 Stephan: "Ein deutscher Forschungsbericht 1990/91," p. 129; "Abolished were [...] almost all books and authors from the GDR: returnees from exile and anti-Fascists of the early period as well as the reformers of the middle years, the eternally-backwards people among the expatriated and the environmentally 'tainted' alternatives from the Prenzlauer Berg."

74 Ibid., pp. 130–32.

75 See Andreas Huyssen: "Das Versagen der deutschen Intellektuellen." Deiritz and Krauss, eds., *Der deutsch-deutsche Literaturstreit*, pp. 78–94, esp. pp. 91–4.

The culture debate of 1990 is also embedded in a wider debate about the role of a new Germany which is attempting to step out from under the shadow of Auschwitz. The "Historikerstreit" of 1986 was a first attempt, now followed by the debates about culture and literature, the gulf war, the participation of German soldiers in actions beyond NATO, the asylum problem, publications of books and articles about Jewish involvement with Fascist and Bolshevist crimes, or Helke Sander's film "BeFreier und Befreite" ("Liberators and Liberated") about the rape of German women by Red Army soldiers.[76] In his book *Deutschland, was nun?* (Germany, what now?) the historian Arnulf Baring sees Germany return to its "hereditary" place in central Europe: "Wir erleben jetzt die Wiederkehr Deutschlands. Es kehrt zurück auf seinen angestammten Platz in Europas Mitte."[77] This "hereditary" place is the place Bismarck once secured for Germany with the first unification in 1871, and which was given its republican mold by Konrad Adenauer:

> Das heutige Deutschland ist eine geglückte Synthese aus Bismarcks Reich und Adenauers Rheinbund. Anders gesagt: Wir leben noch immer im Deutschland Bismarcks, aber in der weltoffenen, republikanischen Form, die ihm die Ära Adenauer gegeben hat.[78]

The SPD-dominated era of Willy Brandt and Helmut Schmidt is simply omitted in this scenario. It is perhaps not surprising that this climate of revisionism provides encouragement even for right wing rock groups such as "Störkraft" or "Böhsen Onkelz" with lines like "Wir müssen kämpfen für unsere Rasse / Deutsches Volk, beweise Deine Klasse."[79]

An objective assessment of East and West German literature and the effect of the unification of 1990 on its future development is still to come; the present efforts to occupy vacant positions and the mutual exchange of accusations is hardly conducive to an objective evaluation. We do not know what the future will hold for the literature and culture in a united Germany but what seems certain is that little of the present cultural debate will

---

76 See, for example, Volker Ulrich's article "Die neue Dreistigkeit." *Die Zeit* No. 45, October 30, 1992, p. 73.
77 Baring: *Deutschland, was nun?*, p. 202; "We now experience Germany's comeback. It is returning to its hereditary place in central Europe."
78 Ibid., p. 203. "The Germany of today is a successful synthesis of Bismarck's Reich and Adenauer's 'Rheinbund.' In other words: We still live in Bismarck's Germany but in a more open republic as shaped by Adenauer."
79 Quoted from Habermas: "Die zweite Lebenslüge der Bundesrepublik." *Die Zeit* No. 51, December 11, 1992, p. 48. "We have to fight for our Race/ German Volk go find your place."

survive – just as the debate between those who stayed and those who left, between Walter von Molo or Frank Thiess and Thomas Mann after 1945 is virtually forgotten. However, it seems equally certain that much of forty years of GDR and FRG literature will survive the test of time, including a number of works by Christa Wolf. "Was bleibet aber, stiften die Dichter."

Philip Brady
University of London

"Wir hausen im Prenzlauer Berg":
On the Very Last Generation of GDR Poets

Abstract: In the late-1970s artists, musicians and writers in East Germany were drawn to the run-down tenement district of East Berlin known as Prenzlauer Berg. Here they began to devise forms of collaboration and of multi-media work: theatre, recitals to music, combinations of words and pictures. Beginning in the early 1980s periodicals were published, devoted either to literary work or to theory. There were under observation by State Security but enjoyed a measure of circumscribed freedom. The paper attempts to summarize this cooperative activity which finally came to an end with end of the GDR.

It is a familiar, perhaps not altogether unwelcome fact – part of what Walter Benjamin has called the "Verlegenheiten der Literaturhistoriker"[1] that literary values change, that judgement is fallible. And it is a yet more familiar fact that judgement is even more insecure when its subject is topical, when neither the contours nor the contexts of a work can be seen from a distance. The work of the writers and artists living in and around the Prenzlauer Berg district of East Berlin in the 1980s is inevitably topical, but any attempt to survey that work faces uncertainties that involve more than the question of insufficient distance.[2] One of those involved, Jan Faktor, has underlined one obvious difficulty: "Der Begriff 'Szene' ist natürlich problematisch."[3] How far does the locality simply provide a convenient label, more neat than revealing? How far are we entitled to speak of a genuine group-enterprise and, if so, how far is literary judgement a judgement on cooperative endeavour and on public performance? Nor can such questions be divorced from the Kulturpolitik of the

---

1 Benjamin: "Gottfried Keller." Benjamin: Gesammelte Schriften vol. 2, 1, pp. 283–85, here p. 284: "The embarrassments of the literary historians."
2 Peter Böthig: "die verlassene sprache." Arnold, ed., *Die andere Sprache*, pp. 38–48.
3 Jan Faktor: "Sechzehn Punkte zur Prenzlauer-Berg-Szene." Böthig and Michael, eds., *Macht-Spiele*, pp. 91–111, here p. 91: "The concept 'scene' is naturally problematic."

GDR. How far, it has frequently been asked, were the writers and artists of the Prenzlauer Berg exploiting their alternative strategies with state support? Were they no more than "Glasnost-Hätschelkinder"[4] or were they a "frei gewählte kreative Enklave" marked by "ungeschliffene Ursprünglichkeit" and "spielerische Spontaneität"?[5]

Questions about literary and cultural-political credentials assumed a quite different tone from the autumn of 1991. The State Security had, it appeared, infiltrated the Prenzlauer Berg scene. The documentation was still incomplete, but for Wolf Biermann the evidence sufficed. In his Büchner-Prize-Speech, published in October 1991, he dismissed all opposition groups in the GDR, reserving his most poisonous venom for Sascha Anderson, a key figure in the Prenzlauer Berg scene, living in West Berlin since 1986, and, as was becoming ever clearer, a Stasi-informer:

> Aber alle Oppositionsgruppen waren von Stasimetastasen zerfressen. Rechtsanwalt Schnur, Waisenkind Böhme, Jutta Braband, Heimkind Monika Haeger, der hochbegabte Poet Heinz Kahlau, der sich nun entblößt und beknirscht hat, der unbegabte Schwätzer Sascha Arschloch, ein Stasispitzel, der immer noch cool den Musensohn spielt und hofft, daß seine Akten nie auftauchen.[6]

Biermann returned to the attack in November, again going beyond the available evidence, alleging that the proven perfidy of the one – Anderson – was reason enough for a sweeping condemnation of the entire alternative scene: "Nun erfahren wir, daß die bunte Kulturszene am Prenzlauer Berg ein blühender Schrebergarten der Stasi war. Jedes Radieschen numeriert an seinem Platz. Spätdadaistische Gartenzwerge mit Bleistift und Pinsel."[7]

---

4 Seiler: "Heute lesen wir vor fünfzehn Muttis am Stadtrand. Priviligiert, korrumpiert, wirkungslos – wie sich DDR-Schriftsteller vom Staat die Wut abkaufen liessen." *Die Weltwoche* No. 34, August 24, 1989, 59: "the pampered children of Glasnost."
5 Arnold: "Die andere Sprache." Arnold, ed., *Die andere Sprache*, p. 12: "a freely chosen enclave […] unpolished originality […] playful spontaneity."
6 Biermann: "Der Lichtblick im gräßlichen Fatalismus der Geschichte: Büchner-Preis-Rede." Biermann: *Der Sturz des Dädalus*, pp. 48–63, here p. 56: "But all oppositional groups were eaten away by Stasi-metastases. Lawyer Schnur, orphan Böhme, Jutta Braband, hostel-child Monika Haeger, the highly gifted poet Heinz Kahlau, who has now revealed himself and repented, the ungifted gasbag Sascha Arsehole, a Stasi-spy, who carries on cooly playing the Muses' darling, hoping his files won't show up."
7 Biermann: "Laß, o Welt, o laß mich sein! Eduard-Mörike-Preis-Rede." Biermann: *Der Sturz des Dädalus*, pp. 64–9, here p. 71: "And now we learn that the colourful cultural scene on the Prenzlauer Berg was one luxuriant Stasi-allotment. Every little radish in its numbered place. Latterday Dada-garden-gnomes with pencil and brush." A second key-figure on the Prenzlauer Berg was revealed – or revealed himself – to have collaborated with State Security (Rainer Schedlinski: "Dem Druck, immer mehr sagen zu sollen").

Biermann represents perhaps the most extreme position in the debate about the connections between GDR writers and the Stasi. The need for more balance and for discrimination was argued at an early stage in the debate by Hajo Steinert:

> Wenn sie doch nur alle "Gartenzwerge" waren, warum denn so riesige Worte? Hatte der Liedermacher nur ein Buch von Bert Papenfuß-Gorek, Jan Faktor, Stefan Döring, Andreas Koziol, Detlev Opitz, Durs Grünbein oder Johannes Jansen gelesen, so hätte ihm auffallen müssen, daß deren Texte keineswegs "angestrengt unpolitisch" sind, sondern verspielt politisch. […] Die Prenzlpoeten machten sich zwar alle irgendwelche sprachexperimentellen, sprachreflektorischen Gedanken. Doch sind ihre Bücher im einzelnen so unterschiedlich, daß man die Autoren kaum über einen Kamm scheren kann.[8]

Despite Steinert's misgivings, the debate continued to focus more on moral issues rather than on questions of literary quality. By now, however, the debate has lost much of its urgency – the unequivocal title of a recent essay – "A Plea for an end to the Stasi-debate" – suggests that it has indeed run its course.[9]

The aim of the following paper is not to refuel the debate but to outline the work of the Prenzlauer Berg writers themselves, in particular varieties of cooperative work that indicate that the notion of a Prenzlauer Berg "scene" was neither an abstraction nor the invention of non-sympathisers bent on root-and-ranch condemnation.

That the run–down, crumbling neighbourhood north of the Alexanderplatz was more than a locality was recognised at the beginning of the 1980s by Ingrid and Klaus-Dieter Hähnel:

> Man fühlt sich unnütz in dieser Gesellschaft, resigniert, zieht sich zurück – zumindest läßt sich von vielen Gedichten darauf schließen. Das entstehende Weltgefühl findet seine Entsprechung vorwiegend bei anderen Jungen. So entsteht Gemeinschaft, die im Zusammenhalt dieses Weltgefühl festigt. Prenzlauer Berg ist – und das alles ist hier ohne jede Ironie gesagt – längst nicht mehr nur eine Wohngegend,

---

8   Hajo Steinert: "Die Szene und die Stasi. Muß man die literarischen Texte der Dichter vom Prenzlauer Berg jetzt anders lesen?" Böthig and Michael, eds., *MachtSpiele*, pp. 329–33, here pp. 330–1: "If they were all just 'garden-gnomes' why the big noise? If the song-maker had read just one book by Bert Papenfuß-Gorek, Jan Faktor, Stefan Döring, Andreas Koziol, Detlev Opitz, Durs Grünbein or Johannes Jansen, he would have noticed that their texts are by no means 'strenuously unpolitical' but playfully political. The Prenzlauer poets indeed had all kinds of ideas about language and language-experiments. But their books are all so different that the authors can hardly be lumped together."

9   Greiner: "Plädoyer für Schluß der Stasi-Debatte." *Die Zeit* No. 6, February 5, 1993, p. 60.

sondern eine "Haltung": Die Risse in den Wänden der Hinterhof-Häuser erscheinen nicht selten als die Korrelate für die "Risse" und "Nöte" des Ichs.[10]

The "Risse in den Wänden" echoes the opening of a poem by Uwe Kolbe[11] which both captures the physical reality of the Prenzlauer Berg and mythologises the poet who lives there. "Wir leben mit Rissen in den Wänden, / ist es dir aufgefallen?" ("We live with cracks in the walls, / have you noticed?") – the poem hints at a general dilapidation and hints at the poet's affinities: "Wir wohnen illegal" ("We live illegally") – the outlawed poet; "Wir hausen im Prenzlauer Berg, / vier Treppen hoch unter dem Dach" ("We live in Prenzlauer Berg, / four floors up under the roof") – the poet in his garret; "laut / schlage ich ein Zupfinstrument" ("I strike loud on my guitar") – the poet as maker of music; "und lache noch im Hagelrauschen, / wenn der Himmel finstrer wird" ("I still laugh in the rush of hail, / when the sky grows darker") – the poet facing the elemental, revelling in the exposure and responding, like Brecht's own garret outlaw-poet, Baal, in his own sexuality: "Im Staub der Körperdünstung lach ich" ("I laugh in the dust of the steaming of bodies") – it is hints and echoes such as these that set the poet in his East Berlin garret in a broader context. Self-consciousness, it seems, means for Kolbe's poet consciousness of ancestry, of a typology. Kolbe's poem was much quoted in the 1980s, acquiring a kind of emblematic status as the portrayal not of the poet's ancestry but of his life-style, "vier Treppen hoch" in the Prenzlauer Berg. And there is another dimension to the poem, understated and yet not easily ignored: the poem opens with the ambiguously – and, therefore, in context, politically – metaphorical cracks in the walls and it concludes with an equally ambiguous, equally political reference to security and to unspecified dangers: "genießend unter Kraftaufwand / die uns gebotne Sicherheit" ("enjoying in mid-effort / the security offered us").

The world of Kolbe's poet is, it might be said, peopled from the past and threatened by the present. This is not, in other words, a withdrawal into solitude and solipsism. It is, however, a life lived at a distance from events and, seemingly, from community. Others – and these we shall now examine – pursued modes of cooperation; the value of Kolbe's poet is that what he

---

10 Hähnel: "Junge Lyrik," p. 129: "They feel useless in this society, resigned, so they withdraw – at least that is what a lot of poems suggest. The attitude to life that emerges is then taken up by other young people. A community emerges that stays together and strengthens this feeling. Prenzlauer Berg – and this is in no sense meant ironically – is no longer merely a place to live but an 'attitude' – the cracks in the walls of the tenement-houses are often the equivalents of the cracks and the needs of the individual."
11 Heukenkamp, Kahlau and Kirsten, eds., *Die eigene Stimme*, pp. 380–1.

expresses precedes cooperation, so to speak, and is shared by most writers around the Prenzlauer Berg – namely, a pronounced self-awareness and self-imaging as a poet.

The best organised and indeed the best documented cooperative enterprise began in 1980. In that year Dieter Kraft and six other puppeteers founded a group-theatre that came to be called Zinnober. What began as puppet-theatre soon changed direction: "im laufe der zeit aber standen ihnen die puppen mehr und mehr im weg, und sie rückten als darsteller selbst in den vordergrund."[12] The shift from puppets to humans was in no sense intended as a move towards conventional theatre. Their brand of theatre takes as its starting-point the group itself, actors whose own recollections, dreams, traumas, impulses are articulated first within the group and only later in performance. What starts as self-analysis, as a "Seelenzergliederung"[13] that sounds more therapeutic than theatrical, can acquire in performance a more general relevance, as a member of the group explained:

> Die Gruppe "Zinnober" stellt sich dem Problem, daß seelische Vereinsamung, psychische Verzweiflung oder Schwermut sehr wesentlich in das Leben intelligenter (also geistig gesunder) Menschen eingreifen und zerstörerisch werden kann. Im Verlauf des Abends [...] bot die Gruppe Lösungen an, um individuelle Schranken überspringen zu können.[14]

Surveying the early work of the group, Dieter Kraft, writing in 1983, argued that a focus on individual psyches did not exclude a political perspective:

> Das Individuelle ist nicht zwangsläufig und in jedem Fall auch politisch, wenn auch durch die Bedrohungen der Gegenwart mehr und mehr. Aber das Individuelle der Frau, das Individuelle nicht von Siegern, sondern Unterlegenen, dieses Individuelle ist politisch, sowohl als Zeichen als auch als Aktion.[15]

---

12 Rainer Schedlinski: "zinnober." Arnold, ed., *Die andere Sprache*, pp. 78–80, here p. 78: "in the course of time the puppets got more and more in the way, so the actors themselves took over."
13 Kraft: *traumhaft*, p. 46.
14 Ibid., p. 282: "The Zinnober-group is engaged with the problem that emotional isolation, psychic despair or melancholy can invade and work destructively on the lives of intelligent (ie mentally healthy) people. In the course of an evening the group offered solutions to help people surmount individual barriers."
15 Ibid., p. 86: "Individuality is not inevitably and in every case political, even though present-day threats make it increasingly so. But the individuality of woman, the individuality not of victors but of the defeated, this individuality is political both intrinsically and actively."

Work centring in a woman's predicament, as many of the Zinnoberpieces do, is "ein politischer Akt, der genau das Gegenteil ist vom Einordnen und Gleichberechtigen; es ist ein Akt der Revolte, ein Akt des Widerstands, ein Akt der Alternativsuche, und es ist ein Stück gelebte Utopie."[16]

The utopia, in this case ambivalent in its details, is exemplified in an early monologue, improvised in 1982 and entitled September. In it the wishes of a woman are enumerated in a seemingly random sequence, mixing the personal, the domestic and the political

> [...]
> – im eigenen bett ins ausland fahren
> – reine haut haben
> – ein duschraum sein, mitten im wald, das schmutzwasser ohne rest und umweg versickert
> – einen monat in westberlin leben
> – ab und zu löwe sein, dann eine zikade
> [...]
> – kontraste
> – in einem land wohnen, wo man nicht erschossen wird, falls man flieht
> – morgens das gefühl, kraft zu haben
> [...][17]

The theme – wishes and, inevitably, frustrations hinting at internal and external constraints – yielded variations. An improvisation of 1985, entitled *Vor dem Spiegel*, consists of a woman alone on stage with a mirror and a suitcase, who remains silent while her situation is narrated on tape:

> Sie wartet wieder. Und wieder wartet sie. Sie wartet nicht, bis sie aufhört zu warten. Sie wartet einfach. Sie steht vor ihrem Koffer und wartet. Sie möchte nicht nachdenken, was in ihrem Koffer ist und wozu sie sich auf die Reise gemacht hat. [...] Alle Bewegungen sind erstarrt. Alles Denken ist gehemmt.[18]

---

16 Ibid., p. 86: "a political act that is the exact opposite of categorising and equalising; it is an act of rebellion, of resistance, an active search for alternatives, and it is a piece of lived out utopia."

17 Ibid., pp. 7–8: "to go abroad in my own bed – to have clear skin – to be a shower-room in the middle of a wood and the dirty water seeps away completely and simply – to live a month in West Berlin – to be a lion now and again, then a cicada – contrasts – to live in a country where you are not shot if you try to leave – to feel strength in the morning."

18 Ibid., p. 211: "She's waiting again. Again she's waiting. She's not waiting till she stops waiting. She's just waiting. She's standing in front of her suitcase waiting. She doesn't want to think what's in the suitcase and why she's setting off. Every movement is paralysed. Every thought is blocked."

"Nie mehr will ich ein Gebäude, nie mehr einen Korridor betreten. Ich will auf keinem Stuhl mehr sitzen. Ich will ins Weite laufen. Leer leer leer von Menschen"[19] – thus the close of another brief scene.

Clearly talk of wide open spaces acquires a political overtone in the East Berlin context. It could indeed be said that the recurrent ingredient in Zinnober performances – the individual improvising or appearing to improvise on stage – subverts in however mild a fashion a system which rejects improvisation and operates through constraint and prohibition. Political pressures are, however, no more than hinted at, the emphasis lies elsewhere: "Mit Hilfe von Darstellungen erinnerter Träume und Kindheitserlebnisse, die natürlich zum Teil verzerrt oder sehr überhöht gezeigt wurden, sollte dem Zuschauer Einblick in die psychologische Biografie der sich vorstellenden Figur […] gegeben werden."[20] To offer insights into the psychological biography of an individual sounds like a recipe for monologue. That the Zinnober-group was also trying out more complex kinds of performance is shown by what is possibly their most important work, the scene-sequence *traumhaft*, first staged in 1985.

"über ein jahr arbeiteten sie an einem neuen stück, das aus den auseinandersetzungen mit ihren ddr-erfahrungen, den konflikten innerhalb der gruppe und ihren theaterunzufriedenheiten überhaupt entstanden ist"[21] – Rainer Schedlinski's comment suggests that a variety of problems motivated the group in its work on *traumhaft*. An explanatory note preceding the printed text puts the emphasis differently, describing in some detail the interaction of individual and group on stage:

> das stück ist die produktion einer gruppe.
> ziel war die gestalt individueller texte.
> die aufführung lebt vom freien umgang mit diesem material.
> die bühne ist ein dreiteiliges podest.
> jeder spieler der gruppe hat seinen auftritt.
> jeder auftritt zerfällt in kurze szenen,
> fingierte dialoge, clownerien, monologe, lieder.

---

19 Ibid., p. 109: "I'll never enter a building or a corridor again. I'll not sit on another chair. I want to run far away. Empty empty empty of people."
20 Ibid., pp. 281–2: "by performing remembered dreams and childhood-experiences, which were of course partly shown in a distorted or highly exaggerated way, the spectator was to be offered insight into the psychological biography of the performer."
21 Rainer Schedlinski: "zinnober," Arnold, ed., *Die andere Sprache*, pp. 78–80, here p. 78: "for over a year they worked at a new play which arose out of their confrontation with their GDR-experiences, the conflicts within the group and their general dissatisfaction with current theatre."

> eine wichtige rolle spielt die musik.
> alle sind von anfang bis ende anwesend.
> sie stehen, liegen, sitzen am podest, laufen herum,
> geben hilfestellungen, räumen, bereiten sich vor,
> oder verfolgen kühl und unbeteiligt,
> manchmal neugierig mit distanz,
> wie der einzelne in der mitte
> arbeitet und sich entblößt.[22]

Clearly – and the title suggests as much – the dream is crucial. The waking dream recapitulates the past and those who then enact that past are "unguarded prisoners, in the ambivalence of a daydream" ("eingesperrte ohne bewachung, in der ambivalenz eines tagtraums"[23]). For a Prenzlauer Berg audience any notion of imprisonment would surely be charged with extra resonance. Indeed the notion is reinforced in the opening to the printed version where *traumhaft* is printed as two words, "traum" and "haft," dream and prison.

The close-up on an individual reaching an audience via his/her biography is still central. But *traumhaft* exploits the groupwork more intensively. Music – saxophone, tuba, piano, violin – accompanies many scenes, the violin in particular creating a thread throughout the work as a musical accompaniment to surreal texts ("einen steinwurf weitab / pfeift der captain / kranke katzen durch die straßen / eisenrad der lahmen alten […]"[24]). Actors themselves resort to song – a scene entitled *Die Singstimme* has the stage-direction:

> Sie wird auf das Podest gehoben. Vor ihr geöffnet, zwei Gräben. Sie ist vermummt. Sie hat die Augen geschlossen. Sie breitet die Arme aus. Sie singt. Grosse Oper. Ariengesten. Liedfetzen. Vokalimprovisation. Reise der Singstimme in den Innenraum […].[25]

---

22 Kraft: *traumhaft*, p. 220: "the play is a group production. the aim was to shape individual texts. performance lives through free work on this material. the stage is a triple platform, every actor in the group has a scene. every scene falls into short scenes, imaginary dialogues, clowning, monologues, songs. music has an important role. everybody is present from start to finish. they stand, they lie, they sit on the platform, run around, get ready to help, clear up, get themselves ready, or follow in a cool, dispassionate way, often with a distanced curiosity, how the individual in the middle is working and revealing him/herself."
23 Ibid., p. 219.
24 Ibid., p. 226: "a stone's throw off / the captain is whistling / sick cats along the streets / iron wheel of the lame old."
25 Ibid., p. 239: "She is lifted onto the platform. In front of her are two open ditches. She is cloaked. Her eyes are closed. She opens her arms. She sings. Grand opera. Aria-gestures. Scraps of song. Vocal improvisation. The singing-voice travelling into inner space."

Her song begins with gibberish – "o forsygon tuk taam vandrere" and ends with Negro spiritual – "i want to cross over / into campground." Starkly contrasting styles and registers of language are a feature of many of the scenes that make up the work. *Der Idiot mit dem Rad* is one such scene. An accompanying photograph depicts a figure in white behind an upturned bicycle watched by two women in white on one side and by two musicians in black on the other. The performance is divided into half-page sections whose tone varies markedly from the colloquial:

>   steffen
>   komm wir wolln
>   zum impfen fahrn
>   nein
>   natürlich
>   zieh dir die hosen an […][26]

to the loftily metaphorical:

>   ins tal der ahnungslosen
>   da verfinsterte es sich und
>   wirbelte schwarzen gewitter
>   schlamm durch die luft […][27]

or the parodistic:

>   also ich meine da müßte man
>   drüber reden oder das problem an
>   einem punkt und dann oder in der
>   geschichte ich meine ja […][28]

Performance is plainly going far beyond confessional improvisation – actors are engaged in a group, and the encounter with the audience is not reducible to a one-to-one exchange. There were indeed various ways of avoiding the self-absorption that might have threatened Uwe Kolbe's poet cooped up in his Prenzlauer garret. They could, moreover, take simpler forms than the complex work of the Zinnober-theatre. Elke Erb summarised a multitude of collaborative activities and a welter of individual cases of multi-media versatility in 1985:

---

26 Ibid., p. 269: "Steffen come on we've got to go for your injection no yes get your trousers on."

27 Ibid., p. 269 : "into the valley of the unsuspecting ones it grew dark swirling black thunder mud through the air."

28 Ibid., p. 271: "Well I think we'd have to talk about it or tackle the problem at one point and then or I think in this matter."

sie schreiben, malen, musizieren, sie produzieren ein neues […] Denken, eine neue Musik, eine neue Literatur und bildende Kunst. Fiedler, Palma und Bozenhard sind Musiker, schreiben aber auch, Cornelia Schleime ist Malerin, schreibt und filmt, Anderson malt und tritt in Bands auf, Tohm di Roes, Lorek und Papenfuß tragen in Gemeinschaft mit musikalischen Produktionen vor …[29]

One form of collaboration is familiar and has been fully documented – the combination of graphic work and text, variously dubbed visual poetry or "Dichtergrafiken, bei denen Schrift und Bild eine Einheit eingegangen sind."[30] Gerrit-Jan Berendse has pointed out that this was a form of collaboration born of political danger: "Die Dichter zogen bildende Künstler hinzu oder fingen an, selbst zu zeichnen und zu malen, damit auf halbwegs legale Weise Texte gedruckt werden konnten, die angesichts des seit 1979 verschärften Druckgesetzes den Eindruck von Nebenprodukten graphischer Arbeit vermitteln sollten."[31] To mix words and pictures was, whether political or not, a way out of what one poet called "der sprache / engpaß."[32] It is, however, impossible even to summarise the possible combinations: poems may be illustrated; pictures may contain, even conceal, poems (poems visible when a drawing is held against the light); poems themselves become concrete or figural. In all cases the reader is engaged in a kind of complicity, holding text against image. The commonest form of all depends less on a poet working with an artist than on the poet devising a concrete, figured shape for his own text – not, in other words, a collaboration between two creators but a single poet working within two modes. The reader reads out a new verbal emphasis from a visible shape: "Visuelle Poesie," as the editors of the *wortBILD* anthology conclude, "baut auf neugierige, unvoreingenommene Leser, die bereit sind, sich gemeinsam mit den Dichtern auf ungesichertes Gebiet vorzuwagen, um Unbekanntes wahrzunehmen und Gewohntes in neuem Licht zu

---

29 Anderson and Erb, eds., *Berührung*, p. 12: "they write, paint, make music, produce new ideas, new music and visual art. Fiedler, Palma and Bozenhard are musicians, but they also write, Cornelia Schleime is a painter who writes and makes films, Anderson paints and plays in bands, Tohm di Roes, Lorek and Papenfuß give readings in conjunction with musical productions."
30 Arnold, ed., *Die andere Sprache*, p. 250: "poets' graphics in which text and picture form a unity." Documented in Deisler and Kowalski, eds., *wortBILD*.
31 Gerrit-Jan Berendse: "Wandlose Werkstätten: Elke Erbs Rolle in der 'Prenzlauer-Berg-connection.'" Arnold and Meyer-Gosau, eds., *Literatur in der DDR*, pp. 210–19, here p. 215: "The poets brought artists in or they themselves started drawing and painting, so that texts could be printed in a more or less legal fashion which in response to the stricter print-law of 1979 looked like by-products of graphic work."
32 Schedlinski, quoted Wolf: *Sprachblätter*, p. 24: "the bottleneck of language."

sehen."³³ Thus a carmen quadratum in which "wahr" ("true") recurs, contains at its centre the word "Poesie." Thus – and a political undertone is apparent – scraps of repeated incomplete text encircle a single central "schnauze voll" ("fed up"); a circle of repeated spaced-out "welt offen" ("open to the world") entraps a single "welt zu" ("closed to the world"); a rectangle of bureaucratic jargon-words ("Entwicklung," Zentralisierung," etc., – "development," "centralisation") are typographically reduced towards a centre which consists only of the repeated "ung ung ung."

Experiments in the interaction of verbal and visual, of which the above-quoted are the simplest, need not reach a wider public. Indeed, one of the most experimental of all, the highly gifted poet and draughtsman flanzendörfer (pseudonym for Frank Lanzendörfer), who restlessly wandered about the Prenzlauer Berg before killing himself at the age of twenty-five in 1988, was one of the most desperate seekers after privacy. Others sought modes of collaborative work that guaranteed a certain publicity, even if, on the Prenzlauer Berg, every public venture was at least half clandestine. Perhaps the most persistent, certainly the most obvious proof of an impulse towards cooperation, is the publication throughout the 1980s of a variety of periodicals. One of the first, *Der Kaiser ist nackt*, first appeared in 1981, was re-named *Mikado* in 1983 and ran until 1987. Its three editors, one of whom was Uwe Kolbe, surveyed the achievement later, emphasising the incalculable value of working-together:

> Freiwillige kollektive Arbeit war eine neue Erfahrung für uns. Wichtigster Punkt bei der Entstehung jeder neuen Ausgabe war nicht das Sammeln von Texten, nicht der technische Ablauf – schwierig genug in einem Land in dem angeblich jeder siebente ein Telefon besitzt (wir kannten nicht genug siebente Bürger). Wesentlicher Teil der Arbeit waren die Zusammenkünfte, bei denen die Texte in einen von uns gemeinsam akzeptierten, gegenseitigen Zusammenhang gebracht wurden […] gemeinsam war uns die Suche nach einer erfrischenderen Form des Zusammenlebens, die hinausgeht über trostloses Zusammensitzen in Kneipen, über unnützes Herumdiskutieren hinter verschlossenen Türen.³⁴

---

33 Deisler and Kowalski, eds., *wortBILD*, p. 6: "depends on inquisitive, unprejudiced readers who are prepared to venture with the poets into uncertain terrain in order to perceive what was unknown and to see familiar things in a new light."

34 Kolbe, Trolle and Wagner, eds., *Mikado*, p. 8: "Voluntary collective work was something new for us. The most important point with every new issue was not collecting the texts or the technical process – hard enough in a country where apparently every seventh person has a telephone (we didn't know enough seventh persons). The crucial part of the work was the meetings, where we got the texts into a coherent sequence that we could all accept. We were all in search of a more refreshing form of living-together that went beyond the dreary sitting-together in pubs or the useless endless discussions behind closed doors."

Out of the cooperative editorial work there emerged coherence, a "Zusammenhang" that clearly mattered. It could take many forms, depending on the group and on the express aims of the periodical concerned. Space permits only a brief comparison between two extremes, illustrating sharply contrasting praatices: *Mikado* and *Ariadnefabrik*. Characteristic of *Mikado*, in particular of its early numbers from the years 1983/4, is an absence of theorising and a tendency to avoid overt politicising and to appeal to a readership capable of reading hints and finding common denominators. One noticeably prominent ingredient can, however, be seen as a piece of transparent political strategy, namely, the items which play with varieties of humorous-ironic distance. Thus, Adolf Endler – for Helmut Heissenbüttel the "Vaterfigur des Prenzlauer Berg"[35] – is represented in an early number by an ironic piece attempting to characterise the Prenzlauer-Berg-scene and entitled "Wir Jungs von Ypsilon-Acht oder Der Lagebesprechungswimpel." This is no straightforward group-portrayal, unless group-portrayal may be felt to lie in the playful non-involvement of an essay couched in a mixture of the party-bureaucratic and spirited reportage. Opposition – of sorts – is taking the form of an outbreak of House-Book-Cannibalism, an act of sacrilege whose dimensions are hinted at in the opening quotation from offialdom: "Betrifft: *Benutzen der Wasch- und Trockenräume und das Ein- und Austragen in das Hausbuch* / Es ist bekannt, Daß Herr Frischke ins Haus 2 gezogen ist. Der Waschraum- und die Trockenraumschlüssel sind ab heute bei mir abzuholen bzw. abzugeben."[36] An all-too-recognisable system has prompted a grotesque form of protest. In the same number Uwe Kolbe in a lengthy poem entitled "Vorstellung des Artisten" proclaims in a rhetoric that echoes other kinds of declaration "Es lebe das kommende Klopapier. / Seiner Heiligkeit, dem deutschen Arsch, zur nobelen Abfuhr."[37] Jürgen Hultenreich, on the other hand, plays with autumnal moods and non-sequiturs in a poem entitled "Mich hat der Herbst erwischt," introducing a note of surreal despair that makes a far from surreal point:

> Mich hat der Herbst erwischt.
> Meine Unterhosen sind auf dem Flug nach Süden.
> Alte Geschichten reißen ihr Maul auf

---

35 Helmut Heissenbüttel: "Hinweis auf einen Dichter. Über Bert Papenfuß-Gorek." Arnold, ed., *Die andere Sprache*, pp. 125–130, here p. 127.
36 Kolbe, Trolle and Wagner, ed., *Mikado*, p. 11: "Item: Use of wash- and drying-rooms, entries in tenants' book / It is known that Herr Frischke has moved into No. 2. The washroom- and the drying-room key should be collected or returned to me as from today."
37 Ibid., p. 20: "Long live German toilet-paper. For stylish removals from His Holiness the German Arse."

> und schnauzen mich an.
> Im Radio stottern die Nachlaßverwalter
> der Oktoberrevolution. Ich versuche mit der Zunge
> in eine Steckdose reinzukommen.
> Mich hat der Herbst
> erwischt.
> [...]³⁸

It would be misleading to suggest that Mikado cultivated the ironic posture in preference to others. It is indeed impossible to summarise a variety that ranges from satire via travel-report to autobiography or a child's monologue. If a coherent point is being made it resides in this variety, a declaration through demonstration rather than polemic that a multitude of voices is itself a strategy against edicts and uniformity.

Ariadnefabrik, founded in 1986, inhabits a different corner of the Prenzlauer Berg enterprise. It arose – thus its two editors Rainer Schedlinski and Andreas Koziol – out of a "Theoriebedürfnis," a need for theory sensed at a point when dialectics had run out of momentum.³⁹ The result was a periodical in which theoretical debate proliferates, a debate owing much to French post-structuralism (and acknowledging on occasion the debt) whilst at the same time having a specifically East German perspective not simply because theoretical positions were being introduced to a public hitherto unaware of them but also because questions about the nature of language and discourse had particular point in a context where language was determined – and impoverished – by official usage. *Ariadnefabrik* was declaring open war on public rhetoric, on rigidly ordered official discourse.⁴⁰ And the open war was to be waged in unison, for there was a common purpose – individuals cooperating to form a coherent thread through the labyrinth.⁴¹ But within the common purpose individual accents were held to be decisive: "je stereotyper eine sprache, das heißt, je mehr ihre zeichen dem sozialen kanon angehören und sich der variation durch den einzelnen entziehen, umso weniger kann sie gesprochen werden."⁴² Variation – and it is a mild term for many of the extremes that individual poets pursued – signalled a recovery of meanings in words.

---

38 Ibid., p. 38: "The autumn's got me. My underpants are flying south. Old stories are opening their mouths and snapping at me. On the radio the executors of the October Revolution are stammering away. I try to stick my tongue in an electric plug. The autumn's got me."
39 Koziol and Schedlinski, eds., *Abriß*, p. 7.
40 Ibid., p. 232.
41 Ibid., pp. 324–5
42 Ibid., p. 232: "the more stereotype a language, that is to say, the more its signs are a part of the social canon and resist variation through the individual, the less it can be spoken."

A poet rejecting jargon-meanings in favour of some kind of authenticity is hardly a lone voice. Almost inevitably, indeed, the poets of the Prenzlauer Berg, however varied their styles, are, even as poets, voices in a long-established chorus. Thus, when Bert Papenfuß-Gorek raises his voice – the date is 1987 – at the opening of a poem entitled "ausdrückliche klage aus der inneren immigration" we catch none-too-distant echoes of other, earlier Sturm-und-Drang outbursts:

> aus sieche, schimpf & scham erhebe ich meine klage
> aus meiner wunden wildem fleisch, aus wildem blut
> aus zank, glut & brunst stieben lange melodiebögen
> schriller töne arrhythmie die trostlose elevation
> stockenden pulses.[43]

And the rejection of bogus communities can have a second-hand ring:

> Geh, wo es geht,
> das hieß: Geh auf eigenen Füßen!
> Angst riß mich aus der Sicherheit.
>   aus der geglaubten Sicherheit.
>   aus der falschen (überholten) Sicherheit.
> Jahrelang vor dieser Zeit
> hatte ich das 19. Jahrhundert verdammt:
>
> Dieses Kaisertum. Diesen Goethe-, Schiller-Verein, Diesen Kriegerverein. Diesen Weltpostverein.
>
> […]
> Jetzt verfluchte ich die Seßhaftigkeit, meine.[44]

There are, then, shared impulses – the stereotype gestures of past rebel-poets. But it is important to stress the extreme character of what resulted. For Rainer Schedlinski, in a programmatic postscript to his own poems, there can be no compromise. On the one hand there is a prevailing "sprachlosigkeit" ("speechlessness"), on the other there is poetic language, out of reach of official languages.[45] And poetic language, with its own inner rhetoric, is not a tool

---

43 Hesse, ed., *Sprache & Antwort*, p. 200: "Out of sickness, scorn and shame I raise my lament / out of my wounded wild flesh, out of wild blood / out of strife, fire and heat long arches of melody fly up / arrhythmia the dreary elevation of a hesitant pulse."
44 Elke Erb: "Angehn, Angriff." Arnold, ed., *Die andere Sprache*, p. 182: "Go where you can, that means: go on your own feet! Fear dragged me out of security. out of security believed in. out of false (outdated) security. For years before this time I had condemned the 19th century: the Empire. The Goethe-, Schiller-Association. The War Veterans' Association. The World-Post Association. Now I curse sedentariness, mine."
45 Schedlinski: *die rationen*, p. 136.

for understanding: it is, Schedlinski argues, an illusion to suggest otherwise, poetic language renders enigmatic – "verschlüsselt die dinge"[46] A poem from this same volume seems to illustrate the retreat from signifiers:

> Alibi oder Libido
> oder die worte Undank und Krimsekt
> Transvestit und Wladiwostok
> oder der satz:
> WER BANKNOTEN NACHMACHT ODER VERFÄLSCHT ODER
> NACHGEMACHTE ODER VERFÄLSCHTE SICH VERSCHAFFT
> UM SIE IN VERKEHR ZU BRINGEN, WIRD BESTRAFT.
> hat etwa den gleichen phonetischen reizwert
> wie das wort
> DESOXYRIBONUKLEINSÄURE
> für mich[47]

Schedlinski, it could be said, has found a kind of coherence faute de mieux, a phonetic "reizwert" beyond meaning, and it is – the final stress is unmistakeable – "für mich." Theory has not displaced personal emphasis. Indeed, the poets of the Prenzlauer Berg seem at one level to be bent on varieties of self-assertion, rejecting conventions of language in order to release other, less anonymous energies. Elke Erb puts matters simply in a long poem, "Start," published in 1988 in *Ariadnefabrik*. Having left the "Zirkel der mir überlieferten Poesie-Münzen, / der poesietümlichen Wörter, wie Stein, Wind, Stunde,"[48] she found a kind of security in "Das Text-Molekül als Treffpunkt und Ansatz. / Als erste Sicherheit: das jedenfalls ist sicher."[49]

In the case of Schedlinski's co-editor on *Ariadnefabrik*, Andreas Koziol, similar gestures of rejection can produce a different kind of poem. The old aim of poetry – "begreifen" ("understanding") is obsolete, he notes in one poem,[50] adding in another that the old theme autumn is nonsense ("wahnsinn").[51] Old techniques are likewise unusable – "ein knirschen mitten im vers

---

46 Ibid., p. 140
47 Ibid., p. 30: "Alibi or Libido or the words ingratitude or Kremlinsekt Transvestite and Vladivostok or the sentence ANY PERSON FORGING OR FALSIFYING BANKNOTES OR OBTAINING FORGED OR FALSIFIED NOTES IN ORDER TO CIRCULATE THEM WILL BE PROSECUTED. has about the same phonetic stimulus as DIOXYRIBONUCLEICACID for me."
48 Koziol and Schedlinski, eds., *Abriß*, p. 197: "the circle of the poetic coinage handed down to me, of the pop-poetic words like stone, wind, hour."
49 Ibid., p. 199: "The text-molecule as meeting-point and starting-point. The first secure point: that at least is secure."
50 Koziol: *mehr über rauten*, p. 77.
51 Ibid., p. 76.

/ ließ horchen" ("a grinding in mid-line / made you listen").[52] Grandpa's metrics[53] ("opas metrik") – lyric rheumatism, as he calls the result, is to be banished. But the result can be extreme. Thus a poem entitled "stenograffitti 1":

> löschpapier für tintenbrände,
> leistungsleichenschauhausmoden,
> mondbeatmung, tatenwende,
> sinnerei der richtschnurknoten
>
> tobsucht in den biotopen,
> lenzbetrieb im heimwehachter,
> finsternis aus horoskopen,
> konsternierte sternbetrachter,
>
> tranquillizer, transzendenzen,
> dieser alptraum macht karriere,
> pendelpappen, wahnsinnsgrenzen
> schluß der zombiezotenserie.[54]

The poem is untranslatable, but there is an emerging, shaped sense in the sequence "leichenschauhaus" ("mortuary") – "tobsucht" ("madness") – "finsternis" ("darkness") – "alptraum" ("nightmare") – "wahnsinn" ("madness") – "zombie."

There are risks in this – poetry can signal a withdrawal into something akin to private language (Koziol) or private associations (Schedlinski). And for the less experimentally-minded Volker Braun this was irresponsible escape into monologue: "Unsere jungen Dichter, Kinder der administrativen Beamten, suchen auch das Loch in der Mauer. Sie verbrauchen ihre Fantasie an Tunnels und Fesselballons [...]."[55]

Braun's attack – like Wolf Biermann's more recent, more vituperative polemic – has an unintended value: any attempt to defend the poets of the Prenzlauer Berg against the charge of self-indulgence or escapism cannot rest on evidence of unambiguous engagement but on hints, associations and on a cooperative reader: "daß gerade die exklusiv aussehenden Texte – exklusiv, gemessen an den üblichen Standards der Rezeption – in Wahrheit auf den

---

52 Ibid., p. 77.
53 Ibid., p. 86.
54 Ibid., p. 39.
55 Braun: "Rimbaud," p. 983: "Our young poets, children of administrators, are looking also for the hole in the wall. They waste their imagination on tunnels and captive balloons."

mitwirkenden Leser oder Hörer zählen."[56] Thus, Jan Faktor – in Adolf Endler's view "der Schalksnarr, der Schwejk dieser Landschaft"[57] – is no less subversive for leaving his reader with empty spaces to fill:

> es gibt immer mehr wörter die man nicht anfassen kann
> die man nicht aussprechen kann
> die man sich nicht mehr ruhig ansehen kann
> es sind zum Beispiel
> (Pause)
> und weiterhin
> (Pause)
> und
> (Pause)
> und
> (Pause)
> und
> (Pause)
> außerdem sind stark abgenutzt Wörter wie
> (Pause)
> und
> (Pause)
> [...][58]

Much clearly depends on the weight that attaches to Faktor's pauses or to other poets' understatements. To the poets themselves that weight was crucial. Bert Papenfuß-Gorek, one of the most prominent of the writers of the Prenzlauer Berg, rejected the argument that experiments with language were an end in themselves. They were, he claimed in an interview in 1987, part of an "Umgang mit Sinnlosigkeit" – "das ist mein Leben, mit dem ich experimentiere, ich sehe mich nicht als Experimentator an der Sprache."[59] To entitle a section of twenty-five poems wortflug – word-flight – is to prompt as many questions about flight as about words. The questions may remain unan-

---

56 Manfred Jäger: "'Wem schreibe ich?' Adressen und Botschaften in Gedichten jüngerer Autoren aus der DDR seit dem Beginn der achtziger Jahre." Arnold, ed., *Die andere Sprache*, pp. 61–71, here p. 63: "that precisely the texts that look exclusive – judged by prevailing standards of reception – that in reality are counting on a reader or listener who is collaborating."
57 Endler: *Den Tiger reiten*, p. 25: "the rogue, the Schweyk on this landscape."
58 Faktor: *Georgs Versuche*, p. 76: "there are more and more words that one cannot touch, that one cannot utter, that one can no longer look at calmly, like for example (pause) and then (pause) [...] and then as well there are much overused words like (pause)."
59 Hesse, ed., *Sprache & Antwort*, p. 220: "living with meaninglessness – that is my life that I'm experimenting with, I don't see myself as an experimenter with language."

swered, but, as the following few lines suggest, there are associations and allusions ("bekwehmlichkeiten [...] trott [...] gleichgeschalt [...] strammstand") within the surface play with orthography and syntax:

> gegen ferfestigungen
> ferfestigter zungen
> & bekwehmlichkeiten
> trott zu beschreiten
> dergestalt gleichgeschalt
> ist selbst in blutgeflut
> strammstand noch der anstand
> so wortschritt um schritt
> flugs ich wortflog[60]

When Jan Faktor surveyed the Prenzlauer Berg scene after the dramas of 1989 he still recollected with admiration Papenfuß-Gorek's ability to be politically disengaged at one level and involved at another: "Er ist beim Schreiben mit einer für mich damals verblüffenden Leichtigkeit mit der 'Politik' klargekommen. [...] Dabei ist er, und nicht nur durch die rein sprachliche Radikalität, immer auch politisch gewesen."[61]

There were, it could be said, as many strategies for refuting charges of irrelevance as there were poets writing poetry. It is, of course, impossible to cover those strategies comprehensively, but it is worth illustrating the variety not simply for its own sake but because there are overlapping themes around questions of words and communication that reinforce our impression that here too there was a kind of cooperative venture. Indeed it is the unemphatic presence of "wir," replacing "ich" and "ihr," that seems to make the second stanza of Stefan Döring's short poem "willelei" point away from the non-communication with which the poem begins:

> ich habe euch nichts zu sagen
> ihr habt mir nichts zu sagen
> ihr macht was ihr wollt
> ich mache was ich will
>
> niemand hat uns was zu sagen
> wir haben niemandem was zu sagen

---

60 Papenfuß-Gorek: *dreizehntanz*, p. 123: "to go against the hardenings of hardened tongues and the lined-up routine easy-ways-out means standing stiff and upright in one's very blood so wordstep by step I swiftly wordflew."

61 Faktor: *Henry's Jupitergestik*, p. 103: "In his writing he seemed to come to terms with 'politics' with an ease that I at the time found baffling, And yet he has always been political – and not just through his purely linguistic radicalism."

> wir machen was wir wollen
> niemand macht was er will[62]

How resonant that emerging "wir" was in its East Berlin context it is impossible to say, it is, however, the allusion to a common purpose that gives the poem its closing point.

Only Döring's title echoes the play with verbal invention that is crucial for Papenfuß-Gorek, for the rest Döring stays close to the language of everyday discourse. He too, however, pursues more extreme effects, producing in a poem entitled "jede untermauerung ist eine unterwanderung" an unusually sharp polemic against the anonymous self-interested hypocrites who have their own way of using language ("es gibt so viele lügen wie lagen / es gibt so viele wahrheiten wie waren"[63] – thus another poet, almost summarising Döring):

> und jeder kopf sein geld wert
> sein kopfgeld
> dass er leugnete was er erlog
> sowie auch die auf nichts bestehen
> mit ihren bodenlosen behauptungen
> denen beweise ein dreck sind
> rechnen ab mit vermutungen
> doch nie ganz wutlos in ihrem mut
> der warwahrheit eines zu geben
> wie sie mutmassung in anmassung wandeln
> und anmassend in mutmassungen vergehen
> erlügen sie das ohnehin falsche
> dass diese felsenfesten fallen
> je überfüllter desto unterhöhlter
> in den grund aus dem sie hier sind[64]

---

62   Hesse, ed., *Sprache & Antwort*, p. 91: "I have nothing to say to you / you have nothing to say to me / you do what you want / I do what I want / nobody has anything to tell us / we have nothing to say to anybody / we do what we want / nobody does what he wants."

63   Gabriele Kachold, in Wolf: *Sprachblätter*, p. 157: "there are as many lies as places / as many truths as wares."

64   Döring: *Heutmorgestern*, p. 33: "and every head has his price / his head-price / for denying his own lies / like those who insist on nothing with their groundless assertions / who don't care a damn about proofs / but work with suspicions / but are never quite angerfree when they boldly / think / of hitting at a dead truth / how they change suspicion into presumption / passing from presumption into suspicion / they lie about what's false from the start / and the rock-solid fall / the more overfull they are the more undermined / down from where they came."

Whether the play with words threatens to blunt Döring's attack is debatable – certainly the play and the attack are connected, indeed, language inventively re-organised is forming the vehicle for articulated opposition.

Attitudes to party-ideology, to party-language as well as to poetry and its own traditions are, it seems, creating a volatile mix. The result – fortunately – was not a narrowing-down of the concerns of poetry to issues of language. But those issues at least prompted poems, and it is worth adding one further example, partly because it is the work of Schedlinski, perhaps the key figure in *Ariadnefabrik*, and partly because it rigorously isolates individual words, patterning them visually in the manner of concrete poetry, the brand of multi-media collaboration to which we have already referred, Again it is the "lichtung," the opening-up of space, that releases meanings, meanings which move from the sunset on a prospectus via memory to words charged with more sinister meaning, where lines, here broken up, are prison-bars, language an open prison:

```
     diese unvordenkliche
                         lichtung
dort                                     der worte
          zwischen den
                      worten
  den dingen                die dinge
            die sonnen                    ausser
                      schälen
sonnen                         sich
        untergangs                      aus den
                  prospekten
schält bis               auch die
          nur noch                  erinnerung
                     erinnerung
alles andere                      abfällt
           damit                          und
                  verdeckt
schwarzen                 siehst du
          schnee                        den
                    auf den
                            seiten
sind gitter                         die zeilen
           des menschen
                         sprache
  gefängnis                       ein offnes
                dort
                     gibt es
                             kein
                                   draussen[85]
```

---

65 Schedlinski: *die rationen*, p. 107: "this immemorial opening-up of words there between the words the things beyond the things the suns peel off from the sun set brochures and memory peels off until only memory falls away and everything else is covered with it do

For tendentious reasons Volker Braun and, later, Wolf Biermann, are in pursuit of common denominators which ignore individual accents. Which is not to deny, however, that the individual accents, varied though they were, risked on occasion isolation and the charge of obscurantism. The tensions between a public, group commitment and more private concerns existed for some, and they were not easily resolved. Gabriele Kachold puts the tension clearly in a poem published in early 1989 in another journal, *Kontext*, under the title "The Law of the Scene – Das Gesetz der Szene." There is a collision in the poem between that law – "das gesetz der szene ist klatsch / das gesetz der szene ist alle wissen alles / das gesetz der szene ist gruppe"[66] and the conflicting claims of the individual, emphasised in the reiterated "mein" in a line such as "meine kraft ist meine frische meine wut meine klarheit."[67]

To many the linguistic ideas within the Prenzlauer Berg scene, facing in a multitude of ways the paralysing rhetoric of State and Party, were a guarantee of relevance and solidarity. In one case, however, reflection about poetry and a sense of the activity underpinning poetry came to be a part of poems as published. The poet in question is the direct object of Volker Braun's polemic – "unsere Flip-out-Elke," he dubs her – in other words, Elke Erb, of the same generation as Adolf Endler and often linked with him as general guide and mentor to the poets of the 1980s. Unlike Endler, however, Erb's viewpoint is that of the practising poet, and what Berendse sees as her special role resides in her notion, deriving, as she sees it, from Franz Fühmann, of a "wandlose Werkstatt" within which poetry is set.[68] Gerhard Wolf characterises the result as "prozessuales Schreiben, bei dem weder ein Ziel noch der Weg dahin festgelegt oder vorgegeben sind. Und der Leser wird […] angeregt, sich mit ihr auf einem solchen 'Prozeß,' der ins Unerwartete, auch ins Unbestimmbare, Nichtvorhersehbare führt, einzulassen."[69]

The results of Erb's involvement with her reader are most apparent in a volume of poems-plus-commentaries, first published in 1987 and containing work from 1981 onwards. The title, *Kastanienallee*, signals the Prenzlauer-Berg-

---

you see the black snow on the pages the lines are bars the language of man an open prison there is no outside."

66 Metelka, ed., *Alles ist im Untergrund obenauf*, p. 67: "the law of the scene is gossip / the law of the scene is everybody knows everything / the law of the scene is group."
67 Ibid., p. 71: "my strength is my vigour my rage my clarity."
68 Gerrit-Jan Berendse: "Wandlose Werkstätten: Elke Erbs Rolle in der 'Prenzlauer-Berg-connection.'" Arnold and Meyer-Gosau, eds., *Literatur in der DDR*, pp. 210–19, here p. 212.
69 Wolf: *Sprachblätter*, p. 120: "a writing-in-progress in which neither a goal nor a route are fixed or declared. And the reader is encouraged to enter with her into a 'process' which leads to what is unexpected, indeterminable, unpredictable."

connection since it is the street in the district where the poet lived. The first poem in the volume illustrates Erb's practice and intentions in their most extreme form. It is dated "1. 1. 1981" and, save for one word, conveniently italicised, is of almost provokingly incidental character:

> KASTANIENALLEE, bewohnt
>
> Im Treppenhaus Kastanienallee 30 nachmittags
> um halb fünf roch es flüchtig
> nach toten, *selbstvergessenen* Mäusen.[70]

The three lines are followed by six pages of comments, recollections, general statements in small print. Rather than attempting what at this stage is impossible, namely a summary of the first of many such commentaries, it is better to emphasise the revelatory character of the whole: Erb is disclosing the aims which underlie the laconic three line-opening, shares with her reader thoughts and misgivings about the opening of a volume of poems and is at the same time disclosing aims which inform the volume as a whole. She decided at the outset to support ("beizustehen") the as yet incomplete volume, to be present alongside her texts, so that a text should no longer stand alone in a white desert, staking its claim unaided:

> [...]
> dem Band, dem zum Buch die Vollendung (Abrundung/Einheit) fehlt,
> beizustehen,
> bei meinen Texten (den Sachen, die mir im Leben 'aufgefallen' sind)
> zugegen zu bleiben,
> [...]
> Nicht mehr der ausschließliche Text, allein auf weißer Wüste
>   sein autistisch behinderter Alleinvertretungsanspruch,
>   umgeben von Unaussprechlichem[71]

Commentary will, she hopes, enable a text to acquire an extra presence "als Wirklichkeit zu wirken" – thus illustrating not a finished product but a process of speech and silence ("Reden und Schweigen"):

> Mir schwebt vor, den Denkprozeß zu erfassen,
> dessen Ausdruck das Reden und Schweigen der Texte ist.
> Vermutlich wird er sich als Schreibprozeß darstellen,
> [...][72]

---

70 Erb: *Kastanienallee*, p. 5: "Kastanienallee, inhabited / In the staircase of Kastanienallee 30 in the afternoon / at half past four it smelled briefly / of dead, absent-minded mice."
71 Ibid., p. 7.
72 Ibid., p. 8.

Some are bound to object, claiming that commentary destroys the independent text – "die Selbständigkeit verdirbt," a charge that Erb, however, rejects.

After what amounts to a declaration of general intent around her first poem Erb proceeds to append to subsequent poems notes about origins, versions, questions of substance, relating more directly to the individual text. The reader is encouraged to trace creative processes, to resolve alternatives. Thus an artifical dividing-line between writing and living, between writer and reader, may be overcome.

Erb in her *Kastanienallee* may seem remote from our starting-point, Uwe Kolbe's poet up under the roof, invoking poetic typologies. But she is not remote from the shared concerns that surface so frequently in the work of the Prenzlauer Berg writers and artists. *Kastanienallee* is indeed an appropriate work on which to conclude a brief survey of those varied activities because it explicitly develops in print some of the encounters that elsewhere remain understated, encounters with an "unmistakeable public" ("erleuchtet von jener Öffentlichkeit, / die man als Unverkennbarkeit bezeichnen kann"[73]). And yet there is irony and ambiguity in this: in emphasising complex processes Erb may seem to restore to poetry some of its hermetic, esoteric character, may seem simultaneously to be underlining and undermining traditional mysteries.

It is perhaps appropriate to end with ambiguity, or at least uncertainty. A final judgement on this last generation is clearly not – or not yet – possible, although an impression of variety, such as this essay has attempted briefly to convey, may help guard against snap labelling. Adolf Endler's sharp response to the charge of recycled avantgardism – a common label – is worth noting: "Als ob auch nur das früheste der Programme und Konzepte der Moderne als 'endgültig abgegolten' ins Schubfach getan werden könnte – so sehr der deutsche Ordnungssinn dazu neigt"[74]). They have been seen as a nameless "ism" ("der 'namenlose ismus'"[75]), as outsiders who resist categorisation (the now discontinued series published by the East Berlin Aufbau publishing house bore the title Außer der Reihe). Gerhard Wolf, the key figure in the Aufbau series and, therefore, in rendering accessible the work of many Prenzlauer Berg writers, finds a variety of unexplained motives and a wealth of activity:

> Man wird eine ganze Reihe von Motiven herzählen können, […] aber wie es dazu kam, daß sich etwa seit Mitte der siebziger Jahre eine ganze Reihe junger Leute, alle um die Mitte der fünfziger Jahre geboren, vor allem in Berlin trafen, um sich

---

73 Ibid., p. 84.
74 Endler: *Den Tiger reiten*, p. 47: "As if only the earliest modernist programme can be filed away under 'Account settled' – however the German sense of order inclines that way."
75 Böthig: "die verlassene sprache." Arnold, ed., *Die andere Sprache*, pp. 38–48, here p. 38.

ihre Texte vorzulesen, sich nach Malern und Zeichnern umsahen, deren Bilder ihnen zu diesen Texten zu passen schienen […], daß sie Musiker fanden, die zu ihren Versen – oft sie übertönend – die entsprechende Instrumentalisierung vornahmen […] – kurz: dies alles findet sich nicht alle Tage, noch dazu in einem bevorzugten Stadtteil, Prenzlauer Berg genannt […]."[76]

One of the lengthiest and most illuminating retrospective summaries of what was involved and what was accomplished has come recently from one of the participants, Jan Faktor. Faktor makes no grandiose claims, nor does he, however, seek to minimise what was undertaken. To him should belong, perhaps, the last word:

Das, was in den 80ern in der DDR und vor allem in Berlin entstanden ist, waren nicht Spinnereien, waren nicht Spinnereien von einzelnen; neben dem Geschriebenen ist dort ein produktives, eigenständiges Milieu geschaffen worden, in dem es vielen möglich wurde, sich zu artikulieren und zu entwickeln. Das ist an sich schon – die Umstände waren nicht ungünstig, aber auch nicht einfach – eine gewisse Leistung; zumal dieses Geflecht in ziemlich relevanter Beziehung zu dem stand, was die Zeit zu bieten hatte.[77]

---

76 Wolf: *Sprachblätter*, p. 14: "one could invoke a whole range of motives, but how it came about that from about the mid-seventies a whole crowd of young people, all born around the mid-fifties, began to meet mainly in Berlin to read their texts, to look around for painters and artists whose pictures seemed to suit the texts, who found musicians who provided music to accompany – sometimes to drown – the words […] in short all this does not happen every day, certainly not in a special neighbourhood called Prenzlauer Berg."

77 Faktor: *Henry's Jupitergestik*, p. 102: "What arose in the 1980's in the GDR and especially in Berlin were not just the crazy ideas of individuals; alongside what was written a productive, autonomous milieu was created in which it was possible for many to express themselves and to develop. That in itself – circumstances were not unfavourable, but they were not simple either – is something of an achievement, especially as this entire network was distinctly relevant to what happening all around at the time."

KEITH BULLIVANT
University of Florida

The End of the Dream of the "Other Germany": The "German Question" in West German Letters

Abstract: After a brief survey of the dominant attitudes amongst West German writers to the "German Question" since 1945, this essay concentrates in detail on statements made in the second half of the Eighties by prominent writers such as Grass and Walser. Particular attention is paid to debates in the turbulent months after the opening of the Berlin Wall in November 1989 and the first two years of unification. In a final section Bullivant examines the treatment of unification and its consequences in the first literary works published after the collapse of the GDR.

The writers of the so-called "younger generation" that made its literary debut after the end of the Second World War were strongly influenced by their experience of childhood and adolescence in the Third Reich and by the war, be it – as with a number of major German writers – through their reluctant service in that war, or as children old enough to have conscious memories of that time. Those experiences led to a large number of these writers sharing a vision of a new Germany born specifically of an awareness of the political mistakes of the Nazi past, one that would tread the "third" or "middle" way between political and economic extremes and thus help to ensure world peace, rather than endangering it yet again. This was something that transcended the political division of the country that was already taking place. If we look back at the short-lived periodicals *Der Ruf, Ost und West, Aufbau* and *Die Wandlung*, the early issues of the *Frankfurter Hefte* and the proceedings of what Alfred Kantorowicz called the "Parlament des Geistes", the first Congress of German Writers, held in East Berlin in 1947 (the second took place in Travemünde in June 1991) a consensus as to the sort of Germany they wanted emerged clearly. It was to be, as Alfred Andersch put it, "die freie Brücke zwischen den divergierenden Kräften," that was to help prevent future wars. As far as internal politics were concerned, it was important "die Gefahr des Auseinanderlebens zu bannen" and "am erneuten, wahren und freiheitlichen Deutschland zu bauen."[1] Their fundamental idea was that the new country should be demilitarized, neutral and undivided, its politics a humanistic blend of liberal democracy and socialism: these were ideas that continued to have some considerable currency in subsequent decades and, above all, were to emerge with briefly renewed vigour after the collapse of the GDR in the winter of 1989–90. However, in the Cold War atmosphere that rapidly developed in the late Forties, particularly as a result of the Berlin Blockade and the creation of separate currencies in the Western and Eastern Zones (the "Währungsreform") in 1948, this dream rapidly became unrealizable. After the founding of the two separate German republics in 1949 Alfred Kantorowicz, then living in East Berlin, made the following, somewhat rueful, entry in his diary:

> Unser Traum von einer Erneuerung Deutschlands ist zu Ende. Die Politiker von Vorgestern haben das Heft nun wieder fest in der Hand hüben und drüben. Staatsmänner, Denker, Dichter, geistig schöpferische Menschen ganz allgemein, sind "draußen vor der Tür".[2]

Peter Rühmkorf and others have since argued that this conclusion was premature, that as late as 1955 all-German elections still lay on the table, and there is much to this, with hindsight, but it is nevertheless equally clear that the path of separate development of the Federal Republic, as pursued by the Adenauer Government, the thrust for rearmament and the membership of NATO, together with the more or less simulataneous integration of the German Democratic Republic into the Eastern alliance, made any alternative to separate development impossible. Another decisive turn came in 1961, when the building of the Wall through Berlin, perhaps more than anything else, seemed to signify the final separation of the two German states, the end of hopes of rapprochement. The only West German statement of note on the question of unification was Enzensberger's "Katechismus zur deutschen Frage" ("Catechism of the German Question", 1966), in which he, as so often somewhat ahead of his time, explored possible common ground between the two Germanies and the benefits of confederation.

---

1 "[…] the free bridge between the divergent powers […]." Andersch: "Die freie deutsche Republik als Brücke." Quoted in Wagenbach et al., eds., *Vaterland, Muttersprache*, pp. 65–6, here p. 66; "to prevent the two halves of the country drifting apart and to help build the new, true, democratic Germany". Ibid., p. 75 ("Drei Manifeste des Ersten Deutschen Schriftstellerkongresses, 1947").

2 "Our dream of the regeneration of Germany is at an end. Yesterday's politicians have once again got the reins tight in their hands, both here and over there. True statesmen, thinkers and poets, every sort of intellectually creative person, are all 'out in the cold'." Kantorowicz: *Deutsches Tagebuch* part 1, p. 647.

With the election victory of Willy Brandt in 1969 the possibility of some normalcy in relations with the GDR and other Eastern Block states was in the air. And Brandt's policy towards the East (his "Ostpolitik") did not disappoint. His successful drive for the normalization of relationships with the GDR seemed nevertheless to set the final seal on the post-war political division of the country; now that division, long a theme – for propagandistic purposes – in the literature of the GDR and of the GDR exile Uwe Johnson (with quite different accentuation) entered the wider domain of West German literature.[3] It was also not insignificant that Grass first started to talk of Germany being defined by its cultural unity at this time (the notion of the "Kulturnation"). In the Eighties Grass's friend Peter Schneider, much in the way that Enzensberger had done in the Sixties, was exploring the possibility of the emergence of a post-Wall alliance that might be called the "BDDR" ("FGDR") and which, as with the original hopes of the late Forties, was to achieve a just society from a fusion of the competing systems.[4]

While Schneider's views do not seem to have been widely received, another well-known writer was making the headlines from the mid-Eighties onwards, and, more significantly, being strongly criticized for his views on the "German Question". In his novella of 1987, *Dorle und Wolf*, then in a highly controversial interview in the Springer Press's *Die Welt* (which was in itself seen by many as an act of betrayal) and a number of other speeches, Martin Walser addressed the difficulty for someone of his generation (b. 1927) of accepting the division of the country in the long term. It had clearly escaped attention that this was by no means a new departure in Walser's thinking. As early as 1962 he had declared the unlikelihood of reunification,[5] but the late Seventies found him twice addressing the topic at length. He was aware of all the problems, especially those centering on Auschwitz (and all it symbolized), but, given his age and consequent personal experience, he now had to concede: "Aus meinem historischen Bewußtsein ist Deutschland nicht zu tilgen. Sie können neue Landkarten drucken, aber sie können mein Bewußtsein nicht neu herstellen. [...] Ich weigere mich, an der Liquidierung von Geschichte teilzunehmen."[6] These statements from the late Seventies aroused

---

3 Prominent examples here were Peter Schneider's *Der Mauerspringer*, Dieter Lattmann's *Die Brüder*, and Walser's *Dorle und Wolf*. On GDR literature see here Hutchinson: *Literary Representations of Divided Germany*.

4 "Geschichte einer Trennung." Schneider: *Deutsche Ängste*, pp. 28–9.

5 Walser: "Deutsches Mosaik", p. 8. He later (1986) declared the term "Wiedervereinigung" to be an "Adenauervokabel": "Deutschländer oder Brauchen wir eine Nation?", pp. 219 and 223.

6 "Germany cannot be erradicated from my consciousness. They can print new maps, but they cannot change my consciousness. I refuse to take part in the liquidation of history." In

no great interest, but a decade later things were quite different: one speech by Walser in particular, "Über Deutschland reden" ("Talking about Germany"), delivered in Munich in the autumn of 1988 and then reprinted in the weekly *Die Zeit*, unleashed a furious controversy. As he conceded with great perceptiveness in the speech, Walser appreciated that his views would be difficult to grasp for younger people, those who had grown up in the Federal Republic. But it was, given the then widespread acceptance of the absolute separation of the two states and, in the light of a number of rather unfortunate formulations, inevitably older writers who attacked him. Jurek Becker went as far as to claim that Walser had "lost his mind."[7] The concern with Walser's apparent forgetfulness of the legacy of recent German history, his refusal to accept the view that division was the permanent price of Germany's earlier sins, together with the notion that Walser had deserted the Left and now moved in increasingly conservative, and therefore extremely dubious, circles, undoubtedly went some way towards explaining why critics overlooked key aspects of Walser's argument, which was essentially little different from their own. An important point for him was that the dangerous concentration of weapons of mass destruction on German soil was "eine Folge der Teilung". "Schlimmer als diese zwei waffenstarrenden Deutschlandfragmente", he continued, "könnte ein vereintes Deutschland, österreichischer oder schweizerischer Zugewandtheit, nicht sein."[8] The hope of a neutral, demilitarized Germany, such as had been the dream of the first Congress of German Writers, was still in place. Moreover, in this speech Walser identified himself with the 60th and 61st Articles of Enzensberger's "Katechismus zur deutschen Frage" of 1966, in which he hadstressed the desirablity of a German Federation, within which context the two German states would be able to learn from each other and benefit accordingly. In addition, it seemed entirely to escape the notice of Walser's critics that he had quoted from a speech he had given in Bergen-Enkheim in

---

Walser's speech in Bergen-Enkheim, 1977, quoted in Horst Ehmke: "Was ist des Deutschen Vaterland?" Habermas, ed., *Stichworte zur "geistigen Situation der Zeit"* vol. 1, pp. 51–76, here p. 67. The volume also contained a lengthy essay by Dieter Wellershoff, also indicating his sense of loss, brought about by the seemingly permanent division of the country ("Deutschland – ein Schwebezustand." Ibid., pp. 77–114). Ehmke also, interestingly enough, quoted a speech by veteran GDR writer Stephan Hermlin, held at the Writers' Congress in 1978, which expressed similar views.

7   Becker: "Gedächtnis verloren – Verstand verloren." *Die Zeit* No. 47, November 18, 1988, p. 61.
8   "[…] a consequence of the division of the country". "A united Germany, perhaps along the lines of Austria or Switzerland, could in no way be worse than these two sabre-rattling fragments of Germany." Walser: "Über Deutschland reden." *Die Zeit* No. 45, November 4, 1988, pp. 65–7.

1977, his first major public pronouncement on the "German Question", in which the nature of his vision of the reunited country was clearly formulated:

> In mir hat ein anderes Deutschland immer noch eine Chance [...], eines nämlich, das seinen Sozialismus nicht von einer Siegermacht draufgestülpt bekommt, sondern ihn ganz und gar selber entwickeln darf; und eines, das seine Entwicklung zur Demokratie nicht ausschließlich nach dem kapitalistischen Krisenrhythmus stolpern muß. Dieses andere Deutschland könnte man, glaube ich, heute brauchen.[9]

A comparison of this statement with ones of Günter Grass in the same year of 1977 makes it difficult to understand why Grass now dismissed this speech out of hand. It should also be stressed that, even after the opening of the Wall, Walser – contrary to the impression given in the comments of others – continued to stress that his idea of unification excluded the idea of the Federal Republic swallowing up the GDR. He argued instead for "ein in Europa völlig integrierter Deutscher Bund" which, through the inevitable breaking down of the military confrontation between East and West, would "der Welt ein friedfertiges, friedvolles Deutschland [...] bieten."[10] In much the same tone Dieter Wellershoff, who, like Walser, also explained his attitude towards unification in terms of generational experience and his continued belief in the hopes of the immediate post-war years, also argued in favour of a united country with a strong federal component.[11] While others were now urging separate development of the two German states, Walser and Wellershoff remained essentially true to the earlier dream of the "other Germany."

It is now somewhat difficult to grasp, but in the autumn of 1988 Walser's plea that his fellow-countrymen should "die Wunde Deutschland offen [...] halten," provocative though it was,[12] seemed nothing but an extreme case of

---

9 "Deep in my heart another Germany still has a chance. It is one that doesn't have its socialism imposed upon it by one of the victors, but can develop it entirely on its own. And it's one that doesn't have to stumble along on its path towards democracy exclusively according to the rhythm of the crises of capitalism. We could do with this other Germany today, I believe." Ibid.

10 "A German Federation fully integrated into Europe" which would "present the world with a peaceable and peaceful Germany." Walser: "Zum Stand der deutschen Dinge." *Frankfurter Allgemeine Zeitung* No. 282, December 5, 1989, pp. L1–2.

11 Cf. Wellershoff: "Gerade noch kreuzungsfähige Unterarten. Votum für die deutsche Vereinigung", paper given at the Literarisches Colloquium, West Berlin, February 24, 1990 (unpublished).

12 "[...] keep the German wound open". Consciously or unconsciously Walser was using here a phrase first used in 1984 by Stefan Heym in his speech "Über Deutschland": "Der Schrägstrich durch Deutschland markiert eine offene Wunde; wir können noch soviel Antibiotika darauf streuen, sie wird weiter eitern." Heym: *Einmischung*, p. 40. Cf. further in this context Wallmann: "Streitbar und umstritten." *Der Tagesspiegel* No. 13, 574, May 20, 1990, p. 13.

wishful thinking. The separation of the two German states had long since been accepted by all parties and during the Eighties the normal relationship between the two regimes had been strengthened, as the visit of Franz-Josef Strauß to the GDR in 1984, which intensified trading links, and, above all, the state visit of Erich Honecker to Bonn in 1987 indicated. The rapid changes in Eastern Europe in the summer of 1989, culminating in the German Revolution, as we may call it, of November 1989, suddenly placed the "German Question" at the top of the political agenda for all Germans. The recently emerged opposition groups in the GDR, who had been at the forefront of the campaign for change, argued for the restoration of human rights and the transition to democracy within a separate state, and once again the notion of the "third way" surfaced. [13] The hopes of intellectuals in what was still the GDR were supported by a considerable number of left-wing and liberal intellectuals in the (old) Federal Republic. While Grass and Walter Jens were the most prominent Western supporters of a separate GDR, it should not be forgotten that a volume on the question of the future of the nation, published in 1990, clearly indicated that the majority of the older generation of writers in the West opposed unification.[14]

Grass's vision of the shape of the post-Cold War Germany was based on a notion that he had first expressed in the early Seventies, when the likelihood of the long-term separation of the two German states first began to seem ever greater, and which reached its first full expression in his "narrative essay" *Kopfgeburten oder Die Deutschen sterben aus* of 1980. An alliance between the two Germanies based entirely on traditional cultural ties would, in Grass's view, in no way disturb the political or military balance that had seemingly been established in Europe. As such it would not only be "unseren Nachbarn verständlich," it would also be "dem Nationalverständnis der Deutschen angemessen."[15] Given this notion on the one hand and his ideas of "democratic socialism" on the other, it was in no way surprising that in December 1989 Grass was arguing for the continued independence of the GDR, since "es [...] mit keinem Satz bewiesen [ist], daß der Niedergang dieses Wirtschaftssystems [...] auch das Experiment eines demokratischen Sozialismus in Deutschland beendet hat."[16] For reasons of European security the nation

---

13 "Für unser Land", reprinted in Christa Wolf: *Im Dialog*, pp. 170–71.
14 Cf. here Barthélemy and Winckler eds., *Mein Deutschland*, esp. pp. 10, 20 and 52.
15 "[...] understandable to our neighbours" and "appropriate to the Germans' understanding of themselves as a nation". Grass: "Kopfgeburten oder Die Deutschen sterben aus" – *Werkausgabe* vol. 6, pp. 141–20, here p. 150.
16 "[...] it is by no means proved that, with the collapse of this economic system, [...] the experiment of democratic socialism in Germany has also come to an end." Grass: "Viel Ge-

should remain divided, but joined with the Federal Republic in a German Federation, conceived not as a political entity, but as a "cultural nation" ("Kulturnation").

While Grass argued more passionately, above all more publicly, on behalf of such a notion, he was only one of many supporters of it, as was demonstrated by a collection of essays published in 1990, carrying the highly significant title *Mein Deutschland findet sich in keinem Atlas* and which was a plea in unison for the concept of the cultural union of two sovereign German states. It should be stressed that the traditional notion of the "Kulturnation," which predated the establishment of the German Empire in 1871 and included all German-speaking areas, was here nothing but a more or less linguistic starting point; it was crucial, Grass stressed, "den von Johann Gottfried Herder geprägten Begriff der Kulturnation mit neuen Inhalten an[zu]reichern."[17] It became clear that it was, above all, to take due cognisance of the wider political role and obligations of the German states, as Lutz Winckler, the co-editor of *Mein Deutschland findet sich in keinem Atlas*, explained in his introduction to that volume:

> Gemeint war die Besinnung auf gemeinsame sprachliche und kulturelle Wurzeln, ein freier Austausch von Erfahrungen und Gedanken, von Büchern und Kunst zwischen beiden deutschen Staaten und schließlich: die Formulierung gemeinsamer, nicht die Deutschen allein betreffender Ziele, wie sie sich gerade aus der Beschäftigung mit und der Verantwortung für Kultur ergaben. Dabei wurde allen Beteiligten zunehmend deutlich, daß der Begriff der Nation zu eng war, wollte man die aktuellen, die Menschheit insgesamt betreffenden Probleme Frieden und Umwelt thematisieren.[18]

The speed of developments in the winter of 1989–90 was such that *Der Spiegel* was asking as early as December 1989 whether the intellectuals in the East

---

fühl, wenig Bewußtsein." *Der Spiegel* No. 47, November 20, 1989, p. 79, reprinted in Grass: *Lastenausgleich*, pp. 13–25, here p. 19.

17 The title of the collection mentioned translates as "My Germany cannot be found in any atlas"; the subsequent statement by Grass reads: "to enrich the term 'Kulturnation' as defined by […] Herder." Grass: *Lastenausgleich*, p. 10.

18 "It was understood as meaning the concern for common linguistic and cultural roots, a free exchange of experiences and ideas, of books and art between the two German states, then, over and above that, the drawing up of common goals, but goals applying not only to the Germans, ones resulting directly from the concern with, and responsibility for, culture. It became increasingly clear to all concerned that the concept of the nation was too narrow, if we wanted to give expression to all the pressing problems to do with peace and the environment, problems which affect all of mankind." Barthélemy and Winckler, eds., *Mein Deutschland*, p. 8.

and the West hadn't already been left way behind.[19] Hans Magnus Enzensberger, still a most perceptive analyst of political and social trends, quickly put his finger on the unique nature of the "Wende" ("turn"):

> Die hinterbliebenen Eliten sehen [dem] spontanen Treiben mit begreiflichem Mißmut zu; denn was dabei zum Vorschein kommt, ist nicht die ersehnte Tiefe, sondern die Gewöhnlichkeit. Es ist den Deutschen nicht um den geistigen Raum der Nation und nicht um die Idee des Sozialismus zu tun, es geht ihnen überhaupt nicht um Glaubensfragen, sondern um Arbeit, Wohnung, Rente, Lohn, Umsatz, Steuern, Konsum, Schmutz, Luft Müll [...] nicht das Milennium, sondern nur ein Alltag [ist] angebrochen, der ohne Propheten auskommt.[20]

And indeed, the course of events was quite different from what had been envisaged in the petition "Für unser Land," with the election results of March and October 1990 confirming that bitter fact for those with hopes of a renewed "GDR experiment": "Ich hatte freilich anderes im Sinn," said the emigré poet-songwriter Wolf Biermann. "Aber es ist nicht die Aufgabe der Weltgeschichte, den kleinen Biermann zu beglücken."[21] Apparently not. While it was clear that, with the sobering-up after the partying of 1990, the problems that Enzensberger identified were far from being solved, the Currency Union of July 1990, the election results and unification in November 1990 collectively meant the final demise of the long-held utopian hopes of the "other" Germany.

The demise of the GDR and unification seemed to hit right at one of the key aspects of West German literature since 1945: the utopian anti-capitalism, the moral criticism of the human cost of a free market economy. Günter Grass, however, clearly did not agree that this position was no longer tenable. Grass, for many years co-editor of *L 76* (later *L 80*), which championed the idea of "democratic socialism" as the "third way" between the extremes of

---

19 Cf. in this context "Bleibt die Avantgarde zurück?" *Der Spiegel* No. 49, December 4, 1989, pp. 230–33.
20 "The various elites that have been left behind are observing all these spontaneous activities with understandable annoyance, for what has emerged is not the longed-for profundity, but the everyday. Germans aren't concerned with the spiritual domain of the nation, nor with the idea of socialism, they aren't the least bit interested in matters of faith, but in jobs, somewhere to live, pensions, wages, turn-over, taxes, spending, filth, the atmosphere, garbage [...] no milennium has dawned, just workaday normality that can get along without prophets." Enzensberger: "Gangarten – ein Nachtrag zur Utopie." *Frankfurter Allgemeine Zeitung* No. 116, May 19, 1990, "Bilder und Zeiten" supplement, pp. 1–2.
21 "I have to admit that I had something else in mind. But it isn't the concern of world history to make little Biermann happy." Biermann: "Das wars. Klappe zu. Affe lebt." *Die Zeit* No. 10, March 2, 1990, p. 66.

capitalism and communism, joined the editorial board of *Die neue Gesellschaft/ Frankfurter Hefte* in the summer of 1990, along with Carola Stern, a fellow-editor from *L 76/80*. Itrapidly became clear that Grass intended to use this as another platform for his views, with one of the first numbers under his co-editorship containing an interview with him, in which he continued to argue in favor of the "Kulturnation." Over and above that, he expressed in various newspaper articles and speeches, swiftly re-published in paperback editions, his indignation at the "Einigung ohne Einigkeit," as he called it. A particular area of concern to him was the tactics employed by West German firms vis-à-vis run-down East German enterprises, which he viewed as ruthless exploitation: "Nach jahrzehntelanger ideologischer Bevormundung" the citizens of the former GDR were now being confronted with "jene Ausbeutung, deren Fratze vormals die Zuchtmeister leninistischer Schule als Schreckengespenst an die Wand gemalt [hatten]" – a point that Grass was by no means alone in making.[22] "Die menschenverachtende Gewalttätigkeit," as he called it, inherent in the tactics, was doubly disturbing, as it was but one part of a drive for economic expansion by West German industrial power, even in alliance with Japanese firms, that evoked memories of the past:

> nicht mehr im militärischen Bereich liegt die vermutete Bedrohung – wie den Japanern ist den Deutschen die Lust am Krieg vergangen –, wohl aber in der ökonomischen Expansionskraft der einst geschlagenen Achsenmächte, die wenig Hemmung zeigen, ihre Macht abermals zu bündeln, wie neuerdings Daimler-Benz und Mitsubishi, denen eine Technologieachse zwischen Deutschland und Japan planenswert ist. Solch "strategische Allianz" drückt jetzt schon aggressiven Willen nach Zuwachs, Marktbeherrschung, aber auch jene Hemmungslosigkeit aus, die sich in exportierten Giftgasfabriken bewiesen hat.

The trade in war technology with Iraq, the extent of which was later revealed as being even more extensive than at the time of Grass's speech to the Greens and Bündnis 90, could well "nicht nur entsetzliche Folgen haben," but could also serve "vergangene deutsche Schuld gegenwärtig [zu] machen."[23]

---

22 "Unification without unity"; "After decades of ideological regimentation [...] that very exploitation, the face of which had previously been painted on the wall as a bogeyman by Leninist drill-masters." Grass: *Schnäppchen*, pp. 39–60. See too here Cora Stephan, who two years after these remarks by Grass, stated, with regard to the state of the ex-GDR, that "capitalism now looks exactly the way *Neues Deutschland* painted it." "Traum vom Ende der Schuld," p. 47.

23 "The contemptuous violence [...]"; "the sense of threat no longer lies in the military sector – the Germans, like the Japanese, have lost the desire for war – but rather in the forceful economic expansion of the former Axis powers. They show little or no constraint about

These remarks were very much resented in many circles. Gerd Bucerius of *Die Zeit* publicly accused Grass of contempt for the people actually affected by unification and, also, of having little understanding for the real complexities of the process. Grass's opposition and, above all, the terms in which it was expressed, was not all that surprising, however. If we look beyond Grass, then it becomes clear that the most vociferous criticism of the path of unification, especially as far as the treatment of the former GDR was concerned, came from the older guard of Gruppe 47, such as Peter Härtling, Gabriele Wohmann and, above all, Walter Jens – i.e. from writers of Grass's generation. Just as the Currency Reform and the Marshall Plan had blocked the hopes of a democratic, socialist, neutral Germany in 1948, the Currency Union and unification in accordance with Article 23 of the Federal Constitution were seen by the Left as again closing off the chance of the "other Germany" in the GDR after 1989, when it represented, according to Jens, a "basisdemokratische Alternative zu der von der Deutschen Bank unterhaltenen Demokratie der BRD," and without which Europe would be "eine Filiale der USA."[24] This time, though, no Marshall Plan, no foreign capital was necessary, the Federal Republic itself had played the role of a "neuen Besatzungsmacht," claimed Erich Kuby, had bought up the GDR "wie eine Viehherde" and gobbled up the second German state in a manner "die der Eroberung von Feindesland gleichkommt."[25] Two years later Grass, undoubtedly feeling that events had vindicated him, was talking of "einer entsetzlichen Kolonialisierung" of the East, with the West arrogantly carrying out a latter-day Morgenthau Plan "auf dem Rücken von Menschen, die nach 1945 die größte Last zu tragen [...] hatten."[26] Perhaps even more astonishing was the play *Wessis in*

---

joining forces once again, as Daimler-Benz and Mitsubishi have recently done and who consider it in their interests to build up a technological axis between Germany and Japan. A 'strategic alliance' like this is already showing an aggressive, determined desire for expansion and market domination; it is also demonstrating the same ruthlessness that manifested itself in the export of poison-gas factories." "not only horrendous consequences," but also serve "to make past German guilt an issue of the day." Cf. Grass: *Schnäppchen*, pp. 56–7, 51.

24 "[...] a fundamentally democratic alternative to that democracy of the FRG sustained by the Deutsche Bank" and without which "Europe would become a subsidiary of the USA." Jens: "Plädoyer gegen die Preisgabe der DDR-Kultur." *Süddeutsche Zeitung* No. 136, June 16/17, 1990, pp. 14–6. Jens was here, as he acknowledged, quoting Heiner Müller.

25 "[...] a new occupying power that had bought up the GDR like a herd of cattle, much as if it was conquering enemy territory." Quoted in Rainer Zitelmann: "Verzweifelter Unsinn." *Frankfurter Allgemeine Zeitung* No. 282, December 4, 1990, p. 39.

26 "[...] an appalling colonialisation on the backs of the people who had to carry the greatest burden after 1945." Grass, quoted in Niklas Frank: "Der Einzelgänger." *Stern* No. 21, May 14, 1992, p. 214.

Weimar (1992) by the dramatist Rolf Hochhuth, who, while of Grass's generation, is not a writer normally associated with the political stance of Grass, Jens et al. The play, a controversy before even being performed, was to be a series of "Satiren auf ein besetztes Land" attacking the "brutale[n] Wirtschaftsdarwinismus der Treuhand" (the body created to dispose of former state property in the ex-GDR).[27] His basic argument was that "daß der Westen schuld sei an der Verelendung von Menschen in den neuen Bundesländern," with Rohwedder – who was assassinated by, so they had claimed, the RAF on April 1, 1991 – portrayed as a contemporary Gessler, the cruel exploiter of the Swiss in Schiller's *Wilhelm Tell*, but, whereas Gessler had only claimed one tenth (tithe) of their property, Rohwedder was taking 90%. Moreover, he was selling off public property to foreigners, depriving Germans of their soil in a variant of colonialism, and would therefore be executed by a vengeful people. It is not our intention here to enter the controversy over the imputation that the murder of this "great patriot" (Helmut Kohl) was, in fact, a symbolic act of retaliation by the people of the GDR,[28] the important thing in this context is the way in which, even at some time after unification, that process was still being critized for proceding in accordance with centralist economic dictates, rather than in a spirit of federal cooperativeness.

In 1990 the continued ghostly presence of a concept of Germany that, in essence, had its roots back in the immediate post-war years was truly astonishing. Even the increasingly somewhat isolated Martin Walser, in what, tired of controversy and misrepresentation, he claimed were his last pronouncements on the "German Question," expressed his hopes that the new Germany would not be a dynamic, centralized political and economic powerhouse, maintaining: "Je föderalistischer dieses Deutschland sich bildet, um so erträglicher wird es sein," a formulation which, in turn, was not all that far removed from the notion of the "Kulturnation." Moreover, the Germans would for him have to prove themselves acceptable to the rest of the world.[29] But, nevertheless, it has to be said that, despite the general sort of publicity Walser's approval of unification received, this aspect of his views went unno-

---

27 "Satires on an occupied country attacking the brutal economic Darwinism of the Treuhand." The key scene between Rohwedder, the President of the Treuhand, and Hildegard (physically and in terms of her background as the daughter of a pastor, seemingly modelled on Gudrun Ensslin), was printed in *Der Spiegel* No. 23, June 1, 1992, pp. 272–75, as were Hochhuth's remarks quoted here. The premiere of the play is scheduled for January 1993 in the Theater am Schiffbauerdamm, East Berlin.
28 Cf. in this context "Das Streiflicht." *Süddeutsche Zeitung* No. 122, May 27, 1992, p. 1.
29 "The more federal this Germany becomes, the more acceptable it will become." Walser: "Vormittag eines Schriftstellers." *Die Zeit* No. 51, December 14, 1990, p. 54.

ticed, while those of Grass, Jens and others no longer have the representative stature in the Nineties that they once had. Ralf Dahrendorf not only pronounced Grass "unimpressive as a political author,"[30] his more general analysis of intellectuals and unification talked of their "failure" and accused them of sowing seeds of doubt and thus undermining the process, while Henning Ritter argued – with an amazing lack of awareness of their role during the previous several decades – that they had succumbed to the myth of their having an exclusively international calling and thus failed "an ihrer Treue zum Vorurteil gegen das Nationale."[31] There were, however, indications that younger writers in the West were, indeed, in some way prejudiced against the national issue and consequently less than excited by the process of unification, as pronouncements by Peter Sloterdijk and Patrick Süskind made clear. For those, like Süskind, born and raised in the "old" Federal Republic, who had never known anything other than the *status quo*, "war die Einheit der Nation, das Nationale überhaupt unsere Sache nicht. Ob die Deutschen in zwei, drei, vier oder einem Dutzend Staaten lebten, war uns schnuppe."[32] Of that younger generation only Botho Strauß had previously addressed the issue of the divided nation, having some years earlier lamented:

> Kein Deutschland gekannt zeit meines Lebens.
> Zwei fremde Staaten nur, die mir verboten,
> je im Namen eines Volkes der Deutschen zu sein.
> Soviel Geschichte, um so zu enden?[33]

Despite the fact that Martin Walser was later to refer to this poem with considerable emphasis, it remained a curiously isolated statement in the context of Strauß's work and was to contrast greatly with the portrayal of the distressingly plebian reality of the opening of the Wall, as depicted at the end of his 1991 play *Schlußchor* ("Final Chorus").[34]

---

30 Dahrendorf's review of Grass's *Two States – One Nation?*. *The New York Times* No. 48, 374, September 30, 1990, Section 7, p. 9.
31 Cf. Dahrendorf: "Die Sache mit der Nation," pp. 825–26. "[…] because of their loyalty to the prejudice against national issues." Ritter: *"Fallhöhe. Intellektuelle und Nation."* Frankfurter Allgemeine Zeitung No. 283, December 5, 1990, p. N3.
32 "[We] weren't concerned with national unity, with any sort of national issues. We didn't give a damn whether Germans lived in two, three, four or a dozen different states." Süskind: "Deutschland, eine Midlife-crisis." *Der Spiegel* No. 38, September 17, 1990, p. 123. Cf. also Sloterdijk: "Landeskundliche Bemerkung zu den jüngsten deutschen Tränen."
33 "No Germany known in my lifetime. / Only two estranged states, which forbade me / ever in the name of a people to be a German. / So much history, just to end like that?" Strauß: *Diese Erinnerung an einen, der nur einen Tag zu Gast war*, p. 48.
34 Cf. Walser: "Vormittag eines Schriftstellers".

As far as reflections of events of and after 1989 in imaginative literature in general were concerned, there were those who argued that it would take a long time indeed – as long as three generations, claimed Christoph Hein[35] – before writers would be able to deal with them. Two years later younger authors were still maintaining that readers should not expect the treatment of the new experiences after 1989 too quickly.[36] Given that, it has to be said that there have been in the circumstances a surprising number of literary responses of various kinds to the opening up of the border and the move towards unity. The most consistent commentary, apart from the highly flexible, but equally ephemeral, form of the literary cabaret, was undoubtedly in the "Lied," in songs by Wolf Biermann, Franz Josef Degenhardt, Konstantin Wecker and Herbert Grönemeyer in particular, but 1991 saw the first works by a number of other, in some cases fairly established, writers.

The title of "the first post-post-war" work of real significance was undoubtedly won by F. C. Delius with his documentary short text *Die Birnen von Ribbeck*, 1991, set in the early days after the opening of the borders and based on a lengthy statement made by one of the villagers of Ribbeck, to the west of Berlin (also discussed in T. J. Reed's "Another Piece of the Past"[37]). West Berliners, enjoying their new freedom to travel out into the nearby countryside of the March Brandenburg, had gone out to Ribbeck, a village made famous by Fontane in his poem in praise of the local lord of the manor, where they wanted to plant a new pear-tree (the original had had to be felled before 1914) and to celebrate the new unity of the country. Delius's text, through the somewhat truculent views of the elderly Ribbecker he interviewed, provided a counter-balance to that euphoria, both in terms of how the "invasion" felt to *him* and other Ossis like him, and by his contextualizing the recent changes within a life's experience that encompassed working under semi-feudal conditions, the Nazis and the socialist regime of the GDR. He was astonished that "kaum geht die Grenze auf, da hupt es und ihr steht mitten auf dem Hof, latscht durch unsere Gärten wie Besatzer […]."[38] Since Ribbeck lay on an important military route, it had been occupied and reoccupied over the years, and he knew that if people gave them something, there would be a price to pay. He was happy enough to take the Wessis' presents

---

35 Hein: *Die fünfte Grundrechenart*, p. 193.
36 Cf. Wittstock: "Generationswechsel? Ja. Aber wie?," p. 131.
37 Cf. this volume, p. 249.
38 "[…] the border is scarcely open, when there's a honk, and there you are in the yard and strolling through our garden like occupying forces […]." Delius: *Die Birnen von Ribbeck*, p. 32.

and drink their beer, but wondered if they had a bill in their pocket and asked "warum ich für euer Bier im Konsum, in Blech verpackt und schön Farbe auf dem Etikett, nun drei Mark zahlen soll statt sechzig Pfennig für das in der Flasche."[39] He also refused to give the expected black-and-white answers to questions about life in the GDR, was not willing to ignore "den winzigen Stolz nach der Bodenreform, wenn das Getreide gut stand, da hast du dich gefreut, was du geschafft hast mit Frau und Kindern […],"[40] nor to forget the earlier good times in the cooperative, when things seemed to be working. He was concerned that now they would find themselves worse off than ever under the "Western world-champions," with the little farmer having to pay the price of change yet again, still controlled by "den alten Genossen, die Parteibuch und Abzeichen weggeworfen haben und jetzt die neue Unschuld spielen mit dem Zauberwort Effektivität und Markt […]."[41] They were, in terms of the problems that were to face people in the former GDR in the early Nineties, highly perceptive words, and the cynical, low-key comments of the old worldy-wise worker provided a refreshing contrast with the euphoric rhetoric of the time after November 1989, constituting a healthy and necessary scepticism towards the new and, at the same time, a plea for Germans not to lose sight of the lessons and legacies of history.

This sense of the need for an authentic coming to terms with the past (a latter-day "Vergangenheitsbewältigung"), as a precondition for moving forward, was also very much the message of Eva Zeller's volume of short stories *Das Sprungtuch* (1991). The opening piece, "Potsdamer Platz," is set at the time right after the opening of the Wall, with people strolling in the former death-zone amidst the flea markets that were rapidly erected, with the sound of the "Wall Woodpeckers" – those chipping off pieces for sale as souvenirs – in the background. But the story of Ruth Wendt, just returned from exile in South Africa, quickly returns to December 1961, when her husband was shot by border guards while trying to escape through the Potsdamer Platz. The title story also returns to 1961, to the time when it was still possible to jump to freedom from houses on the border; in this case the father escaped, the mother remained – it is another story of the German-German separation that was the consequence of the existence of two German states. "Potsdamer

---

39 "Why do I now have to pay three Marks in the shop for a can of your beer, complete with a smart label, instead of sixty Pfennig for the old one in a bottle?" Ibid., pp. 33–4.
40 "That small sense of pride after the land reform, when the corn had grown tall, you were pleased at what you managed with your wife and children […]." Ibid., p. 50.
41 "The old comrades who've thrown Party card and badge away and now play the new innocents, playing with the magic word efficiency and market […]." Ibid., pp. 65–6.

Platz" and "Wunderwaffen" ("Wonder Weapons") also involve the impact of the "Stasi" on life in the GDR, with the latter telling the particularly nasty story of the infiltration of a university campus by a spy masquerading as a student, whose job it was to deliver "enemies of the State" to the knives of the "Stasi." "Die Tochter" ("The Daughter") is the flip-side of "Das Sprungtuch," where the opening of the Wall triggers off a woman's memories of her ordeal with the "Stasi" after her husband had fled to the West. As in Delius's piece, the key response to unification was the setting in motion of a process of painful remembrance, the implicit stressing of the need for a nation that had essentially suppressed its past in 1945 now to address the wounds inflicted on the nation during the years of division, especially after 1961.

There is no doubt, though, that the largest initial literary response to unification was in the theatre, which offered a series of highly critical readings of the problems this had brought about. The final scene of Botho Strauß's *Schlußchor*, in which Anita tears apart a German eagle, the symbol of the united country, and Herbert Achternbusch's *Auf verlorenem Posten* (1990), which also encompassed the revolutionary changes in Rumania, in many ways set the tone for later dramatic works; Achternbusch's work was, indeed, appositely subtitled a "revolutionary farce." A key scene features a "Trabi" belching smoke coming on to the stage; there it is showered with bananas, which are in turn eaten up "properly" ("brav") by the sixteen Ossis it disgorges. Banners are carried proclaiming the concept of "Deutschland in den Grenzen von 1245 – Neapel ist unser," later "in den Grenzen der Natur – die Welt ist unser." A Rumanian-German family fleeing the country is shown as being understandably fearful of the Germans and contemplates remaining in Northern Italy.[42] Not dissimilar grotesque images to those of Achternbusch were used by Manfred Karge in his *MauerStücke* (1991). Against the euphoria of early 1990 Karge set a grotesque scene involving a border guard and his dog in the days after the opening of the Wall. While the soldier – who had previously "mal ganz anders gesprochen," the dog tells us – now finds it "das Selbstverständlichste auf der Welt" for people to go for a stroll along the Wall, the well-trained dog wants to respond as he's always done. But it has clearly not recognized the extent of change, whereas his opportunistic guard is obsessed with the pros and cons of two offers he has received for the dog – one from a Korean hamburger chain, the other from a Swiss pharmaceutical firm.[43] In another sketch, "Ostfotze,"

---

42 "Germany in the boundaries of 1245 – Naples is ours" and "in the boundaries of nature – the world is ours". The text of the play was published in *Theater heute* 1990, No. 4, pp. 15–20, here pp. 16–7.

43 The soldier had "earlier spoken quite differently," but now finds it "the most natural thing in the world" (to walk along the Wall). Karge: "MauerStücke," p. 73.

Karge depicted unification through a bizarre reworking of the "Nibelungenlied": Gunther, from the Lower Rhine, claims he is going to show Brunhild just what a "Western prick" can achieve, when it is, in fact, Siegfried, a former GDR Hero of Labour, who takes her in a sex act of truly Olympic proportions. When Brunhild discovers from Kriemhild how she had been deceived by "diesem mecklenburgischen Pißbullen" and is merely advised by Kriemhild to go "auf den Strich," where she belongs, she swears revenge.[44] That threat of subsequent internal tension is complemented by the final musical element of the play – the sound of marching, to the tune and words of an infamous Nazi song that evokes the threat of rampant German nationalism: "Denn heute gehört uns Deutschland / Und morgen die ganze Welt."[45]

Elfriede Müller's play *Goldener Oktober* (1991) begins and ends in the "New Moskau," a night-club near the Wall that has rapidly been adapted to reach "Westniveau," It is a sort of post-*Cabaret* piece that evokes the familiar image of Berlin dancing on the edge of the volcano that is change. Two of the guests are the Honeckers, with old Erich showing himself much more adept at change than younger people and always with a cynical comment on things. The loose structure of the play allows for a series of one-liners and sick jokes; all the incipient problems in the East, including the rise of racialist skinheads seem to feature. One dominant motif is that nothing has changed: for the Ossis one lie – the State – has been replaced by another lie, i.e. freedom, and the change in the economic system brings with it unemployment and uncertainty for the majority, with the opportunistic "Wendehälse" ("turn-necks") seizing the advantage.[46] Lola, a young woman from East Berlin, wants nothing to do with this disgusting state of affairs:

> Oben die Säue, unten die Säue. Die alten Arschlöcher. Die neuen Wichser. Einsacken. Austeilen. Gnadenlos. Holen, wo was zu holen ist. Niedermachen […]. Die neue Zeit, hurra. Der wilde Westen, der ist da. Hier grinst der Chef, da lacht die Mark. Gemeinsam, gemeinsam, gemeinsam, sind wir stark. Arbeitslos ist keine Schande. Der Rest ist Ihre eigene Sache. Allzeit bereit. Jetzt kommt die deutsche Gemütlichkeit. Whisky Soda. Porno pur, was hat die olle Fotze nur? […] Wir sind das Geld, sie macht uns mies. Mit mir nicht. Mit mir nicht.[47]

---

44 "[…] this Mecklenburg stud […] on the game". Ibid., p. 76.
45 "For Germany belongs to us today / and tomorrow it'll be the whole world". Karge is by no means alone in misquoting this song, "Es zittern die morschen Knochen" ("Rotten bones tremble"), which should read "hört" ("listens to"), rather than "gehört" ("belongs").
46 At one point one singing group perform the song "Wir sind die Wendehälse" to the tune of "Wir sind die Moorsoldaten", the famous resistance song from the Nazi concentration camps.
47 "Pigs on top and pigs underneath. The same old arseholes. The new wankers. Cash in. Divvy up. Ruthlessly. Grab what you can. Trample people underfoot […] The new age, hur-

A not dissimilar picture emerges in Klaus Pohl's *Karate Billi kehrt zurück* (1991). On the night "they opened up the pig-sty," Billi Kotte, a former GDR decathlon champion who had been imprisoned for thirteen years on suspicion of wanting to defect, has also been released. He is confronted with those who had spied and informed on him at the time immediately before his arrest and is thus an uncomfortable presence at a time when those people are trying to do business with the West. They try to present themselves as victims forced to behave in the way they did or as only having done their duty. They cannot understand Billi's implacable hatred and finally this ghost at the feast is forcibly returned to supervised medical care.[48]

The picture painted by these plays was a uniformly bleak one – "unsubtle but authentic", some claimed,[49] – stressing cynical exploitation by the West, opportunism by former Eastern high-ups, financial suffering and spiritual disorientation by the man or woman in the street, with increased nationalism, rising racial intolerance and the legacy of the "Stasi" past also figuring. Unpleasant though they were, they corresponded very much to the reality of post-unification. Of these plays treating this first troubled phase only one, though, Jochen Berg's *Fremde in der Nacht* (1991)[50] was by an East German writer. One reason for this was undoubtedly the distance that enabled writers from the West to identify disturbing features of the way in which developments in the East were being conducted by the West. But it reflected too a more general situation, in which the opening up of necessary debates in the former GDR at the beginning of the Nineties was initiated by those in the West – by those enjoying the "die Gnade der westlichen Geburt"[51] – and with a prominent role also being played by GDR exiles, who were accused by Heiner Müller of particular responsibility for the gulf between the East and

---

rah. The Wild West is here. The boss grins here, the Mark laughs there. Together, together, together we are strong. It's not a shame to be unemployed. The rest is up to you. Always at the ready. Here comes German joviality. Whisky and soda, porno straight up, what's up with the silly bitch now? [...] We are the money and she spoils things. I want out. I want out." Müller: "Goldener Oktober," p. 55.

48 Printed in *Theater der Zeit* 1991, No. 6, pp. 70–86. This play was produced in 1992 by Stephen Unwin at the Royal Court Theatre, London.
49 Benedict Nightingale: "Unsubtle but authentic." *The Times* No. 328, May 9, 1992, p. 5 (his review of the play's performance at the Royal Court Theatre).
50 In this bleak, somewhat Expressionistic play, in which the focus is on the psychological anguish of a former border-guard unable to cope with the swift changes, use is again made of the Nibelung motif.
51 "The blessing of Western birth" – a clever and cynical play on Chancellor Kohl's term "the blessing of late birth" (with regard to those too young to share any sense of guilt for Nazi attrocities), quoted on 'Deutsche Welle', May 30, 1992.

the West. These plays all touched on issues raised in greater detail and with greater specificity in the media during the critical examination of the role of GDR writers and intellectuals, starting with the criticisms of Christa Wolf and others, then in the examination of the "Stasi" involvement of writers and other important figures. Such issues created an "atmosphere of suspicion," claimed East Berlin theatre director Thomas Langhoff, that placed "a burden on unification", while Stefan Heym detected a smear campaign intended to "rob the eastern Germans of their heroes and their courage to resist."[52] Günter de Bruyn, on the other hand, found it merely "unfortunate" that these debates were initiated only in the West and that one key initial target was Christa Wolf (rather than, for him, Hermann Kant). He admitted to feeling that Biermann's attacks on Sascha Anderson were "wahrhaftig nicht schön"[53] but he nevertheless opposed the suggestion that such debates should not take place; he considered them to be "wahrscheinlich die einzige Möglichkeit, Licht in das Dunkel des Vergessens zu bringen." Silence, the avoidance of awkward questions and retreat were not, he argued, what the state of the German nation demanded in the Nineties. Whatever the pros and cons of a difficult issue, which is by no means unique to Germany,[54] the debate is one that will not go away in a hurry, particularly as further information emerges, but rather one that "will dominate and damage German literature throughout the 1990s."[55] In the literary scene, as in the rest of German society in the early Nineties, the signs seem to be that things are likely to get worse before they get better.

---

52 Both quoted in "States of Mind I: Intellectuals warn of 'atmosphere of suspicion in Germany.'" *The Week in Germany*, December 6, 1991.
53 "[…] not at all pretty". de Bruyn in an interview with Peter Glotz: "Gespräch mit Günter de Bruyn", p. 170. The subsequent quotation, located in the next sentence, translates as: "[…] the only possibility of bringing light into the darkness of people wanting to forget."
54 Cf. Engelberg: "The Velvet Revolution gets rough." *The New York Times* (Magazine) No. 48, 983, May 31, 1992, pp. 30–54.
55 Quoted in anon: "Stasier than thou." *The Economist* (U.K. edition) vol. 321, No. 7734, November 23, 1991, p. 158.

Bibliography

The bibliography contains the full data of all titles cited by the contributors, the footnotes give only short-titles.

Primary Sources

Achternbusch, Herbert: "Auf verlorenem Posten." *Theater heute* 1990, No. 4: 15–20.

Alberti, Conrad: *Die Alten und die Jungen*. Vol. 1–2. Leipzig: Friedrich, 1889.

Alberti, Conrad: "Im Rechtsstaat." Alberti: *Plebs: Novellen aus dem Volke*. Leipzig: Friedrich, 1887. 183–324.

Anderson, Sascha, and Elke Erb, eds., *Berührung ist nur eine Randerscheinung: Neue Literatur aus der DDR*. Köln: Luchterhand, 1985.

Andrä, J. C.: *Erzählungen aus der Deutschen Geschichte: Ein Lehr- und Lesebuch für den ersten Unterricht in der Geschichte*. Ausgabe A. Für evangelische Schulen. Besorgt von L. Sevin. Leipzig: Voigtländer, 1891.

Andrä, J. C.: *Lehrbuch der Weltgeschichte für höhere Mädchenschulen und Lehrerinnen-Bildungsanstalten*. 3. Aufl. Bearb. von L. Sevin. T. 2: *Das Mittelalter und die Neuzeit*. Leipzig: Voigtländer, 1895.

Assmann, W.: *Abriß der Geschichte der neueren Zeit in zusammenhängender Darstellung auf geographischer Grundlage: Ein Leitfaden für Gymnasien und Realschulen*. 9., umgearb. Aufl. von Ernst Meyer. Braunschweig: Vieweg, 1879.

Ball, Hugo: *Die Flucht aus der Zeit*. Luzern: Stocker, 1946.

Barthélemy, Françoise, and Lutz Winckler, eds., *Mein Deutschland findet sich in keinem Atlas: Schriftsteller aus beiden deutschen Staaten über ihr nationales Selbstverständnis*. Frankfurt a. M.: Luchterhand, 1990 (Sammlung Luchterhand. 893).

Baudrillard, Jean: "What Are You Doing After the Orgy?" *Artforum* 22:2, October (1983): 42–6.

Baumgarten, Hermann: *Treitschke's Deutsche Geschichte*. 2. Aufl. Straßburg: Trübner, 1883.

Becker, Jurek: "Gedächtnis verloren – Verstand verloren." *Die Zeit* No. 47, November 18, 1988: 61.

Benjamin, Walter: *Gesammelte Schriften*. Unter Mitwirkung von Theodor W. Adorno und Gershom Scholem hrsg. von Rolf Tiedemann und Hermann Schweppenhäuser. Vol. 1–7 (in 14). Frankfurt a. M.: Suhrkamp, 1974–1989.

Berg, Jochen: "Fremde in der Nacht." *Theater der Zeit* 1991, No. 11: 97–105.

Berkéwicz, Ulla: *Engel sind schwarz und weiß. Roman.* Frankfurt a. M.: Suhrkamp, 1992.

Berlin–Bonn, die Debatte: alle Bundestagsreden vom 20. Juni 1991. Hrsg. vom Deutschen Bundestag, Referat Öffentlichkeitsarbeit. Köln: Kiepenheuer & Witsch, 1991.

Berndt, Johannes: *Präparationen für den Geschichtsunterricht. T. 2: Von den Anfängen des brandenburgisch-preußischen Staates bis auf unsere Zeit.* Osterwieck, Leipzig: Zickfeldt, 1913.

Biermann, Wolf: *Alle Lieder.* Köln: Kiepenheuer & Witsch, 1991. 3. Aufl. 1992.

Biermann, Wolf: "Das wars. Klappe zu. Affe lebt." *Die Zeit* No. 10, March 2, 1990: 65–6. Reprinted under the title: "Duftmarke setzen" in Biermann: *Klartexte im Getümmel.* 315–31.

Biermann: *Klartexte im Getümmel: 13 Jahre im Westen. Von der Ausbürgerung bis zur Novemberrevolution.* Hrsg. von Hannes Stein. Köln: Kiepenheuer & Witsch, 1990.

Biermann, Wolf: *Der Sturz des Dädalus oder Eizes für die Eingeborenen der Fidschi-Inseln über den IM Judas Ischariot und den Kuddelmuddel in Deutschland seit dem Golfkrieg.* Köln: Kiepenheuer & Witsch, 1992.

Bloch, Ernst: *Gesamtausgabe.* Vol. 5,1: *Das Prinzip Hoffnung. In fünf Teilen, Kapitel 1–37.* Frankfurt a.M.: Suhrkamp, 1970.

Bölling, F. A., et al.: "Auch eine Dotation. An alle Deutsche im Vaterland und in der Ferne." *Die Gartenlaube. Illustriertes Familienblatt* 1867, No. 17: 272.

Braun, Volker: "Monströse Banalität." *Die Zeit* No. 48, November 22, 1991: 63.

Braun, Volker: "Rimbaud. Ein Psalm der Aktualität." *Sinn und Form* 37:5 (1985): 978–98.

Braun, Volker: *Unvollendete Geschichte.* Frankfurt a. M.: Suhrkamp, 1977.

Brauneck, Manfred, and Christine Müller, eds., *Naturalismus: Manifeste und Dokumente zur deutschen Literatur 1880–1900.* Stuttgart: Metzler, 1987.

Brecht, Bertolt: *Werke.* Große kommentierte Berliner und Frankfurter Ausgabe. Hrsg. von Werner Hecht, Jan Knopf, Werner Mittenzwei, Klaus-Detlef Müller. Vol. 11–15: Gedichte 1–5. Berlin und Weimar: Aufbau; Frankfurt a. M.: Suhrkamp, 1988–93.

Bruyn, Günter de: "Gespräch mit Günter de Bruyn." *Die Neue Gesellschaft/Frankfurter Hefte* 1992, No. 2: 170.

Bucher, Max, et al., eds., *Realismus und Gründerzeit: Manifeste und Dokumente zur deutschen Literatur 1848–1880.* Mit einer Einführung in den Problemkreis und einer Quellenbibliographie. Vol. 1–2. Stuttgart: Metzler, 1976–75 (Epochen der deutschen Literatur. Materialienbände).

Burckhardt, Jacob: *Briefe.* Vollständige und kritische Ausgabe. Mit Benützung des handschriftlichen Nachlasses bearb. von Max Burckhardt. Vol. 5: *1868 bis März 1871.* Basel, Stuttgart: Schwabe, 1963.

Chiarloni, Anna, and Helga Pankoke, eds., *Grenzfallgedichte: Eine deutsche Anthologie*. Berlin: Aufbau, 1991.

Dahn, Felix: *Ein Kampf um Rom: Historischer Roman*. München: Bong, [1953].

Deisler, Guillermo, and Jörg Kowalski, eds., *wortBILD: Visuelle Poesie in der DDR*. Halle, Leipzig: Mitteldeutscher Verlag, 1990.

Delius, Friedrich Christian: *Die Birnen von Ribbeck: Erzählung*. Reinbek: Rowohlt, 1991.

Dittmar, Heinrich: *Leitfaden der Weltgeschichte für mittlere und untere Gymnasialklassen oder lateinische Schulen, Real- und Bürgerschulen, Pädagogien, Seminare und andere Anstalten*. 8. Aufl., durchges. und bis auf die neueste Zeit fortges. Heidelberg: Winter, 1875.

Döblin, Alfred: *Schriften zur Ästhetik, Poetik und Literatur*. Hrsg. von Erich Kleinschmidt. Olten, Freiburg i. Br.: Walter, 1989 (Ausgewählte Werke in Einzelbänden. [26]).

Döring, Stefan: *heutmorgestern: gedichte*. Berlin, Weimar: Aufbau, 1989 (Ausser der Reihe).

Droysen, Johann Gustav: *Geschichte der preußischen Politik*. T. 1. 2. Aufl. Leipzig: Veit, 1868.

Droysen, Johann Gustav: *Historik*. Historisch-kritische Ausgabe von Peter Leyh. Vol. 1. Stuttgart-Bad Cannstatt: Frommann-Holzboog, 1977.

Droysen, Johann Gustav: *Historik: Vorlesungen über Enzyklopädie und Methodologie der Geschichte*. Hrsg. von Rudolf Hübner. 8., unveränd. Aufl. München: Oldenbourg, 1977.

Dunger, Hermann: *Die deutsche Sprachbewegung und der allgemeine deutsche Sprachverein 1885–1910: Festschrift zur 25. Jahresfeier des allgemeinen deutschen Sprachvereins*. Berlin: Verlag des Allgemeinen deutschen Sprachvereins, 1910.

Egelhaaf, Gottlob: *Grundzüge der Geschichte*. Dritter Teil: *Die Neuzeit*. 3., Aufl. Leipzig: Reisland, 1893.

Endler, Adolf: *Vorbildlich schleimlösend: Nachrichten aus einer Hauptstadt 1972–2008*. Berlin: Rotbuch, 1990.

Enzensberger, Hans Magnus: "Gangarten – ein Nachtrag zur Utopie." *Frankfurter Allgemeine Zeitung* No. 116, May 19, 1990, "Bilder und Zeiten" supplement: 1–2.

Erb, Elke: *Kastanienallee: Texte und Kommentare*. Berlin, Weimar: Aufbau, 1987.

Erb, Elke: *Nachts, halb zwei, zu Hause: Texte aus drei Jahrzehnten*. Leipzig: Reclam, 1991.

Faktor, Jan: *Georgs Versuche an einem Gedicht und andere Positive Texte aus dem Dichtergarten des Grauens*. Berlin, Weimar: Aufbau, 1989 (Ausser der Reihe).

Faktor, Jan: *Henry's Jupitergestik in der Blutlache Nr. 3 und andere positive Texte aus Georgs Besudelungs- und Selbstbesudelungskabinett*. Berlin: Janus, 1991.

Fels, Ludwig: *Blaue Allee, versprengte Tataren: Gedichte*. München, Zürich: Piper, 1988.

Fenske, Hans, ed., *Im Bismarckschen Reich: 1871–1890*. Darmstadt: Wissenschaftliche Buchgesellschaft, 1978 (Quellen zum politischen Denken der Deutschen im 19. und 20. Jahrhundert. 6).

Fenske, Hans, ed., *Der Weg zur Reichsgründung: 1850–1870*. Darmstadt: Wissenschaftliche Buchgesellschaft, 1977 (Quellen zum politischen Denken der Deutschen im 19. u. 20. Jahrhundert. 5).

flanzendörfer (pseud. Franz Lanzendörfer): *unmöglich es leben: texte bilder fotos*. Zusammengestellt von Peter Böthig und Klaus Michael. Berlin: Janus, 1992.

Fontane, Theodor: *Briefe an den Verleger Rudolf von Decker*. Hrsg. von Walter Hettche. Heidelberg: Decker, 1988.

Fontane, Theodor: *Briefe in zwei Bänden*. Ausgew. u. erl. von Gotthard Erler. 2. verbesserte Aufl. Berlin u. Weimar: Aufbau, 1980.

Fontane, Theodor: *Der deutsche Krieg von 1866*. Vol. 1 (in 2): "Der Feldzug in Böhmen und Mähren." Berlin: Decker, 1870. Vol. 2: "Der Feldzug in West- und Mitteldeutschland." Berlin: Decker, 1871. (Faksimiledruck; Fontane: *Sämtliche Werke*. Hrsg. von Kurt Schreinert. Abt. 5. München: Nymphenburger Verlagshandlung, 1971).

Fontane, Theodor: *Der Krieg gegen Frankreich*. Vol. 1: "Der Krieg gegen das Kaiserreich." Berlin: Decker, 1873. Vol. 2: "Der Krieg gegen die Republik." Berlin: Decker, 1875–1876. (Faksimiledruck; Fontane: *Sämtliche Werke*. Hrsg. von Kurt Schreinert. Abt. 5. München: Nymphenburger Verlagshandlung, 1971).

Fontane, Theodor: *Reisebriefe vom Kriegsschauplatz Böhmen 1866*. Hrsg. von Christian Andree. Frankfurt: Propyläen, 1973.

Fontane, Theodor: *Der Schleswig-Holsteinische Krieg im Jahre 1864*. Berlin: Decker, 1866 (Faksimiledruck; Fontane: *Sämtliche Werke*. Hrsg. von Kurt Schreinert. Abt. 5. München: Nymphenburger Verlagshandlung, 1971).

Fontane, Theodor: *Vor dem Sturm*. Hrsg. von Gotthard Erler. Vol. 1–2. 2. Aufl. Berlin, Weimar: Aufbau, 1973 (Romane und Erzählungen in acht Bänden. 1 und 2).

Fontane, Theodor: *Werke, Schriften, Briefe*. (teilweise: *Sämtliche Werke*.) Hrsg. von Walter Keitel und Helmuth Nürnberger. Abt. 1: *Sämtliche Romane, Erzählungen, Gedichte*. Vol. 1–6. Abt. 2: *Wanderungen durch die Mark Brandenburg*. Vol. 1–3. Abt. 3: *Erinnerungen. Ausgewählte Schriften und Kritiken*. Vol. 1–5 (in 6). Abt. 4: *Briefe*. Vol. 1–5,1. München: Hanser, 1962–1988.

François, Luise von, and Conrad Ferdinand Meyer: *Ein Briefwechsel*. Hrsg. von Anton Bettelheim. 2., verm. Aufl. Berlin, Leipzig: de Gruyter, 1920.

Frank, Niklas: "Der Einzelgänger." [interview with Günter Grass] *Stern* No. 21, May 14, 1992: 214–16.

Freiligrath, Ferdinand: *Briefwechsel mit Marx und Engels*. Bearb. und eingel. von Manfred Häckel. Teil 1–2. 2., unveränd. Aufl. Berlin: Akademie-Verlag, 1976.

Freiligrath, Ferdinand: *Werke in sechs Teilen*. Hrsg. von Julius Schwering. Berlin: Bong, 1909.

Freytag, Gustav: *Bilder aus der deutschen Vergangenheit*. Vol. 1–3. Leipzig: Fikentscher, [1925].

Freytag, Gustav: *Erinnerungen aus meinem Leben*. Leipzig: Hirzel, 1887.

Freytag, Gustav: *Gesammelte Werke*. Neue wohlfeile Ausgabe. Ser. 1, Vol. 3–5: *Die Ahnen*. Leipzig: Hirzel; Berlin: Klemm, [1920].

Freytag, Gustav: *Der Kronprinz und die deutsche Kaiserkrone: Erinnerungsblätter*. 7. Aufl. Leipzig: Hirzel, 1889.

[Friedmann, Otto Bernhard:] *X.Y.Z. Satyrisch-literarisches Taschenbuch für 1848*. Unter Mitwirkung des jüngsten Deutschlands hrsg. von einem Unberühmten. Leipzig: Spamer, [1847].

Fritzsche, Richard: *Bausteine für den Geschichtsunterricht in der evangelischen Landschule: Eine Handreichung für Lehrer und Seminaristen*. 2. Kursus (Oberstufe). Altenburg: Pierer, 1897.

Fritzsche, Richard: *Bausteine für den Geschichtsunterricht in der evangelischen Landschule: Eine Handreichung für Lehrer und Seminaristen*. 1. Kursus (Mittelstufe). Altenburg: Pierer, 1896.

Fritzsche, Richard: *Die Deutsche Geschichte in der Volksschule: Präparationen und Entwürfe nach Grundsätzen der neueren Pädagogik für das 5. bis 8. Schuljahr*. T. 2: *Vom Dreißigjährigen Krieg bis zur Gegenwart*. 5. verb. Aufl. Altenburg: Pierer, 1911.

Fröhlich, Elke: *Die Herausforderung des Einzelnen: Geschichten über Widerstand und Verfolgung*. München, Wien: Oldenbourg, 1983 (Bayern in der NS-Zeit. 6).

Frohnmeyer, J.: *Leitfaden der Geschichte für die unteren und mittleren Klassen höherer Lehranstalten*. 5. Aufl. Stuttgart: Bonz, 1909.

Fuchs, Jürgen: "Die Lüge." Fuchs: *Gedächtnisprotokolle, Vernehmungsprotokolle: November '76 bis September '77. Neuausgabe 1990*. Reinbek: Rowohlt, 1990 (rororo-Taschenbuch. 12726).

Fuchs, Jürgen: *"— und wann kommt der Hammer?": Psychologie, Opposition und Staatssicherheit*. Berlin: BasisDruck, 1990.

Geibel, Emanuel: *Werke*. Hrsg. von Wolfgang Stammler. Kritisch durchges. u. erl. Ausgabe. Vol. 1–3. Leipzig: Bibliographisches Institut, 1918.

Geiger, Ludwig, ed., *Aus Adolf Stahrs Nachlaß: Briefe von Stahr nebst Briefen an ihn und von Bettina von Arnim u. a.* Ausgewählt und mit Einleitung und Anmerkungen versehen von L. G. Oldenburg: Schulze, 1903.

Geist, Peter, ed., *Ein Molotow-Cocktail auf fremder Bettkante: Lyrik der siebziger/achtziger Jahre von Dichtern aus der DDR. Ein Lesebuch*. Leipzig: Reclam, 1991.

Goethe, Johann Wolfgang: *Werke*. Hrsg. im Auftrag der Großherzogin Sophie von Sachsen. Abt. IV: *Briefe*. Vol. 1–50. Weimar: Böhlau, 1887–1912.

Grass, Günter: "Aufhören, auf leere Hoffnungen zu setzen: Gespräch mit Günter Grass." *Neue Deutsche Literatur* 40:9 (1992): 7–28.

Grass, Günter: "Gegen den Haß: Osloer Rede." *Neue Deutsche Literatur* 38, No. 455 (1990): 5–8.

Grass, Günter: *Deutscher Lastenausgleich: Wider das dumpfe Einheitsgebot: Reden und Gespräche.* Frankfurt a. M.: Luchterhand Literaturverlag, 1990 (Sammlung Luchterhand. 921).

Grass, Günter: [Interview] see Niklas Frank: "Der Einzelgänger."

Grass, Günter: "Kurze Rede eines vaterlandslosen Gesellen." *Die Zeit* No. 7, February 9, 1990: 60–1.

Grass, Günter: "Nötige Kritik oder Hinrichtung?: *Spiegel*-Gespräch mit Günter Grass über die Debatte um Christa Wolf und die DDR-Literatur." *Der Spiegel* No. 29, July 16, 1990: 138–43.

Grass, Günter: *Ein Schnäppchen namens DDR: Letzte Reden vor dem Glockengeläut.* Frankfurt a. M.: Luchterhand Literaturverlag, 1990 (Sammlung Luchterhand. 963).

Grass, Günter: "Schreiben nach Auschwitz." *Die Zeit* No. 9, February 23, 1990: 17–9.

Grass, Günter: "Treuhand." *Neue Deutsche Literatur* 40, No. 480 (1992): 8–11.

Grass, Günter: *Novemberland: 13 Sonette.* Göttingen: Steidl, 1993. First printed in *Die Woche* 1:9 (February 25, 1993): 30.

Grass, Günter: *Unkenrufe: Eine Erzählung.* Göttingen: Steidl, 1992.

Grass, Günter: *Werkausgabe in zehn Bänden.* Hrsg. von Volker Neuhaus. Darmstadt, Neuwied: Luchterhand, 1987.

Grass, Günter, and Regine Hildebrand: "Werden Sie Präsidentin, Regine! Premiere: Günter Grass trifft Regine Hildebrandt." *Wochenpost* No. 8, February 18, 1993: 20–21.

Grube, A. W.: *Charakterbilder aus der Geschichte und Sage, für einen propädeutischen Geschichtsunterricht.* 22. Aufl. Leipzig: Brandstetter, 1880.

Gutzkow, Karl: *Die neuen Serapionsbrüder.* Vol. 1–3. Breslau: Schottländer, 1877.

Haberl, Johann: *Der geschichtliche Unterricht in der Volksschule: Ausführliche Präparationen nach Lehrplan I und II für Landschulen.* München: Kellerer, 1910.

Haefs, Gisbert: *Alexander.* [Vol. 1:] *Der Roman der Einigung Griechenlands: "Hellas".* Zürich: Haffmans, 1992.

Hahn, Ludwig: *Leitfaden der vaterländischen Geschichte für Schule und Haus.* 49., durchges. Aufl. Berlin: Hertz, 1896.

Handke, Peter: *Versuch über die Jukebox: Erzählung.* Frankfurt a. M.: Suhrkamp, 1990.

Harig, Ludwig: *Ordnung ist das ganze Leben: Roman meines Vaters.* München: Hanser, 1986.

Harig, Ludwig: *Weh dem, der aus der Reihe tanzt: Roman.* München: Hanser, 1990.

Haupert, Bernhard, and Franz Josef Schäfer: *Jugend zwischen Kreuz und Hakenkreuz: Biographische Rekonstruktion als Alltagsgeschichte des Faschismus*. Mit einem Vorwort von Manfred Messerschmidt. Frankfurt a. M.: Suhrkamp, 1992 (suhrkamp taschenbuch wissenschaft. 952).

Hauptmann, Gerhart: *Sämtliche Werke*. Hrsg. von Hans-Egon Hass. Vol. 7: *Autobiographisches*. Berlin: Ullstein, 1962.

Hechelmann, A., ed., *Auszug aus Welters Lehrbuch der Weltgeschichte für Schulen*. 49. Aufl. Münster: Coppenrath, 1907.

Hegel, Friedrich: *Ästhetik*. Nach der zweiten Ausgabe Heinrich Gustav Hothos <1842> redigiert u. mit einem ausführlichen Register vers. von Friedrich Bassenge. Mit einem Essay von Georg Lukács. Vol. 1–2. Frankfurt a. M.: Europäische Verlagsanstalt, 1955.

Heiduczek, Werner: *Im gewöhnlichen Stalinismus: Meine unerlaubten Texte, Tagebücher, Briefe, Essays*. Leipzig, Weimar: Kiepenheuer, 1991.

Hein, Christoph: *Die fünfte Grundrechenart: Aufsätze und Reden 1987–1990*. Frankfurt a. M.: Luchterhand Literaturverlag, 1990.

Heinze-Rosenburg: *Die Geschichte für Lehrerbildungsanstalten*. T. 4: *Neueste Geschichte seit 1815 bis zur Gegenwart*. Selbständig bearb. von Hermann Rosenburg. Für die 1. Seminarklasse. 2., verb. Aufl. Hannover, Berlin: Meyer, 1904.

Herwegh, Georg: *Frühe Publizistik 1837–1841*. Unter Leitung von Bruno Kaiser bearb. von Ingrid Pepperle, Johanna Rosenberg, Agnes Ziegengeist. Berlin: Akademie-Verlag, 1971.

Herwegh, Georg: *Werke in drei Teilen*. Hrsg. und mit einem Lebensbild vers. von Hermann Tardel. Berlin: Bong, 1909.

Hesekiel, Ludovika: *Von Brandenburg zu Bismarck*. Vol. 1–2. Berlin: Wedekind & Schwieger, 1873.

Heukenkamp, Ursula, Heinz Kahlau and Wulf Kirsten, eds., *Die eigene Stimme: Lyrik aus der DDR*. Berlin, Weimar: Aufbau, 1988.

Heym, Stefan: "Ash-Wednesday." *New German Critique* 52 (Winter 1991): 31–2.

Heym, Stefan: *Auf Sand gebaut: Sieben Geschichten aus der unmittelbaren Vergangenheit*. 14 Zeichnungen von Horst Hussel. München: Bertelsmann, 1990.

Heym, Stefan: *Einmischung: Gespräche, Reden, Essays*. Ausgew. und hrsg. von Inge Heym und Heinfried Heiniger. Mit einem Vorw. von Egon Bahr. Gütersloh: Bertelsmann, 1990.

Heym, Stefan: *Filz: Gedanken über das neueste Deutschland*. München: Bertelsmann, 1992.

Heym, Stefan: *Schwarzenberg: Roman*. Frankfurt a. M.: Fischer Taschenbuch Verlag, 1987 (Fischer Taschenbuch. 5999).

Hochhuth, Rolf: *Wessis in Weimar: Szenen aus einem besetzten Land*. Berlin: Volk und Welt, 1993.

Hoffmann, C: *Handbuch für den Geschichtsunterricht in preußischen Volksschulen. Ein Hilfsbuch für Lehrer und Seminaristen.* 6., auf Grund des Allerhöchsten Erlasses vom 1. Mai 1889 umgearb. Aufl. Langensalza: Beyer, 1895.

Hoffmann von Fallersleben, August Heinrich: *An meine Freunde: Briefe.* Hrsg. von H[einrich] Gerstenberg. Berlin: Concordia Deutsche Verlags-Anstalt, 1907.

Hoffmann von Fallersleben, August Heinrich: *Deutsche Gassenlieder. Deutsche Salonlieder.* Mit einem Nachwort herausgegeben von Walter Pape. Braunschweig: Literarische Vereinigung Braunschweig, 1991 [richtig: 1992] (Bibliophile Schriften der Literarischen Vereinigung Braunschweig. Bd. 38. Jahresgabe 1991).

Hoffmann von Fallersleben, August Heinrich: *Gesammelte Werke.* Hrsg. von Heinrich Gerstenberg. Vol. 1–8. Berlin: F. Fontane, 1890–1893.

Hoffmann von Fallersleben, August Heinrich: *Mein Leben: Aufzeichnungen und Erinnerungen.* Vol. 1–6. Hannover: Rümpler, 1868.

Hoffmeyer, L., and W. Hering: *Hilfsbuch für den Geschichtsunterricht in Seminaren.* 3., durchges. und erw. Aufl. Breslau: Hirt, 1905.

Hofmannsthal, Hugo von: *Gesammelte Werke in zehn Einzelbänden.* Hrsg. von Bernd Schoeller in Beratung mit Rudolf Hirsch. Frankfurt a. M.: Fischer Taschenbuch Verlag, 1979–1980. (Fischer-Taschenbuch. 2159–68).

Huret, Jules: *Berlin.* Vingt-troisième mille. Paris: Bibliothèque-Charpentier, 1910 (Huret: En Allemagne. 3).

Huret, Jules: *Berlin: <In Deutschland. Dritter Teil>.* Einzige berechtigte Übersetzung aus dem Französischen von Minna Knoblich. München: Albert Langen, 1909.

Immermann, Karl: *Werke in fünf Bänden.* Unter Mitarb. von Hans Asbeck [u.a.] hrsg. von Benno von Wiese. Vol. 1. Frankfurt a. M.: Athenäum, 1971.

Jacobowski, Ludwig: *Werther der Jude.* Berlin: Hoffschläger, 1893.

Jäger, Oskar: *Abriß der neuesten Geschichte: 1815–1871. Ein Hülfsbuch für den historischen Unterricht in den obersten Klassen höherer Schulen und für den Selbstunterricht.* Mainz: Kunze, 1875.

Jäger, Oskar: *Pro Domo: Reden und Aufsätze.* Berlin: Seehagen, 1894.

Janka, Walter: *Schwierigkeiten mit der Wahrheit.* Berlin, Weimar: Aufbau, 1990.

Jenninger, Philipp: "Von der Verantwortung für das Vergangene. Fünfzig Jahre nach der 'Reichskristallnacht'. Rede bei der Gedenkveranstaltung im Deutschen Bundestag." *Die Zeit* No. 47, November 18, 1988: 4–7.

Jöris, Martin: *Erzählungen für den ersten Geschichtsunterricht. Auf Grund der preußischen Bestimmungen für höhere Mädchenschulen. Ausgabe B: Aus der deutschen Geschichte.* 2. Aufl. Leipzig: Freytag, Wien: Tempsky, 1907.

Joyce, James: *Ulysses.* New York: Vintage, 1986.

Kabisch, Richard: *Erziehender Geschichtsunterricht: Versuch einer preußisch-deutschen Staatsgeschichte für Volksschulen*. Göttingen: Vandenhoeck & Ruprecht, 1913.

Kachold, Gabriele: *zügel los: prosatexte*. Berlin, Weimar: Aufbau, 1989 (Ausser der Reihe).

Kaiser, Bruno, ed., *Die Akten Ferdinand Freiligrath und Georg Herwegh. Aus dem Archiv der Deutschen Schillerstiftung Weimar*. Weimar: Volksverl. in Komm., [1963] (Veröffentlichungen aus dem Archiv der Deutschen Schillerstiftung. H. 5/6).

Kaiser, Bruno, ed., *Der Freiheit eine Gasse: Aus dem Leben und Werk Georg Herweghs*. Berlin: Volk und Welt, 1948.

Kant, Hermann: *Abspann: Erinnerung an meine Gegenwart*. Berlin, Weimar: Aufbau, 1991.

Kantorowicz, Alfred: *Deutsches Tagebuch*. Teil 1. Berlin: Verlag Anpassung und Widerstand, 1978.

Karge, Manfred: "MauerStücke." *Theater der Zeit* 1991, No. 1: 68–83.

Keil, Ernst: "Photographien aus dem Reichstag IV." *Gartenlaube. Illustriertes Familienblatt* 1867: 266–68.

Keller, Gottfried: *Gesammelte Briefe in vier Bänden*. Hrsg. von Carl Helbling. Bern: Benteli, 1950–54.

Kirsch, Sarah: *Erlkönigs Tochter: Gedichte*. Stuttgart: Deutsche Verlags-Anstalt, 1992.

Kleist, Heinrich von: *Sämtliche Werke und Briefe in vier Bänden*. Hrsg. von Ilse-Marie Barth, Klaus Müller-Salget, Stefan Ormanns und Hinrich C. Seeba. Vol. 3: *Erzählungen, Anekdoten, Gedichte, Schriften*. Hrsg. von Klaus Müller-Salget. Frankfurt a. M.: Deutscher Klassiker Verlag, 1990.

Koch, Gottfried: *Lehrbuch der Geschichte für höhere Lehranstalten*. T. II/3 für Untersekunda. Leipzig: Quelle & Meyer, 1911.

Kolbe, Uwe, Lothar Irolle and Bernd Wagner, eds., *Mikado oder Der Kaiser ist nackt: Selbstverlegte Literatur in der DDR*. Darmstadt: Luchterhand, 1988.

Königsdorf, Helga: *Adieu DDR: Protokolle eines Abschied*. Reinbek: Rowohlt, 1990 (rororo aktuell. 12991).

Königsdorf, Helga: *Aus dem Dilemma eine Chance machen: Aufsätze und Reden*. Hamburg: Luchterhand, 1990.

Königsdorf, Helga: *1989 oder Ein Moment Schönheit: Eine Collage aus Briefen, Gedichten, Texten*. Reinbek: Rowohlt, 1991. First edition: Berlin, Weimar: Aufbau, 1990 (Aufbau-Texte zur Zeit).

Koziol, Andreas, and Rainer Schedlinski, eds., *Abriß der Ariadnefabrik*. Berlin: Galrev, 1990.

Koziol, Andreas: *mehr über rauten und türme: gedichte*. Berlin, Weimar: Aufbau, 1991 (Ausser der Reihe).

Kraft, Dieter: *traumhaft theater zinnober improvisationen spiele protokolle*. Berlin, Weimar: Aufbau, 1991 (Ausser der Reihe).

Krüger, Carl A.: *Die Weltgeschichte in Biographien und Skizzen: Ein Lehr- und Lernbuch für gehobene Volksschulen, Bürgerschulen und Präparandenanstalten*. Danzig: Gruihn, 1880.

Kühn, Dieter: *Der Parzival des Wolfram von Eschenbach*. Frankfurt a. M., Leipzig: Insel, 1991 (insel taschenbuch. 1328).

Kunert, Günter: *Der Sturz vom Sockel: Feststellungen und Widersprüche*. München, Wien: Hanser, 1992.

Kunert, Günter: *Vor der Sintflut: Das Gedicht als Arche Noah. Frankfurter Vorlesungen*. München: Hanser, 1985 (Edition Akzente).

Kunze, Reiner: *Deckname "Lyrik": Eine Dokumentation*. Frankfurt a. M.: Fischer Taschenbuch Verlag, 1990 (Fischer Taschenbuch Sachbuch. 10854).

Kunze, Reiner: *Die wunderbaren Jahre: Prosa*. Frankfurt a. M.: Fischer, 1976.

Lämmert, Eberhard, et al., eds., *Romantheorie 1620–1880: Dokumentation ihrer Geschichte in Deutschland*. Frankfurt a. M.: Athenäum, 1988 (Athenäum-Taschenbücher. 2186; Literaturwissenschaft).

Lang, Jack: "Rede zur Verleihung des Titels 'Officier des Arts et des Lettres' an Chista Wolf." *Neue Deutsche Literatur* 38, No. 456 (1990): 146–48.

Lattmann, Dieter: *Die Brüder*. Frankfurt a. M.: Fischer, 1985.

Laube, Heinrich: *Ausgewählte Werke in zehn Bänden*. Hrsg. von Heinrich Hubert Houben. Leipzig: Hesse, 1906.

Laube, Heinrich: *Waldstein: Historischer Roman*. Vol. 1–3. Unter Mitw. von Albert Hänel hrsg. von Heinrich Hubert Houben. Leipzig: Hesse, 1908–09 (Gesammelte Werke in fünfzig Bänden. 18–20).

Lindau, Paul: *Der Zug nach dem Westen*. Berlin: Spemann, 1886.

Lipperheide, Franz, ed., *Lieder zu Schutz und Trutz: Gaben deutscher Dichter aus der Zeit des Krieges in den Jahren 1870 und 1871*. Auswahl für Volk und Heer. 47. Tsd. Berlin: Lipperheide, 1871.

Loest, Erich: *Heute kommt Westbesuch: Zwei Monologe*. Göttingen: Steidl, 1992.

Loest, Erich: *Die Stasi war mein Eckermann. Oder: Mein Leben mit der Wanze*. Göttingen: Steidl; Leipzig: Linden, 1991.

Loest, Erich: *Der Zorn des Schafes: Aus meinem Tagewerk*. Künzelsau, Leipzig: Linden, 1990.

Mann, Heinrich: *Im Schlaraffenland: Ein Roman unter feinen Leuten*. Mit einem Nachwort von Wilfried F. Schoeller und einem Materialanhang, zusammengestellt von Peter-Paul Schneider. Frankfurt a. M.: Fischer Taschenbuch Verlag, 1988 (Mann: Studienausgabe in Einzelbänden. 6; Fischer-Taschenbuch. 5928).

Mann, Heinrich: *Der Untertan*. Mit einem Nachwort und Materialanhang von Peter-Paul Schneider. Frankfurt a. M.: Fischer Taschenbuch Verlag, 1991 (Mann: Studienausgabe in Einzelbänden. 16; Fischer-Taschenbuch. 10168).

Mann, Thomas: *Frühe Erzählungen*. Frankfurt a. M.: S. Fischer, 1981 (Gesammelte Werke in Einzelbänden. Frankfurter Ausgabe. Hrsg. von Peter de Mendelssohn).

Marbach, Oswald: *Das Halljahr Deutschlands: Klänge und Lieder*. Berlin: Lipperheide, November 1870 (Für Straßburgs Kinder! Eine Weihnachtsbescheerung von Deutschlands Dichtern. 9)

Marcuse, Herbert: *Schriften*. Vol. 5: *Triebstruktur und Gesellschaft (Eros and Civilization)*. Frankfurt a. M.: Suhrkamp, 1979.

Maron, Monika: *Stille Zeile Sechs: Roman*. Frankfurt a. M.: Fischer, 1991.

Maron, Monika: "Writers and the People." *New German Critique* 52 (Winter 1991): 36–41.

Maron, Monika: "Zonophobie." *Kursbuch* 109 (1992): 91–6.

Marx, Karl, and Friedrich Engels: *Werke*. Hrsg. vom Institut für Marxismus-Leninismus beim ZK der SED. Vol. 21. Berlin: Dietz, 1981.

Mauer, A., ed., *Geschichts-Bilder: Darstellung der wichtigsten Begebenheiten und berühmtesten Personen aus der alten Geschichte, dem Mittelalter, der neuen und neuesten Zeit*. 8., verm. Aufl. Langensalza: Gessler, 1878.

Mauthner, Fritz: *Der neue Ahasver*. Dresden: Minden, 1882.

Mauthner, Fritz: *Das Quartett*. Dresden: Minden, 1893.

Meinecke, Friedrich: *Erlebtes: 1862–1901*. Leipzig: Koehler und Amelang, 1941.

Metelka, Torsten, ed., *Alles ist im Untergrund obenauf; einmannfrei...: ausgewählte beiträge aus der zeitschrift KONTEXT, 1–7*. Berlin: Kontext, 1990.

Meyer, Conrad Ferdinand: *Sämtliche Werke. Historisch-Kritische Ausgabe*. Hrsg. von Hans Zeller und Alfred Zäch. Vol. 1–15. Bern: Benteli, 1963–85.

Meyer, Conrad Ferdinand, and Julius Rodenberg: *Ein Briefwechsel*. Hrsg. von August Langmesser. Berlin: Paetel, 1918.

Montégut, Émile: "La démocratie et la révolution. Les transformations de l'idée de patrie." *Revue des Deux Mondes* 41, vol. 96 (1871): 415–42.

Müller, David: *Leitfaden zur Geschichte des deutschen Volkes*. Berlin: Bahlen, 1875.

Müller, Elfriede: "Goldener Oktober." *Theater heute* 1991, No. 6: 44–55.

Müller, Heiner: "Bautzen oder Babylon." *Sinn und Form* 43 (1991), p. 664–65.

Müller, Heiner: "'Es gibt ein Menschenrecht auf Feigheit': Ein Gespräch mit dem Dramatiker Heiner Müller über seine Kontakte mit der Staatssicherheit." *Frankfurter Rundschau*, May 22, 1993: ZB 3.

Müller, Heiner: *"Jenseits der Nation": Heiner Müller im Interview mit Frank M. Raddatz*. Berlin: Rotbuch, 1991.

Müller, Heiner: "Mommsens Block." *Drucksache 1: Berliner Ensemble*. Berlin: Alexander Lang, 1993: 1–9.

Müller, Heiner: "Was wird aus dem größeren Deutschland?" *Sinn und Form* 43 (1991): 666–69.

Müller, Wilhelm: *Leitfaden für den Unterricht in der Geschichte mit besonderer Berücksichtigung der neueren deutschen Geschichte*. 8., verb. und verm. Aufl. Heilbronn: Scheurlen, 1873.

Muschg, Adolf: "Rede an einen abgefahrenen Zug. Nachtreten auf bereits Liegende als neue deutsche Feuilleton-Lokerheit." *Frankfurter Rundschau* No. 286/49, December 8, 1990: ZB 3.

Neubauer, Friedrich: *Lehrbuch der Geschichte für höhere Lehranstalten*. T. 5: *Vom westfälischen Frieden bis auf unsere Zeit (Oberprima)*. 8., Aufl. Halle: Verlag der Buchhandlung des Waisenhauses, 1907.

Nietzsche, Friedrich: *Sämtliche Briefe*. Kritische Studienausgabe in 8 Bänden. Hrsg. von Giorgio Colli und Mazzino Montinari. München: Deutscher Taschenbuch Verlag; Berlin: de Gruyter, 1986.

Nietzsche, Friedrich: *Sämtliche Werke*. Kritische Studienausgabe in 15 Bänden. Hrsg. von Giorgio Colli und Mazzino Montinari. München: Deutscher Taschenbuch Verlag; Berlin: de Gruyter, 1980.

Nietzsche, Friedrich: *The Use and Abuse of History*. Translated by Adrian Collins. 2nd ed. Indianapolis: Bobbs-Merrill, 1957.

Nösselt, Friedrich: *Weltgeschichte für Töchterschulen und zum Privatunterricht heranwachsender Mädchen*. 16. Aufl., berichtigt und bis auf die Gegenwart fortgesetzt von Friedrich Kurts. T. 4. Stuttgart: Heitz, 1880.

Papenfuß-Gorek, Bert: *dreizehntanz*. Berlin, Weimar: Aufbau, 1988 (Ausser der Reihe).

Papenfuß-Gorek, Bert: *vorwärts im zorn usw.: gedichte*. Berlin, Weimar: Aufbau, 1990.

Raabe, Wilhelm: "Aus Braunschweiger Briefen Wilhelm Raabes an seinen Bruder Heinrich." *Mitteilungen der Gesellschaft der Freunde Wilhelm Raabes* 16:1 (1926): 15–6.

Raabe, Wilhelm: *Der Dräumling: Mit Dokumenten zur Schillerfeier 1859*. Hrsg. von Anneliese Klingenberg. Textrevision Erika Weber. Berlin, Weimar: Aufbau, 1984.

Raabe, Wilhelm: "Kleist von Nollendorf." *Sämtliche Werke* Ser. 3, Vol. 6. Berlin: Klemm, [1920]. 520–31.

Raabe, Wilhelm: *Die schwarze Galeere*. Edited by Annerose Schimanski and Joachim Buscha. Illustration: Hans Mau. Leipzig: Verlag Enzyklopädie, 1969 [Readers for Foreigners whose Native Tongue is English].

Raabe, Wilhelm: *Sämtliche Werke. Historisch-kritische Ausgabe*. Im Auftrag der Braunschweig. Wiss. Gesellschaft hrsg. von Karl Hoppe und Jost Schillemeit. Vol. 1–20 and 4 suppl. Göttingen: Vandenhoeck & Ruprecht, 1965–83.

Rodenberg, Julius: *Die Grandidiers: Ein Berliner Roman aus der französischen Kolonie*. 4. Aufl. Stuttgart: Deutsche Verlags-Anstalt, 1912.

Roland, Ursula: *Wie eine Feder im Wind: Meine Zeit in Stalins Lagern.* Berlin: Rowohlt, 1991.

Rosenlöcher, Thomas: *Die verkauften Pflastersteine: Dresdener Tagebuch.* Frankfurt a. M.: Suhrkamp, 1990 (edition suhrkamp. 1635).

Rosenlöcher, Thomas: *Die Wiederentdeckung des Gehens beim Wandern: Von Dresden in den Harz.* Frankfurt a. M.: Suhrkamp, 1991 (edition suhrkamp. 1685).

Rousseau, Jean-Jacques: *Schriften zur Kulturpolitik <Die zwei Diskurse von 1750 und 1755>.* Übersetzt und mit Einleitung u. Anmerkungen hrsg. von Kurt Weigand. Unveränd. Nachdruck der Ausgabe 1955. Hamburg: Meiner, 1964 (Philosophische Bibliothek. 243).

Ruprecht, Ernst, ed., *Literarische Manifeste des Naturalismus: 1880–1892.* Stuttgart: Metzler, 1962 (Epochen der deutschen Literatur. Materialienband).

Sattler, M. V.: *Abriß der bayerischen Geschichte für den ersten Unterricht in den Mittelschulen.* München: Lindauer 1889.

Schädlich, Hans Joachim: "Ostwestberlin." Schädlich: *Ostwestberlin.* Reinbek: Rowohlt, 1987. 163–80.

Schedlinski, Rainer: *die rationen des ja und des nein: gedichte.* Berlin, Weimar: Aufbau, 1988 (Ausser der Reihe).

Scheiblhuber, A. Cl.: *Präparationen für den Geschichts-Unterricht in der Volksschule: Achtzig ausführliche Lehrproben.* 3. Aufl. Nürnberg: Korn, 1912.

Schenk, K.: *Lehrbuch der Geschichte für höhere Lehranstalten, in Übereinstimmung mit den neuesten Lehrplänen. 9. Lehraufgabe der Oberprima. Neuere Geschichte von 1648–1888.* Verfaßt von E. Wolff. Leipzig, Berlin: Teubner, 1901.

Schiller: *Sämtliche Werke.* Aufgrund der Originaldrucke hrsg. von Gerhard Fricke und Herbert G. Göpfert. 4., durchges. Aufl. Vol. 1–5. München: Hanser, 1967.

Schiller, Friedrich: *Werke. Nationalausgabe.* Begründet von Julius Petersen. Fortgeführt von Lieselotte Blumenthal und Benno von Wiese. Hrsg. [...] von Norbert Oellers und Siegfried Seidel. [Bisher:] Bd.1; 2, 1–2a; 3–14; 15, 1; 16–17; 18, 2; 20–32; 33, 1; 34, 1; 35–38, 1; 39, 1; 40, 1; 42. Weimar: Böhlau, 1949–1993.

Schillmann, R., and F. Viergutz: *Leitfaden für den Unterricht in der Deutschen Geschichte: Nach dem neuen Grundlehrplane für die Berliner Gemeindeschulen. T. 2: Die brandenburgisch-preußische Geschichte von ihren Anfängen bis zur Gegenwart. (III. und II. Klasse.)* 46. Aufl. Berlin: Nicolaische Verlags-Buchhandlung, 1906.

Schlesinger, Klaus: *Fliegender Wechsel: Eine persönliche Chronik.* Frankfurt a. M.: Fischer, 1990.

Schneider, Peter: *Deutsche Ängste: Essays.* Darmstadt: Luchterhand, 1988 (Sammlung Luchterhand. 782).

Schneider, Peter: *Extreme Mittellage: Eine Reise durch das deutsche Nationalgefühl.* Reinbek: Rowohlt, 1990.

Schneider, Peter: *The German Comedy: Scenes of Life after the Wall.* (*Extreme Mittellage*, engl.) Translated by Philip Boehm and Leigh Hafrey. New York: Farrar, Straus, Giroux, 1990.

Schneider, Peter: *Der Mauerspringer: Erzählung.* Darmstadt, Neuwied: Luchterhand, 1982.

Schneider, Peter: *The Wall Jumper.* Translated by Leigh Hafrey. New York: Pantheon Books, 1983.

Schneider, Rolf: "Volk ohne Trauer." *Der Spiegel* No. 44, October 29, 1990: 264–70.

Schumann, K.: *Vaterländische Geschichtsbilder für evangelische Volksschulen.* Bielefeld, Leipzig: Velhagen & Klasing, 1892.

Spielhagen, Friedrich: "Der Held im Roman." Hartmut Steinecke, ed., *Theorie und Technik des Romans im 19. Jahrhundert.* Tübingen: Niemeyer, 1970 (Deutsche Texte. 18). 96–100.

Spielhagen, Friedrich: *Sämtliche Romane.* Vol. 1–29. Leipzig: Staackmann, 1895–1904.

Spielmann, C.: *Der Geschichtsunterricht in ausgeführten Lektionen: Für die Hand des Lehrers, nach den neueren methodischen Grundsätzen und nach den neuen ministeriellen Bestimmungen. T. 3: Preußisch-deutsche Geschichte vom Ende des Großen Krieges bis zum Beginne des zwanzigsten Jahrhunderts.* Halle: Gesenius, 1902.

Springer, Robert: *Banquier und Schriftsteller: Lebensbild aus der Berliner Gesellschaft.* Berlin: Wedekind & Schwieger, 1877.

Springer, Robert: *Berlin: die deutsche Kaiserstadt.* Darmstadt: Lange, 1878.

Stern, Horst: *Mann aus Apulien: Die privaten Papiere des italienischen Staufers Friedrich II., römisch-deutscher Kaiser, König von Sizilien und Jerusalem, Erster nach Gott, über die wahre Natur der Menschen und Tiere, geschrieben 1245–1250.* München: Knaur, 1988 (Knaur Taschenbücher. 2044).

Storm, Theodor: *Briefe.* Hrsg. von Peter Goldammer. Vol. 1–2. 2., durchges. Aufl. Berlin, Weimar: Aufbau, 1984.

Strauß, Botho: "Anschwellender Bocksgesang." *Der Spiegel* 47 (1993) No. 36, February 8: 202–07.

Strauß, Botho: *Beginnlosigkeit: Reflexionen über Fleck und Linie.* München: Hanser, 1992.

Strauß, Botho: *Diese Erinnerung an einen, der nur einen Tag zu Gast war: Gedicht.* 2. Aufl. München, Wien: Hanser, 1985.

Strauß, Botho: *Schlußchor: Drei Akte.* München, Wien: Hanser, 1991.

Struzyk, Brigitte: "Im Niemandsland." *Neue Deutsche Literatur* 39, No. 468 (1991): 49–59.

Stutzer, Emil: *Übersichten zur preußisch-deutschen Geschichte: Für die oberste Stufe des Geschichtsunterrichts sowie zur Selbstbelehrung.* Hannover: Hahn, 1891.

Süskind, Patrick: "Deutschland, eine Midlife-crisis." *Der Spiegel* No. 38, September 17, 1990: 43–54.

Sybel, Heinrich von Sybel: "Über den Stand der neueren deutschen Geschichtsschreibung." Sybel: *Kleine historische Schriften*. München: Cotta, 1863. 345–59.

Treitschke, Heinrich von: *Politik: Vorlesungen gehalten an der Universität zu Berlin*. Hrsg. von Max Cornicelius. Vol. 1–2. Leipzig: Hirzel, 1897–98.

Verhandlungen über Fragen des höheren Unterrichts. Berlin, 6. bis 8. Juni 1900. Berlin, 1900.

Verhandlungen über Fragen des höheren Unterrichts. Berlin, 4. bis 17. Dezember 1890. Berlin, 1891.

Vinke, Hermann, ed., *Akteneinsicht Christa Wolf: Zerrspiegel und Dialog. Eine Dokumentation*. Hamburg: Luchterhand, 1993.

Wagenbach, Klaus, Winfried Stephan, and Michael Krüger, eds., *Vaterland, Muttersprache: Deutsche Schriftsteller und ihr Staat von 1945 bis heute*. Ein Nachlesebuch für die Oberstufe. Mit einem Vorwort von Peter Rühmkorf. Berlin: Wagenbach, 1979 (Quartheft. 100).

Walser, Martin: "Deutsches Mosaik." Walser: *Erfahrungen und Leseerfahrungen*. Frankfurt a. M.: Suhrkamp, 1965 (edition suhrkamp. 109). 7–28.

Walser, Martin: "Deutschländer oder Brauchen wir eine Nation?" Walser: *Auskunft: 23 Gespräche aus 26 Jahren*. Hrsg. von Klaus Siblewski. Frankfurt a. M.: Suhrkamp, 1991 (suhrkamp taschenbuch. 1871). 218–33.

Walser, Martin: *Dorle und Wolf: Eine Novelle*. Frankfurt a. M.: Suhrkamp, 1985.

Walser, Martin: "Über Deutschland reden." *Die Zeit* No. 45, November 4, 1988: 65–7.

Walser, Martin: *Über Deutschland reden*. Erweit. Neuaufl. Frankfurt a. M.: Suhrkamp, 1989 (edition suhrkamp. 1553).

Walser, Martin: *Die Verteidigung der Kindheit: Roman*. Frankfurt a. M.: Suhrkamp, 1991.

Walser, Martin: "Vormittag eines Schriftstellers." *Die Zeit* No. 51, December 14, 1990: 53–4.

Walser, Martin: "Zum Stand der deutschen Dinge." *Frankfurter Allgemeine Zeitung* No. 282, December 5, 1989: L1–2.

Walther, Joachim, et al., eds., *Protokoll eine Tribunals: Die Ausschlüsse aus dem DDR-Schriftstellerverband 1979*. Reinbek: Rowohlt, 1991 (rororo aktuell. 12992).

Weigand, H[einrich], and A. Tecklenburg: *Deutsche Geschichte: Nach den Forderungen der Gegenwart für Schule und Haus*. 3., verb. Aufl. Hannover: Meyer, 1896.

Weigand, Heinrich: *Der Geschichts-Unterricht nach den Forderungen der Gegenwart: Ein methodisches Handbuch im Anschlusse an die Deutsche Geschichte von H. Weigand und A. Tecklenburg*. T. 1. 3., verb. Aufl. Hannover, Berlin: Meyer, 1906.

Wesuls, Elisabeth: "Landeswechsel: Aus dem Tagebuch 1989–90." *Neue Deutsche Literatur* 39, No. 459 (1991): 156–61.

Wildenbruch, Ernst von: *Gesammelte Werke*. Hrsg. von Berthold Litzmann. Dritte Reihe: *Gedichte und kleine Prosa*. Vol. 15. Berlin: Grote, 1924.

Wolf, Christa: "Blickwechsel." Hans-Jürgen Schmidt, ed., *19 Erzähler der DDR*. Frankfurt a. M.: Fischer, 1972. 91–102.

Wolf, Christa: "Dankrede." [delivered after receiving the title "Officier des Arts et des Lettres"]. *Neue Deutsche Literatur* 38, No. 456 (1990): 148–50.

Wolf, Christa: *Im Dialog: Aktuelle Texte*. Frankfurt a. M.: Luchterhand Literaturverlag, 1990 (Sammlung Luchterhand. 923).

Wolf, Christa: *Kindheitsmuster*. Berlin, Weimar: Aufbau, 1976.

Wolf, Christa: *A Model Childhood* . Translated by Ursule Molinaro and Hedwig Rappolt. New York: Farrar, Straus, Giroux, 1980.

Wolf, Christa: *Nachdenken über Christa T.* Neuwied: Luchterhand, 1969.

Wolf, Christa: "Nagelprobe." *Neue Deutsche Literatur* 40, No. 473 (1992): 34–44.

Wolf, Christa: *Sommerstück*. Frankfurt a. M.: Luchterhand Literaturverlag, 1989.

Wolf, Christa: *Störfall: Nachrichten eines Tages*. Darmstadt, Neuwied: Luchterhand, 1987.

Wolf, Christa: *Accident: A Day's News*. Translated by Heike Schwarzbauer and Rick Takvorian. New York: Farrar, Straus, Giroux, 1989.

Wolf, Christa: *Was bleibt: Erzählung*. Frankfurt a. M.: Luchterhand Literaturverlag, 1990.

Zeitschrift des Allgemeinen Deutschen Sprachvereins. Begründet von Hermann Riegel. 1–8: Braunschweig: Meyer; 9–29: Berlin: Verlag des Allgemeinen Deutschen Sprachvereins, 1886–1914.

Zeller, Eva: *Das Sprungtuch: Erzählungen*. Stuttgart: Deutsche Verlagsanstalt, 1991.

Zimmermann, Karl: *Geschichtlicher Anschauungs- und Erfahrungs-Unterricht auf der Mittelstufe (4. u. 5. Schuljahr) als Einführung in die Heimat- u. Vaterlandsgeschichte*. Bd. II b des Handbuches: *Die Praxis der Volksschule*. Ansbach: Prögel, 1914.

Zurbonsen, Fr.: *Leitfaden der Geschichte für Lyzeen und Höhere Mädchenschulen*. T. 6: *Von der französischen Staatsumwälzung bis zur Gegenwart*. 2., Aufl. Düsseldorf: Schwann, 1914.

Secondary Sources

Adorno, Theodor W.: "Rede über Lyrik und Gesellschaft." Adorno: *Noten zur Literatur*. Hrsg. von Rolf Tiedemann. 2. Aufl. Frankfurt a. M.: Suhrkamp, 1984 (Adorno: Gesammelte Schriften. 11). 49–68.

Ahrends, Martin: "The Great Waiting, or The Freedom of the East: An Obituary for Life in Sleeping Beauty's Castle." *New German Critique* 52 (Winter 1991): 41–9.

Althoff, Gert: "Sinnstiftung und Instrumentalisierung. Zugriffe auf das Mittelalter. Eine Einführung." Gert Althoff, ed., *Die Deutschen und ihr Mittelalter: Themen und Funktionen moderner Geschichtsbilder vom Mittelalter*. Darmstadt: Wissenschaftliche Buchgesellschaft, 1992 (Ausblicke). 1–6.

Ameri, Susan Milantchi: *Die deutschnationale Sprachbewegung im Wilhelminischen Reich*. New York: Lang, 1991.

Anderson, Benedict: *Imagined Communities: Reflections on the Origin and Spread of Nationalism*. London: Verso, 1983.

Andrée, Fritz: *Hoffmann von Fallersleben: Des Dichters Leben, Wirken und Gedenkstätten in Wort und Bild*. 2., neubearb. Aufl. Höxter: Hoffmann-von-Fallersleben-Gesellschaft, 1972.

anon.: "Bleibt die Avantgarde zurück?" *Der Spiegel* No. 48, December 4, 1989: 230–33.

anon.: "Die deutsche Literatur der Gegenwart in Ost und West oder Neuer Nationalismus in der Literatur beider deutscher Staaten." *Neue Deutsche Hefte* 35 (1988): 772–87.

anon.: "Stasier than thou". *The Economist* (U. K. edition) vol. 321, No. 7734, November 23, 1991: 158.

anon.: "States of Mind I: Intellectuals warn of 'atmosphere of suspicion in Germany'." *The Week in Germany*, December 6, 1991.

Anonymus (Rev.): "Unpolitische Lieder von Hoffmann von Fallersleben." *Blätter für literarische Unterhaltung* 1841, I: 26–7.

Anz, Thomas, ed., *"Es geht nicht um Christa Wolf": Der Literaturstreit im vereinten Deutschland*. München: Spangenberg, 1991 (edition Spangenberg).

Arnold, Heinz Ludwig, and Frauke Meyer-Gosau, eds., *Literatur in der DDR: Rückblicke*. München: Edition Text und Kritik, 1991 (Sonderband).

Arnold, Heinz Ludwig, ed., *Die andere Sprache: Neue DDR-Literatur der 80er Jahre*. Hrsg. in Zusammenarbeit mit Gerhard Wolf. München: Edition Text und Kritik, 1990 (Text und Kritik. Sonderband).

Backes, Uwe, Eckhard Jesse and Rainer Zitelmann: "Was heißt 'Historisierung' des Nationalsozialismus?" Backes, Jesse, and Zitelmann, eds., *Die Schatten der Vergangenheit: Impulse zur Historisierung des Nationalsozialismus*. Frankfurt a. M., Berlin: Propyläen, 1990. 25–57.

Bänsch, Dieter: "Preußens und Dreysens Gloria. Zu Fontanes Kriegsbüchern." Heinz Ludwig Arnold, ed., *Theodor Fontane*. München: Edition Text – Kritik, 1989 (Text – Kritik. Sonderband). 30–54.

Baring, Arnulf: *Deutschland, was nun?* Ein Gespräch mit Dirk Rumberg und Wolf Jobst Siedler. Berlin: Siedler, 1991.

Baring, Arnulf: *Unser neuer Größenwahn: Deutschland zwischen Ost und West*. Stuttgart: Deutsche Verlagsanstalt, 1988.

Barner, Wilfried: *Barockrhetorik: Untersuchungen zu ihren geschichtlichen Grundlagen.* Tübingen: Niemeyer, 1970.

Baumhauer, Otto A.: "Kulturwandel. Zur Entwicklung des Paradigmas von der Kultur als Kommunikationssystem. Forschungsbericht." *Deutsche Vierteljahrsschrift für Lit.-wiss. u. Geistesgesch.* 56 (1982) Sonderheft: "Geschichte und Verstehen". 1–167.

Becker, Josef, ed., *Wiedervereinigung in Mitteleuropa: Außen- und Innenansichten zur staatlichen Einheit Deutschlands.* München: Vögel, 1992 (Schriften des Philosophischen Fachbereichs der Universität Augsburg. 43).

Behn, Manfred, ed., *Wirkungsgeschichte von Christa Wolfs "Nachdenken über Christa T."* Königstein/Ts.: Athenäum, 1978 (Athenäum-Taschenbücher. 2140; Literaturwissenschaft).

Bell, Andrew: *The General German Language Association: A Study of Radical Nationalism, 1886–1914.* M.A. Thesis, University of Oregon, 1993.

Berdahl, Robert M.: "New Thoughts on German Nationalism." *American Historical Review* 77 (1972): 65–80.

Berg, Christa, et al., eds., *Handbuch der Bildungsgeschichte.* Vol. 3: *1800–1870: Von der Neuordnung Deutschlands bis zur Reichsgründung.* Hrsg. von Karl-Ernst Jeismann und Peter Lundgreen. Vol. 4: *1870–1918: Von der Reichsgründung bis zum Ende des Ersten Weltkriegs.* Hrsg. von Christa Berg. München: Beck, 1987–1991.

Berg, Christa: *Die Okkupation der Schule: Eine Studie zur Aufhellung gegenwärtiger Schulprobleme an der Volksschule Preußens (1872–1900).* Heidelberg: Quelle & Meyer, 1973.

Berliner Autoren-Stadtbuch: 111 von A bis Z. Berlin: Akademie der Künste, 1985 (Schriftenreihe der Akademie der Künste. 17).

Berlin um 1900. Ausstellung der Berlinischen Galerie in Verb. mit der Akademie der Künste zu den Berliner Festwochen 1984. Akademie der Künste 9. September bis 28. Oktober 1984. Redaktion u. Gestaltung: Gesine Asmus. Berlin: Nicolai (i. Komm.), 1984.

Bernsmeier, Helmut: "Der Allgemeine Deutsche Sprachverein in seiner Gründungsphase." *Die Muttersprache* 87 (1977): 369–95.

Bernsmeier, Helmut: "Der Allgemeine Deutsche Sprachverein in der Zeit von 1912 bis 1932." *Die Muttersprache* 90 (1980): 117–40.

Bernsmeier, Helmut: "Der Deutsche Sprachverein im Dritten Reich." *Die Muttersprache* 93 (1983): 35–58.

Blessing, Werner K.: *Staat und Kirche in der Gesellschaft: Institutionelle Autorität und mentaler Wandel in Bayern während des 19. Jahrhunderts.* Göttingen: Vandenhoeck & Ruprecht, 1982.

Bohnen, Klaus: "'Tendenzwende': Zu einer Kulturkontroverse der siebziger Jahre." Schöne, Albrecht, ed., *Kontroversen, alte und neue: Akten des VII. Internationalen Germanistenkongresses, Göttingen 1985.* Vol. 10. Tübingen: Niemeyer, 1986. 171–77.

Bohrer, Karl Heinz: "Kulturschutzgebiet DDR?" *Merkur. Deutsche Zeitschrift für europäisches Denken* 44 (1990): 1015–18.

Bölling, Klaus: "'Kleine Schritte statt großer Sprünge'. Über Stefan Heyms 'Schwarzenberg'." *Der Spiegel* No. 34, August 20, 1984: 34–6.

Born, Karl Erich: *Von der Reichsgründung bis zum Ersten Weltkrieg*. München: Deutscher Taschenbuch Verlag, 1975 (Gebhardt. Handbuch der deutschen Geschichte. 16; dtv. 4216).

Böthig, Peter, and Klaus Michael: *MachtSpiele: Literatur und Staatssicherheit im Fokus Prenzlauer Berg*. Leipzig: Reclam, 1993.

Brackert, Helmut, and Fritz Wefelmeyer, eds., *Naturplan und Verfallskritik: Zu Begriff und Geschichte der Kultur*. Frankfurt a. M.: Suhrkamp, 1984 (edition suhrkamp. 1211).

Brather, Fritz: "Unsere Feinde im Spiegel der Dichtung Wilhelm Raabes." *Mitteilungen der Gesellschaft der Freunde Wilhelm Raabes* 6:1 (1916): 1–22.

Brather, Fritz: "Wilhelm Raabes Erzählung 'Des Reiches Krone' im deutschen Unterricht." *Lehrproben und Lehrgänge aus der Praxis der höheren Lehranstalten* H. 141 (1919): 25–41.

Brather, Fritz: "Wilhelm Raabes Erzählung 'Die schwarze Galeere', eine zeitgemäße Lektüre." *Lehrproben und Lehrgänge aus der Praxis der höheren Lehranstalten* H. 130 (Halle) (1917): 68–72.

Brather, Fritz: "Wilhelm Raabes Erzählung 'Im Siegeskranze' im deutschen Unterricht der 2. Lyzeumsklasse." *Die höheren Mädchenschulen* 32:18 (1919): 273–79; 32:19: 287–90.

Breuer, Stefan: *Anatomie der Konservativen Revolution*. Darmstadt: Wissenschaftliche Buchgesellschaft, 1993.

Brewster, Philip James: *Wilhelm Raabes historische Fiktion im Kontext: Beitrag zur Rekonstruktion der Gattungsproblematik zwischen Geschichtsschreibung und Poesie im 19. Jahrhundert*. Cornell Univ. Ph.D., 1983.

Briegleb, Klaus: "Vergangenheit in der Gegenwart." Briegleb, ed., *Gegenwartsliteratur seit 1986*. München: Hanser, 1992 (Hansers Sozialgeschichte der deutschen Literatur. 12). 73–116.

Briesen, Detlef: *Berlin, die überschätzte Metropole: Über das System der deutschen Hauptstädte von 1850 bis 1940*. Bonn: Bouvier, 1992.

Brockmann, Stephen: "Introduction: The Reunification Debate." *New German Critique* 52 (Winter 1991): 3–30.

Brode, Hanspeter: *Die Zeitgeschichte im erzählenden Werk von Günter Grass: Versuch einer Deutung der "Blechtrommel" und der "Danziger Trilogie"*. Frankfurt a. M., Bern: Lang, 1977 (Regensburger Beiträge zur deutschen Sprach- und Literaturwissenschaft. Reihe B. 11).

Broszat, Martin: *Nach Hitler: Der schwierige Umgang mit unserer Geschichte.* Hrsg. von Hermann Graml und Klaus-Dietmar Henke. München: Oldenbourg, 1986.

Broszat, Martin, and Saul Friedländer: "Um die 'Historisierung des Nationalsozialismus'. Ein Briefwechsel." *Vierteljahrshefte für Zeitgeschichte* 36 (1988): 339–72.

Buch, Hans-Christoph: "Die Stunde der Dichter." *Die Zeit* No. 50, December 4, 1992: Literaturbeil. 3.

Buchner, Wilhelm: *Ferdinand Freiligrath: Ein Dichterleben in Briefen.* Vol. 1–2. Lahr: Schauenburg, 1882.

Busch, Günter, Elisabeth Ruge, Uwe Wittstock: "Editorial." *Neue Rundschau* 104 (1993) H. 3: "Literatur im Abseits – und wie sie herauskommt." 5–6.

Chickering, Roger: "Der 'Deutsche Wehrverein' und die Reform der deutschen Armee 1912–1914." *Militärgeschichtliche Mitteilungen* 1 (1979): 7–33.

Chickering, Roger: *Karl Lamprecht: A German Academic Life (1856–1914).* Atlantic Highlands, N. J.: Humanities Press International, 1993.

Chickering, Roger: *We Men Who Feel Most German: A Cultural Study of the Pan-German League, 1886–1914.* London: Allen and Unwin, 1984.

Childers, Thomas: "The Social Language of Politics in Germany: The Sociology of Political Discourse in the Weimar Republic." *American Historical Review* 95 (1990): 331–58.

Corino, Karl: "Vor und nach der Wende: Die Rezeption der DDR-Literatur in der Bundesrepublik und das Problem einer einheitlichen deutschen Literatur." *Neue deutsche Literatur* 39, No. 464 (1991): 146–64.

Craig, Gordon: "Fontane als Historiker." Vorwort to Fontane: *Der Krieg gegen Frankreich 1870–1871.* Vol. 1. Zürich: Manesse, 1985 (Manesse-Bibliothek der Weltgeschichte). xv–xxxii.

Craig, Gordon A.: *Germany 1866–1945.* Oxford: Clarendon Press, 1978 (Oxford History of Modern Europe. 5).

Craig, Gordon A.: *Die Politik der Unpolitischen: Deutsche Schriftsteller und die Macht 1770–1871.* Aus dem Engl. von Karl Heinz Siber. München: Beck, 1993.

Daemmrich, Horst S.: "Raabe's View of Historical Prosesses." Leo Lensing and Hans-Werner Peter, eds., *Wilhelm Raabe: Studien zu seinem Leben und Werk.* Braunschweig: pp-Vlg., 1981. 99–114.

Dahrendorf, Ralf: "Review of Grass's *Two States – One Nation.*" *New York Times* No. 48, 374, September 30, 1990, Section 7: 9.

Dahrendorf, Ralf: "Die Sache mit der Nation." *Merkur* 44 (1990): 825–26.

Dann, Otto: *Nation und Nationalismus in Deutschland 1770–1990.* München: Beck, 1993 (Beck'sche Reihe. 494).

Deiritz, Karl, and Hannes Krauss, eds., *Der deutsch-deutsche Literaturstreit oder "Freunde, es spricht sich schlecht mit gebundener Zunge": Analysen und Materialien.* Hamburg: Luchterhand Literaturverlag, 1991 (Sammlung Luchterhand. 1002).

Deiritz, Karl, and Hannes Krauss, eds., *Verrat an der DDR-Kunst? Rückblicke auf die DDR-Literatur.* Berlin: Aufbau Taschenbuch Verlag, 1993.

Demetz, Peter: *Formen des Realismus.* München: Hanser, 1964.

Demetz, Peter: "Das Kriegsbuch eines Romantikers: Theodor Fontane als Chronist der Feldzüge von 1866." *Frankfurter Allgemeine Zeitung* No. 177, August 2, 1980: Beilage "Bilder und Zeiten" [5].

Demetz, Peter: "Weißer Sklave Fontane. Kriegsberichterstatter und Selbstinterpret." *Frankfurter Allgemeine Zeitung* No. 70, March 23, 1974: Beilage "Bilder und Zeiten" [5].

Denkler, Horst: *Wilhelm Raabe: Legende – Leben – Literatur.* Tübingen: Niemeyer, 1989.

Denkler, Horst: "Zwischen Julirevolution (1830) und Märzrevolution (1848/49)." Walter Hinderer, ed., *Geschichte der politischen Lyrik in Deutschland.* Stuttgart: Reclam, 1976. 179–209.

Derrida, Jacques: *Grammatologie (De la grammatologie, dt.).* Übersetzt von Hans-Jörg Rheinberger und Hanns Zischler. Frankfurt a.M.: Suhrkamp, 1983 (suhrkamp taschenbuch wissenschaft. 417).

Dieckmann, Christoph: "Ali Baba und die Mörder." *Die Zeit* No. 1, January 1, 1993: 54.

Dieckmann, Christoph: "Mit uns zieht die neue Zeit: Zehn Kapitelchen zum 1. Republikgeburtstag." *Neue Deutsche Literatur* 39, No. 463 (1991): 73–88.

Dieckmann, Friedrich: *Glockenläuten und offene Fragen: Berichte und Diagnosen aus dem anderen Deutschland.* Frankfurt a. M.: Suhrkamp, 1991 (edition suhrkamp. 1644).

Dieckmann, Friedrich: "Kulturaustausch." *Neue deutsche Literatur* 39, No. 457 (1991): 38–41.

Dieckmann, Friedrich: "Staatsräume im Innern Berlins: Ein Streifzug." *Sinn und Form* 44 (1992): 548–65.

Dieckmann, Friedrich: "Unsere oder eine andere Geschichte?" *Der Berliner Tagesspiegel*, July 31, 1991.

Diere, Horst: "Zur Geschichtspropaganda der herrschenden Klassen im preußisch-deutschen Geschichtsunterricht zwischen 1848/49 und 1917." *Geschichtsunterricht und Staatsbürgerkunde* 13 (1971): 979–91.

Doerry, Martin: *Übergangsmenschen: Die Mentalität der Wilhelminer und die Krise des Kaiserreichs.* [Hauptbd. u. Erg.bd.] Weinheim, München: Juventa, 1986.

Domdey, Horst: "Feindbild: BRD." *Kursbuch* 109 (1992): 63–79.

Drescher, Angela, ed., *Christa Wolf: Ein Arbeitsbuch: Studien-Dokumente-Bibliographie.* Berlin, Weimar: Aufbau, 1989.

Drescher, Angela, ed., *Dokumentation zu Christa Wolf "Nachdenken über Christa T."* Hamburg: Luchterhand Literaturverlag, 1991.

Düding, Dieter: *Organisierter gesellschaftlicher Nationalismus in Deutschland (1808–1847): Bedeutung und Funktion der Turner- und Sängervereine für die deutsche Nationalbewegung.* München: Oldenbourg, 1984.

Durzak, Manfred: "Geschichte ist absurd. Eine Antwort auf Hegel. Ein Gespräch mit Günter Grass." Manfred Durzak, ed., *Zu Günter Grass: Geschichte auf dem poetischen Prüfstand.* Stuttgart: Klett, 1985 (Literaturwissenschaft – Gesellschaftswissenschaft. 68; LGW-Interpretationen). 9–19.

Eagleton, Terry: *Ideology: An Introduction.* London, New York: Verso, 1991.

Eggert, Hartmut: "Der historische Roman des 19. Jahrhunderts." Helmut Koopmann, ed., *Handbuch des deutschen Romans.* Düsseldorf: Bagel, 1983. 342–55.

Eggert, Hartmut: *Studien zur Wirkungsgeschichte des deutschen historischen Romans 1850–1870.* Frankfurt a. M.: Klostermann, 1971 (Studien zur Philosophie und Literatur des 19. Jahrhunderts. 14).

Eley, Geoff: *Reshaping the German Right: Radical Nationalism and Political Change after Bismarck.* Ann Arbor: University of Michigan Press, 1991.

Eley, Geoff: "What Produces Fascism: Preindustrial Traditions or a Crisis of the Capitalist State?" Michael N. Dobkowski and Isidor Wallimann, eds., *Radical Perspectives on the Rise of Fascism in Germany, 1919–1945.* New York: Monthly Review Press, 1989. 69–99.

Endler, Adolf: *Den Tiger reiten: Aufsätze, Polemiken und Notizen zur Lyrik der DDR.* Frankfurt a. M.: Luchterhand, 1990.

Engel, Eduard: *Geschichte der Deutschen Literatur von den Anfängen bis zur Gegenwart.* Vol. 2: *Von Goethe bis in die Gegenwart.* 2. Aufl. Leipzig: Freytag; Wien: Tempsky, 1907.

Engelberg, Stephen: "The Velvet Revolution gets rough." *The New York Times, Magazine* No. 48, 983, May 31, 1992: 30–54.

Ergang, Robert R.: *Herder and the Foundations of German Nationalism.* New York: Columbia University Press, 1931.

F., B.: "Herr Friedrich Nietzsche und die deutsche Cultur." *Die Grenzboten* 32:4 (1873): 104–10.

Faden, Eberhard: "Berlin: Hauptstadt – seit wann und wodurch?" *Jahrbuch für brandenburgische Landesgeschichte* 1 (1950): 17–34.

Faulenbach, Bernd: *Ideologie des deutschen Weges: Die deutsche Geschichte in der Historiographie zwischen Kaiserreich und Nationalsozialismus.* München: Beck, 1980.

Fehrenbach, Elisabeth: *Wandlungen des deutschen Kaisergedankens 1871–1918.* München: Oldenbourg, 1969 (Studien zur Geschichte des Neunzehnten Jahrhunderts. 1).

Fehrenbach, Elisabeth: "Über die Bedeutung der politischen Symbole im Nationalstaat." *Historische Zeitschrift* 213 (1971): 296–357.

Fontane, Friedrich: "Theodor Fontanes 'Akademiezeit.' Nach ungedruckten Briefen, Konzepten und Dokumenten." *Märkische Zeitung* Beilage 10 (1928).

Forderer, Christof: *Die Großstadt im Roman: Berliner Großstadtdarstellungen zwischen Naturalismus und Moderne.* Wiesbaden: Deutscher Universitäts-Verlag, 1992.

Frank, Horst Joachim: *Dichtung, Sprache, Menschenbildung: Geschichte des Deutschunterrichts von den Anfängen bis 1945.* München: Deutscher Taschenbuch Verlag, 1973.

Franke, Konrad: *Die Literatur der Deutschen Demokratischen Republik.* Mit einem einführenden Essay von Heinrich Vormweg. Aktualisierte Ausgabe. Vol. 1–2. Frankfurt a. M.: Fischer Taschenbuch Verlag, 1980 (Kindlers Literaturgeschichte der Gegenwart. 3–4).

Freund, Winfried: "Der späte Freiligrath – ein Dichter des Friedens. Zum 175. Geburtstag Ferdinand Freiligraths am 17. Juni 1985." *Grabbe-Jahrbuch* 4 (1985): 46–57.

Fricke, Hermann: "Theodor Fontanes 'Der deutsche Krieg 1866' und seine militärgeschichtlichen Helfer." *Jahrbuch für die Geschichte Mittel- und Ostdeutschlands* 15 (1967): 203–224.

Fricke, Hermann: "Theodor Fontanes Kriegsgefangenschaft 1870. Quellenmäßig dargestellt." *Der Bär von Berlin* 5 (1955): 53–73.

Fricke, Hermann: "Theodor Fontanes Parole d'honneur von 1870." *Der Bär von Berlin* 15 (1965): 59–70.

Friedrich, Gerhard: *Fontanes preußische Welt: Armee – Dynastie – Staat.* Herford: Mittler, 1988.

Fuhrmann, Horst: *Das Interesse am Mittelalter in heutiger Zeit: Betrachtungen und Vermutungen.* Theodor-Schieder-Gedächtnisvorlesung; Lothar Gall: *Theodor Schieder 1908–1984.* München: Oldenbourg, 1987 (Schriften des Historischen Kollegs. Dokumentationen. 2).

Funk, Holger, and Reinhard G. Wittman: *Literatur Hauptstadt: Schriftsteller in Berlin heute.* Berlin: Berlin Verlag, 1983.

Gall, Lothar: *Bismarck: Der weiße Revolutionär.* Berlin: Propyläen, 1980.

Gellner, Ernest: *Nations and Nationalism.* Ithaca, N.Y., London: Cornell University Press, 1983.

Geppert, Hans Vilmar: *Der "andere" historische Roman: Theorie und Strukturen einer diskontinuierlichen Gattung.* Tübingen: Niemeyer, 1976 (Studien zur deutschen Literatur. 42).

Geyer, Dietrich: "Die DDR auf dem Weg zu einer eigenen historischen Identität? DDR-Geschichte und Geschichtswissenschaft zwischen Ost und West." Gerd Meyer and Jürgen Schröder, eds., *DDR heute: Wandlungstendenzen und Widersprüche in einer sozialistischen Industriegesellschaft.* Tübingen: Narr, 1988. 39–51.

Glass, Derek, Dietmar Rösler, and John J. White, eds., *Berlin: Literary Images of a City/Eine Großstadt im Spiegel der Literatur.* Berlin: Schmidt, 1989.

Glockner, Eckhard: *Zur Schulreform im preußischen Imperialismus: Preußische Schul- und Bildungspolitik im Spannungsfeld der Schulkonferenzen von 1890, 1900 und 1920.* Glashütten: Auvermann, 1976.

Gödeke, Karl: *Deutschlands Dichter von 1813 bis 1843: Eine Auswahl von 872 charakteristischen Gedichten aus 131 Dichtern, mit biographisch-literarischen Bemerkungen und einer einleitenden Abhandlung über die technische Bildung poetischer Formen.* Hannover: Hahn'sche Hofbuchhdlg., 1843.

Goebel, Klaus: "Des Kaisers neuer Geschichtsunterricht." *Geschichte in Wissenschaft und Unterricht* 25 (1974): 709–17.

Gottschall, Rudolf von: "Georg Herwegh. Ein Essay." *Unsere Zeit* 11 (1875): 721–35.

Grasskamp, Walter: "Die unästhetische Demokratie. Zusammenwachsen wird auch, was nicht zusammengehört." *Die Zeit* No. 40, September 28, 1990: 71–2.

Grawe, Christian: "Schillers Gedichtentwurf 'Deutsche Größe': 'Ein Nationalhymnus im höchsten Stil'? Ein Beispiel ideologischen Mißbrauchs in der Germanistik seit 1871." *Jahrbuch der deutschen Schillergesellschaft* 36 (1992): 166–96.

Grawe, Christian: "Von Krieg und Kriegsgeschrei: Fontanes Kriegsdarstellungen im Kontext." *Theodor Fontane im literarischen Leben seiner Zeit.* Beiträge zur Fontane-Konferenz vom 17. bis 20. Juni 1986 in Potsdam. Mit einem Vorwort von Otfried Keiler. Berlin: Theodor-Fontane-Archiv, 1987 (Beiträge aus der Deutschen Staatsbibliothek). 67–106.

Greiner, Ulrich: "Die deutsche Gesinnungsästhetik. Noch einmal: Christa Wolf und der deutsche Literaturstreit. Eine Zwischenbilanz." *Die Zeit* No. 45, November 2, 1990: 59–60.

Greiner, Ulrich: "Kassandra, arbeitslos: Günter Grass verläßt die SPD." *Die Zeit* No. 2, January 8, 1993: 41.

Greiner, Ulrich: "Mangel an Feingefühl." *Die Zeit* No. 23, June 1, 1990: 63.

Greiner, Ulrich: "Plädoyer für Schluß der Stasi-Debatte." *Die Zeit* No. 6, February 5, 1993: 60.

Groß, Werner: *Die ersten Schritte: Der Kampf der Antifaschisten in Schwarzenberg während der unbesetzten Zeit Mai/Juni 1945.* Berlin: Rütten & Loening, 1961 (Studien zur Zeitgeschichte. 1).

Grosser, Johannes Franz Gottlieb, ed., *Die grosse Kontroverse: Ein Briefwechsel um Deutschland.* Hamburg, Genf, Paris: Nagel, 1963.

Groys, Boris: *Über das Neue: Versuch einer Kulturökonomie.* München, Wien: Hanser, 1992 (Edition Akzente).

Günther-Arndt, Hilke: "Monarchische Präventivbelehrung oder curriculare Reform? Zur Wirkung des Kaiser-Erlasses vom 1. Mai 1889 auf den Geschichtsunterricht." Karl-Ernst Jeismann, ed., *Bildung, Staat, Gesellschaft im 19. Jahrhundert: Mobilisierung und Disziplinierung.* Stuttgart: Steiner, 1989 (Nassauer Gespräche der Freiherr-vom-Stein-Gesellschaft. 2). 256–75.

Haase, Horst: "Individuum und Geschichte. Aspekte in neuerer DDR-Literatur." *Weimarer Beiträge* 35 (1989): 1720–25.

Habermas, Jürgen, ed., *Stichworte zur "geistigen Situation der Zeit"*. Vol. 1–2. Frankfurt a. M.: Suhrkamp, 1979 (edition suhrkamp. 1000).

Habermas, Jürgen: "Die andere Zerstörung der Vernunft. Über die Defizite der deutschen Vereinigung und über die Rolle der intellektuellen Kritik." *Die Zeit* No. 20, May 10, 1991: 63–4.

Habermas, Jürgen: "Die zweite Lebenslüge der Bundesrepublik: Wir sind wieder 'normal' geworden." *Die Zeit* No. 51, December 11, 1992: 48.

Hacker, Jens: *Deutsche Irrtümer: Schönfärber und Helfershelfer der SED-Diktatur im Westen*. Berlin, Frankfurt a. M.: Ullstein, 1992.

Hage, Volker: "Kunstvolle Prosa." *Die Zeit* No. 23, June 1, 1990: 63–4.

Hage, Volker: "Versprengte Tataren: 'Gedichte sind im Aussterben begriffen' – Schreckensmeldung, Polemik, Abgesang? Eine Situationsbeschreibung zeitgenössischer Lyrik." *Die Zeit* No. 50, December 8, 1989, suppl. "Literatur": 8.

Hähnel, Ingrid, and Klaus-Dieter: "Junge Lyrik am Ende der siebziger Jahre." *Weimarer Beiträge* 7 (1979): 127–54.

Handler, Richard: *Nationalism and the Politics of Culture in Quebec*. Madison: University of Wisconsin Press, 1988.

Hanke, Irma: "Sozialistischer Neohistorismus? Aspekte der Identitätsdebatte in der DDR." Gert-Joachim Glaeßner, ed., *Die DDR in der Ära Honecker: Politik – Kultur – Gesellschaft*. Opladen: Westdeutscher Verlag, 1988 (Schriften des Zentralinstituts für sozialwissenschaftliche Forschung der Freien Universität Berlin. 56). 56–76.

Hankel, Wilhelm: *Die sieben Todsünden der Vereinigung: Wege aus dem Wirtschaftsdesaster*. Berlin: Siedler, 1993.

Hansen, Wilhelm: *Nationaldenkmäler und Nationalfeste im 19. Jahrhundert*. Lüneburg: Niederdeutscher Verband für Volks- und Altertumskunde, Museum, 1976 (Niederdeutscher Verband für Volks- und Altertumskunde. 1).

Hardtwig, Wolfgang, and Harm-Hinrich Brandt, eds., *Deutschlands Weg in die Moderne: Politik, Gesellschaft und Kultur im 19. Jahrhundert*. München: Beck, 1993.

Hardtwig, Wolfgang: *Geschichtskultur und Wissenschaft*. München: Deutscher Taschenbuch Verlag, 1990 (dtv wissenschaft. 4539).

Harlan, David: "Intellectual History and the Return of Literature." *American Historical Review* 94 (1989): 581–609.

Hartmann, Fritz: "Gutmanns Reisen: Raabes politischer Roman." *Mitteilungen der Gesellschaft der Freunde Wilhelm Raabes* (1931): 156–71.

Hartung, Klaus: "Ein Spaziergang der Demokraten." *Die Zeit* No. 47, November 13, 1992: 2.

Das Hauptstadtproblem in der Geschichte. Festgabe zum 90. Geb. für Friedrich Meinecke. Gewidmet vom Friedrich-Meinecke-Institut an der Freien Universität Berlin. Tübingen: Niemeyer, 1952 (Jahrbuch für Geschichte des deutschen Ostens. 1).

Haverkamp, Anselm, Renate Lachmann, and Reinhart Herzog, eds., *Memoria: Vergessen und Erinnern*. München: Fink, 1993 (Poetik und Hermeneutik. 15).

Haxthausen, Charles W., and Heidrun Suhr, eds., *Berlin: Culture and Metropolis*. Minneapolis: University of Minnesota Press, 1990.

Hayes, Carlton J. H.: *The Historical Evolution of Modern Nationalism*. New York: Russell and Russell, 1968.

Heinel, Jürgen: *Die deutsche Sozialpolitik des 19. Jahrhunderts im Spiegel der Schulgeschichtsbücher*. Braunschweig: Limbach, 1962.

Hellfaier, Karl-Alexander, ed., *Ferdinand Freiligrath – Ein Dichter des 19. Jahrhunderts. Eine Ausstellung zur Wiederkehr seines 100. Todesjahres*. Detmold: Selbstverl. der Lippischen Landesbibliothek Detmold, 1976 (Auswahl- u. Ausstellungskataloge der Lippischen Landesbibliothek Detmold. 3).

Henke, Klaus-Dietmar, and Claudio Natoli, eds., *Mit dem Pathos der Nüchternheit: Martin Broszat, das Institut für Zeitgeschichte und die Erforschung des Nationalsozialismus*. Frankfurt a. M., New York: Campus, 1991.

Henrich, Friedhelm: "'Wunsiedel und die Gründung des Deutschen Nationalvereins.' Polarität und Komplexität in Wilhelm Raabes 'Gutmanns Reisen.'" *Jahrbuch der Raabe-Gesellschaft* (1991): 6–32.

Herrmann, Renate: *Gustav Freytag: Bürgerliches Selbstverständnis und preußisch-deutsches Nationalbewußtsein. Ein Beitrag zur Geschichte des national-liberalen Bürgertums der Reichsgründungszeit*. Würzburg, Phil. Diss., 1974.

Herzinger, Richard: *Masken der Lebensrevolution: Vitalistische Zivilisations- und Humanismuskritik in Texten Heiner Müllers*. München: Fink, 1992.

Herzinger, Richard: "Naturschützer im Reich der Transsubstantiation: Zur literaturtheoretischen Einhegung ehemaliger DDR-Schriftsteller." *Frankfurter Rundschau* No. 137, June 17, 1993.

Herzinger, Richard: "Die obskuren Inseln der kultivierten Gemeinschaft: Heiner Müller, Christa Wolf, Volker Braun – deutsche Zivilisationskritik und das deutsche Antiwestlertum." *Die Zeit* No. 23, June 4, 1993: L 8.

Hesse, Egmont, ed., *Sprache & Antwort: Stimmen und Texte einer anderen Literatur aus der DDR*. Frankfurt a. M.: Fischer, 1988.

Heydemann, Günther: "Partner oder Konkurrent? Das britische Deutschlandbild während des Wiedervereinigungsprozesses 1989–1991." Franz Bosbach, ed., *Feindbilder: Die Darstellung des Gegners in der politischen Publizistik des Mittelalters und der Neuzeit*. Köln, Weimar, Wien: Böhlau, 1992. 201–34.

Heydick, Lutz, Günther Hoppe and Jürgen John, eds., *Historischer Führer: Stätten und Denkmale der Geschichte in den Bezirken Leipzig, Karl-Marx-Stadt*. Leipzig, Jena, Berlin: Urania, 1981.

Hinck, Walter: "Epigonendichtung und Nationalidee. Zur Lyrik Emanuel Geibels." Hinck: *Von Heine zu Brecht: Lyrik im Geschichtsprozeß*. Frankfurt a. M.: Suhrkamp, 1978 (suhrkamp taschenbuch. 481). 60–82.

Hinneberg, Paul, ed., *Die Kultur der Gegenwart*. Teil 1, Abt. 1: *Die allgemeinen Grundlagen der Kultur der Gegenwart*. Berlin, Leipzig: Teubner, 1906.

"Historikerstreit": Die Dokumentation der Kontroverse um die Einzigartigkeit der nationalsozialistischen Judenvernichtung. Texte von Rudolf Augstein [u.a.]. München, Zürich: Piper, 1987 (Serie Piper. 816).

Hobsbawm, Eric: "Inventing Traditions." Eric Hobsbawm and Terence Ranger, eds., *The Invention of Tradition*. New York: Cambridge University Press, 1983. 1–14.

Höfele, Karl Heinrich: *Geist und Gesellschaft der Bismarckzeit (1870–1890)*. Göttingen [u.a.]: Musterschmidt, 1967.

Hoffmann, Christa: *Stunden Null? Vergangenheitsbewältigung in Deutschland 1945 und 1989*. Mit einem Vorw. von Alfred Streim. Bonn, Berlin: Bouvier, 1992 (Schriftenreihe Extremismus & Demokratie. 2).

Hoffmann, Gerd E.: "Die schiefen Türme: Stasi-Diktatur und Geldstromland. Anmerkungen eines Wessis zu den Ossis und unseren gemeinsamen Problemen." *Neue Deutsche Literatur* 40, No. 478 (1992): 144–50.

Hoffmann, Hilmar, ed., *"Kulturzerstörung?" 10. Römerberggespräche in Frankfurt am Main*. Mit Beiträgen von Jurek Becker u. a. Königstein/Ts.: Athenäum, 1983.

Holz, Claus: *Flucht aus der Wirklichkeit: "Die Ahnen" von Gustav Freytag. Untersuchungen zum realistischen Roman der Gründerzeit 1872–1880*. Frankfurt a. M., Bern: Lang, 1983 (Europäische Hochschulschriften. Reihe 1: Deutsche Sprache und Literatur. 624).

Honolka, Harro: *Schwarzrotgrün: Die Bundesrepublik auf der Suche nach ihrer Identität*. München: Beck, 1987 (Beck'sche Reihe. 346).

Hoppe, Karl: "Aphorismen Raabes. Chronologisch geordnet." Karl Hoppe: *Wilhelm Raabe: Beiträge zum Verständnis seiner Person und seines Werkes*. Göttingen: Vandenhoeck & Ruprecht, 1966. 87–129.

Hörnigk, Therese: *Christa Wolf*. Göttingen: Steidl, 1989.

Huder, Walther, ed., *Theodor Fontane und die preußische Akademie der Künste*. Berlin: Berliner Handpresse, 1971.

Huesmann, Michael: "'…sie wissen nicht was sie tun': 'Jungdeutsches' Bildungsbewußtsein und bürgerliche Krisenerfahrung als biographische Grundlagen Heinrich Laubes." *Wirkendes Wort* 41 (1991): 27–47.

Hughes, Henry Stuart: Consciousness and Society. The Reorientation of European Social Thought 1890–1930. Brighton: Harvester Press 1979.

Humann, Klaus, ed., *Wir sind das Geld: Wie die Westdeutschen die DDR aufkaufen*. Reinbek: Rowohlt, 1991 (rororo aktuell. 12925).

Humphrey, Richard: "The Napoleonic Wars in the Historical Fiction of the 'Gründerjahre'. Fontane and his Contemporaries in European Perspective." Gisela Brude-Firnau and Karin J. MacHardy, eds., *Fact and Fiction: German History and Literature, 1848–1924*. Tübingen: Francke, 1990 (Edition Orpheus. 2). 111–22.

Hutchinson, Peter: *Literary Representations of Divided Germany: The Development of a Central Theme in East German Fiction 1945–1970*. Cambridge: Cambridge University Press, 1977.

Huyssen, Andreas: *After the Great Divide: Modernism, Mass Culture, Postmodernism*. Houndmills, London: Macmillan, 1988 (Language, Discourse, Society).

Huyssen, Andreas: "After the Wall: The Failure of German Intellectuals." *New German Critique* 52 (Winter 1991): 109–42.

Iggers, Georg G.: *The German Conception of History: The National Tradition of Historical Thought from Herder to the Present*. Middletown, Conn.: Wesleyan University Press, 1966.

Jacobson, Manfred R.: "*Jürg Jenatsch*. The Narration of History." *Amsterdamer Beiträge zur neueren Germanistik* 9 (1979): 73–88.

Jäger, Friedrich, and Jörn Rüsen: *Geschichte des Historismus: Eine Einführung*. München: Beck, 1992.

James, Harold: *A German Identity: 1770–1970*. New York: Routledge, 1989.

Jameson, Frederic: *The Political Unconscious: Narrative as a Socially Symbolic Act*. Ithaca, N.Y.: Cornell University Press, 1981.

Janssen-Aimmermann, Antje: "Perspektiven. Perspektiven? Positionen deutschsprachiger Literatur nach dem Ende der DDR." *Neue Deutsche Literatur* 39, No. 461 (1991): 154–61.

Jarausch, Konrad: "The Failure of East German Anti-Fascism. Some Ironies of History as Politics." *German Studies Review* 14 (1991): 85–102.

Jarausch, Konrad, ed., *Zwischen Parteilichkeit und Professionalität: Bilanz der Geschichtswissenschaft der DDR*. Berlin: Akademie-Verlag, 1991.

Jens, Walter: "Plädoyer gegen die Preisgabe der DDR-Kultur. Fünf Forderungen an die Intellektuellen im geeinten Deutschland." *Süddeutsche Zeitung* No. 136, June 16, 1991: 14–6.

Joas, Hans, and Martin Kohli, eds., *Der Zusammenbruch der DDR: Soziologische Analysen*. Frankfurt a. M.: Suhrkamp, 1993 (edition suhrkamp. 1777).

Jolles, Charlotte: *Fontane und die Politik*. Berlin: Bernburg, 1936.

Kaufmann, Walter: "A Cultural Clearout." *Index on Censorship* 21:1 (1992): 20–21.

Kebbel, Gerhard: *Geschichtengeneratoren: Lektüren zur Poetik des historischen Romans*. Tübingen: Niemeyer, 1992 (Communicatio. 2).

Kellner, Hans: "Triangular Anxieties: The Present State of European Intellectual History." Kellner: *Language and Historical Representation: Getting the Story Crooked*. Madison: University of Wisconsin Press, 1989. 267–93.

Kennedy, Katharine D.: *Lessons and Learners: Elementary Education in Southern Germany, 1871–1914*. Stanford Ph.D., 1981.

Kennedy, Katharine D.: "Regionalism and Nationalism in South German History Lessons, 1871–1914." *German Studies Review* 12 (1989): 11–33.

Kiaulehn, Walter: *Berlin: Schicksal einer Weltstadt*. München: Biederstein, 1958.

Killy, Walter, ed., *Literatur-Lexikon: Autoren und Werke deutscher Sprache*. Vol. 1–15. München: Bertelsmann, 1989–1993.

Kocka, Jürgen: *Klassengesellschaft im Krieg 1914–1918*. Göttingen: Vandenhoeck & Ruprecht, 1973.

Kocka, Jürgen: "Probleme der politischen Integration der Deutschen 1867 bis 1945." Otto Büsch and James J. Sheehan, eds., *Die Rolle der Nation in der deutschen Geschichte und Gegenwart*. Beiträge zu einer internat. Konf. in Berlin (West) von 16. bis 18. Juni 1983. Mit Beiträgen von Karl Otmar von Aretin [u.a.]. Berlin: Colloquium, 1985. (Einzelveröffentlichungen der Historischen Kommission zu Berlin. 50). 119–36.

Kocka, Jürgen: "Revolution und Nation 1989. Zur historischen Einordnung der gegenwärtigen Ereignisse." *Tel Aviver Jahrbuch für deutsche Geschichte* 19 (1990): 479–99.

Kocka, Jürgen: "Zurück zur Erzählung? Plädoyer für historische Argumentation." *Geschichte und Gesellschaft* 10 (1984): 395–408.

Kohn, Hans: *The Idea of Nationalism: A Study in Its Origins and Background*. New York: Macmillan, 1944.

König, Helmut: *Imperialistische und militaristische Erziehung in den Hörsälen und Schulstuben Deutschlands 1870–1960*. Berlin: Volk und Wissen, 1962.

Konrád, György: *Die Melancholie der Wiedergeburt*. Aus dem Ungarischen von Hans-Henning Paetzke. Frankfurt a. M.: Suhrkamp, 1992 (edition suhrkamp. 1720).

Korte, Karl-Rudolf: *Über Deutschland schreiben: Schriftsteller sehen ihren Staat*. München: Beck, 1992 (Perspektiven und Orientierungen. 12).

Koshar, Rudy: "Playing the Cerebral Savage: Notes on Writing German History before the Linguistic Turn." *Central European History* 22 (1989): 343–59.

Krenzlin, Norbert, ed., *Zwischen Angstmetapher und Terminus: Theorien der Massenkultur seit Nietzsche*. Berlin: Akademie-Verlag, 1992.

Kügler, Hans: "Positionen – Schriftsteller zur deutschen Einheit. Über die Verarbeitung politischer Erfahrungen." *Praxis Deutsch* 112 (1992): 4–14.

Kultur und Macht – Deutsche Literatur 1949–1989. Hrsg. vom Sekretariat für kulturelle Zusammenarbeit nichttheatertragender Städte und Gemeinden in Nordrhein-Westfalen, Gütersloh. Red. Leitung: Sabine Kyora. Bielefeld: Aisthesis, 1992.

Lange, Annemarie: *Berlin zur Zeit Bebels und Bismarcks: Zwischen Reichsgründung und Jahrhundertwende.* Berlin: Dietz, 1972.

Langewiesche, Dieter: *Liberalismus in Deutschland.* Frankfurt a. M.: Suhrkamp, 1988 (Neue Historische Bibliothek; edition suhrkamp. 1286).

Langguth, Gerd, ed., *Berlin: Vom Brennpunkt der Teilung zur Brücke der Einheit.* Köln: Kemmer, 1990.

Langsam, Walter Consuelo: "Nationalism and History in the Prussian Elementary Schools under William II." Edward Mead Earle, ed., *Nationalism and Internationalism: Essays Inscribed to Carlton J. H. Hayes.* New York: Columbia University Press, 1950. 241–60.

Lehnert, Herbert: "Fiktionalität und autobiographische Motive: Zu Christa Wolfs Erzählung *Was bleibt*." *Weimarer Beiträge* 37 (1991): 423–44.

Lemmermann, Heinz: *Kriegserziehung im Kaiserreich: Studien zur politischen Funktion von Schule und Schulmusik 1890–1918.* Vol. 1–2. Lilienthal, Bremen: Eres Edition, 1984.

Lepenies, Wolf: "Alles rechtens – nichts mit rechten Dingen." *Die Zeit* No. 51, December 11, 1992: 87–8.

Lepenies, Wolf: *Folgen einer unerhörten Begebenheit: Die Deutschen nach der Vereinigung.* Berlin: Siedler, 1992 (Corso bei Siedler).

Lepsius, M. Rainer: "Parteiensystem und Sozialstruktur: Zum Problem der Demokratisierung der deutschen Gesellschaft." Wilhelm Abel, et al., eds., *Wirtschaft, Geschichte und Wirtschaftsgeschichte: Festschrift zum 65. Geburtstag von Friedrich Lütge.* Stuttgart: Fischer, 1966. 371–93.

Lieser-Triebnigg, Erika, and Siegfried Mampel, eds., *Kultur im geteilten Deutschland.* Berlin: Duncker & Humblot, 1984 (Schriftenreihe der Gesellschaft für Deutschlandforschung. 9).

Limlei, Michael: *Geschichte als Ort der Bewährung: Menschenbild und Gesellschaftsverständnis in den deutschen historischen Romanen (1820–1890).* Frankfurt a. M. [u.a.]: Lang, 1988 (Studien zur Deutschen Literatur des 19. und 20. Jahrhunderts. 5).

Lingg, Hermann: "Über moderne Lyrik." *Die Gegenwart* 1, no. 4, February 17 (1872): 57–8.

Loewy, Hanno, ed., *Holocaust: Die Grenzen des Verstehens: Eine Debatte über die Besetzung der Geschichte.* Reinbek: Rowohlt Taschenbuch Verlag, 1992 (rororo sachbuch. 9367).

Loster-Schneider, Gudrun: *Der Erzähler Fontane: Seine politischen Positionen in den Jahren 1864–1898 und ihre ästhetische Vermittlung.* Tübingen: Narr, 1986 (Mannheimer Beiträge zur Sprach- und Literaturwissenschaft. 11).

Loster-Schneider, Gudrun: "Zur Neuauflage eines Kriegs- und Antikriegsbuches. Theodor Fontanes 'Der Krieg gegen Frankreich 1870–1871'." *Francia* 14 (1986): 610–17.

Löwenthal, Leo: *Erzählkunst und Gesellschaft: Die Gesellschaftsproblematik in der deutschen Literatur des 19. Jahrhunderts*. Neuwied, Berlin: Luchterhand, 1971.

Lübeck, Wilfried: *Die Rolle der Kriegervereine im System des preußisch-deutschen Militarismus bis zum Ausbruch des I. Weltkrieges*. Halle, Diss., 1974.

Lutz, Sabine Beate: *Vom Ereignis zur Erzählung: Ein Vergleich zwischen Conrad Ferdinand Meyers Geschichtsdichtung und der zeitgenössischen Geschichtsschreibung*. University of California, Davis, Ph. D., 1986.

Mangoldt, Renate von: *Berlin Literarisch: 120 Autoren aus Ost und West*. Berlin: Argon, 1988.

Manthey, Jürgen: "Wilhelm Raabe und das Scheitern des deutschen Liberalismus." *Jahrbuch der Raabe-Gesellschaft* 1976: 69–106.

Marcus, J. S.: "Berlin: Into the Future." *New York Times Magazine* Part 2, October 18, 1992: 16, 84–93.

Martin, Nicolas: *Les Poètes contemporains de l'Allemagne*. Paris: J. Renouard, 1846.

Martini, Fritz: "Über die gegenwärtigen Schwierigkeiten des historischen Erzählens." Oswald Hauser, ed., *Geschichte und Geschichtsbewußtsein. 19 Vorträge*. Göttingen, Zürich: Muster-Schmidt, 1981. 246–69.

Matt, Peter von: "Theodor Fontane als Langweiler." *Frankfurter Allgemeine Zeitung* No. 74, March 28, 1987.

Mayer, Hans: *Der Turm von Babel: Erinnerung an eine Deutsche Demokratische Republik*. Frankfurt a. M.: Suhrkamp, 1991.

Mayer, Hans: "Nachdenken über Kultur im heutigen Deutschland." *Neue deutsche Literatur* 40, No. 471 (1992): 68–90.

Megill, Allan: "Foucault, Structuralism, and the Ends of History." *Journal of Modern History* 51 (1989): 451–503.

Mehden, Heilwig von der, ed., *Vor allem eins, mein Kind… Was deutsche Mädchen und Knaben zur Kaiserzeit gelesen haben*. Hamburg: Hoffmann und Campe, 1972.

Meier, Christian: *Die Nation, die keine sein will*. München: Hanser, 1991 (Aktuelle Reihe).

Meier, Christian: "Die deutsche Einheit als Herausforderung." *Frankfurter Allgemeine Zeitung* No. 95, April 24, 1990: 36.

Meinecke, Friedrich: *Die Idee der Staatsräson in der neueren Geschichte*. Hrsg. u. eingeleitet von Walther Hofer. 3. Aufl. München: Oldenbourg, 1963 (Meinecke: *Werke*. 1).

Menne, Angelika: *Einigkeit und Unité: Die Legitimation politischer Vorgänge mit lyrischen Mitteln in den deutschen und französischen Kriegsgedichten 1870–71*. Berlin (FU), Diss., 1980.

Meran, Josef: *Theorien in der Geschichtswissenschaft: Die Diskussion um die Wissenschaftlichkeit der Geschichte*. Göttingen: Vandenhoeck & Ruprecht, 1985 (Kritische Studien zur Geschichtswissenschaft. 66).

Mercer, Wendy: "From Idyll to Arsenal: The Changing Image of Germany in France As Seen through the Work of Xavier Marmier (1808–1892)." *New Comparison: A Journal of Comparative and General Studies* 6 (1988): 176–93.

Merschmeier, Michael: "'Guten Abend, wir sinken. Darf ich mich setzen?' Glanz und Elend des Hauptstadttheaters – Kunst und Kasse, alte Kämpen und neue Stars." *Theater Heute* No. 3, 1992: 7–17, 20–2.

Meyer, Folkert: *Schule der Untertanen: Lehrer und Politik in Preußen 1848–1900*. Hamburg: Hoffmann und Campe, 1976.

Meyer, Richard M.: *Die deutsche Litteratur des Neunzehnten Jahrhunderts*. Berlin: Bondi, 1900 (Das Neunzehnte Jahrhundert in Deutschlands Entwicklung. 3).

Meyer-Krentler, Eckhardt: *Der Bürger als Freund: Ein sozialethisches Programm und seine Kritik in der neueren deutschen Erzählliteratur*. München: Fink, 1984.

Meyer-Krentler, Eckhardt: "Elektronische Einsichten: Neue Zugänge zu Raabes Tagebuch." *Jahrbuch der Raabe-Gesellschaft* (1991): 33–59.

Meyer-Krentler, Eckhardt: "Homerisches und wirkliches Blau. Wilhelm Raabe und sein Wetter." *Jahrbuch der Raabe-Gesellschaft* 1986: 50–82.

Meyer-Krentler, Eckhardt: "Stopfkuchen – Ein Doppelgänger: Wilhelm Raabe erzählt Theodor Storm." *Jahrbuch der Raabe-Gesellschaft* (1987): 179–204.

Meyer-Krentler, Eckhardt: *"Unterm Strich": Literarischer Markt, Trivialität und Romankunst in Raabes "Der Lar."* Paderborn: Schöningh, 1986 (Schriften der Universität Gesamthochschule Paderborn, Reihe Sprach- und Literaturwissenschaft. 8).

Meyer-Krentler, Eckhardt: "'Wir vom Handwerk': Raabe als Berufsschriftsteller." Harro Segeberg, ed., *Vom Wert der Arbeit: Zur literarischen Wahrnehmung des Wertkomplexes "Arbeit" in der deutschen Literatur (1770–1930)*. Dokumentation einer interdisziplinären Tagung in Hamburg vom 16. bis 18. März 1988. Tübingen: Niemeyer, 1991 (Studien und Texte zur Sozialgeschichte der Literatur. 34). 204–229.

Middell, Eike: *Literatur zweier Kaiserreiche: Deutsche und österreichische Literatur der Jahrhundertwende*. Berlin: Akademie-Verlag, 1993.

Mitter, Armin: "Die Aufarbeitung der DDR-Geschichte." Eckhard Jesse and Armin Mitter, eds., *Die Gestaltung der deutschen Einheit: Geschichte – Politik – Gesellschaft*. Bonn, Berlin: Bouvier, 1992. 365–87.

Modrow, Hans O.: *Berlin 1900: Querschnitt durch die Entwicklung einer Stadt um die Jahrhundertwende*. Berlin: Hobbing, 1936.

Mommsen, Wolfgang J.: "Wandlungen der nationalen Identität." Werner Weidenfeld, ed., *Die Identität der Deutschen*. München, Wien: Hanser, 1983. 170–192.

Mönninger, Michael, ed., *Das neue Berlin: Baugeschichte und Stadtplanung der deutschen Hauptstadt*. Frankfurt, Leipzig: Insel, 1991 (insel-taschenbuch. 1395).

Moos, Carlo: *Dasein als Erinnerung: Conrad Ferdinand Meyer und die Geschichte*. Bern, Frankfurt a. M.: Lang, 1973 (Geist und Werk der Zeiten. 35).

Muller, Jerry Z.: *The Other God That Failed: Hans Freyer and the Deradicalization of German Conservatism*. Princeton: Princeton University Press, 1987.

Muschg, Walter: *Die Zerstörung der deutschen Literatur*. 3., erw. Aufl. Bern: Francke, 1958.

Muschg, Walter: *Tragische Literaturgeschichte*. 4., gegenüber der dritten unveränd. Aufl. Bern, München: Francke, 1969.

Muschter, Gabriele, and Rüdiger Thomas, eds., *Jenseits der Staatskultur: Traditionen autonomer Kunst in der DDR*. München: Hanser, 1992.

Naimark, Norman: "'Ich will hier raus': Emigration and the Collapse of the German Democratic Republic." Ivo Banac, ed., *Eastern Europe in Revolution*. Ithaca, N. Y., London: Cornell University Press, 1992. 72–95.

Nawrocki, Joachim: "Angst vor Schutt und toten Zonen: Streit um die Hauptstadt: Die Berliner betrachten die Neubauwut und Abrißideen der Bonner Regierung mit Skepsis." *Die Zeit* No. 1, January 1, 1993: 22.

Neubert, Werner: "Raub bei Schiller." *Die Weltbühne* 39 (1984): 921–23.

Neuhaus, Volker: *Günter Grass*. 2., überarb. u. erw. Aufl. Stuttgart: Metzler, 1993 (Sammlung Metzler. 179).

Nipperdey, Thomas: *Deutsche Geschichte 1866–1918*. Vol. 2: *Machtstaat vor der Demokratie*. München: Beck, 1992.

Noltenius, Rainer: *Dichterfeiern in Deutschland: Rezeptionsgeschichte als Sozialgeschichte am Beispiel der Schiller- und Freiligrath-Feiern*. München: Fink, 1984

Noltenius, Rainer: "Die Einheit Deutschlands unter einem Schriftsteller als Führer: Raabes Schiller-Gedicht 1859 als politisches Glaubensbekenntnis." *Jahrbuch der Raabe-Gesellschaft* (1991): 60–81.

Nürnberger, Helmuth: *Der frühe Fontane: Politik, Poesie, Geschichte*. Frankfurt a. M.: Ullstein, 1975.

Nürnberger, Helmuth: *Theodor Fontane in Selbstzeugnissen und Bilddokumenten*. Reinbek: Rowohlt, 1968 (rowohlts monographien. 145).

Olson, James M.: "Nationalistic Values in Prussian Schoolbooks prior to World War I." *Canadian Review of Studies in Nationalism* 1 (1973): 47–59.

Olson, James M.: "The Social Values of Prussian Primary School Teachers During the Wilhelmian Era." *Paedagogia Historica* 15 (1975): 73–89.

Olt, Reinhard: *Wider das Fremde? Das Wirken des Allgemeinen Deutschen Sprachvereins in Hessen 1885–1944. Mit einer einleitenden Studie über Sprachreinigung und Fremdwortfrage in Deutschland und Frankreich seit dem 16. Jahrhundert*. Darmstadt, Marburg: Hessische Historische Kommission Darmstadt und Historische Kommission für Hessen, 1991.

Ören, Aras: *Wie die Spree in den Bosporus fließt: Briefe zwischen Istanbul und Berlin, 1990–1991*. Berlin: Verlag, 1991.

Osborne, John: *Meyer or Fontane: German Literature after the Franco-Prussian War 1870/71*. Bonn: Bouvier, 1983 (Abhandlungen zur Kunst-, Musik- und Literaturwissenschaft. 341).

Osborne, John: "Theodor Fontane und die Mobilmachung der Kultur: Der Krieg gegen Frankreich 1870–1871." *Fontane-Blätter* 5 (1982/84): 421–35.

Palmer, Bryan: *Descent into Discourse: The Reification of Language and the Writing of Social History*. Philadelphia: Temple University Press, 1990.

Pape, Walter: "'Ein Orpheus – mit den Liedern Andrer!' Ferdinand Freiligraths Anthologie poetologischer Lyrik *Dichtung und Dichter*." *Grabbe-Jahrbuch* 6 (1987): 82–104.

Pape, Walter: "'Die Wüsten- und Löwenpoesie war im Grunde auch nur revolutionair.' Ästhetischer Ursprung und ethische Legitimation von politischer Lyrik im 19. Jahrhundert am Beispiel Ferdinand Freiligraths." Schöne, Albrecht, ed., *Kontroversen, alte und neue: Akten des VII. Internationalen Germanistenkongresses, Göttingen 1985*. Vol. 8. Tübingen: Niemeyer, 1986. 66–77.

Paret, Peter: *The Berlin Secession: Modernism and Its Enemies in Imperial Germany*. Cambridge, MA: Harvard University Press; London: Belknap Press, 1980.

Parr, Rolf: *"Zwei Seelen wohnen, ach! In meiner Brust": Strukturen und Funktionen der Mythisierung Bismarcks (1860–1918)*. München: Fink, 1992.

Peisl, Anton, and Armin Mohler, eds., *Die Deutsche Neurose: Über die beschädigte Identität der Deutschen*. Frankfurt a. M.: Ullstein, 1980 (Schriften der Carl-Friedrich-von-Siemens-Stiftung. 3).

Peter, Hans-Werner: "'Wilhelm Raabe kommt in den bundesdeutschen Lehrplänen nicht vor.' Oder: Hat Raabe Bücher geschrieben, die gewonnen haben, da das Geschlecht, das sie jetzt liest, andere Röcke und Hosen trägt?" *Mitteilungen der Raabe-Gesellschaft* 66 (1979): 13–18.

Pinckney, Darryl: "Nicht länger Hongkong." *Neue Rundschau* 102:3 (1991): 14–7.

Pinson, Koppel S.: *A Bibliographical Introduction to Nationalism*. New York: Columbia University Press, 1935.

Pinson, Koppel S.: *Pietism as a Factor in the Rise of German Nationalism*. New York: Columbia University Press, 1934.

Pommerin, Reiner: *Von Berlin nach Bonn: Die Alliierten, die Deutschen und die Hauptstadtfrage nach 1945*. Köln: Böhlau, 1989.

Prause, Gerhard: "'Und so bleib' es in alle Zeit!' Warum Theodor Fontanes Bücher über die preußischen Kriege den Patrioten nicht gefielen." *Die Zeit* No. 42, October 11, 1985: Literaturbeilage 32.

Protokoll der Anhörung zum Forum für Geschichte und Gegenwart. Berlin, 1983–84.

Protzman, Ferdinand: "Germany Slow to Embrace Its Eastern Artists." *The New York Times* vol. 140, No. 48, 469, January 3, 1991: 15–6.

Prutz, Robert [Eduard]: *Die deutsche Literatur der Gegenwart: 1848–1858*. 2. Aufl. Vol. 1. Leipzig: Voigt & Günther, 1860.

Raddatz, Fritz J.: "Von der Beschädigung der Literatur durch ihre Urheber: Bemerkungen zu Heiner Müller und Christa Wolf." *Die Zeit* No. 5, January 29, 1993: 51–2.

Rammstedt, Otthein, and Gert Schmidt, eds., *BRD ade! Vierzig Jahre in Rück-Ansichten von Sozial- und Kulturwissenschaftlern*. Hrsg. unter Mitwirkung von Klaus Frerichs und Angela Rammstedt. Frankfurt a. M.: Suhrkamp, 1992 (edition suhrkamp. 1773).

Reed, Terence James: "Disconnections in the 1990 *Literaturstreit*." Peter Skrine, Rosemary E. Wallbank-Turner and Jonathan West, eds., *Connections: Essays in Honour of Eda Sagarra on the Occasion of her 60th Birthday*. Stuttgart: Heinz, 1993 (Stuttgarter Arbeiten zur Germanistik. 281). 211–18.

Reed, Terence James: "Ecclesia militans: Weimarer Klassik als Opposition." Barner, Wilfried, Eberhard Lämmert, and Norbert Oellers, eds., *Unser Commercium: Goethes und Schillers Literaturpolitik*. Stuttgart: Cotta, 1984 (Veröffentlichungen d. deutschen Schillergesellschaft. 42). 37–53.

Retzlaw, Karl: *Spartacus. Aufstieg und Niedergang: Erinnerungen eines Parteiarbeiters*. Frankfurt a. M.: Verlag Neue Kritik, 1979.

Reulecke, Jürgen: "Das Berlinbild: Was ist Imagination, was Wirklichkeit?" Gerhard Brunn and Jürgen Reulecke, eds., *Berlin: Blicke auf die deutsche Metropole*. Essen: Hobbing, 1989.

Reuter, Hans Heinrich: *Fontane*. Vol. 1–2. Berlin: Verlag der Nation, 1968.

Richter, Joachim Burkhard: *Hans Ferdinand Maßmann: Altdeutscher Patriotismus im 19. Jahrhundert*. Berlin, New York: de Gruyter, 1992 (Quellen und Forschungen. N. S. 100).

Richter, Werner: *Kaiser Friedrich III*. Erlenbach-Zürich, Leipzig: Rentsch, 1938.

Riha, Karl: "Georg Herwegh in rezeptionsgeschichtlicher Sicht. Ein Kapitel politischer Ästhetik." Walter Veit, ed., *Antipodische Aufklärungen: Antipodean Enlightenments. Festschrift für Leslie Bodi*. Frankfurt a. M., Bern, New York: Lang, 1987. 389–401.

Ritter, Gerhard A., and Jürgen Kocka, eds., *Deutsche Sozialgeschichte: Dokumente und Skizzen*. Vol. 2: *1870–1914*. München: Beck, 1974.

Ritter, Henning: "Fallhöhe. Intellektuelle und Nation." *Frankfurter Allgemeine Zeitung* No. 283, December 5, 1990: N3.

Ritter, Joachim, and Karlfried Gründer, eds., *Historisches Wörterbuch der Philosophie*. [Bisher] Vol. 1–8 [A-Sc]. Darmstadt: Wissenschaftliche Buchgesellschaft, 1971–1992.

Roberts, David, and Philip Thomson, eds., *The Modern German Historical Novel: Paradigms, Problems, Perspectives*. New York, Oxford: Berg 1991 (Berg European Studies Series).

Roper, Katherine: *German Encounters with Modernity: Novels of Imperial Berlin*. New Jersey: Humanities Press, 1991.

Rosellini, Jay: "Zur Funktionalisierung des historischen Romans in der DDR-Literatur." *Amsterdamer Beiträge zur Neueren Germanistik* 11/12 (1981): 61–100.

[Ruge, Arnold:] *Die politischen Lyriker unserer Zeit: Ein Denkmal mit Portraits und kurzen historischen Charakteristiken.* Leipzig: Verlagsbureau (Arnold Ruge), 1847.

Rüsen, Jörn: *Lebendige Geschichte. Grundzüge einer Historik III: Formen und Funktionen des historischen Wissens.* Göttingen: Vandenhoeck & Ruprecht, 1989 (Kleine Vandenhoeck-Reihe. 1542).

Saalmann, Dieter: "'Deconstructing' the Berlin Wall: Reflections on the Current State of German-German Relations." *Germanic Notes* 20: 1 (1989): 19–28.

Sack, Manfred: "Das Berliner Schloßgespenst." *Die Zeit* No. 52, December 18, 1992: 43–4.

Sack, Manfred: "Schmelzendes Packeis." *Die Zeit* No. 38, September 11, 1992: 61–2.

Sagave, Pierre-Paul: "Krieg und Bürgerkrieg in Frankreich. Erlebnis und Dichtung bei Theodor Fontane." *Fontane Blätter* 4 (1979): 452–471.

Sammons, Jeffrey L.: *Wilhelm Raabe: The Fiction of the Alternative Community.* Princeton: U.P., 1987.

Schafer, Boyd C.: *Nationalism: Myth and Reality.* New York: Harcourt, Brace, and World, 1955.

Schäfer, Hermann: "Das Haus der Geschichte der Bundesrepublik Deutschland. Strukturgeschichtliche Darstellung im Museum." *Aus Politik und Zeitgeschichte* 38 (1988) No. B 2, January 8: 27–34.

Schallenberger, Horst: *Untersuchungen zum Geschichtsbild der Wilhelminischen Ära und der Weimarer Zeit: Eine vergleichende Schulbuchanalyse deutscher Schulgeschichtsbücher aus der Zeit von 1888 bis 1933.* Ratingen: Henn, 1964.

Scheffler, Karl: *Berlin: Ein Stadtschicksal.* Berlin: Reiss, 1910.

Scherr, Johannes: *Poeten der Jetztzeit in Briefen an eine Frau.* Stuttgart: Franckh'sche Verlagsbuchhandlung, 1844.

Scheuer, Helmut, ed., *Dichter und ihre Nation.* Frankfurt a. M.: Suhrkamp, 1993 (suhrkamp taschenbuch materialien. 2117).

Schieder, Theodor: *Das deutsche Kaiserreich von 1871 als Nationalstaat.* Köln, Opladen: Westdeutscher Verlag, 1961 (Wissenschaftliche Abhandlungen der Arbeitsgemeinschaft für Forschung des Landes Nordrhein-Westfalen. 20).

Schieder, Theodor, and Ernst Deuerlein: *Reichsgründung 1870/71: Tatsachen – Kontroversen – Interpretationen.* Stuttgart: Seewald, 1970.

Schirrmacher, Frank: "Dem Druck des härteren, strengeren Lebens standhalten." Auch eine Studie über den autoritären Charakter: Christa Wolfs Aufsätze, Reden und ihre jüngste Erzählung *Was bleibt.*" *Frankfurter Allgemeine Zeitung* No. 27, June 2, 1990: Beil. "Bilder und Zeiten".

Schleier, Hans: "Zur Auswirkung der Reichsgründung auf historisch-politische und methodologische Konzeptionen der bürgerlichen deutschen Geschichtsschreibung bis 1914." Horst Bartel and Ernst Engelberg, eds., *Die großpreußisch-militaristische Reichsgründung 1871: Voraussetzungen und Folgen*. Vol. 2. Berlin: Akademie-Verlag, 1971 (Deutsche Akademie der Wissenschaften zu Berlin. Schriften des Zentralinstituts für Geschichte. Reihe 1: Allgemeine und deutsche Geschichte. 36). 515–81.

Schlesak, Dieter: "Zweimal Deutschland: Beobachtet von einem Deutschen der dritten Art." *Neue Deutsche Literatur* 40, No. 476 (1992): 128–42.

Schleunes, Karl A.: *Schooling and Society: The Politics of Education in Prussia and Bavaria 1750–1900*. Oxford, New York, München: Berg, 1989.

Schmidt, Elli, ed., *Der erste Augenblick der Freiheit*. Rostock: Hinstorff, 1970.

Schmidt, Julian: "Friedrich Spielhagen." *Westermann's Illustrierte Deutsche Monatshefte* 29 (N. S. 13) (1870/71): 422–49.

Schmidt, Julian: *Geschichte der deutschen Nationalliteratur im neunzehnten Jahrhundert*. Vol. 1–3. 3., verb. Aufl. Leipzig: Herbig, 1856.

Schmitt, Hans-Jürgen, ed., *Die Literatur der DDR*. München, Wien: Hanser, 1983 (Hansers Sozialgeschichte der deutschen Literatur. 11).

Schnell, Ralf: "Zwischen Geschichtsphilosophie und 'Posthistoire'. Geschichte im deutschen Gegenwartsroman." *Weimarer Beiträge* 37 (1991): 342–55.

Schoefer, Christine: "The Attack on Christa Wolf." *The Nation* No. 251, October 22, 1990: 446–49.

Schoeps, Karl-Heinz: "Wandel und Erinnerung: Christa Wolfs Erzählung 'Blickwechsel' als Paradigma ihrer Erzählstruktur." *The German Quarterly* 52 (1979): 518–525.

Schönemann, Bernd: "Nationale Identität als Aufgabe des Geschichtsunterrichts nach der Reichsgründung." *Internationale Schulbuchforschung* 11 (1989): 107–28.

Schrade, Dorothea: *Kontinuität und Veränderung in Wilhelm Raabes Weltanschauung und Werk um 1871: Der Roman "Drei Federn" und die "Krähenfelder Geschichten."* Leipzig, Diss. masch., 1986.

Schridde, Rudolph: *Zum Bismarckbild im Geschichtsunterricht: Eine historisch-didaktische Analyse deutscher Schulgeschichtsbücher*. Unter Mitarb. von Lutz Stadtler. Ratingen, Kastellaun, Düsseldorf: Henn, 1974.

Schutte, Sabine: "Zur Kritik der Volkslied-Ideologie in der zweiten Hälfte des 19. Jahrhunderts." *Jahrbuch für Volksliedforschung* 20 (1975): 37–52.

Seibt, Gustav: "Wer mit dem Meißel schreibt, hat keine Handschrift: Ein neuer Anfang lyrischen Sprechens am Ausgang einer Epoche. Aus Anlaß eines Gedichts von Heiner Müller." *Frankfurter Allgemeine Zeitung* No. 124, June 1, 1993: 1.

Seiler, Christian: "Heute lesen wir vor fünfzehn Muttis am Stadtrand. Privilegiert, korrumpiert, wirkungslos – wie sich DDR-Schriftsteller vom Staat die Wut abkaufen ließen." *Die Weltwoche* No. 34, August 24, 1989: 59.

Sengle, Friedrich: *Biedermeierzeit: Deutsche Literatur im Spannungsfeld zwischen Restauration und Revolution 1815–1848*. Vol. 1–3. Stuttgart: Metzler, 1971–1980.

Sheehan, James J.: "The Problem of the Nation in German History." Otto Büsch and James J. Sheehan, eds., *Die Rolle der Nation in der deutschen Geschichte und Gegenwart*. Berlin: Colloquium, 1985. 3–20.

Sheehan, James J.: "What is German History? Reflections on the Role of the *Nation* in German History and Historiography." *Journal of Modern History* 53:1 (1981): 1–23.

Sheehan, James: "Zukünftige Vergangenheit. Das deutsche Geschichtsbild in den neunziger Jahren." Gottfried Korff and Martin Roth, eds., *Das historische Museum: Labor, Schaubühne, Identitätsfabrik*. Frankfurt a. M., New York: Campus; Paris: Edition de la Maison des Sciences de l'Homme, 1990. 277–86.

Siemann, Wolfram: "Bilder der Polizei und Zensur in Raabes Werken." *Jahrbuch der Raabe-Gesellschaft* (1987): 84–109.

Siemann, Wolfram: *Die deutsche Revolution von 1848/49*. Frankfurt a. M.: Suhrkamp, 1985 (Neue Historische Bibliothek; edition suhrkamp. 1266).

Sittner, Gernot: *Politik und Literatur 1870/71: Die Spiegelung des politischen Geschehens zur Zeit des deutsch-französischen Krieges in der zeitgenössischen deutschen Literatur*. München, Phil. Diss., 1966.

Sloterdijk, Peter: "Landeskundliche Bemerkungen zu den jüngsten deutschen Tränen." *Psychologie Heute* March 1990: 43–54.

Sommer, Theo: "Noch nicht daheim im deutschen Haus." *Die Zeit* No. 26, June 21, 1991: 1.

Spitzer, Paul Gerd: *Untersuchungen zur Geschichtsdichtung C. F. Meyers: Das Verhältnis von politisch-geschichtlicher Wirklichkeit und individuellen Motiven in den historischen Erzählungen*. Köln, Phil. Diss., 1980.

Springer, Anton: "Unsere Friedensziele." *Im neuen Reich* 1, vol. 1 (1871): 689–98.

Springer, Reinhart K.: "'Strahlte die Jugend für den heiligen Kampf.' Der 'Turnvater' Jahn in deutschen Schulgeschichtsbüchern 1871–1933." *Internationale Schulbuchforschung* 8 (1986): 9–28.

Steinecke, Hartmut: *Romanpoetik von Goethe bis Thomas Mann: Entwicklungen und Probleme der "demokratischen Kunstform" in Deutschland*. München: Fink 1987 (Uni-Taschenbücher. 1435).

Steinfeld, Thomas, and Heidrun Suhr: "Die Wiederkehr des Nationalen. Zur Diskussion um das deutschlandpolitische Engagement in der Gegenwartsliteratur." *The German Quaterly* 62 (1989): 345–56.

Stephan, Alexander: "Ein deutscher Forschungsbericht 1990/91: Zur Debatte um das Ende der DDR-Literatur und den Anfang einer gesamtdeutschen Kultur." *The Germanic Review* 67:3 (1992): 126–134.

Stephan, Cora: "Traum vom Ende der Schuld." *Der Spiegel* No. 18, April 27, 1992: 46–48.

Stern, Fritz: *The Politics of Cultural Despair: A Study in the Rise of Germanic Ideology*. Berkeley, Los Angeles: University of California Press, 1961.

Stölzl, Christoph, and Verena Tafel: "Das Deutsche Historische Museum in Berlin: Perspektiven und Ziele, Entstehung und gegenwärtiger Stand." *Aus Politik und Zeitgeschichte* 38 (1988) No. B 2, January 8: 17–26.

Straube, Edith: "Die Einführung des obligatorischen Geschichtsunterricht als selbständiges Unterrichtsfach an den preußischen Volksschulen." *Wissenschaftliche Zeitschrift der Friedrich-Schiller-Universität Jena* 12 (1963): 153–57.

Theweleit, Klaus: *Männerphantasien: Frauen, Fluten, Körper, Geschichte*. Frankfurt a. M.: Verlag Roter Stern, 1977.

Thiele, Eberhard: "Engagiert – wofür?" Heinz-Ludwig Arnold, ed., *Christoph Hein*. München: edition text – kritik, 1991 (Text – Kritik. 111). 74–80.

Thunecke, Jörg: "Verhinderte Dichter: Wilhelm Buschs Balduin Bählamm und Wilhelm Raabes Dr. Neubauer. Ein Beitrag zur Sozialkritik der Gründerzeit." *Jahrbuch der Raabe-Gesellschaft* (1983): 71–95

Tiemann, Dieter: *Die Vorgeschichte des Krieges von 1870/71 in deutschen und französischen Schulgeschichtsbüchern*. Wuppertal, Diss., 1976.

Toews, John E.: "Intellectual History after the Linguistic Turn: The Autonomy of Meaning and the Irreducibility of Experience." *American Historical Review* 92 (1987): 879–907

Townson, Michael: *Mother-Tongue and Fatherland: Language and Politics in Germany*. Manchester, New York: University of Manchester Press, 1992.

Trapp, Walter: *Der Einfluß der Regierungsform der Monarchie auf den Geschichtsunterricht in den bayerischen Volksschulen (1806–1918)*. München, Phil. Diss., 1971.

Treitschke, Heinrich von: *Deutsche Geschichte im Neunzehnten Jahrhundert*. 5. Theil: *Bis zur Märzrevolution*. Leipzig: Hirzel, 1894 (Staatengeschichte der neuesten Zeit. 28).

Ueding: Gert: "Massenware oder stille Kirche: Über falsche Alternativen in der deutschen Literatur." *Neue Rundschau* 104 (1993) H. 3: "Literatur im Abseits – und wie sie herauskommt." 36–43.

Ullwer, Sigrid: *Der Geschichtsunterricht in der Volksschule nach der Vorstellungen der bayerischen Regierung und des Bayerischen Lehrervereins von der Gründung des Bayerischen Lehrervereins 1861 bis zum Ende des Zweiten Weltkrieges*. Bern, Frankfurt a. M.: Lang, 1976.

Ulrich, Volker: "Die neue Dreistigkeit." *Die Zeit* No. 45, October 30, 1992: 73.

Volkov, Shulamit: "Das geschriebene und das gesprochene Wort. Über Kontinuität und Diskontinuität im deutschen Antisemitismus." Volkov: *Jüdisches Leben und Antisemitismus im 19. und 20. Jahrhundert: Zehn Essays*. München: Beck, 1990. 54–75.

Voltmer, Ernst: "Das Mittelalter ist noch nicht vorbei... Über die merkwürdige Wiederentdeckung einer längst vergangenen Zeit und die verschiedenen Wege, sich ein Bild davon zu machen." Alfred Haverkamp and Alfred Heit, eds., *Ecos Rosenroman: Ein Kolloquium*. München: Deutscher Taschenbuch Verlag, 1987 (dtv. 4449). 185–228.

Wallace, Ian: "Zu Volker Braun." *Neue deutsche Literatur* 39, No. 459 (1991): 155.

Wallmann, Jürgen P.: "Streitbar und umstritten." *Der Tagesspiegel* No. 13, 574, May 20, 1990: 13.

Warm, Günter: "Zum Verhältnis von Vergangenheit und Gegenwart in einigen Werken der zeitgenössischen sowjetischen und der DDR-Epik." Manfred Diersch and Walfried Hartinger, eds., *Literatur und Geschichtsbewußtsein: Entwicklungstendenzen der DDR-Literatur in den sechziger und siebziger Jahren*. Berlin, Weimar: Aufbau, 1976. 51–72.

Weber, A[lbrecht]: "Lehrerfiguren in Raabes 'Horacker.'" Jörg Thunecke, ed., *Formen realistischer Erzählkunst*. Festschrift for Charlotte Jolles. In Honour of her 70th Birthday. In Conjunction with Eda Sagarra. Nottingham: Sherwood Press Agencies 1979. 216–32.

Weber, Bernd: *Pädagogik und Politik vom Kaiserreich zum Faschismus: Zur Analyse politischer Optionen von Pädagogikhochschullehrern von 1914–1933*. Königstein: Scriptor, 1979.

Weber, Ernst: "Zur bibliographischen Darstellung gesellschaftspolitischer Meinungsbildung durch Literatur. Die publizistisch eingesetzte Lyrik in der Zeit der Befreiungskriege und der Reichsgründung." Wolfgang Martens, et al., eds., *Bibliographische Probleme im Zeichen eines erweiterten Literaturbegriffes*. 2. Kolloquium zur bibliogr. Lage in der germanist. Literaturwiss. Weinheim: VCH, 1988 (Mitt. der Komm. für Germanist. Forschung. 4). 5–51.

Weber, Max: *Der Nationalstaat und die Volkswirtschaftspolitik: Akademische Antrittsrede*. Freiburg i. Br., Leipzig: Mohr, 1895.

Weber, Max: "Roscher und Knies und die logischen Probleme der historischen Nationalökonomie." Weber: *Gesammelte Aufsätze zur Wissenschaftslehre*. Hrsg. von Johannes Winckelmann. 5. Aufl. Tübingen: Siebeck, 1982. 1–145.

Wehler, Hans-Ulrich: *Bismarck und der Imperialismus*. Köln, Berlin: Kiepenheuer & Witsch, 1969.

Weidenfeld, Werner: "Politische Kultur und deutsche Frage." Weidenfeld, ed., *Politische Kultur und deutsche Frage: Materialien zum Staats- und Nationalbewußtsein in der Bundesrepublik Deutschland*. Mit Beiträgen von Wilhelm Bleck [u.a.]. Köln: Verlag Wissenschaft und Politik, 1989. 13–38.

Weindling, Paul: *Health, Race and German Politics between National Unification and Nazism, 1870–1945*. Cambridge: Cambridge University Press, 1989.

Welsch, Wolfgang, ed., *Wege aus der Moderne: Schlüsseltexte der Postmoderne-Diskussion*. Weinheim: VCH, Acta humaniora, 1988.

Wengst, Udo, ed., *Historiker betrachten Deutschland: Beiträge zum Vereinigungsprozeß und zur Hauptstadtdiskussion (Februar 1990 – Juni 1991)*. Bonn, Berlin: Bouvier, 1992.

Wenzel, Frank: "Sicherung von Massenloyalität und Qualifikation der Arbeitskraft als Aufgabe der Volksschule." Ursula Aumüller, et al., ed., *Schule und Staat im 18. und 19. Jahrhundert: Zur Sozialgeschichte der Schule in Deutschland*. 2. Aufl. Frankfurt a. M.: Suhrkamp, 1979. 323–86.

Wertheimer, Mildred: *The Pan-German League, 1890–1914*. New York: Columbia University Press, 1924.

Weymar, Ernst: *Das Selbstbildnis der Deutschen: Ein Bericht über den Geist des Geschichtsunterrichts der höheren Schulen im 19. Jahrhundert*. Stuttgart: Klett, 1961.

White, Hayden: *Metahistory: The Historical Imagination in Nineteenth-Century Europe*. Baltimore, London: The John Hopkins University Press, 1973.

Wichert, J., and K. Heinemann: "Zwischen den Zeiten. Geschichte und Gegenwart in der Bundesrepublik der achtziger Jahre. Eine Einführung." Landeszentrale für politische Bildung Nordrhein-Westfalen, ed., *Streitfall deutsche Geschichte: Geschichts- und Gegenwartsbewußtsein in den 80er Jahren*. Essen: Hobbing 1988. 1–16.

Wiese, Benno von: "Dichtertum. Zum Selbstverständnis des deutschen Autors im 19. Jahrhundert und heute." Wiese: *Perspektiven. 1: Studien zur deutschen Literatur und Literaturwissenschaft*. Berlin: Erich Schmidt, 1978. 6–23.

William, Arthur, Stuart Parkes, and Roland Smith, eds., *Literature on the Threshold: The German Novel in the 1980's*. New York, Oxford, München: Berg, 1990.

Williams, Arthur, Stuart Parker, and Roland Smith, eds., *German Literature at a Time of Change 1989–1990: German Unity and German Identity in Literary Perspective*. Bern [u.a.]: Lang, 1991.

Winckler, Arthur: *Die deutschen Reichskleinodien*. Berlin: Lüderitz, 1872 (Sammlung gemeinverständlicher wissenschaftlicher Vorträge. Serie 7, H. 154).

Winckler, Lutz: "Kulturnation DDR – ein intellektueller Gründungsmythos." *Das Argonautenschiff* 1 (1992): 141–49.

Windelband, Wilhelm: "Über Friedrich Hölderlin und sein Geschick." Windelband: *Präludien*. 5., erw. Aufl. Vol. 1. Tübingen: Mohr, 1915. 230–59.

Wittstock, Uwe: "Ab in die Nische? Über neueste deutsche Literatur und was sie vom Publikum trennt." *Neue Rundschau* 104 (1993) H. 3: "Literatur im Abseits – und wie sie herauskommt." 45–58

Wittstock, Uwe: "Generationswechsel? Ja. Aber wie?" *Neue Rundschau* 103:2 (1992): 131–33.

Wittstock, Uwe: *Von der Stalinallee zum Prenzlauer Berg: Wege der DDR-Literatur 1949–1989*. München: Piper, 1989.

Wolf, Gerhard: *Sprachblätter. Wortwechsel: Im Dialog mit Dichtern*. Leipzig: Reclam, 1992.

Wruck, Peter: "Theodor Fontane in der Rolle des vaterländischen Schriftstellers." *Fontane-Blätter* 44 (1987): 644–662.

Zang, Gert: *Die unaufhaltsame Annäherung an das Einzelne: Reflexionen über den theoretischen und praktischen Nutzen der Regional- und Alltagsgeschichte.* Konstanz: Eigenverlag, 1985 (Schriftenreihe des Arbeitskreises für Regionalgeschichte. 6).

Zantop, Susanne M., and W. Daniel Wilson: "Das Kind mit dem Bade: Amerikanische Germanisten solidarisieren sich mit Christa Wolf." *Die Zeit* No. 25, June 18, 1993: 56.

Ziegler, Klaus: "Die Berliner Gesellschaft und die Literatur." Hans Rothfels, ed., *Berlin in Vergangenheit und Gegenwart.* Tübingen: Mohr, 1961 (Tübinger Studien zur Geschichte und Politik. 14). 35–48.

Zimmer, Hasko: *Auf dem Altar des Vaterlandes: Religion und Patriotismus in der deutschen Kriegslyrik des 19. Jahrhunderts.* Frankfurt a. M.: Thesen-Verlag, 1971 (Germanistik. 3).

Zinken, Rosa-Maria: *Der Roman als Zeitdokument: Bürgerlicher Realismus in Friedrich Spielhagens "Die von Hohenstein."* Frankfurt a. M. [u. a.]: Lang, 1991 (Kölner Studien zur Literaturwissenschaft. 4).

Zitelmann, Rainer: "Verzweifelter Unsinn." *Frankfurter Allgemeine Zeitung* No. 282, December 4, 1990: 39.

Zucker, Renée: "Marktplatz Berlin." *Kursbuch* 102 (1990): 179–88.

Notes on Contributors

PHILIP BRADY,
educated at the Universities of Cambridge, Göttingen and London, with a Ph.D. from London University for a study of 16th-century German literature. Teaches sixteenth-, seventeenth- and twentieth-century German literature at Birkbeck College in the University of London, regular reviewer for the Times Literary Supplement, for the B.B.C and for D/S Kultur Berlin. Has published numerous articles on the Baroque sermon, on literature in the Weimar Republic, and on post-war poets and dramatists. Has co-edited a volume of essays (1990) on Günter Grass's *The Flounder*.

KEITH BULLIVANT,
born 1941 in Derby, England. Studies at the University of Birmingham and in Mainz. Until 1990 Professor of German Studies at the University of Warwick (England), since 1989 Professor of German at the University of Florida. Visiting appointments in New Mexico and Paderborn. *Selected publications*: *Literature in Upheaval* (1974, with R. H. Thomas; German ed. 1975); *Industrie und deutsche Literatur 1830–1914* (1976, with H. R. Ridley); *Realism Today. Aspects of the contemporary West German novel* (1987); *The Future of German Literature* (1993). As editor: *Culture and Society in the Weimar Republic* (1977), *The Modern German Novel* (1987), *After the 'Death of Literature'. West German Writing of the 1970s* (1989), *Englische Lektionen* (1989), *Das Werk des Schriftstellers Dieter Wellershoff* (1990). Numerous essays in English and German on German literature and society of the 19th and 20th centuries. Co-editor of Berg Monographs in German, member of the editorial board of *The South-Atlantic Review*.

ROGER CHICKERING
has published on the German peace movement in the era before the First World War, German patriotic societies in the same era, and on the historian Karl Lamprecht. He is now studying the history of Freiburg i. Br. during the First World War. He is currently Professor of History at the Center for German and European Studies at Georgetown University in Washington, D.C.

JOHN S. CORNELL
received his Ph. D. from Yale University in 1990 and is Assistant Professor of history at Butler University, Indianapolis.

DANIEL FULDA,
born 1966 in Frankfurt a. M., studies in German Literature and History; currently working on a Ph. D. Dissertation *Telling History in Historiography and the Historical Novel, 1760–1860*, lecturing at the University of Cologne.

ALFRED KELLY
is Professor of History at Hamilton College. He received his BA from the University of Chicago in 1969 and his PhD from the University of Wisconsin in 1975. He is the author of *The Descent of Darwin: The Popularization of Darwinism in Germany, 1860–1914* (1981) and the editor and translator of *The German Worker: Working-Class Autobiographies from the Age of Industrialization* (1987). Currently he is writing a book entitled *Images of War: The German Memories of 1870/71*, from which the essay in this volume is adapted.

ECKHARDT MEYER-KRENTLER,
born 1946 in Westphalia, is Professor of German Literature at the Ruhr-Universität Bochum. Special fields of research: Social history of literature, literature and jurisprudence, electronic editions of literature (Raabe: works, correspondence, diaries), the eighteenth century, Realism, theory and history of prose narrative. His books include works on Christian Fürchtegott Gellert and the novel in the eighteenth century; the subject of friendship in German literature, Wilhelm Raabe; lyrics and penalty; research techniques in philology; techniques of electronic editing.

VOLKER NEUHAUS,
born 1943 in Breslau, educated at the Universities of Zürich and Bonn, received his Dr. phil. at Bonn University with a study of multiple viewpoint in European and American fiction. Habilitation Cologne 1975 with a thesis on the right-wing sensational novelist Sir John Retcliffe alias H. O. F. Goedsche (1815–1878). Professor of German and Comparative Literature at the University of Cologne, Guest Professor at State University of New York at Buffalo, University of Wisconsin-Parkside, University of California, San Diego, Monash University Melbourne. Special fields of research: nineteenth-century novel, mystery- and detective-fiction, postwar German literature, Günter Grass. Editor of the revised and annotated edition *Günter Grass. Werkausgabe in zehn Bänden* (1987).

WALTER PAPE,
born 1945 in Burg (Magdeburg), educated at the Universities of Heidelberg and Cologne, is University Professor of German Literature at the University of Cologne. Habilitation Cologne 1980. Guest Professor at the University of

California, San Diego (1983), and Santa Barbara (1985); Resident Fellow at the University of California Humanities Research Institute, Irvine (1991). His books include *Joachim Ringelnatz: Parodie und Selbstparodie in Leben und Werk* (1974), *Wilhelm Busch* (1977), *Das literarische Kinderbuch* (1981). He is the co-editor of *Aesthetic Illusion: Theoretical and Historical Approaches* (1990, together with Frederick Burwick). In addition he has edited the eight volume edition of works and letters of Ringelnatz (1982–1988), Lessing's *Æesop's Fables* (1987), Mendelssohn's translation of the Psalms (1991), Hoffmann von Fallersleben's *Deutsche Gassenlieder. Deutsche Salonlieder* (1992). Numerous articles on German literature from the seventeenth century to the present time.

TERENCE JAMES REED
is Taylor Professor of the German Language and Literature at the University of Oxford and Fellow of the Queen's College. His books are: *Thomas Mann: the Uses of Tradition* (Oxford 1974); *The Classical Centre: Goethe and Weimar 1775–1832* (London 1980; German version Stuttgart 1982); *Goethe* (Oxford 1984); *Schiller* (Oxford 1991); editions of Thomas Mann, *Der Tod in Venedig* (Oxford 1971 and Munich 1983); and a verse translation of Heine's *Deutschland ein Wintermärchen* (London 1986). He is co-founder and editor of the yearbook *Oxford German Studies*. He became a Fellow of the British Academy in 1987.

KATHERINE ROPER
is Professor of Modern European History at Saint Mary's College of California in Moraga, California. She is the author of *German Encounters with Modernity: Novels of Imperial Berlin* (Humanities Press, 1991) and of articles analyzing historical implications of nineteenth- and twentieth-century German fiction and literary culture. Currently she is working on a study of the political engagement of German novelists.

KARL-HEINZ JOACHIM SCHOEPS,
born 1935 in Dinslaken, Germany, studied Anglistik and Germanistik at the universities of Freiburg, Innsbruck, Bonn, London (King's College), Kansas and Wisconsin (Madison); Staatsexamen 1962 (Bonn), PhD 1971 (Wisconsin). He is Professor of German at the University of Illinois, where he has been teaching since 1971. His publications include articles on Gruppe 47, Bertolt Brecht, Christa Wolf, the GDR novel, and books such as *Bertolt Brecht and Bernard Shaw* (1974), *Bertolt Brecht* (1977), *Bertolt Brecht: Life, Work, and Criticism* (1989), and *Literatur im Dritten Reich* (1992). In addition he is the co-editor of two books: *DDR-Literatur im Tauwetter* (1985; with Richard Zipser), and *"Was*

in den alten Büchern steht": *Neue Interpretationen von der Aufklärung zur Moderne* (1991; with Christopher J. Wickham).

JAMES J. SHEEHAN,
born 1937 in San Francisco, California, educated at Stanford University and at the University of California, Berkeley. 1964–79 Assistant, Associate Professor Professor Northwestern University, since 1979 Professor of History, Stanford University. Fellowships: Visiting Fellow, Wolfson College, Oxford 1981; Wissenschaftskolleg, Berlin, 1989–90; American Academy of Arts and Sciences, 1992–. His books include *The Career of Lujo Brentano: A Study of Liberalism and Social Reform in Imperial Germany* (1966), *German Liberalism in the Nineteenth Century* (1978, Paperback 1982; German translation 1983), *German history, 1766–1866* (1989, repr. 1991). In addition he is the editor of *Imperial Germany* (1976) and the co-editor (with Otto Büsch) of *Die Rolle der Nation in der deutschen Geschichte* (1985), *The Boundaries of Humanities: Humans, Animals, and Machines* (together with Morton Sosna) and *An Interrupted Past: German Speaking Refugee Historians in the United States after 1933* (together with Hartmut Lehmann, 1991).

Index

Page numbers refer to text and footnotes,
numbers with 'n' (e. g. Adorno, Theodor W. 109n.) to notes only.

Achternbusch, Herbert 316
  Auf verlorenem Posten 316
Adenauer, Konrad 276
Adorno, Theodor W. 109n.
Aesthetic experiment
  in the decade of unification 216
Aesthetics 197
  postmodern 12
Aesthetics and politics 10–3, 20, 53, 55,
  72, 109, 112, 174, 193, 195, 211, 248
  see also Christa Wolf
Alberti, Conrad 184, 191
  Die Alten und die Jungen 191
  Im Rechtsstaat 183
Alexis, Willibald 202
  Die Hosen des Herrn von Bredow 201
  Isegrimm 201
Allgemeiner Deutscher Sprachverein
  see Sprachverein, Allgemeiner
  Deutscher
Alsace-Lorraine 93, 97, 98
Ameri, Susan Milantchi 69n., 71n.
Andersch, Alfred 274, 302
Anderson, Benedict 27n.
Anderson, Sascha 279, 287, 319
Andrä, J. C. 57
Andrée, Fritz 113n.
Anecdote
  in historical fiction 211
Anti-fascism 28, 29, 222, 226, 229,
  253, 256
Anti-foreigner sentiment 192
Anti-Semitism 36, 191
Ariadnefabrik (periodical) 289, 290, 292,
  297

Arndt, Ernst Moritz 50n.
Arnold, Heinz-Ludwig 279n.
Asylum debate 3, 132, 276
Asylum seekers 174, 190, 193
Auerbach, Berthold 112, 120, 138
Aufbau-Verlag 300
Auschwitz 73, 131, 132, 224, 255, 276
Austria 80, 89, 90
Austro-Prussian War, 1866 88, 148
  Fontane's analysis of cause of 89, 91
  Königgrätz 91
Autonomy
  of fiction 228
  of language 65, 78
Avant-garde 11
  in the GDR 278–301

Ball, Hugo 18n.
Baring, Arnulf 30, 276
Bartsch, Kurt 271
Baselitz, Georg 274n.
Basic Law (Grundgesetz) 7, 29, 190
Baudrillard, Jean 12, 20
Baumbach, Rudolf 134
Baumgarten, Hermann 204
  Selbstkritik des deutschen Liberalismus
    204n.
Bavaria, education in 43, 44, 47n.
Bazaine, Marshal François Achille 51,
  58
Becher, Johannes R. 238
Becker, Jurek 305
Beethoven, Ludwig van 182

Befreiungskriege 1813/1814 (Wars of National Liberation) 83, 87, 154, 156
  political poetry 111
Behn, Manfred 256
Bell, Andrew 76n.
Benedetti, Vincent 46
Benedict, Ruth 8n.
Benjamin, Walter 13, 17, 278
Berdahl, Robert M. 62n.
Berendse, Gerrit-Jan 287n.
Berg, Christa 134n.
Berg, Jochen
  Fremde in der Nacht 318
Berkéwicz, Ulla 227
  Engel sind schwarz und weiß 220
Berlin 171–94
  after 1871 127
  Alexanderplatz 178
  as a capital 31, 32
  as cultural capital 172, 173, 183
  as political capital 172, 173, 183
  Berlin Wall 175
  Brandenburg Gate 98, 190, 192
  demolition of the Wall 184
  East vs. West 186, 188, 189, 193
  Flora Establishment 185, 186
  Hohenzollern Palace 186, 190
  imagery of 172, 181, 187, 191
  immigration to 180, 190
  Kantstraße 191
  Kreuzberg 177, 178, 184, 190, 192
  Kurfürstendamm 175, 189
  old vs. new 177, 178, 183
  opening of the Wall 177–79, 182, 189
  Palace of the Republic 186, 189
  physical transformation of 182, 184, 185
  political and cultural capital 173
  Potsdamer Platz 171, 185
  Wall 175, 184, 185, 302–04, 306, 313, 315–17
  Wilhelmstraße 177
Berndt, Johannes 53, 55, 56, 59
Bernsmeier, Helmut 70n., 73n.

Biermann, Wolf 132, 245, 257, 265, 266, 270–72, 279, 280, 293, 298, 309, 314, 319
  Dideldum 132
Bildung 76, 77, 200
  and state 126
Bildungsbürger 76
  after 1871 5
Bildungsroman 156
Birken, Sigmund von 10
Bismarck, Otto Fürst von 6, 16, 37, 47, 48, 58, 59, 89, 90, 94, 102, 109, 116, 118, 122, 124, 138–41, 165, 177, 180, 183, 203, 207, 209, 212, 276
  and Raabe 147, 148, 149, 165
  unification of 1871 35
  unification politics 3
Bloch, Ernst 21, 268
Bohemia 92, 93
Bohley, Bärbel 252
Böhme, Ibrahim 279
Bohrer, Karl Heinz 264, 266, 274, 275
Die Böhsen Onkelz 276
Böll, Heinrich 274
Böthig, Peter 278n.
Braband, Jutta 279
Brady, Philip 12
Brandt, Willy 3, 250, 276
Brather, Friedrich 153n., 156n.
Braun, Karl 111
Braun, Volker 17, 240, 248, 265, 293, 298
  "Nachruf" 236
Bräunig, Werner 257
Brecht, Bertolt 236, 238, 281
  Baal 281
  "Deutschland" 121
  "Deutschland, Du Blondes, Bleiches" 121
  "Ich benötige keinen Grabstein" 235
  "Radwechsel" 244
Breuer, Stefan 17
Brewster, Philip James 214
Broszat, Martin 217, 219, 220
Bruyn, Günter de 224, 265, 319
Buch, Hans-Christoph 108, 172n.
Buchhändler 160

Bullivant, Keith 3n., 98n., 173n., 182n., 188n., 224n., 226n.
Bungee cord, imagery of 171, 173, 193
Burckhardt, Jacob 112, 211n.
Busch, Wilhelm 183

Carriere, Moriz 129n.
Catholicism 76
Catholics 76, 77
Censorship 258
  in the GDR 235
Central Committee of the SED 257, 259, 266, 271
Chernobyl 263n., 266
Chickering, Roger 9n., 67n., 74n., 76n., 77n., 99n.
Childers, Thomas 63–6
Civilization, see also culture 16
  criticism of 17
Class enemy 259, 271
Classes, Lower
  against Honoratiorenpolitik 64
  and culture 11
  and unification 3, 4
  working 140
  yearning for consumption 4
Cold War 35, 188, 249, 303, 307
Colonization, images of 188, 190, 269, 311
Comical literary entertainer 164
Communist 227, 254
Communist dangers
  after 1871 39
Communist governments
  breakdown 3, 190, 241
Community, German 174, 177, 180, 181, 193
Concentration camps 253, 254, 256
Concrete Poetry 287, 297
Conservatism, see also Culture, conservative
  and German unifications 3, 273
  cultural, 4, 10, 13, 16, 17, 122, 177
  literary criticism 275
  upper classes 49
Corino, Karl 19n.

Cornell, John S. 9n., 180n., 181n., 196n.
Craig, Gordon 81n., 125, 126n., 130, 134
Crash of 1873, see Gründerkrach
Cultural criticism 18
  conservative 16
Cultural despair 14
  after 1871 5
  after 1989 6
Cultural nation, see Kulturnation
Cultural politics 9, 258, 270, 278
Cultural skepticism, see Cultural despair
Cultural unity 4, 5, 8, 37–78, 107, 126, 202, 304, 314
Culture 16, 18, 19, 202
  1990 debate 276
  a problem of a minority 13
  aesthetic and moral 15
  affirmative 246
  Alsace 97
  Americanization 16, 19
  and authority 78
  and civilization 16
  and classes 68
  and despotism 15
  and dictatorship 14
  and freedom 14
  and language 61–78
  and nation 123
  and order 77
  and progress 18
  and public order 77
  and the state 14
  as control 75
  authentic 63
  authority 77
  Berlin as cultural capital 173
  borders of German culture 156
  civilizing mission of German culture 102
  conflict between politics and culture 134
  conservatism 17
  criticism 18
  cultural disintegration 4

debate of 1990 274
destruction of GDR culture 18
for the learned 11
forces 62
French 9
German 27
German language as a metaphor 75
German opposed to French 98
middle-class 202
national 26
notion of 8
of foreign peoples 92
opposed to civilization 8
political culture of the FRG 30
popular notion 11
postmodern 11
Prussia dangerous to culture 127
representational function 9
'right' and 'left' culture 10
supermarket culture 188
supremacy of German culture 2
symbols 74
unity of national culture 202
values 78, 95, 98
western as opposed to eastern 16, 18, 188
world culture 2
Customs Union 146
Czechowski, Heinz
  "Historical Reminiscence" 241

Dahlmann, Friedrich Christoph 120
Dahn, Felix 228
  Ein Kampf um Rom 204n., 214
Dahrendorf, Ralf 313
Damaschke, Adolf 5, 133
Danish-German War 110
Dann, Otto 62n., 225
Decker, Rudolf 80
Deiritz, Karl 273n., 275n.
Delius, Friedrich Christian 229, 316
  Die Birnen von Ribbeck 225, 249, 250, 314–316
Demetz, Peter 81n., 92n.

Demonstration
  Berlin 178
Demonstrations
  Leipzig 251
  Leipzig and Berlin 33, 171
Denkler, Horst 115n.
Denmark 80, 83, 86
Derrida, Jacques 20
Deutsche Partei 147
Deutsche Schillerstiftung 122
Dieckmann, Christoph 190, 192n.
Dieckmann, Friedrich 15n., 34n., 179, 186, 187
Dingelstedt, Franz 122
Discourse analysis 208n.
Döblin, Alfred
  November 1918 234
Döring, Stefan 280, 295–97
Dostojéwski, Fedor 17
Drescher, Angela 256, 258n., 259n.
Droysen, Johann Gustav 204, 206
  Geschichte Alexanders des Großen 201, 222
Düding, Dieter 62n.
Dunger, Hermann 70n.
Dwinger, Edwin Erich 265

Eagleton, Terry 77
Eastern Marches Society 76
Ebeling, Theodor 114, 115n., 117n.
Ebers, Georg 198
  Die ägyptische Königstochter 207
Elbers, Ludwig 118n.
Eley, Geoff 64–66, 68
Ems Dispatch 46–48
Endler, Adolf 271, 289, 294, 298, 300
Engagé artists 11
Engel, Eduard 1, 108, 134
Engels, Friedrich 16, 17
Enlightenment
  failure of the project of 10, 11
Enzensberger, Hans Magnus 274, 304, 309
  "Katechismus zur deutschen Frage" 303, 305
Erb, Elke 286, 292, 298–300
  Kastanienallee 299, 300

Ergang, Robert 61
Erk, Ludwig 113n.
Ethnic minorities 77
Everyday life 162
Evolution 201

Faktor, Jan 278, 280, 294, 295, 301
Falk, Adalbert von 38
Fascination of power 209
Fascism, see also National socialism 253–256, 274–276
Faulenbach, Bernd 27n.
Federal Republic of Germany
  historical identity 29
Fehrenbach, Elisabeth 156n.
Fels, Ludwig 108
Feminists 77
Fichte, Johann Gottlieb 50n.
Flanzendörfer see Frank Lanzendörfer
Folk-dialects 71
Fontane, Emilie 81, 97, 100, 101
Fontane, Theodor 79–103, 134, 135, 196n., 207, 225, 228, 229, 234, 249
  as novelist 83, 85, 100, 101
  as secretary of Academy of Arts 101
  Aus den Tagen der Okkupation 97
  Der deutsche Krieg von 1866 81, 88–93
  Der Krieg gegen Frankreich 81, 93–96, 101, 212, 213
  Der Schleswig-Holsteinische Krieg im Jahre 1864 80, 86–88, 99
  German identity of 79, 82–5, 102, 103
  histories of wars of unification 80–83, 99, 100
  Kriegsgefangen 95, 96
  middle years of 85, 86
  revolution of 1848 84
  Schach von Wuthenow 212
  Vor dem Sturm 100, 101, 209–12
  Wanderungen durch die Mark Brandenburg 210, 211
  youth 83
Foreign policy 72
  discourse on 72, 73
Foreign words 61, 70–5, 77

Förster, Ernst 123n.
Fortschrittspartei 135
Foucault, Michel 68
Foundation of the Reich, see also Unification German 10, 35, 156, 165, 166, 199, 202, 228
  'second' 1878 5, 203–05
  literary effect 151, 207, 212
  novel 203
Fourier, Charles 16, 17
Franco-Prussian War 37–60, 93, 96, 109, 114, 115, 119–21, 124, 144, 180, 181, 182, 195, 203
  Fontane's analysis of cause of 80, 94, 95
François, General Bruno von 52, 53
Franke, Konrad 257n.
Freedom, see also Culture, and freedom
  and GDR 227
  and literature 235
  and socialism 223
  and unity 117, 120, 173, 200
  as a lie 317
  German 173–75, 177, 180
  to travel 314
  transvaluation of 120
  western notion 246
Freiligrath, Ferdinand 45, 112, 115, 117–20, 122, 124, 125, 128–30, 136
  "An Deutschland" 121
  complete edition 121
  "Die Toten an die Lebenden" 117
  "Die Trompete von Gravelotte" 122
  "Hurra, Germania" 119, 120
  museum 130
  political poems 1844–1848/49 119
  Treitschke on Freiligrath 128
Fremdwörtertum 71
Fremdwörterunwesen 71, 73
Freund, Winfried 120n.
Freytag, Gustav 126, 136, 137, 157, 196n., 199, 202, 209, 210, 214, 215, 222, 228
  Bilder aus der deutschen Vergangenheit 199, 200, 203

Die Ahnen 195, 199, 200, 203, 204, 206, 212, 229
Soll und Haben 156, 202, 207, 212
Fricke, Hermann 81n.
Fried, Erich 274
Friedmann, Otto Bernhard 115n.
Friedrich III, German Emperor 135, 136, 141, 156
Friedrich der Große 33
Friedrich Wilhelm IV, King of Prussia 115
Friedrich Wilhelm, Great Elector 181
Friedrich, Gerhard 102n.
Fuchs, Jürgen 193
Führmann, Franz 298
Fukuyama, Francis 20
Fulda, Daniel 2n., 5n., 6n., 102n., 112n.

Gall, Lothar 139, 141
Geibel, Emanuel 109, 111, 114, 125, 134
  "Am dritten September" 121
  "Zur Antwort" 110, 111
Gellner, Ernest 27n.
Genre style 211n.
Geppert, Hans Vilmar 197n., 214
German 'Volk,' see Volk
German Colonial Society 76
German Democratic Republic (GDR) 302–04, 306, 307, 309–12, 314–19
  dissident manifestos 223
  economic politics 247
  economic problems 3
  guest workers 190
  historical identity of 28, 29
  national identity 7, 9, 28
  'other Germany' 34, 252, 302–19
  political structure 7
  state socialism 130
German Empire, see also Unification, German
  inner unity 204, 222
German identity, see Identity, national
German Literature courses 153
German nation 159, 160, 164, 166
German Navy League 64

German School Association 76
German-Austrian War 111
German-Danish War 114
Germania 119, 183
Germany
  as civilizing principle 98
  division of 34, 224
  Zerrissenheit (disunity) 173, 180, 181, 192
Gersdorff, Carl von 125n.
Gerstenberg, Heinrich 116
Gesinnung 73, 109, 114, 117
Gesinnungsästhetik 11, 12, 274
Gesinnungskitsch 266
Geyer, D. 29n.
Giesebrecht, Wilhelm 222
Glaßbrenner, Adolf 119n.
Glasnost 279
Göbelbecker, L. F. 41
Gödeke, Karl 129n.
Goethe, Johann Wolfgang 1, 16, 194, 216
Gohr, Siegfried 274n.
Gordimer, Nadine 246
Görlich, Günter 271
Gotsche, Otto 245n.
Gottschall, Rudolf von 123
  Blätter für litterarische Unterhaltung 109
Gräf, Carl 114n.
Grass, Günter 3, 7, 8, 9, 108, 133, 134, 172, 187, 193, 215, 224, 229, 255, 266, 269, 274, 275, 302, 304, 306–13
  Die Blechtrommel 215, 234
  Die Rättin 216
  Kopfgeburten 8, 307
  Novemberland 132
  Unkenrufe 2, 225
Gravelotte/St. Privat, Battle of 49n., 51, 53–55
Grawe, Christian 124n.
Greiner, Ulrich 11–3, 193, 247n., 264–66, 274, 280n.
Grosse, Julius 123
Grosser, J. F. G. 273n.
Grünbein, Durs 280
Gründerkrach (crash) 1873 3, 138, 141, 186, 187

Gründerzeit (The Founders' Era) 80, 140, 152, 166–68, 187
Grundgesetz, see Basic Law
Grünewald, Matthias 268
Gruppe 47 274, 275
Gutzkow, Karl 202
  Die neuen Serapionsbrüder 187
Gymnasiallehrer 76

Habermas, Jürgen 33, 130, 217, 276n.
Haefs, Gisbert
  Alexander 222
Haeger, Monika 279
Hage, Volker 108n., 266
Hahn, Ludwig 51
Hähnel, Ingrid 281n.
Handke, Peter 229
  Versuch über die Jukebox 195
Handler, Richard 62–6
Hankel, Wilhelm 3n.
Harig, Ludwig 219, 221, 226
  Ordnung ist das ganze Leben 218
  Weh dem, der aus der Reihe tanzt 218, 219
Harlan, David 62n.
Hart, Heinrich and Julius 6, 135, 137
Härtling, Peter 311
Hartung, Klaus 192n.
Haupert, Bernhard
  Jugend zwischen Kreuz und Hakenkreuz 219
Hauptmann, Gerhart 38
Häusser, Ludwig 204
Havemann, Robert 260, 265
Hayes, Carlton J. H. 61, 62, 65
Hegel, Georg Wilhelm Friedrich 67, 68, 109
Heidelberger-Leonard, Irene 273n.
Hein, Christoph 192, 252, 314
Heine, Heinrich 122
Heisig, Bernhard 274n.
Heissenbüttel, Helmut 289
Henckell, Karl 6
Henrich, Friedhelm 165n.
Herder, Johann Gottfried 197
Hermann, Ulrich 134n.
Hermlin, Stefan 271

Herwegh, Georg 3, 111, 112, 122–30, 132, 134
  "An die deutschen Dichter" 110
  "Antwort an Geibel" 111
  archives 130
  "Bundeslied für den Allgemeinen Deutschen Arbeiterverein" 110, 122
  "Den Siegestrunkenen" 126
  "Der schlimmste Feind" 126
  "Endlich!" 124
  "Epilog zum Kriege" 124, 125
  Gedichte eines Lebendigen 123
  "Groß" 126
  Neue Gedichte 123
  tomb 130
  Treitschke's verdict 128
  "Tristia" 111, 124
Herzinger, Richard 16
Hesekiel, Ludovika
  Von Brandenburg zu Bismarck 177, 178
Heym, Stefan 178, 183, 187, 188, 241, 257, 265, 270, 271, 275, 306n.
  Auf Sand gebaut 240, 241
  Schwarzenberg 222–24
Hildebrand, Regine 7
Hildebrandt, Dieter 185
Hildesheimer, Wolfgang
  Marbot 216
Hinck, Walter 109n.
Hintze, Otto 209n.
Hirsche, Karl 114n.
Historical fiction 214
  'realistic' 213
Historical narrative 196, 203, 228
  and reunification 229
  genre-model 197, 215
Historical novel 225
  and the foundation of the Reich 202
  autonomy 199
  criticism 214
  genre 196
  ideological function 214
  in the GDR 226
  introspective 220
  national liberal 228

poetics 200, 204, 206, 207, 212, 213, 228, 230
political intention 201
research 198
subject-matter 205
theory 197
Historical progress 14, 15, 17, 18, 20, 140, 216, 228
Historicism 197, 201
Historikerstreit 216, 218, 273, 276
Historiography 198, 199, 209, 216, 218, 219
and fiction 214, 228
linguistic turn 65, 66
method 219
national liberal 204, 228
poetics 211
History 195–97, 199–216, 218–30
as 'narrative argument' 229
constructivistic character 211
end of 2, 20
function 197
individual memory of 219, 226
national 25–36, 203
of mentalities 200
teleology 14
History textbooks 37–60
Hitler, Adolf 62, 218, 253, 273
Hobsbawm, Eric J. 10, 11
Hochhuth, Rolf 224
Wessis in Weimar 3, 312
Hoffmann von Fallersleben, August Heinrich 112–16, 121, 122, 129
"Breslauer Schillerfest" 115
complete edition 116
"Frisch auf, frisch auf!" 115
"Herbstlied" 116
"Das Lied der Deutschen" 9, 117, 139
museum 130
Unpolitische Lieder 112, 115, 116
"Wer ist der greise Siegesheld" 114
Hofmannsthal, Hugo von 18
Hohenzollern, Schloß 33
Hölderlin, Friedrich 264
Holy Roman Empire 156

Honecker, Erich 236, 257, 258, 260, 270
Honoratioren 64, 77
Hörnigk, Therese 259
House of History (Haus der Geschichte, Bonn) 30
Hughes, Henry Stuart 67n.
Hultenreich, Jürgen 289
Huret, Jules
En Allemagne 127
Huyssen, Andreas 11n., 193, 275n.

Ideal-type 67
Identity
Bavarian 43
Berlin's 188
Berlin's Prussian 177
crisis of (after 1871) 5
cultural 7, 8, 26
Fontane's German identity 79–103
German, role of Berlin 181
German, rooted in the Gründerzeit 152
language 74
national 9 (GDR), 50, 59, 124, 146, 156, 216, 222, 228
self-identity 261
social 69
West German 216, 222
Illusion 213
of objectivity 202
Illusionism 200, 226, 228
anti-illusionism 218
Immigration, imagery of 181, 191
Imperial Treasures 156
Imperialism 3, 118
Improvisation
Vor dem Spiegel (Prenzlauer Berg) 283
Intellectuals 4–6, 20, 31, 131, 223, 243, 247, 251–77, 307, 308, 313, 319

Jacobowski, Ludwig
Werther der Jude 191n.
Jäger, Georg 112n.
Jäger, Manfred 294n.
Jäger, Oskar 42
Jahn, Friedrich Ludwig 50n.

Jakobs, Karl-Heinz 271
Jameson, Frederic 69n., 77
Janka, Walter 238
Jansen, Johannes 280
Jarausch, Konrad 29n.
Jenninger, Philipp 217n.
Jens, Walter 249n., 269, 275, 307, 311–13
Jews 77
Johnson, Uwe 304
Johst, Hanns 265
Journalism, see also Christa Wolf
  and East German writers 244
  cultural 18
Joyce, James 36
  Ulysses 26
Jünger, Ernst 275

Kachold, Gabriele 298
Kahlau, Heinz 279
Kaiser ist nackt, Der (periodical) 288
Kaiser, Bruno 123n., 124n., 130n.
Kant, Hermann 265, 269, 272, 319
  Abspann 269, 272
Kant, Immanuel 248n.
Kantorowicz, Alfred 302, 303
Karge, Manfred 317
  MauerStücke 316, 317
Kaufmann, Walter 241n.
Kebbel, Gerhard 198n.
Keil, Ernst 138
Keller, Gottfried 4, 123
Kellner, Hans 62n.
Kelly, Alfred 80n., 82n., 88n., 93n., 94n., 95n., 96n., 180n., 181n.
Kiaulehn, Walter 183n.
Kipphardt, Heinar 274
Kirsch, Sarah 132, 262n.
  Erlkönigs Tochter 107, 108, 131
Kleindeutsch 109, 139, 201, 202, 205
Kleist, Heinrich von 275
  "Germania an ihre Kinder" 119
Klepper, Jochen 273
Koch, Gottfried 52, 53
Kocka, Jürgen 36n., 68
Kohl, Helmut 241, 243, 251, 275, 312, 318n.

Kohn, Hans 62n.
Kolbe, Uwe 281, 286, 288, 289, 300
Königsdorf, Helga 193
Konrád, György 131n.
Kontext (periodical) 298
Koshar, Rudy 62, 63n.
Koziol, Andreas 280, 290, 292, 293
Kraft, Dieter 282, 285n.
Krauss, Hannes 273n., 275n.
Kuba (Kurt Barthel) 265
Kuby, Erich 311
Kühn, Dieter
  Der Parzival des Wolfram von Eschenbach 229
Kulturkampf 4, 141
Kulturnation 5, 8, 9, 17, 222, 229, 304, 308, 310, 312
Kunert, Günter 108, 224
Kunze, Reiner 240
  Deckname "Lyrik" 239, 240
  Die wunderbaren Jahre 235

Lang, Jack 9, 269
Language
  and nationalism 61–78
  of the Berufsstand 63, 66
  of nationality 27
Lanzendörfer, Frank 288
Lasker, Eduard 135
Lassalle, Ferdinand 142, 175
Lattmann, Dieter
  Die Brüder 304n.
Laube, Heinrich 206
  Waldstein 205, 206
Lehnert, Herbert 261
Lenin, Vladimir 183
Lenz, Siegfried 274
Lepenies, Wolf 4, 6, 265n.
Lepsius, M. Rainer 78n.
Lerche, Peter 30
Liberalism, see also National Liberalism
  64, 199, 203, 206, 215, 257, 270
Liberals
  reconciliation with the Prussian state 118
  self-renunciation in 1878 114
Liberation of the Netherlands 153

Liliencron, Detlev von 134
Limlei, Michael 197n., 198n., 204n.
Lindau, Paul
  Der Zug nach dem Westen 188, 189
Lingg, Hermann 108
Linguistic theory 65–9, 74, 78
  nationalism 62
Lipperheide, Franz
  Lieder zu Schutz und Trutz 112n., 127
Literary engagement, see Aesthetics and politics
Literary establishment 10, 124, 136
Literary life 149, 151
Literary market 154, 158, 161, 166
Literary modernism 221
Literary public 154
Literary theory 199
Literature and historiography 197, 213, 220
  parallel development 202, 209, 217, 221, 228
Literaturstreit 273n.
  see Christa Wolf
Loest, Erich
  Heute kommt Westbesuch 20, 21
Loss, sense of 177
Love story 153, 156, 165
Löwenthal, Leo 136, 138
Ludwig II, King of Bavaria 43, 59
Luise, Queen of Prussia 50
Lyric
  after 1871 134
  nineteenth century 107
  political 107–34
  Prenzlauer Berg 281, 289–300
  present condition 108
  representational function 134
  since the 'Wende' 131
  twentieth century 108

Macpherson, C. B.
  possessive individualism 63
Mann, Heinrich 234
  Der Untertan 129, 243
  Im Schlaraffenland 137

Mann, Thomas 273, 277
  Der Tod in Venedig 20
  Doktor Faustus 234, 238
Manthey, Jürgen 167n.
Marbach, Oswald 121
  Das Halljahr Deutschlands 121
Marcks, Erich 27n.
Marcuse, Herbert 21
Marmier, Xavier 127
Maron, Monika 179, 224
  Stille Zeile Sechs 227
Marx, Karl 62, 128
  Das Kapital 128
Marxism
  equated with National Socialism 273
Masur, Kurt 252
Materialism, authors' fears of 174, 184, 186, 188
Mattheuer, Wolfgang 274n.
Mauthner, Fritz
  Das Quartett 191
  Der neue Ahasver 191n.
Mayer, Hans 238n.
Media
  role of the media 12, 266, 271, 319
Meier, Christian 36n.
Meinecke, Friedrich 167, 120n.
Menne, Angelika 120n.
Menzel, Wolfgang 196
Metz, August 111
Meyer, Conrad Ferdinand 134, 196n., 209, 213, 228, 229
  Huttens letzte Tage 212
  Jürg Jenatsch 207, 209, 212
Meyer, Richard M. 1
Meyer-Krentler, Eckhardt 12n., 85n., 152n., 162n., 163n., 164n., 168n., 215n.
Middle-class 63, 76, 168, 199, 203, 205n., 215
  Christa Wolf 255
  culture 202
  hero in Freytag's novels 204
  historical narrative 205
  in Freytag's novels 229
  Martin Walser 209

Raabe as poet of the middle-class 199
Raabe's *Odfeld* 215
Mikado (periodical) 288–90
Militarism 37–60, 71, 97
Mitscherlich, Alexander 273n.
Mitscherlich, Margarete 273n.
Molo, Walter von 273, 277
Moltke, Helmuth von 39, 48, 53–5, 90, 102
Mommsen, Theodor 16, 204
Mönninger, Michael 32n.
Montégut, Emile 133n.
Monuments
  monument problem after 1989 183
  of victory 184
Monuments, historical 32, 33
  restauration 29
Mühler, Heinrich von 116
Müller, David 59
Müller, Elfriede
  Goldener Oktober 317
Müller, Heiner 13, 15, 16, 17, 20, 188n., 193, 237, 238, 248, 249n., 257, 318
  "Fernsehen 3: Selbstkritik" 237
  "Mommsens Block" 16
Muller, Jerry Z. 68n.
Mumford, Lewis 32
Muschg, Adolf 249n.
Muschg, Walter 13, 18
Museum for German History (Berlin/East) 28
Museum of German History (Berlin/West)
  plan of 30

Naimark, Norman 34n.
Napoleon I 210
Napoleon III 46, 94
Napoleonic period 154
Narrative technique 199, 210, 211n., 217, 221
Nation 25, 144–68, 225
  cultural notion 26
  evolution accompanied by literature 230

legal notion 26
normative notion 26
Nation, cultural, see Kulturnation
Nation-state 148, 202
National community 171, 179, 187
National consciousness 154
National history 195, 224
  interpretation 205
National idea 152, 153
National-liberal historical fiction 207
National-liberal historiography 212
National-liberal poetics 204
National-liberal standard style 201, 204
National Liberalism 201
National Liberals 135, 137, 140, 142
National Socialism 27, 28, 35, 215, 216, 219, 221, 228, 253, 265, 273
  fascination 218
  historicization 217, 218, 221
Nationalism 37–60
  Austrian 90
  Danish 86
  French 94, 96
  German 87–89, 95, 96
  language 61–78
  Québécois 62
  Study 61
Nationalistic pathos 163
Nationalverein 146, 147, 152, 153, 165
Nawrocki, Joachim 184n.
Nero 16
Neubauer, Friedrich 53
Neuhaus, Volker 10n., 85n., 102n., 130n., 174n.
Neutsch, Erik 265
New Forum 252
Nietzsche, Friedrich 18, 59, 60, 67, 125, 126, 197
  Unzeitgemäße Betrachtungen 60, 112, 125
Nightingale, Benedict 318n.
Nobles 76
Noll, Dieter 270, 271, 275
Nolte, Ernst 273
Noltenius, Rainer 118n., 146n.
North German Federation 148

Novel
    autobiographical 218
    Einheitsroman 211
    protagonist 200, 202, 207, 209, 219, 221, 226
    realistic 202
    Vielheitsroman 202, 211
Novella 153, 154, 156, 157
November 9, 1989 (opening of the Berlin Wall) 172, 177, 179, 181, 189, 190

Oetker, Friedrich 122n.
Olt, Reinhard 69n.
Opitz, Detlev 280
Ören, Aras 192
    Wie die Spree in den Bosporus fließt 192n.
Osborne, John 97n., 211n.
Ostpolitik 247, 304

Pacifists 77
Palmer, Bryan 66n.
Pan-German League 64, 76
Pape, Walter 102n., 113n., 180n., 181n.
Papenfuß-Gorek, Bert 280, 287, 291, 294–296
Parsons, Talcott 8
Patriotic affirmation 196, 228
Patriotism, see also Nationalism
    cultural 6
    Fontane's war books 86, 88
    Hegel's notion of lyric 109
    "Hurra-Patriotismus" 80, 92
    language 49
    lyric 109
    of beer and shouting 178
    Raabe's critique of 162
    religious language 41
    republican 133
    treated ironically by Raabe 163
Perpeet, Wilhelm 8n.
Philistinism 157
Pinckney, Darryl 184, 192
Pinson, Koppel 61
Plenzdorf, Ulrich
    Die neuen Leiden des jungen W. 235
Poche, Klaus 271

Poet
    and the state 128–30, 132, 134
Poetic exaltation 162
Poetic Realism 162
Pohl, Klaus
    Karate Billi kehrt zurück 318
Poppe, Gerhard 252
Post-modernism 18
Post-structuralism 290
Post-unification, German 1989/90 318
Posthistoire 20
Power, political 73
Preen von, Friedrich 112
Prenzlauer Berg 278–301
Principle of Hope 19, 21, 22, 268
Profession
    as a writer 146, 259
    civic profession and poetic profession 128
    Prussia's 201
    teaching 76
Protestant
    "Sprachbewegung" 76
Protestantism 28, 59, 76, 206, 218
    'Kulturkampf' 141
    Prussian 156
Prussia, see also Franco-Prussian War 38, 79–103, 125, 126, 157, 177, 180, 195, 201, 206, 210, 212, 222, 226, 234
    and Nietzsche 125
    and Raabe 146, 148
    curricular plan 38
    dangerous to culture 127
    death of Prussia 84
    education 38–41, 43, 45, 47–9
    hegemony 111, 126
    mentality 234
    pro-Prussian narrative 198
    school of Prussian historians 204
Prussian historical novel 212
Prussian identity 80, 85
    Berlin 177
Prussian tendencies
    Willibald Alexis 201
Prussian traditions 33
Prussianism 127

Prutz, Robert 111n.
Raabe, Wilhelm 12, 196n., 228
   Abu Telfan oder die Heimkehr vom Mondgebirge 157
   Die Akten des Vogelsangs 167, 168
   Christoph Pechlin 163
   Die Chronik der Sperlingsgasse 154
   Deutscher Adel 164
   Deutscher Mondschein 164
   Der Dräumling 157, 158, 163
   Gutmanns Reisen 165
   Horacker 167
   Der Hungerpastor 156
   Im alten Eisen 161, 168
   Im Siegeskranze 156, 163
   Der Lar 163, 164
   Meister Autor 167
   Das Odfeld 213–15
   Pfisters Mühle 161, 167
   Poetic concept 162
   Des Reiches Krone 156, 163
   Die Schwarze Galeere 153
   Stopfkuchen 168
   Zum wilden Mann 167
Raddatz, Fritz J. 193n.
Ranke, Leopold von 200
Reactionary phase after 1848/49 154
Reading public 11, 88, 108, 109, 136, 137, 152, 157, 158, 160, 267, 288
Realists
   jungdeutsche 137
   jüngstdeutsche 137
Realpolitik 201, 206
Red Army 254, 276
Reed, Terence James 11n., 12, 20, 176n., 188n., 193n., 227n., 261n., 314
Reich-Ranicki, Marcel 245, 258, 259, 266
Reim, C. 40, 41
Reuter, Hans Heinrich 86n., 87, 90n.
Revolution of 1848 84, 110, 117, 135, 138, 142, 173, 175, 177, 180, 201, 204n.
Revolution of 1989 33
Rhoden, A. von 38
Richter, Joachim Burkhard 124n.
Riegel, Hermann 70

Riehl, Wilhelm 198
Ritter, Henning 313
Rodenberg, Julius 179–82, 191
   Die Grandidiers 179, 180, 182
Roper, Katherine 3, 6n., 85n., 127n., 180n., 191n.
Rosenberg, H. 40
Rosenlöcher, Thomas
   Die verkauften Pflastersteine 242–44
Round table 252
Rousseau, Jean-Jacques 14
Ruge, Arnold 115n.
Rühmkorf, Peter 303

Saalmann, Dieter 175n.
Sack, Manfred 185n., 186n.
Sagave, Pierre-Paul 81n.
Sander, Helke
   BeFreier und Befreite 276
Schädlich, Hans Joachim 189
   Ostwestberlin 189
Schafer, Boyd C. 62n.
Schäfer, Franz Josef
   Jugend zwischen Kreuz und Hakenkreuz 219
Schäfer, Hermann 30n.
Schedlinski, Rainer 282n., 284, 290–93, 297
Scheffel, Joseph Viktor von 198
   Ekkehard 207
Scheffler, Karl
   Berlin: Ein Stadtschicksal 188n.
Schenk, K. 53
Scherr, Johannes 115n.
Scheuch, Erwin K. 9n.
Schieder, Theodor 62, 157n.
Schiller Festival 146
Schiller, Friedrich 8, 15
   "Deutsche Größe" 123
   Über die ästhetische Erziehung des Menschen 14
   Wilhelm Tell 312
Schirrmacher, Frank 246n., 264–266, 273, 274
Schlesak, Dieter 179n.
Schlesinger, Klaus 271
   Fliegender Wechsel 176n.

Schleswig-Holstein War 88
    Fontane's analysis of causes of 86, 87
Schlosser, Friedrich Christoph 202
Schmidt, Elli 254n.
Schmidt, Helmut 276
Schmidt, Julian 137, 163, 199
Schneckenburger, Max
    "Die Wacht am Rhein" 49
Schneider, Peter 174–76, 184, 188, 304
    Der Mauerspringer 175, 304n.
Schneider, Reinhold 273
Schneider, Rolf 270–273, 275
Schnur, Wolfgang 279
Schoefer, Christine 3n., 273, 274
Schoeps, Karl-Heinz J. 7, 11n., 176n., 188n., 193n., 251, 254n.
Schoolmaster 167
Schopenhauer, Arthur 151
Schubert, Dieter 271
Schulz, Max Walter 259
Schumann, Gerhard 265
Schutte, Sabine 107n., 133n.
Scott, Walter 196, 205
SED, see Socialist Unity Party
Sedan, Battle of 41, 52, 57
Seghers, Anna 238, 257
    Das siebte Kreuz 275
Seiler, Christian 279n.
Sengle, Friedrich 124
Seyppel, Joachim 270, 271, 275
Sheehan, James J. 7n., 173n., 186n.
Siemann, Wolfram 110n., 154n.
Sindermann, Horst 256
Sittner, Gernot 109n.
Skepticism 134, 139, 152, 158, 164, 180, 215, 242, 256, 257, 315
Sloterdijk, Peter 313
Social Democracy 39–41
Social Democrats 77, 140, 141
Socialist Unity Party (SED) 252, 256, 258–61, 264–66, 269, 270, 272, 273
Sommer, Theo 32n.
Sonderweg, German (special path) 35, 63, 66
South Germany, education in 44n., 47n.

Soviet Occupation Zone 253
Spichern Heights, Battle of 52, 57
Spielhagen, Friedrich 174–76, 183
    Ein neuer Pharao 138, 139, 141, 142
    Finder und Erfinder 136
    Freigeboren 135, 142
    In Reih und Glied 174
    Sturmflut 136, 138, 139, 141, 183, 187
    Was will das werden 137, 138, 141
Sprachbewegung 70, 76, 78
Sprachgesellschaften 69
Sprachverein, Allgemeiner Deutscher 61, 70–8
Springer, Anton 126
Springer, Robert 185, 186
    Banquier und Schriftsteller 185
Stalin, Joseph 273
Stalinism 34, 235, 273, 274, 275n.
Stasi (State Security Police) 239, 240, 244, 245, 261, 266, 272
Steenhuis, Aafke 255
Steinert, Hajo 280
Steinmetz, Karl Friedrich von 53
Stephan, Alexander 275n.
Stern, Fritz 4n., 5n., 10n.
Stern, Horst
    Mann aus Apulien 230
Sternberger, Dolf 30
Stöcker, Adolf 141
Stölzl, Christoph 30n.
Störkraft 276
Storm, Theodor 84, 119, 127
Strauß, Botho 18, 179, 181, 182, 313
    "Anschwellender Bocksgesang" 18
    Beginnlosigkeit 19
    "Diese Erinnerung an einen" 313
    Schlußchor 179, 181, 182, 313, 316
Struzyk, Brigitte 171–73, 193
Stürmer, Michael 30
Subjectivism 257
Superiority, German feeling of
    (1870/71) 27, 93, 98, 121, 125–27, 130
Süskind, Patrick 313
Sybel, Heinrich von 201, 202n., 204, 209

System of petty states 148
Tafel, Verena 30n.
Tecklenburg, August 48, 58
Ten-point plan 251
Theatre
  group-theatre "Zinnober" 282–84, 286
Theweleit, Klaus 77n.
Thiers, Adolphe 94
Thiess, Frank 277
Third Reich, see also National Socialism 216, 217, 220, 221, 229, 302
Third way 222, 224
Thirty Years War 205
Thunecke, Jörg 167n.
Toews, John E. 62n.
Townson, Michael 69n., 74n.
Treitschke, Heinrich von 128, 204
  Deutsche Geschichte im 19. Jahrhundert 204
Treuhandanstalt 3, 187, 188
Triviality 162, 164, 165

Uecker, Günther 268
Ueding, Gert 10
Ulbricht, Walter 258, 259
Ulrich, Volker 275n.
Unification, German
  1870/71 29, 35, 69, 79, 80, 83, 85, 96, 102, 111, 112, 114, 116, 122, 125, 126, 128, 130, 133, 138, 148, 149
  and language 69
  cultural 1–21, 131
  cultural idea 123
  efforts after 1848 124
  economic problems 3
  in German history schoolbooks 37–60
  kleindeutsch 146–147
  novels 138
  transvaluation of 120
  1989/90 2, 34, 35, 131, 132, 133, 302, 303, 304, 306, 307, 309, 311, 316, 317, 319
  economic porblems 3, 33

  and cultural patriotism 6
  and intellectuals 6
  and West Germans 31
  as "Verfassungsbeuge" (Grass) 7
  cultural 1–21, 131
  dividing people 234
  historical assessment 225
  prejudices against it 313
  Walser's approval 312
  impact of both unifications on historical narratives 195–230
  of 1938 131
  parallels between both unifications 3, 4, 9, 131, 133, 134, 171–94
Utopia 11, 16, 20, 111, 131, 134, 223, 224, 229, 236, 241, 249
  political 145, 157, 163

Väterliteratur 216, 218, 226
Vegesack, Thomas von 260n.
Vergangenheitsbewältigung (coming to terms with the past) 174, 181, 182, 215, 217, 218, 226, 228, 229
Vierordt, Heinrich 134
Vincke, Gisbert von 115
Vischer, Friedrich Theodor 122, 134
Vischer-Bilfinger, Wilhelm 125n.
Visual Poetry 287
Volk 115, 117, 118, 145, 149, 155, 158–62, 165, 166
  and cultural unity 126
  and GDR writers 13
  and German unification of 1870/71 107
  and German writers 154, 155, 159, 160
  and literature 10
  and poetry 6
  and revolution 113
  as readers 145
  criticism of the people en masse 149
  criticism of the Volk after 1871 158–62, 165, 166, 168
  "Denkervolk" 126
  der Dichter und Denker 159
  entire German Volk and the Basic Law 29

hopes in the unified Volk 151
in contrast to others 92
Kulturvolk 126
right-wing extremists 276
rural 76
unified 118
Wir sind das Volk/Wir sind ein Volk 171, 172, 236, 241, 251
Volkskammer 256
Vormärz 136, 137

Wall, see Berlin
Wallenstein 205, 208n.
Walser, Martin 30, 224, 229, 274, 302, 304–06, 312, 313
  Die Verteidigung der Kindheit 225
  Dorle und Wolf 304
Walther, Joachim 270
Wander, Maxi 262n.
War with Denmark in 1864 149
Wars of National Liberation, see Befreiungskriege
Warsaw Pact 255, 259, 265, 266
Weber, Ernst 109n.
Weber, Max 3, 4, 62, 67, 68
Wehler, Hans-Ulrich 62n., 221
Weibert, Ferdinand 123n.
Weidig, Ludwig
  Der Hessische Landbote 112
Weigand, Heinrich 48, 53–55, 58
Weimar Germany 63
Weindling, Paul 73n.
Weiss, Peter 274
Wellershoff, Dieter 306
Wende 13, 195, 223, 309
  see also November 9 and Unification
"Wendehälse" 247, 317
Wertheimer, Mildred 61
Wesuls, Elisabeth 179
Wiechert, Ernst 273
Wiesel, Elie 269
Wiesner, Herbert 258
Wildenbruch, Ernst von
  Sedan 107

Wilhelm I, King of Prussia, German Emperor 38, 46–48, 50, 57–59, 91, 94, 114, 115, 118, 135
Wilhelm II, German Emperor 39–41, 47, 135, 141
Winckler, Lutz 308
Windelband, Wilhelm 17
Wohmann, Gabriele 311
Wolf, Christa 7, 12, 13, 17, 193, 244–48, 251–72, 274, 275, 277, 319
  "Blickwechsel" 254
  Der geteilte Himmel 256
  Kassandra 216
  Kindheitsmuster 226, 253, 254
  Nachdenken über Christa T. 244, 256, 257, 266
  "Nagelprobe" 269
  "Prinzip Hoffnung" 21, 268
  Störfall 266
  Was bleibt 244, 245, 256, 262, 263, 265, 266, 273
Wolf, Gerhard 298, 300
Wolff, Julius 134
Women 64, 73, 76, 254, 274, 276
  woman writer 245
Workaday world 162
Workers 76, 136, 179, 180, 190, 218, 249, 253, 315
Wörth, Battle of 52n.
Wruck, Peter 82n.

Young German Movement 135, 137
Youngest German Movement (Jüngstdeutsche) 137

Zeller, Eva 315
  Das Sprungtuch 315, 316
Zentrumspartei 141
Zettel, Karl 112
Ziegler, Klaus 193
Zimmer, Hasko 112n.
Zinken, Rosa-Maria 137n., 138
Zinnober 282–84, 286
  traumhaft 284, 285
Zöberlein, Hans 265
Zucker, Renée 191
Zuckmayer, Carl 41